Finance and Accounting
for Project Managers

Charles T. Horngren, Gary L. Sundem, William O. Stratton, Arthur J. Keown,
David F. Scott, Jr., John D. Martin, J. William Petty, Frank Toney

UNIVERSITY OF PHOENIX
School of Undergraduate Business and Management

SIMON & SCHUSTER
CUSTOM PUBLISHING

Excerpts taken from:

Introduction to Management Accounting, Tenth Edition
by Charles T. Horngren, Gary L. Sundem, and William O. Stratton
Copyright © 1996, 1993, 1990, 1987, 1984, 1981, 1978, 1974, 1970, 1965 by Prentice-Hall, Inc.
Simon & Schuster Company / A Viacom Company
Upper Saddle River, New Jersey 07458

Basic Financial Management, Seventh Edition
by Arthur J. Keown, David F. Scott, Jr., John D. Martin, and J. William Petty
Copyright © 1996 by Prentice-Hall, Inc.

Copyright © 1999 by Simon & Schuster Custom Publishing
All rights reserved.

All rights reserved. No part of this book may be reproduced, in any form
or by any means, without permission in writing from the publisher.

This special edition published in cooperation with
Simon & Schuster Custom Publishing.

Printed in the United States of America

10 9 8 7 6 5 4 3 2 1

Please visit our website at www.sscp.com

ISBN 0–536–01649–6

BA 98452

SIMON & SCHUSTER CUSTOM PUBLISHING
160 Gould Street/Needham Heights, MA 02494
Simon & Schuster Education Group

Copyright Acknowledgments

Grateful acknowledgment is made to the following sources for permission to reprint material copyrighted or controlled by them:

Chapter 11: "Integrating Cost and Schedule Control," of New Project Management, by J. Davidson Frame, 1994, reprinted by permission of Jossey-Bass Publishers, Inc.

Excerpt from Chapter 10: "Standard Costs and Performance Evaluation," of Managerial Accounting, Third edition, by Calvin Engler. Irwin Publishing.

CONTENTS

CHAPTER 5   **EVALUATING AND RANKING PROJECTS   179**

CHAPTER 6

PROJECT PORTFOLIO RISK ANALYSIS   241

SECTION III: PROJECT FINANCIAL PLANNING

SECTION V: PROJECT TERMINATION AND FOLLOW UP

SECTION I
FOUNDATION CONCEPTS

CHAPTER 1

INTRODUCTION

1.1. TEXT OBJECTIVE

The objective of this text is to address accounting and finance topics that will assist the project manager in achieving the project's goals. In achieving this objective, the author recognizes that accounting and finance are intimidating subjects for most people. If this description includes yourself, don't worry, the book will lead you through the learning process hand-in-hand.

1.2. BENEFITS OF ACCOUNTING & FINANCE KNOWLEDGE FOR THE PROJECT MANAGER

There are many important reasons why the project manager needs to be thoroughly versed in project accounting and finance.

IT IS A CORE ELEMENT THAT RESULTS IN PROJECT GOAL ACHIEVEMENT

The figure below is the result of over three years of research by the Fortune 500 Project Management Benchmark Forum. The Forum is a group of 60 large companies that meet every quarter to address project management problems, identify best practices, and support project management related research. The group strongly supports increased emphasis on accounting and finance as a core knowledge area for superior project managers. In support of this judgment, the figure summarizes all the factors that have a scientifically validated, positive impact on project goal achievement. The influence of accounting and financial tools and analytical techniques permeates every area.

FACTORS IMPACTING PROJECT GOAL ACHIEVEMENT

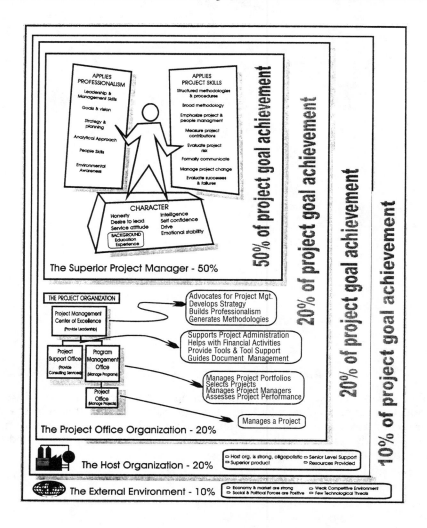

Project goal achievement is impacted by several factors. The factors are categorized in order of importance as the superior project manager, the project office organization, the host organization, and the external environment.

The Superior Project Manager

To obtain the highest degree of potential project success, the single most important element is the selection of a superior project manager. Various studies conclude that the leader is directly responsible for 45 to 75% of an organization's success. Experienced project executives testify that a superior project manager has the ability to overcome almost any obstacle to project success. The project office organization might be nonexistent, the host organization could be weak, and adverse conditions could be encountered in the external environment. Nevertheless, the superior project manager will give the project the highest probability of success.

To achieve the project's objectives, the superior project manager relies upon a large toolkit of accounting and financial analysis aids and managerial approaches. They assist in setting the budgets that ensure the project meets its cost and performance targets. Use of analytical problem-solving methods results in correct decisions being made. Truthfulness is supported by numerically supporting proposals and project control reports. Accounting and financial tools lend themselves to the structured methodologies that are key to project success. They make possible the pragmatic evaluation of project risks as well as the ability to measure the overall successes and failures of the team's efforts.

It is important to recognize that even a superior project manager can not overcome all obstacles. A project that is doomed to failure will still be doomed to failure no matter what quality its leader. Studies note that approximately 25 to 55 percent of the factors impacting project success are outside the sphere of control of the project manager.

The Project Office Organization

The project office organization increases the probability of project success by providing direct support to the project manager. Although the project office organizational structure varies in most companies, it generally consists of a single element or combination of a project manager center of an excellent project support office, program management office, and project office.

In general, the project office organization supports the project manager by providing project focused leadership within the host organization. It serves as an advocate for the project management process by promoting the benefits of project management to senior management and other functional areas. It develops project group strategies and ensures that the strategy supports the host organization's strategy. The project office organization coordinates and directs the building of professionalism and generates standardized methodologies, templates, and project tools.

All of these goal achieving activities depend upon the professional application of accounting and financial tools and management techniques. Portfolios of projects are managed predominantly by the use of accounting and finance performance measurements and summarizing techniques. Project selection involves financial and risk ranking. Development of the project group's strategy often focuses upon the financial contributions of the group and its portfolio of projects.

The Host Organization

Project goal achievement is impacted by the host organization. Higher project success can be predicted if the project and project organization receives senior level support and adequate resources are provided, the host organization is financially strong, is oligopolistic with few competitors, and the project group is assigned a superior product or service to develop. The relationship of the host organization with the project office organization and/or specific projects is generally strategic and financial in nature. Specifically, the projects being performed have been approved primarily because they achieve financial and strategic objectives. Typically, the view of the host organization to specific projects is heavily biased toward bottom line performance. Ability to use and communicate financial and accounting conclusions is paramount when making presentations or preparing reports for executive offices.

The External Environment

There are many remote forces outside the influence of the organization that impact project success. A strong economy and market give support to all the organization's activities, as does a favorable social and political environment. A weak competitive arena combined with few external technological threats have a positive impact on project goal achievement. All of these forces shape the external environment and can seriously impact or support the project manager's ability to attain his/her goals.

It is the duty of the superior project manager to be cognizant of factors in the external environment and their possible impact on the project's success. From this knowledge base, modifications can be made to budgets and financial forecasts. Reports and recommendations can be submitted to project stakeholders.

IT IS A KEY ENTREPRENEURIAL SKILL

Project managers essentially perform the same role as the entrepreneurial chief executive officer. In fact, many organizations use the project manager role as a training ground for future executives. As the project leader progresses higher within the functional organization, or through increasingly larger projects, he/she will be required to increasingly rely upon accounting and finance.

IT HELPS TO MAKE THE <u>RIGHT</u> DECISION

The most successful organizational leaders rely on analytical processes to make the right decisions. The superior project manager strives to make the *right decision rather than simply to build support for a preconceived opinion*. The analytical decision-making approach is heavily dependent on accounting and finance tools.

PROJECT CONTROL IS MAINTAINED

There is an old saying in the world of finance that the person who controls the project budget controls the project. If the project manager professes no knowledge of accounting and finance there is an inclination to delegate these critical leadership functions to other people.

PROJECT MANAGER CREDIBILITY IS INCREASED

The need for accounting and finance knowledge can be as simple as understanding the language of accounting and finance. This is particularly important when making presentations to executive level boards who are focused on the bottom line. There is a tendency to assume that if a person is speaking accounting and finance terminology that the data is founded on more solid decision-making principles.

1.3.   THE NEED FOR A PROJECT FINANCE TEXT

In discussions with project managers and executives in project organizations it is common to hear that there is little emphasis on the accounting and financial aspects of projects. Even the Project Management Institute's *Guide to the Project Management Body of Knowledge* limits its discussion of project accounting and finance to elementary earned value and risk analysis subjects. One result is that there are no comprehensive texts written about the application of accounting and finance techniques to the management of projects. To provide support for project management students, this text is a compilation of selected chapters from several accounting and finance books. The chapters' key project implications for project managers are explained. Even so, some chapters and paragraphs do not flow as smoothly as if the text had been written as a unit. It is hoped the reader will be sympathetic, since this compilation is necessary to achieve access to the great accounting and financial thinkers in one project-focused document.

1.4. TEXT OVERVIEW

This text explores accounting and finance topics as they relate to the achievement of project goals. Topics are addressed in a sequential or methodological order, much in the same manner they would be encountered on an actual project. Specifically, the book addresses the financial tools that are used to *select* a single project from a portfolio of projects. It discusses the type of decision-making information that is used and details how projects are ranked based on forecasted financial return and expected risk factors, and then evaluated in light of pertinent subjective factors. Once a project is selected, it is necessary to address the accounting and financial factors that are used during the *project-planning phase*. Financial forecasting and budgeting are explored in detail. Risk elements specific to an individual project are identified and a mitigation plan developed. The effective leverage of funds, personnel, and equipment are explained. Once the project is underway, a new set of financial tools is used for *monitoring and controlling* the project. Cost and schedule tracking using earned value and other industry costing techniques are explained. The use of variance analysis as a control tool is explored. Associated subjects such as make or buy, leasing versus purchase, and effective stewardship of project assets are investigated and discussed. As the project reaches maturity, it is necessary to plan for *project termination*. Pricing strategy and termination planning are covered. Finally, the process of *following up* on the project's results concludes the process. Warranty estimation and measurement is explained. Project performance evaluation and lessons learned conclude the investigation.

1.5. SPECIFIC OBJECTIVES

Project managers of the most successful project groups critically analyze alternatives and control the performance of their organization by relying heavily on accounting and financial tools. The project management role also includes responsibilities for the efficient and effective allocation of resources as well as the measurement and control of project costs, schedules, and performance. This requires specific skills in evaluating projects according to their economic, financial, and strategic fit with the resources of the enterprise. This text explores the skills required to analyze, evaluate, and control programs and projects. It provides an overview of key budgeting and financial analysis and control skills used by the project manager to achieve these ends. Topics include presenting project resource requirements to management, estimating, scheduling cost control, and cost optimization. The approach taken is one of managerial accounting and finance as opposed to a pure accounting or a "bookkeeping" approach.

By learning the material in the text, the reader will understand, be able to apply the concepts to his/her own workplace, and use them to enhance his/her personal career. The following concepts will be discussed in the text:

- How the use of accounting and finance techniques maximize the probability of project goal achievement.
- Techniques and tools to reduce risk, maximize return, and consider the numerous subjective factors that result in personal and organizational success.

- An understanding of the need to view project financing as competing for corporate financial resources.
- Fundamental skills in determining the congruence of investment alternatives with corporate strategies and core competencies.
- The methods by which a project manager uses estimates and schedules to control the cost of a project.
- The importance of cost optimization.
- Identification of major opportunities and techniques for achieving improved resource utilization, method studies, economic analysis, and productivity improvements.
- The concept of project simulation.

1.6. INTERNATIONAL PROJECT FINANCE AND ACCOUNTING

The professional management of international projects tends to be similar rather than different in most global locations. After all, the study of project management methodology is an ancient endeavor dating at least to the time of the pyramids. Over the millenniums a reasonably universal approach to building a project has evolved. In addition, most project management texts originate in the United States and generally take a common approach to managing projects.

There is a much less universal approach to the financial and accounting management of projects in the international arena. Virtually no two independent countries of the world have the same accounting system and financial reporting requirements. Currencies differ in value and inflation rates vary widely. There is a dramatic impact on project budgeting, control, procurement, and performance evaluation. Variations in cultural views about secrecy affect public availability of the financial details of a project. It may be difficult or even impossible to remove funds and equipment from some countries after the project is terminated. Generally speaking, the users of the information have a direct impact on the quality of information.

CHAPTER 2

Basic Accounting and Finance Concepts for Projects

2.1 COMMON FINANCIAL STATEMENTS

The world of project management is permeated with accounting and financial factors and variables. The project manager must understand the finances of the project itself as well as how the project financially interfaces with the host organization and other stakeholder groups. The fundamentals of accounting are necessary to ensure the project manager is familiar with common accounting and finance terminology and financial statements. The income statement, balance sheet, and cash flow statement are reviewed. Of these, the income statement is most appropriate to project management. The income statement represents the basic approach used by most project managers to develop project forecasts. By modifying the income statement approach to show cash flow coming in at the top of the page and cash expenses below, the income statement is converted effectively to a cash flow projection, budget, or forecast.

The balance sheet is used to show what an organization possesses (assets) and where the money came from to purchase those assets (liabilities and owner's equity). Normally it has fewer applications to projects than the income statement.

2.2 ACCOUNTING COMPARED TO FINANCIAL MANAGEMENT OF PROJECTS

Financial management is concerned with the creation and maintenance of monetary value or wealth. Accounting is generally defined as the process of identifying, measuring, and communicating monetary information. With these definitions setting the stage, it is timely to note that many people approach the discipline of accounting with the visual image in their mind of the stereotypical bookkeeper.

Their view of the discipline is often dominated by the mechanical tasks such as record keeping and number crunching. The emphasis of this text is on the managerial aspects of accounting and finance as they apply to project management.

The distinction between a mechanical and a managerial approach to finance and accounting is an important one. It can have a major impact on the way the day-to-day activities of the project manager are performed. As evidence, consider the findings of the Fortune 500 Project Management Benchmarking Forum. Their surveys determined that beginning project managers spend an average of 70% of their time on project software, templates, reports, and procedures. Only 30% of their time was dedicated to face-to-face communications with project team members.

At the other end of the project management spectrum, experienced "superior" project managers spent 70% of their time on personal communications and only 30% on project management tools. The respondents stressed that the high emphasis on tools is important to new project managers because it disciplines them to build a strong methodological foundation for their projects.

The danger is that the tools can become an end unto themselves, and the project manager can ignore the personal management aspects of the role. An extreme mode of this behavior occurs when the project manager starts thinking that the project plan or budget represents reality and that somehow the project and team members should be conforming to this artificial perception.

One anecdotal story of such behavior is contained in the cultural archives of Caterpillar Tractor Company. Over a period of years, a few workers at the company product demonstration area began illicitly selling tractor parts to dealers and customers. The theft and resale group expanded over the years until eventually someone recognized the loss. The FBI was called in and several people were fired. As can be imagined, there was general hysteria within this old company that prided itself on integrity. Certain employees became very sensitive to any issue related to theft and spent considerable amounts of time closing the barn door even though all the horses had already run away. Consider the following example.

"Bob" was appointed project manager to get the demonstration area under control and functioning smoothly. "Charlie," one of the project team members, was assigned the duty of reviewing the asset listings in an attempt to identify potentially stolen items. A few weeks after taking the new position, Bob was sitting in his office when the telephone rang. It was Charlie, who immediately blurted out, "Bob, we've got a big problem. Someone has stolen a D9 Tractor." Note that in those days the D9 tractor was the largest tractor made by Caterpillar and roughly the size of a typical garage. To this announcement Bob responded, "Really? What's its serial number and how do you know it's missing?" Charlie gave Bob the serial number and stated that the tractor was missing because he couldn't locate it in the asset listing: "It's missing from the books." Bob responded to Charlie, "I think that tractor is here. In fact I can see it out the window. I am looking at it as we speak!" Charlie replied, "No! You can't see it! It's gone! It's missing from the books!"

Charlie regarded the asset ledger as reality. He was attempting to force the tractor (or lack thereof) to match his ledger-defined world of reality. The financial manager, Bob, on the other hand, saw the physical tractor as reality and immediately diagnosed the asset ledger as incorrect. The lesson for project managers is that the project and project personnel are always reality. It is important to never let the numbers, project plans, budgets, or templates overshadow reality or be viewed as the ultimate reality in themselves.

2.3   ACCRUAL VS. CASH FLOW ACCOUNTING

Most people enter the world of project management in an accrual accounting mind set. Particularly if they have taken accounting courses in school, there is a tendency to think the world is measured by accrual accounting procedures. The reality is that project management follows the premise that "cash is king!" Virtually all project management and accounting is cash flow based. The world of accrual accounting is basically focused on external reporting in the form of financial statements for the Internal Revenue Service. For the purposes of project management selection processes, planning, implementation, control, and evaluation, cash flow is the method of choice.

2.4   SKEPTICISM AND THE PROJECT MANAGER. WHY FINANCIAL STATEMENTS RARELY PRESENT AN ACCURATE PICTURE OF THE ORGANIZATION

The project manager takes the view that financial statements are rarely if ever entirely accurate. This surprises many people new to the study of accounting and finance. Many view the disciplines of accounting and finance as rigidly controlled with tight guidelines (Generally Accepted Accounting Principles) and a highly structured reporting format. In fact, the United States has the most flexible accounting and financial guidelines in the world. Inversely, the least flexible systems are found in socialistic and communistic countries.

The advantage to management of a flexible accounting system is that every organization is different and a flexible system is needed to present the appropriate portrait. On the other hand, governments' accounting systems are accused of existing to simply satisfy various legal reporting requirements by "filling in the blanks."

The flexible accounting approach has the advantage that it can be applied to different organizations and projects. Its major disadvantage is that a higher degree of knowledge is needed to apply and to interpret the accounting knowledge and information. In addition, it is easy to present a biased picture or to flavor the presentation with a slanted view. Consequently, the project manager soon learns to view any accounting or financial statement with a critical eye.

Asset Valuation

A cornerstone of accounting philosophy in the United States is that assets are recorded on the balance sheet at the original price paid. Some of the prices of established companies may represent assets purchased forty or fifty years ago. In no way do the values represent current market worth. For example, Ford Motor Company has factories that were originally built in the 1920s. Their River Rouge Steel is valued on the financial statement at the original price Ford paid for it in the 1920s. The lesson is that asset values are almost always misleading; the older the organization, the more misleading the asset values.

REASONS WHY FINANCIAL STATEMENTS MAY NOT PRESENT A TRUE PICTURE OF A FIRM

- **Asset valuation**
- **Accrual accounting**
  - Assets expensed or capitalized.
  - Sales—when recognized.
  - Accounts receivable—may have high uncollectibles.
  - Depreciation—items expensed, method of calculation.
  - Inventory valuation—quality, method of measurement.
- **Comparability**
- **Diversification of firms**
- **Hidden assets**
- **Non-measurable items**
- **Data lumped together**
- **Unethical**
- **Inflation**
- **Management perks**
- **Auditor's opinion**
- **Gobbledygook**
- **Errors**
- **Non-current information**
- **Estimates**
- **Atypical data**

Accrual Accounting

The premise of accrual accounting is that revenues and expenses are allocated to the period in which they occurred rather than the time that money changes hands. Under accrual accounting cash rarely equals profit. The movement of revenues and expenses between different periods provides management the capability to alter the image or portrait of the company. It also makes it necessary to understand accrual accounting procedures and their potential impact on the financial statements.

Expense or Capitalize Assets

There is a broad range of purchased items that can be written off as expenses or capitalized as assets. The choice made has an impact on the accrual based profits of the company. For example, pretend that you are a partner in the ownership of a sporting goods retail store. On December 1st you visit the store. Your partner, the store manager, announces that he has completed the monthly income statement forecast and it appears there will be a profit of about $10,000 for the year. Although this would certainly be a joyous occasion, it also presents a business dilemma.

The problem is that the $10,000 profit will necessitate paying taxes to the IRS—say in the neighborhood of $3000 or so. After some discussion, you also realize that you could take the $10,000 and buy two top-of-the-line computers with the money. Profits would be reduced to zero but the two of you would each have a new computer.

The choice confronting you is whether you prefer to send a $3000 check to the IRS or to obtain new computers.

Seemingly the choice would be easy, but other factors could influence the decision. For example, your spouses might think that a business venture such as your sporting goods store should show a profit. This might represent incentive to investigate a second alternative. The computers could still be bought for $10,000. However, rather than write them off as expenses, now they can be shown as assets on the balance sheet. If the computers are shown as assets, they can be depreciated. The yearly depreciation is listed as an expense that reduces net income. Reduced net income in turn reduces taxes payable. In this way, the two partners can obtain the computers they desire as well as show profits and minimize taxes.

Sales Recognition Timing

Under accrual accounting, sales are recognized when they are earned and realized. In some companies sales are recognized when the order is received. In others, the sale is not recognized until cash payment is obtained. The span of time between these two methods of sales recognition could be several months.

Accounts receivable may have high uncollectibles.
Depreciation is a method of calculation.
Inventory valuation is a quality method of measurement.

Comparability

A company may be dramatically different than it was a year ago. Inflation, mergers, and accounting changes all significantly change a company and make it difficult to compare existing operations with former operations.

Diversification of Firms

Many large firms are so widely diversified and distributed geographically that there are no similar firms with which to compare them.

Hidden Assets

What is the monetary value of patents, copyrights, inventions, employee experience, a good reputation, and market penetration? Most observers would agree that the value of these items is considerable. Nevertheless, the values can not be shown on a balance sheet. For example, pretend we are sitting in our office and the company's brilliant engineer comes in. The brilliant engineer says, "You won't believe what I just invented! I have discovered a way to defy gravity. In other words, we can levitate any item. Furthermore, we can get a patent on the whole process." Is this invention worth anything? Sure! Easily, at least a billion dollars. How much of our new found wealth can be entered on the balance sheet? Nothing, other than the incidental research costs and expenses in obtaining the patent. A similar example would be the value of employee training. Although a few companies are beginning to show training as an asset, most simply write it off as an expense when it occurs.

Non-Measurable Risk

Companies are often subject to high-risk and non-measurable liabilities that never appear on the balance sheet or income statement. An example could be an airline. Assume a news account announces today that a plane from airline X has crashed and the cause appears to be faulty maintenance. Undoubtedly there will be a drop in the number of people flying the airline but it would probably remain in business. Now assume that next week another plane from the same airline goes down. It is announced that the cause is faulty maintenance. Most would predict that at this point the company is going to be fighting for its survival. Although this scenario could happen to almost any airline, it is never listed as a liability on the financial statements of the airline companies.

Unethical Behavior

Sometimes financial statements are intentionally misleading. A recent study indicates that 12 percent of large companies evaluated over a twelve-month period had been convicted of criminal activities. Generally, when an investor has a loss, it is virtually impossible to get the funds back. The best solution is to evaluate every investment and its associated documentation with a critical eye.

Inflation

Even though inflation has averaged 3 to 3.5 percent for years, assets continue to be shown on balance sheets at their original values.

Management Perks

In closely held companies, a strategy is to minimize stockholder taxes by paying low salaries and dividends. The stockholders receive pay indirectly in the form of benefits or perquisites, such as expense accounts, company vehicles, club memberships, a company airplane, board meetings in exotic locations, and extensive retirement and medical benefits. All of these should be added to reported profits to obtain a true picture of the organizations' profitability.

Auditor's Opinion

Historically, readers of financial statements assumed that an auditor's statement meant the financials were valid and the company was in good financial condition. This is no longer true as numerous companies have received "clean" audits only to file bankruptcy a short time later. Astute readers are now aware that the auditor's statement may be misleading or stated with reservations. Auditors are taking less responsibility for the accuracy of the financial statements and always state that the information is presented as the representation of management. The auditor may not have the full picture of the organization. Bias may be a factor since the auditor's employer is the company that is being audited.

Gobbledygook

Often, financial statements contain hard to understand, misleading, or confusing terms. In the world of project finance, if there are words in the financial statements that are difficult to understand, it is wise to investigate. Many times people simply try to impress others by using a complicated word when a simple word would do just as well. As a case in point, an associate retired from a Fortune 500 company and started a franchise hardware store. After a few months an accountant was hired to prepare a financial statement. Upon reviewing the new balance sheet the hardware store owner noticed an item on the statement labeled "capitalized rolling stock" at $15,000. It finally dawned on the owner that the item pertained to his truck. The lesson is that if the statements describe a truck, call it a truck.

Errors

Accounting software programs reject any entry that does not balance. People get very creative when they try to force the accounts to balance. As a result, there could be more errors than before the advent of computers, but now they are much harder to find.

Non-current Information

There may be rapidly occurring events that are major in nature. A group of students in an investment class planned to present a stock analysis of the convenience store chain, Circle K. Two days before the presentation was due, Circle K filed bankruptcy. During the presentation the students took the view that Circle K was a superb company, well run, and financially viable. They gave a strong "buy" recommendation. To everyone's embarrassment, they were totally unaware the company was bankrupt.

Estimates

Financial statements contain numerous estimates such as allowances for uncollectible accounts, periodic depreciation, warranty costs, and contingent losses.

Atypical Data

The company's fiscal year end may not be typical of the financial picture of the company for other periods of the year. Often fiscal years are chosen to coincide with the lowest or slowest period of the year. As a result, some account balances such as cash, accounts receivable, accounts payable, and inventories may not be representative of the rest of the year.

2.5 ETHICS

The major reason to be ethical from a project management view is that ethical organizations and people are consistently more profitable than unethical organizations and people. Ethics has a direct impact on project success and efficiency. The cornerstone of ethics is truthfulness.

The characteristics of honesty and ethics are of paramount importance. There is a high correlation between the degree of honesty and successful goal achievement. Studies indicate that honesty is of such importance that it compensates for other major shortcomings in project leadership. When interviewing team members, one hears statements such as, "My project manager has shortcomings, but I am always given an honest answer. I admire that!"

WHY ETHICAL COMPANIES MAKE MORE MONEY

- Strengthens sales. People like and prefer to deal with ethical people. Inversely, many customers refuse to buy from companies considered unethical.
- **Costs are reduced.** The organization is more efficient.
  - The company pays fewer fines and legal expenses.
  - Less time is spent handling disputes.
  - Codes of Ethics give people guidelines for behavior. They make the organization more efficient and reduce the amount of supervision required. Employees don't have to ask, "What should I do?" so often.
- **It results in more durable relationships.** It isn't necessary to constantly start from scratch. The strength of personal networks is increased.
- **Top quality employees** are attracted to ethical companies.
- **It makes life simpler.** Being ethical makes it easier to stay out of trouble.

The following reading is from *An Introduction to Management Accounting* by Horngren, Sundem, and Stratton. It provides an overview of fundamental accounting concepts.

2.6   BASIC ACCOUNTING: CONCEPTS, TECHNIQUES, AND CONVENTIONS

THE NEED FOR ACCOUNTING

Most people think of accountants as scorekeepers who determine whether a business is making money (and how much, if any). In fact, all kinds of organizations (sometimes called *entities*)—government agencies, nonprofit organizations, and others—rely on accounting to gauge their progress.

Managers, investors, and other interest groups usually want the answers to two important questions about an organization: How well did the organization perform for a given period? Where does the organization stand at a given point? Accountants answer these questions with two major financial statements: an *income statement* and a *balance sheet*. To obtain these statements, accountants continually record the history of an organization. Through the financial accounting process, the accountant accumulates, analyzes, quantifies, classifies, summarizes, and reports events and their effects on the organization.

The accounting process focuses on transactions. A **transaction** is any event that affects the financial position of an organization and requires recording. Through the years, many concepts, conventions, and rules have been developed regarding what events are to be recorded as *accounting transactions* and how their financial impact is measured.

FINANCIAL STATEMENTS

Financial statements are summarized reports of accounting transactions. They can apply to any point in time and to any span of time.

An efficient way to learn about accounting is to study a specific illustration. Suppose King Hardware Company began business as a corporation on March 1. An opening *balance sheet* follows:

King Hardware Company
Balance Sheet (Statement of Financial Position) as of March 1, 19X1

Assets	Equities
Cash $100,000	Paid-in capital $100,000

The **balance sheet** (more accurately called **statement of financial position** or **statement of financial condition**) is a snapshot of financial status at an instant of time. It has two counterbalancing sections—assets and equities. **Assets** are economic resources that are expected to benefit future activities. **Equities** are the claims against, or interests in, the assets.

The accountant conceives of the balance sheet as an equation:

$$\text{assets} = \text{equities}$$

The equities side of this fundamental equation is often divided as follows:

$$\text{assets} = \text{liabilities} + \text{owners' equity}$$

Liabilities are the entity's economic obligations to nonowners. **Owners' equity** is the excess of the assets over the liabilities. For a **corporation**—a business organized as a separate legal entity and owned by its stockholders—the owners' equity is called **stockholders' equity.** In turn, the stockholders' equity is composed of the ownership claim against, or interest in, the total assets arising from any paid-in investment (**paid-in capital**), plus the ownership claim arising as a result of profitable operations (**retained income** or **retained earnings**):

$$\text{assets} = \text{liabilities} + \text{stockholders' equity}$$
$$= \text{liabilities} + (\text{paid-in capital} + \text{retained earnings})$$

Consider a summary of King Hardware's *transactions* in March:

1. Initial investment by owners, $100,000 cash.
2. Acquisition of inventory for $75,000 cash.
3. Acquisition of inventory for $35,000 on open account. A purchase (or a sale) on open account is an agreement whereby the buyer pays cash some time after the date of sale, often in 30 days. Amounts owed on open accounts are usually called **accounts payable,** liabilities of the purchasing entity.

4. Merchandise carried in inventory at a cost of $100,000 was sold on open account for $120,000. These open customer accounts are called **accounts receivable,** assets of the selling entity.

5. Cash collections of accounts receivable, $30,000.

6. Cash payments of accounts payable, $10,000.

7. On March 1, $3,000 cash was disbursed for store rent for March, April, and May. Rent is $1,000 per month, payable quarterly in advance, beginning March 1.

Note that these are indeed *summarized* transactions. For example, all the sales did not occur at once, nor did all purchases of inventory, collections from customers, or disbursements to suppliers. Many repetitive transactions occur in practice, and specialized data collection techniques are used to measure their effects on the organization.

The foregoing transactions can be analyzed using the balance sheet equation, as shown in Exhibit 2-1.

Transaction 1, the initial investment by owners, increases assets and increases equities. That is, cash increases and so does paid-in capital—the claim arising from the owners' total initial investment in the corporation.

Transactions 2 and 3, the purchases of inventory, are steps toward the ultimate goal—the earning of a profit. But stockholders' equity is unaffected. That is, no profit is recorded until a sale is made.

Transaction 4 is the sale of $100,000 of inventory for $120,000. Two things happened simultaneously: a new asset, Accounts Receivable, is acquired (4a) in exchange for the giving up of Inventory (4b), and Stockholders' Equity is increased by the amount of the asset received ($120,000) and decreased by the amount of the asset given up ($100,000). The increase in Stockholders' Equity is called *revenue* or *sales*, and the decrease is an *expense* called *cost of goods sold*.

Transaction 5, cash collection of accounts receivable, is an example of an event that has no impact on stockholders' equity. Collections are merely the transformation of one asset (Accounts Receivable) into another (Cash).

Transaction 6, cash payment of accounts payable, also does not affect stockholders' equity—it affects assets and liabilities only. In general, collections from customers and payments to suppliers have no direct impact on stockholders' equity, unless part of the payment represents *interest expense.*

Transaction 7, the cash disbursement for rent, is made to acquire the right to use store facilities for the next 3 months. On March 1, the $3,000 measured the future benefit from these services, so the asset *Prepaid Rent* was created (7a). Prepaid rent is an asset even though you cannot see or touch it as you can such assets as cash or inventory. Assets also include legal rights to future services such as the use of facilities.

Transaction 7b recognizes that one-third of the rental services has expired during March, so the asset is reduced and stockholders' equity is also reduced by $1,000 as rent expense for March. This recognition of *rent expense* means that $1,000 of the asset Prepaid Rent has been "used up" (or has flowed out of the entity) in the conduct of operations during March.

For simplicity, we have assumed no expenses other than *cost of goods sold* and *rent*. Based on this information, King's accountant can prepare at least two financial statements—the balance sheet and the income statement—as follows:

King Hardware Company
Income Statement for the Month Ended March 31, 19X1

Sales (revenue)		$120,000
Expenses		
Cost of goods sold	$100,000	
Rent	1,000	
Total expenses		101,000
Net income		$ 19,000

King Hardware Co.
Balance Sheet as of March 31, 19X1

Assets		Liabilities and Stockholders' Equity		
Cash	$ 42,000	Liabilities: accounts payable		$ 25,000
Accounts receivable	90,000	Stockholders' equity		
Inventory	10,000	Paid-in capital	$100,000	
Prepaid rent	2,000	Retained income	19,000	119,000
Total	$144,000	Total		$144,000

Relationship of Balance Sheet and Income Statement

The **income statement** measures the performance of an organization by matching its accomplishments (revenue from customers, which is usually called *sales*) and its efforts (*cost of goods sold* and other expenses). The balance sheet shows the organization's financial position at an instant of time, but the income statement measures performance for a span of time, whether it be a month, a quarter, or longer. Thus, the income statement is the major link between balance sheets:

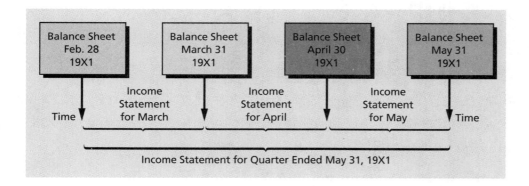

Examine the changes in retained income in Exhibit 2-1. The accountant records *revenue* and *expense* to indicate increases (revenues) and decreases (expenses) in the owners' claims. At the end of a given period, these items are summarized in the form of an income statement. The heading of a balance sheet indicates a *single date*. The heading of an income statement indicates a specific *period*. A balance sheet is a destination; an income statement is a journey.

Exhibit 2-1 King Hardware Co. Analysis of Transactions (in Dollars) for March 19X1

Transactions	Assets					Liabilities +	Stockholders' Equity	
	Cash +	Accounts Receivable +	Inventory +	Prepaid Rent	=	Accounts Payable +	Paid-in Capital +	Retained Income
1. Initial investment	+100,000				=		+100,000	
2. Acquire inventory for cash	− 75,000		+ 75,000		=			
3. Acquire inventory for credit			+ 35,000		=	+35,000		
4a. Sales on credit		+120,000			=			+120,000 (revenue)
4b. Cost of inventory sold			−100,000		=			−100,000 (expense)
5. Collect from customers	+ 30,000	− 30,000			=			
6. Pay accounts of suppliers	− 10,000				=	−10,000		
7a. Pay rent in advance	− 3,000			+3,000	=			
7b. Recognize expiration of rental services				−1,000	=			− 1,000 (expense)
Balance, 3/31/X1	+ 42,000	+ 90,000	+ 10,000	+2,000	=	+25,000	+100,000	+ 19,000
	144,000						144,000	

Each item in a financial statement is frequently called an **account**. In the preceding example, the outflows of assets are represented by decreases in the inventory and prepaid rent accounts and corresponding decreases in stockholders' equity in the form of cost of goods sold and rent expense. Expense accounts are basically negative elements of stockholders' equity. Similarly, the sales (revenue) account is a positive element of stockholders' equity.

Revenues and Expenses

Return to Exhibit 2-1, and review transaction 4. Notice that this transaction has two phases, a revenue phase (4a) and an expense phase (4b) (dollar signs omitted):

Description of Transactions		Assets	=	Equities	
Balances after transaction 3 in Exhibit 2-1			135,000* =		135,000*
4a. Sales on account (inflow)	Accounts receivable		+120,000 =	Stockholders' equity	+120,000
4b. Cost of inventory sold (outflow)	Inventory		−100,000 =	Stockholders' equity	−100,000
Balances, after transaction 4			155,000 =		155,000

* Cash of $100,000 − $75,000	=	$ 25,000	Accounts payable	$ 35,000
Inventory of $75,000 + $35,000	=	110,000	Paid-in capital	100,000
		$135,000		$135,000

Transaction 4a illustrates the recognition of revenue. **Revenues** generally arise from gross increases in assets from delivering goods or services. To be recognized (i.e., formally recorded in the accounting records as revenue during the current period), revenue must ordinarily meet two tests. First, revenues must be *earned*. That is, the goods must be delivered or services must be fully rendered to customers. Second, revenues must be *realized*. That is, an exchange of resources evidenced by a market transaction must occur (e.g., the buyer pays or promises to pay cash and the seller delivers merchandise). If cash is not received directly, the collectibility of the asset (e.g., an account receivable) must be reasonably assured.

Transaction 4b illustrates the incurrence of an expense. **Expenses** generally arise from gross decreases in assets from delivering goods or services.

Transactions 4a and 4b also illustrate the fundamental meaning of **profits** or **earnings** or **income,** which is the excess of revenues over expenses.

As the Retained Income column in Exhibit 2-1 shows, increases in revenues also increase stockholders' equity. In contrast, increases in expenses decrease stockholders' equity.

Transactions 2 and 3 were purchases of merchandise inventory. They were steps toward the ultimate goal—the earning of a profit. But by themselves purchases earn no profit; remember that stockholders' equity was unaffected by the inventory acquisitions in transactions 2 and 3. That is, no profit is recognized until a sale is actually made to customers.

Transaction 4 is the $120,000 sale on open account of inventory that had cost $100,000. Two things happen simultaneously: a $120,000 inflow of assets in the form of accounts receivable (4a) in exchange for a $100,000 outflow of assets in the form of inventory (4b). Liabilities are completely unaffected, so owners' equity increases by $120,000 – $100,000, or $20,000.

Users of financial statements desire an answer to the question: How well did the organization perform for a given period? The income statement helps answer this question. King Hardware Co. has a positive change in stockholders' equity attributable solely to operations. This change is measured by the revenue and expenses that constitute income for the specific period.

For an example of a real company, consider Childrobics, Inc., the company that owns and operates "Play Centers" for children and families in the New York City metropolitan area. The company was incorporated in 1993 and at the end of its first year (on February 28, 1994) it reported:

Revenues	$250,393
Expenses	247,877
Net income	$ 2,516

The company paid no dividends, so its retained earnings increased from $0 to $2,516 during the year.

The Analytical Power of the Balance Sheet Equation

The balance sheet equation can highlight the link between the income statement and balance sheet. Indeed, the entire accounting system is based on the simple balance sheet equation:

$$\text{assets (A)} = \text{liabilities (L)} + \text{stockholders' equity (SE)} \tag{1}$$

SE equals the original ownership claim plus the increase in ownership claim because of profitable operations. That is, SE equals the claim arising from paid-in capital plus the claim arising from retained income. Therefore:

$$A = L + \text{paid-in capital} + \text{retained income} \tag{2}$$

Then, because retained income equals revenue minus expenses (see Exhibit 2-1):

$$A = L + \text{paid-in capital} + \text{revenue} - \text{expenses} \tag{3}$$

Revenue and *expense accounts* are nothing more than subdivisions of stockholders' equity—temporary stockholders' equity accounts. Their purpose is to summarize the volume of sales and the various expenses, so that management is kept informed of the reasons for the continual increases and decreases in stockholders' equity in the course of ordinary operations. In this way, managers can make comparisons, set standards or goals, and exercise better control.

Notice in Exhibit 2-1 that for each transaction the equation is *always* kept in balance. If the items affected are confined to one side of the equation, you will find the total amount added equal to the total amount subtracted on that side. If the items affected are on both sides, then equal amounts are simultaneously added or subtracted on each side.

The striking feature of the balance sheet equation is its universal applicability. No transaction has ever been conceived, no matter how simple or complex, that cannot be analyzed via the equation. The top technical partners in the world's largest professional accounting firms, when confronted with the most intricate transactions of multinational companies, will inevitably discuss and think about their analyses in terms of the balance sheet equation. They focus on its major components: assets, liabilities, and owners' equity (including the explanations of changes in owners' equity that most often take the form of revenues and expenses in an income statement).

ACCRUAL BASIS AND CASH BASIS

Measurements of income and financial position are anchored to the accrual basis of accounting, as distinguished from the cash basis. The **accrual basis** recognizes the impact of transactions on the financial statements in the periods when revenues and expenses occur instead of when cash is received or disbursed. That is, revenue is recorded as it is earned, and expenses are recorded as they are incurred—not necessarily when cash changes hands.

Transaction 4a in Exhibit 2-1, page 20, shows an example of the accrual basis. Revenue is recognized when sales are made on credit, not when cash is received. Similarly, transactions 4b and 7b (for cost of goods sold and rent) show that expenses are recorded as efforts are expended or services are used to obtain the revenue (regardless of when cash is disbursed). Therefore, income is often affected by measurements of noncash resources and obligations. The accrual basis is the principal conceptual framework for relating accomplishments (revenues) with efforts (expenses).

More than 95% of all business is conducted on a credit basis; cash receipts and disbursements are not the critical transactions as far as the recognition of revenue and expense is concerned. Thus, the accrual basis evolved in response to a desire for a more complete, and, therefore, more accurate report of the financial impact of various events.

If the **cash basis** of accounting were used instead of the accrual basis, revenue and expense recognition would occur when cash is received and disbursed. In March, King Hardware would show $30,000 of revenue, the amount of cash collected from customers. Similarly, cost of goods sold would be the $10,000 cash payment for the purchase of inventory, and rent expense would be $3,000 (the cash disbursed for rent) rather than the $1,000 rent applicable to March. A cash measurement of net income or net loss is obviously ridiculous in this case and it could mislead those unacquainted with the fundamentals of accounting.

Ponder the rent example. Under the cash basis, March must bear expenses for the entire quarter's rent of $3,000 merely because cash outflows occurred then. In contrast, the accrual basis measures performance more sharply by allocating the rental expenses to the operations of each of the 3 months that benefited from the use of the facilities. In this way, the economic performance of each month will be comparable. Most accountants maintain that it is nonsense to say that March's rent expense was $3,000 and April's and May's was zero.

The major deficiency of the cash basis of accounting is that it is incomplete. It fails to match efforts and accomplishments (expenses and revenues) in a manner that properly measures economic performance and financial position. Moreover, it omits key assets (such as accounts receivable and prepaid rent) and key liabilities (such as accounts payable) from balance sheets.

Nonprofit Organizations

The examples in this chapter are focused on profit-seeking organizations, but balance sheets and income statements are also used by nonprofit organizations. For example, hospitals and universities have income statements, although they are called *statements of revenue and expense*. The "bottom line" is frequently called "excess of revenue over expense" rather than "net income."

The basic concepts of assets, liabilities, revenues, and expenses are applicable to all organizations, whether they be utilities, symphony orchestras, private, public, American, Asian, and so forth. However, some nonprofit organizations have been slow to adopt several ideas that are widespread in progressive companies. For example, many government organizations still use the cash basis of accounting. The lack of accrual-based financial statements has hampered the evaluation of the performance of such organizations.

ADJUSTMENTS TO THE ACCOUNTS

To measure income under the accrual basis, accountants use adjustments at the end of each reporting period. **Adjustments** record *implicit transactions*, in contrast to the *explicit transactions* that trigger nearly all day-to-day routine entries.

Earlier we defined a *transaction* as any economic event that should be recorded by the accountant. Note that this definition is not confined to market transactions, which are actual exchanges of goods and services between the entity and another party. For instance, the losses of assets from fire or theft are also transactions even though no market exchange occurs.

To illustrate, entries for explicit transactions such as credit sales, credit purchases, cash received on account, and cash disbursed on account are supported by explicit evidence, usually in the form of **source documents** (e.g., sales slips, purchase invoices, employee time records). On the other hand, adjustments for implicit transactions, such as unpaid wages, prepaid rent, interest owed, and the like, are prepared from special schedules or memorandums that recognize events (such as the passage of time) that are temporarily ignored in day-to-day recording procedures. Adjustments refine the accountant's accuracy and provide a more complete and significant measure of efforts, accomplishments, and financial position. Hence, they are an essential part of accrual accounting. They are generally made when the financial statements are about to be prepared.

The principal adjustments may be classified into four types:

1. Expiration of Unexpired Costs
2. Recognition (Earning) of Unearned Revenues
3. Accrual of Unrecorded Expenses
4. Accrual of Unrecorded Revenues

ADJUSTMENT TYPE I: EXPIRATION OF UNEXPIRED COSTS

Assets frequently expire because of the passage of time. This first type of adjustment was illustrated in Exhibit 2-1 by the recognition of rent expense in transaction 7b.

Assets may be viewed as bundles of economic services awaiting future use or expiration. It is helpful to think of assets, other than cash and receivables, as prepaid or stored costs that are carried forward to future periods rather than immediately charged against revenue:

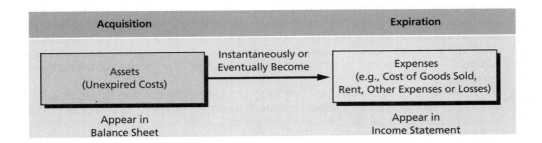

Expenses are used-up assets. An **unexpired cost** is any asset that ordinarily becomes an expense in future periods. Examples in our King Hardware Co. illustration are inventory and prepaid rent. Other examples are equipment and various prepaid expenses such as prepaid insurance and prepaid property taxes. When costs expire, accountants often say they are *written off* to expenses.

The analysis of the inventory and rent transactions in Exhibit 2-1 maintains this distinction of acquisition and expiration. The unexpired costs of inventory and prepaid rent are assets until they are used up and become expenses.

Timing of Asset Expiration

Sometimes services are acquired and used almost instantaneously. Examples are advertising services, interest services (the cost of money, which is a service), miscellaneous supplies, and sales salaries and commissions. Conceptually, these costs should, at least momentarily, be viewed as assets on acquisition before being written off as expenses. For example, suppose there was an eighth transaction in Exhibit 2-1, whereby newspaper advertising was acquired for $1,000 cash. To abide by the acquisition-expiration sequence, the transaction might be analyzed in two phases:

	Assets			= Liabilities +	Stockholders' Equity	
Transaction	Cash +	Other Assets +	Unexpired Advertising =		Paid-in Capital +	Retained Income
8a. Acquire advertising services	−1,000		+1,000 =			
8b. Use advertising services			−1,000 =			−1,000 (expense)

However, services are often acquired and used up so quickly that accountants do not bother recording an asset, such as Unexpired Advertising or Prepaid Rent, for them. Instead, they take a shortcut:

Transaction	Cash	+ Other Assets	= Liabilities	+ Paid-in Capital	+ Retained Income
8 (a) and (b) together	−1,000		=		−1,000 (expense)

Making the entry in two steps instead of one may seem cumbersome, and it is—from a practical bookkeeping viewpoint. But our purpose is not to teach you to be efficient bookkeepers. We want you to develop an orderly way of thinking about what the manager does. The manager acquires goods and services, not expenses per se. These goods and services become expenses as they are used in obtaining revenue.

When does an asset expire and become an expense? Sometimes this question is not easily answered. For example, some accountants believe that research and development costs should be accounted for as assets (listed on balance sheets as "Deferred Research and Development Costs") and written off (charged as an expense) in some systematic manner over a period of years. But the regulators of financial accounting in the United States have ruled that such costs have vague future benefits that are difficult to measure reliably. Thus research costs must be written off as expenses immediately. In cases like this, research costs are not found in balance sheets. This is not always the case, however. Outside the United States, many countries, such as Japan and France, allow research and development to be recorded as an asset.

Depreciation

To keep the expense-adjustment illustration simple, until now we have deliberately ignored the accounting for long-lived assets, such as equipment. Suppose King Hardware Co. had acquired some store equipment for $14,000 on March 1. Equipment is really a bundle of future services that will have a limited useful life. Accountants usually (1) predict the length of the useful life, (2) predict the ultimate **residual value** (the predicted sales value of a long-lived asset at the end of its useful life), and (3) allocate the *cost* of the equipment to the years of its useful life in some systematic way. This process is called the recording of depreciation expense; it applies to physical assets such as buildings, equipment, furniture, and fixtures owned by the entity. (Land is not subject to depreciation.)

The most popular depreciation method for financial reporting is the *straight-line method*, which depreciates an asset by the same amount each year. Suppose the predicted life of the equipment is 10 years and the estimated residual value is $2,000:

$$\text{straight-line depreciation} = \frac{\text{original cost} - \text{estimated residual value}}{\text{years of useful life}}$$

$$= \frac{\$14,000 - \$2,000}{10}$$

$$= \$1,200 \text{ per year, or } \$100 \text{ per month}$$

The essence of the general concept of expense should be clear by now. The purchases and uses of goods and services (e.g., inventories, rent, equipment) ordinarily consist of two basic steps: (1) the *acquisition* of the *assets* (transactions 2, 3, and 7a) and (2) the *expiration* of the assets as *expenses* (transactions 4b and 7b). When these assets expire, the total assets and owners' equity are decreased.

Summary Problem for Your Review

This is an unusually long chapter, so pause. If you have never studied accounting before, or if you studied it long ago, do not proceed until you have solved the following problem. There are no shortcuts. Pushing a pencil is an absolute necessity for becoming comfortable with accounting concepts. The cost-benefit test will easily be met; the value of your gain in knowledge will exceed your investment of time. Another suggestion is to do the work on your own. In particular, do not ask for help from any professional accountants if they introduce any new terms beyond those already covered.

Problem One

The King Hardware Co. transactions for March were analyzed in Exhibit 2-1, page 20. The balance sheet showed the following balances as of March 31, 19X1:

	Assets	Equities
Cash	$ 42,000	
Accounts receivable	90,000	
Inventory	10,000	
Prepaid rent	2,000	
Accounts payable		$ 25,000
Paid-in capital		100,000
Retained income		19,000
	$144,000	$144,000

The following is a summary of the transactions that occurred during the next month, April:

1. Cash collections of accounts receivable, $88,000.
2. Cash payments of accounts payable, $24,000.
3. Acquisitions of inventory on open account, $80,000.
4. Merchandise carried in inventory at a cost of $70,000 was sold on open account for $85,000.
5. Adjustment for recognition of rent expense for April.
6. Some customers paid $3,000 in advance for merchandise that they ordered but did not expect in inventory until mid-May. (What asset must rise? Does this transaction increase liabilities or stockholders' equity?)
7. Total wages of $6,000 (which were ignored for simplicity in March) were paid on four Fridays in April. These payments for employee services were recognized by increasing Wages Expense and decreasing Cash.
8. Wages of $600 were incurred near the end of April, but the employees had not been paid as of April 30. Accordingly, the accountant increased Wages Expense and increased a liability, Accrued Wages Payable.

9. Cash dividends declared by the board of directors and disbursed to stockholders on April 29 equaled $18,000. (What account besides Cash is affected?) As will be explained on page 657, Cash and Retained Income are each decreased by $18,000.

Required

1. Using the *accrual basis* of accounting, prepare an analysis of transactions, employing the equation approach demonstrated in Exhibit 2-1. Be sure to leave plenty of columns for new accounts.
2. Prepare a balance sheet as of April 30, 19X1, and an income statement for the month of April.
3. Prepare a new report, the Statement of Retained Income, which should show the beginning balance in the Retained Income account, followed by a description of any major changes, and end with the balance as of April 30, 19X1.

   Note: Entries 6 through 9 and the statement of retained income have not been explained. However, as a learning step, try to respond to the requirements here anyway. Explanations follow almost immediately.

Solution to Problem One

Part 1. ANALYSIS OF TRANSACTIONS. The answer is in Exhibit 2-2. The first five transactions are straightforward extensions or repetitions of the March transactions, but the rest of the transactions are new. They are discussed in the sections that follow the solution to the second part of this problem.

Parts 2 and 3. PREPARATION OF FINANCIAL STATEMENTS. See Exhibits 2-3, 2-4, and 2-5. The first two of these exhibits show financial statements already described in this chapter: the balance sheet and the income statement. Exhibit 2-5 presents a new statement, the *statement of retained income*, which is merely a formal presentation of the changes in retained income during the reporting period. It starts with the beginning balance, adds net income for the period in question, and deducts cash dividends to arrive at the ending balance. Frequently, this statement is tacked on to the bottom of an income statement. If so, the result is a *combined* statement of income and statement of retained income.

ADJUSTMENT TYPE II: RECOGNITION (EARNING) OF UNEARNED REVENUES

Transaction 6 in Exhibit 2-2 is $3,000 collected in advance from customers for merchandise they ordered. This transaction is an example of **unearned revenue,** sometimes called **deferred revenue.** It is a liability because the retailer is obligated to deliver the goods ordered or to refund the money if the goods are not delivered. Some companies call this account *advances from customers* or *customer deposits*, but it is an unearned revenue account no matter what its label. That is, it is revenue collected in advance that has not yet been earned. Advance collections of rent and magazine subscriptions are other examples.

Exhibit 2-2   King Hardware Co.   Analysis of Transactions (in Dollars) for April 19X1

| | Assets | | | | | Equities | | | | |
| | | | | | | Liabilities | | | Stockholders' Equity | |
Transaction	Cash	+ Accounts Receivable	+ Inventory	+ Prepaid Rent	=	Accounts Payable	+ Accrued Wages Payable	+ Unearned Sales Revenue*	+ Paid-in Capital	+ Retained Income
Bal. 3/31/X1	+42,000	+90,000	+10,000	+2,000	=	+25,000			+100,000	+19,000
1.	+88,000	−88,000			=					
2.	−24,000				=	−24,000				
3.			+80,000		=	+80,000				
4a.		+85,000			=					+85,000 (revenue)
4b.			−70,000		=					−70,000 (expense)
5.				−1,000	=					− 1,000 (expense)
6.	+ 3,000				=			+3,000*		
7.	− 6,000				=					− 6,000 (expense)
8.					=		+600			− 600 (expense)
9.	−18,000				=					−18,000 (dividend)
4/30/X1	+85,000	+87,000	+20,000	+1,000	=	+81,000	+600	+3,000	+100,000	+ 8,400
	193,000				=				193,000	

* Some accountants would call this account "Customer Deposits," "Advances from Customers," "Deferred Sales Revenue," or "Unrealized Sales Revenue."

Exhibit 2-3 King Hardware Company Balance Sheet as of April 30, 19X1

Assets		Liabilities and Stockholders' Equity		
Cash	$ 85,000	Liabilities		
Accounts receivable	87,000	Accounts payable	$ 81,000	
Inventory	20,000	Accrued wages payable	600	
Prepaid rent	1,000	Unearned sales revenue	3,000	$ 84,600
		Stockholders' equity		
		Paid-in capital	$100,000	
		Retained income	8,400	108,400
Total assets	$193,000	Total equities		$193,000

Exhibit 2-4

King Hardware Company

Income Statement (Multiple-Step)*

for the Month Ended April 30, 19X1

Sales		$85,000
Cost of goods sold		70,000
Gross profit		$15,000
Operating expenses		
Rent	$1,000	
Wages	6,600	7,600
Net income		$ 7,400

* A *"single-step" statement* would not draw the gross profit figure but would merely list all the expenses—including cost of goods sold—and deduct the total from sales. *Gross profit* is defined as the excess of sales over the cost of the inventory that was sold. It is sometimes called *gross margin*.

Exhibit 2-5

King Hardware Company

Statement of Retained Income

for the Month Ended April 30, 19X1

Retained income, March 31, 19X1	$19,000
Net income for April	7,400
Total	$26,400
Dividends	18,000
Retained income, April 30, 19X1	$ 8,400

Sometimes it is easier to see how accountants analyze transactions by visualizing the financial positions of both parties to a contract. For instance, consider the rent transaction of March 1. Compare the financial impact on King Hardware Co. with the impact on the landlord who received the rental payment:

	Owner of Property (Landlord, Lessor)				King Hardware Co. (Tenant, Lessee)			
	A	=	L	+	SE	A	= L +	SE
	Cash		Unearned Rent Revenue		Rent Revenue	Cash	Prepaid Rent	Rent Expense
(a) Explicit transaction (advance payment of three months' rent)	+3,000	=	+3,000			−3,000	+3,000 =	
(b) March adjustment (for one month's rent)		=	−1,000		+1,000		−1,000 =	−1,000
(c) April adjustment (for one month's rent)		=	−1,000		+1,000		−1,000 =	−1,000
(d) May adjustment (for one month's rent)		=	−1,000		+1,000		−1,000 =	−1,000

You are already familiar with the King Hardware analysis. The $1,000 monthly entries for King Hardware are examples of the first type of adjustments, the expiration of unexpired costs.

Now study the transactions from the viewpoint of the owner of the rental property. The first transaction recognizes *unearned revenue*, which is a *liability* because the lessor is obligated to deliver the rental services (or to refund the money if the services are not delivered).

As you can see from the preceding table, adjustments for the expiration of unexpired costs (Type I) and for the realization of unearned revenues (Type II) are really mirror images of each other. If one party to a contract has a prepaid expense, the other has unearned revenue. A similar analysis could be conducted for, say, a 3-year fire insurance policy or a 3-year magazine subscription. The buyer recognizes a prepaid expense (asset) and uses adjustments to spread the initial cost to expense over the life of the services. In turn, the seller, such as a magazine publisher, must initially recognize its liability, unearned subscription revenue. The *unearned* revenue is then systematically recognized as *earned* revenue as magazines are delivered throughout the life of the subscription.

You have now seen how two types of adjustments might occur: (1) expiration of unexpired costs and (2) recognition (earning) of unearned revenues. Next we consider the third type of adjustment: accrual of unrecorded expenses, as illustrated by wages.

ADJUSTMENT TYPE III: ACCRUAL OF UNRECORDED EXPENSES

Accrue means to accumulate a receivable or payable during a given period even though no explicit transaction occurs. Examples of accruals are the wages of employees for partial payroll periods and the interest on borrowed money before the interest payment date. The receivables or payables grow as the clock ticks or as some services are continuously acquired and used, so they are said to accrue (accumulate).

Computerized accounting systems can make weekly, daily, or even "real-time" recordings in the accounts for many accruals. However, such frequent entries are often costly and unnecessary. Usually, adjustments are made to bring each expense (and corresponding liability) account up to date just before the formal financial statements are prepared.

Accounting for Payment of Wages

Consider wages. Most companies pay their employees at predetermined times. Here is a sample calendar for April:

Suppose King Hardware Co. pays its employees each Friday for services rendered during that week. For example, wages paid on April 26 would be compensation for the week ended April 26. The cumulative total wages paid on the Fridays during April were $6,000. Although day-to-day and week-to-week procedures may differ from entity to entity, a popular way to account for wages expense is the shortcut procedure described earlier for goods and services that are routinely consumed in the period of their purchase:

	Assets (A) =	Liabilities (L) +	Stockholders' Equity (SE)
	Cash		Wages Expense
7. Routine entry for explicit transactions	−6,000 =		−6,000

Accounting for Accrual of Wages

King Hardware Co.'s wages are $300 per day. In addition to the $6,000 already paid, King Hardware owes $600 for employee services rendered during the last 2 days of April. The employees will not be paid for these services until the next regular weekly payday, May 3, so an accrual is necessary. No matter how simple or complex a set of accounting procedures may be in a particular entity, periodic adjustments ensure that the financial statements adhere to accrual accounting. The tabulation that follows repeats entry 7 for convenience and then adds entry 8:

	A	=	L	+	SE
	Cash		Accrued Wages Payable		Wages Expense
7. Routine entry for explicit transactions	−6,000	=			−6,000
8. Adjustment for implicit transaction, the accrual of unrecorded wages		=	+600		− 600
Total effects	−6,000	=	+600		−6,600

Conceptually, entries 7 and 8 could each be subdivided into the asset acquisition-asset expiration sequence, but this two-step sequence is not generally used in practice for such expenses that represent the immediate consumption of services.

Accrued expenses arise when payment *follows* the rendering of services; prepaid expenses arise when payment *precedes* the services. Other examples of accrued expenses include sales commissions, property taxes, income taxes, and interest on borrowed money. Interest is rent paid for the use of money, just as rent is paid for the use of buildings or automobiles. The interest accumulates (accrues) as time unfolds, regardless of when the actual cash for interest is paid.

ADJUSTMENT TYPE IV: ACCRUAL OF UNRECORDED REVENUES

The final type of adjustment, the realization of revenues that have been earned but not yet recorded as such in the accounts, is not illustrated in the "Summary Problem for Your Review." It is the mirror image of the accrual of unrecorded expenses. Suppose Security State Bank lends cash to King Hardware Co. on a 3-month promissory note for $50,000 with interest at 1% per month payable at maturity. The following tabulation shows the mirror-image effect of the adjustment for interest at the end of the first month (.01 × $50,000 = $500):

Security State Bank (Lender)					King Hardware Co. (Borrower)				
A	=	L	+	SE	A	=	L	+	SE
Accrued Interest Receivable				Interest Revenue			Accrued Interest Payable		Interest Expense
+500	=			+500		=	+500		−500

To recapitulate, Exhibit 2-6 summarizes the four major types of adjustments needed to implement the accrual basis of accounting.

Exhibit 2-6   Four Major Types of Accounting Adjustments Before Preparation of Financial Statements

		Expense		Revenue
Payment Precedes Recognition of Expense or Revenue	I	Expiration of unexpired costs. *Illustration:* The write-off of prepaid rent as rent expense (Exhibit 2-2, p. 29, entry 5)	II	Recognition (earning) of unearned revenues. *Illustration:* The mirror image of Type I, whereby the landlord recognizes rent revenue and decreases unearned rent revenue (rent collected in advance)
Recognition of Expense or Revenue Precedes Payment	III	Accrual of unrecorded expenses. *Illustration:* Wage expense for wages earned by employees but not yet paid (Exhibit 2-2, entry 8)	IV	Accrual of unrecorded revenues. *Illustration:* Interest revenue earned but not yet collected by a financial institution

DIVIDENDS AND RETAINED INCOME

Exhibit 2-2 shows how revenues increase and expenses decrease the retained income portion of stockholders' equity. Transaction 9 shows another type of transaction that affects retained income—payment of dividends.

Dividends Are Not Expenses

Dividends are distributions of assets to stockholders that reduce retained income. (Cash dividends are distributions of *cash* rather than some other asset.) Dividends are not expenses like rent and wages. They should not be deducted from revenues because dividends are not directly related to the generation of sales or the conduct of operations.

The ability to pay dividends is fundamentally caused by profitable operations. Retained income increases as profits accumulate and decreases as dividends occur.

The entire right-hand side of the balance sheet equation can be thought of as claims against the total assets. The liabilities are the claims of creditors. The stockholders' equity represents the claims of owners arising out of their initial investment (paid-in capital) and subsequent profitable operations (retained income). As a company grows, the retained income account can soar enormously if dividends are not paid. Retained income is frequently the largest stockholders' equity account. For example, H.J. Heinz, the food products company, had retained income of $3,633 million in 1994 compared to paid-in capital of only $242 million.

Retained Income Is Not Cash

Although retained income is a result of profitable operations, it is not a pot of cash awaiting distribution to stockholders. Consider the following illustration:

Step 1. Assume an opening balance sheet of:

Cash	$100	Paid-in capital	$100

Step 2. Purchase inventory for $50 cash. The balance sheet now reads:

Cash	$50	Paid-in capital	$100
Inventory	50		
	$100		

Steps 1 and 2 demonstrate a fundamental point. Ownership equity (paid-in capital, here) is an undivided claim against the total assets (in the aggregate). For example, half the shareholders do not have a specific claim on cash, and the other half do not have a specific claim on inventory. Instead, all the shareholders have an undivided claim against (or, if you prefer, an undivided interest in) all the assets.

Step 3. Now sell the inventory for $80, which produces a retained income of $80 – $50 = $30:

Cash	$130	Paid-in capital	$100
		Retained income	30
		Total equities	$130

At this stage, the retained income might be related to a $30 increase in cash. But the $30 in retained income connotes only a *general* claim against *total* assets. This may be clarified by the transaction that follows.

Step 4. Purchase equipment and inventory, in the amounts of $70 and $50, respectively. Now cash is $130 – $70 – $50 = $10:

Cash	$ 10	Paid-in capital	$100
Inventory	50	Retained income	30
Equipment	70		
Total assets	$130	Total equities	$130

To what assets is the $30 in retained income related? Is it linked to Cash, to Inventory, or to Equipment? The answer is all three. This example helps to explain the nature of the Retained Income account. It is a claim, not a pot of gold. You cannot buy a loaf of bread with retained income.

Retained income is increased by profitable operations, but the cash inflow from sales is an increment in assets (see step 3). When the cash inflow takes place, management will use the cash, most often to buy more inventory or equipment (step 4). Retained income (and also paid-in capital) is a general claim against, or undivided interest in, total assets, not a specific claim against cash or against any other particular asset. Do not confuse the assets themselves with the claims against the assets.

Nature of Dividends

As stated earlier, dividends are distributions of assets that reduce ownership claims. The cash assets that are disbursed typically arose from profitable operations. Thus dividends or withdrawals are often spoken of as "distributions of profits" or "distributions of retained income." Dividends are often erroneously described as being "paid *out* of retained income." In reality, cash dividends are distributions of assets that liquidate a portion of the ownership claim. The distribution is made possible by profitable operations.

The amount of cash dividends declared by the board of directors of a company depends on many factors, the least important of which is usually the balance in retained income. Although profitable operations are generally essential, dividend policy is also influenced by the company's cash position and future needs for cash to pay debts or to purchase additional assets. It is also influenced by whether the company is committed to a stable dividend policy or to a policy that normally ties dividends to fluctuations in net income. Under a stable policy, dividends may be paid consistently even if a company encounters a few years of little or no net income.

SOLE PROPRIETORSHIPS AND PARTNERSHIPS

This chapter has focused on the accounting for a corporation, King Hardware Co. However, the basic accounting concepts that underlie the owners' equity are unchanged regardless of whether ownership takes the form of a corporation, a **sole proprietorship**—a business entity with a single owner, or a **partnership**—an organization that joins two or more individuals together as co-owners. However, in proprietorships and partnerships, distinctions between paid-in capital (i.e., the investments by owners) and retained income are rarely made. Compare the possibilities for King Hardware Co. as of April 30:

Owners' Equity for a Corporation		
Stockholders' equity		
Capital stock (paid-in capital)	$100,000	
Retained income	8,400	
Total stockholders' equity		$108,400

Owner's Equity for a Sole Proprietorship	
Alice Walsh, capital	$108,400

Owners' Equity for a Partnership	
Susan Zingler, capital	$ 54,200
John Martin, capital	54,200
Total partners' equity	$108,400

In contrast to corporations, sole proprietorships and partnerships are not legally required to account separately for paid-in capital (i.e., proceeds from issuances of capital stock) and for retained income. Instead, they typically accumulate a single amount for each owner's original investments, subsequent investments, share of net income, and withdrawals. In the case of a sole proprietorship, then, the owner's equity will consist of a lone capital account.

Note that although owners' equity is sometimes called **net worth,** owners' equity is not a measure of the "current value" of the business to an outside buyer. The selling price of a business depends on future profit projections that may have little relationship to the existing assets or equities of the entity as measured by its accounting records.

GENERALLY ACCEPTED ACCOUNTING PRINCIPLES

Accounting is more an art than a science. It is based on a set of principles on which there is general agreement, not on rules that can be "proved."

Auditor's Independent Opinion

The financial statements of publicly held corporations and many other corporations are subject to an *independent audit* that forms the basis for a professional accounting firm's opinion, typically including the following key phrasing:

> In our opinion, such financial statements present fairly, in all material respects, the financial position of Microsoft Corporation and subsidiaries as of June 30, 1993 and 1994, and the results of their operations and their cash flows for each of the 3 years in the period ended June 30, 1994, in conformity with generally accepted accounting principles.

An accounting firm must conduct an audit before it can render the foregoing opinion. An **audit** is an "examination" or in-depth inspection that is made in accordance with generally accepted auditing standards, which have been developed primarily by the American Institute of Certified Public Accountants (AICPA), the leading organization of auditors. An audit includes tests of the accounting records, internal control systems, and other procedures as deemed necessary. After auditing a company, an accountant issues an *independent opinion*—the accountant's testimony that *management's* financial statements are in conformity with generally accepted accounting principles.

The auditor's opinion usually appears at the end of annual reports prepared for the stockholders and other external users. Investors often mistakenly rely on the opinion as an infallible guarantee of financial truth. Somehow accounting is thought to be an exact science, perhaps because of the aura of precision that financial statements possess. But, as noted earlier, accounting is more art than science. The financial reports may appear accurate because of their neatly integrated numbers, but they are the result of a complex measurement process that rests on a huge bundle of assumptions and conventions.

The conventions, rules, and procedures that together make up accepted accounting practice at any given time are called generally accepted accounting principles (GAAP). Accounting principles become "generally accepted" by agreement. Such agreement is not influenced solely by formal logical analysis. Experience, custom, usage, and practical necessity contribute to the set of principles. Accordingly, it might be better to call them *conventions* because principles suggest that they are the product of airtight logic.

FASB and SEC

American GAAP is largely the work of the **Financial Accounting Standards Board (FASB)**. The FASB, consisting of seven full-time members, is an independent creation of the private sector. It is financially supported by various companies and professional accounting associations.

By federal law, the **Securities and Exchange Commission (SEC),** a government agency, has the ultimate responsibility for specifying GAAP for U.S. companies whose stock is held by the general investing public. However, the SEC has informally delegated much rule-making power to the FASB. This public-sector–private-sector relationship may be sketched as follows:

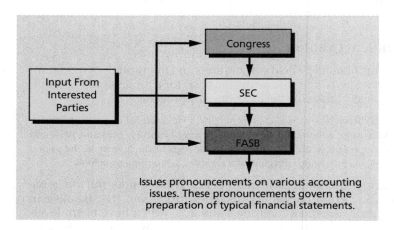

Issues pronouncements on various accounting issues. These pronouncements govern the preparation of typical financial statements.

The FASB issues pronouncements on various accounting issues. These pronouncements govern the preparation of typical financial statements.

Consider this three-tiered structure. Note that Congress can overrule both the SEC and FASB, and the SEC can overrule the FASB. Such undermining of the FASB occurs rarely, but pressure is exerted on all three tiers by corporations and other interested parties if they think an impending pronouncement is "wrong." Hence the setting of accounting principles is a complex process involving heavy interactions among the affected parties: public regulators (Congress and SEC), private regulators (FASB), companies, the public accounting profession, representatives of investors, and other interested groups.

THREE MEASUREMENT CONVENTIONS

Three broad measurement or valuation conventions (principles) underlie accrual accounting: *recognition* (when to record revenue), *matching* and *cost recovery* (when to record expense), and the *stable monetary unit* (what unit of measure to use).

Recognition

The first broad measurement or valuation convention, *recognition*, was discussed earlier in this chapter in the section "Revenues and Expenses." In general, revenue is recognized when the goods or services in question are delivered to customers.

Matching and Cost Recovery

You may often encounter a favorite buzzword in accounting: **matching**. Matching is the relating of accomplishments or revenues (as measured by the selling prices of goods and services delivered) and efforts or expenses (as measured by the cost of goods and services used) to a *particular period* for which a measurement of income is desired. In short, matching is a short description of the accrual basis for measuring income.

Accountants apply matching as follows:

1. Identify the revenue recognized during the period.
2. Link the expenses to the recognized revenue directly (e.g., sales commissions or costs of inventories sold to customers) or indirectly (e.g., wages of janitors and supplies used). The latter expenses are costs of operations during a specific time period that have no measurable benefit for a *future* period.

The heart of recognizing expense is the **cost recovery** concept. That is, assets such as inventories, prepayments, and equipment are carried forward as assets because their costs are expected to be recovered in the form of cash inflows (or reduced cash outflows) in future periods. At the end of each period, the accountant (especially the outside auditor at the end of each year) carefully examines the evidence to be assured that these assets—these unexpired costs—should not be written off as an expense of the current period. For instance, in our chapter example, prepaid rent of $2,000 was carried forward as an asset as of March 31 because the accountant is virtually certain that it represents a future benefit. Why? Because without the prepayment, cash outflows of $2,000 would have to be made for April and May. So the presence of the prepayment is a benefit in the sense that future cash outflows will be reduced by $2,000. Furthermore, future revenue (sales) will be high enough to ensure the recovery of the $2,000.

Stable Monetary Unit

The monetary unit (e.g., the dollar) is the principal means for measuring assets and equities. It is the common denominator for quantifying the effects of a wide variety of transactions. While companies in the United States, Canada, Australia, and New Zealand use the dollar as the mometary unit, in other countries they use the franc, pound, mark, yen, or some other monetary unit.

Such measurement assumes that the monetary unit—the dollar, for example—is an unchanging yardstick. Yet we all know that a 1997 dollar does not have the same purchasing power as a 1987 or 1977 dollar. Therefore, users of accounting statements that include dollars from different years must recognize the limitations of the basic measurement unit.

Accountants have been extensively criticized for not making explicit and formal adjustments to remedy the defects of their measuring unit. In the face of this, some accountants maintain that price-level adjustments would lessen objectivity and would add to the general confusion. They claim that the price-level problem has been exaggerated and that the adjustments would not significantly affect the vast bulk of corporate statements because most accounts are in current or nearly current dollars.

On the other hand, inflation has been steady and its effects are sometimes surprisingly pervasive. Several countries, including Brazil and Argentina, routinely adjust their accounting numbers for the effects of inflation. The most troublesome aspect, however, is how to interpret the results after they are measured. Investors and managers in the United States are accustomed to the conventional statements. The intelligent interpretation of statements adjusted for changes in the price level will require extensive changes in the habits of users.

The body of generally accepted accounting principles contains more than the measurement conventions just discussed. Other major concepts include going concern, objectivity, materiality, and cost benefit. These are discussed in Appendix 2A.

Summary Problem for Your Review

Problem One appeared earlier in this chapter.

Problem Two

The following interpretations and remarks are sometimes encountered regarding financial statements. Do you agree or disagree? Explain fully.

1. "If I purchase 100 shares of the outstanding common stock of General Motors Corporation (or King Hardware Co.), I invest my money directly in that corporation. General Motors must record that transaction."

2. "Sales show the cash coming in from customers and the various expenses show the cash going out for goods and services. The difference is net income."

3. Consider the following recent accounts of Walgreens, the largest U.S. drugstore chain:

Paid-in capital	$ 76,919,000
Retained earnings	1,496,721,000
Total stockholders' equity	$1,573,640,000

A shareholder commented, "Why can't that big drugstore pay higher wages and dividends too? It can use its hundreds of millions of dollars of retained earnings to do so."

4. "The total Walgreens stockholders' equity measures the amount that the shareholders would get today if the corporation were liquidated."

Solution to Problem Two

1. Money is invested directly in a corporation only upon original issuance of the stock by the corporation. For example, 100,000 shares of stock may be issued at $80 per share, bringing in $8 million to the corporation. This is a transaction between the corporation and the stockholders. It affects the corporate financial position:

Cash	$8,000,000	Stockholders' equity	$8,000,000

In turn, 100 shares of that stock may be sold by an original stockholder (A) to another individual (B) for $92 per share. This is a private transaction; no cash comes to the corporation. Of course, the corporation records the fact that 100 shares originally owned by A are now owned by B, but the corporate financial position is unchanged. Accounting focuses on the business entity; the private dealings of the owners have no direct effect on the financial position of the entity and hence are unrecorded except for detailed records of the owners' identities.

2. Cash receipts and disbursements are not the fundamental basis for the accounting recognition of revenues and expenses. Credit, not cash, lubricates the economy. Therefore, if services or goods have been rendered to a customer, a collectible claim to cash in the form of a receivable is deemed sufficient justification for recognizing revenue; similarly, if services or goods have been used up, an obligation in the form of a payable is justification for recognizing expense.

   This approach to the measurement of net income is known as the accrual basis. Revenue is recognized as it is earned and realized. Expenses or losses are recognized when goods or services are used up in the obtaining of revenue (or when such goods or services cannot justifiably be carried forward as an asset because they have no potential future benefit). The expenses and losses are deducted from the revenue, and the result of this matching process is net income, the net increase in stockholders' equity from the conduct of operations.

3. As the chapter indicated, retained earnings is not cash. It is a stockholders' equity account that represents the accumulated increase in ownership claims because of profitable operations. This claim or interest may be partially liquidated by the payment of cash dividends, but a growing company will reinvest cash in sustaining the added investments in receivables, inventories, plant, equipment, and other assets so necessary for expansion. As a result, the ownership claims reflected by retained earnings may become "permanent" in the sense that, as a practical matter, they will never be liquidated as long as the company remains in business.

   This linking of retained earnings and cash is only one example of erroneous interpretation. As a general rule, there is no direct relationship between the individual items on the two sides of the balance sheet. For example, Walgreens had cash of less than $78 million on the above balance sheet date when its retained earnings were nearly $1.5 billion.

4. Stockholders' equity is a difference, the excess of assets over liabilities. If the assets were carried in the accounting records at their liquidating value today, and the liabilities were carried at the exact amounts needed for their extinguishment, the remark would be true. But such valuations would be coincidental because assets are customarily carried at *historical cost* expressed in an unchanging monetary unit. Intervening changes in markets and general price levels in inflationary times may mean that the assets are woefully understated. Investors may make a critical error if they think that balance sheets indicate current values.

   Furthermore, the "market values" for publicly owned shares are usually determined by daily trading conducted in the financial marketplaces such as the New York Stock Exchange. These values are affected by numerous factors including the *expectations* of (a) price appreciation and (b) cash flows in the form of dividends. The focus is on the future; the present and the past are examined only as clues to what may be forthcoming. Therefore the present stockholders' equity is usually of only incidental concern.

   For example, stockholders' equity for Walgreens was $1,573,640,000 ÷ 123,070,536 shares, or $13 per share, while the company's market price per common share fluctuated between $34 and $43.

Highlights to Remember

An underlying structure of concepts, techniques, and conventions provides a basis for accounting practice. Two basic financial statements, the balance sheet (or statement of financial position) and income statement, are presented in this chapter. Their main elements are assets, liabilities, owners' equity, revenues, and expenses. Income statements and balance sheets are linked because the revenues and expenses appearing on income statements are components of stockholders' equity. Revenues increase stockholders' equity; expenses decrease stockholders' equity.

The accrual basis is the heart of accounting. Under accrual accounting revenues are recognized as earned and expenses as incurred rather than as related cash is received or disbursed. Expense should not be confused with the term *cash disbursement*, and revenue should not be confused with the term *cash receipt*.

The balance sheet equation provides a framework for recording accounting transactions. At the end of each accounting period, adjustments must be made so that financial statements may be presented on a full-fledged accrual basis. The major adjustments are for (1) expiration of unexpired costs, (2) recognition (earning) of unearned revenues, (3) accrual of unrecorded expenses, and (4) accrual of unrecorded revenues. After transactions are recorded and adjustments are made, the data can be compiled into financial statements.

Dividends are not expenses; they are distributions of assets that reduce ownership claims. Similarly, retained income is not cash; it is a claim against total assets.

Entities can be organized as corporations, partnerships, or sole proprietorships. The type of organization does not affect most accounting entries. Only the owners' equity section will differ among organizational types.

Three major conventions that affect accounting are recognition, matching and cost recovery, and stable monetary unit. Recognition affects when revenues will be recorded in the income statement; matching and cost recovery specify when expenses will be recorded; and stable monetary units justify use of a unit of currency (the dollar in the United States) to measure accounting transactions.

APPENDIX 2A: ADDITIONAL ACCOUNTING CONCEPTS

This appendix describes several concepts that are prominent parts of the body of generally accepted accounting principles: continuity or going concern, objectivity or verifiability, materiality, conservatism, and cost-benefit.

The Continuity or Going Concern Convention

The **continuity** or **going concern convention** is the assumption that in all ordinary situations an entity persists indefinitely. This notion implies that existing *resources*, such as plant assets, *will be used* to fulfill the general purposes of a continuing entity *rather than sold* in tomorrow's real estate or equipment markets. It also implies that existing liabilities will be paid at maturity in an orderly manner.

Suppose some old specialized equipment has a depreciated cost (i.e., original cost less accumulated depreciation) of $10,000, a replacement cost of $12,000, and a realizable value of $7,000 on the used-equipment market. The continuity convention is often cited as the justification for adhering to acquisition cost (or acquisition cost less depreciation, $10,000 in this example) as the primary basis for valuing assets such as inventories, land, buildings, and equipment. Some critics of these accounting practices believe that such valuations are not as informative as their replacement cost ($12,000) or their realizable values on sale ($7,000). Defenders of using $10,000 as an appropriate asset valuation argue that a going concern will generally use the asset as originally intended. Therefore, the recorded cost (the acquisition cost less depreciation) is the preferable basis for accountability and evaluation of performance. Hence other values are not germane because replacement or disposal will not occur en masse as of the balance sheet date.

The opposite view to this going concern or continuity convention is an immediate-liquidation assumption whereby all items on a balance sheet are valued at the amounts appropriate if the entity's assets were to be sold and its liabilities paid in piecemeal fashion within a few days or months. This liquidation approach to valuation is usually used only when the entity is in severe, near-bankrupt straits.

Objectivity or Verifiability

Users want assurance that the numbers in the financial statements are not fabricated by management or by accountants to mislead or falsify the firm's financial position and performance. Consequently, accountants seek and prize **objectivity** (or **verifiability**) as one of their principal strengths and regard it as an essential characteristic of measurement. A financial statement item is *objective* or *verifiable* if there would be a high extent of consensus among independent measures of the item. For example, the amount paid for assets is usually highly verifiable, but the predicted cost to replace assets often is not.

Many critics of existing accounting practices want to trade objectivity (accuracy) for what they conceive as more relevant or valid information. For example, the accounting literature is peppered with suggestions that accounting should attempt to measure "economic income," even though objectivity may be lessened. This particular suggestion often involves introducing asset valuations at replacement costs when these are higher than historical costs. The accounting profession has generally rejected these suggestions, even when reliable replacement price quotations are available, because no evidence short of a bona fide sale is regarded as sufficient to justify income recognition.

Materiality

Because accounting is a practical art, the practitioner often tempers accounting reports by applying judgments about **materiality.** A financial statement item is not *material* if it is sufficiently small that its omission or misstatement would not mislead a user of the financial statements. Many outlays that should theoretically be recorded as assets are immediately written off as expenses because of their lack of significance. For example, many corporations have a rule that requires the immediate write-off to expense of all outlays under a specified minimum of, say, $100, regardless of the useful life of the asset acquired. In such a case, coat hangers may be acquired that may last indefinitely but may never appear in the balance sheet as assets. The resulting $100 understatement of assets and stockholders' equity would be too trivial to worry about.

When is an item material? There will probably never be a universal clear-cut answer. What is trivial to IBM may be material to Joe's Computer Repair Service. A working rule is that an item is material if its proper accounting would probably affect the decision of a knowledgeable user. In sum, although materiality is an important convention, it is difficult to use anything other than prudent judgment to tell whether an item is material.

The Conservatism Convention

Conservatism has been a hallmark of accounting. In a technical sense, the **conservatism convention** means selecting the method of measurement that yields the gloomiest immediate results. This attitude is reflected in such working rules as "Anticipate no gains, but provide for all possible losses," and "If in doubt, write it off."

Accountants have traditionally regarded the historical costs of acquiring an asset as the ceiling for its valuation. Assets may be written up only upon an exchange, but they may be written down without an exchange. For example, consider *lower-of-cost-or-market* procedures in which inventories are written down when replacement costs decline, but they are never written up when replacement costs increase.

Conservatism has been criticized as being inherently inconsistent. If replacement market prices are sufficiently objective and verifiable to justify write-downs, why aren't they just as valid for write-ups? Furthermore, the critics maintain, conservatism is not a fundamental concept. Accounting reports should try to present the most accurate picture feasible—neither too high nor too low. Accountants defend their attitude by saying that erring in the direction of conservatism would usually have less severe economic consequences than erring in the direction of overstating assets and net income.

Conservatism that leads to understating net income in one period also creates an overstatement of net income in a future period. For example, if a $100 inventory is written down to $80, net income is reduced by $20 in the period of the write-down but *increased* by $20 in the period the inventory is sold.

Cost-Benefit

Accounting systems vary in complexity from the minimum crude records kept to satisfy government authorities to the sophisticated budgeting and feedback schemes that are at the heart of management planning and controlling. As a system is changed, its potential benefits should exceed its additional costs. Often the benefits are difficult to measure but this **cost-benefit criterion** at least implicitly underlies the decisions about the design of accounting systems. Sometimes the reluctance to adopt suggestions for new ways of measuring financial position and performance is because of inertia. More often, it is because the apparent benefits do not exceed the obvious costs of gathering and interpreting the information.

Room for Judgment

Accounting is commonly misunderstood as being a precise discipline that produces exact measurements of a company's financial position and performance. As a result, many individuals regard accountants as little more than mechanical tabulators who grind out financial reports after processing an imposing amount of detail in accordance with stringent predetermined rules. Although accountants take methodical steps with masses of data, their rules of measurement allow much room for judgment. Managers and accountants who exercise this judgment have more influence on financial reporting than is commonly believed. These judgments are guided by the basic concepts, techniques, and conventions called GAAP. Examples of the latter include the basic concepts just discussed. Their meaning will become clearer as these concepts are applied in future chapters.

Chapter 2 focused on the balance sheet equation, the general framework used by accountants to record economic transactions. This appendix focuses on some of the main techniques that accountants use to record the transactions illustrated in the chapter.

The Account

To begin, consider how the accountant would record the King Hardware Co. transactions that were introduced in the chapter. Exhibit 2-1 (p. 20) showed their effects on the elements of the balance sheet equation:

	A		=	L	+	SE
	Cash	Inventory		Accounts Payable		Paid-in Capital
1. Initial investment by owners	+100,000		=			+100,000
2. Acquire inventory for cash	− 75,000	+75,000	=			
3. Acquire inventory on credit		+35,000	=	+35,000		

This balance sheet equation approach emphasizes the concepts, but it can obviously become unwieldy if many transactions occur. You can readily see that changes in the balance sheet equation can occur many times daily. In large businesses, such as in a department store, hundreds or thousands of repetitive transactions occur hourly. In practice, **ledger accounts** must be used to keep track of how these multitudes of transactions affect each particular asset, liability, revenue, expense, and so forth. These accounts used here are simplified versions of those used in practice. These are called T-accounts because they take the form of the capital letter *T*. The preceding transactions would be shown in T-accounts as follows:

Assets		=	Liabilities + Stockholders' Equity	

Cash			**Accounts Payable**	
Increases	Decreases		Decreases	Increases
(1) 100,000	(2) 75,000			(3) 35,000
Bal. 25,000				

Inventory			**Paid-in Capital**	
Increases	Decreases		Decreases	Increases
(2) 75,000				(1) 100,000
(3) 35,000				
Bal. 110,000				

The entries were made in accordance with the rules of a **double-entry system,** whereby each transaction affects at least two accounts. Asset accounts have left-side balances. They are increased by entries on the left side and decreased by entries on the right side.

Liabilities and stockholders' equity accounts have right-side balances. They are increased by entries on the right side and decreased by entries on the left side.

The format of the T-account eliminates the use of negative numbers. Any entry that reduces an account balance is *added* to the side of the account that *decreases* the account balance.

Each T-account summarizes the changes in a particular asset or equity. Each transaction is keyed in some way, such as by the numbering used in this illustration or by date or both. This keying facilitates the rechecking (auditing) process by aiding the tracing of transactions to original sources. A balance of an account is computed by totaling each side of an account and deducting the smaller total amount from the larger. Accounts exist to keep an up-to-date summary of the changes in specific assets and equities.

A balance sheet can be prepared at any time if the accounts are up to date. The necessary information is tabulated in the accounts. For example, the balance sheet after the first three transactions would contain:

	Assets	Liabilities and Stockholders' Equity	
Cash	$ 25,000	Liabilities	
Inventory	110,000	Accounts payable	$ 35,000
		Stockholders' equity	
		Paid-in capital	100,000
Total assets	$135,000	Total equities	$135,000

General Ledger

Exhibit 2-7 is the *general ledger* of King Hardware Co. The **general ledger** is defined as a collection of the group of accounts that supports the items shown in the major financial statements. Exhibit 2-7 is merely a recasting of the facts that were analyzed in Exhibit 2-1. Study Exhibit 2-7 by comparing its analysis of each transaction against its corresponding analysis in Exhibit 2-1.

Debits and Credits

The balance sheet equation has been mentioned often in this chapter. Recall:

A = L + owner's equity	(1)
A = L + paid-in capital + retained income	(2)
A = L + paid-in capital + revenue - expenses	(3)

The accountant often talks about entries in a technical way:

Transposing,

A + expenses = L + paid-in capital + revenue	(4)

Exhibit 2-7 General Ledger of King Hardware Co.

1. Initial investment
2. Acquire inventory for cash
3. Acquire inventory on credit
4a. Sales on credit
4b. Cost of inventory sold
5. Collect from customers
6. Pay accounts of suppliers
7a. Pay rent in advance
7b. Recognize expiration of rental services

Assets
(Increases on Left, Decreases on Right)

Cash

(1)	100,000	(2)	75,000
(5)	30,000	(6)	10,000
		(7a)	3,000
3/31 Bal.	42,000		

Accounts Receivable

(4a)	120,000	(5)	30,000
3/31 Bal.	90,000		

Inventory

(2)	75,000	(4b)	100,000
(3)	35,000		
3/31 Bal.	10,000		

Prepaid Rent

(7a)	3,000	(7b)	1,000
3/31 Bal.	2,000		

Liabilities and Stockholders' Equity
(Decreases on Left, Increases on Right)

Accounts Payable

(6)	10,000	(3)	35,000
		3/31 Bal.	25,000

Paid-In Capital

		(1)	100,000
		3/31 Bal.	100,000

Retained Income

		3/31 Bal.	19,000*

Expense and Revenue Accounts

Sales

		(4a)	120,000

Cost of Goods Sold

(4b)	100,000		

Rent Expense

(7b)	1,000		

* The details of the revenue and expense accounts appear in the income statement. Their net effect is then transferred to a single account, Retained Income, in the balance sheet.

Finally,

$$\text{left side} = \text{right side} \quad (5)$$
$$\text{debit} = \text{credit}$$

Debit means one thing and one thing only—"left side of an account" (not "bad," "something coming," etc.). **Credit** means one thing and one thing only—"right side of an account" (not "good," "something owed," etc.). The word *charge* is often used instead of *debit*, but no single word is used as a synonym for *credit*.

For example, if you asked an accountant what entry to make for transaction 4b, the answer would be: "I would debit (or charge) Cost of Goods Sold for $100,000; and I would credit Inventory for $100,000." Note that the total dollar amounts of the debits (entries on the left side of the account[s] affected) will *always* equal the total dollar amount of credits (entries on the right side of the account[s] affected) because the whole accounting system is based on an equation. The symmetry and power of this analytical debit-credit technique is indeed impressive.

The words *debit* and *credit* have a Latin origin. They were used centuries ago when double-entry bookkeeping was introduced by Pacioli, an Italian monk. Even though *left* and *right* are more descriptive words, *debit* and *credit* are too deeply entrenched to avoid.

Debit and credit are used as verbs, adjectives, or nouns. That is, "debit $1,000 to cash and credit $1,000 to accounts receivable" are examples of uses as verbs, meaning that $1,000 should be placed on the left side of the cash account and on the right side of the accounts receivable account. Similarly, if "a debit is made to cash" or "cash has a debit balance of $12,000," then *debit* is a noun or adjective that describes the status of a particular account.

In our everyday conversation we sometimes use the words *debits* and *credits* in a general sense that may completely diverge from their technical accounting uses. For instance, we may give praise by saying, "She deserves plenty of credit for her good deed" or "That misplay is a debit on his ledger." When you study accounting, forget these general uses and misuses of the words. Merely think right side or left side.

Assets are traditionally carried as left-side balances. Why do assets and expenses both carry debit balances? They carry left-side balances for different reasons. *Expenses* are temporary stockholders' equity accounts. Decreases in stockholders' equity are entered on the left side of the accounts because they offset the normal (i.e., right-side) stockholders' equity balances. Because expenses decrease stockholders' equity, they are carried as left-side balances.

To recapitulate:

Assets		=	Liabilities		+	Stockholders' Equity	
Increase	Decrease		Decrease	Increase		Decrease	Increase
+	–		–	+		–	+
debit	credit		debit	credit		debit	credit
left	right		left	right		left	right

Because revenues increase stockholders' equity, they are recorded as credits. Because expenses decrease stockholders' equity, they are recorded as debits.

Fundamental Assignment Material

2-A1 Balance Sheet Equation

For each of the following independent cases, compute the amounts (in thousands) for the items indicated by letters, and show your supporting computations:

	Case 1	Case 2	Case 3
	1	*2*	*3*
Revenues	$140	$ K	$300
Expenses	110	20	270
Dividends declared	–0–	5	Q
Additional investment by stockholders	–0–	30	35
Net income	E	20	P
Retained income			
Beginning of year	40	60	100
End of year	D	J	110
Paid-in capital			
Beginning of year	15	10	N
End of year	C	H	85
Total assets			
Beginning of year	85	F	L
End of year	95	275	M
Total liabilities			
Beginning of year	A	90	105
End of year	B	G	95

2-A2 Analysis of Transactions, Preparation of Statements

The Ekern Company was incorporated on April 1, 19X5. Ekern had ten holders of common stock. Elke Ekern, who was the president and chief executive officer, held 51% of the shares. The company rented space in chain discount stores and specialized in selling ladies' shoes. Ekern's first location was in a store of Nordic Market Centers, Inc.

The following events occurred during April:

1. The company was incorporated. Common stockholders invested $90,000 cash.
2. Purchased merchandise inventory for cash, $35,000.
3. Purchased merchandise inventory on open account, $25,000.
4. Merchandise carried in inventory at a cost of $37,000 was sold for cash for $25,000 and on open account for $65,000, a grand total of $90,000. Ekern (not Nordic) carries and collects these accounts receivable.
5. Collection of the above accounts receivable, $15,000.
6. Payments of accounts payable, $18,000. See transaction 3.
7. Special display equipment and fixtures were acquired on April 1 for $36,000. Their expected useful life was 36 months with no terminal scrap value. Straight-line depreciation was adopted. This equipment was removable. Ekern paid $12,000 as a down payment and signed a promissory note for $24,000.
8. On April 1, Ekern signed a rental agreement with Nordic. The agreement called for a flat $2,000 per month, payable quarterly in advance. Therefore Ekern paid $6,000 cash on April 1.

9. The rental agreement also called for a payment of 10% of all sales. This payment was in addition to the flat $2,000 per month. In this way, Nordic would share in any success of the venture and be compensated for general services such as cleaning and utilities. This payment was to be made in cash on the last day of each month as soon as the sales for the month were tabulated. Therefore, Ekern made the payment on April 30.

10. Wages, salaries, and sales commissions were all paid in cash for all earnings by employees. The amount was $38,000.

11. Depreciation expense was recognized. See transaction 7.

12. The expiration of an appropriate amount of prepaid rental services was recognized. See transaction 8.

Required

1. Prepare an analysis of Ekern Company's transactions, employing the equation approach demonstrated in Exhibit 2-1. Two additional columns will be needed: Equipment and Fixtures and Note Payable. Show all amounts in thousands.

2. Prepare a balance sheet as of April 30, 19X5, and an income statement for the month of April. Ignore income taxes.

3. Given these sparse facts, analyze Ekern's performance for April and its financial position as of April 30, 19X5.

2-A3 Cash Basis Versus Accrual Basis

Refer to the preceding problem. If Ekern Company measured income on the cash basis, what revenue would be reported for April? Which basis (accrual or cash) provides a better measure of revenue? Why?

2-B1 Balance Sheet Equation

Micron Technology is one of the leading producers of semiconductor components. Its net income grew from $7 million in 1985 to more than $1.6 billion in 1994. The company's actual data (in millions of dollars) follow for its fiscal year ended September 1, 1994:

Assets, beginning of period	$ 965.7
Assets, end of period	E
Liabilities, beginning of period	A
Liabilities, end of period	480.4
Paid-in capital, beginning of period	357.0
Paid-in capital, end of period	D
Retained earnings, beginning of period	282.5
Retained earnings, end of period	C
Revenues	1,628.6
Costs and expenses	B
Net income	400.5
Dividends	12.2
Additional investments by stockholders	21.5

Find the unknowns (in millions), showing computations to support your answers.

2-B2 Analysis of Transactions, Preparation of Statements

Hino Motors has maintained its top position in the sales of medium- and heavy-duty diesel trucks in Japan since 1973. The company's actual condensed balance sheet data, March 31, 1994, follows (in billions of Japanese yen):

Assets		Equities	
Cash	¥ 52	Accounts payable	¥ 84
Accounts receivable	64	Other liabilities	86
Inventories	27		
Prepaid expenses and other assets	60	Paid-in capital	44
Property, plant, and equipment	160	Retained earnings	149
Total	¥ 363	Total	¥ 363

The following summarizes some major transactions during April 1994 (in billions of yen):

1. Trucks carried in inventory at a cost of ¥30 were sold for cash of ¥20 and on open account of ¥50, a grand total of ¥70.
2. Acquired inventory on account, ¥50.
3. Collected receivables, ¥30.
4. On April 2, used ¥25 cash to prepay some rent and insurance for 1995.
5. Payments on accounts payable (for inventories), ¥45.
6. Paid selling and administrative expenses in cash, ¥10.
7. A total of ¥9 of prepaid expenses for rent and insurance expired in April 1994.
8. Depreciation expense of ¥18 was recognized for April.

Required

1. Prepare an analysis of the Hino Motors transactions, employing the equation approach demonstrated in Exhibit 2-1. Show all amounts in billions of yen. (For simplicity, only a few major transactions are illustrated here.)
2. Prepare a statement of earnings for the month ended April 30, 1994, and a balance sheet as of April 30, 1994. Ignore income taxes.

2-B3 Cash Basis Versus Accrual Basis
Refer to the preceding problem. If Hino Motors measured income on the cash basis, what revenue would be reported for April? Which basis (accrual or cash) provides a better measure of revenue? Why?

Additional Assignment Material
Questions

2-1 What types of questions are answered by the income statement and balance sheet?

2-2 Criticize: "Assets are things of value owned by an organization."

2-3 How are the income statement and balance sheet related?

2-4 Criticize: "Net income is the difference in the ownership capital account balances at two points in time."

2-5 Distinguish between the accrual basis and the cash basis.

2-6 How do adjusting entries differ from routine entries?

2-7 Explain why advertising should be viewed as an asset on acquisition.

2-8 Why is it better to refer to the *costs*, rather than *values*, of assets such as plant or inventories?

2-9 "Depreciation is cost allocation, not valuation." Do you agree? Explain.

2-10 Criticize: "As a stockholder, I have a right to more dividends. You have millions stashed away in retained earnings. It's about time that you let the true owners get their hands on that pot of gold."

2-11 Criticize: "Dividends are distributions of profits."

2-12 Explain the relationship between the FASB and the SEC.

2-13 What is the major criticism of the dollar as the principal accounting measure?

2-14 What does the accountant mean by *going concern*?

2-15 What does the accountant mean by *objectivity*?

2-16 What is the role of cost-benefit (economic feasibility) in the development of accounting principles?

2-17 True or False
Use *T* or *F* to indicate whether each of the following statements is true or false.

1. Cash should be classified as a stockholders' equity item.
2. Retained earnings should be accounted for as an asset item.
3. Machinery used in the business should be recorded at replacement cost.
4. The cash balance is the best evidence of stockholders' equity.
5. It is not possible to determine changes in the condition of a business from a single balance sheet.
6. From a single balance sheet, you can find stockholders' equity for a period but not for a specific day.

2-18 Nature of Retained Income
This is an exercise on the relationships among assets, liabilities, and ownership equities. The numbers are small, but the underlying concepts are large.

1. Prepare an opening balance sheet of:

Cash	$1,400	Paid-in capital	$1,400

2. Purchase inventory for $600 cash. Prepare a balance sheet. A heading is unnecessary in this and subsequent requirements.
3. Sell the entire inventory for $850 cash. Prepare a balance sheet. Where is the retained income in terms of relationships within the balance sheet? That is, what is the meaning of the retained income? Explain in your own words.
4. Buy inventory for $400 cash and equipment for $750 cash. Prepare a balance sheet. Where is the retained income in terms of relationships within the balance sheet? That is, what is the meaning of the retained income? Explain in your own words.
5. Buy inventory for $450 on open account. Prepare a balance sheet. Where is the retained income and account payable in terms of the relationships within the balance sheet? That is, what is the meaning of the account payable and the retained income? Explain in your own words.

2-19 Income Statement
Here is a proposed income statement of an antiques dealer:

Rhodes Antiques
Statement of Profit and Loss, December 31, 19X6

Revenues		
Sales	$1,300,000	
Increase in market value of land and building	200,000	$1,500,000
Deduct expenses		
Advertising	$ 100,000	
Sales commissions	60,000	
Utilities	20,000	
Wages	150,000	
Dividends	100,000	
Cost of antiques purchased	800,000	1,230,000
Net profit		$ 270,000

List and describe any shortcomings of this statement.

2-20 Customer and Airline

Suppose Levitz Furniture Company decided to hold a managers' meeting in Hawaii in February. To take advantage of special fares, Levitz purchased airline tickets in advance from American Airlines at a total cost of $90,000. These were acquired on December 1 for cash.

Using the balance sheet equation format, analyze the impact of the December payment and the February travel on the financial position of both Levitz and American.

2-21 Tenant and Landlord

The Handy Hardware Company, a retail hardware store, pays quarterly rent on its store at the beginning of each quarter. The rent per quarter is $9,000. The owner of the building in which the store is located is the Barker Corporation.

Using the balance sheet equation format, analyze the effects of the following on the tenant's and the landlord's financial position:

1. Handy Hardware pays $9,000 rent on July 1.
2. Adjustment for July.
3. Adjustment for August.
4. Adjustment for September.

2-22 Find Unknowns

The following data pertain to Great Barrier Excursions. Total assets at January 1, 19X1, were $100,000; at December 31, 19X1, $120,000. During 19X1, sales were $260,000, cash dividends were $14,000, and operating expenses (exclusive of costs of goods sold) were $50,000. Total liabilities at December 31, 19X1, were $55,000; at January 1, 19X1, $40,000. There was no additional capital paid in during 19X1.

(These need not be computed in any particular order.)
Calculate the following items.

1. Stockholders' equity, for January 1, 19X1
2. Net income for 19X1
3. Cost of goods sold for 19X1

2-23 Balance Sheet Equation; Solving for Unknowns

Compute the unknowns (V, W, X, Y, and Z) in each of the individual cases, Columns 1 through 7.

Given	1	2	3	4	5	6	7
Assets at beginning of period		$9,000				Z	$ 8,200
Assets at end of period		11,000					9,600
Liabilities at beginning of period		6,000				$12,000	4,000
Liabilities at end of period		Y					6,000
Stockholders' equity at beginning of period	$7,000	Z				V	X
Stockholders' equity at end of period	X	5,000				10,000	W
Sales			$15,000		X	14,000	20,000
Inventory at beginning of period			6,000	$ 8,000		Y	
Inventory at end of period			7,000	7,000		7,000	
Purchase of inventory			10,000	12,000		6,000	
Gross profit			Y		3,000	6,000	V
Cost of goods sold*			X	X	4,500	X	Z
Other expenses			4,000			4,000	5,000
Net profit	3,000	X	Z			W	Y
Dividends	2,000	–0–				1,500	400
Additional investments by stockholders						5,000	–0–

* Note that cost of goods sold = beginning inventory + purchases – ending inventory.

2-24 Fundamental Transaction Analysis and Preparation of Statements

Three former college classmates have decided to pool a variety of work experiences by opening a clothing store. The business has been incorporated as The Clothes Hanger. The following transactions occurred during March.

1. On March 1, 19X5, each of the three invested $9,000 in cash in exchange for 1,000 shares of stock each.
2. The corporation quickly acquired $40,000 in inventory, half of which had to be paid for in cash. The other half was acquired on open accounts that were payable after 30 days.
3. A store was rented for $500 monthly. A lease was signed for 1 year on March 1. The first 2 months' rent were paid in advance. Other payments were to be made on the second of each month.
4. Advertising during March was purchased on open account for $3,000 from a newspaper owned by one of the stockholders. Additional advertising services of $6,000 were acquired for cash.

5. Sales were $60,000. Merchandise was sold for twice its purchase cost. Seventy-five percent of the sales were on open account.

6. Wages and salaries incurred in March amounted to $11,000, of which $5,000 was paid.

7. Miscellaneous services paid for in cash were $1,510.

8. On March 1, fixtures and equipment were purchased for $6,000 with a down-payment of $1,000 plus a $5,000 note payable in one year.

9. See transaction 8 and make the March 31 adjustment for interest expense *accrued* at 9.6%. (The interest is not *due* until the note matures.)

10. See transaction 8 and make the March 31 adjustment for depreciation expense on a straight-line basis. The estimated life of the fixtures and equipment is 10 years with no expected terminal scrap value. Straight-line depreciation here would be $6,000 ÷ 10 years = $600 per year, or $50 per month.

11. Cash dividends of $400 were declared and disbursed to stockholders on March 30.

Required

1. Using the accrual basis of accounting, prepare an analysis of transactions, employing the equation approach demonstrated in Exhibit 2-1. Place your analysis sideways; to save space, use abbreviated headings. Work slowly. Use the following headings: Cash, Accounts Receivable, Inventory, Prepaid Rent, Fixtures and Equipment, Accounts Payable, Notes Payable, Accrued Wages Payable, Accrued Interest Payable, Paid-in Capital, and Retained Income.

2. Prepare a balance sheet and a multiple-step income statement. Also prepare a statement of retained income.

3. What advice would you give the owners based on the information compiled in the financial statements?

2-25 Debits and Credits
Study Appendix 2B. Determine for the following transactions whether the account *named in parentheses* is to be debited or credited.

1. Sold merchandise (Merchandise Inventory), $1,000.
2. Paid Johnson Associates $3,000 owed them (Accounts Payable).
3. Paid dividends (Cash), $500.
4. Bought merchandise on account (Merchandise Inventory), $3,000.
5. Received cash from customers on accounts due (Accounts Receivable), $2,000.
6. Bought merchandise on open account (Accounts Payable), $5,000.
7. Borrowed money from a bank (Notes Payable), $12,000.

2-26 True or False
Study Appendix 2B. Use *T* or *F* to indicate whether each of the following statements is true or false. For each false statement, explain why it is false.

1. Decreases in accounts must be shown on the debit side.
2. Both increases in liabilities and decreases in assets should be entered on the right.
3. Equipment purchases for cash should be debited to Equipment and credited to Cash.
4. Asset credits should be on the right and liability credits on the left.
5. Payments on mortgages should be debited to Cash and credited to Mortgages Payable. Mortgages are long-term debts.
6. Debit entries must always be recorded on the left.
7. Money borrowed from the bank should be credited to Cash and debited to Notes Payable.

8. Purchase of inventory on account should be credited to Inventory and debited to Accounts Payable.

9. Decreases in liability accounts should be recorded on the right.

10. Increases in asset accounts must always be entered on the left.

11. Increases in stockholders' equity always should be entered as credits.

2-27 Use of T-Accounts
Study Appendix 2B. Refer to Problem 2-A2. Make entries for April in T-accounts. Key your entries and check to see that the ending balances agree with the financial statements.

2-28 Use of T-Accounts
Study Appendix 2B. Refer to Problem One of the "Summary Problems for Your Review." The transactions are analyzed in Exhibit 2-2, page 29. Make entries in T-accounts and check to see that the ending balances agree with the financial statements in Exhibits 2-3, 2-4, 2-5 on page 30.

2-29 Use of T-Accounts
Study Appendix 2B. Refer to Problem 2-24. Use T-accounts to present an analysis of March transactions. Key your entries and check to see that the ending balances agree with the financial statements.

2-30 Measurement of Income for Tax and Other Purposes
The following are the summarized transactions of Dr. Sally Schwager, a dentist, for 19X5, her first year in practice.

1. Acquired equipment and furniture for $60,000. Its expected useful life is 5 years. Straight-line depreciation will be used, assuming zero terminal disposal value.

2. Fees collected, $81,000. These fees included $2,000 paid in advance by some patients on December 31, 19X5.

3. Rent is paid at the rate of $500 monthly, payable quarterly on the 25th of March, June, September, and December for the following quarter. Total disbursements during 19X5 for rent were $7,500 including an initial payent on January 1.

4. Fees billed but uncollected, December 31, 19X5, $20,000.

5. Utilities expense paid in cash, $600. Additional utility bills unpaid at December 31, 19X5, $100.

6. Salaries expense of dental assistant and secretary, $16,000 paid in cash. In addition, $1,000 was earned but unpaid on December 31, 19X5.

Dr. Schwager may elect either the cash basis or the accrual basis of measuring income for income tax purposes, provided that she uses it consistently in subsequent years. Under either alternative, the original cost of the equipment and furniture must be written off over its 5-year useful life rather than being regarded as a lump-sum expense in the first year.

1. Prepare income statements on both the cash and accrual bases, using one column for each basis.

2. Which basis do you prefer as a measure of Dr. Schwager's performance? Why? What do you think is the justification for the government's allowing the use of the cash basis for income tax purposes?

2-31 Balance Sheet Effects
The Wells Fargo Bank showed the following items (among others) on its balance sheet at January 1, 1994:

Cash	$ 2,644,000,000
Total deposits	$41,644,000,000

1. Suppose you made a deposit of $1,000 in the bank. How would each of the bank's assets and equities be affected? How much would each of your personal assets and equities be affected? Be specific.

2. Suppose Wells Fargo makes an $900,000 loan to a local hospital for remodeling. What would be the effect on each of the bank's assets and equities immediately after the loan is made? Be specific.

3. Suppose you borrowed $10,000 from Wells Fargo on a personal loan. How would such a transaction affect each of your personal assets and equities?

2-32 Preparation of Balance Sheet

Georgia-Pacific Corporation is a large producer of timber, wood products, pulp, and paper. Its annual report included the following balance sheet items at December 31 1994 (in millions of dollars):

Various notes payable	$ 915
Cash	(1)
Total stockholders' equity	(2)
Total liabilities	(3)
Long-term debt	4,157
Accounts receivable	377
Common stock	71
Inventories	1,202
Accounts payable	582
Property, plant, and equipment	5,448
Additional stockholders' equity	2,331
Other assets	3,477
Other liabilities	2,489
Total assets	10,545

Prepare a condensed balance sheet including amounts for

1. Cash. What do you think of its relative size?
2. Total stockholders' equity.
3. Total liabilities.

2-33 Net Income and Retained Income

McDonald's Corporation is a well-known fast-foods restaurant company. The following data are from its 1993 annual report (in thousands):

McDonald's Corporation

Retained earnings,		Dividends paid	$ 197,200
end of year	$7,612,600	General, administrative,	
Revenues	7,408,100	and selling expenses	941,100
Interest and other non-		Retained earnings,	
operating expenses	308,300	beginning of year	6,727,300
Income tax expense	593,200	Other operating expenses	1,456,700
Food and packaging			
expense	1,735,100		
Wages and salaries	1,291,200		

1. Prepare the following for the year:
    a. Income statement. The final three lines of the income statement were labeled as *income before provision for income taxes, provision for income tax expense,* and *net income.*
    b. Statement of retained income.
2. Comment briefly on the relative size of the cash dividend.

2-34 Earnings Statement, Retained Earnings

The Procter & Gamble Company has many well-known products, including Tide, Crest, Jif, and Prell. The following is a reproduction of the terms and amounts in the financial statements contained in a recent annual report regarding the fiscal year ended June 30, 1994 (in millions):

Net sales and other income	$30,544	Retained earnings at	
Cash	2,373	beginning of year	$6,248
Interest expense	482	Cost of products sold	17,355
Income taxes	1,135	Dividends to shareholders	963
Accounts payable—trade	2,604	Marketing, administrative,	
		and other expenses	9,361

Choose the relevant data and prepare (1) the income statement for the fiscal year and (2) the statement of retained income for the fiscal year. The final three lines of the income statement were labeled as *earnings before income taxes, income taxes,* and *net earnings.*

CHAPTER 3

THE MATHEMATICS OF PROJECT FINANCE

3.1 APPLICATION OF FINANCIAL MATH TO PROJECTS

Understanding the time value of money is crucial for the project manager. It is used in all forms of debt and equity project financing. It applies to the evaluation of various project cash flows that occur at differing periods of time and it enables projects to be ranked using a common standard of money measurement.

Many people fear that time value of money calculations are difficult to master and understand. Luckily, the availability of inexpensive financial calculators has resolved these learning dilemmas.

The following reading is from *Basic Financial Management* by Keown, Scott, Martin, and Petty. It provides an overview of the mathematics of project finance. It introduces the concepts and skills needed to apply time value of money concepts to projects. The chapter also assumes that the student will use a financial calculator or the interest tables listed as appendices at the end of the book.

3.2 THE MATHEMATICS OF FINANCE

COMPOUND INTEREST

Most of us encounter the concept of compound interest at an early age. Anyone who has ever had a savings account or purchased a government savings bond has received compound interest. **Compound interest** occurs when interest paid on the investment during the first period is added to the principal, then, during the second period, interest is earned on this new sum.

For example, suppose we place $100 in a savings account that pays 6 percent interest, compounded annually. How will our savings grow? At the end of the first year we have earned 6 percent, or $6 on our initial deposit of $100, giving us a total of $106 in our savings account. The mathematical formula illustrating this phenomenon is

$$FV_1 = PV(1 + i) \tag{3-1}$$

where FV_1 = the future value of the investment at the end of one year
$\quad\quad i$ = the annual interest (or discount) rate
$\quad\quad PV$ = the present value, or original amount invested at the beginning of the first year

In our example

$$
\begin{aligned}
FV_1 &= PV(1 + i) \\
&= \$100(1 + .06) \\
&= \$100(1.06) \\
&= \$106
\end{aligned}
\tag{3-1}
$$

Carrying these calculations one period further, we find that we now earn the 6 percent interest on a principal of $106, which means we earn $6.36 in interest during the second year. Why do we earn more interest during the second year than we did during the first? Simply because we now earn interest on the sum of the original principal, or present value, and the interest we earned in the first year. In effect, we are now earning interest on interest; this is the concept of compound interest. Examining the mathematical formula illustrating the earning of interest in the second year, we find

$$FV_2 = FV_1(1 + i) \tag{3-2}$$

which for our example, gives

$$
\begin{aligned}
FV_2 &= \$106(1.06) \\
&= \$112.36
\end{aligned}
$$

Looking back at equation (3-1) we can see that FV_1, or $106, is actually equal to $PV(1 + i)$, or $100 (1 + .06). If we substitute these values into equation (3-2), we get

$$
\begin{aligned}
FV_2 &= PV(1 + i)(1 + i) \\
&= PV(1 + i)^2
\end{aligned}
\tag{3-3}
$$

Carrying this forward into the third year, we find that we enter the year with $112.36 and we earn 6 percent, or $6.74 in interest, giving us a total of $119.10 in our savings account. Expressing this mathematically

$$
\begin{aligned}
FV_3 &= FV_2(1 + i) \\
&= \$112.36(1.06) \\
&= \$119.10
\end{aligned}
\tag{3-4}
$$

If we substitute the value in equation (3-3) for FV_2 into equation (3-4), we find

$$
\begin{aligned}
FV_3 &= PV(1 + i)(1 + i)(1 + i) \\
&= PV(1 + vi)^3
\end{aligned}
\tag{3-5}
$$

By now a pattern is beginning to be evident. We can generalize this formula to illustrate the value of our investment if it is compounded annually at a rate of i for n years to be

$$FV_n = PV(1 + i)^n \tag{3-6}$$

Table 3-1 Illustration of Compound Interest Calculations			
Year	Beginning Value	Interest Earned	Ending Value
1	$100.00	$ 6.00	$106.00
2	106.00	6.36	112.36
3	112.36	6.74	119.10
4	119.10	7.15	126.25
5	126.25	7.57	133.82
6	133.82	8.03	141.85
7	141.85	8.51	150.36
8	150.36	9.02	159.38
9	159.38	9.57	168.95
10	168.95	10.13	179.08

where FV_n = the future value of the investment at the end of n years

n = the number of years during which the compounding occurs

i = the annual interest (or discount) rate

PV = the present value or original amount invested at the beginning of the first year

Table 3-1 illustrates how this investment of $100 would continue to grow for the first ten years at a compound interest rate of 6 percent. Notice how the amount of interest earned annually increases each year. Again, the reason is that each year interest is received on the sum of the original investment plus any interest earned in the past.

When we examine the relationship between the number of years an initial investment is compounded for and its future value graphically, as shown in Figure 3-1, we see that we can increase the future value of an investment by increasing the number of years we let it compound or by compounding it at a higher interest rate.

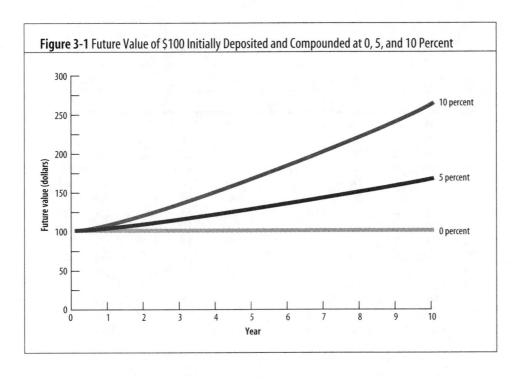

Figure 3-1 Future Value of $100 Initially Deposited and Compounded at 0, 5, and 10 Percent

We can also see this from equation (3-6), since an increase in either i or n while PV is held constant will result in an increase in FV_n.

EXAMPLE

If we place $1,000 in a savings account paying 5 percent interest compounded annually, how much will our account accrue to in ten years? Substituting $PV = \$1000$, $i = 5$ percent, and $n = 10$ years into equation (3-6), we get

$$FV_n = PV(1 + i)^n \qquad (3\text{-}6)$$
$$= \$1000(1 + .05)^{10}$$
$$= \$1000(1.62889)$$
$$= \$1628.89$$

Thus, at the end of ten years, we will have $1,628.89 in our savings account.

As the determination of future value can be quite time consuming when an investment is held for a number of years, **the future-value interest factor** for i and n (**FVIF$_{i,n}$**), defined as $(1 + i)^n$, has been compiled in the back of the book for various values of i and n. An abbreviated compound interest or future-value interest factor table appears in Table 3-2, with a more comprehensive version of this table appearing in Appendix B at the back of this book. Alternatively, the FVIF$_{i,n}$ values could easily be determined using a calculator. Note that the compounding factors given in these tables represent the value of $1 compounded at rate i at the *end* of the nth period. Thus, to calculate the future value of an initial investment, we need only determine the FVIF$_{i,n}$ using a calculator or the tables in Appendix B at the end of the text and multiply this times the initial investment. In effect, we can rewrite equation (3-6) as follows:

$$FV_n = PV(FVIF_{i,n}) \qquad (3\text{-}6a)$$

Table 3-2 $FVIF_{i,n}$ or the Compound Sum of $1

n	1%	2%	3%	4%	5%	6%	7%	8%	9%	10%
1	1.010	1.020	1.030	1.040	1.050	1.060	1.070	1.080	1.090	1.100
2	1.020	1.040	1.061	1.082	1.102	1.124	1.145	1.166	1.188	1.210
3	1.030	1.061	1.093	1.125	1.158	1.191	1.225	1.260	1.295	1.331
4	1.041	1.082	1.126	1.170	1.216	1.262	1.311	1.360	1.412	1.464
5	1.051	1.104	1.159	1.217	1.276	1.338	1.403	1.469	1.539	1.611
6	1.062	1.126	1.194	1.265	1.340	1.419	1.501	1.587	1.677	1.772
7	1.072	1.149	1.230	1.316	1.407	1.504	1.606	1.714	1.828	1.949
8	1.083	1.172	1.267	1.369	1.477	1.594	1.718	1.851	1.993	2.144
9	1.094	1.195	1.305	1.423	1.551	1.689	1.838	1.999	2.172	2.358
10	1.105	1.219	1.344	1.480	1.629	1.791	1.967	2.159	2.367	2.594
11	1.116	1.243	1.384	1.539	1.710	1.898	2.105	2.332	2.580	2.853
12	1.127	1.268	1.426	1.601	1.796	2.012	2.252	2.518	2.813	3.138
13	1.138	1.294	1.469	1.665	1.886	2.133	2.410	2.720	3.066	3.452
14	1.149	1.319	1.513	1.732	1.980	2.261	2.579	2.937	3.342	3.797
15	1.161	1.346	1.558	1.801	2.079	2.397	2.759	3.172	3.642	4.177

If we invest $500 in a bank where it will earn 8 percent compounded annually, how much will it be worth at the end of seven years? Looking at Table 3-2 in the row $n = 7$ and column $i = 8\%$, we find that $FVIF_{8\%, 7yr}$ has a value of 1.714. Substituting this in equation (3-6a), we find

$$FV_n = PV(FVIF_{8\%,\ 7yr}) \qquad\qquad (3\text{-}6a)$$
$$= \$500(1.714)$$
$$= \$857$$

Thus we will have $857 at the end of seven years.

In the future we will find several uses for equation (3-6); not only will we find the future value of an investment, but we can also solve for *PV, i,* or *n*. In any case, we will be given three of the four variables and will have to solve for the fourth.

How many years will it take for an initial investment of $300 to grow to $774 if it is invested at 9 percent compounded annually? In this problem we know the initial investment, $PV = \$300$; the future value, $FV_n = \$774$; the compound growth rate, $i = 9$ percent, and we are solving for the number of years it must compound for, $n = ?$ Substituting the known values in equation (3-6), we find

$$FV_n = PV(1 + i)^n \qquad\qquad (3\text{-}6)$$
$$\$774 = \$300(1 + .09)^n$$
$$2.58 = (1 + .09)^n$$

Thus, we are looking for a value of 2.58 in the $FVIF_{i,n}$ tables, and we know it must be in the 9% column. Looking down the 9% column for the value closest to 2.58, we find that it occurs in the $n = 11$ row. Thus it will take eleven years for an initial investment of $300 to grow to $774 if it is invested at 9 percent compounded annually.

At what rate must $100 be compounded annually for it to grow to $179.10 in ten years? In this case we know the initial investment, $PV = \$100$; the future value of this investment at the end of *n* years, $FV_n = \$179.10$; and the number of years that the initial investment will compound for, $n = 10$ years. Substituting into equation (3-6), we get

$$FV_n = PV(1 + i)^n \qquad\qquad (3\text{-}6)$$
$$\$179.10 = \$100(1 + i)^{10}$$
$$1.791 = (1 + i)^{10}$$

We know we are looking in the $n = 10$ row of the $FVIF_{i,n}$ tables for a value of 1.791, and we find this in the $i = 6\%$ column. Thus, if we want our initial investment of $100 to accrue to $179.10 in 10 years, we must invest it at 6 percent.

Moving Money Through Time with the Aid of a Financial Calculator

Time value of money calculations can be made simple with the aid of a *financial calculator.* In solving time value of money problems with a financial calculator, you will be given three of four variables and will have to solve for the fourth. Before presenting any solutions using a financial calculator, we will introduce the calculator's five most common keys. (In most time value of money problems, only four of these keys are relevant.) These keys are:

Menu Key	Description
N	Stores (or calculates) the total number of payments or compounding periods.
I/Y	Stores (or calculates) the interest or discount rate.
PV	Stores (or calculates) the present value of a cash flow or series of cash flows.
FV	Stores (or calculates) the future value, that is, the dollar amount of a final cash flow or the compound value of a single flow or series of cash flows.
PMT	Stores (or calculates) the dollar amount of each annuity payment deposited or received at the end of each year.

When you use a financial calculator, remember that outflows generally have to be entered as negative numbers. In general, each problem will have two cash flows: one an outflow with a negative value, and one an inflow with a positive value. The idea is that you deposit money in the bank at some point in time (an outflow), and at some other point in time you take money out of the bank (an inflow). Also, every calculator operates a bit differently with respect to entering variables. Needless to say, it is a good idea to familiarize yourself with exactly how your calculator functions.

As stated above, in any problem you will be given three of four variables. These four variables will always include *N* and *I/Y*; in addition, two out of the final three variables *PV, FV,* and *PMT* will also be included. To solve a time value of money problem using a financial calculator, all you need to do is enter the appropriate numbers for three of the four variables and then press the key of the final variable to calculate its value. It is also a good idea to enter zero for any of the five variables not included in the problem in order to clear that variable.

Now let's solve the previous example using a financial calculator. We were trying to find at what rate must $100 be compounded annually for it to grow to $179.10 in ten years. The solution using a financial calculator would be as follows:

Step 1: Input Values of Known Variables

Data Input	Function Key	Description
10	N	Stores $N = 10$ years
−100	PV	Stores $PV = -\$100$
179.10	FV	Stores $FV = \$179.10$
0	PMT	Clears PMT to $= 0$

Step 2: Calculate the value of the unknown variable

Function Key	Answer	Description
CPT I/Y	6.00%	Calculates $I/Y = 6.00\%$

Any of the problems in this chapter can easily be solved using a financial calculator; the solutions to many examples using a Texas Instrument BAII Plus financial calculator are provided in the margins. If you are using the TI BAII Plus, make sure that you have selected both the "END MODE" and "one payment per year" ($P/Y = 1$). This sets the payment conditions to a maximum of one payment per period occurring at the end of the period. One final point, you will notice that solutions using the present-value tables versus solutions using a calculator may vary slightly—a result of rounding errors in the tables.

COMPOUND INTEREST WITH NONANNUAL PERIODS

Until now, we have assumed that the compounding period is always annual; however, it need not be, as evidenced by savings and loan associations and commercial banks that compound on a quarterly and, in some cases, daily basis. Fortunately, this adjustment of the compounding period follows the same format as that used for annual compounding. If we invest our money for five years at 8 percent interest compounded semiannually, we are really investing our money for ten six-month periods during which we receive 4 percent interest each period. If it is compounded quarterly, we receive 2 percent interest per period for twenty three-month periods. Table 3-3 illustrates the importance of nonannual compounding. This process can easily be generalized, giving us the following formula for finding the future value of an investment for which interest is compounded in nonannual periods:

(3-7)

$$FV_n = PV\left(1 + \frac{i}{m}\right)^{mn}$$

where FV_n = the future value of the investment at the end of n years
 n = the number of years during which the compounding occurs
 i = annual interest (or discount) rate
 PV = the present value or original amount invested at the beginning of the first year
 m = the number of times compounding occurs during the year

Table 3-3 The Value of $100 Compounded at Various Intervals

For One Year at i Percent i =	2%	5%	10%	15%
Compounded annually	$102.00	$105.00	$110.00	$115.00
Compounded semiannually	102.01	105.06	110.25	115.56
Compounded quarterly	102.02	105.09	110.38	115.87
Compounded monthly	102.02	105.12	110.47	116.08
Compounded weekly (52)	102.02	105.12	110.51	116.16
Compounded daily (365)	102.02	105.13	110.52	116.18

For 10 Years at i Percent i =	2%	5%	10%	15%
Compounded annually	$121.90	$162.89	$259.37	$404.56
Compounded semiannually	122.02	163.86	265.33	424.79
Compounded quarterly	122.08	164.36	268.51	436.04
Compounded monthly	122.12	164.70	270.70	444.02
Compounded weekly (52)	122.14	164.83	271.57	447.20
Compounded daily (365)	122.14	164.87	271.79	448.03

If we place $100 in a savings account that yields 12 percent compounded quarterly, what will our investment grow to at the end of five years? Substituting $n = 5$, $m = 4$, $i = 12$ percent, and $PV = \$100$ into equation (3-7), we find

$$FV_5 = \$100\left(1 + \frac{.12}{4}\right)^{4 \cdot 5}$$

$$= \$100(1 + .03)^{20}$$

$$= \$100(1.806)$$

$$= \$180.60$$

Thus we will have $180.60 at the end of five years. Notice that the calculator solution is slightly different because of rounding errors in the tables, as explained in the previous section, and that it also takes on a negative value.

Calculator Solution

DATA INPUT	FUNCTION KEY
20	N
3	I/Y
100	PV
0	PMT

FUNCTION KEY	ANSWER
CPT	
FV	−180.61

PRESENT VALUE

Up until this point, we have been moving money forward in time; that is, we know how much we have to begin with and are trying to determine how much that sum will grow in a certain number of years when compounded at a specific rate. We are now going to look at the reverse question: What is the value in today's dollars of a sum of money to be received in the future? The answer to this question will help us determine the desirability of investment projects. In this case, we are moving future money back to the present. We will be determining the **present value** of a lump sum, which in simple terms is the current value of a future payment. What we will be doing is, in fact, nothing other than inverse compounding. The differences in these techniques come about merely from the investor's point of view. In compounding, we talked about the compound interest rate and the initial investment; in determining the present value, we will talk about the discount rate and present value. Determination of the discount rate can be defined as the rate of return available on an investment of equal risk to what is being discounted. Other than that, the technique and the terminology remain the same, and the mathematics are simply reversed. In equation (3-6), we were attempting to determine the future value of an initial investment. We now want to determine the initial investment or present value. By dividing both sides of equation (3-6) by $(1 + i)^n$, we get

$$PV = FV_n \left[\frac{1}{(1 + i)^n} \right] \qquad (3\text{-}8)$$

where PV = the present value of the future sum of money
FV_n = the future value of the investment at the end of n years
n = the number of years until the payment will be received
i = the annual discount (or interest) rate

Because the mathematical procedure for determining the present value is exactly the inverse of determining the future value, we also find that the relationships among n, i, and PV are just the opposite of those we observed in future value. The present value of a future sum of money is inversely related to both the number of years until the payment will be received and the discount rate. Graphically, this relationship can be seen in Figure 3-2.

EXAMPLE

What is the present value of $500 to be received ten years from today if our discount rate is 6 percent? Substituting FV_{10} = $500, n = 10, and i = 6 percent into equation (3-8), we find

$$PV = \$500 \left[\frac{1}{(1 + .06)^{10}} \right]$$

$$= \$500 \left(\frac{1}{1.791} \right)$$

$$= \$500(.558)$$

$$= \$279$$

Thus the present value of the $500 to be received in ten years is $279.

Calculator Solution

DATA INPUT	FUNCTION KEY
10	N
6	I/Y
500	FV
0	PMT

FUNCTION KEY	ANSWER
CPT	
PV	−279.20

To aid in the computation of present values, the **present-value interest factor** for i and n or $PVIF_{i,n}$, which is equal to $[1/(1 + i)^n]$, has been compiled for various combinations of i and n and appears in Appendix B at the back of this book. An abbreviated version of Appendix B appears in Table 3-4. A close examination shows that the values in Table 3-4 are merely the inverse of those found in Appendix A. This, of course, is as it should be, as the values in Appendix B are $(1 + i)^n$ and those in Appendix B are $[1/(1 + i)^n]$. Now, to determine the present value of a sum of

Figure 3-2 Present Value of $100 to Be Received at a Future Date and Discounted Back to the Present at 0, 5, and 10 Percent

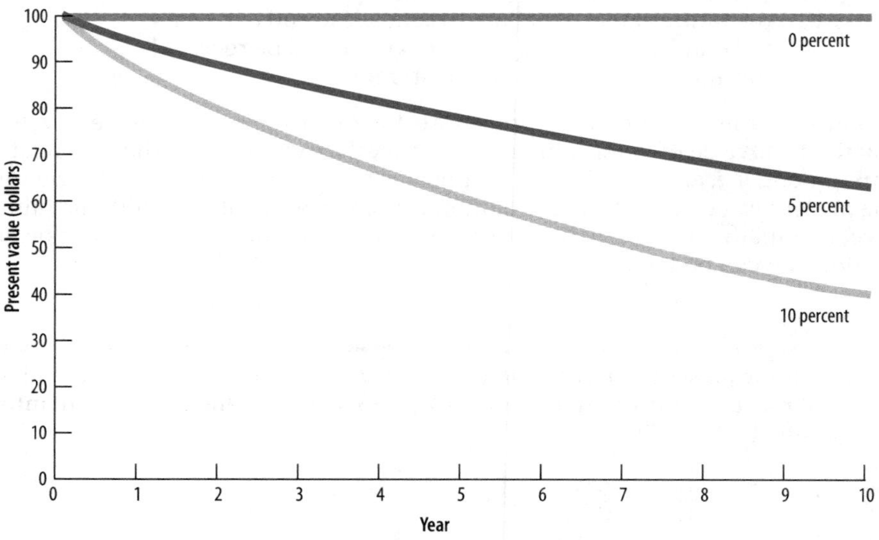

money to be received at some future date, we need only determine the value of the appropriate $PVIF_{i,n}$, either by using a calculator or consulting the tables, and multiply it by the future value. In effect, we can use our new notation and rewrite equation (3-8) as follows:

$$PV = FV_n(PVIF_{i,n})\tag{3-8a}$$

EXAMPLE

What is the present value of $1,500 to be received at the end of ten years if the discount rate is 8 percent? By looking at the $n = 10$ row and $i = 8\%$ column of Table 3-4, we find the $PVIF_{8\%,10yr}$ is .463. Substituting this value into equation (3-8), we find

$$PV = \$1500(.463)$$
$$= \$694.50$$

Thus the present value of this $1,500 payment is $694.50.

Calculator Solution

DATA INPUT	FUNCTION KEY
10	N
8	I/Y
1500	FV
0	PMT

FUNCTION KEY	ANSWER
CPT	
PV	–694.79

Table 3-4 $PVIF_{i,n}$ or the Present Value of $1

n	1%	2%	3%	4%	5%	6%	7%	8%	9%	10%
1	.990	.980	.971	.962	.952	.943	.935	.926	.917	.909
2	.980	.961	.943	.925	.907	.890	.873	.857	.842	.826
3	.971	.942	.915	.889	.864	.840	.816	.794	.772	.751
4	.961	.924	.888	.855	.823	.792	.763	.735	.708	.683
5	.951	.906	.863	.822	.784	.747	.713	.681	.650	.621
6	.942	.888	.837	.790	.746	.705	.666	.630	.596	.564
7	.933	.871	.813	.760	.711	.655	.623	.583	.547	.513
8	.923	.853	.789	.731	.677	.627	.582	.540	.502	.467
9	.914	.837	.766	.703	.645	.592	.544	.500	.460	.424
10	.905	.820	.744	.676	.614	.558	.508	.463	.422	.386
11	.896	.804	.722	.650	.585	.527	.475	.429	.388	.350
12	.887	.789	.701	.625	.557	.497	.444	.397	.356	.319
13	.879	.773	.681	.601	.530	.469	.415	.368	.326	.290
14	.870	.758	.661	.577	.505	.442	.388	.340	.299	.263
15	.861	.743	.642	.555	.481	.417	.362	.315	.275	.239

Again, we only have one present-value–future-value equation; that is, equations (3-6) and (3-8) are identical. We have introduced them as separate equations to simplify our calculations; in one case, we are determining the value in future dollars and in the other case, the value in today's dollars. In either case, the reason is the same: To compare values on alternative investments and to recognize that the value of a dollar received today is not the same as that of a dollar received at some future date, we must measure the dollar values in dollars of the same time period. Since all present values are comparable (they are all measured in dollars of the same time period), we can add and subtract the present value of inflows and outflows to determine the present value of an investment.

EXAMPLE

What is the present value of an investment that yields $500 to be received in five years and $1,000 to be received in ten years if the discount rate is 4 percent? Substituting the values of $n = 5$, $i = 4$ percent, and $FV_5 = \$500$; and $n = 10$, $i = 4$ percent, and $FV_{10} = \$1,000$ into equation (3-8) and adding these values together, we find

$$PV = \$500\left[\frac{1}{(1 + .04)^5}\right] + \$1000\left[\frac{1}{(1 + .04)^{10}}\right]$$

$$= \$500\left(PVIF_{4\%,5\text{yr}}\right) + \$1000\left(PVIF_{4\%,10\text{yr}}\right)$$

$$= \$500(.822) + \$1000(.676)$$

$$= \$411 + \$676$$

$$= \$1087$$

Again, present values are comparable because they are measured in the same time period's dollars.

ANNUITIES

An **annuity** is a series of equal dollar payments for a specified number of years. Because annuities occur frequently in finance—for example, as bond interest payments—we will treat them specially. Although compounding and determining the present value of an annuity can be dealt with using the methods we have just described, these processes can be time consuming, especially for larger annuities. Thus, we have modified the formulas to deal directly with annuities.

While all annuities involve a series of equal dollar payments for a specified number of years, there are two basic types of annuities: an **ordinary annuity** and an **annuity due.** With an ordinary annuity, we assume that the payments occur at the end of each period; with an annuity due, the payments occur at the beginning of each period. Because an annuity due provides the payments earlier (at the beginning of each period instead of the end as with an ordinary annuity), it has a greater present value. After we master ordinary annuities, we will examine annuities due. However, in finance, ordinary annuities are used much more frequently than are annuities due. Thus, in this text whenever the term "annuity" is used, you should assume that we are referring to an ordinary annuity unless otherwise specified.

Compound Annuities

A **compound annuity** involves depositing or investing an equal sum of money at the end of each year for a certain number of years and allowing it to grow. Perhaps we are saving money for education, a new car, or a vacation home. In any case, we want to know how much our savings will have grown by some point in the future.

Actually, we can find the answer by using equation (3-6), our compounding equation, and compounding each of the individual deposits to its future value. For example, if to provide for a college education we are going to deposit $500 at the end of each year for the next five years in a bank where it will earn 6 percent interest, how much will we have at the end of five years? Compounding each of these values using equation (3-6), we find that we will have $2,818.50 at the end of five years.

$$FV_5 = \$500(1 + .06)^4 + \$500(1 + .06)^3 + \$500(1 + .06)^2 + \$500(1 + .06) + \$500$$
$$= \$500(1.262) + \$500(1.191) + \$500(1.124) + \$500(1.060) + \$500$$
$$= \$631.00 + \$595.50 + \$562.00 + \$530.00 + \$500.00$$
$$= \$2818.50$$

Calculator Solution

DATA INPUT	FUNCTION KEY
5	N
6	I/Y
0	PV
500	PMT

FUNCTION KEY	ANSWER
CPT	
FV	–2,818.55

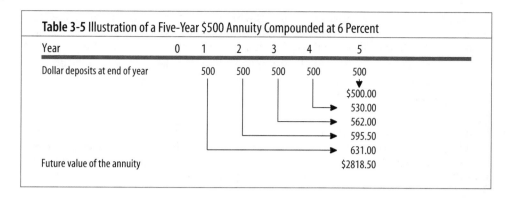

Table 3-5 Illustration of a Five-Year $500 Annuity Compounded at 6 Percent

Year	0	1	2	3	4	5
Dollar deposits at end of year		500	500	500	500	500
						$500.00
						530.00
						562.00
						595.50
						631.00
Future value of the annuity						$2818.50

Table 3-6 $FVIFA_{i,n}$ or the Sum of an Annuity of $1 for n Years

n	1%	2%	3%	4%	5%	6%	7%	8%	9%	10%
1	1.000	1.000	1.000	1.000	1.000	1.000	1.000	1.000	1.000	1.000
2	2.010	2.020	2.030	2.040	2.050	2.060	2.070	2.080	2.090	2.100
3	3.030	3.060	3.091	3.122	3.152	3.184	3.215	3.246	3.278	3.310
4	4.060	4.122	4.184	4.246	4.310	4.375	4.440	4.506	4.573	4.641
5	5.101	5.204	5.309	5.416	5.526	5.637	5.751	5.867	5.985	6.105
6	6.152	6.308	6.468	6.633	6.802	6.975	7.153	7.336	7.523	7.716
7	7.214	7.434	7.662	7.898	8.142	8.394	8.654	8.923	9.200	9.487
8	8.286	8.583	8.892	9.214	9.549	9.897	10.260	10.637	11.028	11.436
9	9.368	9.755	10.159	10.583	11.027	11.491	11.978	12.488	13.021	13.579
10	10.462	10.950	11.464	12.006	12.578	13.181	13.816	14.487	15.193	15.937
11	11.567	12.169	12.808	13.486	14.207	14.972	15.784	16.645	17.560	18.531
12	12.682	13.412	14.192	15.026	15.917	16.870	17.888	18.977	20.141	21.384
13	13.809	14.680	15.618	16.627	17.713	18.882	20.141	21.495	22.953	24.523
14	14.947	15.974	17.086	18.292	19.598	21.015	22.550	24.215	26.019	27.975
15	16.097	17.293	18.599	20.023	21.578	23.276	25.129	27.152	29.361	31.772

From examining the mathematics involved and the graph of the movement of money through time in Table 3-5, we can see that this procedure can be generalized to

$$FV_n = PMT\left[\sum_{t=0}^{n-1}(1 + i)^t\right] \tag{3-9}$$

where FV_n = the future value of the annuity at the end of the nth year
PMT = the annuity payment deposited or received at the end of each year
i = the annual interest (or discount) rate
n = the number of years for which the annuity will last

To aid in compounding annuities, the **future-value interest factor for an annuity** for i and n ($FVIFA_{i,n}$), defined as $\left[\sum_{t=0}^{n-1}(1 + i)^t\right]$ is provided in Appendix C for various combinations of n and i; an abbreviated version is shown in Table 3-6.

Using this new notation, we can rewrite equation (3-9) as follows:

$$FV_n = PMT(FVIFA_{i,n}) \tag{3-9a}$$

Reexamining the previous example, in which we determined the value after five years of $500 deposited at the end of each of the next five years in the bank at 6 percent, we would look in the $i = 6\%$ column and $n = 5$ year row and find the value of the $FVIFA_{6\%,5\text{yrs}}$ to be 5.637. Substituting this value into equation (3-9a), we get

$FV_5 = \$500(5.637)$
$\quad\ = \$2818.50$

This is the same answer we obtained earlier.

Rather than asking how much we will accumulate if we deposit an equal sum in a savings account each year, a more common question is how much we must deposit each year to accumulate a certain amount of savings. This problem frequently occurs with respect to saving for large expenditures and pension funding obligations.

For example, we may know that we need $10,000 for education in eight years; how much must we deposit at the end of each year in the bank at 6 percent interest to have the college money ready? In this case, we know the values of n, i, and FV_n in equation (3-9); what we do not know is the value of PMT. Substituting these example values in equation (3-9), we find

$$\$10,000 = PMT\left[\sum_{t=0}^{8-1}\left(1 + .06\right)^t\right]$$

$$\$10,000 = PMT\left(FVIFA_{6\%,8\text{yrs}}\right)$$

$$\$10,000 = PMT(9.897)$$

$$\frac{\$10,000}{9.897} = PMT$$

$$PMT = \$1010.41$$

Calculator Solution

DATA INPUT	FUNCTION KEY
8	N
6	I/Y
10,000	FV
0	PV

FUNCTION KEY	ANSWER
CPT	
PMT	−1,010.36

Thus we must deposit $1,010.41 in the bank at the end of each year for eight years at 6 percent interest to accumulate $10,000 at the end of eight years.

WALL STREET JOURNAL APRIL 22, 1994

Make a Child a Millionaire

Just Take Your Time

Thanks a million.

Even if you haven't got a lot of money, you can easily give $1 million or more to your children, grandchildren, or favorite charity. All it takes is a small initial investment and a lot of time.

Suppose your 16-year old daughter plans to take a summer job, which will pay her at least $2,000. Because she has earned income, she can open an individual retirement account. If you would like to help fund her retirement, Kenneth Klegon, a financial planner in Lansing. Michigan, suggests giving her $2,000 to set up the IRA. He then advises doing the same in each of the next five years, so that your daughter stashes away a total of $12,000.

Result? If the money is invested in stocks, and stocks deliver their historical average annual return of 10%, your daughter will have more than $1 million by the time she turns 65. **(A)**

Because of the corrosive effect of inflation, that $1 million will only buy a quarter of what $1 million buys today, presuming the cost of living rises at 3% a year. Nonetheless, your $12,000 gift will go a long way toward paying for your daughter's retirement. **(B)** The huge gain is possible because of the way stock-market compounding works, with money earned each year not only on your initial investment, but also on the gains accumulated from earlier years.

"The beauty of this strategy is that it will grow tax-deferred," Klegon says. "There's no cost. You can set up an IRA with a no-load mutual fund for nothing." Similarly, Mr. Klegon says, once your children enter the work force full time, you can encourage them to participate in their company's 401(k) plan by reimbursing them for their contributions.

SOURCE: Jonathan Clements, "Make a Child a Millionaire," *The Wall Street Journal*, April 22, 1994, page C1. Reprinted by permission *The Wall Street Journal*, copyright 1994 Dow Jones & Co., Inc. All Rights Reserved.

ANALYSIS AND IMPLICATIONS...

A. Using the principles and techniques set out in this chapter, we can easily see how much this IRA investment will accumulate to. We can first take the $2,000 six-year annuity and determine its future value—that is, its value when your daughter is twenty-one and receives the last payment. This would be done as follows:

$FV = PMT(FVIFA_{10\%, 6yrs})$
   $= \$2000(FVIFA_{10\%, 6yrs})$
   $= \$15,431.22$

We could then take this amount that your daughter has when she is twenty-one and compound it out forty-four years to when she is sixty-five, as follows:

$FV = PV(FVIF_{10\%, 44yrs})$
   $= \$15,431.22(FVIF_{10\%, 44yrs})$
   $= \$1,022,535.54$

Thus your daughter's IRA would have accumulated to $1,022,535.54 by age sixty-five if it grew at 10 percent compounded annually.

B. To determine how much this is worth in today's dollars, if inflation increases at an annual rate of 3 percent over this period, we need only calculate the present

value of $1,022,535.54 to be received forty-nine years from now given a discount rate of 3 percent. This would determine the future value of this IRA measured in dollars with the same spending power as those around when your daughter was sixteen. This is done as follows:

$PV = FV(PVIF_{3\%, 49yrs})$
   $= \$1,022,535.54(PVIF_{3\%, 49yrs})$
   $= \$240,245.02$

You can change the growth and inflation rates and come up with all kinds of numbers, but one thing holds: there is incredible power in compounding!

How much must we deposit in an 8 percent savings account at the end of each year to accumulate $5,000 at the end of ten years? Substituting the values $FV_{10} = \$5000$, $n = 10$, and $i = 8$ percent into equation (3-9), we find

$$\$5,000 = PMT\left[\sum_{t=0}^{10-1}(1 + .08)^t\right] = PMT\left(FVIFA_{8\%,10\text{yrs}}\right)$$

$$\$5,000 = PMT(14.487)$$

$$\frac{\$5,000}{14.487} = PMT$$

$$PMT = \$345.14$$

Thus we must deposit $345.14 per year for ten years at 8 percent to accumulate $5,000.

Calculator Solution

DATA INPUT	FUNCTION KEY
10	N
8	I/Y
5,000	FV
0	PV

FUNCTION KEY	ANSWER
CPT	
PMT	−345.15

Present Value of an Annuity

Pension funds, insurance obligations, and interest received from bonds all involve annuities. To compare them, we need to know the present value of each. While we can find this by using the present-value table in Appendix B, this can be time consuming, particularly when the annuity lasts for several years. For example, if we wish to know what $500 received at the end of the next five years is worth to us today given the appropriate discount rate of 6 percent, we can simply substitute the appropriate values into equation (3-8), such that

$$PV = \$500\left[\frac{1}{(1 + .06)^1}\right] + \$500\left[\frac{1}{(1 + .06)^2}\right] + \$500\left[\frac{1}{(1 + .06)^3}\right]$$

$$+ \$500\left[\frac{1}{(1 + .06)^4}\right] + \$500\left[\frac{1}{(1 + .06)^5}\right]$$

$$= \$500(.943) + \$500(.890) + \$500(.840) + \$500(.792) + \$500(.747)$$

$$= \$2106$$

Thus the present value of this annuity is $2,106.00. From examining the mathematics involved and the graph of the movement of these funds through time in Table 3-7, we see that this procedure can be generalized to

$$PV = PMT\left[\sum_{t=1}^{n}\frac{1}{(1 + i)^t}\right]$$

(3-10)

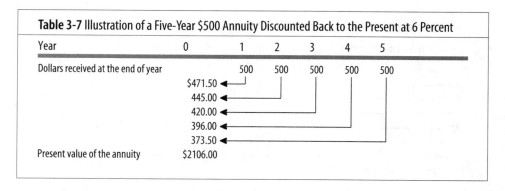

Table 3-7 Illustration of a Five-Year $500 Annuity Discounted Back to the Present at 6 Percent

Year	0	1	2	3	4	5
Dollars received at the end of year		500	500	500	500	500
	$471.50 ←					
	445.00 ←					
	420.00 ←					
	396.00 ←					
	373.50 ←					
Present value of the annuity	$2106.00					

Table 3-8 $PVIFA_{i,n}$ or the Present Value of an Annuity of $1

n	1%	2%	3%	4%	5%	6%	7%	8%	9%	10%
1	0.990	0.980	0.971	0.962	0.952	0.943	0.935	0.926	0.917	0.909
2	1.970	1.942	1.913	1.886	1.859	1.833	1.808	1.783	1.759	1.736
3	2.941	2.884	2.829	2.775	2.723	2.673	2.624	2.577	2.531	2.487
4	3.902	3.808	3.717	3.630	3.546	3.465	3.387	3.312	3.240	3.170
5	4.853	4.713	4.580	4.452	4.329	4.212	4.100	3.993	3.890	3.791
6	5.795	5.601	5.417	5.242	5.076	4.917	4.767	4.623	4.486	4.355
7	6.728	6.472	6.230	6.002	5.786	5.582	5.389	5.206	5.033	4.868
8	7.652	7.326	7.020	6.733	6.463	6.210	5.971	5.747	5.535	5.335
9	8.566	8.162	7.786	7.435	7.108	6.802	6.515	6.247	5.995	5.759
10	9.471	8.983	8.530	8.111	7.722	7.360	7.024	6.710	6.418	6.145
11	10.368	9.787	9.253	8.760	8.306	7.887	7.499	7.139	6.805	6.495
12	11.255	10.575	9.954	9.385	8.863	8.384	7.943	7.536	7.161	6.814
13	12.134	11.348	10.635	9.986	9.394	8.853	8.358	7.904	7.487	7.103
14	13.004	12.106	11.296	10.563	9.899	9.295	8.746	8.244	7.786	7.367
15	13.865	12.849	11.938	11.118	10.380	9.712	9.108	8.560	8.061	7.606

where PMT = the annuity payment deposited or received at the end of each year
i = the annual discount (or interest) rate
PV = the present value of the future annuity
n = the number of years for which the annuity will last

To simplify the process of determining the **present value for an annuity**, the **present-value interest factor for an annuity** for i and n ($PVIFA_{i,n}$), defined as

$$\left[\sum_{t=1}^{n} \frac{1}{(1 + i)^t} \right]$$, has been compiled for various combinations of i and n in Appendix

D with an abbreviated version provided in Table 3-8.

Using this new notation we can rewrite equation (3-10) as follows:

$$PV = PMT(PVIFA_{i,n}) \tag{3-10a}$$

Solving the previous example to find the present value of $500 received at the end of each of the next five years discounted back to the present at 6 percent, we look in the i = 6% column and n = 5 year row and find the $PVIFA_{6\%,5yr}$ to be 4.212. Substituting the appropriate values into equation (3-10a), we find

PV = $500(4.212)
    = $2106

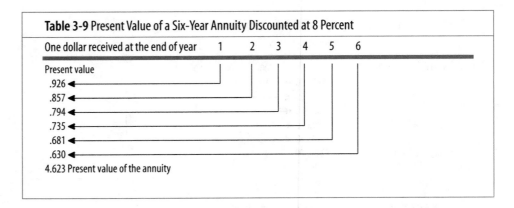

Table 3-9 Present Value of a Six-Year Annuity Discounted at 8 Percent

One dollar received at the end of year	1	2	3	4	5	6

Present value
.926 ◀
.857 ◀
.794 ◀
.735 ◀
.681 ◀
.630 ◀
4.623 Present value of the annuity

This, of course, is the same answer we calculated when we individually discounted each cash flow to the present. The reason is that we really only have one table, all of the tables are derived from Table 3-2; the Table 3-8 value for an *n*-year annuity for any discount rate *i* is merely the sum of the first *n* values in Table 3-4. We can see this by comparing the value in the present-value-of-an-annuity table (Table 3-8) for *i* = 8 percent and *n* = 6 years, which is 4.623, with the sum of the values in the *i* = 8% column and *n* = 1, . . . , 6 rows of the present-value table (Table 3-4), which is equal to 4.623, as shown in Table 3-9.

EXAMPLE

What is the present value of a ten-year $1,000 annuity discounted back to the present at 5 percent? Substituting *n* = 10 years, *i* = 5 percent, and *PMT* = $1,000 into equation (3-10), we find

$$PV = \$1000\left[\sum_{t=1}^{10}\frac{1}{(1 + .05)^t}\right] = \$1000\left(PVIFA_{5\%,10\text{yrs}}\right)$$

Determining the value for the $PVIFA_{5\%,10\text{yr}}$ from Table 3-8, row *n* = 10, column *i* = 5%, and substituting it in, we get

$PV = \$1000(7.722)$
$\quad = \$7722$

Thus the present value of this annuity is $7,722.

Calculator Solution

DATA INPUT	FUNCTION KEY
10	N
5	I/Y
1,000	PMT
0	FV

FUNCTION KEY	ANSWER
CPT	
PV	−7,721.73

As with our other compounding and present-value tables, given any three of the four unknowns in equation (3-10), we can solve for the fourth. In the case of the present-value-of-an-annuity table, we may be interested in solving for *PMT*, if we know *i*, *n*, and *PV*. The financial interpretation of this action would be: How much can be withdrawn, perhaps as a pension or to make loan payments, from an account that earns *i* percent compounded annually for each of the next *n* years if we wish to have nothing left at the end of *n* years? For an example, if we have $5,000 in an account earning 8 percent interest, how large an annuity can we draw out each year if we want nothing left at the end of five years? In this case, the present value, *PV*, of the annuity is $5000, *n* = 5 years, *i* = 8 percent, and *PMT* is unknown. Substituting this into equation (3-10), we find

$5000 = PMT(3.993)$
$1252.19 = PMT$

Thus this account will fall to zero at the end of five years if we withdraw $1,252.19 at the end of each year.

Calculator Solution

DATA INPUT	FUNCTION KEY
5	N
8	I/Y
5,000	PV
0	FV

FUNCTION KEY	ANSWER
CPT	
PMT	−1,252.28

Annuities Due

Because **annuities due** are really just **ordinary annuities** where all the annuity payments have been shifted forward by one year, compounding them and determining their present value is actually quite simple. Remember, with an annuity due, each annuity payment occurs at the beginning of each period rather than at the end of the period. Let's first look at how this affects our compounding calculations.

Since an annuity due merely shifts the payments from the end of the year to the beginning of the year, we now compound the cash flows for one additional year. Therefore the compound sum of an annuity due is simply

$$FV_n(\text{annuity due}) = PMT(FVIFA_{i,n})(1 + i)$$

For example, earlier we calculated the value of a five-year ordinary annuity of $500, invested in the bank at 6 percent to be $2,818.50. If we now assume this to be a five-year annuity due, its future value increases from $2,818.50 to $2,987.61.

$$FV_5 = \$500(FVIFA_{5\%,5yr})(1 + .06)$$
$$= \$500(5.637)(1.06)$$
$$= \$2,987.61$$

Likewise, with the present value of an annuity due, we simply receive each cash flow one year earlier—that is we receive it at the beginning of each year rather than at the end of each year. Thus, since each cash flow is received one year earlier, it is discounted back for one less period. To determine the present value of an annuity due, we merely need to find the present value of an ordinary annuity and multiply that by $(1 + i)$, which in effect cancels out one year's discounting.

$$PV(\text{annuity due}) = PMT(PVIFA_{i,n})(1 + i)$$

Reexamining the earlier example where we calculated the present value of a five-year ordinary annuity of $500 given an appropriate discount rate of 6 percent, we now find that if it is an annuity due rather than an ordinary annuity, the present value increases from $2,106 to $2,232.36.

$$PV = \$500(PVIFA_{6\%,5yrs})(1 + .06)$$
$$= \$500(4.212)(1.06)$$
$$= \$2,232.36$$

The result of all this is that both the future and present values of an annuity due are larger than that of an ordinary annuity because in each case all payments are received earlier. Thus, when *compounding* an annuity due, it compounds for one additional year; while when *discounting* an annuity due, the cash flows are discounted for one less year. While annuities due are used with some frequency in accounting, their usage is quite limited in finance. Therefore, in the remainder of this text, whenever the term annuity is used, you should assume that we are referring to an ordinary annuity.

Amortized Loans

The procedure of solving for *PMT* is also used to determine what payments are associated with paying off a loan in equal installments over time. Loans that are paid off this way, in equal periodic payments, are called **amortized loans**. For example, suppose a firm wants to purchase a piece of machinery. To do this, it borrows $6,000 to be repaid in four equal payments at the end of each of the next four years, and the interest rate that is paid to the lender is 15 percent on the outstanding portion of the loan. To determine what the annual payment associated with the repayment of this debt will be, we simply use equation (3-10) and solve for the value of *PMT*, the annual annuity. Again, we know three of the four values in that equation, *PV*, *i*, and *n*. *PV*, the present value of the future annuity, is $6,000; *i*, the annual interest rate, is 15 percent; and *n*, the number of years for which the annuity will last, is four years. *PMT*, the annuity payment received (by the lender and paid by the firm) at the end of each year, is unknown. Substituting these values into equation (3-10), we find

$$\$6000 = PMT\left[\sum_{t=1}^{4}\frac{1}{(1 + .15)^t}\right]$$

$$\$6000 = PMT\left(PVIFA_{15\%,4yr}\right)$$

$$\$6000 = PMT(2.855)$$

$$\$2101.58 = PMT$$

Calculator Solution

DATA INPUT	FUNCTION KEY
4	N
15	I/Y
6,000	PV
0	FV

FUNCTION KEY	ANSWER
CPT	
PMT	−2,101.59

To repay the principal and interest on the outstanding loan in four years, the annual payments would be $2,101.58. The breakdown of interest and principal payments is given in the **loan amortization schedule** in Table 3-10, with very minor rounding errors. As you can see, the interest payment declines each year as the loan outstanding declines.

Table 3-10 Loan Amortization Schedule Involving a $6,000 Loan at 15 Percent to Be Repaid in Four Years

Year	Annuity	Interest Portion of the Annuity[a]	Repayment of the Principal Portion of the Annuity[b]	Outstanding Loan Balance after the Annuity Payment
1	$2101.58	$900.00	$1201.58	$4798.42
2	2101.58	719.76	1381.82	3416.60
3	2101.58	512.49	1589.09	1827.51
4	2101.58	274.07	1827.51	

[a]The interest portion of the annuity is calculated by multiplying the outstanding loan balance at the beginning of the year by the interest rate of 15 percent. Thus, for year 1 it was $6000.00 x .15 = $900.00, for year 2 it was $4798.42 x .15 = $719.76, and so on.
[b]Repayment of the principal portion of the annuity was calculated by subtracting the interest portion of the annuity (column 2) from the annuity (column 1).

Present Value of an Uneven Stream

While some projects will involve a single cash flow and some annuities, many projects will involve uneven cash flows over several years. Later we will be comparing not only the present value of cash flows between projects, but also the cash inflows and outflows within a particular project, trying to determine that project's present value. However, this will not be difficult because the present value of any cash flow is measured in today's dollars and thus can be compared, through addition for inflows and subtraction for outflows, to the present value of any other cash flow also measured in today's dollars. For example, if we wished to find the present value of the following cash flows

Year	Cash Flow	Year	Cash Flow
1	$500	6	$500
2	200	7	500
3	−400	8	500
4	500	9	500
5	500	10	500

given a 6 percent discount rate, we would merely discount the flows back to the present and total them by adding in the positive flows and subtracting the negative ones. However, this problem is complicated by the annuity of $500 that runs from years 4 through 10. To accommodate this, we can first discount the annuity back to the beginning of period 4 (or end of period 3) by multiplying it by the value of $PVIFA_{6\%,7yr}$ and get its present value at that point in time. We then multiply this value times the $PVIF_{6\%,3yr}$ in order to bring this single cash flow (which is the present value of the seven-year annuity) back to the present. In effect, we discount twice—

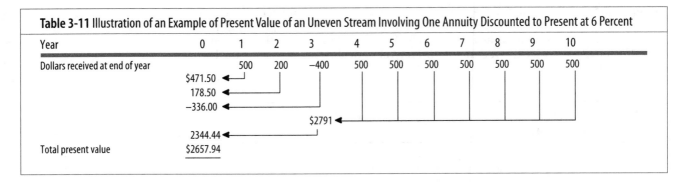

Table 3-11 Illustration of an Example of Present Value of an Uneven Stream Involving One Annuity Discounted to Present at 6 Percent

Year	0	1	2	3	4	5	6	7	8	9	10
Dollars received at end of year		500	200	−400	500	500	500	500	500	500	500
	$471.50										
	178.50										
	−336.00										
				$2791							
	2344.44										
Total present value	$2657.94										

Table 3-12 Determination of the Present Value of an Uneven Stream Involving One Annuity Discounted to Present at 6 Percent

1.	Present value of $500 received at the end of one year = $500(.943) =	$471.50
2.	Present value of $200 received at the end of two years = $200(.890) =	178.00
3.	Present value of a $400 outflow at the end of three years = −$400(.840) =	−336.00
4.	(a) Value at the end of year 3 of a $500 annuity, years 4 through 10 = $500(5.582) = $2791	
	(b) Present value of $2791 received at the end of year 3 = $2,791(.840) =	2344.44
5.	Total present value =	$2657.94

first back to the end of period 3, then back to the present. This is shown graphically in Table 3-11 and numerically in Table 3-12. Thus the present value of this uneven stream of cash flows is $2,657.94.

EXAMPLE

What is the present value of an investment involving $200 received at the end of years 1 through 5, a $300 cash outflow at the end of year 6, and $500 received at the end of years 7 through 10, given a 5 percent discount rate? Here we have two annuities, one that can be discounted directly back to the present by multiplying it by the value of the $PVIFA_{5\%,5yr}$ and one that must be discounted twice to bring it back to the present. This second annuity, which is a four-year annuity, must first be discounted back to the beginning of period 7 (or end of period 6) by multiplying it by the value of the $PVIFA_{5\%,4yr}$. Then the present value of this annuity at the end of period 6 (which can be viewed as a single cash flow) must be discounted back to the present by multiplying it by the value of the $PVIF_{5\%,6yr}$. To arrive at the total present value of this investment, we subtract the present value of the $300 cash outflow at the end of year 6 from the sum of the present value of the two annuities. Table 3-13 shows this graphically; Table 3-14 gives the calculations. Thus, the present value of this series of cash flows is $1,964.66.

Perpetuities

A **perpetuity** is an annuity that continues forever; that is, every year from its establishment this investment pays the same dollar amount. An example of a perpetuity

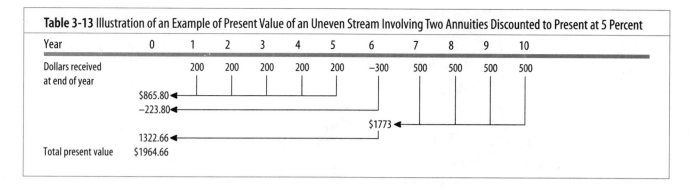

Table 3-13 Illustration of an Example of Present Value of an Uneven Stream Involving Two Annuities Discounted to Present at 5 Percent

Year	0	1	2	3	4	5	6	7	8	9	10
Dollars received at end of year		200	200	200	200	200	−300	500	500	500	500

$865.80
−223.80
$1773
1322.66

Total present value $1964.66

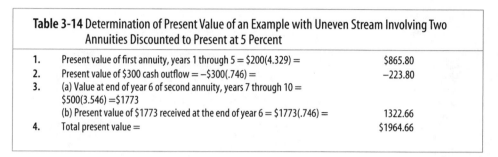

Table 3-14 Determination of Present Value of an Example with Uneven Stream Involving Two Annuities Discounted to Present at 5 Percent

1.	Present value of first annuity, years 1 through 5 = $200(4.329) =	$865.80
2.	Present value of $300 cash outflow = −$300(.746) =	−223.80
3.	(a) Value at end of year 6 of second annuity, years 7 through 10 = $500(3.546) =$1773	
	(b) Present value of $1773 received at the end of year 6 = $1773(.746) =	1322.66
4.	Total present value =	$1964.66

is preferred stock that yields a constant dollar dividend infinitely. Determining the present value of a perpetuity is delightfully simple; we merely need to divide the constant flow by the discount rate. For example, the present value of a $100 perpetuity discounted back to the present at 5 percent is $100/.05 = $2000. Thus the equation representing the present value of a perpetuity is

$$PV = \frac{PP}{i}$$ (3-11)

where *PV* = the present value of the perpetuity
   PP = the constant dollar amount provided by the perpetuity
   i = the annual interest (or discount) rate

EXAMPLE

What is the present value of a $500 perpetuity discounted back to the present at 8 percent? Substituting *PP* = $500 and *i* = .08 into equation (3-11), we find

$$PV = \frac{\$500}{.08} = \$6250$$

Thus the present value of this perpetuity is $6,250.

MAKING INTEREST RATES COMPARABLE

In order to make intelligent decisions on where to invest or borrow money, it is important that we make the stated interest rates comparable. Unfortunately, some rates are quoted as compounded annually, while others are quoted as compounded

THE WASHINGTON POST, MAY 10, 1994

LATEST INFLATION SLAYER HOLDS BRAZIL'S ATTENTION

By now, Brazilian economic plans are a dime a dozen—less if you factor in the 40 percent-a-month inflation rate. But the latest attempt at bringing some order to the country's economic affairs is being met with cautious optimism.

For the first time since Brazil began its current phase of rear guard action against inflation—eight years, six plans, and more than 150-million clicks on the consumer price index ago(A) —analysts say the country finally is standing up to the painful task of cutting the causes of its ingrained inflation.

The failure of previous plans makes success all the more cru-

cial. Although Brazil has Latin America's largest and most industrialized economy, its stabilization and liberalization efforts have lagged behind those of such fast-growing neighbors as Chile and Argentina.(B)

With Brazil claiming more than half of South America's economic output, its stability and prosperity are seen by many analysts as necessary ingredients for regional economic health, integration of South American markets and hemispheric free trade.

"This is the best plan Brazil has ever devised." said Richard Foster, editor of *Brazil Watch*, an economic and political newsletter based in Brasilia. "The govern-

ment has convinced the business community that it has a good chance of success."

Perhaps by mid-April, Brazil is to get a new currency to replace the exhausted current one. This happens periodically in Brazil. But this time the new tender is to be pegged to the dollar and defended by Brazil's ample $31 billion in foreign exchange reserves.

SOURCE: Jeb Blount "Latest Inflation Slayer Hold's Brazil's Attention," May 10, 1994, page C3. Copyright, 1994, *The Washington Post*. Reprinted with permission.

ANALYSIS AND IMPLICATIONS...

A. In 1992, Brazil's inflation had reached 1,100 percent, up from 426 percent in 1991. It had reached the point where the stack of money needed to buy a candy bar was bigger than the candy bar itself. Needless to say, if we were to move Brazilian currency through time, we would have to use an extremely high interest or discount rate. Unfortunately, in countries suffering from hyperinflation, inflation rates tend to fluctuate dramatically, and this makes estimating the appropriate interest rate even more difficult. Imagine how hard it would be to plan

in a country like Serbia where the percentage change in the inflation rate in 1993 was 363,000,000,000,000,000 percent.

B. From Axiom 1, **"The Risk-Return Tradeoff—We Won't Take on Additional Risk Unless We Expect to Be Compensated with Additional Return,"** we learned that investors demand a return for delaying consumption as well as an additional return for taking on added risk. The discount rate that we use to move money through time should reflect

anticipated inflation. In the United States anticipated inflation is quite low, although it does tend to fluctuate over time. Elsewhere in the world, however, the inflation rate is difficult to predict because it can be dramatically high and undergo huge fluctuations. In Brazil, this difficulty in determining the appropriate discount rate to use in moving money through time has made it very difficult for companies to analyze new investment projects and thus has discouraged investments.

quarterly or compounded daily. But we already know that it is not fair to compare interest rates with different compounding periods to each other. Thus, the only way interest rates can logically be compared is to convert them to some common compounding period and then compare them. That is what is done with the **annual percentage yield.** In order to understand the process of making different interest rates comparable, it is first necessary to define the **nominal** or **quoted interest rate.**

The nominal or quoted rate is the rate of interest stated on the contract. For example, if you shop around for loans and are quoted 8 percent compounded annually and 7.85 percent compounded quarterly, then 8 percent and 7.85 percent would both be nominal rates. Unfortunately, because on one the interest is compounded annually while on the other interest is compounded quarterly, they are not comparable. In fact, it is never appropriate to compare nominal rates *unless* they include the same number of compounding periods per year. To make them comparable, we must calculate their equivalent rate at some common compounding period. We do this by calculating the **annual percentage yield (APY)** or **effective annual rate.** This is the annual compound rate that produces the same return as the nominal or quoted rate.

Let's assume that you are considering borrowing money from a bank at 12 percent compounded monthly. To convert this to an APY, we must determine the annual rate that would produce the same return as the nominal rate. In the case of a 12 percent loan compounded monthly, by looking in the *FVIF* Table in the back of the book, we see that the future value of $1 in one year at 12 percent compounded monthly (that is compounded at 1 percent per month for 12 one-month periods) is $1.1268 ($FVIF_{1\%12\text{periods}}$ = 1.1268). This tells us that 12.68 percent is the APY because if we compound $1 at the nominal rate of 12 percent compounded monthly, we would have $1.1268 after one year.

Generalizing on this process, we can calculate the APY using the following equation:

$$APY = (1 + i/m)^m - 1 \qquad\qquad\qquad (3\text{-}12)$$

where APY is the annual percentage yield, i is the nominal rate of interest per year, and m is the number of compounding periods within a year. Given the wide variety of compounding periods used by business and banks, it is important to know how to make these rates comparable so that logical decisions can be made.

BOND VALUATION: AN ILLUSTRATION OF THE TIME VALUE OF MONEY

Bond valuation illustrates a combination of several discounting techniques and procedures, including an annuity, a single cash flow, and the use of semiannual compounding periods. Thus, as we will see, the present value of a bond can change dramatically as the discount rate changes. When a bond is purchased, the owner receives two things: (1) interest payments, which are generally made semiannually; and (2) repayment at maturity of the full principal, regardless of the price the investor pays for the bond. For example, let us look at a bond that pays $45 semiannually and comes due in twenty years; that is, at the end of twenty years the bondholder will receive $1,000, the return of the principal, and the bond will terminate. What is this bond worth? It is worth the present value of the cash flows it provides. Thus, as the corresponding interest rate changes, the value of the bond changes. Let us examine the value of this bond, assuming medium, low, and high interest rates—say, 10, 6, and 14 percent, respectively.

Bond Value at 10 Percent

The bond value is the sum of the present value of the interest payment annuity that the bondholder receives and the present value of the return of bond principal at maturity computed at the interest rate of 10 percent paid semiannually; that is,

$$\begin{matrix} \text{bond value} \\ \text{at 10\%} \\ \text{compounded} \\ \text{semiannually} \end{matrix} = \begin{pmatrix} \text{present value} \\ \text{of interest} \\ \text{payments} \end{pmatrix} + \begin{pmatrix} \text{present value of} \\ \text{the return of} \\ \text{the principal} \end{pmatrix} \qquad (3\text{-}13)$$

$$= PMT\left[\sum_{t=1}^{nm}\frac{1}{(1+i/m)^t}\right] + FV_{nm}\left[\frac{1}{(1+i/m)^{nm}}\right]$$

$$= \$45\left[\sum_{t=1}^{40}\frac{1}{(1+.05)^t}\right] + \$1000\left[\frac{1}{(1+.05)^{40}}\right]$$

$$= \$45(17.159) + \$1000(.142)$$

$$= \$772.16 + \$142$$

$$= \$914.16$$

Calculator Solution

DATA INPUT	FUNCTION KEY
40	N
5	I/Y
45	PMT
1,000	FV

FUNCTION KEY	ANSWER
CPT	
PV	−914.20

Thus, the value of this bond that pays $45 semiannually, given an interest rate of 10 percent, is $914.16.

Bond Value at 6 Percent

If the interest rate drops to 6 percent paid semiannually, the procedure for determining the bond value remains the same, and the only change is that i now equals 6 percent. Logically, since the value of i appears only in the denominators of the present value of interest payments and the return of principal, the bond value should increase as i drops. Intuitively this makes sense; the cash flows to the bondholder all occur in the future, and they are now discounted back to the present at a lower discount rate, so their present value should increase. The value of this bond at a 6 percent interest rate becomes

$$\begin{matrix} \text{bond value} \\ \text{at 6\% compounded} \\ \text{semiannually} \end{matrix} = \$45\left[\sum_{t=1}^{40}\frac{1}{(1+.03)^t}\right] + \$1000\left[\frac{1}{(1+.03)^{40}}\right]$$

$$= \$45(23.115) + \$1000(.307)$$

$$= \$1040.18 + \$307$$

$$= \$1347.18$$

Calculator Solution

DATA INPUT	FUNCTION KEY
40	N
3	I/Y
45	PMT
1,000	FV

FUNCTION KEY	ANSWER
CPT	
PV	−1,346.72

If the interest rate drops from 10 percent to 6 percent, the value of this bond will climb from \$914.16 to \$1,374.18.

Bond Value at 14 Percent

If the interest rate climbs to 14 percent paid semiannually, the bond value will drop, as the future cash flows to the bondholder are now discounted back to the present at a higher discount rate

$$
\begin{aligned}
\text{bond value at 14\% compounded semiannually} &= \$45\left[\sum_{t=1}^{40}\frac{1}{(1+.07)^t}\right] + \$1000\left[\frac{1}{(1+.07)^{40}}\right] \\
&= \$45(13.332) + \$1000(.067) \\
&= \$599.94 + \$67 \\
&= \$666.94
\end{aligned}
$$

Calculator Solution

DATA INPUT	FUNCTION KEY
40	N
7	I/Y
45	PMT
1,000	FV

FUNCTION KEY	ANSWER
CPT	
PV	−666.71

If the interest rate climbs from 10 percent to 14 percent, the value of this bond will drop from \$914.16 to \$666.94. This illustrates the inverse relationship between interest rates and bond prices. When the interest rate goes up, bond values go down, and vice versa.

Table 3-15 Summary of Time Value of Money Equations*

Calculation	Equation
Future value of a single payment	$FV_n = PV(1 + i)^n = PV(FVIF_{i,n})$
Future value of a single payment with nonannual compounding	$FV_n = PV\left(1 + \dfrac{i}{m}\right)^{mn}$
Present value of a single payment	$PV = FV_n\left[\dfrac{1}{(1 + i)^n}\right] = FV_n(PVIF_{i,n})$
Future value of an annuity	$FV_n = PMT\left[\displaystyle\sum_{t=0}^{n-1}(1 + i)^t\right] = PMT(FVIFA_{i,n})$
Present value of an annuity	$PV = PMT\left[\displaystyle\sum_{t=1}^{n}\dfrac{1}{(1 + i)^t}\right] = PMT(PVIFA_{i,n})$
Present value of a perpetuity	$PV = \dfrac{PP}{i}$

Notation: FV_n = the future value of the investment at the end of n years

n = the number of years until payment will be received or during which compounding occurs

i = the annual interest or discount rate

PV = the present value of the future sum of money

m = the number of times compounding occurs during the year

PMT = the annuity payment deposited or received at the end of each year

PP = the constant dollar amount provided by the perpetuity

*Related tables appear in Appendices B through E at the end of the book.

SUMMARY

To make decisions, financial managers must compare the costs and benefits of alternatives that do not occur during the same time period. Whether to make profitable investments or to take advantage of favorable interest rates, financial decision making requires an understanding of the time value of money. Managers who use the time value of money in all of their financial calculations assure themselves of more logical decisions. The time value process first makes all dollar values comparable; since money has a time value, it moves all dollar flows either back to the present or out to a common future date. All time value formulas presented in this chapter actually stem from the single compounding formula $FV_n = PV(1 + i)^n$. The formulas are used to deal simply with common financial situations, for example, discounting single flows, compounding annuities, and discounting annuities. Table 3-15 provides a summary of these calculations.

STUDY QUESTIONS

3-1. What is the time value of money? Why is it so important?

3-2. The processes of discounting and compounding are related. Explain this relationship.

3-3. How would an increase in the interest rate (i) or a decrease in the holding period (n) affect the future value (FV_n) of a sum of money? Explain why.

3-4. Suppose you were considering depositing your savings in one of three banks, all of which pay 5 percent interest; bank A compounds annually, bank B compounds semiannually, and bank C compounds daily. Which bank would you choose? Why?

3-5. What is the relationship between the $PVIF_{i,n}$ (Table 3-4) and the $PVIFA_{i,n}$ (Table 3-8)? What is the $PVIFA_{10\%,10yr}$? Add up the values of the $PVIF_{10\%,n}$ for $n = 1, \ldots, 10$. What is this value? Why do these values have the relationship they do?

3-6. What is an annuity? Give some examples of annuities. Distinguish between an annuity and a perpetuity.

SELF-TEST PROBLEMS

ST-1. You place $25,000 in a savings account paying annual compound interest of 8 percent for three years and then move it into a savings account that pays 10 percent interest compounded annually. How much will your money have grown at the end of six years?

ST-2. You purchase a boat for $35,000 and pay $5,000 down and agree to pay the rest over the next ten years in ten equal annual payments that include principal payments plus 13 percent of compound interest on the unpaid balance. What will be the amount of each payment?

ST-3. For an investment to grow eightfold in nine years, at what rate would it have to grow?

ST-4. You have the opportunity to buy a bond for $1,000 that will pay no interest during its ten-year life and have a value of $3,106 at maturity. What rate of return or yield does this bond pay?

STUDY PROBLEMS (SET A)

3-1A. (Compound Interest) To what amount will the following investments accumulate?
   a. $5,000 invested for ten years at 10 percent compounded annually
   b. $8,000 invested for seven years at 8 percent compounded annually
   c. $775 invested for twelve years at 12 percent compounded annually
   d. $21,000 invested for five years at 5 percent compounded annually

3-2A. (Compound Value Solving for n) How many years will the following take?
   a. $500 to grow to $1,039.50 if invested at 5 percent compounded annually
   b. $35 to grow to $53.87 if invested at 9 percent compounded annually
   c. $100 to grow to $298.60 if invested at 20 percent compounded annually
   d. $53 to grow to $78.76 if invested at 2 percent compounded annually

3-3A. (Compound Value Solving for i) At what annual rate would the following have to be invested?
  a. $500 to grow to $1,948.00 in twelve years
  b. $300 to grow to $422.10 in seven years
  c. $50 to grow to $280.20 in twenty years
  d. $200 to grow to $497.60 in five years

3-4A. (Present Value) What is the present value of the following future amounts?
  a. $800 to be received ten years from now discounted back to present at 10 percent
  b. $300 to be received five years from now discounted back to present at 5 percent
  c. $1,000 to be received eight years from now discounted back to present at 3 percent
  d. $1,000 to be received eight years from now discounted back to present at 20 percent

3-5A. (Compound Annuity) What is the accumulated sum of each of the following streams of payments?
  a. $500 a year for ten years compounded annually at 5 percent
  b. $100 a year for five years compounded annually at 10 percent
  c. $35 a year for seven years compounded annually at 7 percent
  d. $25 a year for three years compounded annually at 2 percent

3-6A. (Present Value of an Annuity) What is the present value of the following annuities?
  a. $2,500 a year for ten years discounted back to the present at 7 percent
  b. $70 a year for three years discounted back to the present at 3 percent
  c. $280 a year for seven years discounted back to the present at 6 percent
  d. $500 a year for ten years discounted back to the present at 10 percent

3-7A. (Compound Value) Brian Mosallam, who recently sold his Porsche, placed $10,000 in a savings account paying annual compound interest of 6 percent.
  a. Calculate the amount of money that will have accrued if he leaves the money in the bank for one, five, and fifteen years.
  b. If he moves his money into an account that pays 8 percent or one that pays 10 percent, rework part (a) using these new interest rates.
  c. What conclusions can you draw about the relationship between interest rates, time, and future sums from the calculations you have done above?

3-8A. (Compound Interest with Nonannual Periods) Calculate the amount of money that will be in each of the following accounts at the end of the given deposit period:

Account	Amount Deposited	Annual Interest Rate	Compounding Period (Compounded Every ___ Months)	Deposit Period (Years)
Theodore Logan III	$ 1,000	10%	12	10
Vernell Coles	95,000	12	1	1
Thomas Elliott	8,000	12	2	2
Wayne Robinson	120,000	8	3	2
Eugene Chung	30,000	10	6	4
Kelly Cravens	15,000	12	4	3

3-9A. (Compound Interest with Nonannual Periods)
  a. Calculate the future sum of $5,000, given that it will be held in the bank five years at an annual interest rate of 6 percent.
  b. Recalculate part (a) using a compounding period that is (1) semiannual and (2) bimonthly.

c. Recalculate parts (a) and (b) for a 12 percent annual interest rate.

d. Recalculate part (a) using a time horizon of twelve years (annual interest rate is still 6 percent).

e. With respect to the effect of changes in the stated interest rate and holding periods on future sums in parts (c) and (d), what conclusions do you draw when you compare these figures with the answers found in parts (a) and (b)?

3-10A. (Solving for i in Annuities) Nicki Johnson, a sophomore mechanical engineering student, receives a call from an insurance agent who believes that Nicki is an older woman ready to retire from teaching. He talks to her about several annuities that she could buy that would guarantee her an annual fixed income. The annuities are as follows:

Annuity	Initial Payment into Annuity (at $t=0$)	Amount of Money Received per Year	Duration of Annuity (Years)
A	$50,000	$8,500	12
B	$60,000	$7,000	25
C	$70,000	$8,000	20

If Nicki could earn 11 percent on her money by placing it in a savings account, should she place it instead in any of the annuities? Which ones, if any? Why?

3-11A. (Future Value) Sales of a new finance book were 15,000 copies this year and were expected to increase by 20 percent per year. What are expected sales during each of the next three years? Graph this sales trend and explain.

3-12A. (Future Value) Reggie Jackson, formerly of the New York Yankees, hit 41 home runs in 1980. If his home-run output grew at a rate of 10 percent per year, what would it have been over the following five years?

3-13A. (Loan Amortization) Mr. Bill S. Preston, Esq., purchased a new house for $80,000. He paid $20,000 down and agreed to pay the rest over the next twenty-five years in twenty-five equal annual payments that include principal payments plus 9 percent compound interest on the unpaid balance. What will these equal payments be?

3-14A. (Solving for *PMT* in an Annuity) To pay for your child's education, you wish to have accumulated $15,000 at the end of fifteen years. To do this, you plan on depositing an equal amount into the bank at the end of each year. If the bank is willing to pay 6 percent compounded annually, how much must you deposit each year to obtain your goal?

3-15A. (Solving for i in Compound Interest) If you were offered $1,079.50 ten years from now in return for an investment of $500 currently, what annual rate of interest would you earn if you took the offer?

3-16A. (Future Value of an Annuity) In ten years you are planning on retiring and buying a house in Oviedo, Florida. The house you are looking at currently costs $100,000 and is expected to increase in value each year at a rate of 5 percent. Assuming you can earn 10 percent annually on your investments, how much must you invest at the end of each of the next ten years to be able to buy your dream home when you retire?

3-17A. (Compound Value) The Aggarwal Corporation needs to save $10 million to retire a $10 million mortgage that matures on December 31, 2005. To retire this mortgage, the company plans to put a fixed amount into an account at the end of each year for ten years, with the first payment occurring on December 31, 1996. The Aggarwal Corporation expects to earn 9 percent annually on the money in this account. What equal annual contribution must it make to this account to accumulate the $10 million by December 31, 2005?

3-18A. (Compound Interest with Nonannual Periods) After examining the various personal loan rates available to you, you find that you can borrow funds from a finance company at 12 percent compounded monthly or from a bank at 13 percent compounded annually. Which alternative is the most attractive?

3-19A. (Present Value of an Uneven Stream of Payments) You are given three investment alternatives to analyze. The cash flows from these three investments are as follows:

Investment			
End of Year	A	B	C
1	$10,000		$10,000
2	10,000		
3	10,000		
4	10,000		
5	10,000	$10,000	
6		10,000	50,000
7		10,000	
8		10,000	
9		10,000	
10		10,000	10,000

Assuming a 20 percent discount rate, find the present value of each investment.

3-20A. (Present Value) The Kumar Corporation is planning on issuing bonds that pay no interest but can be converted into $1,000 at maturity, seven years from their purchase. To price these bonds competitively with other bonds of equal risk, it is determined that they should yield 10 percent, compounded annually. At what price should the Kumar Corporation sell these bonds?

3-21A. (Perpetuities) What is the present value of the following?
  a. A $300 perpetuity discounted back to the present at 8 percent
  b. A $1,000 perpetuity discounted back to the present at 12 percent
  c. A $100 perpetuity discounted back to the present at 9 percent
  d. A $95 perpetuity discounted back to the present at 5 percent

3-22A. (Present Value of an Annuity Due) What is the present value of a 10 year annuity due of $1,000 annually given a 10 percent discount rate?

3-23A. (Solving for n with Nonannual Periods) About how many years would it take for your investment to grow fourfold if it were invested at 16 percent compounded semiannually?

3-24A. (Bond Values) You are examining three bonds with par value of $1,000 (you receive $1,000 at maturity) and are concerned with what would happen to their market value if interest rates (or the market discount rate) changed. The three bonds are

Bond A— A bond with three years left to maturity that pays 10 percent per year compounded semiannually

Bond B—A bond with seven years left to maturity that pays 10 percent per year compounded semiannually

Bond C—A bond with twenty years left to maturity that pays 10 percent per year compounded semiannually

What would be the value of these bonds if the market discount rate were
  a. 10 percent per year compounded semiannually?
  b. 4 percent per year compounded semiannually?
  c. 16 percent per year compounded semiannually?
  d. What observations can you make about these results?

3-25A. (Complex Present Value) How much do you have to deposit today so that beginning eleven years from now you can withdraw $10,000 a year for the next five years (periods 11 through 15) plus an *additional* amount of $20,000 in the last year (period 15)? Assume an interest rate of 6 percent.

3-26A. (Loan Amortization) On December 31, Beth Klemkosky bought a yacht for $50,000, paying $10,000 down and agreeing to pay the balance in ten equal annual installments that include both the principal and 10 percent interest on the declining balance. How big would the annual payments be?

3-27A. (Solving for *i* in an Annuity) You lend a friend $30,000, which your friend will repay in five equal annual payments of $10,000, with the first payment to be received one year from now. What rate of return does your loan receive?

3-28. (Solving for *i* in Compound Interest) You lend a friend $10,000, for which your friend will repay you $27,027 at the end of five years. What interest rate are you charging your "friend"?

3-29A. (Loan Amortization) A firm borrows $25,000 from the bank at 12 percent compounded annually to purchase some new machinery. This loan is to be repaid in equal annual installments at the end of each year over the next five years. How much will each annual payment be?

3-30A. (Present Value Comparison) You are offered $1,000 today, $10,000 in twelve years, or $25,000 in twenty-five years. Assuming that you can earn 11 percent on your money, which should you choose?

3-31A. (Compound Annuity) You plan on buying some property in Florida five years from today. To do this you estimate that you will need $20,000 at that time for the purchase. You would like to accumulate these funds by making equal annual deposits in your savings account, which pays 12 percent annually. If you make your first deposit at the end of this year and you would like your account to reach $20,000 when the final deposit is made, what will be the amount of your deposits?

3-32A. (Complex Present Value) You would like to have $50,000 in fifteen years. To accumulate this amount you plan to deposit each year an equal sum in the bank, which will earn 7 percent interest compounded annually. Your first payment will be made at the end of the year.

    a. How much must you deposit annually to accumulate this amount?

    b. If you decide to make a large lump-sum deposit today instead of the annual deposits, how large should this lump-sum deposit be? (Assume you can earn 7 percent on this deposit.)

    c. At the end of five years you will receive $10,000 and deposit this in the bank toward your goal of $50,000 at the end of fifteen years. In addition to this deposit, how much must you deposit in equal annual deposits to reach your goal? (Again assume you can earn 7 percent on this deposit.)

3-33A. (Comprehensive Present Value) You are trying to plan for retirement in ten years and currently you have $100,000 in a savings account and $300,000 in stocks. In addition you plan on adding to your savings by depositing $10,000 per year in your *savings account* at the end of each of the next five years and then $20,000 per year at the end of each year for the final five years until retirement.

    a. Assuming your savings account returns 7 percent compounded annually while your investment in stocks will return 12 percent compounded annually, how much will you have at the end of ten years? (Ignore taxes.)

    b. If you expect to live for twenty years after you retire, and at retirement you deposit all of your savings in a bank account paying 10 percent, how much can you withdraw each year after retirement (twenty equal withdrawals beginning one year after you retire) to end up with a zero balance at death?

3-34A. (Loan Amortization) On December 31, Son-Nan Chen borrowed $100,000, agreeing to repay this sum in twenty equal annual installments that include both the principal and 15 percent interest on the declining balance. How large will the annual payments be?

3-35A. (Loan Amortization) To buy a new house you must borrow $150,000. To do this you take out a $150,000, thirty-year, 10 percent mortgage. Your mortgage payments, which are made at the end of each year (one payment each year), include both principal and 10 percent interest on the declining balance. How large will your annual payments be?

3-36A. (Present Value) The state lottery's million-dollar payout provides for one million dollars to be paid over nineteen years in $50,000 amounts. The first $50,000 payment is made immediately and the nineteen remaining $50,000 payments occur at the end of each of the next nineteen years. If 10 percent is the appropriate discount rate, what is the present value of this stream of cash flows? If 20 percent is the appropriate discount what is the present value of the cash flows?

3-37A. (Compounding an Annuity Due) Find the future value at the end of year ten of an annuity due of $1,000 per year for ten years compounded annually at 10 percent. What would be the future value of this annuity if it were compounded annually at 15 percent?

3-38A. (Present Value of an Annuity Due) Determine the present value of an annuity due of $1,000 per year for ten years discounted back to present at an annual rate of 10 percent. What would be the present value of this annuity due if it were discounted at an annual rate of 15 percent?

3-39A. (Present Value of a Future Annuity) Determine the present value of an ordinary annuity of $1,000 per year for ten years with the first cash flow from the annuity coming at the end of year 8 (that is, no payments at the end of years 1 through 7 and annual payments at the end of year 8 through year 17) given a 10 percent discount rate.

3-40A. (Solving for i in Compound Interest—Financial Calculator Needed) In September 1963 the first issue of the comic book *X-MEN* was issued. The original price for the issue was 12 cents. By September 1995, 32 years later, the value of this comic book had risen to $3500. What annual rate of interest would you have earned if you had bought the comic in 1963 and sold it in 1995?

3-41A. (Comprehensive Present Value) You have just inherited a large sum of money and you are trying to determine how much you should save for retirement and how much you can spend now. For retirement you will deposit today (January 1, 1996) a lump sum in a bank account paying 10 percent compounded annually. You don't plan on touching this deposit until you retire in five years (January 1, 2001) and you plan on living for 20 additional years and then dropping dead on December 31, 2020. During your retirement you would like to receive income of $50,000 per year to be received the first day of each year, with the first payment on January 1, 2001, the last payment on January 1, 2020. Complicating this objective is your desire to have one final three-year fling during which time you'd like to track down all the original members of "Leave It to Beaver" and "The Brady Bunch" and get their autographs. To finance this you want to receive $250,000 on January 1, 2016, and *nothing* on January 1, 2017 and January 1, 2018, as you will be on the road. In addition, after you pass on (January 1, 2021), you would like to have a total of $100,000 to leave to your children.

   a. How much must you deposit in the bank at 10 percent on January 1, 1996 to achieve your goal? (Use a timeline to answer this question.)

   b. What kinds of problems are associated with this analysis and its assumptions?

INTEGRATIVE PROBLEM

For your job as the business reporter for a local newspaper, you are given the task of putting together a series of articles that explains the power of the time value of money to your readers. Your editor would like you to address several specific questions in addition to demonstrating for the readership the use of the time value of money techniques by applying them to several problems. What would be your response to the following memorandum from your editor:

TO: Business Reporter

FROM: Perry White, Editor, *Daily Planet*

RE: Upcoming Series on the Importance and Power of the Time Value of Money

In your upcoming series on the time value of money, I would like to make sure you cover several specific points. In addition, before you begin this assignment, I want to make sure we are all reading from the same script, as accuracy has always been the cornerstone of the *Daily Planet*. In this regard, I'd like a response to the following questions before we proceed:

a. What is the relationship between discounting and compounding?

b. What is the relationship between the $PVIF_{i,n}$ and $PVIFA_{i,n}$?

c. (1) What will $5,000 invested for ten years at 8 percent compounded annually grow to?

(2) How many years will it take $400 to grow to $1,671, if it is invested at 10 percent compounded annually?

(3) At what rate would $1,000 have to be invested to grow to $4,046 in ten years?

d. Calculate the future sum of $1,000, given that it will be held in the bank for five years and earn 10 percent compounded semiannually?

e. What is an annuity due? How does this differ from an ordinary annuity?

f. What is the present value of an ordinary annuity of $1,000 per year for seven years discounted back to present at 10 percent? What would be the present value if it were an annuity due?

g. What is the future value of an ordinary annuity of $1,000 per year for seven years compounded at 10 percent? What would be the future value if it were an annuity due?

h. You have just borrowed $100,000, and you agree to pay it back over the next twenty-five years in twenty-five equal end-of-year annual payments that include the principal payments plus 10 percent compound interest on the unpaid balance. What will be the size of these payments?

i. What is the present value of a $1,000 perpetuity discounted back to present at 8 percent?

j. What is the present value of a $1,000 annuity for ten years with the first payment occurring at the end of year 10 (that is, ten $1,000 payments occurring at the end of year 10 through year 19) given an appropriate discount rate of 10 percent?

k. Given a 10 percent discount rate, what is the present value of a perpetuity of $1,000 per year if the first payment does not begin until the end of year 10?

l. What is the annual percentage yield (APY) on an 8 percent bank loan compounded quarterly?

SECTION II
SELECTING THE PROJECT

CHAPTER 4

RELEVANT INFORMATION FOR SELECTING PROJECTS

4.1 PROJECT SELECTION AND THE NEED FOR RELEVANT INFORMATION

To the upper management in most large organizations, the projects selected and approved simply represent financial investments. In the early stages of the selection process all prospective projects are analyzed and ranked according to financial return, risk, and subjective factors. Constraints are always a factor. Rarely is sufficient money available to accept every project proposed.

The trend in many large organizations is to include the project management team in the project selection process; this is termed end-to-end project team involvement. There is a higher probability of project success as well as financial return to the organization when the project team is aware of the relative importance of each project and how it helps achieve the company's strategic objectives.

A significant part of the project manager's time is often occupied by the project selection process. The information available to assist in making the selection decision ranges from almost non-existent to nearly infinite. Consequently, the seasoned participant in the selection process will be selective in requesting only relevant information. The following readings from Horngren address relevant information and the decision making process.

MEANING OF RELEVANCE: THE MAJOR CONCEPTUAL LESSON

What information is relevant depends on the decision being made. Decision making is essentially choosing among several courses of action. The available actions are determined by an often time-consuming formal or informal search and screening process, perhaps carried on by a company team that includes engineers, accountants, and operating executives. Accountants have an important role in the decision-making process, not as decision makers but as collectors and reporters of relevant information. (Although many managers want the accountant to recommend the proper decision, the final choice always rests with the operating executive.) The accountant's role in decision making is primarily that of a technical expert on financial analysis who helps managers focus on relevant data, information that will lead to the best decision.

Relevance Defined

In the final stages of the decision-making process, managers compare two or more alternative courses of action. The decision is based on the predicted difference in future performance under each alternative. The key question is: What difference will the choice make? **Relevant information** is the predicted future costs and revenues that will differ among the alternatives.

Note that relevant information is a prediction of the future, not a summary of the past. Historical (past) data have no *direct* bearing on a decision. Such data can have an *indirect* bearing on a decision because they may help in predicting the future. But past figures, in themselves, are irrelevant to the decision itself. Why? Because the decision cannot affect past data. Decisions affect the future. Nothing can alter what has already happened.

Of the expected future data, only those that will differ from alternative to alternative are relevant to the decision. Any item that will remain the same regardless of the alternative selected is irrelevant. For instance, if a department manager's salary will be the same regardless of the products stocked, the salary is irrelevant to the selection of products.

Accuracy and Relevance

In the best of all possible worlds, information used for decision making would be perfectly relevant and accurate. However, in reality, the cost of such information often exceeds its benefit. Accountants often trade off relevance versus accuracy. Of course, relevant information must be reasonably accurate but not precisely so.

Precise but irrelevant information is worthless for decision making. For example, a university president's salary may be $140,000 per year, to the penny, but may have no bearing on the question of whether to buy or rent data processing equipment. On the other hand, imprecise but relevant information can be useful. For example, sales predictions for a new product may be subject to great error, but they still are helpful to the decision of whether to manufacture the product.

The degree to which information is relevant or precise often depends on the degree to which it is *qualitative* or *quantitative*. Qualitative aspects are those for which measurement in dollars and cents is difficult and imprecise; quantitative aspects are those for which measurement is easy and precise. Accountants, statisticians, and mathematicians try to express as many decision factors as feasible in quantitative terms because this approach reduces the number of qualitative factors to be judged. Just as we noted that relevance is more crucial than precision in decision making, so a qualitative aspect may easily carry more weight than a measurable (quantitative) financial impact in many decisions. For example, the opposition of a militant union to new labor-saving machinery may cause a manager to defer or even reject completely the contemplated installation even if it would save money. Alternatively, to avoid a long-run dependence on a particular supplier, a company may pass up the opportunity to purchase a component from the supplier at a price below the cost of producing it themselves.

On the other hand, managers sometimes introduce new technology (e.g., advanced computer systems or automated equipment) even though the expected quantitative results seem unattractive. Managers defend such decisions on the grounds that failure to keep abreast of new technology will surely bring unfavorable financial results sooner or later.

Examples of Relevance

The following examples will help you clarify the sharp distinctions needed to discriminate between relevant and irrelevant information.

Suppose you always buy gasoline from either of two nearby gasoline stations. Yesterday you noticed that one station was selling gasoline at $1.50 per gallon; the other, at $1.40. Your automobile needs gasoline, and in making your choice of stations, you *assume* that these prices have not changed. The relevant costs are $1.50 and $1.40, the expected future costs that will differ between the alternatives. You use your past experience (i.e., what you observed yesterday) for predicting today's price. Note that the relevant cost is not what you paid in the past or what you observed yesterday, but what you *expect to pay* when you drive in to get gasoline. This cost meets our two criteria: (1) it is the expected future cost, and (2) it differs between the alternatives.

You may also plan to have your car lubricated. The recent price at each station was $12, and this is what you anticipate paying. This expected future cost is irrelevant because it will be the same under either alternative. It does not meet our second criterion.

On a business level, consider the following decision. A manufacturer is thinking of using aluminum instead of copper in a line of ashtrays. The cost of direct material will decrease from 30¢ to 20¢ per ashtray. The analysis in a nutshell is as follows:

	Aluminum	Copper	Difference
Direct material	$.20	$.30	$.10

The cost of copper used for this comparison probably came from historical cost records on the amount paid most recently for copper, but the *relevant* cost in the foregoing analysis is the expected future cost of copper compared with the expected future cost of aluminum.

The direct-labor cost will continue to be 70¢ per unit regardless of the material used. It is irrelevant because our second criterion—an element of difference between the alternatives—is not met.

	Aluminum	Copper	Difference
Direct material	$.20	$.30	$.10
Direct labor	.70	.70	—

Therefore we can safely exclude direct labor from the comparison of alternatives. There is no harm in including irrelevant items in a formal analysis, provided that they are included properly. However, confining the reports to the relevant items provides greater clarity and timesavings for busy managers.

Exhibit 4-1 provides a more elaborate view of this decision than is necessary for this simple decision, but it serves to show the appropriate framework for more complex decisions. Box 1(A) represents historical data from the accounting system. Box 1(B) represents other data, such as price indices or industry statistics, gathered from outside the accounting system. Regardless of their source, the data in step 1 help the formulation of *predictions* in step 2. (Remember that although historical data may act as a guide to predicting, they are irrelevant to the decision itself.)

In step 3 these predictions become inputs to the *decision model*. A **decision model** is defined as any method for making a choice. Such models often require elaborate quantitative procedures, such as a petroleum refinery's mathematical method for choosing what products to manufacture for any given day or week. A decision model, however, may also be simple. It may be confined to a single comparison of costs for choosing between two materials. In this instance our decision model is: Compare the predicted unit costs and select the alternative with the lesser cost.

We will be referring back to Exhibit 4-1 frequently because it displays the major conceptual lesson in this chapter. Above all, note the commonality of the relevant-information approach to the various special decisions explored in this chapter. In all decisions managers should focus on predictions of future outcomes, not dwell on past outcomes. The major difficulty is predicting how revenues and costs will be affected under each alternative. No matter what the decision situation, the key question to ask is, What difference will it make?

THE SPECIAL SALES ORDER

The first decision for which we examine relevant information is the special sales order.

Illustrative Example

As you can see, the two income statements differ somewhat in format (see Exhibit 4-2). The difference in format may be unimportant if the accompanying cost analysis leads to the same set of decisions. However, these two approaches sometimes lead to different *unit* costs that must be interpreted warily.

Exhibit 4-1 Decision Process and Role of Information

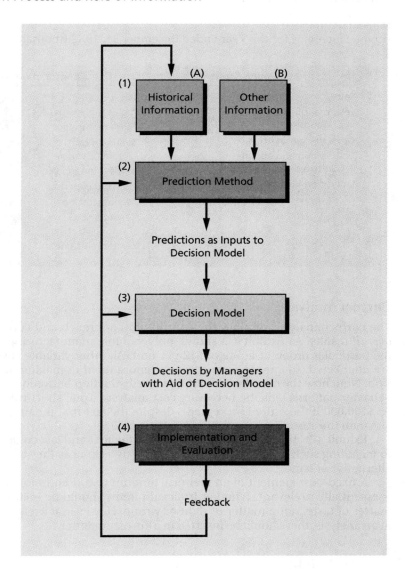

In our illustration, suppose 1 million units of product, such as some automobile replacement part, were made and sold. Under the absorption-costing approach, the unit manufacturing cost of the product would be $15,000,000 ÷ 1,000,000, or $15 per unit. Suppose a mail-order house near year-end offered Samson $13 per unit for a 100,000-unit special order that (1) would not affect Samson's regular business in any way, (2) would not raise any antitrust issues concerning price discrimination, (3) would not affect total fixed costs, (4) would not require any additional variable selling and administrative expenses, and (5) would use some otherwise idle manufacturing capacity. Should Samson accept the order? Perhaps the question should be stated more sharply: What is the difference in the short-run financial results between not accepting and accepting? As usual, the key question is, What difference will it make?

Exhibit 4-2   Absorption and Contribution Forms of the Income Statement

Samson Company
Income Statement for the Year Ended December 31, 19X2 (thousands of dollars)

Absorption Form		Contribution Form		
Sales	$20,000	Sales		$20,000
Less: manufacturing cost		Less: variable expenses		
of goods sold	15,000	Manufacturing	$12,000	
Gross margin or gross profit	$ 5,000	Selling and		
Less: selling and admin-		administrative	1,100	13,100
istrative expenses	4,000	Contribution margin		$ 6,900
Operating income	$ 1,000	Less: fixed expenses		
		Manufacturing	$ 3,000	
		Selling and		
		administrative	2,900	5,900
		Operating income		$ 1,000

Correct Analysis

The correct analysis employs the contribution approach and concentrates on the final *overall* results. As Exhibit 4-3 shows, only variable manufacturing costs are affected by the particular order, at a rate of $12 per unit. All other variable costs and all fixed costs are unaffected, so a manager may safely ignore them in making this special-order decision. Note how the contribution approach's distinction between variable- and fixed-cost behavior patterns aids the necessary cost analysis. Total short-run income will increase by $100,000 if the order is accepted—despite the fact that the unit selling price of $13 is less than the absorption manufacturing cost of $15.

Exhibit 4-3 shows total fixed expenses in the first and last columns. There is no harm in including such irrelevant items in an analysis as long as they are included under every alternative at hand.

A fixed-cost element of an identical amount that is common among all alternatives is essentially irrelevant. Whether irrelevant items should be included in an analysis is a matter of taste, not a matter of right or wrong. However, if irrelevant items are included in an analysis, they should be inserted in a correct manner.

Incorrect Analysis

Faulty cost analysis sometimes occurs because of misinterpreting unit fixed costs. For instance, managers might erroneously use the $15 absorption manufacturing cost per unit to make the following prediction for the year:

Exhibit 4-3 Comparative Predicted Income Statements, Contribution Approach

Samson Company
for Year Ended December 31, 19X2

	Without Special Order, 1,000,000 Units	Effect of Special Order 100,000 Units		With Special Order, 1,100,000 Units
		Total	Per Unit	
Sales	$20,000,000	$1,300,000	$13	$21,300,000
Less: variable expenses				
Manufacturing	$12,000,000	$1,200,000	$12	$13,200,000
Selling and administrative	1,100,000	—	—	1,100,000
Total variable expenses	$13,100,000	$1,200,000	$12	$14,300,000
Contribution margin	$ 6,900,000	$ 100,000	$ 1	$ 7,000,000
Less: fixed expenses				
Manufacturing	$ 3,000,000	—	—	$ 3,000,000
Selling and administrative	2,900,000	—	—	2,900,000
Total fixed expenses	$ 5,900,000	—	—	$ 5,900,000
Operating income	$ 1,000,000	$ 100,000	$ 1	$ 1,100,000

Incorrect Analysis	Without Special Order 1,000,000 Units	Incorrect Effect of Special Order 100,000 Units	With Special Order 1,100,000 Units
Sales	$20,000,000	$1,300,000	$21,300,000
Less: manufacturing cost of goods sold @ $15	15,000,000	1,500,000	16,500,000
Gross margin	5,000,000	(200,000)	4,800,000
Selling and administrative expenses	4,000,000	—	4,000,000
Operating income	$ 1,000,000	$ (200,000)	$ 800,000

The incorrect prediction of a $1.5 million increase in costs results from multiplying 100,000 units by $15. Of course, the fallacy in this approach is that it treats a fixed cost (fixed manufacturing cost) as if it were variable. Avoid the assumption that unit costs may be used indiscriminately as a basis for predicting how total costs will behave. Unit costs are useful for predicting variable costs but often misleading when used to predict fixed costs.

Confusion of Variable and Fixed Costs

Consider the relationship between total fixed manufacturing costs and a fixed manufacturing cost per unit of product:

$$\text{fixed cost per unit of product} = \frac{\text{total fixed manufacturing costs}}{\text{some selected volume level used as the denominator}}$$

$$= \frac{\$3,000,000}{1,000,000 \text{ units}} = \$3 \text{ per unit}$$

The typical cost accounting system serves two purposes simultaneously: *planning and control* and *product costing*. The total fixed cost for *budgetary planning and control purposes* can be graphed as a lump sum:

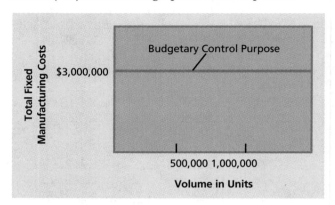

For *product-costing purposes*, however, the absorption-costing approach implies that these *fixed* costs have a *variable*-cost behavior pattern:

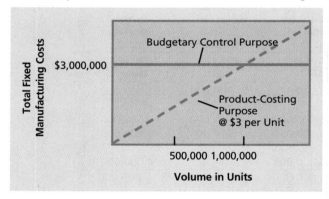

The addition of 100,000 units will not add any *total* fixed costs as long as total output is within the relevant range. The incorrect analysis, however, includes 100,000 × $3 = $300,000 of fixed cost in the predictions of increases in total costs.

In short, the increase in manufacturing costs should be computed by multiplying 1,000,000 units by $12, not by $15. The $15 includes a $3 component that will not affect the total manufacturing costs as volume changes.

Spreading Fixed Costs

As you have just seen, the distinction between unit cost and total cost can become particularly troublesome when analyzing fixed-cost behavior. Assume the same facts concerning the special order as before, except that the order was for 250,000 units at a selling price of $11.50. Then, to avoid the analytical pitfalls of unit-cost analysis, use the contribution approach and concentrate on *totals* instead of units (in thousands of dollars):

	Without Special Order	Effect of Special Order	With Special Order
	1,000,000 Units	*250,000 Units*	*1,250,000 Units*
Sales	20,000	2,875*	22,875
Variable manufacturing costs	12,000	3,000†	15,000
Other variable costs	1,100	—	1,100
Total variable costs	13,100	3,000	16,100
Contribution margin	6,900	(125)‡	6,775

*250,000 × $11.50 selling price of special order.
†250,000 × $12.00 variable manufacturing cost per unit of special order.
‡250,000 × $.50 negative contribution margin per unit of special order.

Short-run income will fall by $125,000 (that is, 250,000 units × $.50) if the special order is accepted. No matter how the fixed manufacturing costs are "unitized" and "spread" over the units produced, their total of $3 million will be *unchanged* by the special order (in thousands of dollars):

	Without Special Order	Effect of Special Order	With Special Order
	1,000,000 Units	*250,000 Units*	*1,250,000 Units*
Contribution margin (as above)	6,900	(125)	6,775
Total fixed costs			
At an average rate of $3.00*:			
1,000,000 × $3.00	3,000		
At an average rate of $2.40†:			
1,250,000 × $2.40		—	3,000
Contribution to other fixed			
costs and operating income	3,900	(125)	3,775

*$3,000,000 ÷ 1,000,000.
†$3,000,000 ÷ 1,250,000.

Notice that no matter how fixed costs are spread for *unit* product-costing purposes, *total* fixed costs are unchanged, even though fixed costs *per unit* fall from $3.00 to $2.40.

The lesson here is important. Do not be deceived. Follow what was called Robert McNamara's First Law of Analysis when he was U.S. Secretary of Defense: "Always start by looking at the grand total. Whatever problem you are studying, back off and look at it in the large." In this context, that law means, "Beware of unit costs. When in doubt, convert all unit costs into the total costs under each alternative to get the big picture." In particular, beware of unit costs when analyzing fixed costs. Think in terms of totals instead.

Multiple-Cost Drivers and Special Orders

To identify costs affected by a special order (or by other special decisions), more and more firms are going a step beyond simply identifying fixed and variable costs. Many different cost drivers may cause companies to incur costs. Businesses that have identified all their significant cost drivers can predict the effects of special orders more accurately.

Suppose Samson Company examined its $12 million of variable costs very closely and identified two significant cost drivers: $9 million that varies directly with *units produced* at a rate of $9 per unit and $3 million that varies with the *number of production setups*. Normally, for production of 1,000,000 units, Samson has 500 setups at a cost of $6,000 per setup, with an average of 2,000 units produced for each setup. Additional sales generally require a proportional increase in the number of setups.

Now suppose the special order is for 100,000 units that vary only slightly in production specifications. Instead of the normal 50 setups, Samson will need only 5 setups, and producing 100,000 units will take only $930,000 of additional variable cost:

Additional unit-based variable cost, 100,000 × $9	$900,000
Additional setup-based variable cost, 5 3 $6,000	30,000
Total additional variable cost	$930,000

Instead of the original estimate of 100,000 × $12 = $1,200,000 additional variable cost, the special order will cost only $930,000, or $270,000 less than the original estimate. Therefore, the special order is $270,000 more profitable than predicted from the simple, unit-based assessment of variable cost.

A special order may also be more costly than predicted by a simple fixed- and variable-cost analysis. Suppose the 100,000-unit special order called for a variety of models and colors delivered at various times, so that 100 setups are required. The variable cost of the special order would be $1.5 million.

Additional unit-based variable cost, 100,000 × $9	$ 900,000
Additional setup-based variable cost, 100 3 $6,000	600,000
Total additional variable cost	$1,500,000

Summary Problem for Your Review

Problem One

1. Return to the basic illustration in Exhibit 4-3. Suppose Samson Co. received a special order like that described in conjunction with Exhibit 4-3 that had the following terms: selling price would be $13.50 instead of $13.00, but a manufacturer's agent who had obtained the potential order would have to be paid a flat fee of $40,000 if the order were accepted. What would be the new special-order difference in operating income if the order were accepted?

2. Assume the original facts concerning the special order, except that the order was for 250,000 units at a selling price of $11.50. Some managers have been known to argue for acceptance of such an order as follows: "Of course, we will lose $.50 each on the variable manufacturing costs, but we will gain $.60 per unit by spreading our fixed manufacturing costs over 1.25 million units instead of 1 million units. Consequently, we should take the offer because it represents an advantage of $.10 per unit."

Old fixed manufacturing cost per unit, $3,000,000 ÷ 1,000,000	$3.00
New fixed manufacturing cost per unit, $3,000,000 4 1,250,000	2.40
"Saving" in fixed manufacturing cost per unit	$ .60
Loss on variable manufacturing cost per unit, $11.50 – $12.00	.50
Net saving per unit in manufacturing cost	$ .10

Explain why this is faulty thinking.

Solution to Problem One

1. Focus on the *differences* in revenues and costs. In this problem, in addition to the difference in variable costs, there is a difference in fixed costs between the two alternatives.

Additional revenue, 100,000 units @ $13.50 per unit	$1,350,000
Less additional costs	
Variable costs, 100,000 units @ $12 per unit	1,200,000
Fixed costs, agent's fee	40,000
Increase in operating income from special order	$ 110,000

2. The faulty thinking comes from attributing a "savings" to the decrease in unit fixed costs. Regardless of how the fixed manufacturing costs are "unitized" or "spread" over the units produced, their total of $3 million will be unchanged by the special order. As the tabulation on page 175 indicates, short-run income will fall by 250,000 units 3 ($12.00 – $11.50) = $125,000 if the second special order is accepted.

DELETION OR ADDITION OF PRODUCTS OR DEPARTMENTS

The same principles of relevance applied to special orders apply—albeit in slightly different ways—to decisions about adding or deleting products or departments.

Avoidable and Unavoidable Costs

Consider a discount department store that has three major departments: groceries, general merchandise, and drugs. Management is considering dropping groceries, which have consistently shown a net loss. The following table reports the present annual net income (in thousands of dollars).

	Total	Groceries	Departments General Merchandise	Drugs
Sales	$1,900	$1,000	$800	$100
Variable cost of goods sold and expenses*	1,420	800	560	60
Contribution margin	$ 480 (25%)	$ 200 (20%)	$240 (30%)	$ 40 (40%)
Fixed expenses (salaries, depreciation, insurance, property taxes, etc.):				
Avoidable	$ 265	$ 150	$100	$ 15
Unavoidable	180	60	100	20
Total fixed expenses	$ 445	$ 210	$200	$ 35
Operating income	$ 35	$ (10)	$ 40	$ 5

*Examples of variable expenses include paper bags and sales commissions.

Notice that the fixed expenses are divided into two categories, *avoidable* and *unavoidable*. **Avoidable costs**—costs that will *not* continue if an ongoing operation is changed or deleted—are relevant. Avoidable costs include department salaries and other costs that could be eliminated by not operating the specific department. **Unavoidable costs**—costs that continue even if an operation is halted—are not relevant because they are not affected by a decision to delete the department. Unavoidable costs include many **common costs**, which are defined as those costs of facilities and services that are shared by users. Examples are store depreciation, heating, air conditioning, and general management expenses.

Assume first that the only alternatives to be considered are dropping or continuing the grocery department, which shows a loss of $10,000. Assume further that the total assets invested would be unaffected by the decision. The vacated space would be idle and the unavoidable costs would continue. Which alternative would you recommend? An analysis (in thousands of dollars) follows:

Income Statements	Total Before Change (a)	Effect of Dropping Groceries (b)	Total After Change (a) – (b)	Store as a Whole
Sales	$1,900	$1,000	$900	
Variable expenses	1,420	800	620	
Contribution margin	$ 480	$ 200	$280	
Avoidable fixed expenses	265	150	115	
Profit contribution to common space and other unavoidable costs	$ 215	$ 50	$165	
Common space and other unavoidable costs	180	—	180	
Operating income	$ 35	$ |50	$ (15)	

The preceding analysis shows that matters would be worse, rather than better, if groceries were dropped and the vacated facilities left idle. In short, as the income statement shows, groceries bring in a contribution margin of $200,000, which is $50,000 more than the $150,000 fixed expenses that would be saved by closing the grocery department. The grocery department showed a loss in the first income statement because of the unavoidable fixed costs charged to it.

Assume now that the space made available by the dropping of groceries could be used to expand the general merchandise department. The space would be occupied by merchandise that would increase sales by $500,000, generate a 30% contribution-margin percentage, and have avoidable fixed costs of $70,000. The $80,000 increase in operating income of general merchandise more than offsets the $50,000 decline from eliminating groceries, providing an overall increase in operating income of $65,000 − $35,000 = $30,000.

(In thousands of dollars)	Effects of Changes			
	Total Before Change (a)	Drop Groceries (b)	Expand General Merchandise (c)	Total After Changes (a) − (b) + (c)
Sales	$1,900	$1,000	$500	$1,400
Variable expenses	1,420	800	350	970
Contribution margin	$ 480	$ 200	$150	$ 430
Avoidable fixed expenses	265	150	70	185
Contribution to common space and other unavoidable costs	$ 215	$ 50	$ 80	$ 245
Common space and other unavoidable costs*	180	—	—	180
Operating income	$ 35	$ 50	$ 80	$ 65

*Includes the $60,000 of former grocery fixed costs, which were allocations of unavoidable common costs that will continue regardless of how the space is occupied.

As the following summary analysis demonstrates, the objective is to obtain, from a given amount of space or capacity, the maximum contribution to the payment of those unavoidable costs that remain unaffected by the nature of the product sold (in thousands of dollars):

	Profit Contribution of Given Space		
	Groceries	Expansion of General Merchandise	Difference
Sales	$1,000	$500	$500 U
Variable expenses	800	350	450 F
Contribution margin	$ 200	$150	$ 50 U
Avoidable fixed expenses	150	70	80 F
Contribution to common space and other unavoidable costs	$ 50	$ 80	30 F

F = Favorable difference resulting from replacing groceries with general merchandise.
U = Unfavorable difference.

In this case, the general merchandise will not achieve the dollar sales volume that groceries will, but the higher contribution margin percentage and the lower wage costs (mostly because of the diminished need for stocking and checkout clerks) will bring more favorable net results.

This illustration contains another lesson. Avoid the idea that relevant-cost analysis merely says, "Consider all variable costs, and ignore all fixed costs." In this case, *some* fixed costs are relevant because they differ under each alternative.

OPTIMAL USE OF LIMITED RESOURCES

When a multiproduct plant is being operated at capacity, managers often must decide which orders to accept. The contribution approach also applies here because the product to be emphasized or the order to be accepted is the one that makes the biggest *total* profit contribution per unit of the limiting factor. A **limiting factor** or **scarce resource** restricts or constrains the production or sale of a product or service. Limiting factors include labor-hours and machine-hours that limit production and, hence, sales in manufacturing firms and square feet of floor space or cubic meters of display space that limit sales in department stores.

The contribution approach must be used wisely, however. Managers sometimes mistakenly favor those products with the biggest contribution margin or gross margin per sales dollar without regard to scarce resources.

Assume that a company has two products: a plain portable heater and a fancier heater with many special features. Unit data follow:

	Plain Heater	Fancy Heater
Selling price	$20	$30
Variable costs	16	21
Contribution margin	$ 4	$ 9
Contribution-margin ratio	20%	30%

Which product is more profitable? On which should the firm spend its resources? The correct answer is: It depends. If sales are restricted by demand for only a limited *number* of heaters, fancy heaters are more profitable. Why? Because sale of a plain heater adds $4 to profit; sale of a fancy heater adds $9. If the limiting factor is *units* of sales, the more profitable product is the one with the higher contribution *per unit*.

Now suppose annual demand for heaters of both types is more than the company can produce in the next year. Productive capacity is the limiting factor. If 10,000 hours of capacity are available, and three plain heaters can be produced per hour in contrast to one fancy heater, the plain heater is more profitable. Why? Because it contributes more profit *per hour* of capacity:

	Plain Heater	Fancy Heater
1. Units per hour	3	1
2. Contribution margin per unit	$4	$9
Contribution margin per hour (1) × (2)	$12	$9
Total contribution for 10,000 hours	$120,000	$90,000

The criterion for maximizing profits when one factor limits sales is to obtain the greatest possible contribution to profit for each unit of the limiting or scarce factor. The product that is most profitable when one particular factor limits sales may be the least profitable if a different factor restricts sales.

When there are capacity limitations, the conventional contribution-margin or gross-margin-per-sales-dollar ratios provide an insufficient clue to profitability. Consider an example of two department stores. The conventional gross profit percentage (gross profit ÷ selling price) is an insufficient clue to profitability because profits also depend on the space occupied and the **inventory turnover** (number of times the average inventory is sold per year). Discount department stores such as Wal-Mart, Target, and K-Mart have succeeded while using lower markups than traditional department stores because they have been able to increase turnover and thus increase the contribution to profit per unit of space. Exhibit 4-4 illustrates the same product, taking up the same amount of space, in each of two stores. The contribution margins per unit and per sales dollar are less in the discount store, but faster turnover makes the same product a more profitable use of space in the discount store. In general, companies seek faster inventory turnover. A survey of retail shoe stores showed that those with above-average financial performance had an inventory turnover of 2.6 compared to an industry average of 2.0.

Notice that throughout this discussion fixed costs have been correctly ignored. They are irrelevant unless their total is affected by the choices.

Exhibit 4-4 Effect of Turnover on Profit

	Regular Department Store	Discount Department Store
Retail price	$4.00	$3.50
Cost of merchandise and other variable costs	3.00	3.00
Contribution to profit per unit	$1.00 (25%)	$ .50 (14%)
Units sold per year	10,000	22,000
Total contribution to profit, assuming the same space allotment in both stores	$10,000	$11,000

ROLE OF COSTS IN PRICING DECISIONS

One of the major decisions managers face is pricing. Actually, pricing can take many forms. Among the many pricing decisions to be made are:

1. Setting the price of a new product
2. Setting the price of products sold under private labels
3. Responding to a new price of a competitor
4. Pricing bids in both sealed and open bidding situations

The pricing decision is extensively covered in the literature of economics and marketing. Our purpose here is not to provide a comprehensive review of that literature, but simply to highlight a few important points that help define the role of costs in pricing.

Economic Theory and Pricing

Pricing decisions depend on the characteristics of the market a firm faces. In **perfect competition**, a firm can sell as much of a product as it can produce, all at a single market price. If it charges more, no customer will buy. If it charges less, it sacrifices profits. Therefore, every firm in such a market will charge the market price, and the only decision for managers is how much to produce.

Although costs do not directly influence prices in perfect competition, they affect the production decision. Consider the marginal cost curve in Exhibit 4-5. The **marginal cost** is the additional cost resulting from producing and selling one additional unit. The marginal cost often decreases as production increases up to a point because efficiencies are possible with larger production amounts. At some point, however, marginal costs begin to rise with increases in production because facilities begin to be overcrowded, resulting in inefficiencies.

Exhibit 4-5 also includes a *marginal revenue curve*. The **marginal revenue** is the additional revenue resulting from the sale of an additional unit. In perfect competition, the marginal revenue curve is a horizontal line equal to the price per unit at all volumes of sales.

As long as the marginal cost is less than the price, additional production and sales are profitable. When marginal cost exceeds price, however, the firm loses money on each additional unit. Therefore, the profit-maximizing volume is the quantity at which marginal cost equals price. In Exhibit 4-5, the firm should produce V_0 units. Producing fewer units passes up profitable opportunities; producing more units reduces profit because each additional unit costs more to produce than it generates in revenue.

In imperfect competition, a firm's price will influence the quantity it sells. At some point, price reductions are necessary to generate additional sales. Exhibit 4-6 contains a demand curve (also called the average revenue curve) for imperfect competition that shows the volume of sales at each possible price. To sell additional units, the price of all units sold must be reduced. Therefore, the marginal revenue curve, also shown in Exhibit 4-6, is below the demand curve. That is, the marginal revenue for selling one additional unit is less than the price at which it is sold because the price of all other units falls as well. For example, suppose 10 units can be sold for $50 per unit. The price must be dropped to $49 per unit to sell 11 units, to $48 to sell 12 units, and to $47 to sell

13 units. The fourth column of Exhibit 4-7 shows the marginal revenue for units 11 through 13. Notice that the marginal revenue decreases as volume increases.

Exhibit 4-5 Marginal Revenue and Cost in Perfect Competition

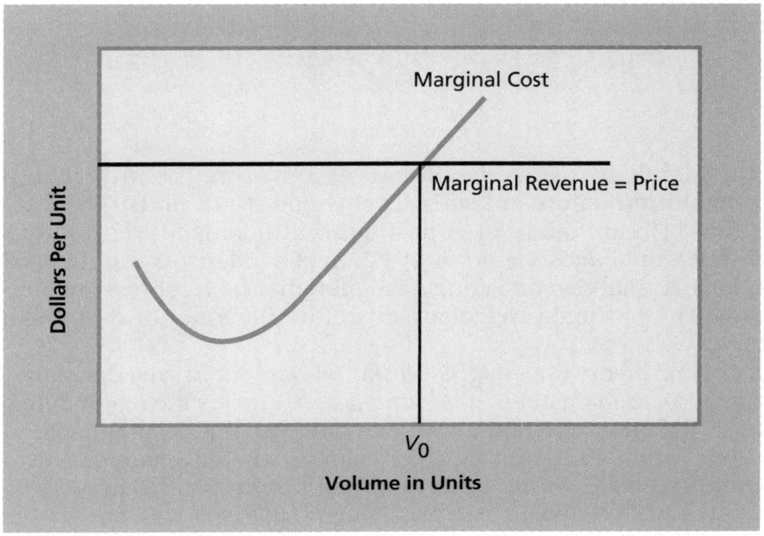

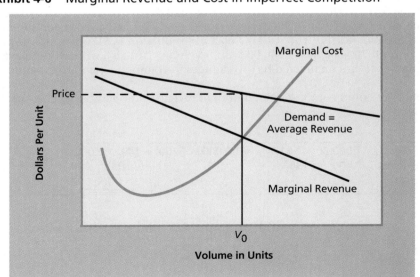

To estimate marginal revenue, managers must predict the effect of price changes on sales volume, which is called **price elasticity**. If small price increases cause large volume declines, demand is highly *elastic*. If prices have little or no effect on volume, demand is highly *inelastic*.

Exhibit 4-6 Marginal Revenue and Cost in Imperfect Competition

Exhibit 4-7 Profit Maximization in Imperfect Competition

Units Sold	Price per Unit	Total Revenue	Marginal Revenue	Marginal Cost	Profit from Production and Sale of Additional Unit
10	$50	10 × $50 = $500			
11	49	11 × 49 = 539	$539 − $500 = $39	$35	$39 − $35 = $4
12	48	12 × 48 = 576	576 − 539 = 37	36	37 − 36 = 1
13	47	13 × 47 = 611	611 − 576 = 35	37	35 − 37 = (2)

Now suppose the marginal cost of the units is as shown in the fifth column of Exhibit 4-7. The optimal production and sales level would be 12 units. The last column illustrates that the 11th unit adds $4 to profit, the 12th adds $1, but production and sale of the 13th unit would *decrease* profit by $2. In general, firms should produce and sell units until the marginal revenue equals the marginal cost, represented by volume V_0 in Exhibit 4-6. The optimal price charged will be the amount that creates a demand for V_0 units.

Notice that in economic theory the *marginal cost* is relevant for pricing decisions. The accountant's approximation to marginal cost is *variable cost*. What is the major difference between the economist's marginal cost and the accountant's variable cost? Variable cost is assumed to be constant within a relevant range of volume, whereas marginal cost may change with each unit produced. Within large ranges of production volume, however, changes in marginal cost are often small. Therefore, using variable cost can be a reasonable approximation to marginal cost in many situations.

Maximization of Total Contribution

Managers seldom compute marginal revenue curves and marginal cost curves. Instead, they use estimates based on judgment to predict the effects of additional production and sales on profits. In addition, they examine selected volumes, not the whole range of possible volumes. Such simplifications are justified because the cost of a more sophisticated analysis would exceed the benefits.

Consider a division of General Electric (GE) that makes microwave ovens. Suppose market researchers estimate that 700,000 ovens can be sold if priced at $200 per unit, but 1,000,000 could be sold at $180. The variable cost of production is $130 per unit at production levels of both 700,000 and 1,000,000. Both volumes are also within the relevant range so that fixed costs are unaffected by the changes in volume. Which price should be charged?

The GE manager could compute the additional revenue and additional costs of the 300,000 additional units of sales at the $180 price:

Additional revenue: (1,000,000 × $180) − (700,000 × $200) = $40,000,000
− Additional costs: 300,000 × $130   = 39,000,000
Additional profit: $ 1,000,000

Alternatively, the manager could compare the total contribution for each alternative:

Contribution at $180: ($180 − $130) × 1,000,000 = $50,000,000
Contribution at $200: ($200 − $130) ×   700,000 =   49,000,000
Difference: $ 1,000,000

Notice that comparing the total contributions is essentially the same as computing the additional revenues and costs. Further, both approaches correctly ignore fixed costs, which are unaffected by this pricing decision.

INFLUENCES ON PRICING IN PRACTICE

Several factors interact to shape the environment in which managers make pricing decisions. Legal requirements, competitors' actions, costs, and customer demands all influence pricing.

Legal Requirements

Pricing decisions must be made within constraints imposed by U.S. and international laws. In addition to prohibiting out-and-out collusion in setting prices, these laws generally prohibit prices that are *predatory* or *discriminatory*.

Predatory pricing is establishing prices so low that competitors are driven out of the market so that the predatory pricer then has no significant competition and can raise prices dramatically. For example, Wal-Mart has been accused of predatory pricing—selling at low cost to drive out local competitors. U.S. courts have generally ruled that pricing is predatory only if companies set prices below average variable cost.

Discriminatory pricing is charging different prices to different customers for the same product or service. For example, a large group of neighborhood pharmacies sued several large drug companies, alleging that their practice of allowing discounts to mail-order drug companies, health maintenance organizations, and other managed-care entities constitutes discriminatory pricing. However, pricing is not discriminatory if it reflects a cost differential incurred in providing the good or service.

Businesses can defend themselves against charges of either predatory or discriminatory pricing by citing their costs as a basis for their prices. Therefore, a good understanding of the cost of a product or service, especially the activities that cause additional costs to be incurred, is useful in avoiding legal pitfalls. Our discussion here assumes that pricing practices do not violate legal constraints.

Competitors' Actions

Competitors usually react to the price changes of their rivals. Many companies will gather information regarding a rival's capacity, technology, and operating policies. In this way, managers make more informed predictions of competitors' reactions to a company's prices. The study of game theory, for which two economists won the 1994 Nobel Prize, focuses on predicting and reacting to competitors' actions.

Tinkering with prices is often most heavily affected by the price setter's expectations of competitors' reactions and of the overall effects on the total industry demand for the good or service in question. For example, an airline might cut prices even if it expects price cuts from its rivals, hoping that total customer demand for the tickets of all airlines will increase sufficiently to offset the reduction in the price per ticket.

Competition is becoming increasingly international. Overcapacity in some countries often causes aggressive pricing policies, particularly for a company's exported goods.

Costs

Costs influence the deliberate setting of prices in some industries, but not in others. Frequently, the market price is regarded as a given. Examples include the prices of metals and agricultural commodities. Consider gold. A mining company sells at the established market prices. Whether profits or losses are forthcoming depends on how well the company controls its costs and volume. Here cost data help managers decide on the level and mix of outputs.

The influence of costs on the setting of prices is often overstated. Nevertheless, many managers say that their prices are set by cost-plus pricing. For example, consider the construction and automobile industries. Their executives describe the procedure as computing an average unit cost and then adding a "reasonable" **markup** (i.e., the amount by which price exceeds cost) that will generate a target return on investment. The key, however, is the "plus" in cost plus. It is rarely an unalterable markup. Its magnitude depends on the behavior of competitors and customers.

Prices are most directly related to costs in industries where revenue is based on cost reimbursement. A prime example is defense contracting. Cost-reimbursement contracts generally specify how costs should be measured and what costs are allowable. For example, only coach-class (not first-class) fares are reimbursable for business air travel on government projects.

Ultimately, though, the market sets prices after all. Why? Because the price as set by a cost-plus formula is inevitably adjusted "in light of market conditions." The maximum price that may be charged is the one that does not drive the customer away. The minimum price might be considered to be zero (e.g., companies may give out free samples to gain entry into a market). A more practical guide is that, in the short run, the minimum price to be quoted, *subject to consideration of long-run effects*, should be equal to the costs that may be avoided by not landing the order—often all variable costs of producing, selling, and distributing the good or service. In the long run, the price must be high enough to cover all costs including fixed costs.

Customer Demands and Target Costing

More than ever before, managers are recognizing the needs of customers. Pricing is no exception. If customers believe a price is too high, they may turn to other sources for the product or service, substitute a different product, or decide to produce the item themselves.

Most companies have traditionally started with costs and added a markup to get prices. However, a growing number of companies are turning the equation around and developing costs based on prices. Companies that use **target costing** first determine the price at which they can sell a new product or service and then design a product or service that can be produced at a low enough cost to provide an adequate profit margin.

Product designers thus become aware of the cost impacts of the design of both the product itself and the process used to produce it.

For example, market research may indicate that Toyota could sell 100,000 units of one model of a sports car annually at a list price of $35,000. The engineers who design the product might consider several different combinations of features bearing different costs. If the total product cost is sufficiently low, the product may be launched. Conversely, if the total product cost is too high, the product may be unjustified. Of course, the point here is that the customer helps determine the price. The product designers and the management accountants work together to see if a product can be developed at a target cost that will provide room for an attractive profit.

Target costing originated in Japan, but now it is used by many companies worldwide, including Chrysler, Mercedes-Benz, Procter & Gamble, and Caterpillar. Even some hospitals use target costing.

Whether a company sets prices based on costs or costs based on prices, it is inevitable that prices and costs interact. If the focus is on prices that are influenced primarily by market forces, managers must make sure that all costs can be covered in the long run. If prices are based on a markup of costs, managers must examine the actions of customers and competitors to ensure that products or services can be sold at the determined prices.

Choice of Cost Words and Terms

Each organization has its own cost vocabulary, which often contains cost definitions that clash with their meanings in management accounting literature. In a specific situation, be sure to obtain the exact meaning of the terms used.

Exhibit 4-8 displays how the costs of products and services are usually described. Note particularly that **full cost** or **fully allocated cost** means the total of all manufacturing costs plus the total of all selling and administrative costs.

Exhibit 4-8   Variety of Cost Terms

	Cost per Unit of Product		
Variable manufacturing cost	$12.00	$12.00	$12.00
Variable selling and administrative cost	1.10		1.10
Total variable cost	$13.10		
Fixed manufacturing cost		3.00*	3.00
Absorption cost		$15.00†	
Fixed selling and administrative cost			2.90*
Full cost (often called fully allocated cost)			$19.00

* Fixed manufacturing costs, $3,000,000 ÷ 1,000,000 = $3.00.
  Fixed selling and administrative costs, $2,900,000 ÷ 1,000,000 units = $2.90.

† This amount must be used by U.S. companies for inventory valuation in reports to shareholders.

Target Costing, ABC, and Service Companies

Many companies use target costing together with an activity-based-costing (ABC) system. Target costing requires a company to first determine what a customer will pay for a product and then work backwards to design the product and production process that will generate a desired level of profit. ABC provides data on the costs of the various activities needed to produce the product. Knowing the costs of activities allows product and production process designers to be able to predict the effects of their designs on the product's cost. Target costing essentially takes activity-based costs and uses them for strategic product decisions.

For example, Culp, Inc., a North Carolina textile manufacturer, uses target costing and ABC to elevate cost management into one of the most strategically imperative areas of the firm. Culp found that 80% of its product costs are predetermined at the design stage, but earlier cost control efforts had focused only on the other 20%. By shifting cost management efforts to the design stage and getting accurate costs of the various activities involved in production, cost management became an integral part of the strategic decisions of the firm.

Cost management at Culp evolved into a process of cutting costs when a product is being designed, not identifying costs that are out of line after the production is complete. A basic goal of target costing is to reduce costs before they occur. After all, once costs have been incurred they cannot be changed. Such a strategy is especially important if product life cycles are short—and, since most product life cycles are shrinking, use of target costing is expanding. Target costing focuses on reducing costs in the product design and development stages—when costs can really be affected. For example, Chrysler's design of the low-priced Neon was heavily influenced by the company's use of target costing, and Procter & Gamble's CEO credits target costing for help-

ing eliminate costs that could lead products to be priced too high for the market.

Target costing has traditionally been applied in manufacturing companies. However, its use in service and nonprofit companies is growing. For example, a process nearly identical to target costing is being used in some hospitals. Development of treatment protocols, the preferred treatment steps for a patient with a particular diagnosis, is the "product design" phase for a hospital. Treatment protocols have short life cycles because of rapid advances in medical technology and knowledge. Therefore, with increased attention to cost containment in health care, it is important to consider the costs of the various activities in a treatment protocol at the time of designing the protocol.

Measuring the costs of a particular treatment protocol after it is in use was the best that could be done until recently, even in the most cost-conscious hospitals. But identifying cost overruns after the fact, although better than never measuring them, did not lead to good cost control. By using target costing techniques, that is, identifying the maximum amount that would be paid for a treatment, protocols can be designed to point out potential cost overruns before a treatment begins. This focuses cost containment on the patient level, where most decisions are made, not at the department level, where identifying the causes of cost overruns is more difficult. ■

Sources: J. Bohn, "Chrysler Cuts Costs by Nurturing Links with Suppliers," Automotive Age, *January 17, 1994, p.18; J. Brausch, "Target Costing for Profit Enhancement,"* Management Accounting, *November 1994, pp. 45–49; G. Hoffman, "Future Vision,"* Grocery Marketing, *March 1994, p. 6; D. Young, "Managing the Stages of Hospital Cost Accounting,"* Healthcare Financial Management, *April 1993, p. 58.*

Target Pricing

Cost plus is often the basis for target prices. The size of the "plus" depends on target (desired) operating incomes, which in turn, frequently depend on the target return on investment for a division, a product line, or a product. For simplicity here, we work with a target operating income.

Target prices can be based on a host of different markups based on a host of different definitions of cost. Thus, there are many ways to arrive at the *same target price*. They simply reflect different arrangements of the components of the same income statement.

Exhibit 4-9 displays the relationships of costs to target selling prices, assuming a target operating income of $1 million. The percentages there represent four popular markup formulas for pricing: (1) as a percentage of variable manufacturing costs, (2) as a percentage of total variable costs, (3) as a percentage of full costs, and (4) as a percentage of absorption costs.

Exhibit 4-9 Relationships of Costs to Same Target Selling Prices

		Alternative Markup Percentages to Achieve Same Target Sales Prices
Target sales price	$20.00	
Variable costs		
(1) Manufacturing	$12.00*	($20.00 – $12.00) ÷ $12.00 = 66.67%
Selling and administrative	1.10	
(2) Unit variable costs	$13.10	($20.00 – $13.10) ÷ $13.10 = 52.67%
Fixed costs		
Manufacturing	$ 3.00*	
Selling and administrative	2.90	
Unit fixed costs	$ 5.90	
(3) Full costs	$19.00	($20.00 – $19.00) ÷ $19.00 = 5.26%
Target operating income	$ 1.00	

* (4) A frequently used formula is based on absorption costs:
[$20.00 – ($12.00 + $3.00)] ÷ $15.00 = 33.33%.

Of course, the percentages differ. For instance, the markup on variable manufacturing costs is 66.67%, and on absorption costs it is 33.33%. Regardless of the formula used, the pricing decision maker will be led toward the *same* target price. For a volume of 1 million units, assume that the target selling price is $20 per unit. If the decision maker is unable to obtain such a price consistently, the company will not achieve its $1 million operating income objective.

ADVANTAGES OF VARIOUS APPROACHES TO PRICING DECISIONS

We have seen that prices can be based on various types of cost information, from variable costs to absorption costs to full costs. Each approach has advantages and disadvantages.

Contribution Approach Provides Detailed Information

Prices based on variable costs represent a contribution approach to pricing. When used intelligently, the contribution approach has some advantages over the absorption-costing and full-cost approaches because the latter often fail to highlight different cost behavior patterns.

Obviously, the contribution approach offers more detailed information because it displays variable- and fixed-cost behavior patterns separately. Because the contribution approach is sensitive to cost-volume-profit relationships, it is a helpful basis for developing pricing formulas. Consequently, this approach makes it easier for managers to prepare price schedules at different volume levels.

The correct analysis in Exhibit 4-10 shows how changes in volume affect operating income. The contribution approach helps managers with pricing decisions because it readily displays the interrelationships among variable costs, fixed costs, and potential changes in selling prices.

Exhibit 4-10   Analyses of Effects of Changes in Volume on Operating Income

	Correct Analysis			Incorrect Analysis		
Volume in units	900,000	1,000,000	1,100,000	900,000	1,000,000	1,100,000
Sales @ $20.00	$18,000,000	$20,000,000	$22,000,000	$18,000,000	$20,000,000	$22,000,000
Total variable costs @ $13.10*	11,790,000	13,100,000	14,410,000			
Contribution margin	6,210,000	6,900,000	7,590,000			
Fixed costs[†]	5,900,000	5,900,000	5,900,000			
Full costs @ $19.00*			17,100,000	19,000,000	20,900,000	
Operating income	$ 310,000	$ 1,000,000	$ 1,690,000	$ 900,000	$ 1,000,000	$ 1,100,000

* From Exhibit 4-8.
[†] Fixed manufacturing costs $3,000,000
   Fixed selling and administrative costs ... 2,900,000
   Total fixed costs $5,900,000

In contrast, target pricing with absorption costing or full costing presumes a given volume level. When volume changes, the unit cost used at the original planned volume may mislead managers. As our "incorrect analysis" on page 103 showed, managers sometimes erroneously assume that the change in total costs may be computed by multiplying any change in volume by the full unit cost.

The incorrect analysis in Exhibit 4-10 shows how managers may be misled if the $19 full cost per unit is used to predict effects of volume changes on operating income. Suppose a manager uses the $19 figure to predict an operating income of $900,000 if the company sells 900,000 instead of 1,000,000 units. If actual operating income is $310,000 instead, as the correct analysis predicts, that manager may be stunned—and possibly looking for a new job.

Other Advantages of Contribution Approach

Two other advantages of the contribution approach deserve mention. First, a normal or target-pricing formula can be developed as easily by the contribution approach as by absorption-costing or full-costing approaches, as Exhibit 4-9 showed.

Second, the contribution approach offers insight into the short-run versus long-run effects of cutting prices on special orders. For example, assume the same cost behavior patterns as at the Samson Co. (Exhibit 4-3). The 100,000-unit order added $100,000 to operating income at a selling price of $13, which was $7 below the target selling price of $20 and $2 below the absorption manufacturing cost of $15. Given all the stated assumptions, accepting the order appeared to be the better choice. No general answer can be given, but the relevant information was more easily generated by the contribution approach. Consider the contribution and absorption-costing approaches:

	Contribution Approach	Absorption-Costing Approach
Sales, 100,000 units @ $13	$1,300,000	$1,300,000
Variable manufacturing costs @ $12	1,200,000	
Absorption manufacturing costs @ $15		1,500,000
Apparent change in operating income	$ 100,000	($ 200,000)

Under the absorption approach, the decision maker has no direct knowledge of cost-volume-profit relationships. The decision maker must make the decision by hunch. On the surface, the offer is definitely unattractive because the price of $13 is $2 below absorption costs.

Under the contribution approach, the decision maker sees a short-run advantage of $100,000 from accepting the offer. Fixed costs will be unaffected by whatever decision is made and operating income will increase by $100,000. Still, there often are long-run effects to consider. Will acceptance of the offer undermine the long-run price structure? In other words, is the short-run advantage of $100,000 more than offset by highly probable long-run financial disadvantages? The decision maker may think so and may reject the offer. But—and this is important—by doing so the decision maker is, in effect, forgoing $100,000 now to protect certain long-run market advantages. Generally, the decision maker can assess problems of this sort by asking whether the probability of long-run benefits is worth an "investment" equal to the forgone contribution margin ($100,000 in this case). Under absorption approaches, the decision maker must ordinarily conduct a special study to find the immediate effects. Under the contribution approach, the manager has a system that will routinely and more surely provide such information.

Advantages of Absorption-Cost or Full-Cost Approaches

Our general theme of focusing on relevant information also extends into the area of pricing. To say that either a contribution approach or an absorption-cost approach or a full-cost approach provides the "best" guide to pricing decisions is a dangerous oversimplification of one of the most perplexing problems in business. Lack of understanding and judgment can lead to unprofitable pricing regardless of the kind of cost data available or cost accounting system used.

Frequently, managers do not employ a contribution approach because they fear that variable costs will be substituted indiscriminately for full costs and will therefore lead to suicidal price cutting. This problem should *not* arise if the data are used wisely. However, if top managers perceive a pronounced danger of underpricing when variable-cost data are revealed, they may justifiably prefer an absorption-costing approach or a full-cost approach for guiding pricing decisions.

Cost-plus pricing based on absorption costs or full costs entails circular reasoning. That is, price, which influences sales volume, is often based on an average absorption cost per unit, which in turn is partly determined by the underlying volume of sales.

Despite the criticism, absorption costs or full costs are far more widely used in practice than is the contribution approach. Why? In addition to the reasons already mentioned, the following have been offered:

1. In the long run, all costs must be recovered to stay in business. Sooner or later fixed costs do indeed fluctuate as volume changes. Therefore, it is prudent to assume that all costs are variable (even if some are fixed in the short run).
2. Computing target prices based on cost plus may indicate what competitors might charge, especially if they have approximately the same level of efficiency as you and also aim at recovering all costs in the long run.
3. Absorption-cost or full-cost formula pricing meets the cost-benefit test. It is too expensive to conduct individual cost-volume tests for the many products (sometimes thousands) that a company offers.
4. There is much uncertainty about the shape of the demand curves and the correct price-output decisions. Absorption-cost or full-cost pricing copes with this uncertainty by not encouraging managers to take too much marginal business.
5. Absorption-cost or full-cost pricing tends to promote price stability. Managers prefer price stability because it eases their professional lives, primarily because planning is more dependable.
6. Absorption-cost pricing or full-cost pricing provides the most defensible basis for justifying prices to all interested parties including government antitrust investigators.
7. Absorption-cost or full-cost pricing provides convenient reference (target) points to simplify hundreds or thousands of pricing decisions.

No single method of pricing is always best. An interview study of executives reported use of *both* full-cost and variable-cost information in pricing decisions: "The full-vs.-variable-cost pricing controversy is not one of either black or white. The companies we studied used both approaches."[1]

The history of accounting reveals that most companies' systems have gathered costs via some form of full-manufacturing-cost system because this is what is required for financial reporting. In recent years, when systems are changed, variable costs and fixed costs are often identified. But managers have regarded this change as an addition to the existing full-manufacturing-cost system. That is, many managers insist on having information regarding both variable costs per unit and the allocated fixed costs per unit before setting selling prices. If the accounting system routinely gathers data regarding both variable and fixed costs, such data can readily be provided. However, most absorption-costing systems in practice do not organize their data collection so as to distinguish between variable and fixed costs. As a result, special studies or special guessing must be used to designate costs as variable or fixed.

Managers are especially reluctant to focus on variable costs and ignore allocated fixed costs when their performance evaluations, and possibly their bonuses, are based on income shown in published financial statements. Why? Because such statements are based on absorption costing and, thus, are affected by allocations of fixed costs.

---

[1] T. Bruegelmann, G. Haessly, C. Wolfangel, and M. Schiff, "How Variable Costing is Used in Pricing Decisions," *Management Accounting*, Vol. 65, no. 10, p. 65.

Cost-Based Pricing for International Telephone Calls

Accounting has a direct effect on the revenue of many government contractors because prices are often simply costs plus a profit margin. Accounting costs also can directly affect the revenues of other companies, especially those subject to regulation.

An intriguing area of cost-based pricing is international telephone calls. When a customer in the United States calls someone (or receives a call from someone) in another country, the revenue from the call must be split between the telephone companies in the two countries. Under international agreements, revenues should be shared according to the costs of the two telephone companies, so that there is an equitable division of profits.

In the early 1990s the U.S. Federal Communications Commission (FCC) proposed changing the way revenues on international calls are shared among companies. Under current rules, U.S. firms pay foreign carriers about $.75 out of every dollar collected on overseas calls. The FCC suspected that payments above the foreign carriers' costs amounted to an overpayment of $1 billion a year. To ensure equitable revenues for U.S. telephone companies, the FCC wanted "to learn about the true costs, levels of profits, and how those costs and profits are shared among U.S. telephone companies and foreign telecommunications authorities."

At least two factors make the FCC's task difficult. First, it has no authority over foreign companies. Only U.S. companies must meet reporting requirements specified by the FCC. Second, accounting systems differ by country. For example, many South American countries explicitly adjust their accounting numbers for inflation, but U.S. companies do not. International cost comparisons will not be easy, but if cost-based pricing is to be used for international telephone calls, some method of comparison is necessary. This type of situation is leading many authorities to support more standardization of accounting measurement and reporting rules throughout the world. ■

Source: Adapted from "Accounting Changes on International Calls Proposed by the FCC," The Wall Street Journal, *July 13, 1990, p. A2.*

Formats for Pricing

Exhibit 4-9 showed how to compute alternative general markup percentages that would produce the same selling prices if used day after day. In practice, the format and arithmetic of quote sheets, job proposals, or similar records vary considerably.

Exhibit 4-11 is from an actual quote sheet used by the manager of a small job shop that bids on welding machinery orders in a highly competitive industry. The Exhibit 4-11 approach is a tool for informed pricing decisions. Notice that the *maximum* price is not a matter of cost at all; it is what you think you can obtain. The *minimum* price is the total variable cost.

Exhibit 4-11 Quote Sheet for Pricing

Direct materials, at cost	$25,000
Direct labor and variable manufacturing overhead, 600 direct-labor-hours × $30	18,000
Sales commission (varies with job)	2,000
Total variable costs—minimum price*	45,000
Add fixed costs allocated to job, 600 direct-labor-hours × $20	12,000
Total costs	57,000
Add desired markup	30,000
Selling price—maximum price that you think you can obtain*	$87,000

* This sheet shows two prices, maximum and minimum. Any amount you can get above the minimum price is a contribution margin.

Of course, the manager will rarely bid the minimum price. To do so regularly would virtually ensure eventual bankruptcy. Still, the manager wants to know the effect of a job on the company's total variable costs. Occasionally, a bid near that minimum price may be justified because of idle capacity or the desire to establish a presence in new markets or with a new customer.

Note that Exhibit 4-11 classifies costs especially for the pricing task. Pricing decisions may be made by more than one person. The accountant's responsibility is to prepare an understandable format that involves a minimum of computations. Exhibit 4-11 combines direct labor and variable manufacturing overhead. All fixed costs, whether manufacturing, selling, or administrative, are lumped together and applied to the job using a single fixed-overhead rate per direct-labor-hour. Obviously, if more accuracy is desired, many more detailed cost items and overhead rates could be formulated. To obtain the desired accuracy, many companies are turning to activity-based costing.

Some managers, particularly in construction and service industries, such as auto repair, compile separate categories of costs of (1) direct materials, parts, and supplies and (2) direct labor. These managers then use different markup rates for each category. These rates are developed to provide revenue for both related overhead costs and operating profit. For example, an automobile repair shop might have the following format for each job:

	Billed to Customers
Auto parts ($200 cost plus 40% markup)	$280
Direct labor (Cost is $20 per hour. Bill at 300% to recover overhead and provide for operating profit. Billing rate is $20 × 300% = $60 per hour. Total billed for 10 hours is $60 × 10 = $600)	600
Total billed to customer	$880

Another example is an Italian printing company in Milan that wants to price its jobs so that each one generates a margin of 28% of revenues—14% to cover selling and administrative expenses and 14% for profit. To achieve this, the manager uses a pricing formula of 140% times predicted materials cost plus 25,000 Italian Lira (abbreviated Lit.) per hour of production time. The latter covers labor and overhead costs of Lit.18,000 per hour. For a product with Lit.400,000 of materials cost and 30 hours of production time, the price would be Lit.1,310,000:

	Cost	Price	Profit
Materials	Lit. 400,000	Lit. 560,000	Lit. 160,000
Labor and overhead	540,000	750,000	210,000
Total	Lit. 940,000	Lit. 1,310,000	Lit. 370,000

The profit of Lit.370,000 is approximately 40% of the cost of Lit.940,000 and 28% of the price of Lit.1,310,000.

Thus, there are numerous ways to compute selling prices. However, some general words of caution are appropriate here. Managers are better able to understand their options and the effects of their decisions on profits if they know their costs. That is, it is more informative to pinpoint costs first, before adding markups, than to have a variety of markups already embedded in the "costs" used as guides for setting selling prices. For example, if materials cost $1,000, they should be shown on a price quotation guide at $1,000, not at, say, a marked-up $1,400 because that is what the seller hopes to get.

Highlights to Remember

The accountant's role in decision making is primarily that of a technical expert on financial analysis. The accountant's responsibility is to help the manager use relevant data as guidance for decisions. Accountants and managers must have a penetrating understanding of relevant information, especially costs.

To be relevant to a particular decision, a cost must meet two criteria: (1) it must be an expected *future* cost, and (2) it must have an element of *difference* among the alternatives. All *past* (*historical* or *sunk*) costs are in themselves irrelevant to any *decision* about the future, although they often provide the best available basis for the *prediction* of expected future data.

The combination of the relevant-costing and contribution approaches provides a commonality of approach, a fundamental framework, based on economic analysis, that applies to a vast range of problems. The following generalizations apply to a variety of decisions:

1. Whenever feasible, think in terms of total costs rather than unit costs. Too often, unit costs are regarded as an adequate basis for predicting changes in total costs. This assumption is satisfactory when analyzing variable costs but it is frequently misleading when analyzing fixed costs.
2. A common error is to regard all unit costs indiscriminately, as if all costs were variable costs. In the short run, changes in volume will affect *total* variable costs but not *total* fixed costs. The danger then is to predict total costs assuming that all unit costs are variable. The correct relationships are:

	Behavior as Volume Fluctuates	
	Variable Cost	*Fixed Cost*
Cost per unit	No change	Change
Total cost	Change	No change

Decisions to accept or reject a special sales order should focus on the *additional* revenues and *additional* costs of the order. Decisions on whether to delete a department or a product require analysis of the revenues forgone and the costs saved from the deletion. The key to obtaining the maximum profit from a given capacity is to obtain the greatest possible contribution to profit per unit of the limiting or scarce factor.

Pricing decisions are influenced by economics, the law, customers, competitors, and costs. Profit markups can be added to a variety of cost bases, including variable manufacturing costs, all variable costs, absorption (full manufacturing) cost, or all costs. The contribution approach to pricing has the advantage of providing detailed information that is consistent with cost-volume-profit analysis.

Summary Problem for Your Review

Problem One appeared earlier in the chapter.

Problem Two

Custom Graphics is a Chicago printing company that bids on a wide variety of design and printing jobs. The owner of the company, Janet Solomon, prepares the bids for most jobs. Her cost budget for 19X6 is:

Materials		$ 350,000
Labor		250,000
Overhead		
Variable	$300,000	
Fixed	150,000	450,000
Total production cost of jobs		1,050,000
Selling and administrative expenses		
Variable	$ 75,000	
Fixed	125,000	200,000
Total costs		$1,250,000

Solomon has a target profit of $250,000 for 19X6.

Compute the average target markup percentage for setting prices as a percentage of:

1. Prime costs (materials plus labor)
2. Variable production cost of jobs
3. Total production cost of jobs
4. All variable costs
5. All costs

Solution to Problem Two

The purpose of this problem is to emphasize that many different approaches to pricing might be used that, properly employed, would achieve the *same* target selling prices. To achieve $250,000 of profit, the desired revenue for 19X6 is $1,250,000 + $250,000 = $1,500,000. The target markup percentages are

1. Percent of prime cost $= \dfrac{(\$1,500,000 - \$600,000)}{(\$600,000)} = 150\%$

2. Percent of variable production cost of jobs $= \dfrac{(\$1,500,000 - \$900,000)}{(\$900,000)} = 66.7\%$

3. Percent of total production cost of jobs $= \dfrac{(\$1,500,000 - \$1,050,000)}{(\$1,050,000)} = 42.9\%$

4. Percent of all variable costs $= \dfrac{(\$1,500,000 - \$975,000)}{(\$975,000)} = 53.8\%$

5. Percent of all costs $= \dfrac{(\$1,500,000 - \$1,250,000)}{(\$1,250,000)} = 20\%$

Fundamental Assignment Material

4-A1   Special Order

Consider the following details of the income statement of the Moinpour Pen Company for the year ended December 31, 19X6:

Sales	$10,000,000
Less manufacturing cost of goods sold	6,000,000
Gross margin or gross profit	$ 4,000,000
Less selling and administrative expenses	3,300,000
Operating income	$ 700,000

Moinpour's fixed manufacturing costs were $2.4 million and its fixed selling and administrative costs were $2.5 million. Sales commissions of 3% of sales are included in selling and administrative expenses.

The company had sold 2 million pens. Near the end of the year, Pizza Hut Corporation offered to buy 150,000 pens on a special order. To fill the order, a special clip bearing the Pizza Hut emblem would have had to be made for each pen. Pizza Hut intended to use the pens in special promotions in an eastern city during early 19X7.

Even though Moinpour had some idle plant capacity, the president rejected the Pizza Hut offer of $660,000 for the 150,000 pens. He said:

> The Pizza Hut offer is too low. We'd avoid paying sales commissions, but we'd have to incur an extra cost of $.20 per clip for the emblem and its assembly with the pens. If Moinpour sells below its regular selling prices, it will begin a chain reaction of competitors' price cutting and of customers wanting special deals. I believe in pricing at no lower than 8% above our full costs of $9,300,000 ÷ 2,000,000 units = $4.65 per unit plus the extra $.20 per clip less the savings in commissions.

1. Using the contribution approach, prepare an analysis similar to that in Exhibit 4-3, page 103. Use four columns: without the special order, the effect of the special order (total and per unit), and totals with the special order.
2. By what percentage would operating income increase or decrease if the order had been accepted? Do you agree with the president's decision? Why?

4-A2   Choice of Products

The Skill-Craft Company has two products: a plain electric mixer and a fancy electric mixer. The plain mixer sells for $64 and has a variable cost of $48. The fancy mixer sells for $100 and has a variable cost of $70.

1. Compute contribution margins and contribution-margin ratios for plain and fancy mixers.
2. The demand is for more units than the company can produce. There are only 20,000 machine-hours of manufacturing capacity available. Two plain mixers can be produced in the same average time (1 hour) needed to produce one fancy mixer. Compute the

total contribution margin for 20,000 hours for plain mixers only and for fancy mixers only.

3. Use two or three sentences to state the major lesson of this problem.

4-A3   Formulas for Pricing

Zeke Podolsky, a building contractor, constructs houses in tracts, often building as many as 20 homes simultaneously. Podolsky has budgeted costs for an expected number of houses in 19X7 as shown at the top of the next page.

Direct materials	$3,500,000
Direct labor	1,000,000
Job construction overhead	1,500,000
Cost of jobs	$6,000,000
Selling and administrative costs	1,500,000
Total costs	$7,500,000

The job construction overhead includes approximately $600,000 of fixed costs, such as the salaries of supervisors and depreciation on equipment. The selling and administrative costs include $300,000 of variable costs, such as sales commissions and bonuses that depend fundamentally on overall profitability.

Podolsky wants an operating income of $1.5 million for 19X7.

Compute the average target markup percentage for setting prices as a percentage of

1. Prime costs (direct materials plus direct labor)
2. The full "cost of jobs"
3. The variable "cost of jobs"
4. The full "cost of jobs" plus selling and administrative costs
5. The variable "cost of jobs" plus variable selling and administrative costs

4-B1   Terminology and Straightforward Interpretations of Unit Costs

Following is the income statement of a manufacturer of blue jeans:

DANUBE COMPANY
Income Statement for the Year Ended December 31, 19X4

	Total	Per Unit
Sales	$40,000,000	$20.00
Less manufacturing cost of goods sold	24,000,000	12.00
Gross margin	$16,000,000	$ 8.00
Less selling and administrative expenses	15,000,000	7.50
Operating income	$ 1,000,000	$ .50

Danube had manufactured 2 million pairs of jeans, which had been sold to various clothing wholesalers and department stores. At the start of 19X5, the president, Rosemary Munoz, died from a stroke. Her son, Hector, became the new president. Hector had worked for 15 years in the marketing phases of the business. He knew very little about accounting and manufacturing, which were his mother's strengths. Hector has several questions for you including inquiries regarding the pricing of special orders.

1. To prepare better answers, you decide to recast the income statement in contribution form. Variable manufacturing cost was $19 million. Variable selling and administrative expenses, which were mostly sales commissions, shipping expenses, and advertising allowances paid to customers based on units sold, were $9 million.
2. Hector asks, "I can't understand financial statements until I know the meaning of various terms. In scanning my mother's assorted notes, I found the following pertaining to both total and unit costs: *absorption cost, full manufacturing cost, variable cost, full cost, fully allocated cost, gross margin, contribution margin*. Using our data for 19X4, please give me a list of these costs, their total amounts, and their per-unit amounts."
3. "Near the end of 19X4 I brought in a special order from Sears for 100,000 jeans at $17 each. I said I'd accept a flat $20,000 sales commission instead of the usual 6% of selling price, but my mother refused the order. She usually upheld a relatively rigid pricing policy, saying that it was bad business to accept orders that did not at least generate full manufacturing cost plus 80% of full manufacturing cost.

    "That policy bothered me. We had idle capacity. The way I figured, our manufacturing costs would go up by 100,000 × $12 = $1,200,000, but our selling and administrative expenses would go up by only $20,000. That would mean additional operating income of 100,000 × ($17 − $12) minus $20,000, or $500,000 minus $20,000, or $480,000. That's too much money to give up just to maintain a general pricing policy. Was my analysis of the impact on operating income correct? If not, please show me the correct additional operating income."
4. After receiving the explanations offered in requirements 2 and 3, Hector said: "Forget that I had the Sears order. I had an even bigger order from J. C. Penney. It was for 500,000 units and would have filled the plant completely. I told my mother I'd settle for no commission. There would have been no selling and administrative costs whatsoever because J. C. Penney would pay for the shipping and would not get any advertising allowances.

    "J. C. Penney offered $9.20 per unit. Our fixed manufacturing costs would have been spread over 2.5 million instead of 2 million units. Wouldn't it have been advantageous to accept the offer? Our old fixed manufacturing costs were $2.50 per unit. The added volume would reduce that cost more than our loss on our variable costs per unit.

    "Am I correct? What would have been the impact on total operating income if we had accepted the order?"

4-B2 Unit Costs and Capacity

(CMA, adapted.) Moorhead Manufacturing Company produces two industrial solvents for which the following data have been tabulated. Fixed manufacturing cost is applied to products at a rate of $1.00 per machine-hour.

Per Unit	XY-7	BD-4
Selling price	$6.00	$4.00
Variable manufacturing costs	3.00	1.50
Fixed manufacturing cost	.80	.20
Variable selling cost	2.00	2.00

The sales manager has had a $160,000 increase in her budget allotment for advertising and wants to apply the money on the most profitable product. The solvents are not substitutes for one another in the eyes of the company's customers.

1. How many machine-hours does it take to produce one XY-7? To produce one BD-4? (*Hint:* Focus on applied fixed manufacturing cost.)

2. Suppose Moorhead has only 100,000 machine-hours that can be made available to produce XY-7 and BD-4. If the potential increase in sales units for either product resulting from advertising is far in excess of these production capabilities, which product should be produced and advertised and what is the estimated increase in contribution margin earned?

4-B3 Dropping a Product Line

Hambley's Toy Store is on Regent Street in London. It has a magic department near the main door. Suppose that management is considering dropping the magic department, which has consistently shown an operating loss. The predicted income statements, in thousands of pounds (£), follow (for ease of analysis, only three product lines are shown):

	Total	General Merchandise	Electronic Products	Magic Department
Sales	£6,000	£5,000	£400	£600
Variable expenses	4,090	3,500	200	390
Contribution margin	£1,910 (32%)	£1,500 (30%)	£200 (50%)	£210 (35%)
Fixed expenses (compensation, depreciation, property taxes, insurance, etc.)	1,110	750	50	310
Operating income	£ 800	£ 750	£150	£(100)

The £310,000 of magic department fixed expenses include the compensation of employees of £100,000. These employees will be released if the magic department is abandoned. All equipment is fully depreciated, so none of the £310,000 pertains to such items. Furthermore, disposal values of equipment will be exactly offset by the costs of removal and remodeling.

If the magic department is dropped, the manager will use the vacated space for either more general merchandise or more electronic products. The expansion of general merchandise would not entail hiring any additional salaried help, but more electronic products would require an additional person at an annual cost of £25,000. The manager thinks that sales of general merchandise would increase by £300,000; electronic products, by £200,000. The manager's modest predictions are partially based on the fact that she thinks the magic department has helped lure customers to the store and thus improved overall sales. If the magic department is closed, that lure would be gone.

Should the magic department be closed? Explain, showing computations.

Additional Assignment Material

Questions

4-1 "The distinction between precision and relevance should be kept in mind." Explain.

4-2 Distinguish between the quantitative and qualitative aspects of decisions.

4-3 Describe the accountant's role in decision making.

4-4 "Any future cost is relevant." Do you agree? Explain.

4-5 Why are historical or past data irrelevant to special decisions?

4-6 Describe the role of past or historical costs in the decision process. That is, how do these costs relate to the prediction method and the decision model?

4-7 "There is a commonality of approach to various special decisions." Explain.

4-8 "No matter what the decision situation, the key question to ask is: What difference does it make?" Explain the nature of the difference.

4-9 "In relevant-cost analysis, beware of unit costs." Explain.

4-10 "Increasing sales will decrease fixed costs because it spreads them over more units." Do you agree? Explain.

4-11 "The key to decisions to delete a product or department is identifying avoidable costs." Do you agree? Explain.

4-12 "Avoidable costs are variable costs." Do you agree? Explain.

4-13 Give four examples of limiting or scarce factors.

4-14 Compare and contrast *marginal cost* and *variable cost*.

4-15 Describe four major factors that influence pricing decisions.

4-16 Why are customers one of the factors influencing price decisions?

4-17 "Basing pricing on only the variable costs of a job results in suicidal underpricing." Do you agree? Why?

4-18 Provide three examples of pricing decisions other than the special order.

4-19 List four popular markup formulas for pricing.

4-20 Describe two long-run effects that may lead to managers rejecting opportunities to cut prices and obtain increases in short-run profits.

4-21 Give two reasons why full costs are far more widely used than variable costs for guiding pricing.

4-22 Why do most executives use both full-cost and variable-cost information for pricing decisions?

4-23 "Target costing is the opposite of target pricing." Do you agree? Explain.

Exercises

4-24 Pinpointing of Relevant Costs
Today you are planning to see a motion picture and you can attend either of two theaters. You have only a small budget for entertainment, so prices are important. You have attended both theaters recently. One charged $6 for admission; the other charged $7. You habitually buy popcorn in the theater—each theater charges $2. The motion pictures now being shown are equally attractive to you, but you are virtually certain that you will never see the picture that you reject today.

Identify the relevant costs. Explain your answer.

4-25 Information and Decisions
Suppose Radio Shack's historical costs for the manufacture of a calculator were as follows: direct materials, $4.60 per unit; direct labor, $3.00 per unit. Management is trying to decide whether to replace some materials with different materials. The replacement should cut material costs by 5% per unit. However, direct-labor time will increase by 5% per unit. Moreover, direct-labor rates will be affected by a recent 10% wage increase.

Prepare an exhibit like Exhibit 4-1 (p. 101), showing where and how the data about direct material and direct labor fit in the decision process.

4-26 Identification of Relevant Costs
Paul and Paula Petrocelli were trying to decide whether to go to the symphony or to the baseball game. They already have two nonrefundable tickets to "Pops Night at the Symphony" that cost $40 each. This is the only concert of the season they considered attending because it is the only one with the type of music they enjoy. The baseball game is the last one of the season, and it will decide the league championship. They can purchase tickets for $20 each.

The Petrocellis will drive 50 miles round trip to either event. Variable costs for operating their auto are $.14 per mile, and fixed costs average $.13 per mile for the 18,000 miles they drive annually. Parking at the symphony is free, but it costs $6 at the baseball game.

To attend either event, Paul and Paula will hire a baby-sitter at $4 per hour. They expect to be gone 5 hours to attend the baseball game but only 4 hours to attend the symphony.

Compare the cost of attending the baseball game to the cost of attending the symphony. Focus on relevant costs. Compute the difference in cost, and indicate which alternative is more costly to the Petrocellis.

4-27 Straightforward Special-Order Decision
The Ventura Sport Shop makes game jerseys for athletic teams. The F. C. Strikers soccer club has offered to buy 100 jerseys for the teams in its league for $15 per jersey. The team price for

such jerseys normally is $18, an 80% markup over Ventura's purchase price of $10 per jersey. Ventura adds a name and number to each jersey at a variable cost of $2 per jersey. The annual fixed cost of equipment used in the printing process is $6,000 and other fixed costs allocated to jerseys is $2,000. Ventura makes about 2,000 jerseys per year, making the fixed cost $4 per jersey. The equipment is used only for printing jerseys and stands idle 75% of the usable time.

The manager of Ventura Sport Shop turned down the offer, saying, "If we sell at $15 and our cost is $16, we lose money on each jersey we sell. We would like to help your league, but we can't afford to lose money on the sale."

1. Compute the amount by which the operating income of Ventura Sport Shop would change if the F. C. Striker's offer were accepted.
2. Suppose you were the manager of Ventura Sport Shop. Would you accept the offer? In addition to considering the quantitative impact computed in requirement 1, list two qualitative considerations that would influence your decision—one qualitative factor supporting acceptance of the offer and one supporting rejection.

4-28 Unit Costs and Total Costs

You are a bank vice president who belongs to a downtown luncheon club. Annual dues are $120. You use the club solely for lunches, which cost $6 each. You have not used the club much in recent years and you are wondering whether to continue your membership.

1. You are confronted with a variable-cost plus a fixed-cost behavior pattern. Plot each on a graph, where the vertical axis is total cost and the horizontal axis is annual volume in number of lunches. Also plot a third graph that combines the previous two graphs.
2. What is the cost per lunch if you pay for your own lunch once a year? Twelve times a year? Two hundred times a year?
3. Suppose the average price of lunches elsewhere is $10. (a) How many lunches must you have at the luncheon club so that the total costs of the lunches would be the same regardless of where you ate for that number of lunches? (b) Suppose you ate 250 lunches a year at the club. How much would you save in relation to the total costs of eating elsewhere?

4-29 Advertising Expenditures and Nonprofit Organizations

Many colleges and universities have been extensively advertising their services. For example, a university in Philadelphia used a biplane to pull a sign promoting its evening program, and one in Mississippi designed bumper stickers and slogans as well as innovative programs.

Suppose Central State University (CSU) charges a comprehensive annual fee of $14,000 for tuition, room, and board, and it has capacity for 2,500 students. Costs per student for the 19X1 academic year are:

	Variable	Fixed	Total
Educational programs	$4,000	$4,200	$ 8,200
Room	1,300	2,200	3,500
Board	2,600	600	3,200
	$7,900	$7,000*	$14,900

* Based on 2,000 to 2,500 students for the year.

The admissions department predicts enrollment of 2,000 students for 19X1. The assistant director of admissions has proposed a two-month advertising campaign, however, using radio and television advertisements together with an extensive direct mailing of brochures.

1. Suppose the advertising campaign will cost $1.83 million. What is the minimum number of additional students the campaign must attract to make the campaign break even?

2. Suppose the admissions department predicts that the campaign will attract 350 additional students. What is the most CSU should pay for the campaign and still break even?

3. Suppose a three-month (instead of two-month) campaign will attract 450 instead of 350 additional students. What is the most CSU should pay for the one-month extension of the campaign and still break even?

4-30 Variety of Cost Terms
Consider the following data:

Variable selling and administrative costs per unit	$ 4.00
Total fixed selling and administrative costs	$2,900,000
Total fixed manufacturing costs	$3,000,000
Variable manufacturing costs per unit	$ 9.00
Units produced and sold	500,000

1. Compute the following per unit of product: (a) total variable costs, (b) absorption cost, (c) full cost.

2. Give a synonym for *full cost*.

4-31 Profit per Unit of Space
1. Several successful chains of warehouse stores have merchandising policies that differ considerably from those of traditional department stores. Name some characteristics of these warehouse stores that have contributed to their success.

2. Food chains have typically regarded approximately 20% of selling price as an average target gross profit on canned goods and similar grocery items. What are the limitations of such an approach? Be specific.

4-32 A&P's Closing of Stores
A major U.S. grocery chain, A&P, recently ran into profit difficulties and closed many of its stores.

1. After the closures the company's labor costs as a percentage of sales increased in some markets, such as the Long Island and Pittsburgh divisions, even after allowing for normal increases in wage rates. How could this effect occur?

2. The company manufactured many of its own products in 46 company-operated plants. Twenty-one were bakeries. The others manufactured a variety of goods, from frozen potatoes to mouthwash. What impact would the store closings probably have on the manufacturing plants and on the total operating income?

4-33 Deletion of Product Line
Country Day School is a private elementary school. In addition to regular classes, after-school care is provided between 3:00 and 6:00 P.M. at $3 per child per hour. Financial results for the after-school care for a representative month are:

Revenue, 600 hours @ $3 per hour		$1,800
		Less
Teacher salaries	1,300	
Supplies	200	
Depreciation	325	
Sanitary engineering	25	
Other fixed costs	50	1,900
Operating income (loss)		$ (100)

The director of Country Day School is considering discontinuing the after-school care services because it is not fair to the other students to subsidize the after-school care program. He thinks that eliminating the program will free up $100 a month to be used in the regular classes.

1. Compute the financial impact on Country Day School from discontinuing the after-school care program.
2. List three qualitative factors that would influence your decision.

4-34 Acceptance of Low Bid

The Hernandez Company, a maker of a variety of metal and plastic products, is in the midst of a business downturn and is saddled with many idle facilities. The National Hospital Supply Company has approached Hernandez to produce 300,000 nonslide serving trays. National will pay $1.20 each.

Hernandez predicts that its variable costs will be $1.30 each. Its fixed costs, which had been averaging $1 per unit on a variety of other products, will now be spread over twice as much volume, however. The president commented, "Sure we'll lose $.10 each on the variable costs, but we'll gain $.50 per unit by spreading our fixed costs. Therefore, we should take the offer, because it represents an advantage of $.40 per unit."

Suppose the regular business had a current volume of 300,000 units, sales of $600,000, variable costs of $390,000, and fixed costs of $300,000. Do you agree with the president? Why?

4-35 Pricing by Auto Dealer

Many automobile dealers have an operating pattern similar to that of Ranch Motors, a dealer in Texas. Each month, Ranch initially aims at a unit volume quota that approximates a break-even point. Until the break-even point is reached, Ranch has a policy of relatively lofty pricing, whereby the "minimum deal" must contain a sufficiently high markup to ensure a contribution to profit of no less than $400. After the break-even point is attained, Ranch tends to quote lower prices for the remainder of the month.

What is your opinion of this policy? As a prospective customer, how would you react to this policy?

4-36 Target Selling Prices

Consider the following data from Blackmar Company's budgeted income statement (in thousands of dollars):

Target sales	$60,000
Variable costs	
Manufacturing	30,000
Selling and administrative	6,000
Total variable costs	36,000
Fixed costs	
Manufacturing	8,000
Selling and administrative	6,000
Total fixed costs	14,000
Total of all costs	50,000
Operating income	$10,000

Compute the following markup formulas that would be used for obtaining the same target sales as a percentage of (1) total variable costs, (2) full costs, (3) variable manufacturing costs, and (4) absorption costs.

4-37 Competitive Bids

Rimmer, Coles, and Diaz, a CPA firm, is preparing to bid for a consulting job. Although Alice Rimmer will use her judgment about the market in finalizing the bid, she has asked you to prepare a cost analysis to help in the bidding. You have estimated the costs for the consulting job to be:

Materials and supplies, at cost	$ 30,000
Hourly pay for consultants, 2,000 hours @ $35 per hour	70,000
Fringe benefits for consultants, 2,000 hours @ $12 per hour	24,000
Total variable costs	124,000
Fixed costs allocated to the job	
Based on labor, 2,000 hours @ $10 per hour	20,000
Based on materials and supplies, 80% of 30,000	24,000
Total cost	$168,000

Of the $44,000 allocated fixed costs, $35,000 will be incurred even if the job is not undertaken.

Alice normally bids jobs at the sum of (1) 150% of the estimated materials and supplies cost and (2) $80 per estimated labor-hour.

1. Prepare a bid using the normal formula.
2. Prepare a minimum bid equal to the additional costs expected to be incurred to complete the job.
3. Prepare a bid that will cover full costs plus a markup for profit equal to 20% of full cost.

4-38 Pricing, Ethics, and the Law

Mega Pharmaceuticals, Inc., (MPI) produces both prescription and over-the-counter medications. In January MPI introduced a new prescription drug, Rythestan, to relieve the pain of arthritis. The company spent more than $50 million over the last five years developing the drug, and advertising alone during the first year of introduction will exceed $10 million. Production cost for a bottle of 100 tablets is approximately $12. Sales in the first three years are predicted to be 500,000, 750,000, and 1,000,000 bottles, respectively. To achieve these sales, MPI plans to distribute the medicine through three sources: directly from physicians, through hospital pharmacies, and through retail pharmacies. Initially, the bottles will be given free to physicians to give to patients, hospital pharmacies will pay $25 per bottle, and retail pharmacies will pay $40 per bottle. In the second and third year, the company plans to phase out the free distributions to physicians and move all other customers toward a $50 per bottle sales price.

Comment on the pricing and promotion policies of MPI. Pay particular attention to the legal and ethical issues involved.

4-39 Pricing and Contribution Approach

The Concord Trucking Company has the following operating results to date for 19X3:

Operating revenues	$100,000,000
Operating costs	80,000,000
Operating income	$ 20,000,000

A large Boston manufacturer has inquired about whether Concord would be interested in trucking a large order of its parts to Atlanta. Steve Minkler, operations manager, investigated the situation and estimated that the "fully allocated" costs of servicing the order would be $40,000. Using his general pricing formula, he quoted a price of $50,000. The manufacturer replied: "We'll give you $37,000, take it or leave it. If you do not want our business, we'll truck it ourselves or go elsewhere."

A cost analyst had recently been conducting studies of how Concord's operating costs tended to behave. She found that $64 million of the $80 million could be characterized as variable costs. Minkler discussed the matter with her and decided that this order would probably generate cost behavior little different from Concord's general operations.

1. Using a contribution format, prepare an analysis for Minkler.
2. Should Concord accept the order? Explain.

4-40 Cost Analysis and Pricing

The budget for the University Park Printing Company for 19X5 follows:

Sales		£1,100,000
Direct material	£280,000	
Direct labor	320,000	
Overhead	400,000	1,000,000
Net income		£ 100,000

The company typically uses a so-called cost-plus pricing system. Direct material and direct labor costs are computed, overhead is added at a rate of 125% of direct labor, and 10% of the total cost is added to obtain the selling price.

Carol Rosenthal, the sales manager, has placed a £22,000 bid on a particularly large order with a cost of £5,600 direct material and £6,400 direct labor. The customer informs her that she can have the business for £19,800, take it or leave it. If Rosenthal accepts the order, total sales for 19X5 will be £1,119,800.

Rosenthal refuses the order, saying: "I sell on a cost-plus basis. It is bad policy to accept orders at below cost. I would lose £200 on the job."

The company's annual fixed overhead is £160,000.

1. What would net income have been with the order? Without the order? Show your computations.
2. Give a short description of a contribution approach to pricing that Rosenthal might follow. Include a stipulation of the pricing formula that Rosenthal should routinely use if she hopes to obtain a target net income of £100,000.

4-41 Pricing of Education

You are the director of continuing education programs for a well-known university. Courses for executives are especially popular, and you have developed an extensive menu of one-day and two-day courses that are presented in various locations throughout the nation. The performance of these courses for the current fiscal year, excluding the final course which is scheduled for the next Saturday, is:

Tuition revenue	$2,000,000
Costs of courses	800,000
Contribution margin	1,200,000
General administrative expenses	400,000
Operating income	$ 800,000

The costs of the courses include fees for instructors, rentals of classrooms, advertising, and any other items, such as travel, that can be easily and exclusively identified as being caused by a particular course.

The general administrative expenses include your salary, your secretary's compensation, and related expenses, such as a lump-sum payment to the university's central offices as a share of university overhead.

The enrollment for your final course of the year is 40 students, who have paid $200 each. Two days before the course is to begin, a city manager telephones your office. "Do you offer discounts to nonprofit institutions?" he asks. "If so, we'll send 10 managers. But our budget will not justify our spending more than $100 per person." The extra cost of including these ten managers would entail lunches at $20 each and course materials at $40 each.

1. Prepare a tabulation of the performance for the full year including the final course. Assume that the costs of the final course for the 40 enrollees' instruction, travel, advertising, rental of hotel classroom, lunches, and course materials would be $4,600. Show a tabulation in four columns: before final course, final course with 40 registrants, effect of 10 more registrants, and grand totals.
2. What major considerations would probably influence the pricing policies for these courses? For setting regular university tuition in private universities?

4-42   Use of Passenger Jets

In 19X5 Continental Air Lines, Inc. filled about 50% of the available seats on its flights, a record about 15 percentage points below the national average.

Continental could have eliminated about 4% of its runs and raised its average load considerably. The improved load factor would have reduced profits, however. Give reasons for or against this elimination. What factors should influence an airline's scheduling policies?

When you answer this question, suppose that Continental had a basic package of 3,000 flights per month that had an average of 100 seats available per flight. Also suppose that 52% of the seats were filled at an average ticket price of $200 per flight. Variable costs are about 70% of revenue.

Continental also had a marginal package of 120 flights per month that had an average of 100 seats available per flight. Suppose that only 20% of the seats were filled at an average ticket price of $100 per flight. Variable costs are about 50% of this revenue. Prepare a tabulation of the basic package, marginal package, and total package, showing percentage of seats filled, revenue, variable expenses, and contribution margin.

4-43   Effects of Volume on Operating Income

The Brownell Division of Victoria Sports Company manufactures boomerangs, which are sold to wholesalers and retailers. The division manager has set a target of 250,000 boomerangs for next month's production and sales. The manager, however, has prepared an analysis of the effects on operating income of deviations from the target:

Volume in units	200,000	250,000	300,000
Sales @ $3.00	$600,000	$750,000	$900,000
Full costs @ $2.50	500,000	625,000	750,000
Operating income	$100,000	$125,000	$150,000

The costs have the following characteristics. Variable manufacturing costs are $1.00 per boomerang; variable selling costs are $.20 per boomerang. Fixed manufacturing costs per month are $275,000; fixed selling and administrative costs, $50,000.

1. Prepare a correct analysis of the changes in volume on operating income. Prepare a tabulated set of income statements at levels of 200,000, 250,000, and 300,000 boomerangs. Also show percentages of operating income in relation to sales.

2. Compare your tabulation with the manager's tabulation. Why is the manager's tabulation incorrect?

4-44   Pricing of Special Order

The Drosselmeier Corporation makes Christmas Nutcrackers and has an annual plant capacity of 2,400 product units. Its predicted operations for the year are:

Production and sales of 2,000 units, total sales	$90,000
Manufacturing costs	
Fixed (total)	$30,000
Variable (per unit)	$13
Selling and administrative expenses	
Fixed (total)	$15,000
Variable (per unit)	$5

Compute the following, ignoring income taxes:

1. If the company accepts a special order for 300 units at a selling price of $20 each, how would the *total* predicted net income for the year be affected, assuming no effect on regular sales at regular prices?
2. Without decreasing its total net income, what is the lowest *unit price* for which the Drosselmeier Corporation could sell an additional 100 units not subject to any variable selling and administrative expenses, assuming no effect on regular sales at regular prices?
3. List the numbers given in the problem that are irrelevant (not relevant) in solving requirement 2.
4. Compute the expected annual net income (with no special orders) if plant capacity can be doubled by adding additional facilities at a cost of $250,000. Assume that these facilities have an estimated life of 5 years with no residual scrap value, and that the current unit selling price can be maintained for all sales. Total sales are expected to equal the new plant capacity each year. No changes are expected in variable costs per unit or in total fixed costs except for depreciation.

4-45   Pricing and Confusing Variable and Fixed Costs

Goldwyn Electronics had a fixed factory overhead budget for 19X2 of $10 million. The company planned to make and sell 2 million units of the product, a communications device. All variable manufacturing costs per unit were $10. The budgeted income statement contained the following:

Sales	$40,000,000
Manufacturing cost of goods sold	30,000,000
Gross margin	10,000,000
Deduct selling and administrative expenses	4,000,000
Operating income	$ 6,000,000

For simplicity, assume that the actual variable costs per unit and the total fixed costs were exactly as budgeted.

1. Compute Goldwyn's budgeted fixed factory overhead per unit.
2. Near the end of 19X2 a large computer manufacturer offered to buy 100,000 units for $1.2 million on a one-time special order. The president of Goldwyn stated: "The offer is a bad

deal. It's foolish to sell below full manufacturing costs per unit. I realize that this order will have only a modest effect on selling and administrative costs. They will increase by a $10,000 fee paid to our sales agent." Compute the effect on operating income if the offer is accepted.

3. What factors should the president of Goldwyn consider before finally deciding whether to accept the offer?

4. Suppose the original budget for fixed manufacturing costs was $10 million, but budgeted units of product were 1 million. How would your answers to requirements 1 and 2 change? Be specific.

4-46 Demand Analysis

(SMA, adapted.) Ross Manufacturing Limited produces and sells one product, a three-foot American flag. During 19X4 the company manufactured and sold 50,000 flags at $24 each. Existing production capacity is 60,000 flags per year.

In formulating the 19X5 budget, management is faced with a number of decisions concerning product pricing and output. The following information is available:

1. A market survey shows that the sales volume is largely dependent on the selling price. For each $1 drop in selling price, sales volume would increase by 10,000 flags.

2. The company's expected cost structure for 19X5 is as follows:
   a. Fixed cost (regardless of production or sales activities), $360,000
   b. Variable costs per flag (including production, selling, and administrative expenses), $15

3. To increase annual capacity from the present 60,000 to 90,000 flags, additional investment for plant, building, equipment, and the like, of $200,000 would be necessary. The estimated average life of the additional investment would be 10 years, so the fixed costs would increase by an average of $20,000 per year. (Expansion of less than 30,000 additional units of capacity would cost only slightly less than $200,000.)

Indicate, with reasons, what the level of production and the selling price should be for the coming year. Also indicate whether the company should approve the plant expansion. Show your calculations. Ignore income tax considerations and the time value of money.

4-47 Choice of Products

Florida Fashions sells both designer and moderately priced women's wear in Sarasota. Profits have been volatile. Top management is trying to decide which product line to drop. Accountants have reported the following relevant data:

	Per Item	
	Designer	Moderately Priced
Average selling price	$240	$140
Average variable expenses	120	75
Average contribution margin	$120	$ 65
Average contribution-margin percentage	50%	46%

The store has 8,000 square feet of floor space. If moderately priced goods are sold exclusively, 400 items can be displayed. If designer goods are sold exclusively, only 300 items can be displayed. Moreover, the rate of sale (turnover) of the designer items will be two-thirds the rate of moderately priced goods.

1. Prepare an analysis to show which product to drop.
2. What other considerations might affect your decision in requirement 1?

4-48 Analysis of Unit Costs

The Sunlight Company manufactures small appliances, such as electric can openers, toasters, food mixers, and irons. The peak season is at hand, and the president is trying to decide whether to produce more of the company's standard line of can openers or its premium line that includes a built-in knife sharpener, a better finish, and a higher-quality motor. The unit data follow:

	Product	
	Standard	Premium
Selling price	$26	$34
Direct material	$ 8	$12
Direct labor	2	1
Variable factory overhead	2	3
Fixed factory overhead	6	9
Total cost of goods sold	$18	$25
Gross profit per unit	$ 8	$ 9

The sales outlook is very encouraging. The plant could operate at full capacity by producing either product or both products. Both the standard and the premium products are processed through the same departments. Selling and administrative costs will not be affected by this decision, so they may be ignored.

Many of the parts are produced on automatic machinery. The factory overhead is allocated to products by developing separate rates per machine-hour for variable and fixed overhead. For example, the total fixed overhead is divided by the total machine-hours to get a rate per hour. Thus the amount of overhead allocated to products is dependent on the number of machine-hours allocated to the product. It takes one hour of machine time to produce one unit of the standard product.

Direct labor may not be proportionate with overhead because many workers operate two or more machines simultaneously.

Which product should be produced? If more than one should be produced, indicate the proportions of each. Show computations. Explain your answers briefly.

4-49 Use of Available Facilities

The Higashi Company manufactures electronic subcomponents that can be sold directly or can be processed further into "plug-in" assemblies for a variety of intricate electronic equipment. The entire output of subcomponents can be sold at a market price of $2 per unit. The plug-in assemblies have been generating a sales price of $5.50 for three years, but the price has recently fallen to $5.10 on assorted orders.

Nancy Ng, the vice-president of marketing, has analyzed the markets and the costs. She thinks that production of plug-in assemblies should be dropped whenever the price falls below $4.50 per unit. The total available capacity should currently be devoted to producing plug-in assemblies. She has cited the data at the top of the next page.

Direct-materials and direct-labor costs are variable. The total overhead is fixed; it is allocated to units produced by predicting the total overhead for the coming year and dividing this total by the total hours of capacity available.

The total hours of capacity available are 600,000. It takes 1 hour to make 60 subcomponents and 2 hours of additional processing and testing to make 60 plug-in assemblies.

		Sub-components
Selling price, after deducting relevant selling costs		$2.00
Direct materials	$ .90	
Direct labor	.30	
Manufacturing overhead	.60	
Cost per unit		1.80
Operating profit		$ .20

		Plug-In Assemblies
Selling price, after deducting relevant selling costs		$5.10
Transferred-in variable cost for subcomponents	$1.20	
Additional direct materials	1.45	
Direct labor	.45	
Manufacturing overhead	1.20*	
Cost per unit		4.30
Operating profit		$ .80

* For additional processing to make and test plug-in assemblies.

1. If the price of plug-in assemblies for the coming year is going to be $5.10, should sales of subcomponents be dropped and all facilities devoted to the production of plug-in assemblies? Show computations.
2. Prepare a report for the vice president of marketing to show the lowest possible price for plug-in assemblies that would be acceptable.
3. Suppose 40% of the manufacturing overhead is variable with respect to processing and testing time. Repeat requirements 1 and 2. Do your answers change? If so, how?

4-50 Target Costing

Knoxville Electrical, Inc., makes small electric motors for a variety of home appliances. Knoxville sells the motors to appliance makers, who assemble and sell the appliances to retail outlets. Although Knoxville makes dozens of different motors, it does not currently make one to be used in garage-door openers. The company's market research department has discovered a market for such a motor.

The market research department has indicated that a motor for garage-door openers would likely sell for $23. A similar motor currently being produced has the following manufacturing costs:

Direct materials	$12.00
Direct labor	5.00
Overhead	8.00
Total	$25.00

Knoxville desires a gross margin of 15% of the manufacturing cost.

1. Suppose Knoxville used cost-plus pricing, setting the price 15% above the manufacturing cost. What price would be charged for the motor? Would you produce such a motor if you were a manager at Knoxville? Explain.
2. Suppose Knoxville uses target costing. What price would the company charge for a garage-door-opener motor? What is the highest acceptable manufacturing cost for which Knoxville would be willing to produce the motor?

3. As a user of target costing, what steps would Knoxville managers take to try to make production of this product feasible?

4-51 Review

The Disposable Camera division of Saari Optics Co. has the following cost behavior patterns:

Production range in units	0–5,000	5,001–10,000	10,001–15,000	15,001–20,000
Fixed costs	$15,000	$22,000	$25,000	$27,000

Maximum production capacity is 20,000 cameras per year. Variable costs per unit are $5 at all production levels.

Each situation described below is to be considered independently.

1. Production and sales are expected to be 11,000 cameras for the year. The sales price is $7 per camera. How many additional cameras need to be sold, in an unrelated market, at $6 per camera to show a total overall net income of $900 for the year?

2. The company has orders for 23,000 cameras at $7. If it desired to make a minimum overall net income of $14,500 on these 23,000 cameras, what unit purchase price would it be willing to pay a subcontractor for 3,000 cameras? Assume that the subcontractor would act as Saari's agent, deliver the cameras to customers directly, and bear all related costs of manufacture, delivery, etc. The customers, however, would pay Saari directly as goods were delivered.

3. Production is currently expected to be 7,000 cameras for the year at a selling price of $7. By how much may advertising or special promotion costs be increased to bring production up to 14,500 cameras and still earn a total net income of 2% of dollar sales?

4. Net income is currently $12,500. Nonvariable costs are $25,000. Competitive pressures are mounting, however. A 5% decrease in price will not affect sales volume but will decrease net income by $4,750. What is the present volume, in units? What is the correct selling price? (Note: It is not $7.)

Cases

4-52 Use of Capacity

(CMA, adapted.) St. Tropez S. A. manufactures several different styles of jewelry cases in southern France. Management estimates that during the third quarter of 1996 the company will be operating at 80% of normal capacity. Because the company desires a higher utilization of plant capacity, it will consider a special order.

St. Tropez has received special-order inquiries from two companies. The first is from JCP, Inc., which would like to market a jewelry case similar to one of St. Tropez's cases. The JCP jewelry case would be marketed under JCP's own label. JCP, Inc., has offered St. Tropez FF57.5 per jewelry case for 20,000 cases to be shipped by October 1, 1996. The cost data for the St. Tropez jewelry case, which would be similar to the specifications of the JCP special order, are as follows:

Regular selling price per unit	FF90
Costs per unit:	
Raw materials	FF25
Direct labor .5 hr @ FF60	30
Overhead .25 machine-hr @ FF40	10
Total costs	FF65

According to the specifications provided by JCP, Inc., the special-order case requires less expensive raw materials, which will cost only FF22.5 per case. Management has estimated that the remaining costs, labor time, and machine time will be the same as those for the St. Tropez jewelry case.

The second special order was submitted by the Cannes Co. for 7,500 jewelry cases at FF75 per case. These cases would be marketed under the Cannes label and would have to be shipped by October 1, 1996. The Cannes jewelry case is different from any jewelry case in the St. Tropez line; its estimated per-unit costs are as follows:

Raw materials	FF32.5
Direct labor .5 hr @ FF60	30
Overhead .5 machine-hr @ FF40	20
Total costs	FF82.5

In addition, St. Tropez will incur FF15,000 in additional setup costs and will have to purchase a FF25,000 special device to manufacture these cases; this device will be discarded once the special order is completed.

The St. Tropez manufacturing capabilities are limited by the total machine-hours available. The plant capacity under normal operations is 90,000 machine-hours per year, or 7,500 machine-hours per month. The budgeted *fixed* overhead for 1996 amounts to FF2.16 million, or FF24 per hour. All manufacturing overhead costs are applied to production on the basis of machine-hours at FF40 per hour.

St. Tropez will have the entire third quarter to work on the special orders. Management does not expect any repeat sales to be generated from either special order. Company practice precludes St. Tropez from subcontracting any portion of an order when special orders are not expected to generate repeat sales.

Should St. Tropez accept either special order? Justify your answer and show your calculations. (*Hint*: Distinguish between variable and fixed overhead.)

4-53 Review

The Lopez Company is a processor of a Bacardi-mix concentrate. Sales are made principally to liquor distributors throughout the country.

The company's income statements for the past year and the coming year are being analyzed by top management and are shown at the top of the next page.

Consider each requirement independently.

Unless otherwise stated, assume that all unit costs of inputs such as material and labor are unchanged. Also, assume that efficiency is unchanged—that is, the labor and quantity of material consumed per unit of output are unchanged. Unless otherwise stated, assume that there are no changes in fixed costs.

1. The president has just returned from a management conference at a local university, where he heard an accounting professor criticize conventional income statements. The professor had asserted that knowledge of cost behavior patterns was of key importance in determining managerial strategies. The president now feels that the income statement should be recast to harmonize with cost-volume-profit analysis—that is, the statement should have three major sections: sales, variable costs, and fixed costs. Using the 1995 data, prepare such a statement, showing the contribution margin as well as operating income.

2. Comment on the changes in each item in the 1996 income statement compared to the 1995 statement. What are the most likely causes for each increase? For example, have selling prices been changed for 1996? How do sales commissions fluctuate in relation to units sold or in relation to dollar sales?

LOPEZ COMPANY
Income Statements

	For the Year 1995 Just Ended		For the Year 1996 Tentative Budget	
Sales 1,500,000 units in 1995		$900,000		$1,000,000
Cost of goods sold				
Direct material	$450,000		$495,000	
Direct labor	90,000		99,000	
Factory overhead				
Variable	18,000		19,800	
Fixed	50,000	608,000	50,000	663,800
Gross margin		$292,000		$ 336,200
Selling expenses				
Variable				
Sales commissions (based on dollar sales)	$ 45,000		$ 50,000	
Shipping and other	90,000		99,000	
Fixed				
Salaries, advertising, etc.	110,000		138,000	
Administrative expenses				
Variable	12,000		13,200	
Fixed	40,000	297,000	40,000	340,200
Operating income		$ (5,000)		$ (4,000)

3. The president is unimpressed with the 1996 budget: "We need to take a fresh look in order to begin moving toward profitable operations. Let's tear up the 1996 budget, concentrate on 1995 results, and prepare a new comparative 1996 budget under each of the following assumptions:

    a. A 5% average price cut will increase unit sales by 20%.

    b. A 5% average price increase will decrease unit sales by 10%.

    c. A sales commission rate of 10% and a 3⅓% price increase will boost unit sales by 10%.

Prepare the budgets for 1996, using a contribution-margin format and three columns. Assume that there are no changes in fixed costs.

4. The advertising manager maintains that the advertising budget should be increased by $125,000 and that prices should be increased by 10%. Resulting unit sales will soar by 25%. What would be the expected operating income under such circumstances?

5. A nearby distillery has offered to buy 300,000 units in 1996 if the unit price is low enough. The Lopez Company would not have to incur sales commissions or shipping costs on this special order, and regular business would be undisturbed. Assuming that 1996's regular operations will be exactly like 1995's, what unit price should be quoted in order for the Lopez Company to earn an operating income of $10,000 in 1996?

6. The company chemist wants to add a special ingredient, an exotic flavoring that will add $.02 per unit to the Bacardi-mix costs. He also wants to replace the ordinary grenadine now used, which costs $.03 per unit of mix, with a more exquisite type costing $.04 per unit. Assuming no other changes in cost behavior, how many units must be sold to earn an operating income of $10,000 in 1996?

OPPORTUNITY, OUTLAY, AND DIFFERENTIAL COSTS

The concept of opportunity cost is often used by decision makers. An **opportunity cost** is the maximum available contribution to profit forgone (or passed up) by using limited resources for a particular purpose. This definition indicates that opportunity cost is not the usual outlay cost recorded in accounting. An **outlay cost**, which requires a cash disbursement sooner or later, is the typical cost recorded by accountants.

An example of an opportunity cost is the salary forgone by a person who quits a job to start a business. Consider Maria Morales, a certified public accountant employed by a large accounting firm at $60,000 per year. She is yearning to have her own independent practice.

Maria's alternatives may be framed in more than one way. A straightforward comparison follows:

	Alternatives Under Consideration		
	Remain as Employee	Open an Independent Practice	Difference
Revenues	$60,000	$200,000	$140,000
Outlay costs (operating expenses)	—	120,000	120,000
Income effects per year	$60,000	$ 80,000	$ 20,000

The annual difference of $20,000 favors Maria's choosing independent practice.

This tabulation is sometimes called a *differential analysis*. The *differential revenue* is $140,000, the *differential cost* is $120,000, and the *differential income* is $20,000. Each amount is the difference between the corresponding items under each alternative being considered. **Differential cost** and **incremental cost** are widely used synonyms. They are defined as the difference in total cost between two alternatives. For instance, the differential costs or incremental costs of increasing production from 1,000 automobiles to 1,200 automobiles per week would be the additional costs of producing the additional 200 automobiles each week. In the reverse situation, the decline in costs caused by reducing production from 1,200 to 1,000 automobiles per week would often be called *differential* or *incremental savings*.

Returning to Maria Morales, focus on the meaning of opportunity cost. What is the contribution to profit of the best of the rejected alternatives? Independent practice has an opportunity cost of $60,000, the forgone annual salary.

These same facts may also be presented as follows:

		Alternative Chosen: Independent Practice
Revenue		$200,000
Expenses		
Outlay costs (operating expenses)	$120,000	
Opportunity cost of employee salary	60,000	180,000
Income effects per year		$ 20,000

Ponder the two preceding tabulations. Each produces the correct key difference between alternatives, $20,000. The first tabulation does not mention opportunity cost because the economic impacts (in the form of revenues and outlay costs) are individually measured for each of the alternatives (two in this case). Neither alternative has been excluded from consideration. The second tabulation mentions opportunity cost because the $60,000 annual economic impact of the *best excluded* alternative is included as a cost of the chosen alternative. The failure to recognize opportunity cost in the second tabulation will misstate the difference between alternatives.

Suppose Morales prefers less risk and chooses to stay as an employee:

		Alternative Chosen: Remain as Employee
Revenue		$ 60,000
Expenses		
Outlay costs	$ 0	
Opportunity cost of independent practice	80,000	80,000
Decrease in income per year		$(20,000)

If the employee alternative is selected, the key difference in favor of independent practice is again $20,000. The opportunity cost is $80,000, the annual operating income forgone by rejecting the best excluded alternative. Morales is sacrificing $20,000 annually to avoid the risks of an independent practice. In sum, the opportunity cost is the contribution of the best alternative that is excluded from consideration.

The major message here is straightforward: Do not overlook opportunity costs. Consider a homeowner who has made the final payment on the mortgage. While celebrating, the owner says, "It's a wonderful feeling to know that future occupancy is free of any interest cost!" Many owners have similar thoughts. Why? Because no future outlay costs for interest are required. Nevertheless, there is an opportunity cost of continuing to live in the home. After all, an alternative would be to sell the home, place the proceeds in some other investment, and rent an apartment. The owner forgoes the interest in the other investment, so this forgone interest income becomes an opportunity cost of home ownership.

MAKE-OR-BUY DECISIONS

Companies often must decide whether to produce a product or service within the firm or purchase it from an outside supplier. They apply relevant cost analysis to a variety of such make-or-buy decisions, including:

- Boeing's decision whether to buy or make many of the tools used in assembling 747 airplanes.
- IBM's decision whether to develop its own operating system for a new computer or to buy it from a software vendor.

- A local school district's decision whether to use its own personnel or hire a consulting firm to design and implement a new computerized accounting system.

Make-or-Buy and Idle Facilities

To focus on basic principles, we examine relatively straightforward make-or-buy decisions. Consider manufacturers who must often decide whether to make or buy a product. For example, should a firm manufacture its own parts and subassemblies or buy them from vendors? Sometimes qualitative factors dominate quantitative assessments of costs. Some manufacturers always make parts because they want to control quality, others because they possess special know-how, usually skilled labor or rare materials needed in production. Alternatively, some companies always purchase parts to protect mutually advantageous long-run relationships with their suppliers. These companies may deliberately buy from vendors even during slack times to avoid difficulties in obtaining needed parts during boom times, when there may well be shortages of materials and workers but no shortage of sales orders.

What quantitative factors are relevant to the decision of whether to make or buy? The answer, again, depends on the situation. A key factor is whether there are idle facilities. Many companies make parts only when their facilities cannot be used to better advantage.

Assume that the following costs are reported:

General Electric Company
Cost of Making Part No. 900

	Total Cost for 20,000 Units	Cost per Unit
Direct material	$ 20,000	$ 1
Direct labor	80,000	4
Variable factory overhead	40,000	2
Fixed factory overhead	80,000	4
Total costs	$220,000	$11

Another manufacturer offers to sell General Electric (GE) the same part for $10. Should GE make or buy the part?

Although the $11 unit cost shown seemingly indicates that the company should buy, the answer is rarely so obvious. The essential question is the difference in expected future costs between the alternatives. If the $4 fixed overhead per unit consists of costs that will continue regardless of the decision, the entire $4 becomes irrelevant. Examples of such costs include depreciation, property taxes, insurance, and allocated executive salaries.

Again, are only the variable costs relevant? No. Perhaps $20,000 of the fixed costs will be eliminated if the parts are bought instead of made. For example, a supervisor with a $20,000 salary might be released. In other words, fixed costs that may be avoided in the future are relevant.

For the moment, suppose the capacity now used to make parts will become idle if the parts are purchased and the $20,000 supervisor's salary is the only fixed cost that would be eliminated. The relevant computations follow:

	Make		Buy	
	Total	Per Unit	Total	Per Unit
Purchase cost			$200,000	$10
Direct material	$ 20,000	$ 1		
Direct labor	80,000	4		
Variable factory overhead	40,000	2		
Fixed factory overhead that can be avoided by not making (supervisor's salary)	20,000*	1*		
Total relevant costs	$160,000	$ 8	$200,000	$10
Difference in favor of making	$ 40,000	$ 2		

* Note that unavoidable fixed costs of $80,000 – $20,000 = $60,000 are irrelevant. Thus the irrelevant costs per unit are $4 – $1 = $3.

The key to make-or-buy decisions is identifying the *additional costs* for making (or the *costs avoided* by buying) a part or subcomponent. Activity analysis helps identify these costs. Production of a product requires a set of activities. A company with accurate measurements of the costs of its various activities can better estimate the additional costs incurred to produce an item. GE's activities for production of part number 900 were measured by two cost drivers, units of production of $8 per unit and supervision at a $20,000 fixed cost. Sometimes identification and measurement of additional cost drivers, especially non-volume-related cost drivers, can improve the predictions of the additional cost to produce a part or subcomponent.

Essence of Make-or-Buy: Use of Facilities

The choice in our example is not only whether to make or buy; it is how best to use available facilities. Although the data indicate that making the part is the better choice, the figures are not conclusive—primarily because we have no idea of what can be done with the manufacturing facilities if the component is bought. Only if the released facilities will otherwise remain idle are the preceding figures valid.

Suppose the released facilities can be used advantageously in some other manufacturing activity (to produce a contribution to profits of, say, $55,000) or can be rented out (say, for $35,000). These alternatives merit consideration. The two courses of action now become four (figures are in thousands):

	Make	Buy and Leave Facilities Idle	Buy and Rent out Facilities	Buy and Use Facilities for Other Products
Rent revenue	$ —	$ —	$ 35	$ —
Contribution from other products	—	—	—	55
Obtaining of parts	(160)	(200)	(200)	(200)
Net relevant costs	$(160)	$(200)	$(165)	$(145)

The final column indicates that buying the parts and using the vacated facilities for the production of other products would yield the lowest net costs in this case.

In sum, the make-or-buy decision should focus on relevant costs in a particular decision situation. In all cases, companies should relate make-or-buy decisions to the long-run policies for the use of capacity:

> One company does subcontract work for *other* manufacturers during periods when sales of its own products do not fully use the plant, but such work could not be carried on regularly without expansion of its plant. The profit margin on subcontracts would not be large enough to cover the additional costs of operating an expanded plant, and, hence, work is accepted only when other business is lacking. The same company sometimes meets a period of high volume by *purchasing* parts or having them made by subcontractors. Although the cost of such parts is usually higher than the cost to make them in the company's own plant, the additional cost is less than it would be if they were made on equipment which could be used only part of the time.[2]

JOINT PRODUCT COSTS

Nature of Joint Products

When two or more manufactured products (1) have relatively significant sales values and (2) are not separately identifiable as individual products until their split-off point, they are called **joint products**. The **split-off point** is that juncture of manufacturing where the joint products become individually identifiable. Any costs beyond that stage are called **separable costs** because they are not part of the joint process and can be exclusively identified with individual products. The costs of manufacturing joint products before the split-off point are called **joint costs**. Examples of joint products include chemicals, lumber, flour, and the products of petroleum refining and meat packing. A meat-packing company cannot kill a sirloin steak; it has to slaughter a steer, which supplies various cuts of dressed meat, hides, and trimmings.

To illustrate joint costs, suppose Dow Chemical Company produces two chemical products, X and Y, as a result of a particular joint process. The joint processing cost is $100,000. This includes raw material costs and the cost of processing to the point where X and Y go their separate ways. Both products are sold to the petroleum industry to be used as ingredients of gasoline. The relationships follow:

---

[2] *The Analysis of Cost-Profit Relationships*, National Association of Accountants, Research Series No. 17, p. 552.

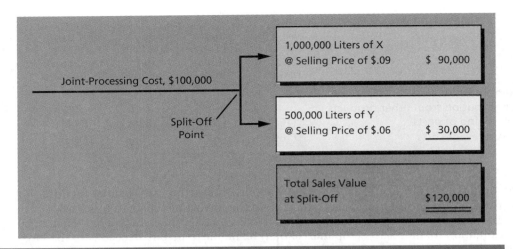

Joint-Processing Cost, $100,000	1,000,000 Liters of X @ Selling Price of $.09 — $ 90,000
Split-Off Point	500,000 Liters of Y @ Selling Price of $.06 — $ 30,000
	Total Sales Value at Split-Off — $120,000

An Example of Make or Buy: Outsourcing

Make-or-buy decisions apply to services as well as to products. One type of make-or-buy decision faced by many companies in the early 1990s was whether to buy data processing and computer network services or to provide them internally. Many companies eliminated their internal departments and "outsourced" (or bought) data processing services and network services from companies such as Electronic Data Systems, a General Motors subsidiary.

One of the first major companies to outsource its data processing was Eastman Kodak. By hiring IBM and Digital Equipment, Kodak was able to eliminate 1,000 jobs and avoid huge capital investments. Another example is J. P. Morgan & Co., which hired BT North America to link 26 Morgan offices in 14 countries. The five-year, $20-million contract is expected to save Morgan $12.5 million. Other outsourcing agreements include Sprint running Unilever's network, MCI handling Sun Microsystem's Pacific Rim network, AT&T working on Chevron's network, and GE Information Services operating the Vatican's global data network. Some companies, such as Sun Microsystems, outsource everything except their core technologies. Sun focuses on hardware and software design and outsources nearly everything else. Its employees do not actually produce any of the products that bear the company's name.

The total value of outsourcing contracts in the United States was about $9 billion in 1995.

The driving forces behind most outsourcing decisions are access to technology and cost savings. As the complexity of data processing and especially networking has grown, companies have found it harder and harder to keep current with the technology.

Instead of investing huge sums in personnel and equipment and diverting attention from the value-added activities of their own businesses, many firms have found outsourcing attractive from a financial standpoint. The big stumbling block has been subjective factors, such as control. To make outsourcing attractive, the services must be reliable, be available when needed, and be flexible enough to adapt to changing conditions. Companies that have successful outsourcing arrangements have been careful to include the subjective factors in their decisions.

Outsourcing has become so profitable that 77% of the Fortune 500 companies outsource some aspect of their business support services. An association, the Outsourcing Institute, was formed to provide "objective, independent information on the strategic use of outside resources." The institute sponsored a 42-page special advertising section in *Fortune* magazine in 1994. ■

Sources: Adapted from "Telecommunications: More Firms 'Outsource' Data Networks," The Wall Street Journal, *March 11, 1992, p. B1; R. Suh, "Guaranteeing that Outsourcing Serves Your Business Strategy,"* Information Strategy: The Executive's Journal, *Spring 1992, pp. 39–42; R. Zahler, "Identifying the Key Issues for Assessing Outsourcing,"* Network World, *March 30, 1992, pp. 21, 23; J. Radigan, "All Wired Up at Morgan,"* Bank Systems & Technology, *March 1992, pp. 25, 27; R.E. Drtina, "The Outsourcing Decision,"* Management Accounting, *March, 1994, pp. 56–62; and M.F. Corbett, "Outsourcing: Redefining the Corporation of the Future,"* Fortune, *December 12, 1994, pp. 51–92.*

Sell or Process Further

Management frequently faces decisions of whether to sell joint products at split-off or to process some or all products further. Suppose the 500,000 liters of Y can be processed further and sold to the plastics industry as product YA, an ingredient for plastic sheeting. The additional processing cost would be $.08 per liter for manufacturing and distribution, a total of $40,000 for 500,000 liters. The net sales price of YA would be $.16 per liter, a total of $80,000.

Product X will be sold at the split-off point, but management is undecided about Product Y. Should Y be sold or should it be processed into YA? The joint costs must be incurred to reach the split-off point: They do not differ between alternatives and are completely irrelevant to the question of whether to sell or process further. The only approach that will yield valid results is to concentrate on the separable costs and revenue *beyond* split-off, as shown in Exhibit 4-1b.

This analysis shows that it would be $10,000 more profitable to process Y beyond split-off than to sell Y at split-off. Briefly, it is profitable to extend processing or to incur additional distribution costs on a joint product *if* the additional revenue exceeds the additional expenses.

Exhibit 4-1b   Illustration of Sell or Process Further

	Sell at Split-Off as Y	Process Further and Sell as YA	Difference
Revenues	$30,000	$80,000	$50,000
Separable costs beyond split-off @ $.08	—	40,000	40,000
Income effects	$30,000	$40,000	$10,000

Exhibit 4-2b illustrates another way to compare the alternatives of (1) selling Y at the split-off point and (2) processing Y beyond split-off. It includes the joint costs, which are the same for each alternative and, therefore, do not affect the difference.

Earlier discussions in this and the preceding chapter have emphasized the desirability of concentrating on totals and being wary of unit costs and allocations of fixed costs. Similarly, the allocation of joint product costs to units of product is fraught with analytical perils.

Exhibit 4-2b   Sell or Process Further Analysis–Firm as Whole

	(1) Alternative One			(2) Alternative Two			(3) Differential Effects
	X	Y	Total	X	YA	Total	
Revenues	$90,000	$30,000	$120,000	$90,000	$ 80,000	$170,000	$50,000
Joint costs			$100,000			$100,000	—
Separable costs			—		40,000	40,000	40,000
Total costs			$100,000			$140,000	$ 40,000
Income effects			$ 20,000			$ 30,000	$ 10,000

The allocation of joint costs would not affect the decision, as Exhibit 4-2b demonstrates. The joint costs are not allocated in the exhibit, but no matter how they might be allocated, the total income effects would be unchanged.

IRRELEVANCE OF PAST COSTS

The ability to recognize and thereby ignore irrelevant costs is sometimes just as important to decision makers as identifying relevant costs. How do we know that past costs, although sometimes predictors, are irrelevant in decision making? Consider such past costs as obsolete inventory and the book value of old equipment to see why they are irrelevant to decisions.

Obsolete Inventory

Suppose General Dynamics has 100 obsolete aircraft parts in its inventory at a manufacturing cost of $100,000. General Dynamics can (1) remachine the parts for $30,000 and then sell them for $50,000 or (2) scrap them for $5,000. Which should it do?

This is an unfortunate situation, yet the $100,000 past cost is irrelevant to the decision to remachine or scrap. The only relevant factors are the expected future revenues and costs:

	Remachine	Scrap	Difference
Expected future revenue	$ 50,000	$ 5,000	$45,000
Expected future costs	30,000	—	30,000
Relevant excess of revenue over costs	$ 20,000	$ 5,000	$15,000
Accumulated historical inventory cost*	100,000	100,000	—
Net overall loss on project	$ (80,000)	$(95,000)	$15,000

* Irrelevant because it is unaffected by the decision.

We can completely ignore the $100,000 historical cost and still arrive at the $15,000 difference, the key figure in the analysis.

Book Value of Old Equipment

Like obsolete parts, the book value of equipment is not a relevant consideration in deciding whether to replace such equipment. When equipment is purchased, its cost is spread over (or charged to) the future periods in which the equipment is expected to be used. This periodic cost is called **depreciation**. The equipment's **book value** (or **net book value**) is the original cost less *accumulated depreciation*, which is the summation of depreciation charged to past periods. For example, suppose a $10,000 machine with a 10-year life has depreciation of $1,000 per year. At the end of 6 years, accumulated depreciation is 6 × $1,000 = $6,000, and the book value is $10,000 − $6,000 = $4,000.

Consider the following data for a decision whether to replace an old machine:

	Old Machine	Replacement Machine
Original cost	$10,000	$8,000
Useful life in years	10	4
Current age in years	6	0
Useful life remaining in years	4	4
Accumulated depreciation	$ 6,000	0
Book value	$ 4,000	Not acquired yet
Disposal value (in cash) now	$ 2,500	Not acquired yet
Disposal value in 4 years	0	0
Annual cash operating costs (maintenance, power, repairs, coolants, etc.)	$ 5,000	$3,000

We have been asked to prepare a comparative analysis of the two alternatives. Before proceeding, consider some important concepts. The most widely misunderstood facet of replacement decision making is the role of the book value of the old equipment in the decision. The book value, in this context, is sometimes called a **sunk cost**, which is really just another term for *historical* or *past cost*, a cost that has already been incurred and, therefore, is irrelevant to the decision-making process. At one time or another, we all try to soothe the wounded pride arising from having made a bad purchase decision by using an item instead of replacing it. It is a serious mistake to think, however, that a current or future action can influence the long-run impact of a past outlay. All past costs are down the drain. Nothing can change what has already happened.

The irrelevance of past costs for decisions does not mean that knowledge of past costs is useless. Often managers use past costs to help predict future costs. In addition, past costs affect future payments for income taxes. However, the past cost *itself* is not relevant. The only relevant cost is the predicted future cost.

In deciding whether to replace or keep existing equipment, four commonly encountered items differ in relevance:

- Book value of old equipment: Irrelevant, because it is a past (historical) cost. Therefore, depreciation on old equipment is irrelevant.
- Disposal value of old equipment: Relevant (ordinarily) because it is an expected future inflow that usually differs among alternatives.
- Gain or loss on disposal: This is the algebraic difference between book value and disposal value. It is, therefore, a meaningless combination of irrelevant and relevant items. The combination form, loss (or gain) on disposal, blurs the distinction between the irrelevant book value and the relevant disposal value. Consequently, it is best to think of each separately.
- Cost of new equipment: Relevant because it is an expected future outflow that will differ among alternatives. Therefore depreciation on new equipment is relevant.

Exhibit 4-3b should clarify the foregoing assertions. It deserves close study. Book value of old equipment is irrelevant regardless of the decision-making technique used. The "difference" column in Exhibit 4-3b shows that the $4,000 book value of the *old* equipment is not an element of difference between alternatives. It should be completely ignored for decision-making purposes. The difference is merely one of timing. The amount written off is still $4,000, regardless of any available alternative. The $4,000 appears on the income statement either as a $4,000 deduction from the $2,500 cash proceeds received to obtain a $1,500 loss on disposal in the first year or as $1,000 of depreciation in each of 4 years. But how it appears is irrelevant to the replacement decision. In contrast, the $2,000 annual depreciation on the new equipment is relevant because the total $8,000 depreciation is a future cost that may be avoided by not replacing. The three relevant items, operating costs, disposal value, and acquisition cost give replacement a net advantage of $2,500.

Examination of Alternatives Over the Long Run

Exhibit 4-3b is the first example that looks beyond one year. Examining the alternatives over the entire lives ensures that peculiar nonrecurring items (such as loss on disposal) will not obstruct the long-run view vital to many managerial decisions.

Exhibit 4-4b concentrates on relevant items only: the cash operating costs, the disposal value of the old equipment, and the depreciation on the new equipment. To demonstrate that the amount of the old equipment's book value will not affect the answer, suppose the book value of the old equipment is $500,000 rather than $4,000. Your final answer will not change. The cumulative advantage of replacement is still $2,500. (If you are in doubt, rework this example, using $500,000 as the book value.)

Sunk Costs and Government Contracts

It is easy to agree that—in theory—sunk costs should be ignored when making decisions. But in practice sunk costs often influence important decisions, especially when a decision maker doesn't want to admit that a previous decision to invest funds was a bad decision.

Consider two examples from the *St. Louis Post Dispatch*: (1) Larry O. Welch, the air force chief of staff, was quoted as saying that "the B-2 already is into production; cancel it and the $17 billion front end investment is lost." (2) Les Aspin, chairman of the House Armed Services Committee, was quoted as stating that "with $17 billion already invested in it, the B-2 is too costly to cancel."

The $17 billion already invested in the B-2 is a sunk cost. It is "lost" regardless of whether production of the B-2 is canceled or not. And whether B-2 production is too costly to continue depends only on the future costs necessary to complete production compared to the value of the completed B-2s. The $17 billion was relevant when the original decision to begin development of the B-2 was made, but now that the money has been spent, it is no longer relevant. No decision can affect it.

Why would intelligent leaders consider the $17 billion relevant to the decision on continuing production of the B-2? Probably because it is difficult to admit that no benefit would be derived from the $17 billion investment. Those who favor canceling production of the B-2 would consider the outcome of the original investment decision to be unfavorable. With perfect hindsight, they believe the investment should not have been made. It is human nature to find unpleasant the task of admitting that $17 billion was wasted. Yet, it is more important to avoid throwing good money after bad—that is, if the value of the B-2 is not at least equal to the *future* investment in it, production should be terminated, regardless of the amount spent to date.

Ignoring sunk costs is not unique to the U.S. government. In reference to Russia's store of bomb-grade plutonium, the country's Minister of Atomic Energy stated, "We have spent too much money making this material to just mix it with radioactive wastes and bury it." Burying the plutonium may or may not be the best decision, but the amount already spent is not relevant to the decision. ∎

Sources: J. Berg, J. Dickhaut, and C. Kanodia, "The Role of Private Information in the Sunk Cost Phenomenon," unpublished paper, November 12, 1991; M. Wald and M. Gordon, "Russia Treasures Plutonium, But U.S. Wants to Destroy It," New York Times, *August 19, 1994, p. A1.*

Exhibit 4-3b Cost Comparison—Replacement of Equipment Including Relevant and Irrelevant Items

	Four Years Together		
	Keep	Replace	Difference
Cash operating costs	$20,000	$12,000	$8,000
Old equipment (book value)			
Periodic write-off as depreciation	4,000	—	
or			—
Lump-sum write-off		4,000*	
Disposal value	—	–2,500*	2,500
New machine			
Acquisition			
Cost	—	8,000†	–8,000
Total costs	$24,000	$21,500	$2,500

The advantage of replacement is $2,500 for the four years together.

* In a formal income statement, these two items would be combined as "loss on disposal" of $4,000 – $2,500 = $1,500.
† In a formal income statement, written off as straight-line depreciation of $8,000 ÷ 4 = $2,000 for each of 4 years.

Exhibit 4-4b Cost Comparison—Replacement of Equipment, Relevant Items Only

	Four Years Together		
	Keep	Replace	Difference
Cash operating costs	$20,000	$12,000	$8,000
Disposal value of old machine	—	–2,500	2,500
New machine, acquisition cost	—	8,000	–8,000
Total relevant costs	$20,000	$17,500	$2,500

IRRELEVANCE OF FUTURE COSTS THAT WILL NOT DIFFER

In addition to past costs, some *future* costs may be irrelevant because they will be the same under all feasible alternatives. These, too, may be safely ignored for a particular decision. The salaries of many members of top management are examples of expected future costs that will be unaffected by the decision at hand.

Other irrelevant future costs include fixed costs that will be unchanged by such considerations as whether machine X or machine Y is selected. However, it is not merely a case of saying that fixed costs are irrelevant and variable costs are relevant. Variable costs can be irrelevant and fixed costs can be relevant. For instance, sales commissions might be paid on an order regardless of whether the order was filled from plant G or plant H. Variable costs are irrelevant whenever they do not differ among the alternatives at hand, and fixed costs are relevant whenever they differ under the alternatives at hand.

BEWARE OF UNIT COSTS

The previous pricing illustration showed that unit costs should be analyzed with care in decision making. There are two major ways to go wrong: (1) the inclusion of irrelevant costs, such as the $3 allocation of unavoidable fixed costs in the make-or-buy example (p. 148) that would result in a unit cost of $11 instead of the relevant unit cost of $8, and (2) comparisons of unit costs not computed on the same volume basis, as the following example demonstrates. Generally, be wary of unit fixed costs. Use total costs rather than unit costs. Then, if desired, the totals may be unitized. Machinery sales personnel, for example, often brag about the low unit costs of using the new machines. Sometimes they neglect to point out that the unit costs are based on outputs far in excess of the volume of activity of their prospective customer.

Assume that a new $100,000 machine with a five-year life can produce 100,000 units a year at a variable cost of $1 per unit, as opposed to a variable cost per unit of $1.50 with an old machine. A sales representative claims that the new machine will reduce cost by $.30 per unit. Is the new machine a worthwhile acquisition?

The new machine is attractive at first glance. If the customer's expected volume is 100,000 units, unit-cost comparisons are valid, provided that new depreciation is also considered. Assume that the disposal value of the old equipment is zero. Because depreciation is an allocation of *historical* cost, the depreciation on the old machine is irrelevant. In contrast, the depreciation on the new machine is relevant because the new machine entails a *future* cost that can be avoided by not acquiring it:

	Old Machine	New Machine
Units	100,000	100,000
Variable costs	$150,000	$100,000
Straight-line depreciation	—	20,000
Total relevant costs	$150,000	$120,000
Unit relevant costs	$ 1.50	$ 1.20

Apparently, the sales representative is correct. However, if the customer's expected volume is only 30,000 units per year, the unit costs change in favor of the old machine:

	Old Machine	New Machine
Units	30,000	30,000
Variable costs	$45,000	$30,000
Straight-line depreciation	—	20,000
Total relevant costs	$45,000	$50,000
Unit relevant costs	$ 1.50	$1.6667

CONFLICTS BETWEEN DECISION MAKING AND PERFORMANCE EVALUATION

We have focused on using relevant information in decision making. To motivate people to make optimal decisions, methods of evaluating the performance of managers should be consistent with the decision analysis.

Consider the replacement decision shown in Exhibit 4-4b, where replacing the machine had a $2,500 advantage over keeping it. To motivate managers to make the right choice, the method used to evaluate performance should be consistent with the decision model—that is, it should show better performance when managers replace the machine than when they keep it. Because performance is often measured by accounting income, consider the accounting income in the first year after replacement compared with that in years 2, 3, and 4.

	Year 1		Years 2, 3, and 4	
	Keep	*Replace*	*Keep*	*Replace*
Cash operating costs	$5,000	$3,000	$5,000	$3,000
Depreciation	1,000	2,000	1,000	2,000
Loss on disposal ($4,000 – $2,500)	—	$1,500	—	—
Total charges against revenue	$6,000	$6,500	$6,000	$5,000

If the machine is kept rather than replaced, first-year costs will be $6,500 – $6,000 = $500 lower, and first-year income will be $500 higher. Because managers naturally want to make decisions that maximize the measure of their performance, they may be inclined to keep the machine. This is an example of a conflict between the analysis for decision making and the method used to evaluate performance.

The conflict is especially severe if managers are transferred often from one position to another. Why? Because the $500 first-year advantage for keeping will be offset by a $1,000 annual advantage of replacing in years 2 to 4. (Note that the net difference of $2,500 in favor of replacement over the 4 years together is the same as in Exhibit 4-4b.) A manager who moves to a new position after the first year, however, bears the entire loss on disposal without reaping the benefits of lower operating costs in years 2 to 4.

The decision to replace a machine earlier than planned also reveals that the original decision to purchase the machine may have been flawed. The old machine was bought 6 years ago for $10,000; its expected life was 10 years. However, if a better machine is now available, then the useful life of the old machine was really 6 years, not 10. This feedback on the actual life of the old machine has two possible effects, the first good and the second bad. First, managers might learn from the earlier mistake. If the useful life of the old machine was overestimated, how believable is the prediction that the new machine will have a 4-year life? Feedback can help avoid repeating past mistakes. Second, another mistake might be made to cover up the earlier one. A "loss on disposal" could alert superiors to the incorrect economic-life prediction used in the earlier decision. By avoiding replacement, the $4,000 remaining book value is spread over the future as "depreciation," a more appealing term than "loss on disposal." The superiors may never find out about the incorrect prediction of economic life. The accounting income approach to performance evaluation mixes the financial effects of various decisions, hiding both the earlier misestimation of useful life and the current failure to replace.

The conflict between decision making and performance evaluation is a widespread problem in practice. Unfortunately, there are no easy solutions. In theory, accountants could evaluate performance in a manner consistent with decision making. In our equipment example, this would mean predicting year-by-year income effects over the planning horizon for 4 years, noting that the first year would be poor, and evaluating actual performance against the predictions.

The trouble is that evaluating performance, decision by decision, is a costly procedure. Therefore, aggregate measures are used. For example, an income statement shows the results of many decisions, not just the single decision of buying a machine. Consequently, in many cases like our equipment example, managers may be most heavily influenced by the first-year effects on the income statement. Thus, managers refrain from taking the longer view that their superiors prefer.

Highlights to Remember

This section has focused on identifying relevant information for a variety of decisions. Relevant costs are future costs that differ among alternatives. Past costs are not relevant, but they might help predict future costs.

Sometimes the notion of an opportunity cost is helpful in cost analysis. An opportunity cost is the maximum sacrifice in rejecting an alternative; it is the maximum earnings that might have been obtained if the productive good, service, or capacity had been applied to some alternative use. The opportunity-cost approach does not affect the important final differences between the courses of action, but the format of the analysis differs. This chapter also introduces differential costs or incremental costs, which are the differences in the total costs under each alternative.

Some generalizations about the decisions in this chapter follow:

- Make-or-buy decisions are, fundamentally, examples of obtaining the most profitable use of given facilities.
- Joint product costs are irrelevant in decisions about whether to sell at split-off or process further.
- The book value of old equipment is always irrelevant in replacement decisions. This cost is often called a sunk cost. Disposal value, however, is generally relevant.

Also, be aware that managers are often motivated to reject desirable economic decisions because of a conflict between the measures used in decision making and those used in performance evaluation.

Summary Problem for Your Review

Problem

Exhibit 4-5b contains data for the Block Company for the year just ended. The company makes industrial power drills. Exhibit 4-5b shows the costs of the plastic housing separately from the costs of the electrical and mechanical components.

Exhibit 4-5b Block Company Cost of Industrial Drills

	A	B	A + B
	Electrical and Mechanical Components*	Plastic Housing	Industrial Drills
Sales: 100,000 units, @ $100			$10,000,000
Variable costs			
Direct material	$4,400,000	$ 500,000	$ 4,900,000
Direct labor	400,000	300,000	700,000
Variable factory overhead	100,000	200,000	300,000
Other variable costs	100,000	—	100,000
Sales commissions, @ 10% of sales	1,000,000	—	1,000,000
Total variable costs	$6,000,000	$1,000,000	$ 7,000,000
Contribution margin			$ 3,000,000
Separable fixed costs	$1,900,000	$ 400,000	$ 2,300,000
Common fixed costs	320,000	80,000	400,000
Total fixed costs	$2,220,000	$ 480,000	$ 2,700,000
Operating income			$ 300,000

* Not including the costs of plastic housing (column B).

1. During the year, a prospective customer in an unrelated market offered $82,000 for 1,000 drills. The latter would be in addition to the 100,000 units sold. The regular sales commission rate would have been paid. The president rejected the order because "it was below our costs of $97 per unit." What would operating income have been if the order had been accepted?
2. A supplier offered to manufacture the year's supply of 100,000 plastic housings for $13.50 each. What would be the effect on operating income if the Block Company purchased rather than made the housings? Assume that $350,000 of the separable fixed costs assigned to housings would have been avoided if the housings were purchased.
3. The company could have purchased the housings for $13.50 each and used the vacated space for the manufacture of a deluxe version of its drill. Assume that 20,000 deluxe units could have been made (and sold in addition to the 100,000 regular units) at a unit variable cost of $90, exclusive of housings and exclusive of the 10% sales commission. The 20,000 extra plastic housings could also be purchased for $13.50 each. The sales price would have been $130. All the fixed costs pertaining to the plastic housings would have continued, because these costs related primarily to the manufacturing facilities used. What would operating income have been if Block had bought the housings and made and sold the deluxe units?

Solution

1. The costs of filling the special order follow:

Direct material	$49,000
Direct labor	7,000
Variable factory overhead	3,000
Other variable costs	1,000
Sales commission @ 10% of $82,000	8,200
Total variable costs	$68,200
Selling price	82,000
Contribution margin	$13,800

Operating income would have been $300,000 + $13,800, or $313,800, if the order had been accepted. In a sense, the decision to reject the offer implies that the Block Company is willing to invest $13,800 in immediate gains forgone (an opportunity cost) in order to preserve the long-run selling-price structure.

2. Assuming that $350,000 of the fixed costs could have been avoided by not making the housings and that the other fixed costs would have been continued, the alternatives can be summarized as follows:

	Make	Buy
Purchase cost		$1,350,000
Variable costs	$1,000,000	
Avoidable fixed costs	350,000	
Total relevant costs	$1,350,000	$1,350,000

If the facilities used for plastic housings became idle, the Block Company would be indifferent as to whether to make or buy. Operating income would be unaffected.

3. The effect of purchasing the plastic housings and using the vacated facilities for the manufacture of a deluxe version of its drill is:

Sales would increase by 20,000 units, @ $130		$2,600,000
Variable costs exclusive of parts would increase by 20,000 units, @ $90	$1,800,000	
Plus: sales commission, 10% of $2,600,000	260,000	2,060,000
Contribution margin on 20,000 units		$ 540,000
Housings: 120,000 rather than 100,000 would be needed		
Buy 120,000 @ $13.50	$1,620,000	
Make 100,000 @ $10 (only the variable costs are relevant)	1,000,000	
Excess cost of outside purchase		620,000
Fixed costs, unchanged		—
Disadvantage of making deluxe units		$ 80,000

Operating income would decline to $220,000 ($300,000 – $80,000). The deluxe units bring in a contribution margin of $540,000, but the additional costs of buying rather than making housings is $620,000, leading to a net disadvantage of $80,000.

Fundamental Assignment Material

4-A1   Replacing Old Equipment

Consider these data regarding Chippewa County's photocopying requirements:

	Old Equipment	Proposed Replacement Equipment
Useful life, in years	5	3
Current age, in years	2	0
Useful life remaining, in years	3	3
Original cost	$25,000	$15,000
Accumulated depreciation	10,000	0
Book value	15,000	Not acquired yet
Disposal value (in cash) now	3,000	Not acquired yet
Disposal value in 2 years	0	0
Annual cash operating costs for power, maintenance, toner, and supplies	14,000	7,500

The county administrator is trying to decide whether to replace the old equipment. Because of rapid changes in technology, she expects the replacement equipment to have only a three-year useful life. Ignore the effects of taxes.

1. Tabulate a cost comparison that includes both relevant and irrelevant items for the next three years together. (*Hint*: See Exhibit 4-3b, page 155)
2. Tabulate a cost comparison of all relevant items for the next three years together. Which tabulation is clearer, this one or the one in requirement 1? (*Hint*: See Exhibit 4-4b, page 155.)
3. Prepare a simple "shortcut" or direct analysis to support your choice of alternatives.

4-A2   Decision and Performance Models

Refer to the preceding problem.

1. Suppose the "decision model" favored by top management consisted of a comparison of a three-year accumulation of cash under each alternative. As the manager of office operations, which alternative would you choose? Why?
2. Suppose the "performance evaluation model" emphasized the minimization of overall costs of photocopying operations for the first year. Which alternative would you choose?

4-A3   Hospital Opportunity Cost

An administrator at University Hospital is considering how to use some space made available when the Family Medical Center moved to a new building. She has narrowed her choices as follows:

a.   Use the space to expand laboratory testing. Expected future annual revenue would be $300,000; future costs, $270,000.

b. Use the space to expand the eye clinic. Expected future annual revenue would be $500,000; future costs, $480,000.

c. The gift shop is rented by an independent retailer who wants to expand into the vacated space. The retailer has offered a $9,000 yearly rental for the space. All operating expenses will be borne by the retailer.

The administrator's planning horizon is unsettled. However, she has decided that the yearly data given will suffice for guiding her decision.

Tabulate the total relevant data regarding the decision alternatives. Omit the concept of opportunity cost in one tabulation, but use the concept in a second tabulation. As the administrator, which tabulation would you prefer to get if you could receive only one?

4-A4 Joint Products: Sell or Process Further

The Visqual Chemical Company produced three joint products at a joint cost of $105,000. These products were processed further and sold as follows:

Chemical Product	Sales	Additional Processing Costs	
A	$260,000	$220,000	
B		330,000	300,000
C	175,000	100,000	

The company has had an opportunity to sell at split-off directly to other processors. If that alternative had been selected, sales would have been: A, $56,000; B, $28,000; and C, $54,000.

The company expects to operate at the same level of production and sales in the forthcoming year.

Consider all the available information, and assume that all costs incurred after split-off are variable.

1. Could the company increase operating income by altering its processing decisions? If so, what would be the expected overall operating income?

2. Which products should be processed further and which should be sold at split-off?

4-B1 Role of Old Equipment Replacement

On January 2, 19X1, the K. Sung Company installed a brand-new $84,000 special molding machine for producing a new product. The product and the machine have an expected life of three years. The machine's expected disposal value at the end of 3 years is zero.

On January 3, 19X1, Jill Swain, a star salesperson for a machine tool manufacturer, tells Mr. Sung: "I wish I had known earlier of your purchase plans. I can supply you with a technically superior machine for $99,000. The machine you just purchased can be sold for $16,000. I guarantee that our machine will save $35,000 per year in cash operating costs, although it too will have no disposal value at the end of three years."

Sung examines some technical data. Although he has confidence in Swain's claims, Sung contends: "I'm locked in now. My alternatives are clear: (a) disposal will result in a loss, (b) keeping and using the 'old' equipment avoids such a loss. I have brains enough to avoid a loss when my other alternative is recognizing a loss. We've got to use that equipment until we get our money out of it."

The annual operating costs of the old machine are expected to be $60,000, exclusive of depreciation. Sales, all in cash, will be $850,000 per year. Other annual cash expenses will be $750,000 regardless of this decision. Assume that the equipment in question is the company's only fixed asset.

Ignore income taxes and the time value of money.

1. Prepare statements of cash receipts and disbursements as they would appear in each of the next 3 years under both alternatives. What is the total cumulative increase or decrease in cash for the 3 years?
2. Prepare income statements as they would appear in each of the next 3 years under both alternatives. Assume straight-line depreciation. What is the cumulative increase or decrease in net income for the 3 years?
3. Assume that the cost of the "old" equipment was $1 million rather than $84,000. Would the net difference computed in requirements 1 and 2 change? Explain.
4. As Jill Swain, reply to Mr. Sung's contentions.
5. What are the irrelevant items in each of your presentations for requirements 1 and 2? Why are they irrelevant?

4-B2 Make or Buy

A Volkswagen executive in Germany is trying to decide whether the company should continue to manufacture an engine component or purchase it from Hanover Corporation for 50 deutsche marks (DM) each. Demand for the coming year is expected to be the same as for the current year, 200,000 units. Data for the current year follow:

Direct material	DM 5,000,000
Direct labor	2,000,000
Factory overhead, variable	1,000,000
Factory overhead, fixed	2,500,000
Total costs	DM10,500,000

If Volkswagen makes the components, the unit costs of direct material will increase 10%.

If Volkswagen buys the components, 40% of the fixed costs will be avoided. The other 60% will continue regardless of whether the components are manufactured or purchased. Assume that variable overhead varies with output volume.

1. Tabulate a comparison of the make-or-buy alternatives. Show totals and amounts per unit. Compute the numerical difference between making and buying. Assume that the capacity now used to make the components will become idle if the components are purchased.
2. Assume also that the Volkswagen capacity in question can be rented to a local electronics firm for DM1,250,000 for the coming year. Tabulate a comparison of the net relevant costs of the three alternatives: make, buy and leave capacity idle, buy and rent. Which is the most favorable alternative? By how much in total?

4-B3 Sell or Process Further

ConAgra, Inc. produces meat products with brand names such as Swift, Armour, and Butterball. Suppose one of the company's plants processes beef cattle into various products. For simplicity, assume that there are only three products: steak, hamburger, and hides, and that the average steer costs $500. The three products emerge from a process that costs $100 per cow to run, and output from one steer can be sold for the following net amounts:

Steak (100 pounds)	$300
Hamburger (500 pounds)	500
Hides (120 pounds)	100
Total	$900

Assume that each of these three products can be sold immediately or processed further in another ConAgra plant. The steak can be the main course in frozen dinners sold under the Healthy Choice label. The vegetables and desserts in the 400 dinners produced from the 100 pounds of steak would cost $120, and production, sales, and other costs for the 400 meals would total $350. Each meal would be sold wholesale for $1.90.

The hamburger could be made into frozen Salisbury Steak patties sold under the Armour label. The only additional cost would be a $200 processing cost for the 500 pounds of hamburger. Frozen Salisbury Steaks sell wholesale for $1.50 per pound.

The hides can be sold before or after tanning. The cost of tanning one hide is $80, and a tanned hide can be sold for $175.

1. Compute the total profit if all three products are sold at the split-off point.
2. Compute the total profit if all three products are processed further before being sold.
3. Which products should be sold at the split-off point? Which should be processed further?
4. Compute the total profit if your plan in requirement 3 is followed.

Additional Assignment Material

Questions

4-1. "Qualitative factors generally favor making over buying a component." Do you agree? Explain.

4-2. "Choices are often mislabeled as *make* or *buy*." Do you agree? Explain.

4-3. Distinguish between an opportunity cost and an outlay cost.

4-4. "I had a chance to rent my summer home for two weeks for $800. But I chose to have it idle. I didn't want strangers living in my summer house." What term in this chapter describes the $800? Why?

4-5. "Accountants do not ordinarily record opportunity costs in the formal accounting records." Why?

4-6. Distinguish between an incremental cost and a differential cost.

4-7. "Incremental cost is the addition to costs from the manufacture of one unit." Do you agree? Explain.

4-8. "The differential costs or incremental costs of increasing production from 1,000 automobiles to 1,200 automobiles per week would be the additional costs of producing the additional 200 automobiles." If production were reduced from 1,200 to 1,000 automobiles per week, what would the decline in costs be called?

4-9. "No technique used to assign the joint cost to individual products should be used for management decisions regarding whether a product should be sold at the split-off point or processed further." Do you agree? Explain.

4-10. "Past costs are indeed relevant in most instances because they provide the point of departure for the entire decision process." Do you agree? Why?

4-11. Which of the following items are relevant to replacement decisions? Explain.
   a. Book value of old equipment
   b. Disposal value of old equipment
   c. Cost of new equipment

4-12. Give an example of a situation in which the performance evaluation model is not consistent with the decision model.

4-13. "Evaluating performance, decision by decision, is costly. Aggregate measures, like the income statement, are frequently used." How might the wide use of income statements affect managers' decisions about buying equipment?

4-14. Explain the one-year-at-a-time approach for acquiring equipment in not-for-profit organizations.

4-15. "The financial consequences of Decision A regarding the acquisition of equipment should be separated from similar Decision B consequences made at a later date." Why?

4-16. "Some expected future costs may be irrelevant." Do you agree? Explain.

4-17. "Variable costs are irrelevant whenever they do not differ among the alternatives at hand." Do you agree? Explain.

4-18. There are two major reasons why unit costs should be analyzed with care in decision making. What are they?

4-19. "Machinery sales personnel sometimes erroneously brag about the low unit costs of using their machines." Identify one source of an error concerning the estimation of unit costs.

Exercises

4-20 Relevant Investment

Rhonda Timm had obtained a new truck with a list price, including options, of $16,000. The dealer had given her a "generous trade-in allowance" of $4,500 on her old truck that had a wholesale price of $3,000. Sales tax was $1,200.

The annual cash operating costs of the old truck were $4,200. The new truck was expected to reduce these costs by one-third.

Compute the amount of the original investment in the new truck. Explain your reasoning.

4-21 Weak Division

Elgin Electronics Company paid $6 million in cash four years ago to acquire a company that manufactures magnetic tape drives. This company has been operated as a division of Elgin and has lost $500,000 each year since its acquisition.

The minimum desired return for this division is that, when a new product is fully developed, it should return a net profit of $500,000 per year for the foreseeable future.

Recently the IBM Corporation offered to purchase the division from Elgin for $4 million. The president of Elgin commented, "I've got an investment of $8 million to recoup ($6 million plus losses of $500,000 for each of four years). I have finally got this situation turned around, so I oppose selling the division now."

Prepare a response to the president's remarks. Indicate how to make this decision. Be as specific as possible.

4-22 Make Or Buy

Assume that a division of Sony makes an electronic component for its speakers. Its manufacturing process for the component is a highly automated part of a just-in-time production system. All labor is considered to be an overhead cost, and all overhead is regarded as fixed with respect to output volume. Production costs for 100,000 units of the component are as follows:

Direct materials		$300,000
Factory overhead		
Indirect labor	$80,000	
Supplies	30,000	
Allocated occupancy cost	40,000	150,000
Total cost		$450,000

A small, local company has offered to supply the components at a price of $3.45 each. If the division discontinued its production of the component, it would save two-thirds of the supplies cost and $30,000 of indirect labor cost. All other overhead costs would continue.

The division manager recently attended a seminar on cost behavior and learned about fixed and variable costs. He wants to continue to make the component because the variable cost of $3.00 is below the $3.45 bid.

1. Compute the relevant cost of (a) making and (b) purchasing the component. Which alternative is less costly and by how much?
2. What qualitative factors might influence the decision about whether to make or buy the component?

4-23 Opportunity Costs

Esther Goldman is an attorney employed by a large law firm at $95,000 per year. She is considering whether to become a sole practitioner, which would probably generate annually $325,000 in operating revenues and $220,000 in operating expenses.

1. Present two tabulations of the annual income effects of these alternatives. The second tabulation should include the opportunity cost of Goldman's compensation as an employee.
2. Suppose Goldman prefers less risk and chooses to stay as an employee. Show a tabulation of the income effects of rejecting the opportunity of independent practice.

4-24 Opportunity Cost of Home Ownership

Jerry Sikma has just made the final payment on his mortgage. He could continue to live in the home; cash expenses for repairs and maintenance (after any tax effects) would be $500 monthly. Alternatively, he could sell the home for $200,000 (net of any income taxes), invest the proceeds in 10% municipal tax-free bonds, and rent an apartment for $18,000 annually. The landlord would then pay for repairs and maintenance.

Prepare two analyses of Sikma's alternatives, one showing no explicit opportunity cost and the second showing the explicit opportunity cost of the decision to hold the present home.

4-25 Opportunity Cost

Jennifer Foucade, M.D., is a psychiatrist who is in heavy demand. Even though she has raised her fees considerably during the past five years, Dr. Foucade still cannot accommodate all the patients who wish to see her.

Foucade has conducted 6 hours of appointments a day, 6 days a week, for 48 weeks a year. Her fee averages $150 per hour.

Her variable costs are negligible and may be ignored for decision purposes. Ignore income taxes.

1. Foucade is weary of working a 6-day week. She is considering taking every other Saturday off. What would be her annual income (a) if she worked every Saturday and (b) if she worked every other Saturday?
2. What would be her opportunity cost for the year of not working every other Saturday?
3. Assume that Dr. Foucade has definitely decided to take every other Saturday off. She loves to repair her sports car by doing the work herself. If she works on her car during half a Saturday when she otherwise would not see patients, what is her opportunity cost?

4-26 Sell or Process Further

A Chevron petrochemical factory produces two products, L and M, as a result of a particular joint process. Both products are sold to manufacturers as ingredients for assorted chemical products.

Product L sells at split-off for $.25 per gallon; M, for $.30 per gallon. Data for April follow:

Joint processing cost	$1,500,000
Gallons produced and sold	
L	4,000,000
M	2,500,000

Suppose that in April the 2,500,000 gallons of M could have been processed further into Super M at an additional cost of $235,000. The Super M output could have been sold for $.38 per gallon. Product L would have been sold at split-off in any event.

Should M have been processed further in April and sold as Super M? Show computations.

4-27 Joint Products, Multiple Choice

(CPA.) From a particular joint process, Watkins Company produces three products, X, Y, and Z. Each product may be sold at the point of split-off or processed further. Additional processing requires no special facilities, and production costs of further processing are entirely variable and traceable to the products involved. In 19X3 all three products were processed beyond split-off. Joint production costs for the year were $60,000. Sales values and costs needed to evaluate Watkins's 19X3 production policy follow:

Product	Units Produced	Net Realizable Values (Sales Values) at Split-Off	Additional Costs and Sales Values if Processed Further	
			Sales Values	*Added Costs*
X	6,000	$25,000	$42,000	$9,000
Y	4,000	41,000	45,000	7,000
Z	2,000	24,000	32,000	8,000

Answer the following multiple-choice questions:

1. For units of Z, the unit production cost most relevant to a sell-or-process-further decision is (a) $5, (b) $12, (c) $4, (d) $9.
2. To maximize profits, Watkins should subject the following products to additional processing (a) X only, (b) X, Y, and Z, (c) Y and Z only, (d) Z only.

4-28 Obsolete Inventory

The local bookstore bought more Sierra Club calendars than it could sell. It was nearly June and 200 calendars remained in stock. The store paid $4.00 each for the calendars and normally sold them for $8.95. Since February, they had been on sale for $6.00, and 2 weeks ago the price was dropped to $5.00. Still, few calendars were being sold. The bookstore manager thought it was no longer worthwhile using shelf space for the calendars.

The proprietor of Mac's Collectibles offered to buy all 200 calendars for $300. He intended to store them a few years and then sell them as novelty items.

The bookstore manager was not sure she wanted to sell for $1.50 calendars that cost $4.00. The only alternative, however, was to scrap them because the publisher would not take them back.

1. Compute the difference in profit between accepting the $300 offer and scrapping the calendars.
2. Describe how the $4.00 × 200 = $800 paid for the calendars affects your decision.

4-29 Replacement of Old Equipment

Three years ago the Broadway Dairy Queen bought a frozen yogurt machine for $8,000. A salesman has just suggested to the Broadway manager that she replace the machine with a new, $10,000 machine. The manager has gathered the following data:

	Old Machine	New Machine
Original cost	$8,000	$10,000
Useful life in years	8	5
Current age in years	3	0
Useful life remaining in years	5	5
Accumulated depreciation	$3,000	Not acquired yet
Book value	$5,000	Not acquired yet
Disposal value (in cash) now	$2,000	0
Disposal value in 5 years	0	0
Annual cash operating cost	$4,500	$2,500

1. Compute the difference in total costs over the next 5 years under both alternatives, that is, keeping the original machine or replacing it with the new machine. Ignore taxes.
2. Suppose the Broadway manager replaces the original machine. Compute the "loss on disposal" of the original machine. How does this amount affect your computation in requirement 1? Explain.

4-30 Hotel Rooms and Opportunity Costs

The Sheraton Corporation operates many hotels throughout the world. Suppose one of its Los Angeles hotels is facing difficult times because of the opening of several new competing hotels.

To accommodate its flight personnel, United Airlines has offered Sheraton a contract for the coming year that provides a rate of $50 per night per room for a minimum of 50 rooms for 365 nights. This contract would assure Sheraton of selling 50 rooms of space nightly, even if some of the rooms are vacant on some nights.

The Sheraton manager has mixed feelings about the contract. On several peak nights during the year, the hotel could sell the same space for $100 per room.

1. Suppose the contract is signed. What is the opportunity cost of the 50 rooms on October 20, the night of a big convention of retailers when every midtown hotel room is occupied? What is the opportunity cost on December 28, when only 10 of these rooms would be expected to be rented at an average rate of $80?
2. If the year-round rate per room averaged $90, what percentage of occupancy of the 50 rooms in question would have to be rented to make Sheraton indifferent about accepting the offer?

4-31 Extension of Preceding Problem

Assume the same facts as in the preceding problem. However, also assume that the variable costs per room per day are $10.

1. Suppose the best estimate is a 53% general occupancy rate for the 50 rooms at an average $90 room rate for the next year. Should Sheraton accept the contract?
2. What percentage of occupancy of the 50 rooms in question would make Sheraton indifferent about accepting the offer?

4-32 Hotel Pricing and Discounts

(A. Wheelock.) A growing corporation in a large city has offered a 200-room Red Lion Motel a 1-year contract to rent 40 rooms at reduced rates of $48 per room instead of the regular rate of $83 per room. The corporation will sign the contract for 365-day occupancy because its visiting manufacturing and marketing personnel are virtually certain to use all the space each night.

Each room occupied has a variable cost of $8 per night (for cleaning, laundry, lost linens, and extra electricity).

The motel manager expects an 85% occupancy rate for the year, so she is reluctant to sign the contract. If the contract is signed, the occupancy rate on the remaining 160 rooms will be 95%.

1. Compute the total contribution margin for the year with and without the contract.
2. Compute the lowest room rate that the motel should accept on the contract so that the total contribution margin would be the same with or without the contract.

4-33 Special Air Fares

The manager of operations of Qantas Airlines is trying to decide whether to adopt a new discount fare. Focus on one 134-seat 737 airplane now operating at a 56% load factor. That is, on the average the airplane has .56 × 134 = 75 passengers. The regular fares produce an average revenue of 12¢ per passenger mile.

Suppose an average 40% fare discount (which is subject to restrictions regarding time of departure and length of stay) will produce three new additional passengers. Also suppose that three of the previously committed passengers accept the restrictions and switch to the discount fare from the regular fare.

1. Compute the total revenue per airplane mile with and without the discount fares.
2. Suppose the maximum allowed allocation to new discount fares is 50 seats. These will be filled. As before, some previously committed passengers will accept the restrictions and switch to the discount fare from the regular fare. How many will have to switch so that the total revenue per mile will be the same either with or without the discount plan?

4-34 Joint Costs and Incremental Analysis

(CMA.) LaFountaine de Paris, a high-fashion women's dress manufacturer, is planning to market a new cocktail dress for the coming season. LaFountaine de Paris supplies retailers in Europe and the United States.

Four yards of material are required to lay out the dress pattern. Some material remains after cutting, which can be sold as remnants. The leftover material could also be used to manufacture a matching cape and handbag. However, if the leftover material is to be used for the cape and handbag, more care will be required in the cutting, which will increase the cutting costs.

The company expects to sell 1,250 dresses if no matching cape or handbag is available. Market research reveals that dress sales will be 20% higher if a matching cape and handbag are available. The market research indicates that the cape and handbag will not be sold individually, but only as accessories with the dress. The various combinations of dresses, capes, and handbags that are expected to be sold by retailers are as follows:

	Percent of Total
Complete sets of dress, cape, and handbag	70%
Dress and cape	6%
Dress and handbag	15%
Dress only	9%
Total	100%

The material used in the dress costs FF62.5 a yard, or FF250 for each dress. The cost of cutting the dress if the cape and handbag are not manufactured is estimated at FF100 a dress, and the resulting remnants can be sold for FF25 for each dress cut out. If the cape and handbag are to be manufactured, the cutting costs will be increased by FF36 per dress. There will be no salable remnants if the capes and handbags are manufactured in the quantities estimated. The selling prices and the costs to complete the three items once they are cut are as follows:

	Selling Price per Unit	Unit Cost to Complete (Excludes Cost of Material and Cutting Operation)
Dress	FF1,000	FF400
Cape	140	100
Handbag	50	30

1. Calculate the incremental profit or loss to LaFountaine de Paris from manufacturing the capes and handbags in conjunction with the dresses.
2. Identify any nonquantitative factors that could influence the company's management in its decision to manufacture the capes and handbags that match the dress.

4-35 Make or Buy

Dana Corporation manufactures automobile parts. It frequently subcontracts work to other manufacturers, depending on whether Dana's facilities are fully occupied. Dana is about to make some final decisions regarding the use of its manufacturing facilities for the coming year.

The following are the costs of making part KZ31, a key component of an emission control system:

	Total Cost for 60,000 Units	Cost per Unit
Direct material	$ 480,000	$ 8
Direct labor	360,000	6
Variable factory overhead	180,000	3
Fixed factory overhead	360,000	6
Total manufacturing costs	$1,380,000	$23

Another manufacturer has offered to sell the same part to Dana for $21 each. The fixed overhead consists of depreciation, property taxes, insurance, and supervisory salaries. All the fixed overhead would continue if Dana bought the component except that the cost of $120,000 pertaining to some supervisory and custodial personnel could be avoided.

1. Assume that the capacity now used to make parts will become idle if the parts are purchased. Should the parts be made or bought? Show computations.
2. Assume that the capacity now used to make parts will either (a) be rented to a nearby manufacturer for $75,000 for the year or (b) be used to make oil filters that will yield a profit contribution of $240,000. Should part KZ31 be made or bought? Show computations.

4-36 New Machine

A new $250,000 machine is expected to have a five-year life and a terminal value of zero. It can produce 40,000 units a year at a variable cost of $4 per unit. The variable cost is $6 per unit with an old machine, which has a book value of $100,000. It is being depreciated on a straight-line basis at $20,000 per year. It too is expected to have a terminal value of zero. Its current disposal value is also zero because it is highly specialized equipment.

The salesman of the new machine prepared the following comparison:

	New Machine	Old Machine
Units	40,000	40,000
Variable costs	$160,000	$240,000
Straight-line depreciation	50,000	20,000
Total cost	$210,000	$260,000
Unit cost	$ 5.25	$ 6.50

He said, "The new machine is obviously a worthwhile acquisition. You will save $1.25 for every unit you produce."

1. Do you agree with the salesman's analysis? If not, how would you change it? Be specific. Ignore taxes.
2. Prepare an analysis of total and unit costs if the annual volume is 20,000 units.
3. At what annual volume would both the old and new machines have the same total relevant costs?

4-37 Conceptual Approach

A large automobile-parts plant was constructed four years ago in an Ohio city served by two railroads. The PC Railroad purchased 40 specialized 60-foot freight cars as a direct result of the additional traffic generated by the new plant. The investment was based on an estimated useful life of 20 years.

Now the competing railroad has offered to service the plant with new 86-foot freight cars, which would enable more efficient shipping operations at the plant. The automobile company has threatened to switch carriers unless PC Railroad buys 10 new 86-foot freight cars.

The PC marketing management wants to buy the new cars, but PC operating management says, "The new investment is undesirable. It really consists of the new outlay plus the loss on the old freight cars. The old cars must be written down to a low salvage value if they cannot be used as originally intended."

Evaluate the comments. What is the correct conceptual approach to the quantitative analysis in this decision?

4-38 Book Value of Old Equipment

Consider the following data:

	Old Equipment	Proposed New Equipment
Original cost	$24,000	$12,000
Useful life in years	8	3
Current age in years	5	0
Useful life remaining in years	3	3
Accumulated depreciation	$15,000	0
Book value	9,000	*
Disposal value (in cash) now	4,000	*
Annual cash operating costs (maintenance, power, repairs, lubricants, etc.)	$ 10,000	$ 6,000

* Not acquired yet.

1. Prepare a cost comparison of all relevant items for the next three years together. Ignore taxes.
2. Prepare a cost comparison that includes both relevant and irrelevant items.
3. Prepare a comparative statement of the total charges against revenue for the first year. Would the manager be inclined to buy the new equipment? Explain.

4-39 Decision and Performance Models
Refer back to problem 4-B1.

1. Suppose the "decision model" favored by top management consisted of a comparison of a three-year accumulation of wealth under each alternative. Which alternative would you choose? Why? (Accumulation of wealth means cumulative increase in cash.)
2. Suppose the "performance evaluation model" emphasized the net income of a subunit (such as a division) each year rather than considering each project, one by one. Which alternative would you expect a manager to choose? Why?
3. Suppose the same quantitative data existed, but the "enterprise" was a city and the "machine" was a computer in the treasurer's department. Would your answers to the first two parts change? Why?

4-40 Relevant Costs
A cable television network is considering canceling the program "San Francisco Attorney" because it is watched by only 2.3% of the audience in its Monday evening time slot. It would be replaced by "Hawaiian Surfers," a new show being created from the same formula as the popular "Baywatch." Market research indicates that "Hawaiian Surfers" would be watched by 4% of the audience in the same time slot. For audiences between 1.5% and 5%, the network believes each 1% of audience in this time slot results in additional advertising revenue of $40,000 per week (including beneficial effects on other programs, both present and future). Replacement would come half-way through the 30-week season.

The network's accounting staff has prepared the following financial information to be used in making the decision:

- Developmental expenses for "San Francisco Attorney" were $600,000, and these are being amortized over the originally projected complete season (30 programs).
- Developmental expenses for "Hawaiian Surfers" were $900,000. If "Hawaiian Surfers" is shown for the second half of this season, the entire development cost must be amortized over those 15 programs. If it is not aired until next season, amortization will take place over 30 programs.
- The cost of a script for one program of "San Francisco Attorney" is $20,000 and for "Hawaiian Surfers" is $24,000. No contract for scripts for "Hawaiian Surfers" has yet been signed, but a contract for 20 programs of "San Francisco Attorney" was signed and the $400,000 was already paid.
- The star of "San Francisco Attorney" is under contract to the network for the entire season at $240,000. If "San Francisco Attorney" is canceled, the star will do one special in the spring; if "San Francisco Attorney" continues, he will not do the special. If the star does not do the special, another person (with completely equivalent audience appeal) will be hired for $40,000 to do the special.
- The star of "Hawaiian Surfers" has been hired for the next season for $180,000. If she does 15 shows this season, she will have to forego a part in a movie. Consequently, she must be paid $120,000 for 15 shows this season.
- Investment in the set for "San Francisco Attorney" was $100,000, which was immediately expensed. Additional expenses for the set average $10,000 per show. If "San Francisco Attorney" is canceled, the set can be sold for $20,000. Another alternative use of the set is for a TV movie the network is planning. Additional set expenses for the movie would be $50,000, but building a completely new set would cost $80,000.

- "Hawaiian Surfers" is filmed on location; thus, there is no investment required for a set. However, $20,000 per show is required to make the location suitable for filming.
- The production crew for "San Francisco Attorney" (including actors other than the star) receive $50,000 per show. Most of these people could be used profitably in other operations at the network. However, two actors must be fired if the show is canceled, and the actors' union requires severance pay of $4,000 each.
- There will be a large start-up cost of production for "Hawaiian Surfers" because it will be needed suddenly, six months ahead of schedule. This will amount to $150,000, only $60,000 of which would be necessary if it were not aired until next season. The production crew is very important for "Hawaiian Surfers," and they receive $80,000 per show.
- The network allocates corporate overhead to each show by a complex formula. Each program of "San Francisco Attorney" was allocated $20,000 of overhead; each program of "Hawaiian Surfers" will be allocated $30,000 of overhead. The only corporate overhead expense that would change if "Hawaiian Surfers" replaced "San Francisco Attorney" is the consultation time that corporate management spends with the production staff. This averages 10% of the total production crew expense.
- This decision is to be made by top management, who will invest about $20,000 of their time and effort in it. In addition, a consultant will be paid $4,000 to review the decision.

Should the network cancel "San Francisco Attorney" and replace it with "Hawaiian Surfers" immediately? Explain. Be sure to describe the information that was relevant to this decision and compute the monetary advantage or disadvantage to switching from "San Francisco Attorney" to "Hawaiian Surfers."

4-41 Relevant Cost and Special Order

Estrada Company's *unit* costs of manufacturing and selling a given item at an activity level of 10,000 units per *month* are:

Manufacturing costs	
Direct materials	$3.90
Direct labor	.60
Variable overhead	.80
Fixed overhead	.90
Selling expenses	
Variable	3.00
Fixed	1.10

Ignore income taxes in all requirements. These four parts have no connection with each other.

1. Compute the *annual* operating income at a selling price of $12 per unit.
2. Compute the expected *annual* operating income if the volume can be increased by 20% when the selling price is reduced to $11. Assume the implied cost behavior patterns are correct.
3. The company desires to seek an order for 5,000 units from a foreign customer. The variable selling expenses will be reduced by 40%, but the fixed costs for obtaining the order will be $6,000. Domestic sales will not be affected. Compute the minimum break-even price per unit to be considered.
4. The company has an inventory of 2,000 units of this item left over from last year's model. These must be sold through *regular channels* at reduced prices. The inventory will be valueless unless sold this way. What unit cost is relevant for establishing the minimum selling price of these 2,000 units?

4-42 Relevant-Cost Analysis

Following are the unit costs of making and selling a single product at a normal level of 5,000 units per month and a current unit selling price of $80:

Manufacturing costs	
Direct material	$25
Direct labor	12
Variable overhead	8
Fixed overhead (total for the year, $300,000)	5
Selling and administrative expenses	
Variable	15
Fixed (total for the year, $480,000)	8

Consider each requirement separately. Label all computations, and present your solutions in a form that will be comprehensible to the company president.

1. This product is usually sold at a rate of 60,000 units per year. It is predicted that a rise in price to $88 will decrease volume by 10%. How much may advertising be increased under this plan without having annual operating income fall below the current level?
2. The company has received a proposal from an outside supplier to make and ship this item directly to the company's customers as sales orders are forwarded. Variable selling and administrative costs would fall 40%. If the supplier's proposal is accepted, the company will use its own plant to produce a new product. The new product would be sold through manufacturer's agents at a 10% commission based on a selling price of $20 each. The cost characteristics of this product, based on predicted yearly normal volume, are as follows:

	Per Unit
Direct material	$ 3
Direct labor	6
Variable overhead	4
Fixed overhead	3
Manufacturing costs	$16
Selling and administrative expenses	
Variable (commission)	10% of selling price
Fixed	$ 1

What is the maximum price per unit that the company can afford to pay to the supplier for subcontracting production of the entire old product? This is not easy. Assume the following:

- Total fixed factory overhead and total fixed selling expenses will not change if the new product line is added.
- The supplier's proposal will not be considered unless the present annual net income can be maintained.
- Selling price of the old product will remain unchanged.
- All $300,000 of fixed manufacturing overhead will be assigned to the new product.

4-43 Relevant Costs on Broadway

The *New York Times* reported that Neil Simon plans to open his latest play, *London Suite*, off Broadway. Why? For financial reasons. Producer Emanuel Azenberg predicted the following costs before the play even opens:

	On Broadway	Off Broadway
Sets, costumes, lights	$ 357,000	$ 87,000
Loading in (building set, etc.)	175,000	8,000
Rehearsal salaries	102,000	63,000
Director and designer fees	126,000	61,000
Advertising	300,000	121,000
Administration	235,000	100,000
Total	$1,295,000	$440,000

Broadway ticket prices average $55, and theaters can seat about 1,000 persons per show. Off-Broadway prices average only $40, and the theaters seat only 500. Normally plays run eight times a week, both on and off Broadway. Weekly operating expenses off Broadway average $82,000; they average an extra $124,000 on Broadway for a weekly total of $206,000.

1. Suppose 400 persons attended each show, whether on or off Broadway. Compare the weekly financial results from a Broadway production to one produced off Broadway.
2. Suppose attendance averaged 75% of capacity, whether on or off Broadway. Compare the weekly financial results from a Broadway production to one produced off Broadway.
3. Compute the attendance per show required just to cover weekly expenses (a) on Broadway and (b) off Broadway.
4. Suppose average attendance on Broadway was 600 per show and off Broadway was 400. Compute the total net profit for a 26-week run (a) on Broadway and (b) off Broadway. Be sure to include the pre-opening costs.
5. Repeat requirement 4 for a 100-week run.
6. Using attendance figures from requirements 4 and 5, compute (a) the number of weeks a Broadway production must run before it breaks even, and (b) the number of weeks an off-Broadway production must run before it breaks even.
7. Using attendance figures from requirements 4 and 5, determine how long a play must run before the profit from a Broadway production exceeds that from an off-Broadway production.
8. If you were Neil Simon, would you prefer *London Suite* to play on Broadway or off Broadway? Explain.

Cases

4-44 Make or Buy

(CMA, adapted.) The Weisbrod Corporation, which produces and sells to wholesalers a highly successful line of summer lotions and insect repellents, has decided to diversify to stabilize sales throughout the year. The company is considering the production of winter lotions and creams to prevent dry and chapped skin.

After considerable research, a winter products line has been developed. Because of the conservative nature of the company management, however, Weisbrod's president has decided to introduce only one of the new products for this coming winter. If the product is a success, further expansion in future years will be initiated.

The product selected (called Chap-Off) is a lip balm that will be sold in a lipstick-type tube. The product will be sold to wholesalers in boxes of 24 tubes for $8 per box. Because of available capacity, no additional fixed charges will be incurred to produce the product. A $100,000 fixed charge will be absorbed by the product, however, to allocate a fair share of the company's present fixed costs to the new product.

Using the estimated sales and production of 100,000 boxes of Chap-Off as the expected volume, the accounting department has developed the following costs per box:

Direct labor	$3.50
Direct material	3.00
Total overhead	1.50
Total	$8.00

Weisbrod has approached a cosmetics manufacturer to discuss the possibility of purchasing the tubes for Chap-Off. The purchase price of the empty tubes from the cosmetics manufacturer would be $1.05 per 24 tubes. If the Weisbrod Corporation accepts the purchase proposal, it is predicted that direct-labor and variable-overhead costs would be reduced by 10% and direct-material costs would be reduced by 20%.

1. Should the Weisbrod Corporation make or buy the tubes? Show calculations to support your answer.
2. What would be the maximum purchase price acceptable to the Weisbrod Corporation for the tubes? Support your answer with an appropriate explanation.
3. Instead of sales of 100,000 boxes, revised estimates show sales volume at 125,000 boxes. At this new volume, additional equipment, at an annual rental of $10,000, must be acquired to manufacture the tubes. This incremental cost would be the only additional fixed cost required even if sales increased to 300,000 boxes. (The 300,000 level is the goal for the third year of production.) Under these circumstances, should the Weisbrod Corporation make or buy the tubes? Show calculations to support your answer.
4. The company has the option of making and buying at the same time. What would be your answer to requirement 3 if this alternative were considered? Show calculations to support your answer.
5. What nonquantifiable factors should the Weisbrod Corporation consider in determining whether they should make or buy the lipstick-type tubes?

4-45   Make or Buy
The Rohr Company's old equipment for making subassemblies is worn out. The company is considering two courses of action: (a) completely replacing the old equipment with new equipment or (b) buying subassemblies from a reliable outside supplier, who has quoted a unit price of $1 on a seven-year contract for a minimum of 50,000 units per year.

Production was 60,000 units in each of the past two years. Future needs for the next seven years are not expected to fluctuate beyond 50,000 to 70,000 units per year. Cost records for the past two years reveal the following unit costs of manufacturing the subassembly:

Direct material	$ .30
Direct labor	.35
Variable overhead	.10
Fixed overhead (including $.10 depreciation and $.10 for direct departmental fixed overhead)	.25
	$1.00

The new equipment will cost $188,000 cash, will last seven years, and will have a disposal value of $20,000. The current disposal value of the old equipment is $10,000.

The sales representative for the new equipment has summarized her position as follows: The increase in machine speeds will reduce direct labor and variable overhead by 35¢ per unit. Consider last year's experience of one of your major competitors with identical equipment. They produced 100,000 units under operating conditions very comparable to yours and showed the following unit costs:

Direct material	$.30
Direct labor	.05
Variable overhead	.05
Fixed overhead, including depreciation of $.24	.40
	$.80

For purposes of this case, assume that any idle facilities cannot be put to alternative use. Also assume that 5¢ of the old Rohr unit cost is allocated fixed overhead that will be unaffected by the decision.

1. The president asks you to compare the alternatives on a total-annual-cost basis and on a per-unit basis for annual needs of 60,000 units. Which alternative seems more attractive?
2. Would your answer to requirement 1 change if the needs were 50,000 units? 70,000 units? At what volume level would Rohr be indifferent between making and buying subassemblies? Show your computations.
3. What factors, other than the preceding ones, should the accountant bring to the attention of management to assist them in making their decision? Include the considerations that might be applied to the outside supplier.

CHAPTER 5

EVALUATING AND RANKING PROJECTS

5.1 PROJECT RANKING CRITERIA

The project selection process generally involves the evaluation of three sets of criteria.

Financial Return

People tend to intuitively rank all investment opportunities by how much money the project will earn. Financial return analysis involves calculating how much money the project will generate compared to its cost. Techniques used commonly involve the calculation of net present values (NPV), internal rates of return (IRR), and payback periods. From these calculations, the projects can be ranked according to those generating the most revenue down to those generating the least.

Risk

It could be tempting to simply select the projects with the highest return. Unfortunately, high financial return projects are often saddled with corresponding high rates of risk. Consequently, the project manager evaluates the risk elements associated with each project. These are then compared with the expected financial returns. Risk analysis is more difficult than the process of financially ranking projects because there are few well-accepted, simple, and easy to understand project risk ranking tools.

Subjective Factors

Even after financial return and risk have been evaluated, the highest ranked project could easily be rejected due to any number of subjective factors (e.g., it might not fit the strategy of the company or there might not be a champion to assure success).

The following readings from Keown deal with the subject of capital budgeting. The subject is particularly appropriate to the project management of large projects. Capital budgeting involves (a) large amounts of money, (b) direct and indirect impacts affecting the organization for years, and (c) poor capital budgeting decisions can be career busters because of the high visibility of the results.

The decisions inherent in capital budgeting will sound very familiar to experienced project management executives. Common capital and project budgeting concerns are (a) whether to purchase labor saving equipment or to perform operations manually, (b) how projects are to be evaluated that have cash flows varying in duration and amount, and (c) how a cutoff can be implemented to eliminate marginal projects.

5.2 CAPITAL BUDGETING TECHNIQUES

FINDING PROFITABLE PROJECTS

Without question, it is easier to *evaluate* profitable projects than it is to *find* them. In competitive markets, generating ideas for profitable projects is extremely difficult. The competition is brisk for new profitable projects, and once they have been uncovered, competitors generally rush in, pushing down prices and profits. For this reason, a firm must have a systematic strategy for generating **capital-budgeting** projects. Without this flow of new projects and ideas, the firm cannot grow or even survive for long, being forced to live off the profits from existing projects with limited lives. So where do these ideas come from for new products, for ways to improve existing products, or for ways to make existing products more profitable? The answer is from inside the firm—from everywhere inside the firm.

Typically, a firm has a research and development department that searches for ways of improving on existing products or finding new products. These ideas may come from within the R&D department or be based on referral ideas from executives, sales personnel, or anyone in the firm. For example, at Ford Motor Company prior to the 1980s, ideas for product improvement had typically been generated in Ford's research and development department. Unfortunately, this strategy was not enough to keep Ford from losing much of its market share to the Japanese. In an attempt to cut costs and improve product quality, Ford moved from strict reliance on an R&D department to seeking the input of employees at all levels for new ideas. Bonuses are now provided to workers for their cost-cutting suggestions, and assembly line personnel who can see the production process from a hands-on point of view are now brought into the hunt for new projects. The effect on Ford has been positive and significant. Although not all suggested projects prove to be profitable, many new ideas generated from within the firm turn out to be good ones. The best way to evaluate new investment proposals is the topic of the remainder of this chapter.

CAPITAL-BUDGETING DECISION CRITERIA

In deciding whether to accept a new project, we will focus on cash flows. Cash flows represent the benefits generated from accepting a capital-budgeting proposal. In this chapter, we will assume a given cash flow is generated by a project and work on determining whether that project should be accepted.

We will consider four commonly used criteria for determining acceptability of investment proposals. The first is the payback period and it is the least sophisticated, in that it does not incorporate the time value of money into its calculations; the remaining three do take it into account. For the time being, the problem of

WALL STREET JOURNAL FEBRUARY 8, 1994

As Capital Spending Grows, Firms Take a Hard Look at Returns From the Effort

NEW YORK—As corporate America ratchets up its capital spending, it's doing so with a much keener eye to profiting from the effort.

"Chief executives are becoming much more disciplined about saying OK" to spending requests, says Ennius Bergsma of McKinsey & Co., the management consulting firm.(A) "They want to know what will happen in year one, two and three, rather than plow money in and realize nothing materialized."

Notably, the sharper scrutiny isn't scaring spending projects away. Economists say that, for the second year in a row, companies this year are expected to boost spending on equipment by more than 12%.(B)

DRI/McGraw Hill, which forecasts economic trends, sees capital spending on equipment in the U.S. reaching a record $457 billion this year. It expects capital spending in total, which includes the construction of new plants, to reach $610 billion, up 11% from 1993.

"We keep seeing new opportunities" for saving money through capital investments," says Reuben Mark, chief executive of Colgate-Palmolive Co., the big maker of household and personal-care products. One recent opportunity involved the company's Italian unit, where Colgate installed $1 million worth of new automated equipment for packaging the company's stand-up toothpaste tubes. The machines replaced some workers. Estimated savings to Colgate in the first year: $250,000.

The company is demanding more of this sort of cost-saving investment from its managers: In 1994, it wants total capital expenditures to equal 6% of sales, up from 5.2% of sales last year.(C)

When Mr. Mark became chief executive in 1984, roughly 13% of Colgate's total capital spending was going towards cost-saving ventures; the rest went into building new plants, among other things. Now the company is demanding that fully 60% of its capital spending be for cost-saving projects. Colgate even has assigned a force of spending police to track the rate of return on capital expenditures.

"This is not misty, Ingmar Bergman stuff," says Mr. Mark. In fact, part of a manager's compensation is determined by how well he or she meets the capital spending guidelines.

SOURCE: Fred R. Bleakley, "As Capital Spending Grows, Firms Take a Hard Look at Returns From the Effort," *The Wall Street Journal* (February 8, 1994): A2. Reprinted by permission of *The Wall Street Journal* © 1994 Dow Jones & Co., Inc. All Rights Reserved.

ANALYSIS AND IMPLICATIONS...

A. Once a project is accepted, its progress is monitored throughout its life. The project's actual results are compared with the forecasted results. If there is a significant deviation between what was expected and what actually occurred, the forecasting process may be reexamined. Moreover, the project's cash flows will be reestimated, and the project may be reworked with cost cuts, modifications, and possibly early termination. The point here is that projects are always being reexamined and reevaluated, and the option to terminate them is always a possibility.

B. Much of the importance of capital-budgeting decisions comes from the amount of money spent on capital projects. The spending on equipment has been growing at an extremely rapid pace, from a level of just over $200 billion per year in 1980 to the expected level of $457 billion in 1994. Given the size of these investments and the difficulty in reversing them once they are made, capital budgeting decisions take on even more importance.

C. In recent years, more and more capital expenditures have been directed at cost-saving and productivity-improving projects, rather than being aimed at introducing new products. For example, in 1994, RJR Nabisco issued a directive to its managers that new capital expenditures were to be made that would result in costs being cut by an amount equivalent of 20 percent of the dollar value of investment.

incorporating risk into the capital-budgeting decision is ignored. In addition, we will assume that the appropriate discount rate, required rate of return, or cost of capital is given.

Payback Period

The **payback period** is the number of years needed to recover the initial cash outlay. As this criterion measures how quickly the project will return its original investment, it deals with cash flows rather than accounting profits. It also ignores the time value of money and does not discount these cash flows back to the present. The accept-reject criterion involves whether the project's payback period is less than or equal to the firm's maximum desired payback period. For example, if a firm's maximum desired payback period is three years and an investment proposal requires an initial cash outlay of $10,000 and yields the following set of annual cash flows, what is its payback period? Should the project be accepted?

	After-Tax Cash Flow
Year 1	$2,000
Year 2	4,000
Year 3	3,000
Year 4	3,000
Year 5	1,000

In this case, after three years the firm will have recaptured $9,000 on an initial investment of $10,000, leaving $1,000 of the initial investment still to be recouped. During the fourth year, a total of $3,000 will be returned from this investment. Assuming cash will flow into the firm at a constant rate over the year, it will take one third of the year ($1,000/$3,000) to recapture the remaining $1,000. Thus the payback period on this project is three and one third years, which is more than the desired payback period. Using the payback period criterion, the firm would reject this project.

Although the payback period is used frequently, it does have some rather obvious drawbacks, which can best be demonstrated through the use of an example. Consider two investment projects, A and B, which involve an initial cash outlay of $10,000 each and produce the annual cash flows shown in Table 5-1. Both projects have a payback period of two years; therefore, in terms of the payback period criterion, both are equally acceptable. However, if we had our choice, it is clear we would select A over B, for at least two reasons. First, regardless of what happens after the payback period, project A returns our initial investment to us earlier within the payback period. Thus, if there is a time value of money, the cash flows occurring within the payback period should not be weighted equally, as they are. In addition, all cash flows that occur after the payback period are ignored. This violates the principle that investors desire more in the way of benefits rather than less—a principle that is difficult to deny, especially when we are talking about money.

To deal with the criticism that the payback period ignores the time value of money, some firms use the **discounted payback period** approach. The discounted payback period method is similar to the traditional payback period except that it uses discounted net cash flows rather than actual undiscounted net cash flows in calculating the payback period. The discounted payback period is defined as the number of years needed to recover the initial cash outlay from the *discounted net cash flows*. The accept-reject criterion then becomes whether the project's discounted payback period is less than or equal to the firm's maximum desired discounted payback period. Using the assumption that the required rate of return on projects A and B illustrated in Table 5-1 is 17 percent, the discounted cash flows from these projects are given in Table 5-2. The discounted payback period for

Table 5-1 Payback Period Example

Projects	A	B
Initial cash outlay	−$10,000	−$10,000
Annual net cash inflows:		
Year 1	$ 6,000	$ 5,000
2	4,000	5,000
3	3,000	0
4	2,000	0
5	1,000	0

Project A is 3.07 years, calculated as follows:

Discounted Payback Period$_A$ = 3.0 + $74 / $1,068 = 3.07 years.

If Project A's discounted payback period was less than the firm's maximum desired discounted payback period, then Project A would be accepted. Project B, on the other hand, does not have a discounted payback period because it never fully recovers the project's initial cash outlay and, thus, should be rejected. The major problem with the discounted payback period comes in setting the firm's maximum desired discounted payback period. This is an arbitrary decision that affects which projects are accepted and which ones are rejected. Thus, while the discounted payback period is superior to the traditional payback period, in that it accounts for the time value of money in its calculations, its use is limited by the arbitrariness of the process used to select the maximum desired payback period. Moreover, as we will soon see, the net present value criterion is theoretically superior and no more difficult to calculate.

Although these deficiencies limit the value of the payback period and discounted payback period as tools for investment evaluation, these methods do have several positive features. First, they deal with cash flows, as opposed to accounting profits, and, therefore, focus on the true timing of the project's benefits and costs, even though the traditional payback period does not adjust the cash flows for the time value of money. Second, they are easy to visualize, quickly understood, and easy to calculate. Finally, although the payback period and discounted payback period methods have serious deficiencies, they are often used as rough screening devices to eliminate projects whose returns do not materialize until later years. These methods emphasize the earliest returns, which in all likelihood are less uncertain, and provide for the liquidity needs of the firm. Although their advantages are certainly significant, their disadvantages severely limit their value as discriminating capital-budgeting criteria.

Net Present Value

The **net present value (NPV)** of an investment proposal is equal to the present value of its annual after tax net cash flows less the investment's initial outlay. The net present value can be expressed as follows:

$$NPV = \sum_{t=1}^{n} \frac{ACF_t}{(1+k)^t} - IO \tag{5-1}$$

where ACF_t = the annual after-tax cash flow in time period t
(this can take on either positive or negative values)
 k = the appropriate discount rate; that is, the required rate of return or cost of capital

$$IO = \text{the initial cash outlay}$$
$$n = \text{the project's expected life}$$

The project's net present value gives a measurement of the *net value* of an investment proposal in terms of today's dollars. Because all cash flows are discounted back to the present, comparing the difference between the present value of the annual cash flows and the investment outlay is appropriate. The difference between the present value of the annual cash flows and the initial outlay determines the net value of accepting the investment proposal in terms of today's dollars. Whenever the project's NPV is greater than or equal to zero, we will accept the project; whenever there is a negative value associated with the acceptance of a project, we will reject the project. If the project's net present value is zero, then it returns the required rate of return and should be accepted. This accept-reject criterion is restated below:

NPV ≥ 0.0: Accept
NPV < 0.0: Reject

The following example illustrates the use of the net present value capital-budgeting criterion.

EXAMPLE

A firm is considering new machinery, for which the after-tax cash flows are shown in Table 5-3. If the firm has a 12 percent required rate of return, the present value of the after-tax cash flows is $47,678, as calculated in Table 5-4. Furthermore, the net present value of the new machinery is $7,678. Because this value is greater than zero, the net present value criterion indicates that the project should be accepted.

Table 5-2 Discounted Payback Period Example Using a 17 Percent Required Rate of Return

Project A

Year	Undiscounted Cash Flows	$PVIF_{17\%,n}$	Discounted Cash Flows	Cumulative Discounted Cash Flows
0	−$10,000	1.0	−$10,000	−$10,000
1	6,000	.855	5,130	− 4,870
2	4,000	.731	2,924	− 1,946
3	3,000	.624	1,872	− 74
4	2,000	.534	1,068	994
5	1,000	.456	456	1,450

Project B

Year	Undiscounted Cash Flows	$PVIF_{17\%,n}$	Discounted Cash Flows	Cumulative Discounted Cash Flows
0	−$10,000	1.0	−$10,000	−$10,000
1	5,000	.855	4,275	− 5,725
2	5,000	.731	3,655	− 2,070
3	0	.624	0	− 2,070
4	0	.534	0	− 2,070
5	0	.456	0	− 2,070

Table 5-3 NPV Illustration of Investment in New Machinery

	After-Tax Cash Flow		After-Tax Cash Flow
Initial outlay	−$40,000	Inflow year 3	13,000
Inflow year 1	15,000	Inflow year 4	12,000
Inflow year 2	14,000	Inflow year 5	11,000

Table 5-4 Calculation for NPV Illustration of Investment in New Machinery

	After-Tax Cash Flow	Present Value Factor at 12 Percent	Present Value
Inflow year 1	$15,000	.893	$13,395
Inflow year 2	14,000	.797	11,158
Inflow year 3	13,000	.712	9,256
Inflow year 4	12,000	.636	7,632
Inflow year 5	11,000	.567	6,237
Present value of cash flows			$47,678
Initial outlay			− 40,000
Net present value			$ 7,678

Note that the worth of the net present value calculation is a function of the accuracy of cash flow predictions. Before the NPV criterion can reasonably be applied, incremental costs and benefits must first be estimated, including the initial outlay, the differential flows over the project's life, and the terminal cash flow.

The NPV criterion is the capital-budgeting decision tool we will find most favorable. First of all, it deals with cash flows rather than accounting profits. Also, it is sensitive to the true timing of the benefits resulting from the project. Moreover, it recognizes that the time value of money allows comparison of the benefits and costs in a logical manner. Finally, because projects are accepted only if a positive net present value is associated with them, the acceptance of a project using this criterion will increase the value of the firm, which is consistent with the goal of maximizing the shareholders' wealth.

The disadvantage of the NPV method stems from the need for detailed, long-term forecasts of the incremental cash flows accruing from the project's acceptance. Despite this drawback, the net present value is the theoretically correct criterion in that it measures the impact of a project's acceptance on the value of the firm's equity. The following example provides an additional illustration of its application.

EXAMPLE

A firm is considering the purchase of a new computer system, which will cost $30,000 initially, to aid in credit billing and inventory management. The incremental after-tax cash flows resulting from this project are provided in Table 5-5. The required rate of return demanded by the firm is 10 percent. To determine the system's net present value, the three-year $15,000 cash flow annuity is first discounted back to the present at 10 percent. From Appendix E in the back of this book, we find that $PVIFA_{10\%,3yr}$ is 2.487. Thus, the present value of this $15,000 annuity is $37,305 ($15,000 × 2.487).

Because the cash inflows have been discounted back to the present, they can now be compared with the initial outlay. This is because both of the flows are now stated in terms of today's dollars. Subtracting the initial outlay ($30,000) from the present value of the cash inflows ($37,305) we find that the system's net present value is $7,305. Because the NPV on this project is positive, the project should be accepted.

Table 5-5 NPV Example Problem of Computer System

	After-Tax Cash Flow		After-Tax Cash Flow
Initial outlay	−$30,000	Inflow year 2	15,000
Inflow year 1	15,000	Inflow year 3	15,000

Profitability Index (Benefit/Cost Ratio)

The **profitability index (PI)**, or **benefit/cost ratio**, is the ratio of the present value of the future net cash flows to the initial outlay. Although the net present value investment criterion gives a measure of the absolute dollar desirability of a project, the profitability index provides a relative measure of an investment proposal's desirability—that is, the ratio of the present value of its future net benefits to its initial cost. The profitability index can be expressed as follows:

$$PI = \frac{\sum_{t=1}^{n} \frac{ACF_t}{(1+k)^t}}{IO}$$

(5-2)

where ACF_t = the annual after-tax cash flow in time period t (this can take on either positive or negative values)

k = the appropriate discount rate; that is, the required rate of return or cost of capital

IO = the initial cash outlay

n = the project's expected life

The decision criterion with respect to the profitability index is to accept the project if the PI is greater than or equal to 1.00, and to reject the project if the PI is less than 1.00.

PI ≥ 1.0: Accept
PI < 1.0: Reject

Looking closely at this criterion, we see that it yields the same accept-reject decision as does the net present value criterion. Whenever the present value of the project's net cash flows is greater than its initial cash outlay, the project's net present value will be positive, signaling a decision to accept. When this is true, the project's profitability index will also be greater than 1, as the present value of the net cash flows (the PI's numerator) is greater than its initial outlay (the PI's denominator). Although these two decision criteria will always yield the same accept/reject decision, they will not necessarily rank acceptable projects in the same order. This problem of conflicting ranking will be dealt with at a later point.

Because the net present value and profitability index criteria are essentially the same, they have the same advantages over the other criteria examined. Both employ cash flows, recognize the timing of the cash flows, and are consistent with the goal of maximization of shareholders' wealth. The major disadvantage of this criterion, similar to the net present value criterion, is that it requires detailed cash flow forecasts over the entire life of the project.

A firm with a 10 percent required rate of return is considering investing in a new machine with an expected life of six years. The after-tax cash flows resulting from this investment are given in Table 5-6. Discounting the project's future net cash flows back to the present yields a present value of $53,667; dividing this value by the initial outlay of $50,000 gives a profitability index of 1.0733, as shown in Table 5-7. This tells us that the present value of the future benefits accruing from this project is 1.0733 times the level of the initial outlay. Because the profitability index is greater than 1.0, the project should be accepted.

Internal Rate of Return

The **internal rate of return (IRR)** attempts to answer this question: What rate of return does this project earn? For computational purposes, the internal rate of return is defined as the discount rate that equates the present value of the project's future net cash flows with the project's initial cash outlay. Mathematically, the internal rate of return is defined as the value of *IRR* in the following equation:

$$IO = \sum_{t=1}^{n} \frac{ACF_t}{(1 + IRR)^t} \tag{5-3}$$

where ACF_t = the annual after-tax cash flow in time period t
  (this can take on either positive or negative values)
  IO = the initial cash outlay
  n = the project's expected life
  IRR = the project's internal rate of return

In effect, the IRR is analogous to the concept of the yield to maturity for bonds. In other words, a project's internal rate of return is simply the rate of return that the project earns.

The decision criterion associated with the internal rate of return is to accept the project if the internal rate of return is greater than or equal to the required rate of return. We reject the project if its internal rate of return is less than this required rate of return. This accept-reject criterion is restated below:

IRR ≥ required rate of return: Accept
IRR < required rate of return: Reject

If the internal rate of return on a project is equal to the shareholders' required rate of return, then the project should be accepted. This is because the firm is earning the rate that its shareholders require. However, the acceptance of a project with an internal rate of return below the investors' required rate of return will decrease the firm's stock price.

If the NPV is positive, then the IRR must be greater than the required rate of return, *k.* Thus all the discounted cash flow criteria are consistent and will give similar accept-reject decisions. In addition, because the internal rate of return is another discounted cash flow criterion, it exhibits the same general advantages and disadvantages as both the net present value and profitability index but has an additional disadvantage of being tedious to calculate if a financial calculator is not available.

An additional disadvantage of the IRR relative to the NPV deals with the implied reinvestment rate assumptions made by these two methods. The NPV method implicitly assumes that cash flows received over the life of the project are reinvested back in projects that earn the required rate of return. That is, if we have a mining project with a ten-year expected life that produces a $100,000 cash flow at the end of the second year, the NPV technique assumes that this $100,000 is reinvested over the period years 3 through 10 at the required rate of return. The use of the IRR, on the other hand, implies that cash flows over the life of the project can be reinvested

Table 5-6 PI Illustration of Investment in New Machinery

	After-Tax Cash Flow		After-Tax Cash Flow
Initial outlay	−$50,000	Inflow year 4	12,000
Inflow year 1	15,000	Inflow year 5	14,000
Inflow year 2	8,000	Inflow year 6	16,000
Inflow year 3	10,000		

Table 5-7 Calculation for PI Illustration of Investment in New Machinery

	After-Tax Cash Flow	Present Value Factor at 10 Percent	Present Value
Initial outlay	−$50,000	1.000	−$50,000
Inflow year 1	15,000	0.909	13,635
Inflow year 2	8,000	0.826	6,608
Inflow year 3	10,000	0.751	7,510
Inflow year 4	12,000	0.683	8,196
Inflow year 5	14,000	0.621	8,694
Inflow year 6	16,000	0.564	9,024

$$
PI = \frac{\displaystyle\sum_{t=1}^{n} \frac{ACF_t}{(1+k)^t}}{IO}
$$

$$
= \frac{\$13,635 + \$6,608 + \$7,510 + \$8,196 + \$8,694 + \$9,024}{\$50,000}
$$

$$
= \frac{\$53,667}{\$50,000}
$$

$$
= 1.0733
$$

at the IRR. Thus, if the mining project we just looked at has a 40 percent IRR, the use of the IRR implies that the $100,000 cash flow that is received at the end of year 2 could be reinvested at 40 percent over the remaining life of the project. In effect, *the NPV method implicitly assumes that cash flows over the life of the project can be reinvested at the firm's required rate of return, whereas the use of the IRR method implies that these cash flows could be reinvested at the IRR.* The better assumption is that one made by the NPV, that cash flows could be reinvested at the required rate of return. The reason being that these cash flows will either be (1) returned in the form of dividends to shareholders who demand the required rate of return on their investment, or (2) reinvested in a new investment project. If these cash flows are invested in a new project, then they are simply substituting for external funding on which the required rate of return is demanded. Thus, the opportunity cost of these funds is the required rate of return. The bottom line to all this is that the NPV method makes the best reinvestment rate assumption and, as such, is superior to the IRR method. Why should we care which method is used if both methods give similar accept-reject decisions? The answer, as we will see later, is that while they may give the same accept-reject decision, they may rank projects differently in terms of desirability.

Computing the IRR with a Financial Calculator

With today's calculators, the determination of an internal rate of return is merely a matter of a few keystrokes. Whenever we were solving time value of money problems for i, we were really solving for the internal rate of return. For instance, when we solved for the rate that $100 must be compounded annually for it to grow to $179.10 in ten years, we were actually solving for that problem's internal rate of return. Thus, with financial calculators we need only input the initial outlay, the cash flows and their timing, and then input the function key **I/Y** or the **IRR** button to calculate the internal rate of return. On some calculators it is necessary to input the compute key, **CPT**, before inputting the function key to be calculated.

Computing the IRR for Even Cash Flows

In this section we are going to put our calculators aside and examine the mathematical process of calculating internal rates of return for a better understanding of the IRR.

The calculation of a project's internal rate of return can either be very simple or relatively complicated. As an example of a straightforward solution, assume that a firm with a required rate of return of 10 percent is considering a project that involves an initial outlay of $45,555. If the investment is taken, the after-tax cash flows are expected to be $15,000 per annum over the project's four-year life. In this case, the internal rate of return is equal to IRR in the following equation:

$$\$45,555 = \frac{\$15,000}{(1 + IRR)^1} + \frac{\$15,000}{(1 + IRR)^2} + \frac{\$15,000}{(1 + IRR)^3} + \frac{\$15,000}{(1 + IRR)^4}$$

From our discussion of the present value of an annuity, we know that this equation can be reduced to

$$\$45,555 = \$15,000 \left[\sum_{t=1}^{4} \frac{1}{(1 + IRR)^t} \right]$$

Appendix D gives values for the $PVIFA_{i,n}$ for various combinations of i and n, which further reduces this equation to

$$\$45,555 = \$15,000 \, (PVIFA_{i, \, 4 \, yr})$$

Dividing both sides by $15,000, this becomes

$$3.037 = PVIFA_{i, \, 4 \, yr}$$

Hence we are looking for a $PVIFA_{i, \, 4 \, yr}$ of 3.037 in the four-year row of Appendix E. This value occurs when i equals 12 percent, which means that 12 percent is the internal rate of return for the investment. Therefore, since 12 percent is greater than the 10 percent required return, the project should be accepted.

Computing the IRR for Uneven Cash Flows

Unfortunately, although solving for the IRR is quite easy when using a financial calculator or spreadsheet, it can be solved directly in the tables only when the future after-tax net cash flows are in the form of an annuity or a single payment. With a calculator, the process is simple: One need only key in the initial cash outlay, the cash flows, and their timing, and press the **IRR** button. When a financial calculator is not available and these flows are in the form of an uneven series of flows, a trial-and-error approach is necessary. To do this, we first determine the present value of the future after-tax net cash flows using an arbitrary discount rate. If the present value of the future cash flows at this discount rate is larger than the initial outlay,

WALL STREET JOURNAL APRIL 20, 1994

Hospitals Rush to Buy a $3 Million Device Few Patients Can Use

CORAL GABLES, FLA.— The Gamma Knife is a medical device that costs $3 million. It emits gamma radiation to treat brain tumors and lesions. But it is used on only a few types of tumors, and most of the 16 Gamma Knives in the U.S. are idle for all but two days a week.**(A)** By some estimates, six of them could have treated all American patients last year.

Doctors covet the prestige of having the best equipment. Desperately sick patients hope for a breakthrough that might save them. And hospitals are in a medical arms race; if they don't have the latest gadget, star doctors and their patients may bolt.**(B)**

For people worried about runaway costs, the Gamma Knife is a troubling case. "It all comes down to a race to see who can have the better toys," charges James Proffitt, health-benefits manager at McDonnell Douglas

Corp. of St. Louis. "If we're ever going to get costs under control, we've got to learn to share the resources that we already have."

Of all the ways to deliver radiation to the brain, the Gamma Knife is the most precise—and most expensive. Per-patient charges typically run $10,000 to $25,000. The machine-related cost is about half the total, the rest going to a surgeon, a radiologist and a physicist.

In Southern Florida, two nearby hospitals are battling to see which can make the most of the Gamma Knife. A midsize community hospital, Doctors Hospital in Coral Gables, acted first, installing one last October. On March 28, Miami's biggest teaching hospital, Jackson Memorial Medical Center, activated its Gamma Knife.

Officials at both facilities concede it is ridiculous to have two such specialized machines

only 10 miles apart. Yet neither would dream of yielding to the other.**(C)** In the words of William Comte, a senior vice president at HealthSouth Rehabilitation Corp., of Birmingham, Ala., which owns Doctors Hospital: "Does this go against everything you're seeing in health care today? Yes. It's crazy. But we think our program has a great deal of credibility."

Most Gamma Knives can pay their way with just 100 patients a year. That means using each machine at less than 30% of capacity, he says. But with reimbursement rates usually at $15,000 or more per patient, it doesn't take many.

SOURCE: George Anders, "Hospitals Rush to Buy a $3 Million Device Few Patients Can Use," *Wall Street Journal* (April 20, 1994), A1. Reprinted by permission of *The Wall Street Journal*, 1994, Dow Jones & Co., Inc. All Rights Reserved.

ANALYSIS AND IMPLICATIONS...

A. Capital budgeting in the not-for-profit area is much more difficult than it is for the typical for-profit firm. One problem is that we have generally assumed that the goal of the firm is maximization of shareholder wealth. For a hospital that might not be the case. The goal may have something to do with saving lives, or providing quality health care to a large number of individuals at a low cost, but the creation of wealth may have nothing to do with their decision making. What is quality health care and how do we place a value on a human life that is saved? That's one of the nice things about decision making in the private sector with a decision rule that states that if the present value of the

benefits are greater than the present value of the costs, the project should be accepted. Using this rule, it is relatively clear what is a good project and what is a bad project. With hospitals, where we are talking about saving lives, the decision-making process becomes much more difficult and, as a result, much more subjective. This is complicated even more by the fact that hospitals have limited funds available for new equipment—that is, when one piece of new equipment is purchased, another is no longer affordable.

B. In the competitive free market, it is what Adam Smith referred to as the "invisible hand"—that in pursuit of their own best

interests, individuals and businesses help to allocate scarce resources to their most efficient use—that assures us that resources are efficiently allocated. However, in the not-for-profit sector, this is not necessarily the case. It is certainly possible that some capital-budgeting decisions in hospitals may be driven by individual doctors attempting to increase the status of their individual departments.

For the hospital, cash flows may be important in assuring that payrolls can be met and operations can continue, but the quality of health care may take on a role of greater importance in the decision-making process.

the rate is increased; if it is smaller than the initial outlay, the discount rate is lowered and the process begins again. This search routine is continued until the present value of the future after-tax cash flows is equal to the initial outlay. The interest rate that creates this situation is the internal rate of return. This is the same basic process that a financial calculator uses to calculate an IRR.

To illustrate the procedure, consider an investment proposal that requires an initial outlay of $3,817 and returns $1,000 at the end of year 1, $2,000 at the end of year 2, and $3,000 at the end of year 3. In this case, the internal rate of return must be determined using trial and error. This process is presented in Table 5-8, in which an arbitrarily selected discount rate of 15 percent was chosen to begin the process. The trial-and-error technique slowly centers in on the project's internal rate of return of 22 percent. The project's internal rate of return is then compared with the firm's required rate of return, and if the *IRR* is the larger, the project is accepted.

Table 5-8 Computing IRR for Uneven Cash Flows Without a Financial Calculator

Initial outlay	−$3,817		Inflow year 2	2,000
Inflow year 1	1,000		Inflow year 3	3,000

Solution:

Step 1: Pick an arbitrary discount rate and use it to determine the present value of the inflows.

Step 2: Compare the present value of the inflows with the initial outlay; if they are equal you have determined the IRR.

Step 3: If the present value of the inflows is larger (less than) than the initial outlay, raise (lower) the discount rate.

Step 4: Determine the present value of the inflows and repeat Step 2.

1. Try $i = 15$ percent:

	Net Cash Flows	Present Value Factor at 15 Percent	Present Value
Inflow year 1	$1,000	.870	$ 870
Inflow year 2	2,000	.756	1,512
Inflow year 3	3,000	.658	1,974
Present value of inflows			$4,356
Initial outlay			−$3,817

2. Try $i = 20$ percent:

	Net Cash Flows	Present Value Factor at 20 Percent	Present Value
Inflow year 1	$1,000	.833	$ 833
Inflow year 2	2,000	.694	1,388
Inflow year 3	3,000	.579	1,737
Present value of inflows			$3,958
Initial outlay			−$3,817

3. Try $i = 22$ percent:

	Net Cash Flows	Present Value Factor at 22 Percent	Present Value
Inflow year 1	$1,000	.820	$ 820
Inflow year 2	2,000	.672	1,344
Inflow year 3	3,000	.551	1,653
Present value of inflows			$3,817
Initial outlay			−$3,817

A firm with a required rate of return of 10 percent is considering three investment proposals. Given the information in Table 5-9, management plans to calculate the internal rate of return for each project and determine which projects should be accepted.

Because project A is an annuity, we can easily calculate its internal rate of return by determining the $PVIFA_{i,4yr}$ necessary to equate the present value of the future cash flows with the initial outlay. This computation is done as follows:

$$IO = \sum_{t=1}^{n} \frac{ACF_t}{(1 + IRR)^t}$$

$$\$10,000 = \sum_{t=1}^{4} \frac{\$3,362}{(1 + IRR)^t}$$

$$\$10,000 = \$3,362\left(PVIFA_{i,4yr}\right)$$

$$2.974 = \left(PVIFA_{i,4yr}\right)$$

We are looking for a $PVIFA_{i,4\,yr}$ of 2.974, in the four-year row of Appendix E, which occurs in the $i = 13$ percent column. Thus, 13 percent is the internal rate of return. Because this rate is greater than the firm's required rate of return of 10 percent, the project should be accepted.

Project B involves a single future cash flow of $13,605, resulting from an initial outlay of $10,000; thus, its internal rate of return can be determined directly from the present-value table in Appendix B, as follows:

$$IO = \frac{ACF_t}{(1 + IRR)^t}$$

$$\$10,000 = \frac{\$13,605}{(1 + IRR)^4}$$

$$\$10,000 = \$13,605\left(PVIF_{i,4yr}\right)$$

$$.735 = \left(PVIF_{i,4yr}\right)$$

This tells us that we should look for a $PVIF_{i,4\,yr}$ of .735 in the four-year row of Appendix B, which occurs in the $i = 8$ percent column. We may therefore conclude that 8 percent is the internal rate of return. Because this rate is less than the firm's required rate of return of 10 percent, project B should be rejected.

The uneven nature of the future cash flows associated with project C necessitates the use of the trial-and-error method. The internal rate of return for project C is equal to the value of IRR in the following equation:

$$\$10,000 = \frac{\$1,000}{(1 + IRR)^1} + \frac{\$3,000}{(1 + IRR)^2} + \frac{\$6,000}{(1 + IRR)^3} + \frac{\$7,000}{(1 + IRR)^4} \tag{5-4}$$

Arbitrarily selecting a discount rate of 15 percent and substituting it into equation (5-4) for IRR reduces the right-hand side of the equation to $11,090, as shown in Table 5-10. Therefore, because the present value of the future cash flows is larger than the initial outlay, we must raise the discount rate to find the project's internal rate of return. Substituting 20 percent for the discount rate, the right-hand side of equation (5-4) now becomes $9,763. As this is less than the initial outlay of $10,000, we must now decrease the discount rate. In other words, we know that the internal rate of return for this project is between 15 and 20 percent. Because the present value of the future flows discounted back to present at

20 percent was only $237 too low, a discount rate of 19 percent is selected. As shown in Table 5-10, a discount rate of 19 percent reduces the present value of the future inflows down to $10,009, which is approximately the same as the initial outlay. Consequently, project C's internal rate of return is approximately 19 percent. Because the internal rate of return is greater than the firm's required rate of return of 10 percent, this investment should be accepted.

Table 5-9 Three IRR Investment Proposal Examples

	A	B	C
Initial outlay	−$10,000	−$10,000	−$10,000
Inflow year 1	3,362	0	1,000
Inflow year 2	3,362	0	3,000
Inflow year 3	3,362	0	6,000
Inflow year 4	3,362	13,605	7,000

Table 5-10 Computing IRR for Project C

Try $i = 15$ percent:

	Net Cash Flows	Present Value Factor at 15 Percent	Present Value
Inflow year 1	$1,000	.870	$ 870
Inflow year 2	3,000	.756	2,268
Inflow year 3	6,000	.658	3,948
Inflow year 4	7,000	.572	4,004
Present value of inflows			$11,090
Initial outlay			−$10,000

Try $i = 20$ percent:

	Net Cash Flows	Present Value Factor at 20 Percent	Present Value
Inflow year 1	$1,000	.833	$ 833
Inflow year 2	3,000	.694	2,082
Inflow year 3	6,000	.579	3,474
Inflow year 4	7,000	.482	3,374
Present value of inflows			$ 9,763
Initial outlay			−$10,000

Try $i = 19$ percent:

	Net Cash Flows	Present Value Factor at 19 Percent	Present Value
Inflow year 1	$1,000	.840	$ 840
Inflow year 2	3,000	.706	2,118
Inflow year 3	6,000	.593	3,558
Inflow year 4	7,000	.499	3,493
Present value of inflows			$10,009
Initial outlay			−$10,000

Complications with IRR: Multiple Rates of Return

Although any project can have only one NPV and one PI, a single project under certain circumstances can have more than one IRR. The reason for this can be traced to the calculations involved in determining the IRR. Equation (5-3) states that the IRR is the discount rate that equates the present value of the project's future net cash flows with the project's initial outlay:

$$IO = \sum_{t=1}^{n} \frac{ACF_t}{(1 + IRR)^t}$$

(5-3)

However, because equation (5-3) is a polynomial of a degree n, it has n solutions. Now, if the initial outlay (*IO*) is the only negative cash flow and all the annual after-tax cash flows (*ACF$_t$*) are positive, then all but one of these n solutions is either a negative or imaginary number and there is no problem. But problems occur when there are sign reversals in the cash flow stream; in fact, there can be as many solutions as there are sign reversals. Thus, a normal pattern with a negative initial outlay and positive annual after-tax cash flows after that (−, +, +, ..., +) has only one sign reversal, hence only one positive IRR. However, a pattern with more than one sign reversal can have more than one IRR. Consider, for example, the following pattern of cash flows.[1]

	After-Tax Cash Flow
Initial outlay	−$1,600
Year 1	+$10,000
Year 2	−$10,000

In this pattern of cash flows, there are two sign reversals, from −$1,600 to +$10,000 and then from +$10,000 to −$10,000, so there can be as many as two positive IRRs that will make the present value of the future cash flows equal to the initial outlay. In fact, two internal rates of return solve this problem, 25 and 400 percent. Graphically what we are solving for is the discount rate that makes the project's NPV equal to zero; as Figure 5-1 illustrates, this occurs twice.

Which solution is correct? The answer is that neither solution is valid. Although each fits the definition of IRR, neither provides any insight into the true project returns. In summary, when there is more than one sign reversal in the cash flow stream, the possibility of multiple IRRs exists, and the normal interpretation of the IRR loses its meaning.

Modified Internal Rate of Return

The primary drawback of the internal rate of return relative to the net present value method is the reinvestment rate assumption made by the internal rate of return. Recently, a new technique, the **modified internal rate of return (MIRR),** has gained popularity as an alternative to the IRR method because it allows the decision-maker to directly specify the appropriate reinvestment rate. As a result, the MIRR provides the decision-maker with the intuitive appeal of the IRR coupled with an improved reinvestment rate assumption.

The driving force behind the MIRR is the assumption that all cash inflows over the life of the project are reinvested at the required rate of return until the termination of

---

[1]This example is taken from James H. Lorie and Leonard J. Savage, "Three Problems in Rationing Capital," *Journal of Business* 28 (October 1955): 229–39.

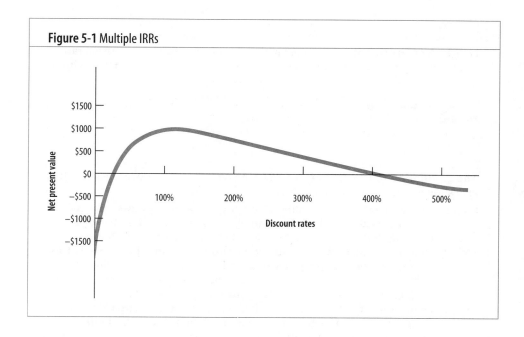

Figure 5-1 Multiple IRRs

the project. Thus, to calculate the MIRR, we take all the annual after-tax cash *in*flows, $ACIF_t$'s, and find their future value at the end of the project's life, compounded at the required rate of return. We will call this the project's *terminal value*, or *TV*. We then calculate the present value of the project's cash *out*flows. We do this by discounting all cash *out*flows, $ACOF_t$, back to the present at the required rate of return. If the initial outlay is the only cash *out*flow, then the initial outlay is the present value of the cash *out*flows. The MIRR is the discount rate that equates the present value of the cash *out*flows with the present value of the project's *terminal value*. Mathematically, the modified internal rate of return is defined as the value of MIRR in the following equation:

$$PV_{outflows} = PV_{inflows} \tag{5-5}$$

$$\sum_{t=0}^{n} \frac{ACOF_t}{(1 + k)^t} = \frac{\sum_{t=0}^{n} ACIF_t(1 + k)^{n-}}{(1 + MIRR)^n}$$

$$PV_{outflows} = \frac{TV}{(1 + MIRR)^n}$$

where $ACOF_t$ = the annual after-tax cash *out*flow in time period t
  $ACIF_t$ = the annual after-tax cash *in*flow in time period t
  TV = the terminal value of the $ACIF$'s compounded at the required rate of return to the end of the project
  n = the project's expected life
  $MIRR$ = the project's modified internal rate of return
  k = the appropriate discount rate; that is, the required rate of return or cost of capital

Let's look at an example of a project with a three-year life and a required rate of return of 10 percent assuming the following cash flows are associated with it:

After-Tax Cash Flows		After-Tax Cash Flows	
Initial outlay	−$6,000	Year 2	3,000
Year 1	2,000	Year 3	4,000

The calculation of the *MIRR* can be viewed as a three-step process, which is also shown graphically in Figure 5-2.

Step 1: Determine the present value of the project's cash *out*flows. In this case, the only *out*flow is the initial outlay of $6,000, which is already at the present; thus, it becomes the present value of the cash *out*flows.

Step 2: Determine the terminal value of the project's cash *in*flows. To do this, we merely use the project's required rate of return to calculate the future value of the project's three cash *in*flows at the termination of the project. In this case, the *terminal value* becomes $9,720.

Step 3: Determine the discount rate that equates the present value of the *terminal value* and the present value of the project's cash *out*flows. Thus, the *MIRR* is calculated to be 17.446 percent.

For our example, the calculations are as follows:

$$\$6000 = \frac{\sum_{t=1}^{3} ACIF_t (1 + k)^{n-t}}{(1 + MIRR)^n}$$

$$\$6000 = \frac{\$2000(1 + .10)^2 + \$3000(1 + .10)^1 + \$4000(1 + .10)^0}{(1 + MIRR)^3}$$

$$\$6000 = \frac{\$2420 + \$3300 + \$4000}{(1 + MIRR)^3}$$

$$\$6000 = \frac{\$9720}{(1 + MIRR)^3}$$

$$MIRR = 17.446\%$$

Thus, the *MIRR* for this project (17.446 percent) is less than its IRR which comes out to 20.614 percent. In this case, it only makes sense that the IRR should be greater than the MIRR because the IRR allows intermediate cash *in*flows to grow at the IRR rather than the required rate of return.

In terms of decision rules, if the project's MIRR is greater than or equal to the project's required rate of return, then the project should be accepted; if not, it should be rejected:

MIRR ≥ required rate of return: Accept
MIRR < required rate of return: Reject

Because of the frequent use of the IRR in the real world as a decision-making tool, and its limiting reinvestment rate assumption, the MIRR has become increasingly popular as an alternative decision-making tool.

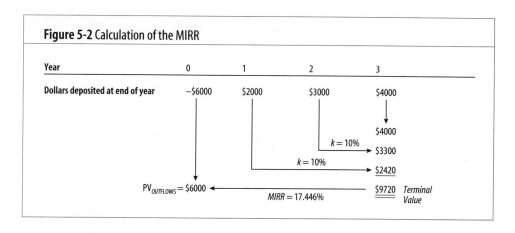

Figure 5-2 Calculation of the MIRR

Year	0	1	2	3
Dollars deposited at end of year	−$6000	$2000	$3000	$4000

$4000

$k = 10\%$ → $3300

$k = 10\%$ → $2420

$PV_{OUTFLOWS} = 6000 $MIRR = 17.446\%$ $9720 *Terminal Value*

ETHICS IN CAPITAL BUDGETING

Although it may not seem obvious, ethics has a role in capital budgeting. Any actions that violate ethical standards can cause a loss of trust which can, in turn, have a negative and long-lasting effect on the firm. The "Bad Apple for Baby" story outlines one such violation. In this case, it deals with ethical lapses at Beech-Nut and demonstrates the consequences of those actions. No doubt the decisions of the Beech-Nut executives were meant to create wealth, but in fact, they cost Beech-Nut tremendously.

A GLANCE AT ACTUAL CAPITAL-BUDGETING PRACTICES

During the past forty years, the popularity of each of the capital-budgeting methods has shifted rather dramatically. In the 1950s and 1960s, the payback period method dominated capital budgeting; but through the 1970s and 1980s, the internal rate of return and the net present value techniques slowly gained in popularity until they are today used by virtually all major corporations in decision making. Table 5-11 provides the results of a 1992 survey of the 100 largest Fortune 500 firms, showing the popularity of the internal rate of return and net present value methods.

Interestingly, although most firms use the NPV and IRR as their primary techniques, most firms also use the payback period as a secondary decision method for capital budgeting. In a sense, they are using the payback period to control for risk. The logic behind this being that because the payback period dramatically emphasizes early cash flows, which are presumably more certain—that is, have less risk—than cash flows occurring later in a project's life, managers believe its use will lead to projects with more certain cash flows.

A reliance on the payback period came out even more dramatically in a study of the capital-budgeting practices of twelve large manufacturing firms. Information for this study was gathered from interviews over one to three days, in addition to an examination of the records of about 400 projects. This study revealed several points of interest. First, firms were typically found to categorize capital investments as mandatory (regulations and contracts, capitalized maintenance, replacement of antiquated equipment, product quality) or discretionary (expanded markets, new businesses, cost cutting), with the decision-making process being different for mandatory and discretionary projects. Second, it was found that the decision-making process was different for projects of differing size. In fact, approval authority tended to rest in different locations, depending on the size of the project. Table 5-12 provides the typical levels of approval authority.

FINANCIAL WORLD, JUNE 27, 1989

Bad Apple for Baby

It's a widely held, but hard-to-prove belief that a company gains because it is perceived as more socially responsive than its competitors.**(A)** Over the years, the three major manufacturers of baby food—Gerber Products, Beech-Nut Nutrition, and H. J. Heinz—had, with almost equal success, gone out of their way to build an image of respectability.

Theirs is an almost perfect zero-sum business. They know, at any given time, how many babies are being born. They all pay roughly the same price for their commodities, and their manufacturing and distribution costs are almost identical. So how does one company gain a market share edge over another, especially in a stagnant or declining market?

The answer for Beech-Nut was to sell a cheaper, adulterated product. Beginning in 1977, the company began buying a chemical concoction, made up mostly of sugar and water, and labeling it as apple juice. Sales of that product brought Beech-Nut an estimated $60 million between 1977 and 1982, while reducing material costs about $250,000 annually.

When various investigators tried to do something about it, the company stonewalled. Among other things, they shipped the bogus juice out of a plant in New York to Puerto Rico, to put it beyond the jurisdiction of federal investigators, and they even offered the juice as a give-away to reduce their stocks after they were finally forced to discontinue selling it.

In the end, the company pleaded guilty to 215 counts of introducing adulterated food into commerce and violating the Federal Food Drug and Cosmetic Act. The FDA fined Beech-Nut $2 million.**(B)**

In addition, Beech-Nut's president, Neils Hoyvald, and its vice president of operations, John Lavery, were found guilty of similar charges. Each faces a year and one day in jail and a $100,000 fine. Both are now out on appeal on a jurisdiction technicality.

Why did they do it? The Fort Washington, Pa.-based company will not comment. But perhaps some portion of motive can be inferred from a report Hoyvald wrote to Nestle, the company which had acquired Beech-Nut in the midst of his cover-up. "It is our feeling that we can report safely now that the apple juice recall has been completed. If the recall had been effectuated in early June [when the FDA had first ordered it], over 700,000 cases in inventory would have been affected; due to our many delays, we were only faced with having to destroy 20,000 cases."

One thing is clear: Two executives of a company with an excellent reputation breached a trust and did their company harm.

SOURCE: Stephen Kindel, "Bad Apple for Baby," *Financial World* (June 27, 1989): 48. Reprinted by permission of *Financial World* © 1989 *Financial World*.

ANALYSIS AND IMPLICATIONS...

A. In this case, we can directly relate unethical behavior to a loss of shareholder wealth.

B. The most damaging event a business can suffer is a loss of the public's confidence in its ethical standards. In the financial world, we have seen this happen with the insider trading scandal at Drexel Burnham Lambert that brought down the firm, and more recently at Salomon Brothers, revolving around the attempt to corner the Treasury bill market. At Beech-Nut, the loss in consumer confidence that accompanied this scandal resulted in a drop of Beech-Nut's share of the overall baby food market from 19.1 percent to 15.8 percent. Thus, while this violation of ethics resulted in a short-run gain for Beech-Nut, much more was lost in the long run for many years to come.

Table 5-11 1992 Survey of Capital-Budgeting Practices of the 100 Largest Fortune 500 Industrial Firms

Investment Evaluation Methods Used:	Percent of Firms		
	A Primary Method	A Secondary Method	Total Using This Method
Payback period	24%	59%	83%
Internal rate of return	88%	11%	99%
Net present value	63%	22%	85%
Profitability index	15%	18%	33%

SOURCE: Harold Bierman, Jr., "Capital Budgeting in 1992: A Survey," *Financial Management* (Autumn 1993): 24.

Table 5-12 Project Size and Decision-Making Authority

Project Size	Typical Boundaries	Primary Decision Site
Very small	Up to $100,000	Plant
Small	$100,000 to $1,000,000	Division
Medium	$1 million to $10 million	Corporate investment committee
Large	Over $10 million	CEO & board

The study also showed that while the discounted cash flow methods are used at most firms, the simple payback criterion was the measure relied on primarily in one third of the firms examined. The use of the payback period seemed to be even more common for smaller projects, with firms severely simplifying the discounted cash flow analysis or relying primarily on the payback period. Thus, although discounted cash flow decision techniques have become more widely accepted, their use depends to an extent on the size of the project and where within the firm the decision is being made.

SUMMARY

Before a profitable project can be adopted, it must be identified or found. Unfortunately, coming up with ideas for new products, for ways to improve existing products, or for ways to make existing products more profitable is extremely difficult. In general, the best source of ideas for these new, potentially profitable products is from within the firm.

The process of capital budgeting involves decision making with respect to investment in fixed assets. We examine four commonly used criteria for determining the acceptance or rejection of capital-budgeting proposals. The first method, the payback period, does not incorporate the time value of money into its calculations, although a variation of it, the discounted payback period, recognizes the time value of money. The discounted methods, net present value, profitability index, and internal rate of return, do account for the time value of money. These methods are summarized in Table 5-13.

Ethics and ethical decisions continuously crop up in capital budgeting. Just as with all other areas of finance, violating ethical considerations results in a loss of public confidence which can have a significant negative effect on shareholder wealth.

Over the past forty years, the discounted capital-budgeting techniques have continued to gain in popularity and today dominate in the decision-making process.

Table 5-13 Capital-Budgeting Criteria

1. Payback period = number of years required to recapture the initial investment
Accept if payback ≤ maximum acceptable payback period
Reject if payback > maximum acceptable payback period

Advantages:
- Uses cash flows.
- Is easy to calculate and understand.
- May be used as rough screening device.

Disadvantages:
- Ignores the time value of money.
- Ignores cash flows occurring after the payback period.
- Selection of the maximum acceptable payback period is arbitrary.

2. Discounted payback period = the number of years needed to recover the initial cash outlay from the *discounted net cash flows*
Accept if discounted payback ≤ maximum acceptable discounted payback period
Reject if discounted payback > maximum acceptable discounted payback period

Advantages:
- Uses cash flows.
- Is easy to calculate and understand.
- Considers time value of money.

Disadvantages:
- Ignores cash flows occurring after the payback period.
- Selection of the maximum acceptable discounted payback period is arbitrary.

3. Net present value = present value of the annual cash flows after taxes less the investment's initial outlay

$$NPV = \sum_{t=1}^{n} \frac{ACF_t}{(1 + k)^t} - IO$$

where ACF_t = the annual after-tax cash flow in time period t (this can take on either positive or negative values)
k = the appropriate discount rate; that is, the required rate of return or the cost of capital
IO = the initial cash outlay
n = the project's expected life

Accept if NPV ≥ 0.0
Reject if NPV < 0.0

Advantages:
- Uses cash flows.
- Recognizes the time value of money.
- Is consistent with the firm goal of shareholder wealth maximization.

Disadvantages:
- Requires detailed long-term forecasts of the incremental benefits and costs.

(Continued on next page)

Table 5-13 Capital-Budgeting Criteria (continued)

4. Profitability index = the ratio of the present value of the future net cash flows to the initial outlay

$$PI = \frac{\displaystyle\sum_{t=1}^{n}\frac{ACF_t}{(1 + k)^t}}{IO}$$

Accept if $PI \geq 1.0$
Reject if $PI < 1.0$

Advantages:
- Uses cash flows.
- Recognizes the time value of money.
- Is consistent with the firm goal of shareholder wealth maximization.

Disadvantages:
- Requires detailed long-term forecasts of the incremental benefits and costs.

5. Internal rate of return = the discount rate that equates the present value of the project's future net cash flows with the project's initial outlay

$$IO = \sum_{t=1}^{n}\frac{ACF_t}{(1 + IRR)^t}$$

where IRR = the project's internal rate of return
Accept if $IRR \geq$ required rate of return
Reject if $IRR <$ required rate of return

Advantages:
- Uses cash flows.
- Recognizes the time value of money.
- Is in general consistent with the firm goal of shareholder wealth maximization.

Disadvantages:
- Requires detailed long-term forecasts of the incremental benefits and costs.
- Possibility of multiple IRRs.
- Assumes cash flows over the life of the project are reinvested at the IRR.

6. Modified internal rate of return = the discount rate that equates the present value of the project's cash *outflows* with the present value of the project's *terminal value*

$$\sum_{t=0}^{n}\frac{ACOF_t}{(1 + k)^t} = \frac{\displaystyle\sum_{t=0}^{n}ACIF_t\,(1 + k)^{n-t}}{(1 + MIRR)^n}$$

$$PV_{\text{OUTFLOWS}} = \frac{TV}{(1 + MIRR)^n}$$

where $ACOF_t$ = the annual after-tax cash *out*flow in time period t.
$ACIF_t$ = the annual after-tax cash *in*flow in time period t.
TV = the terminal value of *ACIF*'s compounded at the required rate of return to the end of the project.

Accept if $MIRR \geq$ the required rate of return
Reject if $MIRR <$ required rate of return

Advantages:
- Uses cash flows.
- Recognizes the time value of money.
- In general, is consistent with the goal of maximization of shareholder wealth.

Disadvantages:
- Requires detailed long-term forecasts of the incremental benefits and costs.

STUDY QUESTIONS

5-1. Why is the capital-budgeting decision such an important process? Why are capital-budgeting errors so costly?

5-2. What are the criticisms of the use of the payback period as a capital-budgeting technique? What are its advantages? Why is it so frequently used?

5-3. In some countries, expropriation of foreign investments is a common practice. If you were considering an investment in one of those countries, would the use of the payback period criterion seem more reasonable than it otherwise might? Why?

5-4. Briefly compare and contrast the NPV, PI, and IRR criteria. What are the advantages and disadvantages of using each of these methods?

5-5. What is the advantage of using the MIRR as opposed to the IRR decision criteria?

SELF-TEST PROBLEMS

ST-1. You are considering a project that will require an initial outlay of $54,200. This project has an expected life of five years and will generate after-tax cash flows to the company as a whole of $20,608 at the end of each year over its five-year life. In addition to the $20,608 cash flow from operations during the fifth and final year, there will be an additional cash inflow of $13,200 at the end of the fifth year associated with the salvage value of the machine, making the cash flow in year 5 equal to $33,808. Thus the cash flows associated with this project look like this:

Year	Cash Flow	Year	Cash Flow
0	−$54,200	3	20,608
1	20,608	4	20,608
2	20,608	5	33,808

Given a required rate of return of 15 percent, calculate the following:

- **a.** Payback period
- **b.** Net present value
- **c.** Profitability index
- **d.** Internal rate of return

Should this project be accepted?

STUDY PROBLEMS (SET A)

5-1A. (IRR Calculation) Determine the internal rate of return on the following projects:
- **a.** An initial outlay of $10,000 resulting in a single cash flow of $17,182 after eight years
- **b.** An initial outlay of $10,000 resulting in a single cash flow of $48,077 after ten years
- **c.** An initial outlay of $10,000 resulting in a single cash flow of $114,943 after twenty years
- **d.** An initial outlay of $10,000 resulting in a single cash flow of $13,680 after three years

5-2A. (IRR Calculation) Determine the internal rate of return on the following projects:
- **a.** An initial outlay of $10,000 resulting in a cash flow of $1,993 at the end of each year for the next ten years
- **b.** An initial outlay of $10,000 resulting in a cash flow of $2,054 at the end of each year for the next twenty years

c. An initial outlay of $10,000 resulting in a cash flow of $1,193 at the end of each year for the next twelve years

d. An initial outlay of $10,000 resulting in a cash flow of $2,843 at the end of each year for the next five years

5-3A. (IRR Calculation) Determine the internal rate of return to the nearest percent on the following projects:

   a. An initial outlay of $10,000 resulting in a cash flow of $2,000 at the end of year 1, $5,000 at the end of year 2, and $8,000 at the end of year 3

   b. An initial outlay of $10,000 resulting in a cash flow of $8,000 at the end of year 1, $5,000 at the end of year 2, and $2,000 at the end of year 3

   c. An initial outlay of $10,000 resulting in a cash flow of $2,000 at the end of years 1 through 5 and $5,000 at the end of year 6

5-4A. (NPV, PI, and IRR Calculations) Fijisawa, Inc., is considering a major expansion of its product line and has estimated the following cash flows associated with such an expansion. The initial outlay associated with the expansion would be $1,950,000 and the project would generate incremental after-tax cash flows of $450,000 per year for six years. The appropriate required rate of return is 9 percent.

   a. Calculate the net present value.

   b. Calculate the profitability index.

   c. Calculate the internal rate of return.

   d. Should this project be accepted?

5-5A. (Payback Period, Net Present Value, Profitability Index, and Internal Rate of Return Calculations) You are considering a project with an initial cash outlay of $80,000 and expected after-tax cash flows of $20,000 at the end of each year for six years. The required rate of return for this project is 10 percent.

   a. What are the project's payback and discounted payback periods?

   b. What is the project's NPV?

   c. What is the project's PI?

   d. What is the project's IRR?

5-6A. (Net Present Value, Profitability Index, and Internal Rate of Return Calculations) You are considering two independent projects, Project A and Project B. The initial cash outlay associated with Project A is $50,000 and the initial cash outlay associated with Project B is $70,000. The required rate of return on both projects is 12 percent. The expected annual after-tax cash flows from each project are as follows:

Year	Project A	Project B
0	−$50,000	−$70,000
1	12,000	13,000
2	12,000	13,000
3	12,000	13,000
4	12,000	13,000
5	12,000	13,000
6	12,000	13,000

Calculate the NPV, PI, and IRR for each project and indicate if the project should be accepted.

5-7A. (Payback Period Calculations) You are considering three independent projects, Project A, Project B, and Project C. The required rate of return is 10 percent on each. Given the following cash flow information calculate the payback period and discounted payback period for each.

Year	Project A	Project B	Project C
0	−$1,000	−$10,000	−$5,000
1	600	5,000	1,000
2	300	3,000	1,000
3	200	3,000	2,000
4	100	3,000	2,000
5	500	3,000	2,000

If you require a three-year payback for both the traditional and discounted payback period methods before an investment can be accepted, which projects would be accepted under each criterion?

5-8A. (NPV with Varying Rates of Return) Dowling Sportswear is considering building a new factory to produce aluminum baseball bats. This project would require an initial cash outlay of $5,000,000 and will generate annual after-tax cash inflows of $1 million per year for eight years. Calculate the project's NPV given:

    a. A required rate of return of 9 percent

    b. A required rate of return of 11 percent

    c. A required rate of return of 13 percent

    d. A required rate of return of 15 percent

5-9A. (Internal Rate of Return Calculations) Given the following cash flows, determine the internal rate of return for the three independent projects A, B, and C.

	Project A	Project B	Project C
Initial Investment:	−$50,000	−$100,000	−$450,000
Cash Inflows:			
Year 1	$10,000	$ 25,000	$200,000
Year 2	15,000	25,000	200,000
Year 3	20,000	25,000	200,000
Year 4	25,000	25,000	—
Year 5	30,000	25,000	—

5-10A. (NPV with Varying Required Rates of Return) Big Steve's, makers of swizzle sticks, is considering the purchase of a new plastic stamping machine. This investment requires an initial outlay of $100,000 and will generate after-tax cash inflows of $18,000 per year for ten years. For each of the listed required rates of return, determine the project's net present value.

    a. The required rate of return is 10 percent.

    b. The required rate of return is 15 percent.

    c. Would the project be accepted under part (a) or (b)?

    d. What is this project's internal rate of return?

5-11A. (MIRR Calculation) Emily's Soccer Mania is considering building a new plant. This project would require an initial cash outlay of $10 million and will generate annual after-tax cash inflows of $3 million per year for ten years.

Calculate the project's MIRR, given:

    a. A required rate of return of 10 percent

    b. A required rate of return of 12 percent

    c. A required rate of return of 14 percent

Your first assignment in your new position as assistant financial analyst at Caledonia Products is to evaluate two new capital-budgeting proposals. Since this is your first assignment, you have been asked not only to provide a recommendation, but also to respond to a number of questions aimed at judging your understanding of the capital-budgeting process. This is a standard procedure for all new financial analysts at Caledonia, and will serve to determine whether you are moved directly into the capital-budgeting analysis department or are provided with remedial training. The memorandum you received outlining your assignment follows:

TO: The New Financial Analysts

FROM: Mr. V. Morrison, CEO, Caledonia Products

RE: Capital-Budgeting Analysis

Provide an evaluation of two proposed projects, both with five-year expected lives and identical initial outlays of $110,000. Both these projects involve additions to Caledonia's highly successful Avalon product line, and as a result, the required rate of return on both projects has been established at 12 percent. The expected after-tax cash flows from each project are as follows:

3	Project A	Project B
Initial Outlay	−$110,000	−$110,000
Year 1	20,000	40,000
Year 2	30,000	40,000
Year 3	40,000	40,000
Year 4	50,000	40,000
Year 5	70,000	40,000

In evaluating these projects, please respond to the following questions:

a. Why is the capital-budgeting process so important?

b. Why is it difficult to find exceptionally profitable projects?

c. What is the payback period on each project? If Caledonia imposes a three-year maximum acceptable payback period, which of these projects should be accepted?

d. What are the criticisms of the payback period?

e. What are the discounted payback periods for each of these projects? If Caledonia requires a three-year maximum acceptable discounted payback period on new projects, which of these projects should be accepted?

f. What are the drawbacks or deficiencies of the discounted payback period? Do you feel either the payback or discounted payback period should be used to determine whether or not these projects should be accepted? Why or why not?

g. Determine the net present value for each of these projects. Should they be accepted?

h. Describe the logic behind the net present value.

i. Determine the profitability index for each of these projects. Should they be accepted?

j. Would you expect the net present value and profitability index methods to give consistent accept/reject decisions? Why or why not?

k. What would happen to the net present value and profitability index for each project if the required rate of return increased? If the required rate of return decreased?

l. Determine the internal rate of return for each project. Should they be accepted?

m. How does a change in the required rate of return affect the project's internal rate of return?

n. What reinvestment rate assumptions are implicitly made by the net present value and internal rate of return methods? Which one is better?

o. Determine the modified internal rate of return for each project. Should they be accepted? Do you feel it is a better evaluation technique than the internal rate of return? Why or why not?

FORD'S PINTO

Ethics Case: The Value of Life

There was a time when the "made in Japan" label brought a predictable smirk of superiority to the face of most Americans. The quality of most Japanese products usually was as low as their price. In fact, few imports could match their domestic counterparts, the proud products of "Yankee know-how." But by the late 1960s, an invasion of foreign-made goods chiseled a few worry lines into the countenance of American industry. And in Detroit, worry was fast fading to panic as the Japanese, not to mention the Germans, began to gobble up more and more of the subcompact auto market.

Never one to take a back seat to the competition, Ford Motor Company decided to meet the threat from abroad head-on. In 1968, Ford executives decided to produce the Pinto. Known inside the company as "Lee's car," after Ford president Lee Iacocca, the Pinto was to weigh no more than 2,000 pounds and cost no more than $2,000.

Eager to have its subcompact ready for the 1971 model year, Ford decided to compress the normal drafting-board-to-showroom time of about three-and-a-half years into two. The compressed schedule meant that any design changes typically made before production-line tooling would have to be made during it.

Before producing the Pinto, Ford crash-tested eleven of them, in part to learn if they met the National Highway Traffic Safety Administration (NHTSA) proposed safety standard that all autos be able to withstand a fixed-barrier impact of 20 miles per hour without fuel loss. Eight standard-design Pintos failed the tests. The three cars that passed the test all had some kind of gas-tank modification. One had a plastic baffle between the front of the tank and the differential housing; the second had a piece of steel between the tank and the rear bumper; and the third had a rubber-lined gas tank.

Ford officials faced a tough decision. Should they go ahead with the standard design, thereby meeting the produc-

tion time table but possibly jeopardizing consumer safety? Or should they delay production of the Pinto by redesigning the gas tank to make it safer and thus concede another year of subcompact dominance to foreign companies?

To determine whether to proceed with the original design of the Pinto fuel tank, Ford decided to use a capital-budgeting approach, examining the expected costs and the social benefits of making the change. Would the social benefits of a new tank design outweigh design costs, or would they not?

To find the answer, Ford had to assign specific values to the variables involved. For some factors in the equation, this posed no problem. The costs of design improvement, for example, could be estimated at eleven dollars per vehicle. But what about human life? Could a dollar-and-cents figure be assigned to a human being?

NHTSA thought it could. It had estimated that society loses $200,725 every time a person is killed in an auto accident. It broke down the costs as follows:

Future productivity losses	
Direct	$132,000
Indirect	41,300
Medical Costs	
Hospital	700
Other	425
Property damage	1,500
Insurance administration	4,700
Legal and court expenses	3,000
Employer losses	1,000
Victim's pain and suffering	10,000
Funeral	900
Assets (lost consumption)	5,000
Miscellaneous accident costs	200
Total per fatality	$200,725[a]

[a]Ralph Drayton, "One Manufacturer's Approach to Automobile Safety Standards," *CTLA News 8* (February 1968): 11.

Ford used NHTSA and other statistical studies in its cost-benefit analysis, which yielded the following estimates:

Benefits	
Savings:	180 burn deaths, 180 serious burn injuries, 2,100 burned vehicles
Unit cost:	$200,000 per death, $67,000 per injury, $700 per vehicle
Total benefit:	(180 x $200,000) + (180 x $67,000) + (2,100 x $700) = $49.5 million
Costs	
Sales:	11 million cars, 1.5 million light trucks
Unit cost:	$11 per car, $11 per truck
Total cost:	12.5 million x $11 = $137.5 million[a]

[a]Mark Dowie, "Pinto Madness," *Mother Jones* (September–October 1977): 20. See also Russell Mokhiber, *Corporate Crime and Violence* (San Francisco: Sierra Club Books, 1988): 373–82, and Francis T. Cullen, William J. Maakestad,and Gray Cavender, *Corporate Crime Under Attack: The Ford Pinto Case and Beyond* (Cincinnati: Anderson Publishing, 1987)

Since the costs of the safety improvement outweighed its benefits, Ford decided to push ahead with the original design. Here is what happened after Ford made this decision:

Between 700 and 2,500 persons died in accidents involving Pinto fires between 1971 and 1978. According to sworn testimony of Ford engineer Harley Copp, 95 percent of them would have survived if Ford had located the fuel tank over the axle (as it had done on its Capri automobiles).

NHTSA's standard was adopted in 1977. The Pinto then acquired a rupture-proof fuel tank. The following year Ford was obliged to recall all 1971–1976 Pintos for fuel-tank modifications.

Between 1971 and 1978, approximately fifty lawsuits were brought against Ford in connection with rear-end accidents in the Pinto. In the Richard Grimshaw case, in addition to awarding over $3 million in compensatory damages to the victims of a Pinto crash, the jury awarded a landmark $125 million in punitive damages against Ford. The judge reduced punitive damages to $3.5 million.

On August 10, 1978, eighteen-year-old Judy Ulrich, her sixteen-year-old sister Lynn, and their eighteen-year-old cousin Donna, in their 1973 Ford Pinto, were struck from the rear by a van near Elkhart, Indiana. The gas tank of the Pinto exploded on impact. In the fire that resulted, the three teenagers were burned to death. Ford was charged with criminal homicide. The judge presiding over the twenty-week trial advised jurors that Ford should be convicted if it had clearly disregarded the harm that might result from its actions and that disregard represented a substantial deviation from acceptable standards of conduct. On March 13, 1980, the jury found Ford not guilty of criminal homicide.

For its part, Ford has always denied that the Pinto is unsafe compared with other cars of its type and era. The company also points out that in every model year the Pinto met or surpassed the government's own standards. But what the company doesn't say is that successful lobbying by it and its industry associates was responsible for delaying for nine years the adoption of NHTSA's 20 miles-per-hour crash standard. And Ford critics claim that there were more than forty European and Japanese models in the Pinto price and weight range with safer gas-tank position. "Ford made an extremely irresponsible decision," concludes auto safety expert Byron Bloch, "when they placed such a weak tank in such a ridiculous location in such a soft rear end."

Questions

1. Do you think Ford approached this question properly?
2. What responsibilities to its customers do you think Ford had? Were their actions ethically appropriate?
3. Would it have made a moral or ethical difference if the $11 savings had been passed on to Ford's customers? Could a rational customer have chosen to save $11 and risk the more dangerous gas tank? Would that have been similar to making air bags optional? What if Ford had told potential customers about its decision?
4. Should Ford have been found guilty of criminal homicide in the Ulrich case?
5. If you, as a financial manager at Ford, found out about what had been done, what would you do?

Reprinted by permission from William Shaw and Vincent Barry, *Moral Issues in Business*, 5th ed. (New York: Wadsworth, 1992), 86–88. © by Wadsworth, Inc.

GUIDELINES FOR CAPITAL BUDGETING

To evaluate investment proposals, we must first set guidelines by which we measure the value of each proposal.

Use Cash Flows Rather than Accounting Profits

We will use cash flows, not accounting profits, as our measurement tool. The firm receives and is able to reinvest cash flows, whereas accounting profits are shown when they are earned rather than when the money is actually in hand. Unfortunately, a firm's accounting profits and cash flows may not be timed to occur together. For example, capital expenses, such as vehicles and plant and equipment, are depreciated over several years, with their annual depreciation subtracted from profit. Cash flows correctly reflect the timing of benefits and costs—that is, when the money is received, when it can be reinvested, and when it must be paid out.

Think Incrementally

Unfortunately, calculating cash flows from a project may not be enough. Decision makers must ask: What new cash flows will the company as a whole receive if the company takes on a given project? What if the company does not take on the project? Interestingly, we may find that not all cash flows a firm expects from an investment proposal are incremental in nature. In measuring cash flows, however, the trick is to *think* incrementally. In doing so, we will see that only *incremental after-tax cash flows* matter. As such, our guiding rule in deciding if a cash flow is incremental will be to look at the company with, versus without, the new product. As you will see in the upcoming sections, this may be easier said than done.

Beware of Cash Flows Diverted from Existing Products

Assume for a moment that we are managers of a firm considering a new product line that might compete with one of our existing products and possibly reduce its sales. In determining the cash flows associated with the proposed project, we should consider only the incremental sales brought to the company as a whole. New-product sales achieved at the cost of losing sales of other products in our line are not considered a benefit of adopting the new product. For example, when General Foods' Post Cereal Division introduced its Dino Pebbles in 1991, the product competed directly with the company's Fruity Pebbles. (In fact, the two were actually the same product, with an addition to the former of dinosaur-shaped marshmallows.) Post meant to target the market niche held by Kellogg's Marshmallow Krispies, but there was no question that sales recorded by Dino Pebbles bit into— literally cannibalized—Post's existing product line.

Remember that we are only interested in the sales dollars to the firm if this project is accepted, as opposed to what the sales dollars would be if the project is rejected. Just moving sales from one product line to a new product line does not bring anything new into the company, but if sales are captured from our competitors or if sales that would have been lost to new competing products are retained, then these are relevant **incremental cash flows**. In each case, these are the incremental cash flows to the firm—looking at the firm as a whole with the new product versus without the new product.

Look for Incidental or Synergistic Effects

Although in some cases a new project may take sales away from a firm's current projects, in other cases, a new effort may actually bring new sales to the existing line. For example, in September 1991 USAir introduced service to Sioux City, Iowa. The new routes connecting this addition to the USAir system not only brought about new ticket sales on those routes, but also fed passengers to connecting routes. If managers were to look at only the revenue from ticket sales on the Sioux City routes, they would miss the incremental cash flow to USAir as a whole that results from taking on the new route. This is called a *synergistic* effect. The cash flow comes from *any* USAir flight that would not have occurred if service to Sioux City had not been available. The bottom line: Any cash flow to any part of the company that may result from the decision at hand must be considered when making that decision.

Work in Working Capital Requirements

Many times, a new project will involve additional investment in working capital. This may take the form of new inventory to stock a sales outlet, additional investment in accounts receivable resulting from additional credit sales, or increased investment in cash to operate cash registers, and more. Working capital requirements are considered a cash flow even though they do not leave the company. How can investment in inventory be considered a cash outflow when the goods are still in the store? Because the firm does not have access to the inventory's cash value, the firm cannot use the money for other investments. Generally, working-capital requirements are tied up over the life of the project. When the project terminates there is usually an offsetting cash inflow as the working capital is recovered.

Consider Incremental Expenses

Just as cash inflows from a new project are measured on an incremental basis, expenses should also be measured on an incremental basis. For example, if introducing a new product line necessitates training the sales staff, the after-tax cash flow associated with the training program must be considered a cash outflow and charged against the project. If accepting a new project dictates that a production facility be reengineered, the after-tax cash flows associated with that capital investment should be charged against the project. Again, any incremental after-tax cash flow affecting the company as a whole is a relevant cash flow whether it is flowing in or flowing out.

Remember That Sunk Costs Are Not Incremental Cash Flows

Only cash flows that are affected by the decision made at the moment are relevant in capital budgeting. The manager asks two questions: (1) Will this cash flow occur if the project is accepted? (2) Will this cash flow occur if the project is rejected? *Yes* to the first question and *no* to the second equals an incremental cash flow. For example, let's assume you are considering introducing a new taste treat called Puddin' in a Shoe. You would like to do some test marketing before production. If you are considering the decision to test market and have not yet done so, the costs associated with the test marketing are relevant cash flows. Conversely, if you have already test marketed, the cash flows involved in test marketing are no longer relevant in project evaluation. It's a matter of timing. Regardless of what you might decide about future production, the cash flows allocated to marketing have already occurred. Cash flows that have already taken place are often referred to as "sunk costs" because they have been sunk into the project and cannot be undone. As a

THE WALL STREET JOURNAL, APRIL 25, 1994

With Remedy in Hand, Drug Firms Get Ready to Popularize an Illness

For years, Fran Sydney Scotch-taped her carpet to pick up specks of dirt, washed her keys, and scrubbed her shoes in the sink. The Connecticut mother of three painstakingly hung all her clothes in sequence by size, and spent half an hour making and remaking her bed. She insisted that her children bathe before entering their room, then stay there to avoid recontamination.

Unknown to Ms. Sydney, she was suffering from a disease of the mind called obsessive compulsive disorder. First reported by incredulous researchers at the turn of the century, OCD remains a medical mystery, and many people haven't even heard of it.

But in coming months, OCD will be talked about everywhere. Brochures about it will sprout in doctors' offices. A prominent Washington scholar will release a study declaring that OCD costs the U.S. economy $8 billion a year. Doctors who specialize in it will start appearing on talk shows and giving newspaper interviews. So will Fran Sydney, offering harrowing sound bites about her ordeal.

OCD's sudden burst into public awareness will result from a careful strategy by two giant drug companies, Upjohn Co. of Kalamazoo, Mich., and the Belgian firm Solvay SA. They make the medicine that finally helped Ms. Sydney, a close cousin of Prozac called Luvox.(A)

The selling of OCD offers a vivid example of how diseases have come to be packaged and marketed. The strategy solves a vexing business problem for drug companies, which increasingly want to market directly to patients but face Food and Drug Administration curbs on advertising.(B)

"The goal is to make the disease better known and make patients seek treatment. Obviously it's not all altruistic—we want to be part of the treatment," says Upjohn public-relations director Philip Sheldon.

Such strategies can make a valuable contribution to public health and education. But most consumers have no idea the studies and public service messages actually are part of a plan to sell drugs. The drug companies typically leave few fingerprints, running their disease campaigns through PR firms, patient groups, "institutes" and other third parties. They may discreetly identify a corporate sponsor, but seldom a specific drug.

"With resources for research and treatment increasingly scarce, do we simply want the marketplace to decide on the basis of who puts how many advertising dollars into raising fears and concern about disease X vs. disease Y in order to promote their particular products?"(C) asks Jay Winsten, associate dean of the Harvard School of Public Health. Dr. Winsten recently led a publicity campaign to promote designated drivers. But he pointedly turned down offers of grants from the alcoholic-beverage industry, worrying they would "inevitably raise questions about the creditability and legitimacy of the message."

SOURCE: Excerpted from Michael W. Miller, "With Remedy in Hand, Drug Firms Get Ready to Popularize an Illness," *Wall Street Journal* (April 25, 1994). © 1994 by Dow Jones & Co. Inc. Reprinted by permission.

ANALYSIS AND IMPLICATIONS...

A. It was extremely difficult to find exceptionally profitable projects. Generally, the process involves developing a product that satisfies a demand. In this case, the product has already been developed and the capital-budgeting process actually involves making an investment that will generate demand for this product. Thus, what we generally refer to as the initial outlay will involve very large marketing expenditures. In other words, in this case, the product development has preceded the demand for the product.

B. Generally, we make an estimate of the future cash flows and use this estimate to determine whether or not investment in the project is justified. In this case, the size of the investment in the project, the marketing and promotional expenditures, will determine the demand. Thus the drug companies no doubt focused on determining that expenditure level at which the increased promotional costs were no longer covered by the revenue associated with the increased demand resulting from those promotional expenditures.

C. Is it ethical to rely on fear and concerns about a disease to influence the allocation of scarce resources in the healthcare area? Obviously, Doctor Winsten questions this. What is your opinion?

rule, any cash flows that are not affected by the accept-reject decision should not be included in capital-budgeting analysis.

Account for Opportunity Costs

Now we will focus on the cash flows that are lost because a given project consumes scarce resources that would have produced cash flows if that project had been rejected. This is the opportunity cost of doing business. For example, a product may use valuable floor space in a production facility. Although the cash flow is not obvious, the real question remains: What else could be done with this space? The space could have been rented out, or another product could have been stored there. The key point is that opportunity-cost cash flows should reflect net cash flows that would have been received if the project under consideration were rejected. Again, we are analyzing the cash flows to the company as a whole, with or without the project.

Decide if Overhead Costs Are Truly Incremental Cash Flows

Although we certainly want to include any incremental cash flows resulting in changes from overhead expenses such as utilities and salaries, we also want to make sure that these are truly incremental cash flows. Many times, overhead expenses—heat, light, rent—would occur whether a given project were accepted or rejected. There is often not a single specific project to which these expenses can be allocated. Thus, the question is not whether the project benefits from overhead items but whether the overhead costs are incremental cash flows associated with the project—and relevant to capital budgeting.

Ignore Interest Payments and Financing Flows

In evaluating new projects and determining cash flows, we must separate the investment decision from the financing decision. Interest payments and other financing cash flows that might result from raising funds to finance a project should not be considered incremental cash flows. If accepting a project means we have to raise new funds by issuing bonds, the interest charges associated with raising funds are not a relevant cash outflow. When we discount the incremental cash flows back to the present at the required rate of return, we are implicitly accounting for the cost of raising funds to finance the new project. In essence, the required rate of return reflects the cost of the funds needed to support the project. Managers first determine the desirability of the project and then determine how best to finance it.

MEASURING A PROJECT'S BENEFITS AND COSTS

In measuring cash flows, we will be interested only in the **incremental,** or differential, **after-tax cash flows** that can be attributed to the proposal being evaluated. That is, we will focus our attention on the difference in the firm's after-tax cash flows *with* versus *without* the project. The worth of our decision depends on the accuracy of our cash flow estimates. For this reason, we first examined the question of what cash flows are relevant. Now we will see that, in general, a project's cash flows will fall into one of three categories: (1) the initial outlay, (2) the differential flows over the project's life, and (3) the terminal cash flow.

Initial Outlay

The **initial outlay** involves the immediate cash outflow necessary to purchase the asset and put it in operating order. This amount includes the cost of installing the asset (the asset's purchase price plus any expenses associated with shipping or installation) and any nonexpense cash outlays, such as increased working capital requirements. If we are considering a new sales outlet, there might be additional cash flows associated with investment in working capital in the form of increased inventory and cash necessary to operate the sales outlet. Although these cash flows are not included in the cost of the asset or even expensed on the books, they must be included in our analysis. The after-tax cost of expense items incurred as a result of new investment must also be included as cash outflows—for example, any training expenses or special engineering expenses that would not have been incurred otherwise.

Finally, if the investment decision is a replacement decision, the cash inflow associated with the selling price of the old asset, in addition to any tax effects resulting from its sale, must be included.

Determining the initial outlay is a complex matter. Table 5-14 summarizes some of the more common calculations involved in determining the initial outlay. This list is by no means exhaustive, but it should help simplify the calculations involved in the example that follows.

Tax Effects—Sale of Old Machine

Potentially, one of the most confusing initial outlay calculations is for a replacement project involving the incremental tax payment associated with the sale of an old machine. There are three possible tax situations dealing with the sale of an old asset:

1. The old asset is sold for a price above the depreciated value. Here the difference between the old machine's selling price and its depreciated value is considered a taxable gain and taxed at the marginal corporate tax rate. If, for example, the old machine was originally purchased for $15,000, had a book value of $10,000, and was sold for $17,000, assuming the firm's marginal corporate tax rate is 34 percent, the taxes due from the gain would be ($17,000 − $10,000) × (.34), or $2,380.
2. The old asset is sold for its depreciated value. In this case no taxes result, as there is neither a gain nor a loss in the asset's sale.
3. The old asset is sold for less than its depreciated value. In this case the difference between the depreciated book value and the salvage value of the asset is a taxable loss and may be used to offset ordinary income and, thus, results in tax savings. For example, if the depreciated book value of the asset is $10,000 and it is sold for $7,000, we have a $3,000 loss. Assuming the firm's marginal corporate tax rate is 34 percent, the cash inflow from tax savings is ($10,000 − $7,000) × (.34), or $1,020.

EXAMPLE

To clarify the calculation of the initial outlay, consider an example of Sibon Beverage in the 34 percent marginal tax bracket. Sibon is considering the purchase of a new machine for $30,000 to be used in bottling. It has a five-year life (according to IRS guidelines) and will be depreciated using the *simplified straight-line method*. (This depreciation method will be explained later.) The useful life of this new machine is also five years. The new machine will replace an existing machine, originally purchased for $30,000 ten years ago, which currently has five more years of expected useful life. The existing machine will generate $2,000 of depreciation expenses for each of the next five years, at which time the book value will be equal to zero. To put the new machine in

Table 5-14 Summary of Calculation of Initial Outlay Incremental After-Tax Cash Flow

1. Installed cost of asset
2. Additional nonexpense outlays incurred (for example, working-capital investments)
3. Additional expenses on an after-tax basis (for example, training expenses)
4. In a replacement decision, the *after-tax* cash flow associated with the sale of the old machine

running order, it is necessary to pay after-tax shipping charges of $2,000 and installation charges of $3,000. Because the new machine will work faster than the old one, it will require an increase in goods-in-process inventory of $5,000. Finally, the old machine can be sold to a scrap dealer for $15,000.

The installed cost of the new machine would be $30,000 plus $2,000 shipping and $3,000 installation fees, for a total of $35,000. Additional outflows are associated with taxes incurred on the sale of the old machine and with increased investment in inventory. Although the old machine has a book value of $10,000, it could be sold for $15,000. The increased taxes from gain on the sale will be equal to the selling price of the old machine less its depreciated book value times the firm's marginal tax rate, or ($15,000–$10,000) × (.34), or $1,700. The increase in goods-in-process inventory of $5,000 must also be considered part of the initial outlay, with an offsetting inflow of $5,000 corresponding to the recapture of this inventory occurring at the termination of the project. In effect, Sibon invests $5,000 in inventory now, resulting in an initial cash outlay, and liquidates this inventory in five years, resulting in a cash inflow at the end of the project. The total outlays associated with the new machine are $35,000 for its installed cost, $1,700 in increased taxes, and $5,000 in investment in inventory, for a total of $41,700. This is somewhat offset by the sale of the old machine for $15,000. Thus, the net initial outlay associated with this project is $26,700. These calculations are summarized in Table 5-15.

Table 5-15 Calculation of Initial Outlay for Sibon Bottling

Outflows:		
Purchase price	$30,000	
Shipping fee	2,000	
Installation fee	3,000	
Installed cost of machine		$ 35,000
Increased taxes from sale of old machine		
($15,000 − $10,000)(.34)		1,700
Increased investment in inventory		5,000
Total outflows		$ 41,700
Inflows:		
Salvage value of old machine		−15,000
Net initial outlay		$ 26,700

Differential Flows over Project's Life

The differential cash flows over the project's life involve the incremental after-tax cash flows resulting from increased revenues, plus savings in labor or material and reductions in selling expenses. Overhead items, such as utilities, heat, light, and executive salaries, are generally not affected. However, any resultant change in any of these categories must be included. Any increase in interest payments incurred as

Table 5-16 Summary of Calculation of Differential Cash Flows on After-Tax Basis
1. Added revenue offset by increased expenses
2. Labor and material savings
3. Increases in overhead incurred
4. Tax savings from an increase in depreciation expense if the new project is accepted
5. Do *not* include interest expenses if the project is financed by issuing debt, as this is accounted for in the required rate of return

a result of issuing bonds to finance the project should *not* be included, as the costs of funds needed to support the project are implicitly accounted for by discounting the project back to the present using the required rate of return. Finally, an adjustment for the incremental change in taxes should be made, including any increase in taxes that might result from increased profits or any tax savings from an increase in depreciation expenses. Increased depreciation expenses affect tax-related cash flows by reducing taxable income and thus lowering taxes. Table 5-16 lists some of the factors that might be involved in determining a project's differential cash flows. However, before looking at an example, we will briefly examine the calculation of depreciation.

Depreciation Calculation—Modified Accelerated Cost Recovery System

The Revenue Reconciliation Act of 1993 largely left intact the modified version of the Accelerated Cost Recovery System introduced in the Tax Reform Act of 1986. This modified version of the old accelerated cost recovery system (ACRS) is used for most tangible, depreciable property placed in service beginning in 1987. Under this method, the life of the asset is determined according to the asset's class life, which is assigned by the IRS; for example, most computer equipment has a five-year asset life. It also allows for only a half-year's deduction in the first year and a half-year's deduction in the year after the recovery period. The asset is then depreciated using the 200 percent declining balance method or an optional straight-line method.

Depreciation Calculation—Simplified Straight-Line Depreciation Method

Depreciation is calculated using a simplified straight-line method. This simplified process ignores the half-year convention that allows only a half-year's deduction in the year the project is placed in service and a half-year's deduction in the first year after the recovery period. By ignoring the half-year convention and assuming a zero salvage value, we are able to calculate annual depreciation by taking the project's initial depreciable value and dividing by its depreciable life as follows:

$$\frac{\text{annual depreciation using}}{\text{the simplified straight-line method}} = \frac{\text{initial depreciable value}}{\text{depreciable life}}$$

The initial depreciable value is equal to the cost of the asset plus any expenses necessary to get the new asset into operating order.

This is not how depreciation would actually be calculated. The reason we have simplified the calculation is to allow you to focus directly on what should and should not be included in the cash flow calculations. Moreover, because the tax laws change rather frequently, we are more interested in recognizing the tax implications of depreciation than in understanding the specific depreciation provisions of the current tax laws.

Table 5-17 Calculation of Depreciation for Sibon Using Simplified Straight-Line Method

New machine purchase price	$ 30,000
Shipping fee	2,000
Installation fee	3,000
Total depreciable value	$ 35,000
Divided by depreciable life	$35,000/5
Equals: Annual depreciation	$ 7,000

Table 5-18 Calculation of Differential Cash Flows for Sibon

		Book Profit	Cash Flow
Savings:	Reduced salary	$10,000	$10,000
	Reduced fringe benefits	1,000	1,000
	Reduced defects ($8,000 − $3,000)	5,000	5,000
Costs:	Increased maintenance expense	−4,000	−4,000
	Increased depreciation expense ($7,000 − $2,000)	−5,000	
Net savings before taxes		$ 7,000	$12,000
Taxes (34%)		−2,380 →	−2,380
Net cash flow after taxes			$ 9,620

Table 5-19 Summary of Calculation of Terminal Cash Flow on After-Tax Basis

1. The after-tax salvage value of the project
2. Cash outlays associated with the project's termination
3. Recapture of nonexpense outlays that occurred at the project's initiation (for example, working capital investments)

If we were to construct a cash flow diagram from this example (Figure 5-2), it would have an initial outlay of $26,700, differential cash flows during years 1 through 5 of $9,620, and an additional terminal cash flow at the end of year 5 of $5,000. The cash flow occurring in year 5 is $14,620, the sum of the differential cash flow in year 5 of $9,620, and the terminal cash flow of $5,000.

Cash flow diagrams similar to Figure 5-2 will be used through the remainder of this chapter with arrows above the time line indicating cash inflows and arrows below the time line denoting outflows.

Although the preceding calculations for determining the incremental, after-tax, net cash flows do not cover all possible cash flows, they do set up a framework in which almost any situation can be handled. To simplify this framework and to provide an overview of the calculations, Table 5-20 summarizes the rules in Tables 5-14, 5-16, and 5-19.

Discounted Cash Flow Criteria: Comprehensive Example

To demonstrate further the computations for the discounted cash flow techniques, assume that a manufacturing firm in the electronic components field is in the 34 percent marginal tax bracket with a 15 percent required rate of return or cost of capital. Management is considering replacing a hand-operated assembly machine with a fully automated assembly operation. Given the information in Table 5-21, we

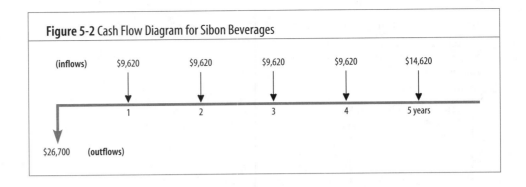

Figure 5-2 Cash Flow Diagram for Sibon Beverages

(inflows) $9,620 $9,620 $9,620 $9,620 $14,620

            1   2   3   4   5 years

$26,700   (outflows)

Table 5-20 Summary of Calculation of Incremental After-Tax Cash Flows

A. Initial Outlay
  1. Installed cost of asset
  2. Additional nonexpense outlays incurred
    (for example, working-capital investments)
  3. Additional expenses, on an after-tax basis (for example, training expenses)
  4. In a replacement decision, the after-tax cash flow associated with the sale of the old machine

B. Differential Cash Flows over the Project's Life
  1. Added revenue offset by increased expenses
  2. Labor and material savings
  3. Increases in overhead incurred
  4. Tax savings from an increase in depreciation if the new project is accepted
  5. Do not include interest expenses if the project is financed by issuing debt,
    as this is accounted for in the required rate of return

C. Terminal Cash Flow
  1. The after-tax salvage value of the project
  2. Cash outlays associated with the project's termination
  3. Recapture of nonexpense outlays that occurred at the project's initiation
    (for example, working capital investments)

---

want to determine the cash flows associated with this proposal, the project's net present value, profitability index, and internal rate of return, and then to apply the appropriate decision criteria.

First, the initial outlay is determined to be $44,680, as reflected in Table 5-22. Next, the differential cash flows over the project's life are calculated as shown in Table 5-23, yielding an estimated $15,008 cash flow per annum. In making these computations, the incremental change in depreciation was determined by first calculating the original depreciable value, which is equal to the cost of the new machine ($50,000) plus any expense charges necessary to get the new machine in operating order (shipping fee of $1,000 plus the installation fee of $5,000). This depreciable amount was then divided by five years. The annual depreciation lost with the sale of the old machine was then subtracted out ($10,000/5 = $2,000 per year for the old machine's remaining five years of life). Once the change in taxes is determined from the incremental change in book profit, it is subtracted from the net cash flow savings before taxes, yielding the $15,008 net cash flow after taxes.

Finally, the terminal cash flow associated with the project has to be determined. In this case, because the new machine is expected to have a zero salvage value, there will be no terminal cash flow. The cash flow diagram associated with this project is shown in Figure 5-3.

Table 5-21 Comprehensive Capital-Budgeting Example

Existing situation:	One part-time operator—salary $12,000
	Variable overtime—$1,000 per year
	Fringe benefits—$1,000 per year
	Cost of defects—$6,000 per year
	Current book value—$10,000
	Expected life—15 years
	Expected salvage value—$0
	Age—10 years
	Annual depreciation—$2,000 per year
	Current salvage value of old machine—$12,000
	Annual maintenance—$0
	Marginal tax rate—34 percent
	Required rate of return—15 percent
Proposed situation:	Fully automated operation—no operator necessary
	Cost of machine—$50,000
	After-tax shipping fee—$1,000
	After-tax installation costs—$5,000
	Expected economic life—5 years
	Depreciation method—simplified straight-line over 5 years
	Salvage value after 5 years—$0
	Annual maintenance—$1,000 per year
	Cost of defects—$1,000 per year

Table 5-22 Calculation of Initial Outlay for Comprehensive Example

Outflows:	Cost of new machine	$50,000
	Shipping fee	1,000
	Installation cost	5,000
	Increased taxes on sale of old machine	
	($12,000–$10,000) (.34)	680
Inflows:	Salvage value–old machine	−12,000
	Net initial outlay	$ 44,680

Table 5-23 Calculation of Differential Cash Flows for Comprehensive Example

		Book Profit	Cash Flow
Savings:	Reduced salary	$12,000	$12,000
	Reduced variable overtime	1,000	1,000
	Reduced fringe benefits	1,000	1,000
	Reduced defects ($6,000 − $1,000)	5,000	5,000
Costs:	Increased maintenance expense	−1,000	−1,000
	Increased depreciation expense		
	($11,200 − $2,000)	−9,200	
Net savings before taxes		$ 8,800	$18,000
Taxes (34%)		−2,992 →	−2,992
Net cash flow after taxes			$15,008

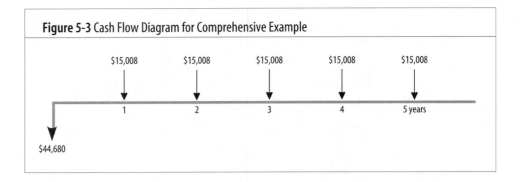

Figure 5-3 Cash Flow Diagram for Comprehensive Example

The net present value for this project is calculated as follows:

$$NPV = \sum_{t=1}^{n} \frac{ACF_t}{(1 + k)^t} - IO$$

$$= \sum_{t=1}^{5} \frac{\$15,008}{(1 + .15)^t} - \$44,680$$

$$= 15,008\left(PVIFA_{15\%,5\,yr}\right) - \$44,680$$

$$= \$15,008(3.352) - \$44,680$$

$$= \$50,307 - \$44,680$$

$$= \$5627$$

Because its net present value is greater than zero, the project should be accepted. The profitability index, which gives a measure of relative desirability of a project, is calculated as follows:

$$PI = \frac{\sum_{t=1}^{n} \dfrac{ACF_t}{(1 + k)^t}}{IO}$$

$$= \frac{\$50,307}{\$44,680}$$

$$= 1.13$$

Because the project's PI is greater than 1, the project should be accepted.

The internal rate of return can be determined directly from the *PVIFA* table, as follows:

$$IO = \sum_{t=1}^{n} \frac{ACF_t}{(1 + IRR)^t}$$

$$\$44,680 = \$15,008\left(PVIFA_{i,5\,yr}\right)$$

$$2.977 = PVIFA_{i,5\,yr}$$

Looking for the value of the $PVIFA_{i,5yr}$ in the 5-year row of the table in Appendix E, we find that the value of 2.977 occurs between the 20 percent column (2.991) and the 21 percent column (2.926). As a result, the project's internal rate of return is between 20 percent and 21 percent, and the project should be accepted.

Applying the decision criteria to this example, we find that each of them indicates the project should be accepted, as the net present value is positive, the profitability index is greater than 1.0, and the internal rate of return is greater than the firm's required rate of return of 15 percent.

CAPITAL RATIONING

The use of our capital-budgeting decision rules implies that the size of the capital budget is determined by the availability of acceptable investment proposals. However, a firm may place a limit on the dollar size of the capital budget. This situation is called **capital rationing.** As we will see, an examination of capital rationing will not only enable us to deal with complexities of the real world but will serve to demonstrate the superiority of the NPV method over the IRR method for capital budgeting.

Using the internal rate of return as the firm's decision rule, a firm accepts all projects with an internal rate of return greater than the firm's required rate of return. This rule is illustrated in Figure 5-4 where projects A through E would be chosen. However, when capital rationing is imposed, the dollar size of the total investment is limited by the budget constraint. In Figure 5-4, the budget constraint of $X precludes the acceptance of an attractive investment, project E. This situation obviously contradicts prior decision rules. Moreover, the solution of choosing the projects with the highest internal rate of return is complicated by the fact that some projects may be indivisible; for example, it is meaningless to recommend that half of project D be acquired.

Rationale for Capital Rationing

We will first ask why capital rationing exists and whether it is rational. In general, three principal reasons are given for imposing a capital rationing constraint. First, management may think market conditions are temporarily adverse. In the period surrounding the stock market crash of 1987, this reason was frequently given. At that time, interest rates were high, and stock prices were depressed. Second, there may be a shortage of qualified managers to direct new projects; this can happen when projects are of a highly technical nature. Third, there may be intangible considerations. For example, management may simply fear debt, wishing to avoid interest payments at any cost. Or perhaps issuance of common stock may be limited to maintain a stable dividend policy.

Despite strong evidence that capital rationing exists in practice, the question remains as to its effect on the firm. In brief, the effect is negative, and to what degree depends on the severity of the rationing. If the rationing is minor and short-lived, the firm's share price will not suffer to any great extent. In this case, capital rationing can probably be excused, although it should be noted that any capital

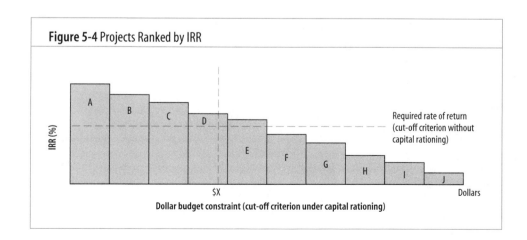

Figure 5-4 Projects Ranked by IRR

rationing that rejects projects with positive net present values is contrary to the firm's goal of maximization of shareholders' wealth. If the capital rationing is a result of the firm's decision to limit dramatically the number of new projects or to limit total investment to internally generated funds, then this policy will eventually have a significantly negative effect on the firm's share price. For example, a lower share price will eventually result from lost competitive advantage if, owing to a decision to limit arbitrarily its capital budget, a firm fails to upgrade its products and manufacturing process.

Capital Rationing and Project Selection

If the firm decides to impose a capital constraint on investment projects, the appropriate decision criterion is to select the set of projects with the highest net present value subject to the capital constraint. This guideline may preclude merely taking the highest-ranked projects in terms of the profitability index or the internal rate of return. If the projects shown in Figure 5-4 are divisible, the last project accepted may be only partially accepted. Although partial acceptances may be possible in some cases, the indivisibility of most capital investments prevents it. If a project is a sales outlet or a truck, it may be meaningless to purchase half a sales outlet or half a truck.

To illustrate this procedure, consider a firm with a budget constraint of $1 million and five indivisible projects available to it, as given in Table 5-24. If the highest-ranked projects were taken, projects A and B would be taken first. At that point there would not be enough funds available to take project C; hence, projects D and E would be taken. However, a higher total net present value is provided by the combination of projects A and C. Thus, projects A and C should be selected from the set of projects available. This illustrates our guideline: to select the set of projects that maximizes the firm's net present value.

Project Ranking

In the past, we have proposed that all projects with a positive net present value, a profitability index greater than 1.0, or an internal rate of return greater than the required rate of return be accepted, assuming there is no capital rationing. However, this acceptance is not always possible. In some cases, when two projects are judged acceptable by the discounted cash flow criteria, it may be necessary to select only one of them, as they are mutually exclusive.

Mutually exclusive projects occur when a set of investment proposals perform essentially the same task; acceptance of one will necessarily mean rejection of the others. For example, a company considering the installation of a computer system may evaluate three or four systems, all of which may have positive net present values; however, the acceptance of one system will automatically mean rejection of the others. In general, to deal with mutually exclusive projects, we will simply rank

Table 5-24 Capital-Rationing Example of Five Indivisible Projects

Project	Initial Outlay	Profitability Index	Net Present Value
A	$200,000	2.4	$280,000
B	200,000	2.3	260,000
C	800,000	1.7	560,000
D	300,000	1.3	90,000
E	300,000	1.2	60,000

them by means of the discounted cash flow criteria and select the project with the highest ranking. On occasion, however, problems of conflicting ranking may arise. As we will see, in general the net present value method is the preferred decision-making tool because it leads to the selection of the project that increases shareholder wealth the most.

Problems in Project Ranking

There are three general types of ranking problems: the size disparity problem, the time disparity problem, and the unequal lives problem. Each involves the possibility of conflict in the ranks yielded by the various discounted cash flow capital-budgeting criteria. As noted previously, when one discounted cash flow criterion gives an accept signal, they will all give an accept signal, but they will not necessarily rank all projects in the same order. In most cases this disparity is not critical; however, for mutually exclusive projects the ranking order is important.

Size Disparity

The *size disparity problem* occurs when mutually exclusive projects of unequal size are examined. This problem is most easily clarified with an example.

EXAMPLE

Suppose a firm is considering two mutually exclusive projects, A and B, both with required rates of return of 10 percent. Project A involves a $200 initial outlay and cash inflow of $300 at the end of one year, whereas project B involves an initial outlay of $1,500 and a cash inflow of $1,900 at the end of one year. The net present value, profitability index, and internal rate of return for these projects are given in Table 5-25.

In this case, if the net present value criterion is used, project B should be accepted, whereas if the profitability index or the internal rate of return criterion is used, project A should be chosen. The question now becomes: Which project is better? The answer depends on whether capital rationing exists. Without capital rationing, project B is better because it provides the largest increase in shareholders' wealth; that is, it has a larger net present value. If there is a capital constraint, the problem then focuses on what can be done with the additional $1,300 that is freed if project A is chosen (costing $200, as opposed to $1,500). If the firm can earn more on project A plus the project financed with the additional $1,300 than it can on project B, then project A and the marginal project should be accepted. In effect, we are attempting to select the set of projects that maximizes the firm's NPV. Thus, if the marginal project has a net present value greater than $154.40 ($227.10 − $72.70), selecting it plus project A with a net present value of $72.70 will provide a net present value greater than $227.10, the net present value for project B.

In summary, whenever the size disparity problem results in conflicting rankings between mutually exclusive projects, the project with the largest net present value will be selected, provided there is no capital rationing. When capital rationing exists, the firm should select the set of projects with the largest net present value.

Time Disparity

The *time disparity problem* and the conflicting rankings that accompany it result from the differing reinvestment assumptions made by the net present value and internal rate of return decision criteria. The NPV criterion assumes that cash flows

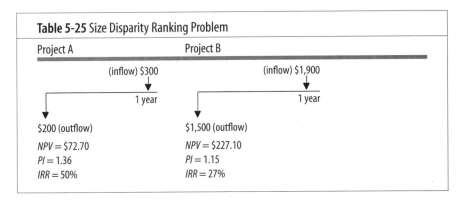

Table 5-25 Size Disparity Ranking Problem

Project A	Project B
(inflow) $300	(inflow) $1,900
1 year	1 year
$200 (outflow)	$1,500 (outflow)
NPV = $72.70	NPV = $227.10
PI = 1.36	PI = 1.15
IRR = 50%	IRR = 27%

over the life of the project can be reinvested at the required rate of return or cost of capital, whereas the IRR criterion implicitly assumes that the cash flows over the life of the project can be reinvested at the internal rate of return. Again, this problem may be illustrated through the use of an example.

EXAMPLE

Suppose a firm with a required rate of return or cost of capital of 10 percent and with no capital constraint is considering the two mutually exclusive projects illustrated in Table 5-26. The net present value and profitability index indicate that project A is the better of the two, whereas the internal rate of return indicates that project B is the better. Project B receives its cash flows earlier than project A, and the different assumptions made as to how these flows can be reinvested result in the difference in rankings. Which criterion should be followed depends on which reinvestment assumption is used. The net present value criterion is preferred in this case because it makes the most acceptable assumption for the wealth-maximizing firm. It is certainly the most conservative assumption that can be made because the required rate of return is the lowest possible reinvestment rate. Moreover, as we have already noted, the net present value method maximizes the value of the firm and the shareholders' wealth. An alternate solution is to use the *MIRR* method.

Unequal Lives

The final ranking problem to be examined centers on the question of whether it is appropriate to compare mutually exclusive projects with different lifespans.

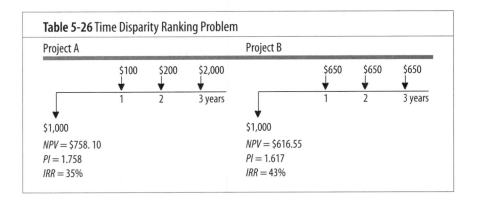

Table 5-26 Time Disparity Ranking Problem

Project A	Project B
$100 $200 $2,000	$650 $650 $650
1 2 3 years	1 2 3 years
$1,000	$1,000
NPV = $758. 10	NPV = $616.55
PI = 1.758	PI = 1.617
IRR = 35%	IRR = 43%

Suppose a firm with a 10 percent required rate of return is faced with the problem of replacing an aging machine and is considering two replacement machines, one with a three-year life and one with a six-year life. The relevant cash flow information for these projects is given in Table 5-27.

Examining the discounted cash flow criteria, we find that the net present value and profitability index criteria indicate that project B is the better project, whereas the internal rate of return favors project A. This ranking inconsistency is caused by the different life spans of the projects being compared. In this case the decision is a difficult one because the projects are not comparable.

The problem of incomparability of projects with different lives arises because future profitable investment proposals may be rejected without being included in the analysis. This can easily be seen in a replacement problem such as the present example, in which two mutually exclusive machines with different lives are being considered. In this case, a comparison of the net present values alone on each of these projects would be misleading. If the project with the shorter life were taken, at its termination the firm could replace the machine and receive additional benefits, whereas acceptance of the project with the longer life would exclude this possibility, a possibility that is not included in the analysis. The key question thus becomes: Does today's investment decision include all future profitable investment proposals in its analysis? If not, the projects are not comparable. In this case, if project B is taken, then the project that could have been taken after three years when project A terminates is automatically rejected without being included in the analysis. Thus, acceptance of project B not only forces rejection of project A, but also forces rejection of any replacement machine that might have been considered for years 4 through 6 without including this replacement machine in the analysis.

There are several methods to deal with this situation. The first option is to assume that the cash inflows from the shorter-lived investment will be reinvested at the required rate of return until the termination of the longer-lived asset. Although this approach is the simplest, merely calculating the net present value, it actually ignores the problem at hand—that of allowing for participation in another replacement opportunity with a positive net present value. The proper solution thus becomes the projection of reinvestment opportunities into the future—that is, making assumptions about possible future investment opportunities. Unfortunately, while the first method is too simplistic to be of any value, the second is extremely difficult, requiring extensive cash flow forecasts. The final technique for confronting the problem is to assume that reinvestment opportunities in the future will be similar to the current ones. The two most common ways of doing this are by creating a replacement chain to equalize life spans or calculating the project's equivalent annual annuity (EAA). Using a replacement chain, the present example would call for the creation of a two-chain cycle for project A; that is, we assume that project A can be replaced with a similar investment at the end of three years. Thus, project A would be viewed as two A projects occurring back to back, as illustrated in Figure 5-4. The net present value on this replacement chain is $426.50, which is comparable with project B's net present value. Therefore, project A should be accepted because the net present value of its replacement chain is greater than the net present value of project B.

One problem with replacement chains is that depending on the life of each project, it can be quite difficult to come up with equivalent lives. For example, if the two projects had 7- and 13-year lives, a 91-year replacement chain would be needed to establish equivalent lives. In this case, it is easier to determine the project's **equivalent annual annuity (EAA)**. A project's EAA is simply an annuity cash flow that yields the same present value as the project's NPV. To

Table 5-27 Unequal Lives Ranking Problem

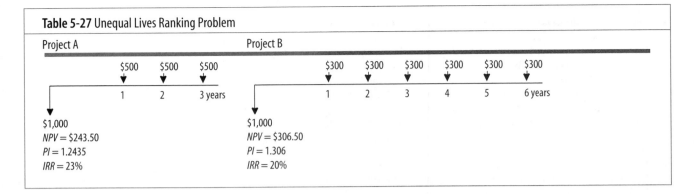

Project A				Project B						

Project A: $500, $500, $500 at years 1, 2, 3 years
$1,000
NPV = $243.50
PI = 1.2435
IRR = 23%

Project B: $300, $300, $300, $300, $300, $300 at years 1, 2, 3, 4, 5, 6 years
$1,000
NPV = $306.50
PI = 1.306
IRR = 20%

calculate a project's EAA, we need only calculate a project's NPV and then divide that number by the $PVIFA_{i,n}$ to determine the dollar value of an *n*-year annuity that would produce the same NPV as the project. This can be done in two steps as follows:

Step 1: *Calculate the project's NPV.* In Table 5-27 we determined that project A had an NPV of $243.50, whereas project B had an NPV of $306.50.

Step 2: *Calculate the EAA.* The EAA is determined by dividing each project's NPV by the $PVIFA_{i,n}$ where *i* is the required rate of return and *n* is the project's life. This determines the level of an annuity cash flow that would produce the same NPV as the project. For project A the $PVIFA_{10\%,3yr}$ is equal to 2.487, whereas the $PVIFA_{10\%, 6yr}$ for project B is equal to 4.355. Dividing each project's NPV by the appropriate $PVIFA_{i,n}$ we determine the EAA for each project:

$$EAA_A = NPV/PVIFA_{i,n}$$ $$= \$243.50/2.487$$ $$= \$97.91$$ $$EAA_B = \$306.50/4.355$$ $$= \$70.38$$

(5-16)

How do we interpret the EAA? For a project with an *n*-year life, it tells us what the dollar value is of an *n*-year annual annuity that would provide the same NPV as the project. Thus, for project A, it means that a three-year annuity of $97.91 given a discount rate of 10 percent would produce a net present value the same as project A's net present value, which is $243.50. We can now compare the equivalent annual annuities directly to determine which project is better. We can do this because we now have found the level of annual annuity that produces an NPV equivalent to the project's NPV. Thus, because they are both annual annuities they are comparable. An easy way to see this is to use the EAAs to create infinite-life replacement chains. To do this, we need only calculate the present value of an infinite stream or perpetuity of equivalent annual annuities. This is done by using the present value of an infinite annuity formula, that is, simply dividing the equivalent annual annuity by the appropriate discount rate. In this case we find:

$$NPV_{\infty, A} = \$97.91/.10$$ $$= \$979.10$$ $$NPV_{\infty, B} = \$70.38/.10$$ $$= \$703.80$$

Here we have calculated the present value of an infinite-life replacement chain. Because the EAA method provides the same results as the infinite-life replacement chain, it really doesn't matter which method you prefer to use.

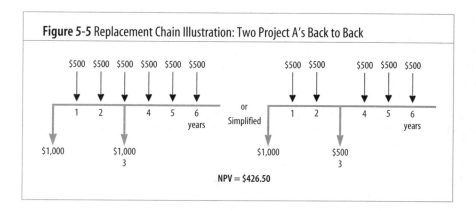

Figure 5-5 Replacement Chain Illustration: Two Project A's Back to Back

SUMMARY

In this chapter, we examine the measurement of incremental cash flows associated with a firm's investment proposals which are used to evaluate those proposals. We focus only on the incremental or different after-tax cash flows attributed to the investment proposal. Care is taken to beware of cash flows diverted from existing products, look for incidental or synergistic effects, consider working capital requirements, consider incremental expenses, ignore sunk costs, account for opportunity costs, examine overhead costs carefully, and ignore interest payments and financing flows.

In general, a project's cash flows fall into one of three categories: (1) the initial outlay, (2) the differential flows over the project's life, and (3) the terminal cash flow. A summary of the typical entries in each of these categories appears in Table 5-7.

Several complications are introduced into the capital-budgeting process as a result of the imposition of a limit on the availability of funds for capital-budgeting projects. In this chapter, we also examine capital rationing and the problems it can create by imposing a limit on the dollar size of the capital budget. Although capital rationing does not, in general, lead to the goal of maximization of shareholders' wealth, it does exist in practice. We also discuss problems associated with the evaluation of mutually exclusive projects. Mutually exclusive projects occur when a set of investment proposals perform essentially the same task. In general, to deal with mutually exclusive projects, we rank them by means of the discounted cash flow criteria and select the project with the highest ranking. Conflicting rankings may arise because of the size disparity problem, the time disparity problem, and unequal lives. The problem of incomparability of projects with different lives is not simply a result of the different lives; rather, it arises because future profitable investment proposals may be rejected without being included in the analysis. Replacement chains and equivalent annual annuities are presented as possible solutions to this problem.

STUDY QUESTIONS

5-1. Why do we focus on cash flows rather than accounting profits in making our capital-budgeting decisions? Why are we interested only in incremental cash flows rather than total cash flows?

5-2. If depreciation is not a cash flow item, does it affect the level of cash flows from a project in any way? Why?

5-3. If a project requires additional investment in working capital, how should this be treated in calculating cash flows?

5-4. How do sunk costs affect the determination of cash flows associated with an investment proposal?

5-5. What are mutually exclusive projects? Why might the existence of mutually exclusive projects cause problems in the implementation of the discounted cash flow capital-budgeting criteria?

5-6. What are common reasons for capital rationing? Is capital rationing rational?

5-7. How should managers compare two mutually exclusive projects of unequal size? Would your approach change if capital rationing existed?

5-8. What causes the time disparity ranking problem? What reinvestment rate assumptions are associated with the net present value and internal rate of return capital-budgeting criteria?

5-9. When might two mutually exclusive projects having unequal lives be incomparable? How should managers deal with this problem?

SELF-TEST PROBLEMS

ST- 1. The Scotty Gator Corporation of Meadville, Pa., maker of Scotty's electronic components, is considering replacing one of its current hand-operated assembly machines with a new fully automated machine. This replacement would mean the elimination of one employee generating salary and benefit savings. Given the following information, determine the cash flows associated with this replacement.

Existing situation:	One full-time machine operator—salary and benefits, $25,000 per year
	Cost of maintenance—$2,000 per year
	Cost of defects—$6,000 per year
	Original depreciable value of old machine—$50,000
	Annual depreciation—$5,000 per year
	Expected life—10 years
	Age—five years old
	Expected salvage value in five years—$0
	Current salvage value—$5,000
	Marginal tax rate—34 percent
Proposed situation:	Fully automated machine—no operator required
	Cost of machine—$60,000
	Installation fee—$3,000
	Shipping fee—$3,000
	Cost of maintenance—$3,000 per year
	Cost of defects—$3,000 per year
	Expected life—five years
	Salvage value—$20,000
	Depreciation method—simplified straight-line method over five years

ST-2. The J. Serrano Corporation is considering signing a one-year contract with one of two computer-based marketing firms. Although one is more expensive, it offers a more extensive program and thus will provide higher after-tax net cash flows. Assume these two options are mutually exclusive and that the required rate of return is 12 percent. Given the following after-tax net cash flows:

Year	Option A	Option B
0	−$50,000	−$100,000
1	70,000	130,000

    a. Calculate the net present value.

    b. Calculate the profitability index.

    c. Calculate the internal rate of return.

    d. If there is no capital-rationing constraint, which project should be selected? If there is a capital-rationing constraint, how should the decision be made?

STUDY PROBLEMS (SET A)

5-1A. (Capital Gains Tax) The J. Harris Corporation is considering selling one of its old assembly machines. The machine, purchased for $30,000 five years ago, had an expected life of ten years and an expected salvage value of zero. Assume Harris uses simplified straight-line depreciation, creating depreciation of $3,000 per year, and could sell this old machine for $35,000. Also assume a 34 percent marginal tax rate.

    a. What would be the taxes associated with this sale?

    b. If the old machine were sold for $25,000, what would be the taxes associated with this sale?

    c. If the old machine were sold for $15,000, what would be the taxes associated with this sale?

    d. If the old machine were sold for $12,000, what would be the taxes associated with this sale?

5-2A. (Cash Flow Calculations) The Winky Corporation, maker of electronic components, is considering replacing a hand-operated machine used in the manufacture of electronic components with a new fully automated machine. Given the following information, determine the cash flows associated with this replacement.

Existing situation:	One full-time machine operator—salary $20,000 per year
	Cost of maintenance—$5000 per year
	Cost of defects—$5000 per year
	Original cost of old machine—$30,000
	Expected life—10 years
	Age—five years old
	Expected salvage value—$0
	Depreciation method—simplified straight-line over 10 years, $3000 per year
	Current salvage value—$10,000
	Marginal tax rate—34 percent
Proposed situation:	Fully automated machine—no operator required
	Cost of machine—$55,000
	Installation fee—$5000
	Cost of maintenance—$6000 per year
	Cost of defects—$2000 per year
	Expected life—five years
	Salvage value—$0
	Depreciation method—simplified straight-line method over five years

5-3A. (Capital-Budgeting Calculation) Given the cash flow information in problem 5-2A and a required rate of return of 15 percent, compute the following for the automated machine:

    a. Payback period

    b. Net present value

    c. Profitability index

    d. Internal rate of return

Should this project be accepted?

5-4A. (New Project Analysis) The Chung Chemical Corporation is considering the purchase of a chemical analysis machine. Although the machine being considered will not produce any increase in sales revenues, it will result in a before-tax reduction of labor costs by $35,000 per year. The machine has a purchase price of $100,000, and it would cost an additional $5,000 to properly install this machine. In addition, to properly operate this machine, inventory must be increased by $5,000. This machine has an expected life of ten years, after which it will have no salvage value. Also, assume simplified straight-line depreciation and that this machine is being depreciated down to zero, a 34 percent marginal tax rate, and a required rate of return of 15 percent.

    a. What is the initial outlay associated with this project?

    b. What are the annual after-tax cash flows associated with this project, for years 1 through 9?

    c. What is the terminal cash flow in year 10 (what is the annual after-tax cash flow in year 10 plus any additional cash flows associated with termination of the project)?

    d. Should this machine be purchased?

5-5A. (New Project Analysis) Raymobile Motors is considering the purchase of a new production machine for $500,000. Although the purchase of this machine will not produce any increase in sales revenues, it will result in a before-tax reduction of labor costs by $150,000 per year. To operate this machine properly, workers would have to go through a brief training session that would cost $25,000. In addition, it would cost $5,000 to install this machine properly. Also, because this machine is extremely efficient, its purchase would necessitate an increase in inventory of $30,000. This machine has an expected life of ten years, after which it will have no salvage value. Assume simplified straight-line depreciation and that this machine is being depreciated down to zero, a 34 percent marginal tax rate, and a required rate of return of 15 percent.

    a. What is the initial outlay associated with this project?

    b. What are the annual after-tax cash flows associated with this project, for years 1 through 9?

    c. What is the terminal cash flow in year 10 (what is the annual after-tax cash flow in year 10 plus any additional cash flows associated with termination of the project)?

    d. Should this machine be purchased?

5-6A. (New Project Analysis) Garcia's Truckin' Inc. is considering the purchase of a new production machine for $200,000. Although the purchase of this machine will not produce any increase in sales revenues, it will result in a before-tax reduction of labor costs by $50,000 per year. To operate this machine properly, workers would have to go through a brief training session that would cost $5,000. In addition, it would cost $5,000 to install this machine properly. Also, because this machine is extremely efficient, its purchase would necessitate an increase in inventory of $20,000. This machine has an expected life of ten years, after which it will have no salvage value. Finally, to purchase the new machine, it appears that the firm would have to borrow $100,000 at 8 percent interest from its local bank, resulting in additional interest payments of $8,000 per year. Assume simplified straight-line depreciation and that this machine is being depreciated down to zero, a 34 percent marginal tax rate, and a required rate of return of 10 percent.

    a. What is the initial outlay associated with this project?

    b. What are the annual after-tax cash flows associated with this project, for years 1 through 9?

    c. What is the terminal cash flow in year 10 (what is the annual after-tax cash flow in year 10 plus any additional cash flows associated with termination of the project)?

    d. Should this machine be purchased?

5-7A. (Cash Flow—Capital-Budgeting Calculation) The C. Duncan Chemical Corporation is considering replacing one of its machines with a new, more efficient machine. The old machine presently has a book value of $100,000 and could be sold for $60,000. The old machine is being depreciated on a simplified straight-line basis down to a salvage value of zero over the next five years, generating depreciation of $20,000 per year. The replacement machine would cost $300,000, and have an expected life of five years, after which it could be sold for $50,000. Because of reductions in defects and material savings, the new machine would produce cash benefits of $90,000 per year before depreciation and taxes. Assuming simplified straight-line depreciation, and that the replacement machine is being depreciated down to zero for tax purposes even though it can be sold at termination for $50,000, a 34 percent marginal tax rate, and a required rate of return of 15 percent, find:

   a. The payback period
   b. The net present value
   c. The profitability index
   d. The internal rate of return

5-8A. (Cash Flow—Capital-Budgeting Calculation) The Sumitomo Chemical Corporation is considering replacing a five-year-old machine that originally cost $50,000, presently has a book value of $25,000, and could be sold for $60,000. This machine is currently being depreciated using the simplified straight-line method down to a terminal value of zero over the next five years, generating depreciation of $5,000 per year. The replacement machine would cost $125,000, and have a five-year expected life over which it would be depreciated down using the simplified straight-line method and have no salvage value at the end of five years. The new machine would produce savings before depreciation and taxes of $45,000 per year. Assuming a 34 percent marginal tax rate and a required rate of return of 10 percent, calculate:

   a. The payback period
   b. The net present value
   c. The profitability index
   d. The internal rate of return

5-9A. (Cash Flow—Capital-Budgeting Calculation) Jabot Cosmetics Corporation is considering replacing a 10-year-old machine that originally cost $30,000, has a current book value of $10,000 with five years of expected life left, and is being depreciated using the simplified straight-line method over its fifteen-year expected life down to a terminal value of zero in five years, generating depreciation of $2,000 per year. The replacement machine being considered would cost $80,000 and have a five-year expected life over which it would be depreciated using the simplified straight-line method down to zero. At termination in five years the new machine would have a salvage value of $40,000. Material efficiencies resulting from the replacement would result in savings of $30,000 per year before depreciation and taxes. Currently, the old machine could be sold for $15,000. Assuming simplified straight-line depreciation, a 34 percent marginal tax rate, and a required rate of return of 20 percent, calculate:

   a. The payback period
   b. The net present value
   c. The profitability index
   d. The internal rate of return

5-10A. (Size Disparity Ranking Problem) The D. Dorner Farms Corporation is considering purchasing one of two fertilizer-herbicides for the upcoming year. The more expensive of the two is the better and will produce a higher yield. Assume these projects are mutually exclusive and that the required rate of return is 10 percent. Given the following after-tax net cash flows:

Year	Project A	Project B
0	−$500	−$5000
1	700	6000

   a. Calculate the net present value.
   b. Calculate the profitability index.

c. Calculate the internal rate of return.

d. If there is no capital-rationing constraint, which project should be selected? If there is a capital-rationing constraint, how should the decision be made?

5-11A. (Time Disparity Ranking Problem) The State Spartan Corporation is considering two mutually exclusive projects. The cash flows associated with those projects are as follows:

Year	Project A	Project B
0	−$50,000	−$50,000
1	15,625	0
2	15,625	0
3	15,625	0
4	15,625	0
5	15,625	$100,000

The required rate of return on these projects is 10 percent.

a. What is each project's payback period?

b. What is each project's net present value?

c. What is each project's internal rate of return?

d. What has caused the ranking conflict?

e. Which project should be accepted? Why?

5-12A. (Unequal Lives Ranking Problem) The B. T. Knight Corporation is considering two mutually exclusive pieces of machinery that perform the same task. The two alternatives available provide the following set of after-tax net cash flows:

Year	Equipment A	Equipment B
0	−$20,000	−$20,000
1	12,590	6,625
2	12,590	6,625
3	12,590	6,625
4		6,625
5		6,625
6		6,625
7		6,625
8		6,625
9		6,625

Equipment A has an expected life of three years, whereas equipment B has an expected life of nine years. Assume a required rate of return of 15 percent.

a. Calculate each project's payback period.

b. Calculate each project's net present value.

c. Calculate each project's internal rate of return.

d. Are these projects comparable?

e. Compare these projects using replacement chains and EAA. Which project should be selected? Support your recommendation.

5-13A. (EAAs) The Andrzejewski Corporation is considering two mutually exclusive projects, one with a three-year life and one with a seven-year life. The after-tax cash flows from the two projects are as follows:

Year	Project A	Project B
0	−$50,000	−$50,000
1	20,000	36,000
2	20,000	36,000
3	20,000	36,000
4	20,000	
5	20,000	
6	20,000	
7	20,000	

a. Assuming a 10 percent required rate of return on both projects, calculate each project's EAA. Which project should be selected?

b. Calculate the present value of an infinite-life replacement chain for each project.

5-14A. (Capital Rationing) Cowboy Hat Company of Stillwater, Oklahoma, is considering seven capital investment proposals, for which the funds available are limited to a maximum of $12 million. The projects are independent and have the following costs and profitability indexes associated with them:

Project	Cost	Profitability Index
A	$4,000,000	1.18
B	3,000,000	1.08
C	5,000,000	1.33
D	6,000,000	1.31
E	4,000,000	1.19
F	6,000,000	1.20
G	4,000,000	1.18

a. Under strict capital rationing, which projects should be selected?

b. What problems are there with capital rationing?

It's been two months since you took a position as an assistant financial analyst at Caledonia Products. While your boss has been pleased with your work, he is still a bit hesitant about unleashing you without supervision. Your next assignment involves both the calculation of the cash flows associated with a new investment under consideration and the evaluation of several mutually exclusive projects. Given your lack of tenure at Caledonia, you have been asked not only to provide a recommendation, but also to respond to a number of questions aimed at judging your understanding of the capital budgeting process. The memorandum you received outlining your assignment follows:

TO: The Financial Analyst

FROM: Mr. V. Morrison, CEO, Caledonia Products

RE: Cash Flow Analysis and Capital Rationing

We are currently considering the purchase of a new fully automated machine to replace an older, manually operated one. The machine being replaced, now five years old, originally had an expected life of ten years. It was being depreciated using the simplified straight-line method from $20,000 down to zero, thus generating $2,000 in depreciation per year, and could be sold for $25,000. The old machine took one operator, who earned $15,000 per year in salary and $2,000 per year in fringe benefits. Since the new machine is fully automated, this worker would no longer be needed. The annual costs of maintenance and defects associated with the old machine were $7,000 and $3,000, respectively. The replacement machine being considered had a purchase price of $50,000, a salvage value after five years of $10,000, and would be depreciated over five years using the simplified straight-line depreciation method down to zero. To get the automated machine in running order, there would be a $3,000 shipping fee and a $2,000 installation charge. In addition, because the new machine would work faster than the old one, investment in raw materials and goods-in-process inventories would need to be increased by a total of $5,000. The annual costs of maintenance and defects on the new machine would be $2,000 and $4,000, respectively. The new machine also requires maintenance workers to be specially trained; fortunately, a similar machine was purchased three months ago, and at that time the maintenance workers went through the $5,000 training program needed to familiarize themselves with the new equipment. Caledonia's management is uncertain whether or not to charge half of this $5,000 training fee toward the new project. Finally, to purchase the new machine, it appears the firm would have to borrow an additional $20,000 at 10 percent interest from its local bank, resulting in additional interest payments of $2,000 per year. The required rate of return on projects of this kind is 20 percent and Caledonia is in the 34 percent marginal tax bracket.

a. Should Caledonia focus on cash flows or accounting profits in making our capital-budgeting decisions? Should we be interested in incremental cash flows, incremental profits, total cash flows or total profits?

b. How does depreciation affect cash flows?

c. How do sunk costs affect the determination of cash flows?

d. What is the project's initial outlay?

e. What are the differential cash flows over the project's life?

f. What is the terminal cash flow?

g. Draw a cash flow diagram for this project.

h. What is its net present value?

i. What is its internal rate of return?

j. Should the project be accepted? Why or why not?

You have *also* been asked for your views on three unrelated sets of projects. Each set of projects involves two mutually exclusive projects. These projects follow:

k. Caledonia is considering two investments with one-year lives. The more expensive of the two is the better and will produce more savings. Assume these projects are mutually exclusive and that the required rate of return is 10 percent. Given the following after-tax net cash flows:

Year	Project A	Project B
0	−$195,000	−$1,200,000
1	240,000	1,650,000

1. Calculate the net present value.
2. Calculate the profitability index.
3. Calculate the internal rate of return.
4. If there is no capital rationing constraint, which project should be selected? If there is a capital rationing constraint, how should the decision be made?

l. Caledonia is considering two additional mutually exclusive projects. The cash flows associated with these projects are as follows:

Year	Project A	Project B
0	−$100,000	−$100,000
1	32,000	0
2	32,000	0
3	32,000	0
4	32,000	0
5	32,000	$200,000

The required rate of return on these projects is 11 percent.
1. What is each project's payback period?
2. What is each project's net present value?
3. What is each project's internal rate of return?
4. What has caused the ranking conflict?
5. Which project should be accepted? Why?

m. The final two mutually exclusive projects that Caledonia is considering involves mutually exclusive pieces of machinery that perform the same task. The two alternatives available provide the following set of after-tax net cash flows:

Year	Equipment A	Equipment B
0	−$100,000	−$100,000
1	65,000	32,500
2	65,000	32,500
3	65,000	32,500
4		32,500
5		32,500
6		32,500
7		32,500
8		32,500
9		32,500

Equipment A has an expected life of three years, whereas equipment B has an expected life of nine years. Assume a required rate of return of 14 percent.
1. Calculate each project's payback period.
2. Calculate each project's net present value.
3. Calculate each project's internal rate of return.
4. Are these projects comparable?
5. Compare these projects using replacement chains and EAAs. Which project should be selected? Support your recommendation.

DANFORTH & DONNALLEY LAUNDRY PRODUCTS COMPANY

Capital Budgeting: Relevant Cash Flows

On April 14, 1996, at 3:00 P.M., James Danforth, president of Danforth & Donnalley (D&D) Laundry Products Company, called to order a meeting of the financial directors. The purpose of the meeting was to make a capital-budgeting decision with respect to the introduction and production of a new product, a liquid detergent called Blast.

D&D was formed in 1971 with the merger of Danforth Chemical Company, headquartered in Seattle, Washington, producers of Lift-Off detergent, the leading laundry detergent on the West Coast, and Donnalley Home Products Company, headquartered in Detroit, Michigan, makers of Wave detergent, a major Midwestern laundry product. As a result of the merger, D&D was producing and marketing two major product lines. Although these products were in direct competition, they were not without product differentiation: Lift-Off was a low-suds, concentrated powder, and Wave was a more traditional powder detergent. Each line brought with it considerable brand loyalty, and by 1996, sales from the two detergent lines had increased tenfold from 1971 levels, with both products now being sold nationally.

In the face of increased competition and technological innovation, D&D spent large amounts of time and money over the past four years researching and developing a new, highly concentrated liquid laundry detergent. D&D's new detergent, which they called Blast, had many obvious advantages over the conventional powdered products. It was felt that with Blast the consumer would benefit in three major areas. Blast was so highly concentrated that only 2 ounces was needed to do an average load of laundry as compared with 8 to 12 ounces of powdered detergent. Moreover, being a liquid, it was possible to pour Blast directly on stains and hard-to-wash spots, eliminating the need for a pre-soak and giving it cleaning abilities that powders could not possibly match. And, finally, it would be packaged in a lightweight, unbreakable plastic bottle with a sure-grip handle, making it much easier to use and more convenient to store than the bulky boxes of powdered detergents with which it would compete.

The meeting was attended by James Danforth, president of D&D; Jim Donnalley, director of the board; Guy Rainey, vice-president in charge of new products; Urban McDonald, controller; and Steve Gasper, a newcomer to D&D's financial staff, who was invited by McDonald to sit in on the meeting. Danforth called the meeting to order, gave a brief statement of its purpose, and immediately gave the floor to Guy Rainey.

Rainey opened with a presentation of the cost and cash flow analysis for the new product. To keep things clear, he passed out copies of the projected cash flows to those present (see Exhibits 1 and 2). In support of this information, he pro-

vided some insights as to how these calculations were determined. Rainey proposed that the initial cost for Blast include $500,000 for the test marketing, which was conducted in the Detroit area and completed in the previous June, and $2 million for new specialized equipment and packaging facilities. The estimated life for the facilities was fifteen years, after which they would have no salvage value. This fifteen-year estimated life assumption coincides with company policy set by Donnalley to not consider cash flows occurring more than fifteen years into the future, as estimates that far ahead "tend to become little more than blind guesses."

Rainey cautioned against taking the annual cash flows (as shown in Exhibit 1) at face value because portions of these cash flows actually are a result of sales that had been diverted from Lift-Off and Wave. For this reason, Rainey also produced the annual cash flows that had been adjusted to include only those cash flows incremental to the company as a whole (as shown in Exhibit 2).

At this point, discussion opened between Donnalley and McDonald, and it was concluded that the opportunity cost on funds is 10 percent. Gasper then questioned the fact that no costs were included in the proposed cash budget for plant facilities, which would be needed to produce the new product.

Exhibit 1. D&D Laundry Products Company Annual Cash Flows from the Acceptance of Blast (Including flows resulting from sales diverted from the existing product lines)

Year	Cash Flows	Year	Cash Flows
1	$280,000	9	350,000
2	280,000	10	350,000
3	280,000	11	250,000
4	280,000	12	250,000
5	280,000	13	250,000
6	350,000	14	250,000
7	350,000	15	250,000
8	350,000		

Exhibit 2. D&D Laundry Products Company Annual Cash Flows from the Acceptance of Blast (Not including flows resulting from sales diverted from the existing product lines)

Year	Cash Flows	Year	Cash Flows
1	$250,000	9	315,000
2	250,000	10	315,000
3	250,000	11	225,000
4	250,000	12	225,000
5	250,000	13	225,000
6	315,000	14	225,000
7	315,000	15	225,000
8	315,000		

Rainey replied that, at the present time, Lift-Off's production facilities were being used at only 55 percent of capacity, and because these facilities were suitable for use in the production of Blast, no new plant facilities other than the specialized equipment and packaging facilities previously mentioned need be acquired for the production of the new product line. It was estimated that full production of Blast would only require 10 percent of the plant capacity.

McDonald then asked if there had been any consideration of increased working capital needs to operate the investment project. Rainey answered that there had and that this project would require $200,000 of additional working capital; however, as this money would never leave the firm and always would be in liquid form it was not considered an outflow and hence was not included in the calculations.

Donnalley argued that this project should be charged something for its use of the current excess plant facilities. His reasoning was that, if an outside firm tried to rent this space from D&D, it would be charged somewhere in the neighborhood of $2 million, and since this project would compete with the current projects, it should be treated as an outside project and charged as such; however, he went on to acknowledge that D&D has a strict policy that forbids the renting or leasing out of any of its production facilities. If they didn't charge for facilities, he concluded, the firm might end up accepting projects that under normal circumstances would be rejected.

From here, the discussion continued, centering on the questions of what to do about the "lost contribution from other projects," the test marketing costs, and the working capital.

Questions

1. If you were put in the place of Steve Gasper, would you argue for the cost from market testing to be included as a cash outflow?
2. What would your opinion be as to how to deal with the question of working capital?
3. Would you suggest that the product be charged for the use of excess production facilities and building?
4. Would you suggest that the cash flows resulting from erosion of sales from current laundry detergent products be included as a cash inflow? If there were a chance of competition introducing a similar product if you do not introduce Blast, would this affect your answer?
5. If debt is used to finance this project, should the interest payments associated with this new debt be considered cash flows?
6. What are the NPV, IRR, and PI of this project, including cash flows resulting from lost sales from existing product lines? What are the NPV, IRR, and PI of this project excluding these flows? Under the assumption that there is a good chance that competition will introduce a similar product if you don't, would you accept or reject this project?

HARDING PLASTIC MOLDING COMPANY

Capital Budgeting: Ranking Problems

On January 11, 1996, the finance committee of Harding Plastic Molding Company (HPMC) met to consider eight capital-budgeting projects. Present at the meeting were Robert L. Harding, president and founder, Susan Jorgensen, comptroller, and Chris Woelk, head of research and development. Over the past five years, this committee has met every month to consider and make final judgment on all proposed capital outlays brought up for review during the period.

Harding Plastic Molding Company was founded in 1968 by Robert L. Harding to produce plastic parts and molding for the Detroit automakers. For the first ten years of operations, HPMC worked solely as a subcontractor for the automakers, but since then has made strong efforts to diversify in an attempt to avoid the cyclical problems faced by the auto industry. By 1996, this diversification attempt has led HPMC into the production of over 1,000 different items, including kitchen utensils, camera housings, and photographic equipment. It also led to an increase in sales of 800 percent during the 1978–1996 period. As this dramatic increase in sales was paralleled by a corresponding increase in production volume, HPMC was forced, in late 1994, to expand production facilities. This plant and equipment expansion involved capital expenditures of approximately $10.5 million and resulted in an increase of production capacity of about 40 percent. Because of this increased production capacity, HPMC has made a concerted effort to attract new business and consequently has recently entered into contracts with a large toy firm and a major discount department store chain. While non-auto-related business has grown significantly, it still only represents 32 percent of HPMC's overall business. Thus HPMC has continued to solicit nonautomotive business, and as a result of this effort and its internal research and development, the firm has four sets of mutually exclusive projects to consider at this month's finance committee meeting.

Over the past ten years, HPMC's capital-budgeting approach has evolved into a somewhat elaborate procedure in which new proposals are categorized into three areas: profit, research and development, and safety. Projects falling into the profit or research and development areas are evaluated using present value techniques, assuming a 10 percent opportunity rate; those falling into the safety classification are evaluated in a more subjective framework. Although research and development projects have to receive favorable results from the present value criteria, there is also a total dollar limit assigned to projects of this category, typically running about $750,000 per year. This limitation was imposed by Harding primarily because of the limited availability of quality researchers in the plastics industry. Harding felt that if more funds than this were allocated, "we simply couldn't find the manpower to administer them properly." The benefits derived from safety projects, on the other hand, are not in terms of cash flows; hence, present value methods are not used at all in their evaluation. The subjective approach used to evaluate safety projects is a result of the pragmatically difficult task of quantifying the benefits from these projects into dollar terms. Thus these projects are subjectively evaluated by a management-worker committee with a limited budget. All eight projects to be evaluated in January are classified as profit projects.

The first set of projects listed on the meeting's agenda for examination involve the utilization of HPMC's precision equipment. Project A calls for the production of vacuum containers for thermos bottles produced for a large discount hardware chain. The containers would be manufactured in five different size and color combinations. This project would be carried out over a three-year period, for which HPMC would be guaranteed a minimum return plus a percentage of the sales. Project B involves the manufacture of inexpensive photographic equipment for a national photography outlet. Although HPMC currently has excess plant capacity, each of these projects would utilize precision equipment of which the excess capacity is limited. Thus, adopting either project would tie up all precision facilities. In addition, the purchase of new equipment would be both prohibitively expensive and involve a time delay of approximately two years, thus making these projects mutually exclusive. (The cash flows associated with these two projects are given in Exhibit 1.)

The second set of projects involves the renting of computer facilities over a one-year period to aid in customer billing and perhaps inventory control. Project C entails the evaluation of a customer billing system proposed by Advanced Computer Corporation. Under this system all the bookkeeping and billing presently being done by HPMC's accounting department would be done by Advanced. In addition to saving costs involved in bookkeeping, Advanced would provide a more efficient billing system and do a credit analysis of delinquent customers, which could be used in the future for in-depth credit analysis. Project D is proposed by International Computer Corporation and includes a billing system similar to that offered by Advanced and, in addition, an inventory control system that will keep track of all raw materials and parts in stock and reorder when necessary, thereby reducing the likelihood of material stockouts, which has become more and more frequent over the past three years. (The cash flows for these projects are given in Exhibit 2.)

The third decision that faces the financial directors of HPMC involves a newly developed and patented process for molding hard plastics. HPMC can either manufacture and market the equipment necessary to mold such plastics or it can sell the patent rights to Polyplastics Incorporated, the world's largest producer of plastics products. (The cash flows

for projects E and F are shown in Exhibit 3.) At present, the process has not been fully tested, and if HPMC is going to market it itself, it will be necessary to complete this testing and begin production of plant facilities immediately. On the other hand, the selling of these patent rights to Polyplastics would involve only minor testing and refinements, which could be completed within the year. Thus, a decision as to the proper course of action is necessary immediately.

The final set of projects up for consideration revolve around the replacement of some of the machinery. HPMC can go in one of two directions. Project G suggests the purchase and installation of moderately priced, extremely efficient equipment with an expected life of five years; project H advocates the purchase of a similarly priced, although less efficient, machine with life expectancy of 10 years. (The cash flows for these alternatives are shown in Exhibit 4.)

As the meeting opened, debate immediately centered on the most appropriate method for evaluating all the projects. Harding suggested that as the projects to be considered were mutually exclusive, perhaps their usual capital-budgeting criteria of net present value was inappropriate. He felt that, in examining these projects, perhaps they should be more concerned with relative profitability or some measure of yield. Both Jorgensen and Woelk agreed with Harding's point of view, with Jorgensen advocating a profitability index approach and Woelk preferring the use of the internal rate of return. Jorgensen argued that the use of the profitability index would provide a benefit-cost ratio, directly implying relative profitability. Thus, they merely need to rank these projects and select those with the highest profitability index. Woelk agreed

Exhibit 2. Harding Plastic Molding Company

| | Cash Flows | |
Year	Project C	Project D
0	$-8,000	$-20,000
1	11,000	25,000

Exhibit 3. Harding Plastic Molding Company

| | Cash Flows | |
Year	Project E	Project F
0	$-30,000	$-271,500
1	210,000	100,000
2		100,000
3		100,000
4		100,000
5		100,000
6		100,000
7		100,000
8		100,000
9		100,000
10		100,000

Exhibit 1. Harding Plastic Molding Company

| | Cash Flows | |
Year	Project A	Project B
0	$-75,000	$-75,000
1	10,000	43,000
2	30,000	43,000
3	100,000	43,000

Exhibit 4. Harding Plastic Molding Company

	Cash Flows	
Year	Project G	Project H
0	$-500,000	$-500,000
1	225,000	150,000
2	225,000	150,000
3	225,000	150,000
4	225,000	150,000
5	225,000	150,000
6		150,000
7		150,000
8		150,000
9		150,000
10		150,000

with Jorgensen's point of view, but suggested that the calculation of an internal rate of return would also give a measure of profitability and perhaps be somewhat easier to interpret. To settle the issue, Harding suggested that they calculate all three measures, as they would undoubtedly yield the same ranking.

From here the discussion turned to an appropriate approach to the problem of differing lives among mutually exclusive projects E and F, and G and H. Woelk argued that there really was not a problem here at all, that as all the cash flows from these projects can be determined, any of the discounted cash flow methods of capital budgeting will work well. Jorgensen argued that although this was true, some

compensation should be made for the fact that the projects being considered did not have equal lives.

Questions

1. Was Harding correct in stating that the NPV, PI, and IRR necessarily will yield the same ranking order? Under what situations might the NPV, PI, and IRR methods provide different rankings? Why is it possible?

2. What are the NPV, PI, and IRR for projects A and B? What has caused the ranking conflicts? Should project A or B be chosen? Might your answer change if project B is a typical project in the plastic molding industry? For example, if projects for HPMC generally yield approximately 12 percent, is it logical to assume that the IRR for project B of approximately 33 percent is a correct calculation for ranking purposes? (*Hint:* Examine the implied reinvestment rate assumption.)

3. What are the NPV, PI, and IRR for projects C and D? Should project C or D be chosen? Does your answer change if these projects are considered under a capital constraint? What return on the marginal $12,000 not employed in project C is necessary to make one indifferent to choosing one project over the other under a capital-rationing situation?

4. What are the NPV, PI, and IRR for projects E and F? Are these projects comparable even though they have unequal lives? Why? Which project should be chosen? Assume that these projects are not considered under a capital constraint.

5. What are the NPV, PI, and IRR for projects G and H? Are these projects comparable even though they have unequal lives? Why? Which project should be chosen? Assume that these projects are not considered under a capital constraint.

CHAPTER 6

PROJECT PORTFOLIO RISK ANALYSIS

6.1 CATEGORIES OF PROJECT RISK

Project management involves two types of risk analysis. The first occurs during the project selection process and involves the overall risk inherent in one project when compared to another. The second application of risk analysis occurs during the project planning process. It involves a detailed risk analysis of a specific project.

Project portfolio risk analysis is much more difficult than the process of estimating and ranking projects according to their amount of financial returns. Various methods of portfolio risk ranking methods are listed below.

High-medium-low

The most common and easily understood method of risk ranking consists of estimating whether the project is high risk, medium risk, or low risk. Projects can then be grouped into categories.

Weighted risk factors

Various key project portfolio risk elements can be listed and given a numerical value. For example, the projects might require new, unproven technology, capital investment could be large and stretch the company's resource base, or there could be stringent delivery time constraints. Each of these factors can be listed on a grid as shown on the next page.

	Unproven Technology	Investment High	Delivery Stringent	TOTAL
Project A	5	5	5	15
Project B	4	4	5	13
Project C	3	3	3	9

* 5 is highest risk, 1 is lowest risk

In the example above, Project C would have the lowest number of risk points. This information would be compared with the amount of potential financial return as well as the subjective factors in making the decision to select the project.

The readings that follow are from Keown and deal with capital budgeting and risk analysis.

6.2   CAPITAL BUDGETING AND RISK ANALYSIS

RISK AND THE INVESTMENT DECISION

Up to this point, we have ignored risk in capital budgeting; that is, we have discounted expected cash flows back to present and ignored any uncertainty there might be surrounding that estimate. In reality, the future cash flows associated with the introduction of a new sales outlet or a new product are estimates of what is expected to happen in the future, not necessarily what will happen in the future. For example, when the Ford Motor Company made its decision to introduce the Edsel, you can bet that the expected cash flows it based its decision on were nothing like the cash flows it realized. In effect, the cash flows we have discounted back to the present have been our best estimate of the expected future cash flows. A cash flow diagram based on the possible outcomes of an investment proposal rather than the expected values of these outcomes appears in Figure 6-1.

In this section, we will assume that under conditions of risk we do not know beforehand what cash flows will actually result from a new project. However, we do have expectations concerning the possible outcomes and are able to assign probabilities to these outcomes. Stated another way, although we do not know the cash flows resulting from the acceptance of a new project, we can formulate the probability distributions from which the flows will be drawn.

Risk occurs when there is some question as to the future outcome of an event. We will now proceed with an examination of the logic behind this definition. Again, risk is defined as the potential variability in future cash flows.

The fact that variability reflects risk can easily be shown with a coin toss. Consider the possibility of flipping a coin—heads you win, tails you lose—for 25 cents with your finance professor. Most likely, you would be willing to take on this game because the utility gained from winning 25 cents is about equal to the utility lost if you lose 25 cents. Conversely, if the flip is for $1,000 you may be willing to play only if you are offered more than $1,000 if you win—say, you win $1,500 if it turns out heads and lose $1,000 if it turns out tails. In each case, the probability of winning and losing is the same; that is, there is an equal chance that the coin will land heads or tails. In each case, however, the width of the dispersion changes, which is why the second coin toss is more risky and why you may not take the chance unless the payoffs are altered. The key here is the fact that only the dispersion changes; the probability of winning or losing is the same in each case. Thus, the potential variability in future returns reflects the risk.

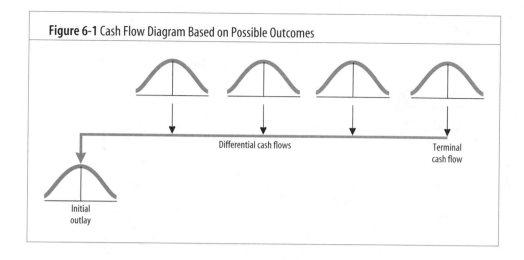

Figure 6-1 Cash Flow Diagram Based on Possible Outcomes

Differential cash flows

Terminal cash flow

Initial outlay

The final question to be addressed is whether or not individuals are in fact risk averse. Although we do see people gambling where the odds of winning are against them, it should be stressed that monetary return is not the only possible return they may receive. A nonmonetary, psychic reward accrues to some gamblers, allowing them to fantasize that they will break the bank, never have to work again, and retire to some offshore island. Actually, the heart of the question is how wealth is measured. Although gamblers appear to be acting as risk seekers, they actually attach an additional nonmonetary return to gambling; the risk is in effect its own reward. When this is considered, their actions seem totally rational. It should also be noted that although gamblers appear to be pursuing risk on the one hand, on the other hand they are also eliminating some risk by purchasing insurance and diversifying their investments.

In the remainder of this chapter we assume that although future cash flows are not known with certainty, the probability distribution from which they come is known. Also, since the dispersion of possible outcomes reflects risk, we are prepared to use a measure of dispersion or variability later in the chapter when we quantify risk.

In the pages that follow, there are only two basic issues that we address: (1) What is risk in terms of capital-budgeting decisions, and how should it be measured? (2) How should risk be incorporated into capital-budgeting analysis?

What Measure of Risk Is Relevant in Capital Budgeting

Before we begin our discussion of how to adjust for risk, it is important to determine just what type of risk we are to adjust for. In capital budgeting, a project's risk can be looked at on three levels. First, there is the **project standing alone risk,** which is a project's risk ignoring the fact that much of this risk will be diversified away as the project is combined with the firm's other projects and assets.

Second, we have the project's **contribution-to-firm risk,** which is the amount of risk that the project contributes to the firm as a whole; this measure considers the fact that some of the project's risk will be diversified away as the project is combined with the firm's other projects and assets, but *ignores* the effects of diversification of the firm's shareholders. Finally, there is **systematic risk,** which is the risk of the project from the viewpoint of a well-diversified shareholder; this measure considers the fact that some of a project's risk will be diversified away as the project is combined with the firm's other projects, and, in addition, some of the remaining risk will be diversified away by shareholders as they combine this stock with other stocks in their portfolio. Graphically, this is shown in Figure 6-2.

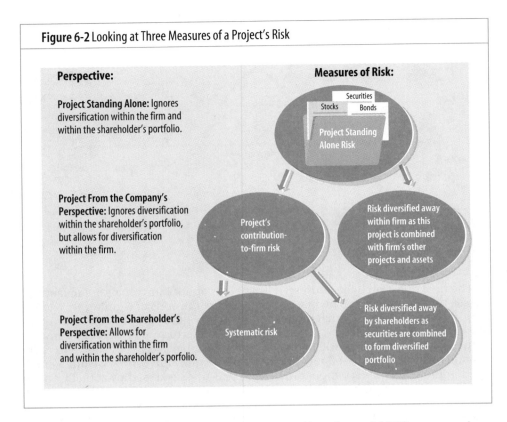

Figure 6-2 Looking at Three Measures of a Project's Risk

Perspective:

Project Standing Alone: Ignores diversification within the firm and within the shareholder's portfolio.

Project From the Company's Perspective: Ignores diversification within the shareholder's portfolio, but allows for diversification within the firm.

Project From the Shareholder's Perspective: Allows for diversification within the firm and within the shareholder's porfolio.

Measures of Risk:

Securities
Stocks   Bonds
Project Standing Alone Risk

Project's contribution-to-firm risk

Risk diversified away within firm as this project is combined with firm's other projects and assets

Systematic risk

Risk diversified away by shareholders as securities are combined to form diversified portfolio

Should we be interested in the project standing alone risk? The answer is no. Perhaps the easiest way to understand why not is to look at an example. Let's take the case of research and development projects at Johnson & Johnson. Each year Johnson & Johnson takes on hundreds of new R&D projects, knowing that they only have about a 10 percent probability of being successful. If they are successful, the profits can be enormous; if they fail, the investment is lost. If the company has only one project, and it is an R&D project, the company would have a 90 percent chance of failure. Thus, if we look at these R&D projects individually and measure their project standing alone risk, we would have to judge them to be enormously risky. However, if we consider the effect of the diversification that comes about from taking on several hundred independent R&D projects a year, all with a 10 percent chance of success, we can see that these R&D projects do not add much in the way of risk to Johnson & Johnson. In short, because much of a project's risk is diversified away within the firm, project standing alone risk is an inappropriate measure of the level of risk of a capital-budgeting project.

Should we be interested in the project's contribution-to-firm risk? Once again, the answer is no, provided investors are well diversified and there is no chance of bankruptcy. As shareholders, if we combined our stocks with other stocks to form a diversified portfolio, much of the risk of our security would be diversified away. Thus, all that affects the shareholders is the systematic risk of the project and, as such, is all that is theoretically relevant for capital budgeting.

Measuring Risk for Capital-Budgeting Purposes and a Dose of Reality—Is Systematic Risk All There Is?

According to the Capital Asset Pricing Model (CAPM), systematic risk is the only relevant risk for capital-budgeting purposes; however, reality complicates this somewhat. In many instances, a firm will have undiversified shareholders, including

WASHINGTON POST MAY 7, 1994

Plight at the End of the Tunnel

FOLKSTONE, ENGLAND—Hailing what they called the engineering marvel of the century, Queen Elizabeth II and French President Francois Mitterrand inaugurated the Channel Tunnel crossing today and formally marked the end of Britain's physical isolation from the continent since the last Ice Age.

In a historic celebration that began in the French seacoast village of Coquelles and ended here near the white cliffs of Dover, the two heads of state pledged that the successful completion of the project that eluded visionary builders since Napoleon's time would now bind Britain irrevocably to Europe.

The queen paid tribute to the 15,000 workers on both sides of the channel who toiled for the past seven years and surmounted countless obstacles in finishing Europe's largest construction project "for the benefit of all humanity." (A)

Mitterrand too saluted the crowning example of French-British cooperation that aides say has been one of the most gratifying events of his presidency.

"We now have a land frontier," Mitterrand said. "This prodigious work, full of imagination and invention, shows what France and Britain can do when they put together their talent, energy and resources. We can achieve even greater things, so let us vow to do more for the cause of Europe."

Yet even before it enters into service, the Channel Tunnel is being lambasted by critics as a potential white elephant. The undersea link, which features two tubular train lines each running for a length of more than 31 miles, cost $16 billion to build, more than twice the original estimate.

The Anglo-French consortium Eurotunnel, the private enterprise in charge of tunnel operations, is already burdened by $10 billion in debt and expects to run out of cash by June unless a bank rescue can be arranged.(B) Eurotunnel was supposed to start service a year ago, but security checks and other delays will postpone regular traffic for at least another four months. Each day lost is costing an extra $2 million.

Ferry companies, fearing possible extinction, have vowed to launch a price war that could sink the tunnel's hopes of breaking even by the year 2000. Round-trip tunnel fares for a single car, which will start at $330 in the winter and run to $460 in summer, are deemed too high by experts to justify crossing the channel in 35 minutes, half the time it takes with the cheaper ferry crossing.(C)

SOURCE: Excerpted from William Drozdiak, "Plight at End of Tunnel," *Washington Post* (May 7, 1994): A1, 14. Copyright 1995 by the *Washington Post*. Reprinted by permission.

ANALYSIS AND IMPLICATIONS...

A. This project illustrates just how large a capital-budgeting project can be. In this case the cost of the Channel Tunnel was $16 billion. Where is the risk? In this case, the risk is that the estimated initial outlay and annual cash flows are not reliable. Given the fact that the initial outlay ran double the estimate, this project could face some serious problems in the years to come.

B. As is evident in this case, not only the future cash flows but the initial outlay estimates can have uncertainty associated with them. Throughout this chapter try to keep in mind that the value of any capital-budgeting decision is dependent on the quality of the inputs. As the old saying goes, "Junk in, junk out."

C. Capital budgeting in the public sector is always difficult. What exactly happens to the Eurotunnel, only time will tell. But as with most capital budgeting projects, it will be difficult to reverse—and if it proves to be unprofitable, it will drain resources for years to come.

owners of small corporations. Because they are not diversified, for those shareholders the relevant measure of risk is the project's contribution-to-firm risk.

The possibility of bankruptcy also affects our view of what measure of risk is relevant. Because the project's contribution-to-firm risk can affect the possibility of bankruptcy, this may be an appropriate measure of risk if there are costs associated with bankruptcy. Quite obviously, in the real world, there is a cost associated with bankruptcy. First, if a firm fails, its assets, in general, cannot be sold for their true economic value. Moreover, the amount of money actually available for distribution to stockholders is further reduced by liquidation and legal fees that must be paid. Finally, the opportunity cost associated with the delays related to the legal process further reduces the funds available to the shareholder. Therefore, because there are costs associated with bankruptcy, reduction of the chance of bankruptcy has a very real value associated with it.

Indirect costs of bankruptcy also affect other areas of the firm, including production, sales, and the quality and efficiency of management. For example, firms with a higher probability of bankruptcy may have a more difficult time recruiting and retaining quality managers because jobs with that firm are viewed as being less secure. Suppliers also may be less willing to sell on credit. Finally, customers may lose confidence and fear that the firm may not be around to honor the warranty or to supply spare parts for the product in the future. As a result, as the probability of bankruptcy increases, the eventual bankruptcy may become self-fulfilling as potential customers and suppliers flee. The end result is that the project's contribution-to-firm risk is also a relevant risk measure for capital budgeting.

Finally, problems in measuring a project's systematic risk make its implementation extremely difficult. As we will see later on in this chapter, it is much easier talking about a project's systematic risk than it is measuring it.

Given all this, what do we use? The answer is that we will give consideration to both measures. We know in theory systematic risk is correct. We also know that bankruptcy costs and undiversified shareholders violate the assumptions of the theory, which brings us back to the concept of a project's contribution-to-firm risk. Still, the concept of systematic risk holds value for capital-budgeting decisions because that is the risk for which shareholders are compensated. As such, we will concern ourselves with both the project's contribution-to-firm risk and the project's systematic risk, and not try to make any specific allocation of importance between the two for capital-budgeting purposes.

METHODS FOR INCORPORATING RISK INTO CAPITAL BUDGETING

Previously we ignored any risk differences between projects. This assumption is simple but not valid; different investment projects do in fact contain different levels of risk. We will now look at two methods for incorporating risk into the analysis. The first technique, the *certainty equivalent approach*, attempts to incorporate the manager's utility function into the analysis. The second technique, the *risk-adjusted discount rate*, is based on the notion that investors require higher rates of return on more risky projects.

Certainty Equivalent Approach

The **certainty equivalent approach** involves a direct attempt to allow the decision maker to incorporate his/her utility function into the analysis. The financial manager is allowed to substitute the certain dollar amount that he/she feels is equivalent to the expected but risky cash flow offered by the investment for that risky cash flow in the capital-budgeting analysis. In effect, a set of riskless cash flows is substituted for the original risky cash flows, between both of which the financial manager is indifferent. To a certain extent this process is like the old television program "Let's Make a Deal." On that show, Monty Hall asked contestants to trade certain outcomes for uncertain outcomes. In some cases, contestants were willing to make a trade, and in some cases they were not; it all depended upon how risk averse they were. The main difference between what we are doing and what was done on "Let's Make a Deal" is that on the TV show contestants were in general not indifferent with respect to the certain outcome and the risky outcome, whereas in the certainty equivalent approach managers are indifferent.

To illustrate the concept of a **certainty equivalent**, let us look at a simple coin toss. Assume you can play the game only once and if it comes out heads, you win $10,000, and if it comes out tails you win nothing. Obviously, you have a 50 percent chance of winning $10,000 and a 50 percent chance of winning nothing, with an expected value of $5,000. Thus, $5,000 is your uncertain expected value outcome. The certainty equivalent then becomes the amount you would demand to make you indifferent with regard to playing and not playing the game. If you are indifferent with respect to receiving $3,000 for certain and not playing the game, then $3,000 is the certainty equivalent.

To simplify future calculations and problems, let us define the certainty equivalent coefficient (α_t) that represents the ratio of the certain outcome to the risky or expected outcome, between which the financial manager is indifferent. In equation form, α_t can be represented as follows:

$$\alpha_t = \frac{\text{certain cash flow}_t}{\text{risky or expected cash flow}_t} \qquad (6\text{-}1)$$

Thus, the alphas (α_t) can vary between 0, in the case of extreme risk, and 1, in the case of certainty. To obtain the value of the equivalent certain cash flow, we need only multiply the risky cash flow in years t times the α_t. When this is done, we are indifferent with respect to this certain cash flow and the risky cash flow. In the preceding example of the simple coin toss, the certain cash flow was $3,000, while the risky cash flow was $5,000, the expected value of the coin toss; thus, the certainty equivalent coefficient is $3000/$5000 = 0.6. In summary, by multiplying the certainty equivalent coefficient (α_t) times the expected but risky cash flow, we can determine an equivalent certain cash flow.

Once this risk is taken out of the project's cash flows, those cash flows are discounted back to present at the risk-free rate of interest, and the project's net present value or profitability index is determined. If the internal rate of return is calculated, it is then compared with the risk-free rate of interest rather than the firm's required rate of return in determining whether or not it should be accepted or rejected. The certainty equivalent method can be summarized as follows:

$$NPV = \sum_{t=1}^{n} \frac{\alpha_t ACF_t}{\left(1 + k_{rf}\right)^t} - IO \qquad (6\text{-}2)$$

where α_t = the certainty equivalent coefficient in period t
ACF_t = the annual after-tax expected cash flow in period t
IO = the initial cash outlay
n = the project's expected life
k_{rf} = the risk-free interest rate

The certainty equivalent approach can be summarized as follows:

Step 1: Risk is removed from the cash flows by substituting equivalent certain cash flows for the risky cash flows. If the certainty equivalent coefficient (α_t) is given, this is done by multiplying each risky cash flow by the appropriate α_t value.

Step 2: These riskless cash flows are then discounted back to the present at the riskless rate of interest.

Step 3: The normal capital-budgeting criteria are then applied, except in the case of the internal rate of return criterion, where the project's internal rate of return is compared with the risk-free rate of interest rather than the firm's required rate of return.

EXAMPLE

A firm with a 10 percent required rate of return is considering building new research facilities with an expected life of five years. The initial outlay associated with this project involves a certain cash outflow of $120,000. The expected cash inflows and certainty equivalent coefficients, α_t are as follows:

Year	Expected Cash Flow	Certainty Equivalent Coefficient, α_t
1	$10,000	0.95
2	20,000	0.90
3	40,000	0.85
4	80,000	0.75
5	80,000	0.65

The risk-free rate of interest is 6 percent. What is the project's net present value?

To determine the net present value of this project using the certainty equivalent approach, we must first remove the risk from the future cash flows. We do so by multiplying each expected cash flow by the corresponding certainty equivalent coefficient, α_t, as shown below:

Expected Cash Flow	Certainty Equivalent Coefficient, α_t	α_t (Expected Cash Flow) = Equivalent Riskless Cash Flow
$10,000	0.95	$ 9,500
20,000	0.90	18,000
40,000	0.85	34,000
80,000	0.75	60,000
80,000	0.65	52,000

The equivalent riskless cash flows are then discounted back to the present at the riskless interest rate, not the firm's required rate of return. The required rate of return would be used if this project had the same level of risk as a typical project for this firm. However, these equivalent cash flows have no risk at all; hence, the appropriate discount rate is the riskless rate of interest. The equivalent riskless cash flows can be discounted back to present at the riskless rate of interest, 6 percent, as follows:

Year	Equivalent Riskless Cash Flow	Present Value Factor at 6 Percent	Present Value
1	$ 9,500	0.943	$ 8,958.50
2	18,000	0.890	16,020.00
3	34,000	0.840	28,560.00
4	60,000	0.792	47,520.00
5	52,000	0.747	38,844.00

NPV = −$120,000 + $8958.50 + $16,020 + $28,560 + $47,520 + $38,844 = $19,902.50

Applying the normal capital-budgeting decision criteria, we find that the project should be accepted, as its net present value is greater than zero.

Risk-Adjusted Discount Rates

The use of risk-adjusted discount rates is based on the concept that investors demand higher returns for more risky projects. This is the basic principle behind the CAPM, and the relationship between risk and return is illustrated graphically in Figure 6-3.

The required rate of return on any investment should include compensation for delaying consumption equal to the risk-free rate of return, plus compensation for any risk taken on. If the risk associated with the investment is greater than the risk involved in a typical endeavor, the discount rate is adjusted upward to compensate for this added risk. Once the firm determines the appropriate required rate of return for a project with a given level of risk, cash flows are discounted back to present at the **risk-adjusted discount rate.** Then the normal capital-budgeting criteria are applied, except in the case of the internal rate of return. For the IRR, the hurdle rate with which the project's internal rate of return is compared now becomes the risk-adjusted discount rate. Expressed mathematically, the net present value using the risk-adjusted discount rate becomes

$$NPV = \sum_{t=1}^{n} \frac{ACF_t}{\left(1 + k^*\right)^t} - IO$$

(6-3)

where ACF_t = the annual after-tax expected cash flow in time period t
IO = the initial cash outlay
k^* = the risk-adjusted discount rate
n = the project's expected life

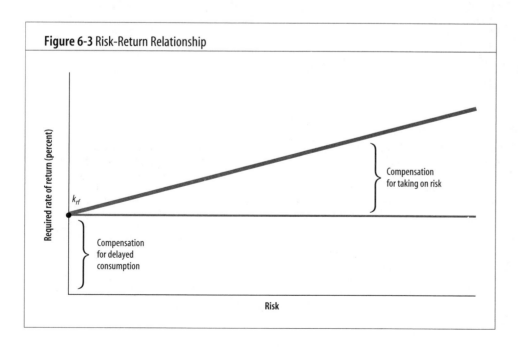

Figure 6-3 Risk-Return Relationship

HARVARD BUSINES REVIEW, JANUARY-FEBRUARY, 1994

Scientific Management at Merck: An Interview with CFO Judy Lewent

"People who don't practice finance properly have done a great disservice to U.S. industry. Too often, when finance people are unleashed on operating people, an unhealthy tension develops between the need to invest in new projects and the need to have tight controls on spending. For that reason, finance people are often viewed as traffic cops: "You can't do this or go there."(A) They keep the records straight, and that's that.

"At Merck, we certainly work with a very sharp pencil. We are not lax. But instead of being an impediment to business, we attempt to work with the operating units and, in many cases, have been accepted as a partner in the business. I think that finance departments can take the nuances, the intuitive feelings

that really fine businesspeople have and quantify them. In that way, they can capture both the hard financials of a project and the strategic intent.

"For example, we had a development project for a non-traditional market segment, an antiparasitic agent called Avid that everyone was excited about. We collected the manufacturing and marketing elements and the research inputs, but the financial evaluation of the model showed a negative net present value for the project.(B) If we had been traffic cops, we would have blown our whistle and gone home.

"But instead, we started to take the project apart and talk more in-depth with marketing and with manufacturing. It turned out that the packaging

costs were eating up the gross margins on the project.(C) This was something that the original sponsors of the project had feared all along, but only on a conceptual level. We were able to give the project's sponsors, the marketing department, and manufacturing people a framework for talking about the product, and it suddenly became clear to all involved that the packaging size had to change. In this case, then, finance was a real resource in problem solving."

SOURCE: Reprinted by permission of *Harvard Business Review*. An excerpt from "Scientific Management at Merck: An Interview with CFO Judy Lewent," by Nancy A. Nichols. Copyright © 1993 by the President and Fellows of Harvard College, all rights reserved.

ANALYSIS AND IMPLICATIONS...

A. For Merck and other pharmaceutical firms, taking on risk is simply part of the game. New products can only be generated through research and there is no guarantee that an R&D project will result in a profitable project. Complicating all this is the fact that after a large investment in research, a good project may not generate profits for ten to fifteen years.

B. In evaluating projects, Merck relies on a simulation approach. In fact, since 1989, every significant research and development project at Merck has been analyzed using a simulation approach over a twenty-year time horizon.

C. Merck uses the simulation approach not only to make decisions, but also to find areas causing financial concern to the project. This is done by performing

sensitivity or "What if?" analysis—changing one input while holding other inputs constant to determine what the effect is on the distribution of possible returns. In this case, Merck was able to spot an area in which the costs were so large as to turn a good project into a bad one. Once the problem area was spotted, it could be corrected. In this way, finance served not only as a method to evaluate and control the project, but also to refine it.

The logic behind the risk-adjusted discount rate stems from the idea that if the level of risk in a project is different from that in the firm's typical project, then management must incorporate the shareholders' probable reaction to this new endeavor into the decision-making process. If the project has more risk than a typical project, then a higher required rate of return should apply. Otherwise, marginal projects will lower the firm's share price—that is, reduce shareholders' wealth. This will occur as the market raises its required rate of return on the firm to reflect the addition of a more risky project, whereas the incremental cash flows resulting from the acceptance of the new project are not large enough to offset this change fully. By the same logic, if the project has less than normal risk, a reduction in the required rate of return is appropriate. Thus, the risk-adjusted discount method attempts to apply more stringent standards—that is, require a higher rate of return—to projects that will increase the firm's risk level.

EXAMPLE

A toy manufacturer is considering the introduction of a line of fishing equipment with an expected life of five years. In the past, this firm has been quite conservative in its investment in new products, sticking primarily to standard toys. In this context, the introduction of a line of fishing equipment is considered an abnormally risky project. Management thinks that the normal required rate of return for the firm of 10 percent is not sufficient. Instead, the minimally acceptable rate of return on this project should be 15 percent. The initial outlay would be $110,000, and the expected cash flows from this project are as given below:

Year	Expected Cash Flow
1	$30,000
2	30,000
3	30,000
4	30,000
5	30,000

Discounting this annuity back to the present at 15 percent yields a present value of the future cash flows of $100,560. Because the initial outlay on this project is $110,000, the net present value becomes –$9,440, and the project should be rejected. If the normal required rate of return of 10 percent had been used as the discount rate, the project would have been accepted with a net present value of $3,730.

In practice, when the risk-adjusted discount rate is used, projects are generally grouped according to purpose, or risk class; then, the discount rate preassigned to that purpose or risk class is used. For example, a firm with an overall required rate of return of 12 percent might use the following rate-of-return categorization:

Project	Required Rate of Return
Replacement decision	12%
Modification or expansion of existing product line	15
Project unrelated to current operations	18
Research and development operations	25

Table 6-1 Computational Steps in Certainty Equivalent
and Risk-Adjusted Discount Rate Methods

Certainty Equivalent		Risk-Adjusted Discount Rate	
STEP 1:	Adjust the expected cash flows, ACF_t, downward for risk by multiplying them by the corresponding certainty equivalent, coefficient, α_t.	STEP 1:	Adjust the discount rate upward for risk.
STEP 2:	Discount the certainty equivalent, riskless, cash flows back to the present using the risk-free rate of interest.	STEP 2:	Discount the expected cash flows back to present using the risk-adjusted discount rate.
STEP 3:	Apply the normal decision criteria, except in the case of the internal rate of return, where the risk-free rate of interest replaces the required rate of return as the hurdle rate.	STEP 3:	Apply the normal decision criteria except in the case of the internal rate of return, where the risk-adjusted discount rate replaces the required rate of return as the hurdle rate.

The purpose of this categorization of projects is to make their evaluation easier, but it also introduces a sense of the arbitrary into the calculations that makes the evaluation less meaningful. The tradeoffs involved in the classification above are obvious; time and effort are minimized, but only at the cost of precision.

Certainty Equivalent Versus Risk-Adjusted Discount Rate Methods

The primary difference between the certainty equivalent approach and the risk-adjusted discount rate approach involves the point at which the adjustment for risk is incorporated into the calculations. The certainty equivalent penalizes or adjusts downward the value of the expected annual after-tax cash flows, ACF_t which results in a lower net present value for a risky project. The risk-adjusted discount rate, conversely, leaves the cash flows at their expected value and adjusts the required rate of return, k, upward to compensate for added risk. In either case the project's net present value is being adjusted downward to compensate for additional risk. The computational differences are illustrated in Table 6-1.

In addition to the difference in point of adjustment for risk, the risk-adjusted discount rate makes the implicit assumption that risk becomes greater as we move further out in time. Although this is not necessarily a good or bad assumption, we should be aware of it and understand it. Let's look at an example in which the risk-adjusted discount rate is used and then determine what certainty equivalent coefficients, α_t, would be necessary to arrive at the same solution.

EXAMPLE

Assume that a firm with a required rate of return of 10 percent is considering introducing a new product. This product has an initial outlay of $800,000, an expected life of fifteen years, and after-tax cash flows of $100,000 each year during its life. Because of the increased risk associated with this project, management is requiring a 15 percent rate of return. Let us also assume that the risk-free rate of return is 6 percent.

If the firm chose to use the certainty equivalent method, the certainty equivalent cash flows would be discounted back to the present at 6 percent, the risk-free rate of interest. The present value of the $100,000 cash flow occurring at the end of the first year discounted back to present at 15 percent is $87,000. The present value of this $100,000 flow discounted back to present at the risk-free rate of 6 percent is $94,300. Thus, if the certainty equivalent approach were used, a certainty equivalent coefficient, α_1, of .9226 ($87,000 ÷ $94,300 =

0.9226) would be necessary to produce a present value of $87,000. In other words, the same results can be obtained in the first year by using the risk-adjusted discount rate and adjusting the discount rate up to 15 percent or by using the certainty equivalent approach and adjusting the expected cash flows by a certainty equivalent coefficient of 0.9226.

Under the risk-adjusted discount rate, the present value of the $100,000 cash flow occurring at the end of the second year becomes $75,600, and to produce an identical present value under the certainty equivalent approach, a certainty equivalent coefficient of 0.8494 would be needed. Following this through for the life of the project yields the certainty equivalent coefficients given in Table 6-2.

What does this analysis suggest? It indicates that if the risk-adjusted discount rate method is used, we are adjusting downward the value of future cash flows that occur further in the future more severely than earlier cash flows.

In summary, the use of the risk-adjusted discount rate assumes that risk increases over time and that cash flows occurring further in the future should be more severely penalized.

Risk-Adjusted Discount Rate and Measurement of a Project's Systematic Risk

When we initially talked about systematic risk or a beta, we were talking about measuring it for the entire firm. As you recall, although we could estimate a firm's beta using historical data, we did not have complete confidence in our results. As we will see, estimating the appropriate level of systematic risk for a single project is even more fraught with difficulties. To truly understand what it is that we are trying to do and the difficulties that we will encounter let us step back a bit and examine systematic risk and the risk adjustment for a project.

What we are trying to do is to use the CAPM to determine the level of risk and the appropriate risk-return tradeoffs for a particular project. We will then take the expected return on this project and compare it to the risk-return tradeoffs suggested by the CAPM to determine whether or not the project should be accepted. If the project appears to be a typical one for the firm, using the CAPM to determine the appropriate risk-return tradeoffs and then judging the project against them may be a warranted approach. But if the project is not a typical project, what do we do? Historical data generally do not exist for a new project. In fact, for some capital investments, for example, a truck or a new building, historical data would not have much meaning. What we need to do is make the best out of a bad situation. We either (1) fake it—that is, use historical accounting data, if available, to substitute for historical price data in estimating systematic risk; or (2) we attempt to find a substitute firm in the same industry as the capital-budgeting project and use the substitute firm's estimated systematic risk as a proxy for the project's systematic risk.

Beta Estimation Using Accounting Data

When we are dealing with a project that is identical to the firm's other projects, we need only estimate the level of systematic risk for the firm and use that estimate as

Table 6-2 Certainty Equivalent Coefficients Yielding Same Results as Risk-Adjusted Discount Rate of 15 Percent in Illustrative Example

Year	1	2	3	4	5	6	7	8	9	10
α_t:	0.9226	0.8494	0.7833	0.7222	0.6653	0.6128	0.5654	0.5215	0.4797	0.4427

a proxy for the project's risk. Unfortunately, when projects are not typical of the firm, this approach does not work. For example, when R. J. Reynolds introduces a new food through one of its food products divisions, this new product most likely carries with it a different level of systematic risk than is typical for Reynolds as a whole.

To get a better approximation of the systematic risk level on this project we could estimate the level of systematic risk for the food division and use that as a proxy for the project's systematic risk. Unfortunately, historical stock price data are available only for the company as a whole, and historical stock return data are generally used to estimate a firm's beta. Thus, we are forced to use *accounting return data* rather than historical stock return data for the division to estimate the division's systematic risk. To estimate a project's beta using accounting data we need only run a time series regression of the division's return on assets (net income/total assets) on the market index (the S&P 500). The regression coefficient from this equation would be the project's accounting beta and would serve as an approximation for the project's true beta or measure of systematic risk. Alternatively, a multiple regression model based on accounting data could be developed to explain betas. The results of this model could then be applied to firms which are not publicly traded to estimate their betas.

How good is the accounting beta technique? It certainly is not as good as a direct calculation of the beta. In fact, the correlation between the accounting beta and the beta calculated on historical stock return data is only about 0.6; however, better luck has been experienced with multiple regression models used to predict betas. Unfortunately, in many cases there may not be any realistic alternative to the calculation of the accounting beta. Owing to the importance of adjusting for a project's risk, the accounting beta method is much preferred to doing nothing.

The Pure Play Method for Estimating a Project's Beta

Whereas the accounting beta method attempts to directly estimate a project or division's beta, the **pure play method** attempts to identify publicly traded firms that are engaged solely in the same business as the project or division. Once the proxy or pure play firm is identified, its systematic risk is determined and then used as a proxy for the project or division's level of systematic risk. What we are doing is looking for a publicly traded firm on the outside that looks like our project and using that firm's required rate of return to judge our project. In doing so, we are presuming that the systematic risk and the capital structure of the proxy firm are identical to those of the project.

In using the pure play method, it should be noted that a firm's capital structure is reflected in its beta. When the capital structure of the proxy firm is different from that of the project's firm, some adjustment must be made for this difference. Although not a perfect approach, it does provide some insights as to the level of systematic risk a project might have.

OTHER APPROACHES TO EVALUATING RISK IN CAPITAL BUDGETING

Simulation

Another method for evaluating risk in the investment decision is through the use of **simulation.** The certainty equivalent and risk-adjusted discount rate approaches provided us with a single value for the risk-adjusted net present value, whereas a simulation approach gives us a probability distribution for the investment's net present value or internal rate of return. Simulation imitates the performance of the project under evaluation. This is done by randomly selecting observations from each of the distributions that affect the outcome of the project, combining those observations to determine the final output of the project, and continuing with this process until a representative record of the project's probable outcome is assembled.

The easiest way to develop an understanding of the computer simulation process is to follow through an example simulation for an investment project evaluation. Suppose Merck is considering a new drug for the treatment of Alzheimers disease. The simulation process is portrayed in Figure 6-4. First, the probability distributions are determined for all the factors that affect the project's returns; in this case, let us assume there are nine such variables:

1. Market size
2. Selling price
3. Market growth rate
4. Share of market (which results in physical sales volume)
5. Investment required
6. Residual value of investment
7. Operating costs
8. Fixed costs
9. Useful life of facilities

Then the computer randomly selects one observation from each of the probability distributions according to its chance of actually occurring in the future. These nine observations are combined and a net present value or internal rate of return figure is calculated. This process is repeated as many times as desired, until a representative distribution of possible future outcomes is assembled. Thus, the inputs to a simulation include all the principal factors affecting the project's profitability, and the simulation output is a probability distribution of net present values or internal rates of return for the project. The decision maker bases the decision on the full range of possible outcomes. The project is accepted if the decision maker feels that enough of the distribution lies above the normal cut-off criteria ($NPV \geq 0$, $IRR \geq$ required rate of return).

Suppose that the output from the simulation of Merck's Alzheimers disease drug project is as given in Figure 6-5. This output provides the decision maker with the probability of different outcomes occurring in addition to the range of possible outcomes. Sometimes called **scenario analysis,** this examination identifies the range of possible outcomes under the worst, best, and most likely case. Merck's management will examine the distribution to determine the project's level of risk and then make the appropriate adjustment.

You'll notice that although the simulation approach helps us to determine the amount of total risk that a project has, it does not differentiate between systematic and unsystematic risk. Because systematic risk cannot be diversified away for free, the simulation approach does not provide a complete method of risk assessment. However, it does provide important insights as to the total risk level of a given investment project. Now we will look briefly at how the simulation approach can be used to perform sensitivity analysis.

Sensitivity Analysis through Simulation Approach

Sensitivity analysis involves determining how the distribution of possible net present values or internal rates of return for a particular project is affected by a change in one particular input variable. This is done by changing the value of one input variable while holding all other input variables constant. The distribution of possible net present values or internal rates of return that is generated is then compared

Figure 6-4 Capital-Budgeting Simulation for Proposed New Alzheimers Drug

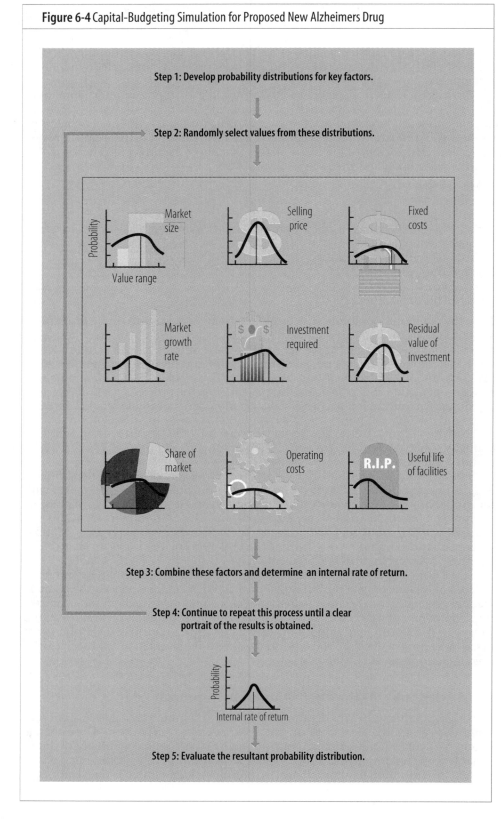

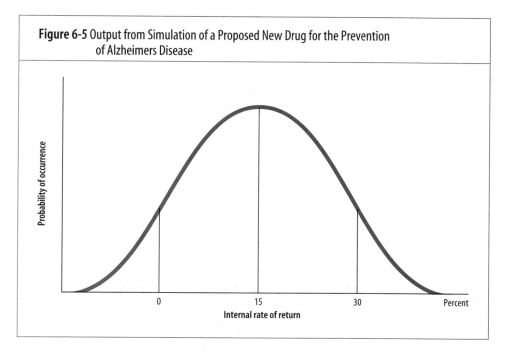

Figure 6-5 Output from Simulation of a Proposed New Drug for the Prevention of Alzheimers Disease

with the distribution of possible returns generated before the change was made to determine the effect of the change. For this reason, sensitivity analysis is commonly called *"What if?" Analysis*.

For example, in analyzing the proposal for a new drug for the prevention of Alzheimers disease, Merck's management may wish to determine the effect of a more pessimistic forecast of the anticipated market growth rate. After the more pessimistic forecast replaces the original forecast in the model, the simulation is rerun. The two outputs are then compared to determine how sensitive the results are to the revised estimate of the market growth rate.

By modifying assumptions made about the values and ranges of the input factors and rerunning the simulation, management can determine how sensitive the outcome of the project is to these changes. If the output appears to be highly sensitive to one or two of the input factors, the financial managers may then wish to spend additional time refining those input estimates to make sure they are accurate.

Probability Trees

A **probability tree** is a graphic exposition of the sequence of possible outcomes; it presents the decision maker with a schematic representation of the problem in which all possible outcomes are pictures. Moreover, the computations and results of the computations are shown directly on the tree, so that the information can be easily understood.

To illustrate the use of a probability tree, suppose a firm is considering an investment proposal that requires an initial outlay of $1 million and will yield cash flows for the next two years. During the first year let us assume there are three possible outcomes, as shown in Table 6-3. Graphically, each of these three possible alternatives is represented on the probability tree in Figure 6-6 as one of the three possible branches.

The second step in the probability tree is to continue drawing branches in a similar manner so that each of the possible outcomes during the second year is represented by a new branch. For example, if outcome 1 occurs in year 1, then

Table 6-3 Possible Outcomes in Year 1

	Probability		
	.5	.3	.2
	Outcome 1	Outcome 2	Outcome 3
Cash flow	$600,00	$700,000	$800,000

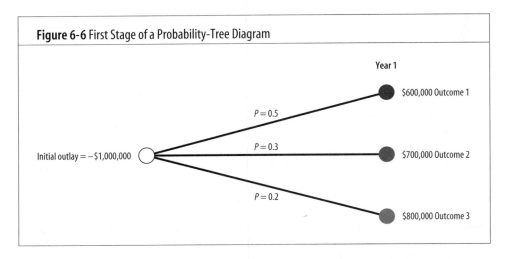

Figure 6-6 First Stage of a Probability-Tree Diagram

Year 1

Initial outlay = –$1,000,000

$P = 0.5$ → $600,000 Outcome 1

$P = 0.3$ → $700,000 Outcome 2

$P = 0.2$ → $800,000 Outcome 3

there would be a 20 percent chance of a $300,000 cash flow and an 80 percent chance of a $600,000 cash flow in year 2 as shown in Table 6-4. Two branches would be sent out from the outcome 1 node, reflecting these two possible outcomes. The cash flows that occur if outcome 1 takes place and the probabilities associated with them are called *conditional outcomes* and *conditional probabilities* because they can occur only if outcome 1 occurs during the first year. Finally, to determine the probability of the sequence of a $600,000 flow in year 1 and a $300,000 outcome in year 2, the probability of the $600,000 flow (.5) is multiplied by the conditional probability of the second flow (.2), telling us that this sequence has a 10 percent chance of occurring; this is called its **joint probability**. Letting the values in Table 6-4 represent the conditional outcomes and their respective conditional probabilities, we can complete the probability tree, as shown in Figure 6-7.

The financial manager, by examining the probability tree, is provided with the expected internal rate of return for the investment, the range of possible outcomes, and a listing of each possible outcome with the probability associated with it. In this case, the expected internal rate of return is 14.74 percent, and there is a 10 percent chance of incurring the worst possible outcome with an internal rate of return of –7.55 percent. There is a 2 percent probability of achieving the most favorable outcome, an internal rate of return of 37.98 percent.

Decision making with probability trees does not mean simply the acceptance of any project with an internal rate of return greater than the firm's required rate of return, because the project's required rate of return has not yet been adjusted for risk. As a result, the financial decision maker must examine the entire distribution of possible internal rates of return. Then, based on that examination, he/she must decide, given her/his aversion to risk, if enough of this distribution is above the appropriate (risk-adjusted) required rate of return to warrant acceptance of the project. Thus, the probability tree allows the manager to quickly visualize the possible future events, their probabilities, and their outcomes. In addition, the calculation

HARVARD BUSINESS REVIEW, JANUARY–FEBRUARY, 1994

Financial Engineering at Merck

Last year Merck & Co., Inc., invested well over $2 billion in R&D and capital expenditures combined. The company spent much of the money on risky, long-term projects that are notoriously difficult to evaluate. Indeed, the critics of modern finance would argue that such projects should not be subjected to rigorous financial analysis, because such analysis fails to reflect the strategic value of long-term investments.(A) Yet at Merck, it is those projects with the longest time horizon that receive the most intense and financially sophisticated analyses. In fact, Merck's financial function is active and influential with a highly quantitative, analytical orientation. The company is seldom, if ever, criticized for being shortsighted.

Why doesn't all this analysis choke off long-term investing, as critics of modern finance theory say it should? In part because Merck is a leader in building financial models of scientific and commercial processes and in using those models to improve business decisions. Rather than relying on static, single-point forecasts, Merck's models use probability distributions for numerous variables and come up with a range of possible outcomes that both stimulate discussion and facilitate decision making.(B)

For example, Merck's Research Planning Model, now ten years old, and its Revenue Hedging Model, now four years old, integrate economics, finance, statistics, and computer science to produce disciplined, quantitative analyses of specific elements of Merck's business. These models do not make decisions. Instead, they provide Merck executives with cogent information both about risks and returns and about financial performance for specific projects and activities.(C)

SOURCE: Reprinted by permission of *Harvard Business Review.* An excerpt from "Financial Engineering at Merck" by Timothy A. Luehrman. *Harvard Business Review* (January–February 1994): 93. Copyright © 1994 by The President and Fellows of Harvard College, all rights reserved.

ANALYSIS AND IMPLICATIONS...

A. The risks that pharmaceutical firms face in product development are great. It costs $359 million and takes ten years to bring a new drug to market. Then, once the drug has reached the market, 70 percent of the new drugs introduced do not cover their costs.

B. Rather than simply using an estimate of the project's expected net present value, Merck relies on a simulation approach. They examine the returns on proposed new drugs over a twenty-year period, allowing for any and all complexities that they can foresee.

C. One of the key aspects of the simulation approach used by Merck is the ability to perform sensitivity analysis by changing the value of specific variables and seeing how the results are affected. In this way, Merck can determine where to spend more time in forecasting and where they should spend time and money trying to improve efficiency.

Table 6-4 Conditional Outcomes and Probabilities for Year 2

	If Outcome 1		If Outcome 2		If Outcome 3	
Year 1	$ACF_1 = \$600,000$		$ACF_1 = \$700,000$		$ACF_1 = \$800,000$	
	Then		Then		Then	
Year 2	ACF_2	Probability	ACF_2	Probability	ACF_2	Probability
	$300,000	.2	$300,000	.2	$400,000	.2
	600,000	.8	500,000	.3	600,000	.7
			700,000	.5	800,000	.1

Figure 6-7 Probability Tree

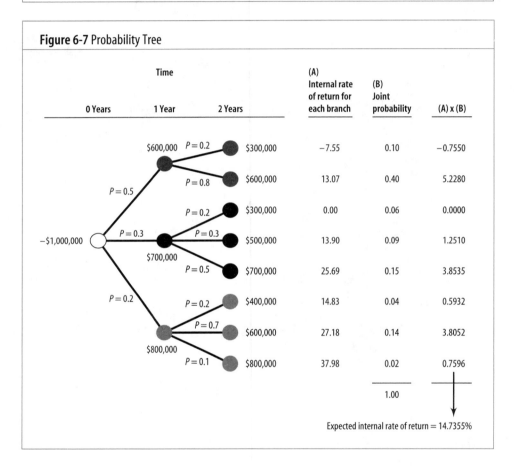

of the expected internal rate of return and enumeration of the distribution should aid the financial manager in determining the risk level of the project.

Other Sources of Risk: Time Dependence of Cash Flows

Up to this point, in all approaches other than the probability tree, we have assumed that the cash flow in one period is independent of the cash flow in the previous period. Although this assumption is appealing because it is simple, in many cases it is also invalid. For example, if a new product is introduced and the initial public reaction is poor, resulting in low initial cash flows, then cash flows in future periods are likely to be low. An extreme example of this is Ford's experience with the Edsel.

Poor consumer acceptance and sales in the first year were followed by even poorer results in the second year. If the Edsel had been received favorably during its first year, it quite likely would have done well in the second year. The end effect of time dependence of cash flows is to increase the risk of the project over time. That is, because large cash flows in the first period lead to large cash flows in the second period, and low cash flows in the first period lead to low cash flows in the second period, the probability distribution of possible net present values tends to be wider than if the cash flows were not dependent over time. The greater the degree of correlation between flows over time, the greater will be the dispersion of the probability distribution.

Other Sources of Risk: Skewness

In all previous approaches other than simulation and probability trees, we have assumed that the distributions of net present values for projects being evaluated are normally distributed. This assumption is not always valid. When it is true, the standard deviation provides an adequate measure of the distribution's dispersion; however, when the distribution is not normally distributed, reliance on the standard deviation can be misleading.

A distribution that is not symmetric is said to be skewed. A **skewed distribution** has either a longer "tail" to the right or to the left. For example, if a distribution is skewed to the right, most values will be clustered around the left end, and the distribution will appear to have a long tail on the right end of the range of values. Graphic illustrations of skewed distributions are presented in Figure 6-8.

The difficulty associated with skewed distributions arises from the fact that the use of the expected value and standard deviation alone may not be enough to differentiate properly between two distributions. For example, the two distributions shown in Figure 6-9 have the same expected value and the same standard deviation; however, distribution A is skewed to the left while B is skewed to the right. If a financial manager were given a choice between these two distributions, assuming they are mutually exclusive, he/she would most likely choose distribution B, because it involves less chance of a negative net present value. Thus, skewness can affect the level of risk and the desirability of a distribution.

SUMMARY

In this chapter, we examine the problem of incorporating risk into the the capital-budgeting decision. First, we explore just what type of risk to adjust for: project standing alone risk, the project's contribution-to-firm risk, or the project's systematic risk. In theory, systematic risk is the appropriate risk measure, but bankruptcy costs and the issue of undiversified shareholders also give weight to considering a project's contribution-to-firm risk as the appropriate risk measure. Both measures of risk have merit and we avoid making any specific allocation of importance between the two in capital budgeting.

Two commonly used methods for incorporating risk into capital budgeting are (1) the certainty equivalent method and (2) risk-adjusted discount rates. The certainty equivalent approach involves a direct attempt to incorporate the decision maker's utility function into the analysis. Under this method, cash flows are adjusted downward by multiplying them by certainty equivalent coefficients, α_t's which transform the risky cash flows into equivalent certain cash flows in terms of desirability. A project's net present value using the certainty equivalent method for adjusting for risk becomes

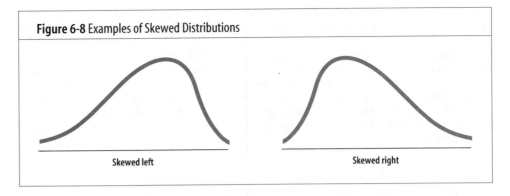

Figure 6-8 Examples of Skewed Distributions

Skewed left

Skewed right

Figure 6-9 Two Distributions with Identical Expected Values and Standard Deviations but Different Skewness

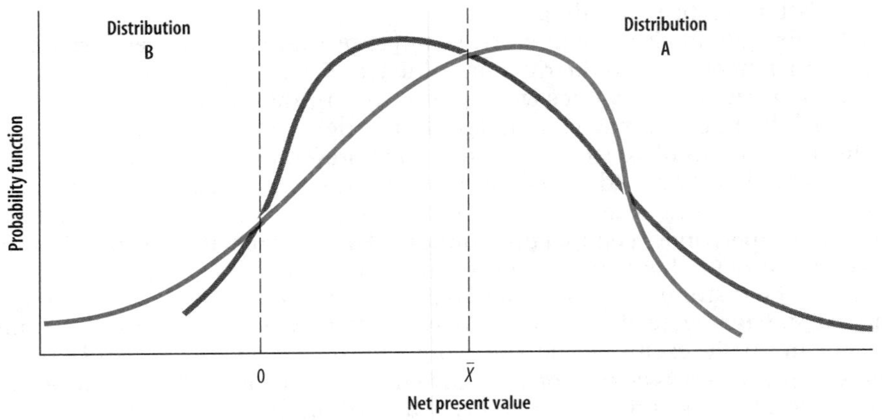

Distribution B

Distribution A

Probability function

0

$\bar{X}$

Net present value

$$NPV = \sum_{t=1}^{n} \frac{\alpha_t ACF_t}{\left(1 + k_{rf}\right)^t} - IO$$

(6-2)

The risk-adjusted discount rate involves an upward adjustment of the discount rate to compensate for risk. This method is based on the concept that investors demand higher returns for riskier projects.

The simulation and probability tree methods are used to provide information as to the location and shape of the distribution of possible outcomes. Decisions could be based directly on these methods, or they could be used to determine input into either certainty equivalent or risk-adjusted discount method approaches.

STUDY QUESTIONS

6-1. Earlier, we examined the payback period capital-budgeting criterion. Often this capital-budgeting criterion is used as a risk-screening device. Explain the rationale behind its use.

6-2. The use of the risk-adjusted discount rate assumes that risk increases over time. Justify this assumption.

6-3. What are the similarities and differences between the risk-adjusted discount rate and certainty equivalent methods for incorporating risk into the capital-budgeting decision?

6-4. What is the value of using the probability tree technique for evaluating capital-budgeting projects?

6-5. Explain how simulation works. What is the value in using a simulation approach?

6-6. What does time dependence of cash flows mean? Why might cash flows be time dependent? Give some examples.

6-7. What does skewness mean? If a distribution is skewed, how does this affect the significance of its standard deviation and mean?

SELF-TEST PROBLEMS

ST-1. G. Norohna and Co. is considering two mutually exclusive projects. The expected values for each project's cash flows are given below.

Year	Project A	Project B
0	−$300,000	−$300,000
1	100,000	200,000
2	200,000	200,000
3	200,000	200,000
4	300,000	300,000
5	300,000	400,000

The company has decided to evaluate these projects using the certainty equivalent method. The certainty equivalent coefficients for each project's cash flows are given below.

Year	Project A	Project B
0	1.00	1.00
1	.95	.90
2	.90	.80
3	.85	.70
4	.80	.60
5	.75	.50

Given that this company's normal required rate of return is 15 percent and the after-tax risk-free rate is 8 percent, which project should be selected?

STUDY PROBLEMS (SET A)

6-1A. (Risk-Adjusted NPV) The Hokie Corporation is considering two mutually exclusive projects. Both require an initial outlay of $10,000 and will operate for five years. The probability distributions associated with each project for years 1 through 5 are given as follows:

Probability Distribution for Cash Flow Years 1–5 (the same cash flow each year)			
Project A		Project B	
Probability	Cash Flow	Probability	Cash Flow
.15	$4,000	.15	$ 2,000
.70	5,000	.70	6,000
.15	6,000	.15	10,000

Because project B is the riskier of the two projects, the management of Hokie Corporation has decided to apply a required rate of return of 15 percent to its evaluation but only a 12 per-cent required rate of return to project A.

    a. Determine the expected value of each project's cash flows.

    b. Determine each project's risk-adjusted net present value.

    c. What other factors might be considered in deciding between these two projects?

6-2A. (Risk-Adjusted NPV) The Goblu Corporation is evaluating two mutually exclusive pro-jects, both of which require an initial outlay of $100,000. Each project has an expected life of five years. The probability distributions associated with the annual cash flows from each pro-ject are given below:

Probability Distribution for Cash Flow Years 1–5 (the same cash flow each year)			
Project A		Project B	
Probability	Cash Flow	Probability	Cash Flow
.10	$35,000	.10	$10,000
.40	40,000	.20	30,000
.40	45,000	.40	45,000
.10	50,000	.20	60,000
		.10	80,000

The normal required rate of return for Goblu is 10 percent, but because these projects are riskier than most, they are requiring a higher-than-normal rate of return on them. On project A they are requiring a 12 percent and on project B a 13 percent rate of return.

    a. Determine the expected value for each project's cash flows.

    b. Determine each project's risk-adjusted net present value.

    c. What other factors might be considered in deciding between these projects?

6-3A. (Certainty Equivalents) The V. Coles Corp. is considering two mutually exclusive pro-jects. The expected values for each project's cash flows are given below:

Year	Project A	Project B
0	−$1,000,000	−$1,000,000
1	500,000	500,000
2	700,000	600,000
3	600,000	700,000
4	500,000	800,000

The management has decided to evaluate these projects using the certainty equivalent method. The certainty equivalent coefficients for each project's cash flows are given below:

Year	Project A	Project B
0	1.00	1.00
1	.95	.90
2	.90	.70
3	.80	.60
4	.70	.50

Given that this company's normal required rate of return is 15 percent and the after-tax risk-free rate is 5 percent, which project should be selected?

6-4A. (Certainty Equivalents) Neustal, Inc., has decided to use the certainty equivalent method in determining whether or not a new investment should be made. The expected cash flows associated with this investment and the estimated certainty equivalent coefficients are as follows:

Year	Expected Values for Cash Flows	Certainty Equivalent Coefficients
0	−$90,000	1.00
1	25,000	0.95
2	30,000	0.90
3	30,000	0.83
4	25,000	0.75
5	20,000	0.65

Given that Neustal's normal required rate of return is 18 percent and that the after-tax risk free rate is 7 percent, should this project be accepted?

6-5A. (Risk-Adjusted Discount Rates and Risk Classes) The G. Wolfe Corporation is examining two capital-budgeting projects with five-year lives. The first, project A, is a replacement project; the second, project B, is a project unrelated to current operations. The G. Wolfe Corporation uses the risk-adjusted discount rate method and groups projects according to purpose and then uses a required rate of return or discount rate that has been preassigned to that purpose or risk class. The expected cash flows for these projects are given below:

	Project A	Project B
Initial Investment:	$250,000	$400,000
Cash inflows:		
Year 1	$ 30,000	$135,000
Year 2	40,000	135,000
Year 3	50,000	135,000
Year 4	90,000	135,000
Year 5	130,000	135,000

The purpose/risk classes and preassigned required rates of return are as follows:

Purpose	Required Rate of Return
Replacement decision	12%
Modification or expansion of existing product line	15
Project unrelated to current operations	18
Research and development operations	20

Determine the project's risk-adjusted net present value.

6-6A. (Certainty Equivalents) Nacho Nachtmann Company uses the certainty equivalent approach when it evaluates risky investments. The company presently has two mutually exclusive investment proposals, with an expected life of four years each, to choose from with money it received from the sale of part of its toy division to another company. The expected net cash flows are given below:

Year	Project A	Project B
0	−$50,000	−$50,000
1	15,000	20,000
2	15,000	25,000
3	15,000	25,000
4	45,000	30,000

The certainty equivalent coefficients for the net cash flows are as follows:

Year	Project A	Project B
0	1.00	1.00
1	.95	.90
2	.85	.85
3	.80	.80
4	.70	.75

Which of the two investment proposals should be chosen, given that the after-tax risk-free rate of return is 6 percent?

6-7A. (Probability Trees) The M. Solt Corporation is evaluating an investment proposal with an expected life of two years. This project will require an initial outlay of $1,200,000. The resultant possible cash flows are given below:

Possible Outcomes in Year 1			
	Probability		
	.6	.3	.1
	Outcome 1	Outcome 2	Outcome 3
Cash flow =	$700,000	$850,000	$1,000,000

Conditional Outcomes and Probabilities for Year 2						
If ACF$_1$ = $700,000		If ACF$_1$ = $850,000		If ACF$_1$ = $1,000,000		
ACF$_2$	Probability	ACF$_2$	Probability	ACF$_2$	Probability	
$ 300,000	.3	$ 400,000	.2	$ 600,000	.1	
700,000	.6	700,000	.5	900,000	.5	
1,100,000	.1	1,000,000	.2	1,100,000	.4	
		1,300,000	.1			

    a. Construct a probability tree representing the possible outcomes.

    b. Determine the joint probability of each possible sequence of events taking place.

    c. What is the expected IRR of this project?

    d. What is the range of possible IRRs for this project?

6-8A. (Probability Trees) V. Janjigian, Inc., is considering expanding its operations into computer-based basketball games. Janjigian feels that there is a three-year life associated with this project, and it will initially involve an investment of $100,000. It also believes there is a 60 percent chance of success and a cash flow of $100,000 in year 1 and a 40 percent chance of failure and a $10,000 cash flow in year 1. If the project fails in year 1, there is a 60 percent chance that it will produce cash flows of only $10,000 in years 2 and 3. There is also a 40 percent chance that it will *really* fail and Janjigian will earn nothing in year 2 and get out of this line of business, with the project terminating and no cash flow occurring in year 3. If, conversely, this project succeeds in the first year, then cash flows in the second year are expected to be $200,000, $175,000, or $150,000 with probabilities of .30, .50, and .20, respectively. Finally, if the project succeeds in the third and final year of operation, the cash flows are expected to be either $30,000 more or $20,000 less than they were in year 2, with an equal chance of occurrence.

    a. Construct a probability tree representing the possible outcomes.

    b. Determine the joint probability of each possible sequence of events.

    c. What is the expected IRR?

    d. What is the range of possible IRRs for this project?

I t's been four months since you took a position as an assistant financial analyst at Caledonia Products. During that time, you've had a promotion and now are working as a special assistant for capital budgeting to the CEO of Caledonia Products. Your latest assignment involves the analysis of several risky projects. Since this is your first assignment dealing with risk analysis, you have been asked not only to provide a recommendation on the projects in question, but also to respond to a number of questions aimed at judging your understanding of analysis and capital budgeting. The memorandum you received outlining your assignment follows:

TO: The Special Assistant for Capital Budgeting

FROM: Mr. V. Morrison, CEO, Caledonia Products

RE: Capital Budgeting and Risk Analysis

Provide a written response to the following questions:

    a. In capital budgeting, risk can be measured from three perspectives. What are those three measures of a project's risk?

    b. According to the CAPM, which measurement of a project's risk is relevant? What complications does reality introduce into the CAPM view of risk and what does that mean for our view of the relevant measure of a project's risk?

    c. What are the similarities and differences between the risk-adjusted discount rate and certainty equivalent methods for incorporating risk into the capital-budgeting decision?

d. Why might we use the probability-tree technique for evaluating capital-budgeting projects?

e. Explain how simulation works. What is the value in using a simulation approach?

f. What is sensitivity analysis and what is its purpose?

g. What does time dependence of cash flows mean? Why might cash flows be time dependent? Give some examples.

h. Caledonia Products is using the certainty equivalent approach to evaluate two mutually exclusive investment proposals with an expected life of four years. The expected net cash flows are given below:

Year	Project A	Project B
0	−$150,000	−$200,000
1	40,000	50,000
2	40,000	60,000
3	40,000	60,000
4	100,000	50,000

The certainty equivalent coefficients for the net cash flows are as follows:

Year	Project A	Project B
0	1.00	1.00
1	.90	.95
2	.85	.85
3	.80	.80
4	.70	.75

Which of the two investment proposals should be chosen, given that the after-tax risk-free rate of return is 7 percent?

i. Caledonia is considering an additional investment project with an expected life of two years and would like some insights on the level of risk this project has using the probability tree method. The initial outlay on this project would be $600,000, and the resultant possible cash flows are given below:

Possible Outcomes in Year 1			
	.4	.4	.2
	Outcome 1	Outcome 2	Outcome 3
Cash flow =	$300,000	$350,000	$450,000

Conditional Outcomes and Probabilities for Year 2					
If $ACF_1 = \$300,000$		If $ACF_1 = \$350,000$		If $ACF_1 = \$450,000$	
ACF_2	Probability	ACF_2	Probability	ACF_2	Probability
$200,000	.3	$ 250,000	.2	$ 300,000	.2
300,000	.7	450,000	.5	500,000	.5
		650,000	.3	700,000	.2
				1,000,000	.1

1. Construct a probability tree representing the possible outcomes.
2. Determine the joint probability of each possible sequence of events taking place.
3. What is the expected IRR of this project?
4. What is the range of possible IRRs for this project?

CASE PROBLEM

MADE IN THE U.S.A.: DUMPED IN BRAZIL, AFRICA . . .

Ethics in Dealing with Uncertainty in Capital Budgeting, or What Happens When a Project Is No Longer Sellable

In an uncertain world, capital budgeting attempts to determine what the future of a new product will bring and how then to act on that forecast. We never know for certain what the future will bring, but we do arrive at some idea of what the distribution of possible outcomes looks like. Unfortunately, when there is uncertainty, the outcome is not always a good one. For example, what happens if the government rules that our product is not safe. The answer is that we must abandon the product. The question then becomes what to do with the inventory we currently have on hand. We certainly want to deal with it in a way that is in the best interests of our shareholders. We also want to obey the law and act ethically. As with most ethical questions, there isn't necessarily a right or wrong answer.

When it comes to the safety of young children, fire is a parent's nightmare. Just the thought of their young ones trapped in their cribs and beds by a raging nocturnal blaze is enough to make most mothers and fathers take every precaution to ensure their children's safety. Little wonder that when fire-retardant children's pajamas hit the market in the mid-1970s, they proved an overnight success. Within a few short years, more than 200 million pairs were sold, and the sales of millions more were all but guaranteed. For their manufacturers, the future could not have been been brighter. Then, like a bolt from the blue, came word that the pajamas were killers.

In June 1977, the U.S. Consumer Product Safety Commission (CPSC) banned the sale of these pajamas and ordered the recall of millions of pairs. Reason: The pajamas contained the flame-retardant chemical Tris (2,3-dibromoprophyl), which had been found to cause kidney cancer in children.

Whereas just months earlier the 100 medium- and small-garment manufacturers of the Tris-impregnated pajamas couldn't fill orders fast enough, suddenly they were worrying about how to get rid of the millions of pairs now sitting in warehouses. Because of its toxicity, the sleepwear couldn't even be thrown away, let alone be sold. Indeed, the CPSC left no doubt about how the pajamas were to be disposed of—buried or burned or used as industrial wiping cloths. All meant millions of dollars in losses for manufacturers.

The companies affected—mostly small, family-run operations employing fewer than 100 workers—immediately attempted to shift blame to the mills that made the cloth. When that attempt failed, they tried to get the big department stores that sold the pajamas and the chemical companies that produced Tris to share the financial losses. Again, no sale. Finally, in desperation, the companies lobbied in Washington for a bill making the federal government partially responsible for the losses. It was the government, they argued, that originally had required the companies to add Tris to pajamas and then had prohibited their sale. Congress was sympathetic; it passed a bill granting companies relief. But President Carter vetoed it.

While the small firms were waging their political battle in the halls of Congress, ads began appearing in the classified pages of *Women's Wear Daily*. "Tris-Tris-Tris ... We will buy any fabric containing Tris," read one. Another said, "Tris—we will purchase any large quantities of garments containing Tris."[1] The ads had been placed by exporters, who began buying up the pajamas, usually at 10 to 30 percent of the normal wholesale price. Their intent was clear: to dump[2] the carcinogenic pajamas on overseas markets.[3]

Tris is not the only example of dumping. In 1972, 400 Iraqis died and 5,000 were hospitalized after eating wheat and barley treated with a U.S.-banned organic mercury fungicide. Winstrol, a synthetic male hormone that had been found to stunt the growth of American children, was made available in Brazil as an appetite stimulant for children. Depo-Provera, an injectable contraceptive known to cause malignant tumors in animals, was shipped overseas to seventy countries where it was used in U.S.-sponsored population control programs. And 450,000 baby pacifiers, of the type known to have caused choking deaths, were exported for sale overseas.

Manufacturers that dump products abroad clearly are motivated by profit or at least by the hope of avoiding financial losses resulting from having to withdraw a product from the market. For government and health agencies that cooperate in the exporting of dangerous products, the motives are more complex.

---

[1]Mark Hosenball, "Karl Marx and the Pajama Game," *Mother Jones* (November 1979): 47.

[2]"Dumping" is a term apparently coined by *Mother Jones* magazine to refer to the practice of exporting to overseas countries products that have been banned or declared hazardous in the United States.

[3]Unless otherwise noted, the facts and quotations reported in this case are based on Mark Dowie, "The Corporate Crime of the Century," *Mother Jones* (November 1971) and Russell Mokhiber, *Corporate Crime and Violence* (San Francisco: Sierra Club Books, 1988), 181–95. See also Jane Kay, "Global Dumping of U.S. Toxics Is Big Business," *San Francisco Examiner* (September 23, 1990): A2.

For example, as early as 1971, the dangers of the Dalkon Shield intrauterine device were well documented.[4] Among the adverse reactions were pelvic inflammation, blood poisoning, pregnancies resulting in spontaneous abortions, tubal pregnancies, and uterine perforations. A number of deaths were even attributed to the device. Faced with losing its domestic market, A. H. Robins Co., manufacturer of the Dalkon Shield, worked out a deal with the Office of Population within the U. S. Agency for International Development (AID), whereby AID bought thousands of the devices at a reduced price for use in population-control programs in forty-two countries.

Why do governmental and population-control agencies approve for sale and use overseas birth control devices proved dangerous in the United States? They say their motives are humanitarian. Since the rate of dying in childbirth is high in Third World countries, almost any birth control device is preferable to none. Third World scientists and government officials frequently support this argument. They insist that denying their countries access to the contraceptives of their choice is tantamount to violating their countries' national sovereignty.

Apparently this argument has found a sympathetic ear in Washington, for it turns up in the "notification" system that regulates the export of banned or dangerous products overseas. Based on the principles of national sovereignty, self-determination, and free trade, the notification system requires that foreign governments be notified whenever a product is banned, deregulated, suspended, or canceled by an American regulatory agency. The State Department, which implements the system, has a policy statement on the subject that reads in part: "No country should establish itself as the arbiter of others' health and safety standards. Individual governments are generally in the best position to establish standards of public health and safety."

Critics of the system claim that notifying foreign health officials is virtually useless. For one thing, other governments rarely can establish health standards or even control imports into their countries. Indeed, most of the Third World countries where banned or dangerous products are dumped lack regulatory agencies, adequate testing facilities, and well-staffed customs departments.

Then there's the problem of getting the word out about hazardous products. In theory, when a government agency such as the Environmental Protection Agency or the Food and Drug Administration (FDA) finds a product hazardous, it is supposed to inform the State Department, which is to notify local health officials. But agencies often fail to inform the State Department of the product they have banned or found harmful. And when it is notified, its communiqués typically go no further than the U.S. embassies abroad. One embassy official even told the General Accounting Office that he "did not routinely forward notification of chemicals not registered in the host country because it may adversely affect U.S. exporting." When foreign officials are notified by U.S. embassies, they sometimes find the communiqués vague or ambiguous or too technical to understand.

In an effort to remedy these problems, at the end of his term in office, President Jimmy Carter issued an executive order that (1) improved export notice procedures; (2) called for publishing an annual summary of substances banned or severely restricted for domestic use in the United States; (3) directed the State Department and other federal agencies to participate in the development of international hazards alert systems; and (4) established procedures for placing formal export licensing controls on a limited number of extremely hazardous substances. In one of his first acts as president, however, Ronald Reagan rescinded the order. Later in his administration, the law that formerly prohibited U.S. pharmaceutical companies from exporting drugs that are banned or not registered in this country was weakened to allow the export to twenty-one countries of drugs not yet approved for use in the United States.

But even if communication procedures were improved or the export of dangerous products forbidden, there are ways that companies can circumvent these threats to their profits—for example, by simply changing the name of the product or by exporting the individual ingredients of a product to a plant in a foreign country. Once there, the ingredients can be reassembled and the product dumped.[5] Upjohn, for example, through its Belgian subsidiary, continues to produce Depo-Provera, which the FDA has consistently refused to approve for use in this country. And the prohibition on the export of dangerous drugs is not that hard to sidestep. "Unless the package bursts open on the dock," one drug company executive observes, "you have no chance of being caught."

Unfortunately for us, in the case of pesticides the effects of overseas dumping are now coming home. The Environmental Protection Agency bans from the United States all crop uses of DDT and Dieldrin, which kill fish, cause tumors in animals, and build up in the fatty tissue of humans. It also bans heptachlor, chlordane, leptophos, endrin, and many other pesticides, including 2,4,5-T (which contains the deadly poison dioxin, the active ingredient in Agent Orange, the notorious defoliant used in Vietnam) because they are dangerous to human beings. No law, however, prohibits the sale of DDT and these other U.S.-banned pesticides overseas, where thanks to corporate dumping they are routinely used in agriculture. The FDA now estimates, through spot checks, that 10 percent of our imported food is contaminated with illegal residues of banned pesticides. And the FDA's most commonly used testing procedure does not even check for 70 percent of the pesticides known to cause cancer.

SOURCE: Adapted by permission from William Shaw and Vincent Barry, *Moral Issues in Business,* 5th ed. (New York: Wadsworth, 1992), 28–31. Copyright © 1992 by Wadsworth Inc.

Questions

1. Was the dumping in this case ethical? Those involved in the dumping might have argued that the people receiving the pajamas would not have otherwise had access to such clothing and were notified of the health and safety haz-

---

[4]See Mark Dowie and Tracy Johnston, "A Case of Corporate Malpractice," *Mother Jones* (November 1976).

[5]Mark Dowie, "A Dumper's Guide to Tricks of the Trade," *Mother Jones* (November 1979): 25.

ards. Does this affect your feelings about the case? What do you think about the exportation of the Dalkon Shield? Can it be justified because the rate of dying during childbirth in Third World countries is extremely high, and, as such, any effective birth control device is better than none?

2. What obligations did the financial managers have to their shareholders to do whatever is possible to avoid major financial losses associated with these products?

3. Is it still immoral or unethical to dump goods when doing so does not violate any U.S. laws? How about when those receiving the goods know the dangers? Why do you think dumpers dump? Do you think they believe what they are doing is ethically acceptable?

SECTION III
PROJECT FINANCIAL PLANNING

CHAPTER 7

FINANCIAL FORECASTING, PLANNING, AND BUDGETING

7.1. THE IMPACT OF FINANCIAL FORECASTING ON PROJECT SUCCESS

Financial forecasting and budgeting is an accounting and financial activity shared by most project managers. The manner in which the task is performed can have a significant impact on the project. Effective financial forecasting impacts and is used by each of the areas that affect project goal achievement (see the text "Introduction" for details). If the forecast is biased it will cloud stakeholder's views of the project leader's integrity as well as the overall knowledge base. For the project organization, it can alter the selection of projects. For the host organization, it could impact the bottom line as well as the attainment of organizational goals. Forecasting should reflect the external environment and expected changes to attain the highest probability of project success.

The following reading from Keown presents a generalized discussion of financial forecasting, planning, and budgeting. All the subjects discussed in the reading apply directly to the project management discipline.

7.2. FINANCIAL FORECASTING, PLANNING, AND BUDGETING

FINANCIAL FORECASTING

Forecasting in financial management is used to estimate a firm's future financial needs. The basic steps involved in predicting those financing needs are the following: **Step 1:** Project the firm's sales revenues and expenses over the planning period. **Step 2:** Estimate the levels of investment in current and fixed assets that are necessary to support the projected sales. **Step 3:** Determine the firm's financing needs throughout the planning period.

Sales Forecast

The key ingredient in the firm's planning process is the *sales forecast*. This projection is generally derived using information from a number of sources. At a minimum, the sales forecast for the coming year would reflect (1) any past trend in sales that is expected to carry through into the new year, and (2) the influence of any events that might materially affect that trend. An example of the latter would be the initiation of a major advertising campaign or a change in the firm's pricing policy.

Forecasting Financial Variables

Traditional financial forecasting takes the sales forecast as a given and makes projections of its impact on the firm's various expenses, assets, and liabilities. The most commonly used method for making these projections is the percent of sales method.

Percent of Sales Method of Financial Forecasting

The **percent of sales method** involves estimating the level of an expense, asset, or liability for a future period as a percent of the sales forecast. The percentage used can come from the most recent financial statement item as a percent of current sales, from an average computed over several years, from the judgment of the analyst, or from some combination of these sources.

Figure 7-1 presents a complete example of the use of the percent of sales method of financial forecasting. In this example each item in the firm's balance sheet that varies with sales is converted to a percentage of 1995 sales of $10 million. The forecast of the new balance for each item is then calculated by multiplying this percentage times the $12 million in projected sales for the 1996 planning period. This method of forecasting future financing is not as precise or detailed as the method using a cash budget, which is presented later; however, it offers a relatively low-cost and easy-to-use first approximation of the firm's financing needs for a future period.

Note that in the example in Figure 7-1, both current and fixed assets are assumed to vary with the level of firm sales. This means that the firm does not have sufficient productive capacity to absorb a projected increase in sales. Thus, if sales were to rise by $1, fixed assets would rise by $ .40, or 40 percent of the projected increase in sales. Note that if the fixed assets the firm currently owns were sufficient to support the projected level of new sales, these assets should not be allowed to vary with sales. If this were the case, then fixed assets would not be converted to a percent of sales and would be projected to remain unchanged for the period being forecast.

Also, we note that accounts payable and accrued expenses are the only liabilities allowed to vary with sales. Both these accounts might reasonably be expected to rise and fall with the level of firm sales, hence, the use of the percent of sales forecast. Because these two categories of current liabilities normally vary directly with the level of sales, they are often referred to as **spontaneous sources of financing.** Notes payable, long-term debt, common stock, and paid-in capital are not assumed to vary directly with the level of firm sales. These sources of financing are termed **discretionary,** in that the firm's management must make a conscious decision to seek additional financing using any one of them. Finally, we note that the level of retained earnings does vary with estimated sales. The predicted change in the level of retained earnings equals the estimated after-tax profits (projected net income) equal to 5 percent of sales or $600,000 less the common stock dividends of $300,000.

Thus, using the example from Figure 7-1, we estimate that firm sales will increase from $10 million to $12 million, which will cause the firm's needs for total

Figure 7-1 Using the Percent of Sales Method to Forecast Future Financing Requirements

Assets	Present (1995)	Percent of Sales (1995 Sales = $10 M)	Projected (Based on 1996 Sales = $12 M)
Current assets	$2.0 M	$\frac{\$2\,M}{\$10\,M} = 20\%$	.2 x $12 M = $2.4 M
Net fixed assets	$4.0 M	$\frac{\$4\,M}{\$10\,M} = 40\%$	.4 x $12 M = $4.8 M
Total	$6.0 M		$7.2 M

Liabilities and Owners' Equity			
Accounts payable	$1.0 M	$\frac{\$1\,M}{\$10\,M} = 10\%$	.10 x $12 M = $1.2 M
Accrued expenses	1.0 M	$\frac{\$1\,M}{\$10\,M} = 10\%$	.10 x $12 M = $1.2 M
Notes payable	.5 M	NA[a]	no change	.5 M
Long-term debt	$2.0 M	NA[a]	no change	2.0 M
Total liabilities	$4.5 M			$4.9 M
Common stock	$.1 M	NA[a]	no change	$ .1 M
Paid-in capital	.2 M	NA[a]	no change	.2 M
Retained earnings	1.2 M		1.2M [.05 x $12 M x (1 – .5)] = 1.5 M[b]	
Common equity	$1.5 M			$1.8 M
Total	$6.0 M		Total financing provided	$6.7 M
			Discretionary financing needed	.5 M[c]
			Total	$7.2 M

[a] Not applicable. These account balances are assumed not to vary with sales.

[b] Projected retained earnings equals the beginning level ($1.2 M) plus projected net income less any dividends paid. In this case net income is projected to equal 5 percent of sales, and dividends are projected to equal half of net income: .05 x $12 M x (1 – .5) = $300,000.

[c] Discretionary financing needed equals projected total assets ($7.2 M) less projected total liabilities ($4.9 M) less projected common equity ($1.8), or $7.2 M – 4.9 M – 1.8 M = $500,000.

assets to rise to $7.2 million. These assets will then be financed by $4.9 million in existing liabilities plus spontaneous liabilities; $1.8 million in owner funds, including $300,000 in retained earnings from next year's sales; and finally, $500,000 in discretionary financing, which can be raised by issuing notes payable, selling bonds, offering an issue of stock, or some combination of these sources.

In summary, we can estimate the firm's needs for discretionary financing, using the percent of sales method of financial forecasting, by following a four-step procedure:

Step 1: Convert each asset and liability account that varies directly with firm sales to a percent of current year's sales.

EXAMPLE

$$\frac{\text{current assets}}{\text{sales}} = \frac{\$2\,M}{\$10\,M} = .2 \text{ or } 20\%$$

Step 2: Project the level of each asset and liability account in the balance sheet using its percent of sales multiplied by projected sales or by leaving the

FORBES, FEBRUARY 9, 1987

Now You See It . . .

Cash flow is at least as important a measure of corporate health as reported earnings. But put a dozen investors in a room and you'll get almost as many different definitions.

After grappling with the problem for more than six years, the Financial Accounting Standards Board has come up with the beginnings of a more precise definition. It would require all companies to use the same format to explain how cash and cash equivalents change from one reporting period to the next. The proposal still leaves companies with room for flexibility but will make investors' lives much easier. Why? Companies will have to show sources and uses of cash in three areas: operations, investing, and financing.

Let's take a specific case: Lowe's Cos., the North Carolina-based retailer of building materials. The company said in its annual report that cash flow amounted to $2.31 per share in 1985 as compared with $2.20 the year before.

An investor looking at these numbers might have assumed Lowe's had plenty of cash left over for dividends and other purposes.

Not necessarily so. Although Lowe's used a generally accepted definition of cash flow, it was not a strict definition. It failed to subtract the cash absorbed by higher inventories and receivables. **(A)** Lowe's ended the year with hardly more cash than it started the year, and its long-term debt almost doubled from 1984 to 1985—despite the positive cash flow.

Does it really matter how you measure cash flow? Very much. While Lowe's is healthy—the increased inventory and receivables simply reflect growth in revenues—there are situations where a company can go broke while reporting positive cash flow. How can this be? Simple.

Suppose inventories and receivables rise faster than sales, reflecting slow pay by customers and unsold goods. Under the simpler method of reporting cash flow (which would not include working-capital components), such a company could report a positive cash flow even while it was fast running out of cash.**(B)**

When the smoke clears, investors will still need to do lots of homework. It's never enough to know just what the numbers are. You still have to figure out what the numbers mean. Again, Lowe's is an example. Even if it were forced to report a negative cash flow, it would still be a very healthy business; it would cease being one only if inventories and receivables increased faster than sales and the company's credit were deteriorating.

When it comes to some things, the more you try simplifying them, the more complicated they become.

Excerpted by permission of Forbes (February 9, 1987): 70. © Forbes Inc. 1987

ANALYSIS AND IMPLICATIONS...

A. A crude way to estimate a firm's cash flow is to add depreciation and other non-cash expenses to a firm's reported net income. This does not measure the cash flow that actually passes through the firm during the period, however. The reason is that firms account for their income using the accrual method of accounting. The accrual method recognizes as income for the period all revenues "earned" during the period and recognizes as expenses all those expenses incurred in generating those revenues. This means, for example, that a firm might sell $4,000,000 worth of merchandise in February that cost it $3,000,000. This generates $1,000,000 in gross profit. Now, let's assume that the items sold during February were actually purchased and paid for in January such that the firm does not pay out any cash during February. Furthermore, let's assume that the items sold in February are all sold on terms of net 60 meaning that no cash will be received for 60 days. What is the firm's cash flow for the period? Zero. The cash flow statement (discussed in Chapter 3) provides a uniform method of accounting for differences in the way that we account for income and the actual flow of cash.

B. Consider the following example: The firm has $100,000 in cash and $825,000 in inventories at the beginning of January. January's sales are collected in equal amounts during the following two months so that all of January's sales end up in accounts receivable. During January the firm purchased and paid for the items it will sell in February (cost of goods sold is 75% of sales so purchases during January for February sales equal .75 × $1,100,000 = $825,000). Note that the firm is highly profitable, earning a gross profit margin of 25% on each dollar of revenues. Now, notice that sales are growing rapidly at a rate of 10% each month. This means that the firm's purchases for inventories (that are paid for immediately) are higher than its collections from sales (which lag sales by 60 days). Consequently its cash position deteriorates and actually becomes negative. Thus, even highly profitable firms that are growing rapidly can experience cash shortages. We will discuss this problem in more depth later when we discuss the Sustainable Rate of Growth concept.

	January	February	March	April	May
Sales Revenues	$1,000,000	$1,100,000	$1,210,000	$1,331,000	$1,464,100
Cash	100,000	(307,500)	(255,750)	(198,825)	(136,208)
Accounts Receivable	1,000,000	600,000	160,000	76,000	193,600
Inventories	825,000	907,500	998,250	1,098,075	1,207,883

account balance unchanged where the account does not vary with the level of sales.

EXAMPLE

$$\text{projected current assets} =$$
$$\text{projected sales} \times \frac{\text{current assets}}{\text{sales}} = \$12 \text{ M} \times .2 = \$2.4 \text{ M}$$

Step 3: Project the addition to retained earnings available to help finance the firm's operations. This equals projected net income for the period less planned common stock dividends.

EXAMPLE

$$\text{projected addition to retained earnings} =$$
$$\text{projected sales} \times \frac{\text{net income}}{\text{sales}} \times \left(1 - \frac{\text{cash dividends}}{\text{net income}}\right)$$
$$= \$12 \text{ M} \times .05 \times [1 - .5] = \$300,000$$

Step 4: Project the firm's need for discretionary financing as the projected level of total assets less projected liabilities and owners' equity.

EXAMPLE

$$\text{discretionary financing needed} =$$
$$\text{projected total assets} - \text{projected total liabilities} - \text{projected owner's equity}$$
$$= \$7.2 \text{ M} - \$4.9 \text{ M} - \$1.8 \text{ M} = \$500,000$$

The Discretionary Financing Needed (DFN) Model

In the preceding discussion, we estimated DFN (discretionary financing needed) as the difference in projected total assets and the sum of projected liabilities and owner's equity. We can estimate DFN directly using the predicted change in sales (ΔS) and corresponding changes in assets, liabilities, and owner's equity as follows:

$$\text{DFN}_{t+1} = \begin{array}{c} \text{projected} \\ \text{change in} \\ \text{assets} \end{array} - \begin{array}{c} \text{projected} \\ \text{change in} \\ \text{liabilities} \end{array} - \begin{array}{c} \text{projected} \\ \text{change in} \\ \text{owners'equity} \end{array} \qquad (7\text{-}1)$$

or

$$\text{DFN}_{t+1} = \left[\frac{\text{assets}_t{}^*}{\text{sales}_t}\Delta\text{sales}_{t+1}\right] - \left[\frac{\text{liabilities}_t{}^*}{\text{sales}_t}\Delta\text{sales}_{t+1}\right] - \left[\text{NPM}_{t+1}(1-b)\text{sales}_{t+1}\right]$$

where

DFN_{t+1} = predicted discretionary financing needed for period $t+1$.

$assets_t{}^*$ = those assets in period t that are expected to change in proportion to the level of sales. In our example we have assumed that all the firm's assets vary in proportion to sales. We will have more to say about this assumption in the next section, where we consider economies of scale and lumpy fixed asset investments.

$sales_t$ = the level of sales for the period t.

$\Delta sales_{t+1}$ = the change in sale projected for period $t+1$, i.e., $sales_{t+1} - sales_t$. Note that "Δ" is the Greek symbol delta which is used here to represent "change."

$liabilities_t^*$ = those liabilities in period t that are expected to change in proportion to the level of sales. In our preceding example we assumed that accounts payable and accrued expenses varied with sales, but notes payable and long-term debt did not.

NPM_{t+1} = the net profit margin (Net Income ÷ sales) projected for period $t+1$.

b = dividends as a percent of net income or the dividend payout ratio such that $(1 - b)$ is the proportion of the firm's projected net income that will be retained and reinvested in the firm (that is, $(1 - b)$ is the retention ratio).

Using the numbers from the preceding example, we estimate DFN_{1996} as follows:

$$DFN_{1996} = \left(\frac{\$2\,M + 4\,M}{\$10\,M}\right)\$2\,M - \left(\frac{\$1\,M + 1\,M}{\$10\,M}\right)\$2\,M - [.05(1 - .5)\$12\,M]$$

$$= \$.5 \text{ million or } \$500,000$$

Analyzing the Effects of Profitability and Dividend Policy on DFN

Using the DFN model we can quickly and easily evaluate the sensitivity of our projected financing requirements to changes in key variables. For example, using the information from the preceding example we evaluate the effect of net profit margins (NPM) equal to 1 percent, 5 percent, and 10 percent in combination with dividend payout ratios of 30 percent, 50 percent, and 70 percent as follows:

Discretionary Financing Needed for Various Net Profit Margins and Dividend Payout Ratios

Net Profit Margin	Dividend Payout Ratios (Dividends ÷ Net Income)		
	30%	50%	70%
1%	$716,000	$740,000	$764,000
5%	380,000	500,000	620,000
10%	(40,000)	200,000	440,000

If these values for the net profit margin represent reasonable estimates of the possible ranges of values the firm might experience, and if the firm is considering dividend payouts ranging from 30 percent to 70 percent, then we estimate that the firm's financing requirements (DFN) will range from ($40,000), which represents a surplus of $40,000, to a situation where it would need to acquire $764,000. Lower net profit margins mean higher fund requirements. Also, higher dividend payout percentages, other things remaining constant, lead to a need for more discretionary financing. This is a direct result of the fact that a high-dividend-paying firm retains less of its earnings.

The Sustainable Rate of Growth

The **sustainable rate of growth** (g^*) represents the rate at which a firm's sales can grow if it wants to maintain its present financial ratios and *does not* want to resort to the sale of new equity shares. We can solve for the sustainable rate of growth directly using the discretionary financing needed formula found in equation 7-1 as

Table 7-1 Harris Electronics Corporation: Sustainable Rate of Growth Calculations

	1995	1994	1993	1992	1991
Sales	$1,500.00	$1,450.00	$1,400.00	$1,150.00	$1,090.00
Net Income	75.00	73.00	70.00	58.00	55.00
Dividends	30.00	29.20	28.00	23.20	22.00
Common equity	$ 725.00	$ 680.00	$ 637.00	$ 595.00	$ 560.00
Liabilities	625.00	625.00	623.00	440.00	421.00
Liabilities & owner's equity	$1,350.00	$1,305.00	$1,260.00	$1,035.00	$ 981.00
Return on equity (ROE)	10.34%	10.74%	10.99%	9.75%	9.82%
Retention ratio (1–b)	60.00%	60.00%	60.00%	60.00%	60.00%
Debt to assets ratio	46.30%	47.89%	49.44%	42.51%	42.92%
New common stock	—	—	—	—	—
Sustainable rate of growth	6.21%	6.44%	6.59%	5.85%	5.89%
Actual growth rate in sales	NA	3.45%	3.57%	21.74%	5.50%

NA—Not available or cannot be calculated without 1996 data.

illustrated below.* Specifically, the sustainable rate of growth is that rate of sales growth for which discretionary financing needed equals zero. The resulting formula is quite simple and relies on the return on equity (ROE) ratio and dividend payout ratio (b).

(7-2)

Sustainable Rate of Growth $(g^*) = \text{ROE} \,(1 - b)$

and we recall that ROE is defined as follows:

$$\text{ROE} = \frac{\text{net income}}{\text{common equity}}$$

Equation 7-2 is deceptively simple. Note that a firm's ROE is determined by a number of factors, including the firm's profit margin, asset turnover and its use of financial leverage. Specifically, recall that we developed the following relationship for ROE:

$\text{ROE} = $ (net profit margin) $\times$ (total asset turnover) $\div$ (1 − debt ratio)

or

$$\text{ROE} = \left(\frac{\text{net income}}{\text{sales}}\right) \times \left(\frac{\text{sales}}{\text{assets}}\right) \div \left(1 - \frac{\text{total debt}}{\text{total assets}}\right).$$

---

*We can evaluate the impact of differing rates of sales growth on DFN by recognizing that the growth in firm sales, g, is simply the ratio of the projected change in sales divided by the most recent past level of sales (Sales_t). Rearranging terms in equation 7-1 and substituting g for $\frac{\Delta\text{sales}_{t+1}}{\text{sales}_t}$ we get the following result:

$\text{DFN}_{t+1} = g \cdot \text{assets}_t - \text{liabilities}_t \cdot g - \text{NPM}\,(1 - b)\,\text{sales}_{t+1}$

Note that the Sustainable Rate of Growth is that growth rate in firm sales (g^*) which makes $\text{DFN}_{t+1} = 0$. Thus setting DFN_{t+1} in the above equation equal to zero and solving for g, we get the Sustainable Rate of Growth equation:

Sustainable Rate of Growth $(g^*) = \text{ROE}\,(1 - b)$

where ROE is the return on equity (Net Income ÷ Common Equity) and b is the fraction of firm earnings paid out in dividends or the Dividend Payout Ratio.

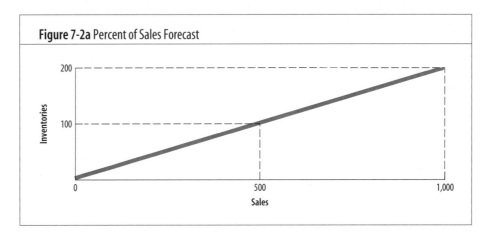

Figure 7-2a Percent of Sales Forecast

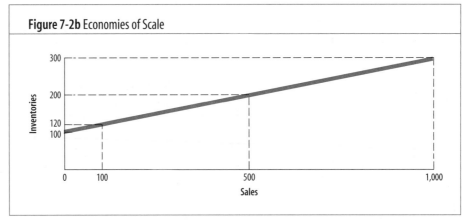

Figure 7-2b Economies of Scale

Hence, the firm's sustainable rate of growth is determined by all the determinants of its return on equity (net profit margin, total asset turnover, and financial leverage) and its choice of a dividend payout ratio (b). To illustrate the calculation of the sustainable rate of growth, consider the financial information for the Harris Electronics Corporation found in Table 7-1.

Harris experienced reasonably stable sustainable rates of growth ranging from a low of 5.85 percent in 1992 to a high of 6.59 percent in 1993. The reasons for the modest variation are easy to see from the data in Table 7-1. The firm's rate of return on common equity (ROE) varied only slightly over the period, from a low of 9.75 percent in 1992 to a high of 10.99 percent in 1993, while the retention ratio (1 – b) remained steady at 60 percent of earnings. Harris's actual rate of sales growth from 1992 to 1993 was 21.74 percent, which was above its sustainable rate for 1993, which was only 5.85 percent. Note that the sustainable rate of growth applicable to 1993 is calculated using data from 1992. In this year, we calculated the firm's sustainable rate of growth for 1993 to be 5.85 percent [9.75 percent (1 – .40)], but its actual increase in sales for the coming year was 21.74 percent [($1,400 – 1,150) / $1,150]. How did Harris accommodate the financing demands during 1993? The answer can be found by examining the firm's debt-to-assets ratio and changes to the firm's common equity. We see that Harris increased its borrowing from 42.56 percent of assets in 1992 to 49.48 percent in 1993 without issuing any new common stock. Thus, Harris has financed its DFN using new debt issues.

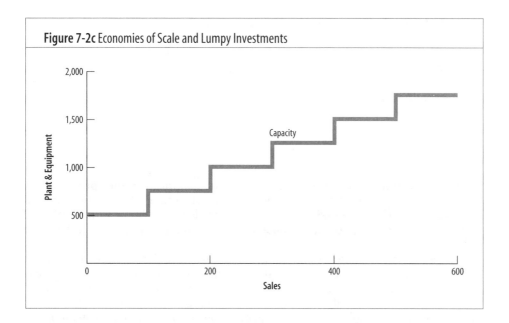

Figure 7-2c Economies of Scale and Lumpy Investments

Limitations of the Percent of Sales Forecast Method

The **percent of sales method** of financial forecasting provides reasonable estimates of a firm's financing requirements only where asset requirements and financing sources can be accurately forecast as a constant percent of sales. For example, predicting inventories using the percent of sales method involves the following predictive equation:

$$\text{inventories}_t = \frac{\text{inventories}_t}{\text{sales}_t} \times \text{sales}_t$$

Figure 7-2a depicts this predictive relationship. Note that the percent-of-sales predictive model is simply a straight line that passes through the origin (that is, has a zero intercept). There are some fairly common instances in which this type of relationship fails to describe the relationship between an asset category and sales. Two such examples involve assets for which there are scale economies and assets that must be purchased in discrete quantities ("lumpy assets").

Economies of scale are sometimes realized from investing in certain types of assets. This means that these assets do not increase in direct proportion to sales. Figure 7-2b reflects one instance in which the firm realizes economies of scale from its investment in inventory. Note that inventories as a percent of sales decline from 120 percent where sales are $100, to 30 percent where sales equal $1,000. This reflects the fact that there is a fixed component of inventories (in this case $100) that the firm must have on hand regardless of the level of sales, plus a variable component (20 percent of sales). In this instance the predictive equation for inventories is as follows:

$$\text{inventories}_t = a + b\ \text{sales}_t$$

In this example, a is equal to 100 and b equals .20.

Figure 7-2c is an example of *lumpy assets,* that is, assets that must be purchased in large, nondivisible components. Consequently, when a block of assets is purchased, it creates excess capacity until sales grow to the point where the capacity is fully used. The result is a step function like the one depicted in Figure 7-2c. Thus, if the firm does not expect sales to exceed the current capacity of its plant and equipment, there would be no projected need for added plant and equipment capacity.

FINANCIAL PLANNING AND BUDGETING

As we noted earlier, the principal virtue of the percent of sales method of financial forecasting is its simplicity. To obtain a more precise estimate of the amount and timing of the firm's future financing needs, we require a cash budget. The percent of sales method of financial forecasting provides a very useful, low-cost forerunner to the development of the more detailed cash budget, which the firm will ultimately use to estimate its financing needs.

Budget Functions

A *budget* is simply a forecast of future events. For example, students preparing for final exams make use of time budgets, which help them allocate their limited preparation time among their courses. Students also must budget their financial resources among competing uses, such as books, tuition, food, rent, clothes, and extracurricular activities.

Budgets perform three basic functions for a firm. First, they indicate the amount and timing of the firm's needs for future financing. Second, they provide the basis for taking corrective action in the event budgeted figures do not match actual or realized figures. Third, budgets provide the basis for performance evaluation. Plans are carried out by people, and budgets provide benchmarks that management can use to evaluate the performance of those responsible for carrying out those plans and, in turn, to control their actions. Thus, budgets are valuable aids in both the planning and controlling aspects of the firm's financial management.

The Cash Budget

The **cash budget** represents a detailed plan of future cash flows and is composed of four elements: cash receipts, cash disbursements, net change in cash for the period, and new financing needed.

EXAMPLE

To demonstrate the construction and use of the cash budget, consider Salco Furniture Company, Inc., a regional distributor of household furniture. Management is in the process of preparing a monthly cash budget for the upcoming six months (January through June 1996). Salco's sales are highly seasonal, peaking in the months of March through May. Roughly 30 percent of Salco's sales are collected one month after the sale, 50 percent two months after the sale, and the remainder during the third month following the sale.

Salco attempts to pace its purchases with its forecast of future sales. Purchases generally equal 75 percent of sales and are made two months in advance of anticipated sales. Payments are made in the month following purchases. For example, June sales are estimated at $100,000, thus April purchases are $.75 \times \$100,000 = \$75,000$. Correspondingly, payments for purchases in May equal $75,000. Wages, salaries, rent, and other cash expenses are recorded in Table 7-2, which gives Salco's cash budget for the six-month period ended in June 1994. Additional expenditures are recorded in the cash budget related to the purchase of equipment in the amount of $14,000 during February and the repayment of a $12,000 loan in May. In June, Salco will pay $7,500 interest on its $150,000 in long-term debt for the period of January–June 1996. Interest on the $12,000 short-term note repaid in May for the period January through May equals $600 and is paid in May.

Table 7-2 Salco Furniture Co., Inc., Cash Budget for the Six Months Ended June 30, 1996

Worksheet	Oct.	Nov.	Dec.	Jan.	Feb.	Mar.	Apr.	May	June	July	Aug.
Sales	$55,000	$62,000	$50,000	$60,000	$75,000	$88,000	$100,000	$110,000	$100,000	$80,000	$75,000
Collections:											
First month (30%)				15,000	18,000	22,500	26,400	30,000	33,000		
Second month (50%)				31,000	25,000	30,000	37,500	44,000	50,000		
Third month (20%)				11,000	12,400	10,000	12,000	15,000	17,600		
Total				$57,000	55,400	62,500	75,900	89,000	100,600		
Purchases (75% of sales in two months)			$56,250	66,000	75,000	82,500	75,000	60,000	56,250		
Payments (one-month lag)				$56,250	66,000	75,000	82,500	75,000	60,000		
Cash budget											
Cash receipts											
Collections (see worksheet)				$57,000	55,400	62,500	75,900	89,000	100,600		
Cash disbursements:											
Payments (see worksheet)				$56,250	66,000	75,000	82,500	75,000	60,000		
Wages and salaries				3,000	10,000	7,000	8,000	6,000	4,000		
Rent				4,000	4,000	4,000	4,000	4,000	4,000		
Other expenses				1,000	500	1,200	1,500	1,500	1,200		
Interest expense on existing debt ($12,000 note and								600			
$150,000 in long-term debt)									7,500		
Taxes						4,460			5,200		
Purchase of equipment					14,000						
Loan repayment ($12,000 note due in May)								12,000			
Total disbursements:				$64,250	94,500	91,660	96,000	99,100	81,900		
Net monthly change				$(7,250)	(39,100)	(29,160)	(20,100)	(10,100)	18,700		
Plus: Beginning cash balance				20,000	12,750	10,000	10,000	10,000	10,000		
Less: Interest on short-term borrowing				—	—	(364)	(659)	(866)	(976)		
Equals: Ending cash balance before short-term no borrowing				$12,750	(26,350)	(19,524)	(10,759)	(966)	27,724		
Financing needed[a]				—	36,350	29,524	20,759	10,966	(17,724)[b]		
Ending cash balance				$12,750	10,000	10,000	10,000	10,000	10,000		
Cumulative borrowing				—	36,350	65,874	86,633	97,599	79,875		

[a]The amount of financing that is required to raise the firm's ending cash balance up to its $10,000 desired cash balance.
[b]Negative financing needed simply means the firm has excess cash that can be used to retire a part of its short-term borrowing from prior months.

Salco currently has a cash balance of $20,000 and wants to maintain a minimum balance of $10,000. Additional borrowing necessary to maintain that minimum balance is estimated in the final section of Table 7-2. Borrowing takes place at the beginning of the month in which the funds are needed. Interest on borrowed funds equals 12 percent per annum, or 1 percent per month, and is paid in the month following the one in which funds are borrowed. Thus, interest on funds borrowed in January will be paid in February equal to 1 percent of the loan amount outstanding during January.

The financing-needed line in Salco's cash budget determines that the firm's cumulative short-term borrowing will be $36,350 in February, $65,874 in March, $86,633 in April, and $97,599 in May. In June the firm will be able to reduce its borrowing to $79,875. Note that the cash budget indicates not only the amount of financing needed during the period, but also when the funds will be needed.

Fixed versus Flexible Budgets

The cash budget given in Table 7-2 for Salco, Inc., is an example of a fixed budget. Cash flow estimates are made for a single set of monthly sales estimates. Thus, the estimates of expenses and new financing needed are meaningful only for the level of sales for which they were computed. To avoid this limitation, several budgets corresponding to different sets of sales estimates can be prepared. Such a flexible budgeting fulfills two basic needs: first, it gives information regarding the firm's possible financing needs; and second, it provides a standard against which to measure the performance of subordinates who are responsible for the various cost and revenue items contained in the budget.

This second function deserves some additional comment. The obvious problem that arises relates to the fact that costs vary with the actual level of sales experienced by the firm. Thus, if the budget is to be used as a standard for performance evaluation or control, it must be constructed to match realized sales and production figures. This can involve much more than simply adjusting cost figures up or down in proportion to the deviation of actual from planned sales; that is, costs may not vary in strict proportion to sales, just as inventory levels may not vary as a constant percent of sales. Thus, preparation of a flexible budget involves reestimating all the cash expenses that would be incurred at each of several possible sales levels. This process might utilize a variation of the percent of sales method discussed earlier.

Budget Period

There are no strict rules for determining the length of the budget period. However, as a general rule, it should be long enough to show the effect of management policies yet short enough so that estimates can be made with reasonable accuracy. Applying this rule of thumb to the Salco example in Table 7-2, it appears that the six-month budget period is too short. The reason is that we cannot tell whether the planned operations of the firm will be successful over the coming fiscal year. That is, for most of the first six-month period, the firm is operating with a cash flow deficit. If this does not reverse in the latter six months of the year, then a reevaluation of the firm's plans and policies is clearly in order.

Longer-range budgets are also prepared in the form of the capital-expenditure budget. This budget details the firm's plans for acquiring plant and equipment over a five-year, ten-year, or even longer period. Furthermore, firms often develop comprehensive long-range plans extending up to ten years into the future. These plans are generally not as detailed as the annual cash budget, but they do consider such major components as sales, capital expenditures, new-product development, capital funds acquisition, and employment needs.

To Bribe or Not to Bribe

In many parts of the world, bribes and payoffs to public officials are considered the norm in business transactions. This raises a perplexing ethical question. If paying bribes is not considered unethical in a foreign country, should you consider it unethical to make these payments?

This situation provides an example of an ethical issue that gave rise to legislation. The Foreign Corrupt Practices Act of 1977 (as amended in the Omnibus Trade and Competitiveness Act of 1988) established criminal penalties for making payments to foreign officials, political parties, or candidates in order to obtain or retain business. Ethical problems are frequently found in the gray areas just outside the boundaries of current legislation and often lead to the passage of new legislation. **(A)**

Consider the following question: If you were involved in negotiating an important business deal in a foreign country, and the success or failure of the deal hinged on whether you paid a local government official to help you consummate the deal, would you authorize the payment? **(B)** Assume that the form of the payment is such that you do not expect to be caught and punished; for example, your company agrees to purchase supplies from a family member of the government official at a price slightly above the competitive price.

ANALYSIS AND IMPLICATIONS...

A. Ethical dilemmas arise in those situations that are not clearly prescribed by law or social custom. It is the gray areas that give us trouble. Ethical behavior is simple to define and difficult to implement. Very simply, ethical behavior is "doing the right thing". The hard part comes when defining what is right for this requires that each of us search our own personal values for guidance. In these situations it is ultimately your own conscience, as dictated by your personal beliefs and system of values, that will serve as your guide to action.

B. What would you do?

COMPUTERIZED FINANCIAL PLANNING

In recent years, a number of developments in both computer hardware (machines) and software (programs) have reduced the tedium of the planning and budgeting process immensely. These include the introduction of "user-friendly" or "easy-to-use" computer programs that are specialized for application to financial planning.

Financial planning software packages (sometimes referred to as electronic spreadsheets) were first made popular on large mainframe computers but quickly spread to personal computers in the early 1980s. These packages allow even a computer novice to use a personal computer to construct budgets and forecasts. The real advantage of the computer is realized when there is a need for different scenarios to be evaluated quickly and easily.

Another major development that has had a significant impact on the extent to which computers are used in the planning and budgeting process is the advent of the personal computer. For mere hundreds of dollars, the financial analyst's desk can contain the computing power it took hundreds of thousands of dollars to buy just a decade ago. The development of financial planning software has paralleled the development of microcomputer technology. The number of spreadsheet packages has mushroomed over the past five years. These packages generally sell for less than $500 and include graphics programs as well as elementary database management capabilities.

SUMMARY

This chapter develops the role of forecasting within the context of the firm's financial planning activities. Forecasts of the firm's sales revenues and related expenses provide the basis for projecting future financing needs. The most popular method for forecasting financial variables is the percent of sales method.

The percent of sales method presumes that the asset or liability being forecast is a constant percent of sales for all future levels of sales. There are instances where this assumption is not reasonable, and, consequently, the percent of sales method does not provide reasonable predictions. One such instance arises where there are economies of scale in the use of the asset being forecast. For example, the firm may need at least $10 million in inventories to open its doors and operate even for sales as low as $100 million per year. If sales double to $200 million, inventories may only increase to $15 million. Thus, inventories do not increase with sales in a constant proportion. A second situation where the percent of sales method fails to work properly is where asset purchases are lumpy. That is, if plant capacity must be purchased in $50 million increments, then plant and equipment will not remain a constant percent of sales.

How serious are these possible problems and should we use the percent of sales method? Even in the face of these problems, the percent of sales method predicts reasonably well where predicted sales levels do not differ drastically from the level used to calculate the percent of sales. For example, if the current sales level used in calculating percent of sales for inventories is $40 million, then we can feel more comfortable forecasting the level of inventories corresponding to a new sales level of $42 million than were sales predicted to rise to $60 million.

A firm's sustainable rate of growth is the maximum rate at which its sales can grow if it is to maintain its present financial ratios and not have to resort to issuing new equity. We calculate the sustainable rate of growth as follows:

sustainable rate of growth $(g^*) = \text{ROE}\,(1 - b)$

where ROE is the return earned on common equity and b is the dividend payout ratio (that is, the ratio of dividends to earnings). Consequently, a firm's sustainable rate of growth increases with ROE and decreases with the fraction of its earnings paid out in dividends.

The cash budget is the primary tool of financial forecasting and planning. It contains a detailed plan of future cash flow estimates and is comprised of four elements or segments: cash receipts, cash disbursements, net change in cash for the period, and new financing needed. Once prepared, the cash budget also serves as a tool for monitoring and controlling the firm's operations. By comparing actual cash receipts and disbursements to those in the cash budget, the financial manager can gain an appreciation for how well the firm is performing. In addition, deviations from the plan serve as an early warning system to signal the onset of financial difficulties ahead.

STUDY QUESTIONS

7-1. Discuss the shortcomings of the percent of sales method of financial forecasting.

7-2. Explain how a fixed cash budget differs from a variable or flexible cash budget.

7-3. What two basic needs does a flexible (variable) cash budget serve?

7-4. What would be the probable effect on a firm's cash position of the following events?
  a. Rapidly rising sales
  b. A delay in the payment of payables
  c. A more liberal credit policy on sales (to the firm's customers)
  d. Holding larger inventories

7-5. How long should the budget period be? Why would a firm not set a rule that all budgets be for a twelve-month period?

7-6. A cash budget is usually thought of as a means of planning for future financing needs. Why would a cash budget also be important for a firm that had excess cash on hand?

7-7. Explain why a cash budget would be of particular importance to a firm that experiences seasonal fluctuations in its sales.

SELF-TEST PROBLEMS

ST-1. (Financial Forecasting) Use the percent of sales method to prepare a pro forma income statement for Calico Sales Co., Inc. Projected sales for next year equal $4 million. Cost of goods sold equals 70 percent of sales, administrative expense equals $500,000, and depreciation expense is $300,000. Interest expense equals $50,000 and income is taxed at a rate of 40 percent. The firm plans to spend $200,000 during the period to renovate its office facility and will retire $150,000 in notes payable. Finally, selling expense equals 5 percent of sales.

ST-2. (Cash Budget) Stauffer, Inc., has estimated sales and purchase requirements for the last half of the coming year. Past experience indicates that it will collect 20 percent of its sales in the month of the sale, 50 percent of the remainder one month after the sale, and the balance in the second month following the sale. Stauffer prefers to pay for half its purchases in the month of the purchase and the other half the following month. Labor expense for each month is expected to equal 5 percent of that month's sales, with cash payment being made in the month in which the expense is incurred. Depreciation expense is $5,000 per month; miscellaneous cash expenses are $4,000 per month and are paid in the month incurred. General and administrative expenses of $50,000 are recognized and paid monthly. A $60,000 truck is to be purchased in August and is to be depreciated on a straight-line basis over ten years with no expected salvage value. The company also plans to pay a $9,000 cash dividend to stockholders in July. The company feels that a minimum cash balance of $30,000 should be maintained. Any borrowing will cost 12 percent annually, with interest paid in the month following the month in which the funds are borrowed. Borrowing takes place at the beginning of the month in which the need for funds arises. For example, if during the month of July the firm should need to borrow $24,000 to maintain its $30,000 desired minimum balance, then $24,000 will be taken out on July 1 with interest owed for the entire month of July. Interest for the month of July would then be paid on August 1. Sales and purchase estimates are shown below. Prepare a cash budget for the months of July and August (cash on hand June 30 was

$30,000, while sales for May and June were $100,000 and purchases were $60,000 for each of these months).

Month	Sales	Purchases
July	$120,000	$50,000
August	150,000	40,000
September	110,000	30,000

STUDY PROBLEMS (SET A)

7-1A. (Financial Forecasting) Zapatera Enterprises is evaluating its financing requirements for the coming year. The firm has only been in business for one year, but its chief financial officer predicts that the firm's operating expenses, current assets, net fixed assets, and current liabilities will remain at their current proportion of sales.

Last year Zapatera had $12 million in sales with net income of $1.2 million. The firm anticipates that next year's sales will reach $15 million with net income rising to $2 million. Given its present high rate of growth, the firm retains all its earnings to help defray the cost of new investments.

The firm's balance sheet for the year just ended is found below:

Zapatera Enterprises, Inc.

Balance Sheet

	12/31/95	% of Sales
Current assets	$3,000,000	25%
Net fixed assets	6,000,000	50%
Total	$9,000,000	

Liabilities and Owner's Equity

Accounts payable	$3,000,000	25%
Long-term debt	2,000,000	NA[6]
Total liabilities	$5,000,000	
Common stock	1,000,000	NA
Paid-in capital	1,800,000	NA
Retained earnings	1,200,000	
Common equity	4,000,000	
Total	$9,000,000	

[6]Not applicable. This figure does not vary directly with sales and is assumed to remain constant for purposes of making next year's forecast of financing requirements.

Estimate Zapatera's total financing requirements (i.e., total assets) for 1996 and its net funding requirements (discretionary financing needed).

Month	Sales	Month	Sales
January	$15,000	March	30,000
February	20,000	April (projected)	40,000

7-2A. (Pro forma accounts receivable balance calculation) On March 31, 1995, the Sylvia Gift Shop had outstanding accounts receivable of $20,000. Sylvia's sales are roughly evenly split between credit and cash sales, with the credit sales collected half in the month after the sale and the remainder two months after the sale. Historical and projected sales for the gift shop are given below:

    a. Under these circumstances, what should the balance in accounts receivable be at the end of April?

    b. How much cash did Sylvia realize during April from sales and collections?

7-3A. (Financial Forecasting) Sambonoza Enterprises projects its sales next year to be $4 million and expects to earn 5 percent of that amount after taxes. The firm is currently in the process of projecting its financing needs and has made the following assumptions (projections):

    1. Current assets will equal 20 percent of sales, while fixed assets will remain at their current level of $1 million.

    2. Common equity is currently $0.8 million, and the firm pays out half its after-tax earnings in dividends.

    3. The firm has short-term payables and trade credit that normally equal 10 percent of sales, and has no long-term debt outstanding.

What are Sambonoza's financing needs for the coming year?

7-4A. (Financial Forecasting—Percent of Sales) Tulley Appliances, Inc., projects next year's sales to be $20 million. Current sales are at $15 million based on current assets of $5 million and fixed assets of $5 million. The firm's net profit margin is 5 percent after taxes. Tulley forecasts that current assets will raise in direct proportion to the increase in sales, but fixed assets will increase by only $100,000. Currently, Tulley has $1.5 million in accounts payable (which vary directly with sales), $2 million in long-term debt (due in ten years) and common equity (including $4 million in retained earnings) totaling $6.5 million. Tulley plans to pay $500,000 in common stock dividends next year.

    a. What are Tulley's total financing needs (that is, total assets) for the coming year?

    b. Given the firm's projections and dividend payment plans, what are its discretionary financing needs?

    c. Based on your projections, and assuming that the $100,000 expansion in fixed assets will occur, what is the largest increase in sales the firm can support without having to resort to the use of discretionary sources of financing?

7-5A. (Pro Forma Balance Sheet Construction) Use the following industry average ratios to construct a pro forma balance sheet for Carlos Menza, Inc.

Total asset turnover	2 times
Average collection period (assume a 365-day year)	9 days
Fixed asset turnover	5 times
Inventory turnover (based on cost of goods sold)	3 times
Current ratio	2 times
Sales (all on credit)	$4.0 million
Cost of goods sold	75% of sales
Debt ratio	50%

Cash		Current liabilities	
		Long-term debt	
Accounts receivable	_____	Common stock plus	
Net fixed assets	_____	Retained earnings	_____
	$ _____		$ _____

7-6A. (Cash Budget) The Sharpe Corporation's projected sales for the first eight months of 1996 are as follows:

January	$ 90,000	May	$300,000
February	120,000	June	270,000
March	135,000	July	225,000
April	240,000	August	150,000

Of Sharpe's sales, 10 percent is for cash, another 60 percent is collected in the month following sale, and 30 percent is collected in the second month following sale. November and December sales for 1995 were $220,000 and $175,000, respectively.

Sharpe purchases its raw materials two months in advance of its sales equal to 60 percent of their final sales price. The supplier is paid one month after it makes delivery. For example, purchases for April sales are made in February and payment is made in March.

In addition, Sharpe pays $10,000 per month for rent and $20,000 each month for other expenditures. Tax prepayments of $22,500 are made each quarter, beginning in March.

The company's cash balance at December 31, 1995, was $22,000; a minimum balance of $15,000 must be maintained at all times. Assume that any short-term financing needed to maintain the cash balance would be paid off in the month following the month of financing if sufficient funds are available. Interest on short-term loans (12 percent) is paid monthly. Borrowing to meet estimated monthly cash needs takes place at the beginning of the month. Thus, if in the month of April the firm expects to have a need for an additional $60,500, these funds would be borrowed at the beginning of April with interest of $605 ($.12 \times 1/12 \times \$60,500$) owed for April and paid at the beginning of May.

    a. Prepare a cash budget for Sharpe covering the first seven months of 1996.

    b. Sharpe has $200,000 in notes payable due in July that must be repaid or renegotiated for an extension. Will the firm have ample cash to repay the notes?

7-7A. (Percent-of-Sales Forecasting) Which of the following accounts would most likely vary directly with the level of firm sales? Discuss each briefly.

	Yes	No		Yes	No
Cash	_____	_____	Notes payable	_____	_____
Marketable securities	_____	_____	Plant and equipment	_____	_____
Accounts payable	_____	_____	Inventories	_____	_____

7-8A. (Financial Forecasting—Percent of Sales) The balance sheet of the Thompson Trucking Company (TTC) follows:

Thompson Trucking Company Balance Sheet, December 31, 1996 ($ millions)

Current assets	$10	Accounts payable	$ 5
Net fixed assets	15	Notes payable	0
Total	$25	Bonds payable	10
		Common equity	10
		Total	$25

TTC had sales for the year ended 12/31/93 of $50 million. The firm follows a policy of paying all net earnings out to its common stockholders in cash dividends. Thus TTC generates no funds from its earnings that can be used to expand its operations. (Assume that depreciation expense is just equal to the cost of replacing worn-out assets.)

a. If TTC anticipates sales of $80 million during the coming year, develop a pro forma balance sheet for the firm for 12/31/97. Assume that current assets vary as a percent of sales, net fixed assets remain unchanged, accounts payable vary as a percent of sales, and use notes payable as a balancing entry.

b. How much "new" financing will TTC need next year?

c. What limitations does the percent of sales forecast method suffer from? Discuss briefly.

7-9A. (Financial Forecasting—Discretionary Financing Needed) The most recent balance sheet for the Armadillo Dog Biscuit Co. is shown in the table following. The company is about to embark on an advertising campaign, which is expected to raise sales from the current level of $5 million to $7 million by the end of next year. The firm is currently operating at full capacity and will have to increase its investment in both current and fixed assets to support the projected level of new sales. In fact, the firm estimates that both categories of assets will rise in direct proportion to the projected increase in sales.

Armadillo Dog Biscuit Co., Inc. ($ millions)			
	Present Level	Percent of Sales	Projected Level
Current assets	$2.0		
Net fixed assets	3.0		
Total	$5.0		
Accounts payable	$0.5		
Accrued expenses	0.5		
Notes payable	—		
Current liabilities	$1.0		
Long-term debt	$2.0		
Common stock	0.5		
Retained earnings	1.5		
Common equity	$2.0		
Total	$5.0		

The firm's net profits were 6 percent of current year's sales but are expected to rise to 7 percent of next year's sales. To help support its anticipated growth in asset needs next year, the firm has suspended plans to pay cash dividends to its stockholders. In past years a $1.50 per share dividend has been paid annually.

Armadillo's payables and accrued expenses are expected to vary directly with sales. In addition, notes payable will be used to supply the funds that are needed to finance next year's operations and that are not forthcoming from other sources.

a. Fill in the table and project the firm's needs for discretionary financing. Use notes payable as the balancing entry for future discretionary financing needed.

b. Compare Armadillo's current ratio and debt ratio (total liabilities/total assets) before the growth in sales and after. What was the effect of the expanded sales on these two dimensions of Armadillo's financial condition?

c. What difference, if any, would have resulted if Armadillo's sales had risen to $6 million in one year and $7 million only after two years? Discuss only; no calculations required.

7-10A. (Forecasting Discretionary Financing Needs) Fishing Charter, Inc., estimates that it invests 30 cents in assets for each dollar of new sales. However, 5 cents in profits are produced by each dollar of additional sales, of which 1 cent can be reinvested in the firm. If sales rise from their current level of $5 million by $500,000 next year, and the ratio of spontaneous liabilities to sales is .15, what will be the firm's need for discretionary financing? *(Hint:* In this situation you do not know what the firm's existing level of assets is, nor do you know how those assets have been financed. Thus you must estimate the change in financing needs and match this change with the expected changes in spontaneous liabilities, retained earnings, and other sources of discretionary financing.)

7-11A. (Preparation of a Cash Budget) Harrison Printing has projected its sales for the first eight months of 1996 as follows:

January	$100,000	April	$300,000	July	$200,000
February	120,000	May	275,000	August	180,000
March	150,000	June	200,000		

Harrison collects 20 percent of its sales in the month of the sale, 50 percent in the month following the sale, and the remaining 30 percent two months following the sale. During November and December of 1995 Harrison's sales were $220,000 and $175,000, respectively.

Harrison purchases raw materials two months in advance of its sales equal to 65 percent of its final sales. The supplier is paid one month after delivery. Thus purchases for April sales are made in February and payment is made in March.

In addition, Harrison pays $10,000 per month for rent and $20,000 each month for other expenditures. Tax prepayments of $22,500 are made each quarter beginning in March. The company's cash balance as of December 31, 1995, was $22,000; a minimum balance of $20,000 must be maintained at all times to satisfy the firm's bank line of credit agreement. Harrison has arranged with its bank for short-term credit at an interest rate of 12 percent per annum (1 percent per month) to be paid monthly. Borrowing to meet estimated monthly cash needs takes place at the end of the month, and interest is not paid until the end of the following month. Consequently, if the firm were to need to borrow $50,000 during the month of April, then it would pay $500 (= .01 x $50,000) in interest during May. Finally, Harrison follows a policy of repaying its outstanding short-term debt in any month in which its cash balance exceeds the minimum desired balance of $20,000.

    a. Harrison needs to know what its cash requirements will be for the next six months so that it can renegotiate the terms of its short-term credit agreement with its bank, if necessary. To evaluate this problem, the firm plans to evaluate the impact of a ± 20 percent variation in its monthly sales efforts. Prepare a six-month cash budget for Harrison and use it to evaluate the firm's cash needs.

    b. Harrison has a $200,000 note due in June. Will the firm have sufficient cash to repay the loan?

7-12A. (Sustainable Rate of Growth) ADP, Inc., is a manufacturer of specialty circuit boards in the personal computer industry. The firm has experienced phenomenal sales growth over its short five-year life. Selected financial statement data are found in the following table:

	19x5	19x4	19x3	19x2	19x1
Sales	$3,000	$2,200	$1,800	$1,400	$1,200
Net income	150	110	90	70	60
Assets	2,700	1,980	1,620	1,260	1,080
Dividends	60	44	36	28	24
Common equity	812	722	656	602	560
Liabilities	1,888	1,258	964	658	520
Liabilities and equity	2,700	1,980	1,620	1,260	1,080

    a. Calculate ADP's sustainable rate of growth for each of the five years of its existence.

    b. Compare the actual rates of growth in sales to the firm's sustainable rates calculated in part a. How has ADP been financing its growing asset needs?

7-13A. (Sustainable Rate of Growth) The Carrera Game Company has experienced a 100% increase in sales over the last five years. The company president, Jack Carrera, has become increasingly alarmed by the firm's rising debt level even in the face of continued profitability.

	19x7	19x6	19x5	19x4	19x3
Sales	$60,000	$56,000	$48,000	$36,000	$30,000
Net income	3,000	2,800	2,400	1,800	1,500
Assets	54,000	50,400	43,200	32,400	27,000
Dividends	1,200	1,120	960	720	600
Common equity	21,000	19,200	17,520	16,080	15,000
Liabilities	33,000	31,200	25,680	16,320	12,000
Liabilities and equity	54,000	50,400	43,200	32,400	27,000

a. Calculate the debt to assets ratio, return on common equity, actual rate of growth in firm sales and retention ratio for each of the five years of data provided above.

b. Calculate the sustainable rates of growth for Carrera for each of the last five years. Why has the firm's borrowing increased so dramatically?

7-14A. (Forecasting Inventories) Findlay Instruments produces a complete line of medical instruments used by plastic surgeons and has experienced rapid growth over the last five years. In an effort to make more accurate predictions of its financing requirements Findlay is currently attempting to construct a financial planning model based on the percent of sales forecasting method. However, the firm's chief financial analyst (Sarah Macias) is concerned that the projections for inventories will be seriously in error. She recognizes that the firm has begun to accrue substantial economies of scale in its inventory investment and has documented this fact in the following data and calculations:

Year	Sales (000)	Inventory (000)	% of Sales
19xl	$15,000	1,150	7.67%
19X2	18,000	1,180	6.56%
19X3	17,500	1,175	6.71%
19X4	20,000	1,200	6.00%
19X5	25,000	1,250	5.00%
		Average	6.39%

a. Plot Findlay's sales and inventories for the last five years. What is the relationship between these two variables?

b. Estimate firm inventories for 19X6 where firm sales are projected to reach $30,000,000. Use the average percent of sales for the last five years, the most recent percent of sales and your evaluation of the true relationship between the sales and inventories from part a to make three predications.

Problem

Phillips Petroleum is an integrated oil and gas company with headquarters in Bartlesville, Oklahoma, where it was founded in 1917. The company engages in petroleum exploration and production worldwide. In addition, it engages in natural gas gathering and processing, as well as petroleum refining and marketing primarily in the United States. The company has three operating groups—Exploration and Production, Gas and Gas Liquids, and Downstream Operations, which encompasses Petroleum Products and Chemicals.

Summary Financial Information for Phillips Petroleum Corporation: 1986–92. (in millions of dollars except for per share figures)							
	1986	1987	1988	1989	1990	1991	1992
Sales	10,018.00	10,917.00	11,490.00	12,492.00	13,975.00	13,259.00	12,140.00
Net income	228.00	35.00	650.00	219.00	541.00	98.00	270.00
EPS	0.89	0.06	2.72	0.90	2.18	0.38	1.04
Current assets	2,802.00	2,855.00	3,062.00	2,876.00	3,322.00	2,459.00	2,349.00
Total assets	12,403.00	12,111.00	11,968.00	11,256.00	12,130.00	11,473.00	11,468.00
Current liabilities	2,234.00	2,402.00	2,468.00	2,706.00	2,910.00	2,603.00	2,517.00
Long-term debt	5,758.00	5,419.00	4,761.00	3,939.00	3,839.00	3,876.00	3,718.00
Total liabilities	10,409.00	10,289.00	9,855.00	9,124.00	9,411.00	8,716.00	8,411.00
Preferred stock	270.00	205.00	0.00	0.00	0.00	0.00	359.00
Common equity	1,724.00	1,617.00	2,113.00	2,132.00	2,719.00	2,757.00	2,698.00
Dividends per share	2.02	1.73	1.34	0.00	1.03	1.12	1.12

SOURCE: Phillips Annual Reports for the years 1987–92.

In the mid-eighties Phillips engaged in a major restructuring following two failed takeover attempts, one led by T. Boone Pickins and the other by Carl Ichan.* The restructuring resulted in a $4.5 billion plan to exchange a package of cash and debt securities for roughly half the company's shares and to sell $2 billion worth of assets. Phillip's long-term debt increased from $3.4 billion in late 1984 to a peak of $8.6 billion in April 1985.

During 1992 Phillips was able to strengthen its financial structure dramatically. Its subsidiary Phillips Gas Company completed an offering of $345 million of Series A 9.32% Cumulative Preferred Stock. As a result of these actions and prior year's debt reductions, the company lowered its long-term debt to capital ratio over the last five years from 75 to 55 percent. In addition, the firm refinanced over a billion dollars of its debt at reduced rates. A company spokesman said that "Our debt-to-capital ratio is still on the high side, and we'll keep working to bring it down. But the cost of debt is manageable, and we're beyond the point where debt overshadows everything else we do."†

Highlights of Phillips' financial condition spanning the years 1986–92 are found above. These data reflect the modern history of the company as a result of its financial restructuring following the downsizing and reorganization of Phillips' operations begun in the mid-eighties.

Phillips' management is currently developing its financial plans for the next five years and wants to develop a forecast of its financing requirements. As a first approximation they have asked you to develop a model that can be used to make "ball park" estimates of the firm's financing needs under the proviso that existing relationships found in the firm's financial statements remain the same over the period. Of particular interest is whether Phillips will be able to further reduce its reliance on debt financing. You may assume that Phillips' projected sales (in millions) for 1993 through 1997 are as follows: $13,000; $13,500; $14,000; $14,500; and $15,500.

a. Project net income for 1993–97 using the percent of sales method based on an average of this ratio for 1986–92.

b. Project total assets and current liabilities for the period 1993–97 using the percent of sales method and your sales projections from part a.

c. Assuming that common equity increases only as a result of the retention of earnings and holding long-term debt and preferred stock equal to their 1992 balances, project Phillips' discretionary financing needs for 1993–97. (*Hint:* Assume that total assets and current liabilities vary as a percent of sales as per your answer to part c above. In addition, assume that Phillips plans to continue to pay its dividend of $1.12 per share in each of the next five years.)

*This discussion is based on a story in the *New York Times*, January 7, 1986.
†From *SEC Online*, 1992.

IMPACT OF LEVERAGE

Financial planning for projects always involves various types of expenditures. One type of expenditure remains constant over the life of the project and is referred to as "fixed." Examples are machines and interest paid on loans. Variable costs are those costs that change as the project requirements vary. The most common example of a variable cost is labor. The selection of the balance between fixed and variable expenses has a significant impact on risk and is entitled "leverage." Basically, the more fixed expenses incurred, the more leverage or risk. The reason is simple. If the project falters or the economy enters a recession, the interest and payments on the machines must still be paid. On the other hand, variable expenses such as labor can be modified to fit the situation. Specifically, in time of recession the labor force can be reduced. The following reading from Keown discusses the analysis and impact of leverage.

BUSINESS AND FINANCIAL RISK

In studying capital-budgeting techniques, we referred to **risk** as the likely variability associated with expected revenue or income streams. As our attention is now focused on the firm's financing decision rather than its investment decision, it is useful to separate the income stream variations attributable to (1) the company's exposure to business risk, and (2) its decision to incur financial risk.

   Business risk refers to the relative dispersion (variability) in the firm's expected earnings before interest and taxes (EBIT). Figure 8-2 shows a subjectively estimated probability distribution of next year's EBIT for the Pierce Grain Company

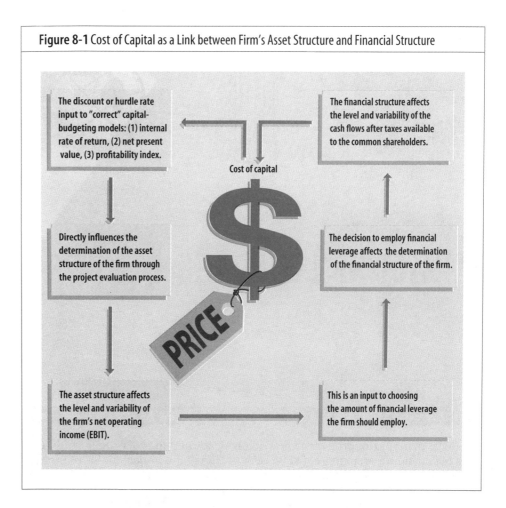

Figure 8-1 Cost of Capital as a Link between Firm's Asset Structure and Financial Structure

The discount or hurdle rate input to "correct" capital-budgeting models: (1) internal rate of return, (2) net present value, (3) profitability index.

The financial structure affects the level and variability of the cash flows after taxes available to the common shareholders.

Cost of capital

Directly influences the determination of the asset structure of the firm through the project evaluation process.

The decision to employ financial leverage affects the determination of the financial structure of the firm.

The asset structure affects the level and variability of the firm's net operating income (EBIT).

This is an input to choosing the amount of financial leverage the firm should employ.

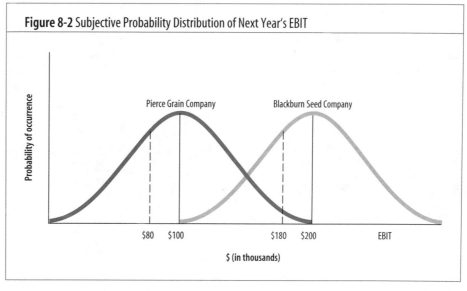

Figure 8-2 Subjective Probability Distribution of Next Year's EBIT

Probability of occurrence

Pierce Grain Company

Blackburn Seed Company

$80 $100 $180 $200   EBIT

$ (in thousands)

Table 8-1 Concept of Business Risk	
Business Risk Attribute	Example[a]
1. Sensitivity of the firm's product demand to general economic conditions	If GNP declines, does the firm's sales level decline by a greater percentage?
2. Degree of competition	Is the firm's market share small in comparison with other firms that produce and distribute the same product(s)?
3. Product diversification	Is a large proportion of the firm's sales revenue derived from a single major product or product line?
4. Operating leverage	Does the firm utilize a high level of operating leverage resulting in a high level of fixed costs?
5. Growth prospects	Are the firm's product markets expanding and (or) changing, making income estimates and prospects highly volatile?
6. Size	Does the firm suffer a competitive disadvantage due to lack of size in assets, sales, or profits that translates into (among other things) difficulty in tapping the capital market for funds?

[a]Affirmative responses indicate greater business risk exposure.

and the same type of projection for Pierce's larger competitor, the Blackburn Seed Company. The expected value of EBIT for Pierce is $100,000, with an associated standard deviation of $20,000. If next year's EBIT for Pierce fell one standard deviation short of the expected $100,000, the actual EBIT would equal $80,000. Blackburn's expected EBIT is $200,000 and the size of the associated standard deviation is $20,000. The standard deviation for the expected level of EBIT is the same for both firms. We would say that Pierce's degree of business risk exceeds Blackburn's because of its larger coefficient of variation of expected EBIT as follows:

$$\text{Pierce's coefficient of variation of expected EBIT} = \frac{\$20,000}{\$100,000} = .20$$

$$\text{Blackburn's coefficient of variation of expected EBIT} = \frac{\$20,000}{\$200,000} = .10$$

The relative dispersion in the firm's EBIT stream, measured here by its expected coefficient of variation, is the *residual* effect of several causal influences. Dispersion in operating income does not *cause* business risk; rather, this dispersion, which we call business risk, is the *result* of several influences. Some of these are listed in Table 8-1, along with an example of each particular attribute. Notice that the company's cost structure, product demand characteristics, and intra-industry competitive position all affect its business risk exposure. Such business risk is a direct result of the firm's investment decision. It is the firm's asset structure, after all, that gives rise to both the level and variability of its operating profits.

Financial risk, conversely, is a direct result of the firm's financing decision. In the context of selecting a proper financing mix, this risk applies to (1) the additional variability in earnings available to the firm's common shareholders; and (2) the additional chance of insolvency borne by the common shareholder caused by the use of financial leverage. **Financial leverage** means financing a portion of the firm's assets with securities bearing a fixed (limited) rate of return in hopes of increasing the ultimate return to the common stockholders. The decision to use debt or preferred stock in the financial structure of the corporation means that those who own the common shares of the firm are exposed to financial risk. Any given level of variability in EBIT will be *magnified* by the firm's use of financial leverage, and such additional variability will be embodied in the variability of earnings available to the common stockholder and earnings per share. If these magnifications are negative, the common stockholder has a higher chance of insolvency than would have existed had the use of fixed charge securities (debt and preferred stock) been avoided.

The closely related concepts of business and financial risk are crucial to the problem of financial structure design. This follows from the impact of these types of risk on the variability of the earnings stream flowing to the company's shareholders. In the rest of this chapter, we study techniques that permit a precise assessment of the earnings stream variability caused by (1) operating leverage and (2) financial leverage. We have already defined financial leverage. Table 8-1 shows that the business risk of the enterprise is influenced by the use of what is called operating leverage. **Operating leverage** refers to the incurrence of fixed operating costs in the firm's income stream. To understand the nature and importance of operating leverage, we need to draw upon the basics of cost-volume-profit analysis, or *breakeven analysis.*

BREAKEVEN ANALYSIS

The technique of breakeven analysis is familiar to legions of businesspeople. It is usefully applied in a wide array of business settings, including both small and large organizations. This tool is widely accepted by the business community for two reasons: It is based on straightforward assumptions, and companies have found that the information gained from the breakeven model is beneficial in decision-making situations.

Objective and Uses

The objective of *breakeven analysis* is to determine the *breakeven quantity of output* by studying the relationships among the firm's cost structure, volume of output, and profit. Alternatively, the firm ascertains the breakeven level of sales dollars that corresponds to the breakeven quantity of output. We will develop the fundamental relationships by concentrating on units of output, and then extend the procedure to permit direct calculation of the breakeven sales level.

What is meant by the breakeven quantity of output? It is that quantity of output, denominated in units, that results in an EBIT level equal to zero. Use of the breakeven model, therefore, enables the financial officer (1) to determine the quantity of output that must be sold to cover all operating costs, as distinct from financial costs, and (2) to calculate the EBIT that will be achieved at various output levels.

The many actual and potential applications of the breakeven approach include the following:

1. **Capital expenditure analysis.** As a complementary technique to discounted cash flow evaluation models, the breakeven model locates in a rough way the sales volume needed to make a project economically beneficial to the firm. It should not be used to replace the time-adjusted evaluation techniques.
2. **Pricing policy.** The sales price of a new product can be set to achieve a target EBIT level. Furthermore, should market penetration be a prime objective, a price could be set that would cover slightly more than the variable costs of production and provide only a partial contribution to the recovery of fixed costs. The negative EBIT at several possible sales prices can then be studied.
3. **Labor contract negotiations.** The effect of increased variable costs resulting from higher wages on the breakeven quantity of output can be analyzed.
4. **Cost structure.** The choice of reducing variable costs at the expense of incurring higher fixed costs can be evaluated. Management might decide to become more capital-intensive by performing tasks in the production process through use of

equipment rather than labor. Application of the breakeven model can indicate what the effects of this tradeoff will be on the breakeven point for the given product.

5. **Financing decisions.** Analysis of the firm's cost structure will reveal the proportion that fixed operating costs bear to sales. If this proportion is high, the firm might reasonably decide not to add any fixed financing costs on top of the high fixed operating costs.

Essential Elements of the Breakeven Model

To implement the breakeven model, we must separate the production costs of the company into two mutually exclusive categories: fixed costs and variable costs. You will recall from your study of basic economics that in the long run all costs are variable. Breakeven analysis, therefore, is a short-run concept.

Assumed Behavior of Costs

Fixed Costs

Fixed costs, also referred to as **indirect costs,** do not vary in total amount as sales volume or the quantity of output changes over some *relevant* range of output. Total fixed costs are independent of the quantity of product produced and equal some constant dollar amount. As production volume increases, fixed cost per unit of product falls as fixed costs are spread over larger and larger quantities of output. Figure 8-3 graphs the behavior of total fixed costs with respect to the company's relevant range of output. This total is shown to be unaffected by the quantity of product that is manufactured and sold. Over some other relevant output range, the amount of total fixed costs might be higher or lower for the same company.

In a manufacturing setting, some specific examples of fixed costs are

1. Administrative salaries
2. Depreciation
3. Insurance
4. Lump sums spent on intermittent advertising programs
5. Property taxes
6. Rent

Variable Costs

Variable costs are sometimes referred to as **direct costs.** Variable costs are fixed per unit of output but vary in total as output changes. Total variable costs are computed by taking the variable cost per unit and multiplying it by the quantity produced and sold. The breakeven model assumes proportionality between total variable costs and sales. Thus, if sales rise by 10 percent, it is assumed that variable costs will rise by 10 percent. Figure 8-4 graphs the behavior of total variable costs with respect to the company's relevant range of output. Total variable costs are seen to depend on the quantity of product that is manufactured and sold. Notice that if zero units of the product are manufactured, then variable costs are zero, but fixed costs are greater than zero. This implies that some contribution to the coverage of fixed costs occurs as long as the selling price per unit exceeds the variable cost per unit. This helps explain why some firms will operate a plant even when sales are temporarily depressed—that is, to provide some increment of revenue toward the coverage of fixed costs.

For a manufacturing operation, some examples of variable costs include

1. Direct labor
2. Direct materials
3. Energy costs (fuel, electricity, natural gas) associated with the production area

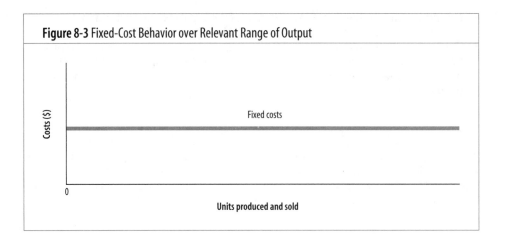

Figure 8-3 Fixed-Cost Behavior over Relevant Range of Output

Costs ($)

Fixed costs

0

Units produced and sold

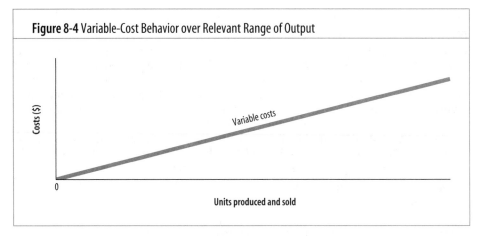

Figure 8-4 Variable-Cost Behavior over Relevant Range of Output

Costs ($)

Variable costs

0

Units produced and sold

4. Freight costs for products leaving the plant
5. Packaging
6. Sales commissions

More on Behavior of Costs

No one believes that all costs behave as neatly as we have illustrated the fixed and variable costs in Figures 8-3 and 8-4. Nor does any law or accounting principle dictate that a certain element of the firm's total costs always be classified as fixed or variable. This will depend on each firm's specific circumstances. In one firm energy costs may be predominantly fixed, whereas in another they may vary with output.

Furthermore, some costs may be fixed for a while, then rise sharply to a higher level as a higher output is reached, remain fixed, and then rise again with further increases in production. Such costs may be termed either **semivariable** or **semifixed.**

The label is your choice, because both are used in industrial practice. An example might be the salaries paid production supervisors. Should output be cut back by 15 percent for a short period, the management of the organization is not likely to lay off 15 percent of the supervisors. Similarly, commissions paid to salespeople often follow a stepwise pattern over wide ranges of success. This sort of cost behavior is shown in Figure 8-5.

To implement the breakeven model and deal with such a complex cost structure, the financial manager must (1) identify the most relevant output range for planning purposes and then (2) approximate the cost effect of semivariable items over this

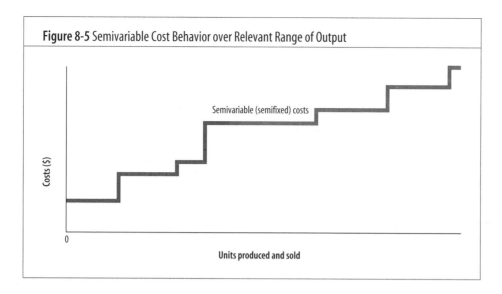

Figure 8-5 Semivariable Cost Behavior over Relevant Range of Output

Semivariable (semifixed) costs

Costs ($)

0

Units produced and sold

range by segregating a portion of them to fixed costs and a portion to variable costs. In the actual business setting this procedure is not fun. It is not unusual for the analyst who deals with the figures to spend considerably more time allocating costs to fixed and variable categories than in carrying out the actual breakeven calculations.

Total Revenue and Volume of Output

Besides fixed and variable costs, the essential elements of the breakeven model include total revenue from sales and volume of output. **Total revenue** means sales dollars and is equal to the selling price per unit multiplied by the quantity sold. The **volume of output** refers to the firm's level of operations and may be indicated either as a unit quantity or as sales dollars.

Finding the Breakeven Point

Finding the breakeven point in terms of units of production can be accomplished in several ways. All approaches require the essential elements of the breakeven model just described. The breakeven model is a simple adaptation of the firm's income statement expressed in the following analytical format:

sales – (total variable cost + total fixed cost) = profit   (8-1)

On a units of production basis, it is necessary to introduce (1) the price at which each unit is sold and (2) the variable cost per unit of output. Because the profit item studied in breakeven analysis is EBIT, we will use that acronym instead of the word "profit." In terms of units, the income statement shown in equation (8-1) becomes the breakeven model by setting EBIT equal to zero:

(sales price per unit) (units sold) – [(variable cost per unit) (units sold)   (8-2)
+ (total fixed cost)] = EBIT = $0

Our task now becomes finding the number of units that must be produced and sold in order to satisfy equation (8-2)—that is, to arrive at an EBIT = $0. This can be done by (1) trial-and-error analysis, (2) contribution-margin analysis, or (3) algebraic analysis. Each approach will be illustrated using the same set of circumstances.

Table 8-2 Pierce Grain Company Sales, Cost, and Profit Schedule

(1) Units Sold	(2) Unit Sales Price	(3) = (1)x(2) Sales	(4) Unit Variable Cost	(5) = (1)x(4) Total Variable Cost	(6) Total Fixed Cost	(7) = (5) + (6) Total Cost	(8) =(3)–(7) EBIT	
1. 10,000	$10	$100,000	$6	$ 60,000	$100,000	$160,000	$–60,000	1.
2. 15,000	10	150,000	6	90,000	100,000	190,000	–40,000	2.
3. 20,000	10	200,000	6	120,000	100,000	220,000	–20,000	3.
4. 25,000	10	250,000	6	150,000	100,000	250,000	0	4.
5. 30,000	10	300,000	6	180,000	100,000	280,000	20,000	5.
6. 35,000	10	350,000	6	210,000	100,000	310,000	40,000	6.

Input Data

Unit sales price = $10

Unit variable cost = $6

Total fixed cost = $100,000

Output Data

Breakeven point in units = 25,000 units produced and sold

Breakeven point in sales = $250,000

Problem Situation

Even though the Pierce Grain Company manufactures several different products, it has observed over a lengthy period that its product mix is rather constant. This allows management to conduct its financial planning by use of a "normal" sales price per unit and "normal" variable cost per unit. The "normal" sales price and variable cost per unit are calculated from the constant product mix. It is like assuming that the product mix is one big product. The selling price is $10 and the variable cost is $6. Total fixed costs for the firm are $100,000 per year. What is the breakeven point in units produced and sold for the company during the coming year?

Trial-and-Error Analysis

The most cumbersome approach to determining the firm's breakeven point is to employ the trial-and-error technique illustrated in Table 8-2. The process simply involves the arbitrary selection of an output level and the calculation of a corresponding EBIT amount. When the level of output is found that results in an EBIT = $0, the breakeven point has been located. Notice that Table 8-2 is just equation (8-2) in worksheet form. For the Pierce Grain Company, total operating costs will be covered when 25,000 units are manufactured and sold. This tells us that if sales equal $250,000, the firm's EBIT will equal $0.

Contribution-Margin Analysis

Unlike trial and error, use of the contribution-margin technique permits direct computation of the breakeven quantity of output. The **contribution margin** is the difference between the unit selling price and unit variable costs, as follows:

Unit sales price

− Unit variable cost

= Unit contribution margin

The use of the word "contribution" in the present context means contribution to the coverage of fixed operating costs. For the Pierce Grain Company, the unit contribution margin is

Unit sales price	$10
Unit variable cost	−6
Unit contribution margin	$ 4

If the annual fixed costs of $100,000 are divided by the unit contribution margin of $4, we find the breakeven quantity of output for Pierce Grain is 25,000 units. With much less effort, we have arrived at the identical result found by trial and error. Figure 8-6 portrays the contribution-margin technique for finding the breakeven point.

Algebraic Analysis

To explain the algebraic method for finding the breakeven output level, we need to adopt some notation. Let

Q = the number of units sold
Q_B = the breakeven level of Q
P = the unit sales price
F = total fixed costs anticipated over the planning period
V = the unit variable cost

Equation (8-2), the breakeven model, is repeated below as equation (8-2a) with the model symbols used in place of words. The breakeven model is then solved for Q, the number of units that must be sold in order that EBIT will equal $0. We label the breakeven point quantity Q_B.

$$(P \cdot Q) - [(V \cdot Q) + (F)] = \text{EBIT} = \$0 \qquad (8\text{-}2a)$$
$$(P \cdot Q) - (V \cdot Q) - F = \$0$$
$$Q(P - V) = F$$
$$Q_B = \frac{F}{P - V} \qquad (8\text{-}3)$$

Observe that equation (8-3) says: divide total fixed operating costs, F, by the unit contribution margin, $P - V$, and the breakeven level of output, Q_B, will be obtained.

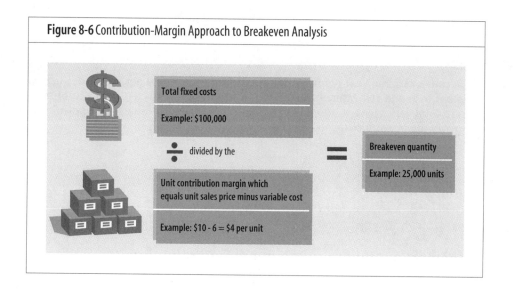

Figure 8-6 Contribution-Margin Approach to Breakeven Analysis

Total fixed costs

Example: $100,000

÷ divided by the

Unit contribution margin which equals unit sales price minus variable cost

Example: $10 - 6 = $4 per unit

= Breakeven quantity

Example: 25,000 units

Table 8-3 Pierce Grain Company Analytical Income Statement	
Sales	$300,000
Less: Total variable costs	180,000
Revenue before fixed costs	$120,000
Less: Total fixed costs	100,000
EBIT	$ 20,000

The contribution-margin analysis is nothing more than equation (8-3) in different garb.

Application of equation (8-3) permits direct calculation of Pierce Grain's breakeven point, as follows:

$$Q_B = \frac{F}{P - V} = \frac{\$100,000}{\$10 - \$6} = 25,000 \text{ units}$$

Breakeven Point in Sales Dollars

In dealing with the multiproduct firm, it is convenient to compute the breakeven point in terms of sales dollars rather than units of output. Sales, in effect, become a common denominator associated with a particular product mix. Furthermore, an outside analyst may not have access to internal unit cost data. He/she may, however, be able to obtain annual reports for the firm. If the analyst can separate the firm's total costs as identified from its annual reports into their fixed and variable components, he/she can calculate a general breakeven point in sales dollars.

We will illustrate the procedure using the Pierce Grain Company's cost structure, contained in Table 8-2. Suppose that the information on line 5 of Table 8-2 is arranged in the format shown in Table 8-3. We will refer to this type of financial statement as an **analytical income statement.** This distinguishes it from audited income statements published, for example, in the annual reports of public corporations. If we are aware of the simple mathematical relationships on which cost-volume-profit analysis is based, we can use Table 8-3 to find the breakeven point in sales dollars for the Pierce Grain Company.

First, let us explore the logic of the process. Recall from equation (8-1) that

sales – (total variable cost + total fixed cost) = EBIT

If we let total sales = S, total variable cost = VC, and total fixed cost = F, the preceding relationship becomes

$S - (VC + F) = \text{EBIT}$

Because variable cost per unit of output and selling price per unit are *assumed* constant over the relevant output range in breakeven analysis, the ratio of total sales to total variable cost, VC/S, is a constant for any level of sales. This permits us to rewrite the previous expression as

$$S - \left[\left(\frac{VC}{S}\right)S\right] - F = \text{EBIT}$$

and

$$S\left(1 - \frac{VC}{S}\right) - F = \text{EBIT}$$

At the breakeven point, however, EBIT = 0, and the corresponding breakeven level of sales can be represented as S^*. At the breakeven level of sales, we have

$$S^* \left(1 - \frac{VC}{S}\right) - F = 0$$

or

$$S^* \left(1 - \frac{VC}{S}\right) = F$$

Therefore,

$$S^* = \frac{F}{1 - \dfrac{VC}{S}} \tag{8-4}$$

The application of equation (8-4) to Pierce Grain's analytical income statement in Table 8-3 permits the breakeven sales level for the firm to be directly computed, as follows:

$$S^* = \frac{\$100,000}{1 - \dfrac{\$180,000}{\$300,000}}$$

$$= \frac{\$100,000}{1 - .60} = \$250,000$$

Notice that this is indeed the same breakeven sales level for Pierce Grain that is indicated on line 4 of Table 8-2.

Graphic Representation, Analysis of Input Changes, and Cash Breakeven Point

In making a presentation to management, it is often effective to display the firm's cost-volume-profit relationships in the form of a chart. Even those individuals who truly enjoy analyzing financial problems find figures and equations dry material at times. Furthermore, by quickly scanning the basic breakeven chart, the manager can approximate the EBIT amount that will prevail at different sales levels.

Such a chart has been prepared for the Pierce Grain Company. Figure 8-7 has been constructed for this firm using the input data contained in Table 8-2. Total fixed costs of $100,000 are added to the total variable costs associated with each production level to form the total costs line. When 25,000 units of product are manufactured and sold, the sales line and total costs line intersect. This means, of course, that the EBIT that would exist at that volume of output is zero. Beyond 25,000 units of output, notice that sales revenues exceed the total costs line. This causes a positive EBIT. This positive EBIT, or profits, is labeled "original EBIT" in Figure 8-7.

The unencumbered nature of the breakeven model makes it possible to quickly incorporate changes in the requisite input data and generate the revised output. Suppose a favorable combination of events causes Pierce Grain's fixed costs to decrease by $25,000. This would put total fixed costs for the planning period at a level of $75,000 rather than the $100,000 originally forecast. Total costs, being the sum of fixed and variable costs, would be lower by $25,000 at all output levels. The revised total costs line in Figure 8-7 reflects Pierce Grain's reduction in fixed costs. Under these revised conditions, the new breakeven point in units would be as follows:

$$Q_B = \frac{\$75,000}{\$10 - \$6} = 18,750 \text{ units}$$

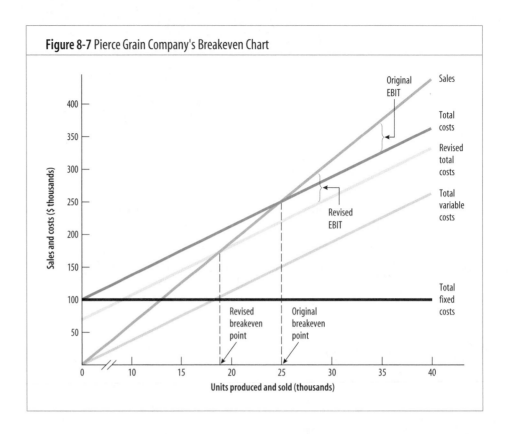

Figure 8-7 Pierce Grain Company's Breakeven Chart

The revised breakeven point of 18,750 units is identified in Figure 8-7, along with the revised EBIT amounts that would prevail at differing output and sales levels. The chart clearly indicates that at any specific production and sales level, the revised EBIT would exceed the original EBIT. This must be the case, as the revised total costs line lies below the original total costs line over the entire relevant output range. The effect on the breakeven point caused by other changes in (1) the cost structure or (2) the pricing policy can be analyzed in a similar fashion.

The data in Figure 8-7 can be used to demonstrate another version of basic cost-volume-profit analysis. This can be called **cash breakeven analysis**. If the company's fixed- or variable-cost estimates allow for any noncash expenses, then the resultant breakeven point is higher on an accounting profit basis than on a cash basis. This means the firm's production and sales levels do not have to be as great to cover the cash costs of manufacturing the product.

What are these noncash expenses? The largest and most significant is depreciation expense. Another category is prepaid expenses. Insurance policies are at times paid to cover a three-year cycle. Thus, the time period for which the breakeven analysis is being performed might *not* involve an actual cash outlay for insurance coverage.

For purposes of illustration, assume that noncash expenses for Pierce Grain amount to $25,000 over the planning period and that all these costs are fixed. We can compare the revised total costs line in Figure 8-7, which implicitly assumes a lower fixed *cash* cost line, with the sales revenue line to find the cash breakeven point. Provided Pierce Grain can produce and sell 18,750 units over the planning horizon, revenues from sales will be equal to cash operating costs.

Limitations of Breakeven Analysis

Earlier we identified some of the applications of breakeven analysis. This technique is a useful tool in many settings. It must be emphasized, however, that breakeven analysis provides a *beneficial guide* to managerial action, not the final answer. The use of cost-volume-profit analysis has limitations, which should be kept in mind. These include the following:

1. The cost-volume-profit relationship is assumed to be linear. This is realistic only over narrow ranges of output.
2. The total revenue curve (sales curve) is presumed to increase linearly with the volume of output. This implies any quantity can be sold over the relevant output range at that *single* price. To be more realistic, it is necessary in many situations to compute *several* sales curves and corresponding breakeven points at differing prices.
3. A constant production and sales mix is assumed. Should the company decide to produce more of one product and less of another, a new breakeven point would have to be found. Only if the variable cost-to-sales ratios were identical for products involved would the new calculation be unnecessary.
4. The breakeven chart and the breakeven computation are static forms of analysis. Any alteration in the firm's cost or price structure dictates that a new breakeven point be calculated. Breakeven analysis is more helpful, therefore, in stable industries than in dynamic ones.

OPERATING LEVERAGE

If *fixed* operating costs are present in the firm's cost structure, so is *operating leverage.* Fixed operating costs do *not* include interest charges incurred from the firm's use of debt financing. Those costs will be incorporated into the analysis when financial leverage is discussed.

So operating leverage *arises* from the firm's use of fixed operating costs. But, what is operating leverage? **Operating leverage** is the responsiveness of the firm's EBIT to fluctuations in sales. By continuing to draw on our data for the Pierce Grain Company, we can illustrate the concept of operating leverage. Table 8-4 contains data for a study of a possible fluctuation in the firm's sales level. It is assumed that Pierce Grain is currently operating at an annual sales level of $300,000. This is referred to in the tabulation as the base sales level at t (time period zero). The question is: How will Pierce Grain's EBIT level respond to a positive 20 percent change in sales? A sales volume of $360,000, referred to as the forecast sales level at $t + 1$, reflects the 20 percent sales rise anticipated over the planning period. Assume that the planning period is one year.

Table 8-4 Concept of Operating Leverage: Increase in Pierce Grain Company Sales		
Item	Base Sales Level, t	Forecast Sales Level, $t + 1$
Sales	$300,000	$360,000
Less: Total variable costs	180,000	216,000
Revenue before fixed costs	$120,000	$144,000
Less: Total fixed costs	100,000	100,000
EBIT	$ 20,000	$ 44,000

Operating leverage relationships are derived within the mathematical assumptions of cost-volume-profit analysis. In the present example, this means that Pierce Grain's variable cost-to-sales ratio of .6 will continue to hold during time period $t + 1$, and the fixed costs will hold steady at $100,000.

Given the forecasted sales level for Pierce Grain and its cost structure, we can measure the responsiveness of EBIT to the upswing in volume. Notice in Table 8-4 that EBIT is expected to be $44,000 at the end of the planning period. The percentage change in EBIT from t to $t + 1$ can be measured as follows:

$$\text{percentage change in EBIT} = \frac{\$44,000_{t+1} - \$20,000_t}{\$20,000_t}$$

$$= \frac{\$24,000}{\$20,000}$$

$$= 120\%$$

We know that the projected fluctuation in sales amounts to 20 percent of the base period, t, sales level. This is verified below:

$$\text{percentage change in sales} = \frac{\$360,000_{t+1} - \$300,000_t}{\$300,000_t}$$

$$= \frac{\$60,000}{\$300,000}$$

$$= 20\%$$

By relating the percentage fluctuation in EBIT to the percentage fluctuation in sales, we can calculate a specific measure of operating leverage. Thus, we have

$$\begin{matrix}\text{degree of operating leverage} \\ \text{from the base sales level(s)}\end{matrix} = DOL_s = \frac{\text{percentage change in EBIT}}{\text{percentage change in sales}} \qquad (8\text{-}5)$$

Applying equation (8-5) to our Pierce Grain data gives

$$DOL_{\$300,000} = \frac{120\%}{20\%} = 6 \text{ times}$$

Unless we understand what the specific measure of operating leverage tells us, the fact that we may know it is equal to six times is nothing more than sterile information. For Pierce Grain, the inference is that for *any* percentage fluctuation in sales from the base level, the percentage fluctuation in EBIT will be six times as great. If Pierce Grain expected only a 5 percent rise in sales over the coming period, a 30 percent rise in EBIT would be anticipated as follows:

$$(\text{percentage change in sales}) \times (DOL_s) = \text{percentage change in EBIT}$$

$$(5\%) \times (6) = 30\%$$

We will now return to the postulated 20 percent change in sales. What if the direction of the fluctuation is expected to be negative rather than positive? What is in store for Pierce Grain? Unfortunately for Pierce Grain, but fortunately for the analytical process, we will see that the operating leverage measure holds in the negative direction as well. This situation is displayed in Table 8-5.

At the $240,000 sales level, which represents the 20 percent decrease from the base period, Pierce Grain's EBIT is expected to be –$4,000. How sensitive is EBIT to this sales change? The magnitude of the EBIT fluctuation is calculated as

$$\text{percentage change in EBIT} = \frac{-\$4,000_{t+1} - \$20,000_t}{\$20,000_t}$$

$$= \frac{-\$24,000}{\$20,000}$$

$$= -120\%$$

Making use of our knowledge that the sales change was equal to −20 percent permits us to compute the specific measure of operating leverage as

$$DOL_{\$300,000} = \frac{-120\%}{-20\%} = 6 \text{ times}$$

What we have seen, then, is that the degree of operating leverage measure works in the positive or negative direction. A negative change in production volume and sales can be magnified severalfold when the effect on EBIT is calculated.

To this point our calculations of the degree of operating leverage have required two analytical income statements: one for the base period and a second for the subsequent period that incorporates the possible sales alteration. This cumbersome process can be simplified. If unit cost data are available to the financial manager, the relationship can be expressed directly in the following manner:

$$DOL_s = \frac{Q(P - V)}{Q(P - V) - F} \tag{8-6}$$

Observe in equation (8-6) that the variables were all previously defined in our algebraic analysis of the breakeven model. Recall that Pierce sells its product at $10 per unit, the unit variable cost is $6, and total fixed costs over the planning horizon are $100,000. Still assuming that Pierce is operating at a $300,000 sales volume, which means output (Q) is 30,000 units, we can find the degree of operating leverage by application of equation (8-6):

$$DOL_{\$300,000} = \frac{30,000(\$10 - \$6)}{30,000(\$10 - \$6) - \$100,000} = \frac{\$120,000}{\$20,000} = 6 \text{ times}$$

Whereas equation (8-6) requires us to know unit cost data to carry out the computations, the next formulation we examine does not. If we have an analytical income statement for the base period, then equation (8-7) can be employed to find the firm's degree of operating leverage:

$$DOL_s = \frac{\text{revenue before fixed costs}}{\text{EBIT}} = \frac{S - VC}{S - VC - F} \tag{8-7}$$

Use of equation (8-7) in conjunction with the base period data for Pierce Grain shown in either Table 8-4 or 8-5 gives

$$DOL_{\$300,000} = \frac{\$120,000}{\$20,000} = 6 \text{ times}$$

The three versions of the operating leverage measure all produce the same result. Data availability will sometimes dictate which formulation can be applied. The crucial consideration, though, is that you grasp what the measurement tells you. For Pierce Grain, a 1 percent change in sales will produce a 6 percent change in EBIT.

Table 8-5 Concept of Operating Leverage: Decrease in Pierce Grain Company Sales

Item	Base Sales Level, t	Forecast Sales Level, t + 1
Sales	$300,000	$240,000
Less: Total variable costs	180,000	144,000
Revenue before fixed costs	$120,000	$ 96,000
Less: Total fixed costs	100,000	100,000
EBIT	$ 20,000	$ −4,000

Implications

As the firm's scale of operations moves in a favorable manner above the breakeven point, the degree of operating leverage at each subsequent (higher) sales base will decline. In short, the greater the sales level, the lower the degree of operating leverage. This is demonstrated in Table 8-6 for the Pierce Grain Company. At the breakeven sales level for Pierce Grain, the degree of operating leverage is *undefined* because the denominator in any of the computational formulas is zero. Notice that beyond the breakeven point of 25,000 units, the degree of operating leverage declines. It will decline at a decreasing rate and asymptotically approach a value of 1.00. As long as some fixed operating costs are present in the firm's cost structure, however, operating leverage exists, and the degree of operating leverage (DOL_S) will exceed 1.00. Operating leverage is present, then, whenever the firm faces the following situation:

$$\frac{\text{percentage change in EBIT}}{\text{percentage change in sales}} > 1.00$$

The data in Table 8-6 are presented in graphic form in Figure 8-8.

The greater the firm's degree of operating leverage, the more its profits will vary with a given percentage change in sales. Thus, operating leverage is definitely an attribute of the business risk that confronts the company. From Table 8-6 and Figure 8-8 we have seen that the degree of operating leverage falls as sales increase past the firm's breakeven point. The sheer size and operating profitability of the firm, therefore, affect and can lessen its business-risk exposure.

The manager considering an alteration in the firm's cost structure will benefit from an understanding of the operating leverage concept. It might be possible to replace part of the labor force with capital equipment (machinery). A possible result is an increase in fixed costs associated with the new machinery and a reduction in variable costs attributable to a lower labor bill. This conceivably could raise the firm's degree of operating leverage at a specific sales base. If the prospects for future sales increases are high, then increasing the degree of operating leverage might be a prudent decision. The opposite conclusion will be reached if sales prospects are unattractive.

FINANCIAL LEVERAGE

We have defined *financial leverage* as the practice of financing a portion of the firm's assets with securities bearing a fixed rate of return in hope of increasing the ultimate return to the common shareholders. In the present discussion, we focus on the responsiveness of the company's earnings per share to changes in its EBIT. For the time being, then, the return to the common stockholder being concentrat-

Table 8-6 Pierce Grain Company Degree of Operating Leverage Relative to Different Sales Bases		
Units Produced and Sold	Sales Dollars	DOL_S
25,000	$ 250,000	Undefined
30,000	300,000	6.00
35,000	350,000	3.50
40,000	400,000	2.67
45,000	450,000	2.25
50,000	500,000	2.00
75,000	750,000	1.50
100,000	1,000,000	1.33

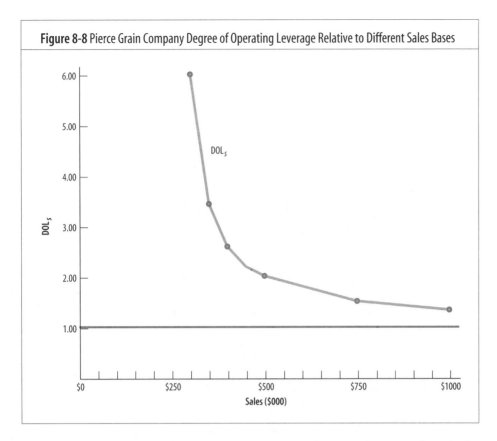

Figure 8-8 Pierce Grain Company Degree of Operating Leverage Relative to Different Sales Bases

ed upon is earnings per share. We are *not* saying that earnings per share is the appropriate criterion for all financing decisions. Rather, the use of financial leverage produces a certain type of *effect*. This effect can be illustrated clearly by concentrating on an earnings-per-share criterion.

Let us assume that the Pierce Grain Company is in the process of getting started as a going concern. The firm's potential owners have calculated that $200,000 is needed to purchase the necessary assets to conduct the business. Three possible financing plans have been identified for raising the $200,000; they are presented in Table 8-7. In plan A, no financial risk is assumed: the entire $200,000 is raised by selling 2,000 common shares, each with a $100 par value. In plan B, a moderate amount of financial risk is assumed: 25 percent of the assets are financed with a debt issue that carries an 8 percent annual interest rate. Plan C would use the most financial leverage: 40 percent of the assets would be financed with a debt issue costing 8 percent.

Table 8-8 presents the impact of financial leverage on earnings per share associated with each fund-raising alternative. If EBIT should increase from $20,000 to $40,000, then earnings per share would rise by 100 percent under plan A. The same positive fluctuation in EBIT would occasion an earnings per share rise of 125 percent under plan B, and 147 percent under plan C. In plans B and C, the 100 percent increase in EBIT (from $20,000 to $40,000) is magnified to a greater than 100 percent increase in earnings per share. The firm is employing financial leverage, and exposing its owners to financial risk, when the following situation exists:

$$\frac{\text{percentage change in earnings per share}}{\text{percentage change in EBIT}} > 1.00$$

By following the same general procedures that allowed us to analyze the firm's use of operating leverage, we can lay out a precise measure of financial leverage.

Table 8-7 Pierce Grain Company Possible Financial Structures

Plan A: 0% debt

		Total debt	$ 0
		Common equity	200,000[a]
Total assets	$200,000	Total liabilities and equity	$200,000

Plan B: 25% debt at 8% interest rate

		Total debt	$ 50,000
		Common equity	150,000[b]
Total assets	$200,000	Total liabilities and equity	$200,000

Plan C: 40% debt at 8% interest rate

		Total debt	$ 80,000
		Common equity	120,000[c]
Total assets	$200,000	Total liabilities and equity	$200,000

[a]2,000 common shares outstanding   [b]1,500 common shares outstanding   [c]1,200 common shares outstanding

---

Table 8-8 Pierce Grain Company Analysis of Financial Leverage at Different EBIT Levels

(1) EBIT	(2) Interest	(3)=(1)−(2) EBT	(4)=(3)X.5 Taxes	(5) = (3)−(4) Net Income to Common	(6) Earnings per Share
Plan A: 0% debt; $200,000 common equity; 2000 shares					
$ 0	$ 0	$ 0	$ 0	$ 0	$ 0
20,000	0	20,000	10,000	10,000	5.00 }100%
40,000	0	40,000	20,000	20,000	10.00
60,000	0	60,000	30,000	30,000	15.00
80,000	0	80,000	40,000	40,000	20.00
Plan B: 25% debt; 8% interest rate; $150,000 common equity, 1500 shares					
$ 0	$4,000	$(4,000)	$(2,000)[a]	$ (2,000)	$ (1.33)
20,000	4,000	16,000	8,000	8,000	5.33 }125%
40,000	4,000	36,000	18,000	18,000	12.00
60,000	4,000	56,000	28,000	28,000	18.67
80,000	4,000	76,000	38,000	38,000	25.33
Plan C: 40% debt; 8% interest rate; $120,000 common equity; 1200 shares					
$ 0	$6,400	$(6,400)	$(3,200)[a]	$ (3,200)	$ (2.67)
20,000	6,400	13,600	6,800	6,800	5.67 }147%
40,000	6,400	33,600	16,800	16,800	14.00
60,000	6,400	53,600	26,800	26,800	22.33
80,000	6,400	73,600	36,800	36,800	30.67

[a]The negative tax bill recognizes the credit arising from the carryback and carryforward provision of the tax code.

Such a measure deals with the sensitivity of earnings per share to EBIT fluctuations. The relationship can be expressed as

$$\text{degree of financial leverage (DFL) from base EBIT level} = DFL_{EBIT} = \frac{\text{percentage change in earnings per share}}{\text{percentage change in EBIT}} \qquad (8\text{-}8)$$

Use of equation (8-8) with each of the financing choices outlined for Pierce Grain is shown subsequently. The base EBIT level is $20,000 in each case.

$$\text{Plan A}: DFL_{\$20,000} = \frac{100\%}{100\%} = 1.00 \text{ time}$$

$$\text{Plan B}: DFL_{\$20,000} = \frac{125\%}{100\%} = 1.25 \text{ times}$$

$$\text{Plan C}: DFL_{\$20,000} = \frac{147\%}{100\%} = 1.47 \text{ times}$$

Like operating leverage, the *degree of financial leverage* concept performs in the negative direction as well as the positive. Should EBIT fall by 10 percent, the Pierce Grain Company would suffer a 12.5 percent decline in earnings per share under plan B. If plan C were chosen to raise the necessary financial capital, the decline in earnings would be 14.7 percent. Observe that the greater the DFL, the greater the fluctuations (positive or negative) in earnings per share. The common stockholder is required to endure greater variations in returns when the firm's management chooses to use more financial leverage rather than less. The DFL measure allows the variation to be quantified.

Rather than taking the time to compute percentage changes in EBIT and earnings per share, the DFL can be found directly, as follows:

$$DFL_{EBIT} = \frac{EBIT}{EBIT - I} \qquad (8\text{-}9)$$

In equation (8-9) the variable, I, represents the total interest expense incurred on *all* the firm's contractual debt obligations. If six bonds are outstanding, I is the sum of the interest expense on all six bonds. If the firm has preferred stock in its financial structure, the dividend on such issues must be inflated to a before-tax basis and included in the computation of I. In this latter instance, I is in reality the sum of all fixed financing costs.

Equation (8-9) has been applied to each of Pierce Grain's financing plans (Table 8-8) at a base EBIT level of $20,000. The results are as follows:

$$\text{Plan A}: DFL_{\$20,000} = \frac{\$20,000}{\$20,000 - 0} = 1.00 \text{ time}$$

$$\text{Plan B}: DFL_{\$20,000} = \frac{\$20,000}{\$20,000 - \$4000} = 1.25 \text{ times}$$

$$\text{Plan C}: DFL_{\$20,000} = \frac{\$20,000}{\$20,000 - \$6400} = 1.47 \text{ times}$$

Figure 8-9 Leverage and Earnings Fluctuations

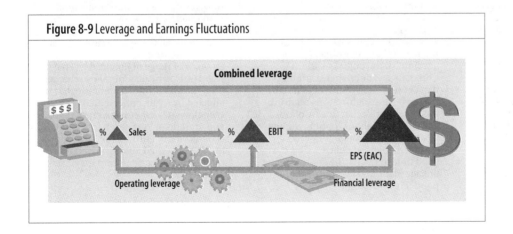

COCA-COLA COMPANY ANNUAL REPORT, 1993

The Coca-Cola Company Financial Policies

Management's primary objective is to maximize share-owner value over time. To accomplish this objective, the Coca-Cola Company and sub-sidiaries (the Company) have developed a comprehensive business strategy that empha-sizes maximizing long-term cash flows. This strategy focuses on continuing aggressive invest-ment in the high-return soft drink business, increasing returns on existing investments and optimizing the cost of capital through appropriate financial policies. **(A)** The success of this strategy is evidenced by the growth in the Company's cash flows and earnings, its increased returns on total capital and equi-ty and the total return to its share

owners over time.

Management seeks invest-ments that strategically enhance existing operations and offer cash returns that exceed the Company's long-term after-tax weighted average cost of capital, estimated by management to be approximately 11 percent as of January 1, 1994. The Company's soft drink business generates inherent high returns on capital, providing an attractive area for continued investment.

Maximizing share-owner value necessitates optimizing the Company's cost of capital through appropriate financial policies.

The Company maintains debt levels considered prudent based on the Company's cash

flows, interest coverage, and the percentage of debt to the Com-pany's total capital. The Compa-ny's overall cost of capital is low-ered by the use of debt financing, resulting in increased return to share owners.**(B)**

The Company's capital structure and financial policies have resulted in long-term credit ratings of "AA" from Standard & Poor's and "Aa3" from Moody's, as well as the highest credit rat-ings available for its commercial paper programs. The Company's strong financial position and cash flows allow for opportunis-tic access to financing in finan-cial markets around the world.

SOURCE: The Coca-Cola Company, *Annual Report* (1993): 44–46.

ANALYSIS AND IMPLICATIONS...

The fact that financial leverage effects can be measured provides manage-ment the opportunity to shape corpo-rate policy formally around the deci-sion to use or avoid the use of leverage-inducing financial instruments. The Coca-Cola Company has very specific policies on the use of financial lever-age. The learning objectives of this chapter, then, comprise more than mere academic, intellectual exercises. The material is, in fact, the stuff of boardroom-level discussion.

A. We stated earlier that the goal of the firm is to maximize shareholder

wealth, and this means maximizing the price of the firm's existing common stock. The Coca-Cola Company has accepted this approach to manage-ment as its "primary objective." To accomplish the objective, the Company has developed a strategy that centers on investment in its core business—the high-return soft drink business. Notice that Coca-Cola also speaks clearly about "optimizing" its cost of capital through properly designed financial policies. This is a good time to review the cost of capital linkage identified in Figure 8-1 and ponder its meaning.

B. Determining an appropriate (opti-mal) financing mix is a crucial activity of financial management. Companies use different approaches to seek an optimal range of financial leverage use. The Coca-Cola Company searches for a "prudent" level of debt use that is affected by (1) its projected cash flows, (2) interest coverage ratios, and (3) ratio of long-term debt to total capitalization. Further, the Company is highly concerned about the bond ratings that it receives from major rat-ing agencies.

Table 8-9 Pierce Grain Company Combined Leverage Analysis

Item	Base Sales Level, t	Forecast Sales Level, $t+1$	Selected Percentage Changes
Sales	$300,000	$360,000	+20
Less: Total variable costs	180,000	216,000	
Revenue before fixed costs	$120,000	$144,000	
Less: Total fixed costs	100,000	100,000	
EBIT	$ 20,000	$ 44,000	+120
Less: Interest expense	4,000	4,000	
Earnings before taxes (EBT)	$ 16,000	$ 40,000	
Less: Taxes at 50%	8,000	20,000	
Net income	$ 8,000	$ 20,000	+150
Less: Preferred dividends	0	0	
Earnings available to common (EAC)	$ 8,000	$ 20,000	+150
Number of common shares	1,500	1,500	
Earnings per share (EPS)	$ 5.33	$ 13.33	+150

$$\text{Degree of operating leverage } = \text{DOL}_{\$300,000} = \frac{120\%}{20\%} = 6 \text{ times}$$

$$\text{Degree of financial leverage } = \text{DFL}_{\$20,000} = \frac{150\%}{120\%} = 1.25 \text{ times}$$

$$\text{Degree of combined leverage } = \text{DCL}_{\$300,000} = \frac{150\%}{20\%} = 7.50 \text{ times}$$

As you probably suspected, the measures of financial leverage shown previously are identical to those obtained by use of equation (8-8). This will always be the case.

COMBINATION OF OPERATING AND FINANCIAL LEVERAGE

Changes in sales revenues cause greater changes in EBIT. Additionally, changes in EBIT translate into larger variations in both earnings per share (EPS) and total earnings available to the common shareholders (EAC), if the firm chooses to use financial leverage. It should be no surprise, then, to find out that combining operating and financial leverage causes further large variations in earnings per share. This entire process is visually displayed in Figure 8-9.

Because the risk associated with possible earnings per share is affected by the use of combined or total leverage, it is useful to quantify the effect. For an illustration, we refer once more to the Pierce Grain Company. The cost structure identified for Pierce Grain in our discussion of breakeven analysis still holds. Furthermore, assume that plan B, which carried a 25 percent debt ratio, was chosen to finance the company's assets. Turn your attention to Table 8-9.

In Table 8-9, an increase in output for Pierce Grain from 30,000 to 36,000 units is analyzed. This increase represents a 20 percent rise in sales revenues. From our earlier discussion of operating leverage and the data in Table 8-9, we can see that this 20 percent increase in sales is magnified into a 120 percent rise in EBIT. From this base sales level of $300,000 the degree of operating leverage is six times.

The 120 percent rise in EBIT induces a change in earnings per share and earnings available to the common shareholders of 150 percent. The degree of financial leverage is therefore 1.25 times.

The upshot of the analysis is that the 20 percent rise in sales has been magnified to 150 percent, as reflected by the percentage change in earnings per share. The formal measure of combined leverage can be expressed as follows:

$$\begin{pmatrix} \text{degree of combined} \\ \text{leverage from the} \\ \text{base sales level} \end{pmatrix} = DCL_s = \begin{pmatrix} \dfrac{\text{percentage change in}}{\text{earnings per share}} \\ \dfrac{}{\text{percentage change in sales}} \end{pmatrix} \qquad (8\text{-}10)$$

This equation was used in the bottom portion of Table 8-9 to determine that the degree of combined leverage from the base sales level of $300,000 is 7.50 times. Pierce Grain's use of both operating and financial leverage will cause any percentage change in sales (from the specific base level) to be magnified by a factor of 7.50 when the effect on earnings per share is computed. A one percent change in sales, for example, will result in a 7.50 percent change in earnings per share.

Notice that the degree of combined leverage is actually the *product* (not the simple sum) of the two independent leverage measures. Thus, we have

$$(DOL_s) \times (DFL_{EBIT}) = DCL_s \qquad (8\text{-}11)$$

or

$$(6) \times (1.25) = 7.50 \text{ times}$$

It is possible to ascertain the degree of combined leverage in a direct fashion, without determining any percentage fluctuations or the separate leverage values. We need only substitute the appropriate values into equation (8-12):

$$DCL_s = \frac{Q(P - V)}{Q(P - V) - F - I} \qquad (8\text{-}12)$$

The variable definitions in equation (8-12) are the same ones that have been employed throughout this chapter. Use of equation (8-12) with the information in Table 8-9 gives

$$\begin{aligned} DCL_{\$300,000} &= \frac{\$30,000(\$10 - \$6)}{\$30,000(\$10 - \$6) - \$100,000 - \$4000} \\ &= \frac{\$120,000}{\$16,000} \\ &= 7.5 \text{ times} \end{aligned}$$

Implications

The total risk exposure the firm assumes can be managed by combining operating and financial leverage in different degrees. Knowledge of the various leverage measures aids the financial officer in determining the proper level of overall risk that should be accepted. If a high degree of business risk is inherent to the specific line of commercial activity, then a low posture regarding financial risk would minimize *additional* earnings fluctuations stemming from sales changes. Conversely, the firm that by its very nature incurs a low level of fixed operating costs might choose to use a high degree of financial leverage in the hope of increasing earnings per share and the rate of return on the common equity investment.

NEW ENGLAND ECONOMIC REVIEW, JANUARY/FEBRUARY 1994

The Relationship Among Sales, Cash Flow, and Leverage

Perhaps it is not surprising that leverage, liquidity, and other variables should influence capital spending so little once the general business climate (represented by sales or cash flow) has been taken into account. The choice of leverage, like capital spending, depends on the prospect for profit. A good business climate can foster both investment and debt financing.(A) In these cases, higher leverage does not deter investment; instead, it may appear to facilitate investment.

At other times, companies may increase their leverage while they reduce their capital spending, if the return on existing capital is great compared to that foreseen on new investments. In these cases, higher leverage may appear to deter investment. In any of these cases, appearances can be deceiving, because investment and leverage jointly depend on business conditions, and this dependency entails no consistent relationship between indebtedness and investment.(B)

For the making of economic policy, the evidence suggests that the familiar macroeconomic incentives for investment would be no less effective today than they have been in the past. In particular, the volume of investment spending would appear to respond to monetary and fiscal policies in the customary way. Profits and cash flow might increase as a result of either rising sales or a tax cut.

SOURCE: R. W. Kopcke with M. M. Howrey, "A Panel Study of Investment: Sales, Cash Flow, the Cost of Capital, and Leverage," *New England Economic Review* (January/February 1994): 23.

ANALYSIS AND IMPLICATIONS...

We spent considerable time in earlier chapters studying capital-budgeting techniques and discussed the search by firms for projects with positive net present values. The spending by firms on real capital projects is an important topic not only for the specific firms involved, but also for the aggregate economy. This is because high levels of real capital spending over time are associated with high levels of societal wealth. Societies that do not invest tend to be poor. So, it follows that national economic policymaking is concerned with what variables do affect the spending by companies on projects.

Mr. Kopcke and Mr. Howrey of the Federal Reserve Bank of Boston studied the investment spending of 396 domestic manufacturing corporations and found some interesting relationships among the variables that seem to influence the size of firm's capital budgets.

A. The authors of this study have put forth a reasonable conclusion concerning the relationship between capital spending and the firm's choice to use or avoid financial leverage. They suggest that *both* capital budgets and financial leverage use depend on expected profits. This is close to asserting that the specific firm's capacity to generate future cash flows is a major determinant of its financing mix. In the present context, the firm's ability to service its debt contracts depends on its ability to generate future cash flows.

B. Also, we see that these researchers suggest that general business conditions (that is, strong or weak) affect not only the size of the firm's capital budget, but also management's decision to use financial leverage in the financing of that capital budget. Such a logical combination of (1) the state of business conditions and (2) the expectation of future profits (cash flows) means that the underlying nature of the business in which the firm operates should be the most important factor affecting its ultimate financing mix. That is, *business risk* and commercial strategy directly affect the specific firm's decision to use financial leverage.

SUMMARY

In this chapter, we begin to study the process of arriving at an appropriate financial structure for the firm. We examine tools that can assist the financial manager in this task. We are mainly concerned with assessing the variability in the firm's residual earnings stream (either earnings per share or earnings available to the common shareholders) induced by the use of operating and financial leverage. This assessment builds on the tenets of breakeven analysis.

Breakeven analysis permits the financial manager to determine the quantity of output or the level of sales that will result in an EBIT level of zero. This means the firm has neither a profit nor a loss before any tax considerations. The effect of price changes, cost structure changes, or volume changes on profits (EBIT) can be studied. To make the technique operational, it is necessary that the firm's costs be classified as fixed or variable. Not all costs fit neatly into one of these two categories. Over short planning horizons, though, the preponderance of costs can be assigned to either the fixed or variable classification. Once the cost structure has been identified, the breakeven point can be found by use of (1) trial-and-error analysis, (2) contribution-margin analysis, or (3) algebraic analysis.

Operating leverage is the responsiveness of the firm's EBIT to changes in sales revenues. It arises from the firm's use of fixed operating costs. When fixed operating costs are present in the company's cost structure, changes in sales are magnified into even greater changes in EBIT. The firm's degree of operating leverage from a base sales level is the percentage change in EBIT divided by the percentage change in sales. All types of leverage are two-edged swords. When sales decrease by some percentage, the negative impact upon EBIT will be even larger.

A firm employs financial leverage when it finances a portion of its assets with securities bearing a fixed rate of return. The presence of debt and/or preferred stock in the company's financial structure means that it is using financial leverage. When financial leverage is used, changes in EBIT translate into larger changes in earnings per share. The concept of the degree of financial leverage dwells on the sensitivity of earnings per share to changes in EBIT. The DFL from a base EBIT level is defined as the percentage change in earnings per share divided by the percentage change in EBIT. All other things equal, the more fixed-charge securities the firm employs in its financial structure, the greater its degree of financial leverage. Clearly, EBIT can rise or fall. If it falls, and financial leverage is used, the firm's shareholders endure negative changes in earnings per share that are larger than the relative decline in EBIT. Again, leverage is a two-edged sword.

Firms use operating and financial leverage in various degrees. The joint use of operating and financial leverage can be measured by computing the degree of combined leverage, defined as the percentage change in earnings per share divided by the percentage change in sales. This measure allows the financial manager to ascertain the effect on total leverage caused by adding financial leverage on top of operating leverage. Effects can be dramatic because the degree of combined leverage is the product of the degrees of operating and financial leverage. Table 8-10 summarizes the salient concepts and calculation formats discussed in this chapter.

Table 8-10 Summary of Leverage Concepts and Calculations

Technique	Description or Concept	Calculation	Text Reference
Breakeven Analysis			
1. Breakeven point quantity	Total fixed costs divided by the unit contribution margin	$Q_B = \dfrac{F}{P-V}$	(8-3)
2. Breakeven sales level	Total fixed costs divided by 1 minus the ratio of total variable costs to the associated level of sales	$S^* = \dfrac{F}{1 - \dfrac{VC}{S}}$	(8-4)
Operating leverage			
3. Degree of operating leverage	Percentage change in EBIT divided by the percentage change in sales; or revenue before fixed costs divided by revenue after fixed costs	$DOL_s = \dfrac{Q(P-V)}{Q(P-V)-F}$	(8-6)
Financial Leverage			
4. Degree of financial leverage	Percentage change in earnings per share divided by the percentage change in EBIT; or EBIT divided by EBT.[a]	$DFL_{EBIT} = \dfrac{EBIT}{EBIT-I}$	(8-9)
Combined Leverage			
5. Degree of combined leverage	Percentage change in earnings per share divided by the percentage change in sales; or revenue before fixed costs divided by EBT.[a]	$DCL_s = \dfrac{Q(P-V)}{Q(P-V)-F-I}$	(8-12)

[a]The use of EBT here presumes no preferred dividend payments. In the presence of preferred dividend payments replace EBT with earnings available to common stock (EAC).

STUDY QUESTIONS

8-1. Distinguish between business risk and financial risk. What gives rise to, or causes, each type of risk?

8-2. Define the term *financial leverage*. Does the firm use financial leverage if preferred stock is present in the capital structure?

8-3. Define the term *operating leverage*. What type of effect occurs when the firm uses operating leverage?

8-4. What is the difference between the (ordinary) breakeven point and the cash breakeven point? Which will be the greater?

8-5. A manager in your firm decides to employ breakeven analysis. Of what shortcomings should this manager be aware?

8-6. What is meant by total risk exposure? How may a firm move to reduce its total risk exposure?

8-7. If a firm has a degree of combined leverage of 3.0 times, what does a negative sales fluctuation of 15 percent portend for the earnings available to the firm's common stock investors?

8-8. Breakeven analysis assumes linear revenue and cost functions. In reality these linear functions over large output and sales levels are highly improbable. Why?

SELF-TEST PROBLEMS

ST-1. (Breakeven Point) You are a hard-working analyst in the office of financial operations for a manufacturing firm that produces a single product. You have developed the following cost structure information for this company. All of it pertains to an output level of 10 million units. Using this information, find the breakeven point in units of output for the firm.

Return on operating assets	= 30%
Operating asset turnover	= 6 times
Operating assets	= $20 million
Degree of operating leverage	= 4.5 times

ST-2. (Leverage Analysis) You have developed the following analytical income statement for your corporation. It represents the most recent year's operations, which ended yesterday. Your supervisor in the financial studies office has just handed you a memorandum that asked for written responses to the following questions:

    a. At this level of output, what is the degree of operating leverage?

    b. What is the degree of financial leverage?

    c. What is the degree of combined leverage?

    d. What is the firm's breakeven point in sales dollars?

    e. If sales should increase by 30 percent, by what percent would earnings before taxes (and net income) increase?

Sales	$20,000,000
Variable costs	12,000,000
Revenue before fixed costs	$ 8,000,000
Fixed costs	5,000,000
EBIT	3,000,000
Interest expense	1,000,000
Earnings before taxes	$ 2,000,000
Taxes (0.50)	1,000,000
Net income	$ 1,000,000

    f. Prepare an analytical income statement that verifies the calculations from part (e) above.

ST-3. (Fixed Costs and the Breakeven Point) Bonaventure Manufacturing expects to earn $210,000 next year after taxes. Sales will be $4 million. The firm's single plant is located on the outskirts of Olean, New York. The firm manufactures a combined bookshelf and desk unit used extensively in college dormitories. These units sell for $200 each and have a variable cost per unit of $150. Bonaventure experiences a 30 percent tax rate.

    a. What are the firm's fixed costs expected to be next year?

    b. Calculate the firm's breakeven point in both units and dollars.

STUDY PROBLEMS (SET A)

8-1A. (Breakeven Point) Napa Valley Winery (NVW) is a boutique winery that produces from organically grown cabernet sauvignon grapes a high-quality nonalcoholic red wine. It sells each bottle for $30. NVW's chief financial officer, Jackie Cheng, has estimated variable costs to be 70 percent of sales. If NVW's fixed costs are $360,000, how many bottles of its wine must NVW sell to break even?

8-2A. (Operating Leverage) In light of a sales agreement that Napa Valley Winery (see description in Problem 8-1A) just signed with a national chain of health food restaurants, NVW's CFO Jackie Cheng is estimating that NVW's sales in the next year will be 50,000 bottles at $30 per bottle. If variable costs are expected to be 70 percent of sales, what is NVW's expected degree of operating leverage?

8-3A. (Breakeven Point and Operating Leverage) Some financial data for each of three firms are given below:

	Jake's Lawn Chairs	Sarasota Sky Lights	Jefferson Wholesale
Average selling price per unit	$ 32.00	$ 875.00	$ 97.77
Average variable cost per unit	$ 17.38	$ 400.00	$ 87.00
Units sold	18,770	2,800	11,000
Fixed costs	$120,350	$850,000	$89,500

a. What is the profit for each company at the indicated sales volume?

b. What is the breakeven point in units for each company?

c. What is the degree of operating leverage for each company at the indicated sales volume?

d. If sales were to decline, which firm would suffer the largest relative decline in profitability?

8-4A. (Leverage Analysis) You have developed the following analytical income statement for your corporation. It represents the most recent year's operations, which ended yesterday.

Sales	$45,750,000
Variable costs	22,800,000
Revenue before fixed costs	$22,950,000
Fixed costs	9,200,000
EBIT	13,750,000
Interest expense	1,350,000
Earnings before taxes	$12,400,000
Taxes (.50)	6,200,000
Net income	$ 6,200,000

Your supervisor in the controller's office has just handed you a memorandum asking for written responses to the following questions:

a. At this level of output, what is the degree of operating leverage?

b. What is the degree of financial leverage?

c. What is the degree of combined leverage?

d. What is the firm's breakeven point in sales dollars?

e. If sales should increase by 25 percent, by what percent would earnings before taxes (and net income) increase?

8-5A. (Breakeven Point and Operating Leverage) Footwear, Inc., manufactures a complete line of men's and women's dress shoes for independent merchants. The average selling price of its finished product is $85 per pair. The variable cost for this same pair of shoes is $58. Footwear, Inc., incurs fixed costs of $170,000 per year.

    a. What is the breakeven point in pairs of shoes for the company?

    b. What is the dollar sales volume the firm must achieve to reach the breakeven point?

    c. What would be the firm's profit or loss at the following units of production sold: 7,000 pairs of shoes? 9,000 pairs of shoes? 15,000 pairs of shoes?

    d. Find the degree of operating leverage for the production and sales levels given in part (c) above.

8-6A. (Breakeven Point and Operating Leverage) Zeylog Corporation manufactures a line of computer memory expansion boards used in microcomputers. The average selling price of its finished product is $180 per unit. The variable cost for these same units is $110. Zeylog incurs fixed costs of $630,000 per year.

    a. What is the breakeven point in units for the company?

    b. What is the dollar sales volume the firm must achieve to reach the breakeven point?

    c. What would be the firm's profit or loss at the following units of production sold: 12,000 units? 15,000 units? 20,000 units?

    d. Find the degree of operating leverage for the production and sales levels given in part (c) above.

8-7A. (Breakeven Point and Operating Leverage) Some financial data for each of three firms are shown below:

	Blacksburg Furniture	Lexington Cabinets	Williamsburg Colonials
Average selling price per unit	$ 15.00	$ 400.00	$40.00
Average variable cost per unit	$ 12.35	$ 220.00	$14.50
Units sold	75,000	4,000	13,000
Fixed costs	$35,000	$100,000	$70,000

    a. What is the profit for each company at the indicated sales volume?

    b. What is the breakeven point in units for each company?

    c. What is the degree of operating leverage for each company at the indicated sales volume?

    d. If sales were to decline, which firm would suffer the largest relative decline in profitability?

8-8. (Fixed Costs and the Breakeven Point) A & B Beverages expects to earn $50,000 next year after taxes. Sales will be $375,000. The store is located near the shopping district surrounding Blowing Rock University. Its average product sells for $27 a unit. The variable cost per unit is $14.85. The store experiences a 40 percent tax rate.

    a. What are the store's fixed costs expected to be next year?

    b. Calculate the store's breakeven point in both units and dollars.

8-9A. (Breakeven Point and Profit Margin) Mary Clark, a recent graduate of Clarion South University, is planning to open a new wholesaling operation. Her target operating profit margin is 26 percent. Her unit contribution margin will be 50 percent of sales. Average annual sales are forecast to be $3,250,000.

  a. How large can fixed costs be for the wholesaling operation and still allow the 26 percent operating profit margin to be achieved?

  b. What is the breakeven point in dollars for the firm?

8-10A. (Leverage Analysis) You have developed the following analytical income statement for your corporation. It represents the most recent year's operations, which ended yesterday. Your supervisor in the controller's office has just handed you a memorandum asking for written responses to the following questions:

  a. At this level of output, what is the degree of operating leverage?

  b. What is the degree of financial leverage?

Sales	$30,000,000
Variable costs	13,500,000
Revenue before fixed costs	$16,500,000
Fixed costs	8,000,000
EBIT	8,500,000
Interest expense	1,000,000
Earnings before taxes	7,500,000
Taxes(.50)	3,750,000
Net income	$ 3,750,000

  c. What is the degree of combined leverage?

  d. What is the firm's breakeven point in sales dollars?

  e. If sales should increase by 25 percent, by what percent would earnings before taxes (and net income) increase?

8-11A. (Breakeven Point) You are a hard-working analyst in the office of financial operations for a manufacturing firm that produces a single product. You have developed the following cost structure information for this company. All of it pertains to an output level of 10 million units. Using this information, find the breakeven point in units of output for the firm.

Return on operating assets	= 25%
Operating asset turnover	= 5 times
Operating assets	= $20 million
Degree of operating leverage	= 4 times

8-12A. (Breakeven Point and Operating Leverage) Allison Radios manufactures a complete line of radio and communication equipment for law enforcement agencies. The average selling price of its finished product is $180 per unit. The variable cost for these same units is $126. Allison Radios incurs fixed costs of $540,000 per year.

  a. What is the breakeven point in units for the company?

  b. What is the dollar sales volume the firm must achieve in order to reach the breakeven point?

  c. What would be the firm's profit or loss at the following units of production sold: 12,000 units? 15,000 units? 20,000 units?

  d. Find the degree of operating leverage for the production and sales levels given in part (c) above.

8-13A. (Breakeven Point and Operating Leverage) Some financial data for each of three firms are given below:

	Oviedo Seeds	Gainesville Sod	Athens Peaches
Average selling price per unit	$ 14.00	$ 200.00	$ 25.00
Average variable cost per unit	$ 11.20	$ 130.00	$ 17.50
Units sold	100,000	10,000	48,000
Fixed costs	$25,000	$100,000	$35,000

    a. What is the profit for each company at the indicated sales volume?

    b. What is the breakeven point in units for each company?

    c. What is the degree of operating leverage for each company at the indicated sales volume?

    d. If sales were to *decline,* which firm would suffer the largest relative decline in profitability?

8-14A. (Fixed Costs and the Breakeven Point) Dot's Quik-Stop Party Store expects to earn $40,000 next year after taxes. Sales will be $400,000. The store is located near the fraternity-row district of Cambridge Springs State University and sells only kegs of beer for $20 a keg. The variable cost per keg is $8. The store experiences a 40 percent tax rate.

    a. What are the Party Store's fixed costs expected to be next year?

    b. Calculate the firm's breakeven point in both units and dollars.

8-15A. (Fixed Costs and the Breakeven Point) Albert's Cooling Equipment hopes to earn $80,000 next year after taxes. Sales will be $2 million. The firm's single plant is located on the edge of Slippery Rock, Pennsylvania, and manufactures only small refrigerators. These are used in many of the dormitories found on college campuses. Refrigerators sell for $80 per unit and have a variable cost of $56. Albert's experiences a 40 percent tax rate.

    a. What are the firm's fixed costs expected to be next year?

    b. Calculate the firm's breakeven point both in units and dollars.

8-16A. (Breakeven Point and Selling Price) Gerry's Tool and Die Company will produce 200,000 units next year. All of this production will be sold as finished goods. Fixed costs will total $300,000. Variable costs for this firm are relatively predictable at 75 percent of sales.

    a. If Gerry's Tool and Die wants to achieve an earnings before interest and taxes level of $240,000 next year, at what price per unit must it sell its product?

    b. Based on your answer to part (a), set up an analytical income statement that will verify your solution.

8-17A. (Breakeven Point and Selling Price) Parks Castings, Inc., will manufacture and sell 200,000 units next year. Fixed costs will total $300,000, and variable costs will be 60 percent of sales.

    a. The firm wants to achieve an earnings before interest and taxes level of $250,000. What selling price per unit is necessary to achieve this result?

    b. Set up an analytical income statement to verify your solution to part (a).

8-18A. (Breakeven Point and Profit Margin) A recent business graduate of Midwestern State University is planning to open a new wholesaling operation. His target operating profit margin is 28 percent. His unit contribution margin will be 50 percent of sales. Average annual sales are forecast to be $3,750,000.

    a. How large can fixed costs be for the wholesaling operation and still allow the 28 percent operating profit margin to be achieved?

    b. What is the breakeven point in dollars for the firm?

8-19A. (Operating Leverage) Rocky Mount Metals Company manufactures an assortment of woodburning stoves. The average selling price for the various units is $500. The associated variable cost is $350 per unit. Fixed costs for the firm average $180,000 annually.

    a. What is the breakeven point in units for the company?

    b. What is the dollar sales volume the firm must achieve to reach the breakeven point?

    c. What is the degree of operating leverage for a production and sales level of 5,000 units for the firm? (Calculate to three decimal places.)

    d. What will be the projected effect upon earnings before interest and taxes if the firm's sales level should increase by 20 percent from the volume noted in part (c) above?

8-20A. (Breakeven Point and Operating Leverage) The Portland Recreation Company manufactures a full line of lawn furniture. The average selling price of a finished unit is $25. The associated variable cost is $15 per unit. Fixed costs for Portland average $50,000 per year.

    a. What is the breakeven point in units for the company?

    b. What is the dollar sales volume the firm must achieve to reach the breakeven point?

    c. What would be the company's profit or loss at the following units of production sold: 4,000 units? 6,000 units? 8,000 units?

    d. Find the degree of operating leverage for the production and sales levels given in part (c) above.

    e. What is the effect on the degree of operating leverage as sales rise above the breakeven point?

8-21A. (Fixed Costs) Detroit Heat Treating projects that next year its fixed costs will total $120,000. Its only product sells for $12 per unit, of which $7 is a variable cost. The management of Detroit is considering the purchase of a new machine that will lower the variable cost per unit to $5. The new machine, however, will add to fixed costs through an increase in depreciation expense. How large can the *addition to* fixed costs be to keep the firm's breakeven point in units produced and sold unchanged?

8-22A. (Operating Leverage) The management of Detroit Heat Treating did not purchase the new piece of equipment (see problem 8-21A). Using the existing cost structure, calculate the degree of operating leverage at 30,000 units of output. Comment on the meaning of your answer.

8-23A. (Leverage Analysis) An analytical income statement for Detroit Heat Treating is shown below. It is based on an output (sales) level of 40,000 units. You may refer to the original cost structure data in problem (8-21A).

Sales	$480,000
Variable costs	280,000
Revenue before fixed costs	$200,000
Fixed costs	120,000
EBIT	$ 80,000
Interest expense	30,000
Earnings before taxes	$ 50,000
Taxes	25,000
Net income	$ 25,000

    a. Calculate the degree of operating leverage at this output level.

    b. Calculate the degree of financial leverage at this level of EBIT.

    c. Determine the combined leverage effect at this output level.

8-24A. (Breakeven Point) You are employed as a financial analyst for a single-product manufacturing firm. Your supervisor has made the following cost structure information available to you, all of which pertains to an output level of 1,600,000 units.

Return on operating assets	= 15%
Operating asset turnover	= 5 times
Operating assets	= $3 million
Degree of operating leverage	= 8 times

Your task is to find the breakeven point in units of output for the firm.

8-25A. (Fixed Costs) Des Moines Printing Services is forecasting fixed costs next year of $300,000. The firm's single product sells for $20 per unit and incurs a variable cost per unit of $14. The firm may acquire some new binding equipment that would lower variable cost per unit to $12. The new equipment, however, would add to fixed costs through the price of an annual maintenance agreement on the new equipment. How large can this increase in fixed costs be and still keep the firm's present breakeven point in units produced and sold unchanged?

8-26A. (Leverage Analysis) Your firm's cost analysis supervisor supplies you with the following analytical income statement and requests answers to the four questions listed below the statement.

Sales	$12,000,000
Variable costs	9,000,000
Revenue before fixed costs	$ 3,000,000
Fixed costs	2,000,000
EBIT	$ 1,000,000
Interest expense	200,000
Earnings before taxes	$ 800,000
Taxes	400,000
Net income	$ 400,000

a. At this level of output, what is the degree of operating leverage?

b. What is the degree of financial leverage?

c. What is the degree of combined leverage?

d. What is the firm's breakeven point in sales dollars?

8-27A. (Leverage Analysis) You are supplied with the following analytical income statement for your firm. It reflects last year's operations.

Sales	$16,000,000
Variable costs	8,000,000
Revenue before fixed costs	$ 8,000,000
Fixed costs	4,000,000
EBIT	$ 4,000,000
Interest expense	1,500,000
Earnings before taxes	$ 2,500,000
Taxes	1,250,000
Net income	$ 1,250,000

a. At this level of output, what is the degree of operating leverage?

b. What is the degree of financial leverage?

c. What is the degree of combined leverage?

d. If sales should increase by 20 percent, by what percent would earnings before taxes (and net income) increase?

e. What is your firm's breakeven point in sales dollars?

8-28A. (Sales Mix and Breakeven Point) Toledo Components produces four lines of auto accessories for the major Detroit automobile manufacturers. The lines are known by the code letters A, B, C, and D. The current sales mix for Toledo and the contribution margin ratio (unit contribution margin divided by unit sales price) for these product lines are as follows:

Product Line	Percent of Total Sales
A	25%
B	$36^2/_3$
C	$33^1/_3$
D	5

Total sales for next year are forecast to be $120,000. Total fixed costs will be $29,400.

a. Prepare a table showing (1) sales, (2) total variable costs, and (3) the total contribution margin associated with each product line.

b. What is the aggregate contribution margin ratio indicative of this sales mix?

c. At this sales mix, what is the breakeven point in dollars?

8-29A. (Sales Mix and Breakeven Point) Because of production constraints, Toledo Components (see problem 8-28A) may have to adhere to a different sales mix for next year. The alternative plan is outlined below:

Product Line	Percent of Total Sales	Contribution Margin Ratio
A	$33^1/_3$%	40%
B	$41^2/_3$	32
C	$16^2/_3$	20
D	$8^1/_3$	60

a. Assuming all other facts in problem 8-28A remain the same, what effect will this different sales mix have on Toledo's breakeven point in dollars?

b. Which sales mix will Toledo's management prefer?

Problem

Imagine that you were hired recently as a financial analyst for a relatively new, highly leveraged ski manufacturer located in the foothills of Colorado's Rocky mountains. Your firm manufactures only one product, a state-of-the-art snow ski. The company has been operating up to this point without much quantitative knowledge of the business and financial risks it faces.

Ski season just ended, however, so the president of the company has started to focus more on the financial aspects of managing the business. He has set up a meeting for next week with the CFO, Maria Sanchez, to discuss matters such as the business and financial risks faced by the company. Accordingly, Maria has asked you to prepare an analysis to assist her in her discussions with the president.

As a first step in your work, you compiled the following information regarding the cost structure of the company.

Output Level	50,000 units
Operating Assets	$2,000,000
Operating Asset Turnover	7 times
Return on Operating Assets	35%
Degree of Operating Leverage	5 times
Interest Expense	$400,000

As the next step, you need to *determine the breakeven point in units of output* for the company. One of your strong points has been that you always prepare supporting workpapers, which show how you arrive at your conclusions. You know Maria would like to see such workpapers for this analysis to facilitate her review of your work.

Thereafter you will have the information you require to *prepare an analytical income statement* for the company. You are sure that Maria would like to see this statement; in addition, you know that you need it to be able to answer the following questions. You also know Maria expects you to prepare, in a format that is presentable to the president, answers to the questions to serve as a basis for her discussions with the president.

a. What is the degree of financial leverage?

b. What is the degree of combined leverage?

c. What is the firm's breakeven point in sales dollars?

d. If sales should increase by 30 percent (as the president expects), by what percent would EBT (earnings before taxes) and net income increase?

e. Prepare another analytical income statement, this time to verify the calculations from part (d) above.

CASE PROBLEM

ERIE GENERAL PRODUCERS

Breakeven Analysis, Operating Leverage, Financial Leverage

Erie General Producers (EGP) is a medium-size public corporation that until recently consisted of two divisions. The Retail Furniture Group (RFG) has eight locations in the northeastern Ohio area, mostly concentrated around Cleveland. These retail outlets generate sales of contemporary, traditional, and early American furniture. In addition, casual and leisure furniture lines are carried by the stores. The other (old) division of EGP is its Concrete Group (CG). The CG operates three plants in the North Tonawanda area of western New York. These plants produce precast concrete wall panels and concrete stave farm silos. The company headquarters of EGP is located in Erie, Pennsylvania. This community touches Lake Erie in northwestern Pennsylvania and is about 140 miles

north of Pittsburgh. Because Erie is almost equidistant from Cleveland and North Tonawanda and is a connecting hub for several interstate highways, it makes a sensible spot for the firm's home offices.

EGP was started ten years ago as Erie Producers by its current president and board chairman, Anthony Toscano. During the firm's existence it has enjoyed periods of both moderate and strong growth in sales, assets, and earnings. Key managerial decisions have always been dominated by Toscano, who openly boasts of the fact that his company has never suffered through a year of negative earnings despite the often cyclical nature of both the retail furniture (RFG) and concrete (CG) divisions.

Recently, Mr. Toscano decided to acquire a third division for his firm. The division manufactures special machinery for the seafood processing industry and is appropriately called the Seafood Industry Group (SIG). The financial settlement for the acquisition took place yesterday. Currently, the SIG consists of one manufacturing plant in Erie. A single product is to be manufactured, assembled, and shipped from the facility. That product, however, represents a design breakthrough and carries with it a projected contribution margin ratio of .4000. This is greater than that enjoyed by either of EGP's other two divisions.

EGP's manufacturing operation in Erie will produce a new machine called "The Picker." The Picker was invented and successfully tested by Ben Pinkerton, the major stockholder and manager of a small seafood processing firm in Morattico, Virginia. Pinkerton plans and supervises all operations at Eastern Shore Processors. Eastern Shore specializes in freezing and pasteurizing crab meat. Freezing and pasteurizing procedures have been a boon to the seafood industry, for they permit the processor to retain a product without spoilage in hopes of higher prices at a later date. In comparing his industry to that of agriculture, Pinkerton aptly states: "The freezer is our grain elevator."

The seafood processing industry is characterized by a notable lack of capital equipment and a corresponding heavy use of human labor. Pinkerton will tell you that at Eastern Shore Processors a skilled crab meat picker will produce about thirty pounds of meat per day. No matter how skilled the human picker, however, he will leave about ten pounds of meat per day in the top piece of the crab shell. This past year, after five years of trying, Pinkerton perfected a machine that would recover about 30 percent of this otherwise lost meat. In exchange for cash, Eastern Shore Processors sold all rights to The Picker to EGP. Thus, Toscano established the SIG and immediately made plans to manufacture The Picker.

Recent income statements for the older divisions of EGP are contained in Exhibits 1 and 2. Toscano has now decided to assess more fully the probable impact of the decision to establish the SIG on the financial condition of EGP. Toscano knew that such figures should have been generated prior to the decision to enter this special field, but his seasoned judgment led him to a quick choice. He has requested several pieces of information, detailed as follows, from his chief financial officer.

Questions and Problems

1. Using last year's results, determine the breakeven point in dollars for EGP (that is, before investing in the new SIG). The breakeven point is defined here in the traditional manner where EBIT = $0. (*Hint:* Use an aggregate contribution-margin ratio in your analysis.)

2. Using last year's results, determine what volume of sales must be reached to cover all before-tax costs.

3. Next year's sales for the SIG are projected to be $4,000,000. Total fixed costs will be $640,000. This division will have no outstanding debt on its balance sheet. EGP uses a 50 percent tax rate in all its financial projections. Using the format of Exhibits 1 and 2, construct a pro forma income statement for the SIG.

4. After the SIG begins operations, what will be EGP's breakeven point in dollars (a) as traditionally defined and (b) reflecting the coverage of *all* before-tax costs? Base the new sales mix on last year's sales performance for the older divisions plus that anticipated next year for the SIG. Using your answer to part (b) of this question, construct an analytical income statement demonstrating that earnings before taxes = $0

5. Using next year's anticipated sales volume for EGP (including the SIG), compute (a) the degree of operating leverage, (b) the degree of financial leverage, and (c) the degree of combined leverage. Comment on the meaning of each of these statistics.

6. Using projected figures, determine whether acquisition of the SIG will increase or decrease the vulnerability of EGP's earnings before interest and taxes (EBIT) to cyclical swings in sales. Show your work.

7. Review the key assumptions of cost-volume-profit analysis.

Exhibit 1 Erie General Producers Retail Furniture Group Income Statement, December 31, Last Year

Sales	$12,000,000
Less: total variable costs	7,920,000
Revenue before fixed costs	$ 4,080,000
Less: total fixed costs	2,544,000
EBIT	$ 1,536,000
Less: interest expense	192,000
Earnings before taxes	$ 1,344,000
Less: taxes @ 50%	672,000
Net profit	$ 672,000

Exhibit 2 Erie General Producers Concrete Group Income Statement, December 31, Last Year

Sales	$8,000,000
Less: total variable costs	5,920,000
Revenue before fixed costs	$2,080,000
Less: total fixed costs	640,000
EBIT	$1,440,000
Less: interest expense	80,000
Earnings before taxes	$1,360,000
Less: taxes @ 50%	680,000
Net profit	$ 680,000

CHAPTER 9

LEASE VS. PURCHASE ANALYSIS

One way to reduce financial and operating leverage on a project is to lease equipment rather than purchase. Keown discusses the various ramifications of the leasing decision in the following section.

We begin our discussion by defining the major types of lease arrangements. Next we briefly renew the history and describe the present practice of the accounting treatment of leases. We examine the lease versus purchase decision, and we conclude by investigating the potential benefits of leasing.

TYPES OF LEASE ARRANGEMENTS

There are three major types of lease agreements: direct leasing, sale and leaseback, and leveraged leasing. Most lease agreements fall into one of these categories. However, the particular lease agreement can take one of two forms. (1) The **financial lease** constitutes a noncancelable contractual commitment on the part of the firm leasing the asset (the lessee) to make a series of payments to the firm that actually owns the asset (the lessor) for use of the asset. (2) The **operating lease** differs from the financial lease only with respect to its cancelability. An operating lease can be canceled after proper notice to the lessor any time during its term. Thus, operating leases are by their very nature sources of short-term financing. The balance of this chapter is concerned with the financial lease, which provides the firm with a form of intermediate-term financing most comparable with debt financing.

Direct Leasing

In a *direct lease,* the firm acquires the services of an asset it did not previously own. Direct leasing is available through several financial institutions including manufacturers, banks, finance companies, independent leasing companies, and special-purpose leasing companies. In the lease arrangement, the lessor purchases the asset and leases it to the lessee. In the case of the manufacturer lessor, however, the acquisition step is not necessary.

Sale and Leaseback

A **sale and leaseback arrangement** arises when a firm sells land, buildings, or equipment that it already owns to a lessor and simultaneously enters into an agreement to lease the property back for a specified period under specific terms. The lessor involved in the sale and leaseback varies with the nature of the property involved and the lease period. When land is involved and the corresponding lease is long term, the lessor is generally a life insurance company. If the property consists of machinery and equipment, then the maturity of the lease will probably be intermediate term, and the lessor could be an insurance company, commercial bank, or leasing company.

The lessee firm receives cash in the amount of the sales price of the assets sold and the use of the asset over the term of the lease. In return, the lessee must make periodic rental payments through the term of the lease and give up any salvage or residual value to the lessor.

Net and Net-Net Leases

In the jargon of the leasing industry, a financial lease can take one of two basic forms: a **net lease** or a **net-net lease.** In a net lease agreement, the lessee firm assumes the risk and burden of ownership over the term of the lease. That is, the lessee must maintain the asset, as well as pay insurance and taxes on the asset. A net-net lease requires that the lessee meet all the requirements of the net lease as well as return the asset, still worth a *preestablished value,* to the lessor at the end of the lease term.

Leveraged Leasing

In the leasing arrangements discussed thus far, only two participants have been identified: the lessor and lessee. In leveraged leasing, a third participant is added: the lender, who helps finance the acquisition of the asset to be leased. From the viewpoint of the lessee, there is no difference in a leveraged lease, direct lease, or sale and leaseback arrangement. However, with a leveraged lease, the method of financing used by the lessor in acquiring the asset receives specific consideration. The lessor generally supplies equity funds up to 20 to 30 percent of the purchase price and borrows the remainder from a third-party lender, which may be a commercial bank or insurance company. In some arrangements, the lessor firm sells bonds, which are guaranteed by the lessee. This guarantee serves to reduce the risk and, thus, the cost of the debt. The majority of financial leases are leveraged leases.

ACCOUNTING FOR LEASES

Before January 1977, most financial leases were not included in the balance sheets of lessee firms. Instead, they were reported in the footnotes to the balance sheet. However, in November 1976, the Financial Accounting Standards Board (FASB) reversed its position with *Statement of Financial Accounting Standards No. 13,* "Accounting for Leases."[1] The board adopted the position that the economic effect of the transaction should govern its accounting treatment.[2] In this regard, the FASB asserted that

---

[1]Financial Accounting Standards Board, *Statement of Accounting Standards No. 13,* "Accounting for Leases" (Stamford, CT: FASB, November 1976).

[2]Financial Accounting Standards Board, *Statement of Accounting Standards No. 13,* 49.

"a lease that transfers substantially all the benefits and risks incident to the owner-ship of property should be accounted for as the acquisition of an asset and the incur-rence of an obligation by the lessee."[3] Specifically, *Statement No. 13* requires that any lease that meets one or more of the following criteria is a *capital lease* and must be included in the body of the balance sheet of the lessee. All other lease agreements are classified as *operating leases* for accounting purposes. In a capital lease

1. The lease transfers ownership of the property to the lessee by the end of the lease term.
2. The lease contains a bargain repurchase option.
3. The lease term is equal to 75 percent or more of the estimated economic life of the leased property.
4. The present value of the minimum lease payments equals or exceeds 90 percent of the excess of the fair value of the property over any related investment tax credit retained by the lessor.[4]

The last two requirements are the most stringent elements in the board's state-ment. The first two have been applicable to most leases for many years because of the Internal Revenue Service's "true" lease requirements. However, the last two apply to most financial leases written in the United States. As a result, the board now requires capitalization of all leases meeting one or more of these criteria.

Figure 9-1 is a sample balance sheet for the Alpha Mfg. Company. Alpha has entered into capital leases whose payments have a present value of $4 million.

Note that the asset "leased property" is matched by a liability, "capital lease obligations." The specific entries recorded for the lease obligation equal the present value of minimum lease payments the firm must pay over the term of the lease. The discount rate used is the lower of either the lessee's incremental borrowing rate or the lessor's implicit interest rate (where that rate can be determined).

Operating leases are not disclosed in the body of the balance sheet. Instead, these lease obligations must be reported in a footnote to the balance sheet.

THE LEASE-VERSUS-PURCHASE DECISION

The lease-versus-purchase decision is a hybrid capital-budgeting problem that forces the analyst to consider the consequences of alternative forms of financing on the investment decision. When we discussed capital budgeting and the cost of cap-ital, we assumed that all new financing would be undertaken in accordance with the firm's optimal capital structure. When analyzing an asset that is to be leased, the analysis must be altered to consider financing through leasing as opposed to the use of the more traditional debt and equity sources of funds. Thus, the lease-versus-purchase decision requires a standard capital-budgeting type of analysis, as well as an analysis of two alternative financing *packages*. The lease-purchase deci-sion involves the analysis of two basic issues:

1. Should the asset be purchased using the firm's optimal financing mix?
2. Should the asset be financed using a financial lease?

The answer to the first question can be obtained through an analysis of the pro-ject's NPV. However, regardless of whether the asset should or should not be pur-chased, it may be advantageous for the firm to lease it. That is, the cost savings accruing through leasing might be great enough to offset a negative net present val-ue resulting from the purchase of an asset. For example, the Alpha Mfg. Co. is con-sidering the acquisition of a new computer-based inventory and payroll system. The computed net present value of the new system based on normal purchase

---

[3]Financial Accounting Standards Board, *Statement of Accounting Standards No. 13*, 19.

[4]Financial Accounting Standards Board, *Statement of Accounting Standards No. 13*, 9–10.

Assets

Current assets	$14
Plant and equipment	20
Leased property (capital leases)	4
Total	$38

Liabilities and stockholders' equity

Current liabilities	$8
Long-term debt	9
Capital lease obligations	4
Stockholders' equity	17
Total	$38

financing is –$40, indicating that acquisition of the system through purchasing or ownership is not warranted. However, an analysis of the cost savings resulting from leasing the system (referred to here as the *net advantage of leasing—NAL*) indicates that the lease alternative will produce a present value cost saving of $60 over normal purchase financing. Therefore, the net present value of the system, if leased, is $20 (the net present value if leased equals the NPV of a purchase *plus* the net advantage of leasing, or – $40 + $60). Thus, the system's services should be acquired via the lease agreement.

In the pages that follow we will (1) review briefly the concept of a project's net present value, which we will refer to as the *net present value of purchase,* or *NPV(P);* (2) introduce a model for estimating the net present value advantage of leasing over normal purchase financing, which we will refer to as the *net advantage of lease financing,* or *NAL;* (3) present a flow chart that can be used in performing lease-purchase analyses based on *NPV(P)* and *NAL,* and (4) provide a comprehensive example of a lease-purchase analysis.

The Lease-Purchase Algorithm

Answers to both questions posed above can be obtained using the two equations found in Table 9-2. The first equation is simply the net present value of purchasing the proposed project. The second equation calculates the net present value advantage of leasing. NAL represents an accumulation of the cash flows (both inflows and outflows) associated with leasing *as opposed* to purchasing the asset. Specifically, through leasing the firm avoids certain operating expenses, O_t, but incurs the after-tax rental expense, $R_t(1 - T)$. By leasing, furthermore, the firm loses the tax-deductible expense associated with interest, $T \cdot I_t$, and depreciation, $T \cdot D_t$. Finally, the firm does not receive the salvage value from the asset, V_n, if it is leased, but it does not have to make the initial cash outlay to purchase the asset, *IO*. Thus, *NAL* reflects the cost savings associated with leasing, net of the opportunity costs of not purchasing.

Note that the before-tax cost of new debt is used to discount the *NAL* cash flows other than the salvage value, V_n. This is justified because the affected cash flows are very nearly riskless and certainly no more risky than the interest and principal accruing to the firm's creditors (which underlie the rate of interest charged to the firm for its debt). Because V_n is not a risk-free cash flow, but depends on the market

Table 9-2 Lease-Purchase Model

Equation One—Net present value of purchase [NPV(P)]:

$$NPV(P) = \sum_{t=1}^{n} \frac{ACF_t}{(1+K)^t} - IO \qquad (9\text{-}3)$$

where ACF_t = the annual after-tax cash flow in period t resulting from the asset's purchase (note that ACF_n also includes any after-tax salvage value expected from the project).

K = the firm's cost of capital applicable to the project being analyzed and the particular mix of financing used to acquire the project.

IO = the initial cash outlay required to purchase the asset in period zero (now).

n = the productive life of the project.

Equation Two—Net Advantage of Leasing (NAL):

$$NAL = \sum_{t=1}^{n} \frac{O_t(1-T) - R_t(1-T) - T \cdot I_t - T \cdot D_t}{(1+r_b)^t} - \frac{V_n}{(1+K_s)^n} + IO \qquad (9\text{-}4)$$

where O_t = any operating cash flows incurred in period t that are incurred only when the asset is purchased. Most often this consists of maintenance expenses and insurance that would be paid by the lessor.

R_t = the annual rental for period t.

T = the marginal tax rate on corporate income.

I_t = the tax-deductible interest expense forfeited in period t if the lease option is adopted. This represents the interest expense on a loan equal to the full purchase price of the asset being acquired.[a]

D_t = depreciation expense in period t for the asset.

V_n = the after-tax salvage value of the asset expected in year n.

K_s = the discount rate used to find the present value of V_n. This rate should reflect the risk inherent in the estimated V_n. For simplicity, the after-tax cost of capital (K) is often used as a proxy for this rate. Also, note that this rate is the same one used to discount the salvage value in $NPV(P)$.

IO = the purchase price of the asset, which is not paid by the firm in the event the asset is leased.

r_b = the after-tax rate of interest on borrowed funds (i.e., $r_b = r(1-T)$ where r is the before-tax borrowing rate for the firm). This rate is used to discount the relatively certain after-tax cash flow savings that accrue through the leasing of the asset.

[a]This analysis makes the implicit assumption that a dollar of lease financing is equivalent to a dollar of loan. This form of equivalence is only one of several that might be used.

price for the leased asset in year n, a rate higher than r is appropriate. Because the salvage value of the leased asset was discounted using the cost of capital when determining *NPV(P)*, we use this rate here when calculating *NAL*.

Figure 9-2 contains a flow chart that can be used in performing lease-purchase analyses. The analyst first calculates *NPV(P)*. If the project's net present value is positive, then the left-hand branch of Figure 9-2 should be followed. Tracing through the left branch we now compute *NAL*. If *NAL* is positive, the lease alternative offers a positive present-value cost advantage over normal purchase financing, and the asset should be leased. Should *NAL* be negative, then the purchase alternative should be selected. Return to the top of Figure 9-2 once again. This time we assume that *NPV(P)*, is negative, and the analyst's attention is directed to the right-hand side of the flow chart. The only hope for the project's acceptance at this point

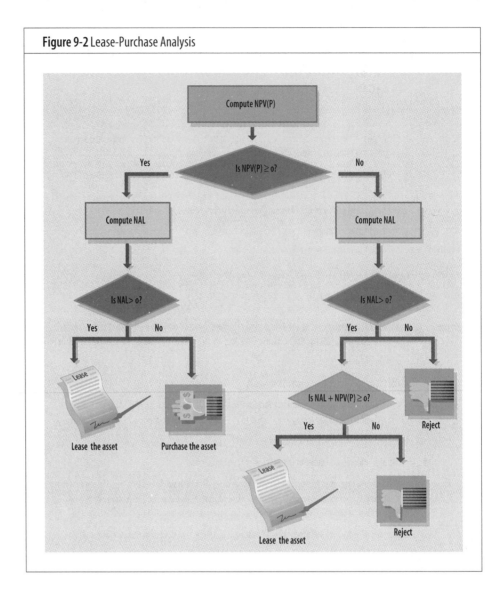

Figure 9-2 Lease-Purchase Analysis

is a favorable set of lease terms. In this circumstance the project would be acceptable and, thus, leased *only* if *NAL* were large enough to offset the negative *NPV(P)* (that is, where *NAL* was greater than the absolute value of *NPV[P]* or, equivalently, where *NAL + NPV[P] ≥ 0)*.

Case Problem in Lease-Purchase Analysis

The Waynesboro Plastic Molding Company (WPM) is now deciding whether to purchase an automatic casting machine. The machine will cost $15,000 and for tax purposes, will be depreciated toward a zero salvage value over a five-year period. However, at the end of five years, the machine actually has an expected salvage value of $2,100. Because the machine is depreciated toward a zero book value at the end of five years, the salvage value is fully taxable at the firm's marginal tax rate of 50 percent. Hence, the after-tax salvage value of the machine is only $1,050.[5] The

---

[5]The problem example is a modification of the well-known example from R. W. Johnson and W. G. Lewellen, "Analysis of the Lease-or-Buy Decision," *Journal of Finance* 27 (September 1972): 815–23.

firm uses the straight-line depreciation method to depreciate the $15,000 asset toward a zero salvage value. Furthermore, the project is expected to generate annual cash revenues of $5,000 per year over the next five years (net of cash operating expenses, but before depreciation and taxes). For projects of this type, WPM has a target debt ratio of 40 percent that is impounded in its after-tax cost-of-capital estimate of 12 percent. Finally, WPM can borrow funds at a before-tax rate of 8 percent.

Step 1: Computing NPV(P)—Should the Asset Be Purchased?

The first step in analyzing the lease-purchase problem involves computing the net present value under the purchase alternative. The relevant cash flow computations are presented in Table 9-3.

The *NPV(P)* is found by discounting the annual cash flows (ACF_t) in Table 9-3 back to the present at the firm's after-tax cost of capital of 12 percent, adding this sum to the present value of the salvage value, and subtracting the initial cash outlay. These calculations are shown in Table 9-4. The project's *NPV(P)* is a positive $15.35, indicating that the asset should be acquired.

The second question concerns whether the asset should be leased. This can be answered by considering the net advantage to leasing (*NAL*).

Step 2: Computing NAL—Should the Asset Be Leased?

The computation of *NAL* is shown in Table 9-5. The resulting *NAL* is a negative $(1,121), which indicates that leasing is not preferred to the normal debt-equity method of financing. In fact, WPM will be $(1,121) worse off, in present value terms, if it chooses to lease rather than purchase the asset.

Calculating *NAL* involves solving equation (9-4) presented earlier in Table 9-2. To do this, we first estimate all those cash flows that are to be discounted at the firm's after-tax cost of debt, r_b. These include $O_t(1 - T)$, $R_t(1 - T)$, $I_t \cdot T$, and $T \cdot D_t$.

The operating expenses associated with the asset that will be paid by the lessor if we lease—that is, the O_t—generally consist of certain maintenance expenses and insurance. WPM estimates them to be $1,000 per year over the life of the project. The annual rental or lease payments, R_t, are given and equal $4,200.

The interest tax shelter lost because the asset is leased and not purchased must now be estimated. This tax shelter is lost because the firm does not borrow any money if it enters into the lease agreement. Table 9-1 contains the principal and interest components for a five-year $15,000 loan. Note that the interest column supplies the needed information for the interest tax shelter that is lost if the asset is leased, I_t.

The next step in calculating *NAL* involves finding the present value of the after-tax salvage value. Earlier when we computed *NPV(P)*, we found this to equal $15.35. Now, substituting the results of our calculations into equation (9-4) produces the *NAL* of $(1,121).

Table 9-3 Computing Project Annual After-Tax Cash Flows (ACF_t) Associated with Asset Purchase

	Year									
	1		2		3		4		5	
	Book Profits	Cash Flow	Book Profits	Cash Flow	Book Profits	Cash Flow	Book Profits	Cash Flow	Book Profits	Cash Flow
Annual cash revenues	$ 5,000	$ 5,000	$ 5,000	$ 5,000	$ 5,000	$ 5,000	$ 5,000	$ 5,000	$ 5,000	$ 5,000
Less: depreciation	(3,000)	—	(3,000)	—	(3,000)	—	(3,000)	—	(3,000)	—
Net revenues before taxes	$ 2,000	$ 5,000	$ 2,000	$ 5,000	$ 2,000	$ 5,000	$ 2,000	$ 5,000	$ 2,000	$ 5,000
Less: taxes (50%)	(1,000) →	(1,000)	(1,000) →	(1,000)	(1,000) →	(1,000)	(1,000) →	(1,000)	(1,000) →	(1,000)
Annual after-tax cash flow		$ 4,000		$ 4,000		$ 4,000		$ 4,000		$ 4,000

Table 9-4 Calculating $NPV(P)$

Year t	Annual CashFlow ACF_t	Discount Factor for 12 Percent	Present Value
1	$4,000	.893	$3,572
2	4,000	.797	3,188
3	4,000	.712	2,848
4	4,000	.636	2,544
5	4,000	.567	2,268
5 (Salvage – V_n)	1,050	.567	595.35

Present value of ACFs and V_n = $15,015.35

$NPV(P)$ = $15.015.35 – $15,000 = $ 15.35

Table 9-5 Computing NAL

Overview: To solve for NAL we use equation (9-4), which was discussed in Table 9-2. This equation contains three terms and is repeated below for convenience.

$$NAL = \sum_{t=1}^{n} \frac{O_t(1-T) - R_t(1-T) - I_t \cdot T - D_t \cdot T}{(1+r_b)^t} - \frac{V_n}{(1+K_s)^n} + IO$$

$$\underbrace{\phantom{\sum_{t=1}^{n} \frac{O_t(1-T)}{(1+r_b)^t}}}_{\text{Term 1}} \quad \underbrace{\phantom{\frac{V_n}{(1+K_s)^n}}}_{\text{Term2}} \quad \underbrace{}_{\text{Term 3}}$$

Step 1: Solving for Term 1 $= \sum_{t=1}^{n} \dfrac{O_t(1-T) - R_t(1-T) - I_t \cdot T - D_t \cdot T}{(1+r_b)^t}$

Year t	After-Tax Operating Expenses Paid by Lessor[a] $O_t(1-T)$	–	After-Tax Rental Expense[b] $R_t(1-T)$	–	Tax Shelter on Loan Interest[c] $I_t T$	–	Tax Shelter on Depreciation[d] $D_t T$	=	Sum	x	Discount Factor[e] DF	=	Present Value PV
1	$500		$2,100		$600		$1,500		–$3,700		.962		–$3,558
2	500		2,100		498		1,500		– 3,598		.925		– 3,326
3	500		2,100		387		1,500		– 3,487		.889		– 3,100
4	500		2,100		268		1,500		– 3,368		.855		– 2,879
5	500		2,100		140		1,500		– 3,240		.822		– 2,662
													–15,525

Step 2: Solving for term 2 $= -\left[\dfrac{V_n}{(1+K_s)^n} \right] = \dfrac{\$1050}{(1+.12)^5} \times -\$1,050 \times .567^f =$ – 596

Step 3: Term 3 = IO $15,000

Step 4: Calculate NAL $13,961 – $595 + $15,000 = –$1,121

---

[a] After-tax lessor-paid operating expenses are found by $O_t(1-T) = \$1000(1-.5) = \$500$.
[b] After-tax rent expense for year 1 is computed as follows: $R_t(1-T) = \$4,200(1-.5) = \$2,100$.
[c] Interest expense figures were calculated in Table 9-1 for a $15,000 loan. For year 1 the interest tax shelter is 0.5 x $1200 = $600.
[d] The tax shelter from depreciation is found as follows: $D_1T = \$3,000 \times 0.5 = \$1,500$.
[e] Based on the after-tax borrowing rate, i.e., $.08(1-.5) = .04$.
[f] K_s was estimated to be the same as the firm's after-tax cost of capital, 12 percent.

Note that the lease payments used in this example were made at the end of each year. In practice, lease payments are generally made at the beginning of each year (that is, they constitute an *annuity due* rather than an ordinary annuity, as used here). The *NAL* for the example used here is even more negative if we assume beginning of year lease payments. That is, with beginning of year payments *NAL* = − $1,495. You can easily verify this result as follows. Note first that changing from a regular annuity to an annuity due affects only the first and last annuity payments. In this example this means that the first lease payment of $2,100(after tax) is paid immediately such that its present value is $2,100. However, the final lease payment is now made at the beginning of year 5 (or at the end of year 4). The present value of the fifth-year after-tax lease payment is therefore $2100 × .822 = $1,726. To summarize, by changing from a regular annuity set of lease payments to an annuity due, we must include a –$2,100 immediate cash flow at time $t = 0$ and we exchange this for the fifth-year present-value after-tax lease payment of $1,726. Therefore, the *NAL* with annuity due lease payments is *NAL* (annuity due) = (1,121) + 1,726 − 2,100 = (1,495). Hence, if the lease payments are an annuity due, the asset should be purchased (because *NPV* [*P*] = $15.35) and not leased (because *NAL* = –$1,495).

Let's recap the lease-purchase analysis. First, the project's net present value was computed. This analysis produced a positive *NPV(P)* equal to $15.35, which indicated that the asset should be acquired. On computing the net advantage to leasing, we found that the financial lease was not the preferred method of financing the acquisition of the asset's services. Thus, the asset's services should be purchased using the firm's normal financing mix.

THE ECONOMICS OF LEASING VERSUS PURCHASING

Let's now review briefly the economic character of leasing and purchasing. Figure 9-3 summarizes the participants and transactions involved in leasing (the

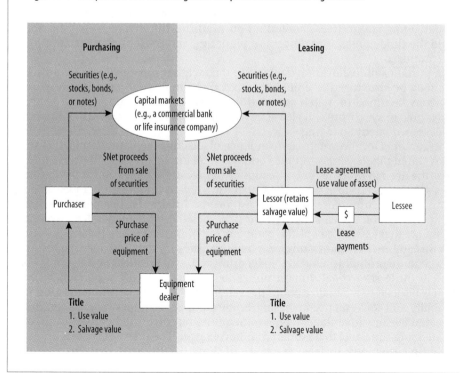

Figure 9-3 Comparison of Purchasing with Simple Financial Lease Agreement

right-hand side of the figure) and purchasing (the left-hand side). In purchasing, the asset is financed via the sale of securities and the purchaser acquires title to the asset (including both the use and salvage value of the asset). In leasing, the lessee acquires the use value of the asset but uses the lessor as an *intermediary* to finance and purchase the asset. The key feature of leasing as opposed to purchasing is the interjection of a financial intermediary (the lessor) into the scheme used to acquire the asset's services. Thus, the basic question that arises in lease-purchase analysis is one of "Why does adding another financial intermediary (the lessor) save the lessee money?" Some of the traditional answers to this question are discussed subsequently. As you read through each, simply remember that the lessee is hiring the lessor to perform the functions associated with ownership that he or she would perform if the asset were purchased. Thus, for the lease to be "cheaper" than owning, the lessor must be able to perform these functions of ownership at a lower cost than the lessee could perform them, and be willing to pass these savings along to the lessee in the form of lower rental rates.

POTENTIAL BENEFITS FROM LEASING

Several purported advantages have been associated with leasing as opposed to debt financing. These benefits include flexibility and convenience, lack of restrictions, avoiding the risk of obsolescence, conservation of working capital, 100 percent financing, tax savings, and availability of credit.

Flexibility and Convenience

A variety of potential benefits are often included under the rubric of flexibility and convenience. It is argued, for example, that leasing provides the firm with flexibility because it allows for piecemeal financing of relatively small asset acquisitions. Debt financing of such acquisitions can be costly and difficult to arrange. Leases, conversely, may be arranged more quickly and with less documentation.

Another flexibility argument notes that leasing may allow a division or subsidiary manager to acquire equipment without the approval of the corporate capital-budgeting committee. Depending on the firm, the manager may be able to avoid the time-consuming process of preparing and presenting a formal acquisition proposal.

A third flexibility advantage relates to the fact that some lease payment schedules may be structured to coincide with the revenues generated by the asset, or they may be timed to match seasonal fluctuations in a given industry. Thus, the firm is able to synchronize its lease payments with its cash cycle—an option rarely available with debt financing.

Arguments for the greater convenience of leasing take many forms. It is sometimes stated that leasing simplifies bookkeeping for tax purposes because it eliminates the need to prepare time-consuming depreciation tables and subsidiary fixed asset schedules. It is also pointed out that the fixed-payment nature of lease rentals allows more accurate forecasting of cash needs. Finally, leasing allows the firm to avoid the "problems" and "headaches" associated with ownership. Executives often note that leasing "keeps the company out of the real estate business." Implicit in this argument is the assumption that the firm's human and material resources may be more profitably allocated to its primary line of business and that it is better to allow the lessor to deal with the obligations associated with ownership.

It is difficult to generalize about the validity of the various arguments for greater flexibility and convenience in leasing. Some companies, under specific conditions, may find leasing advantageous for some of the reasons listed earlier. In practice, the tradeoffs are likely to be different for every firm. The relevant issue is often that of shifting functions. By leasing a piece of capital equipment, the firm may effectively shift bookkeeping, disposal of used equipment, and other functions to the lessor. The lessee will benefit in these situations if the lessor is able to perform the functions at a lower cost than the lessee and is willing to pass on the savings in a lower lease rate.

The arguments that follow should be viewed in a similar vein. The lessee must attempt to determine the price it is paying for greater flexibility and convenience. In many cases the benefits the firm is able to attain are not worth the cost. Compounding the problem is the fact that it is often difficult for a lessee firm to quantify such cost-benefit tradeoffs.

Lack of Restrictions

Another suggested advantage of leasing relates to the lack of restrictions associated with a lease. Unlike term loan agreements or bond indentures, lease contracts generally do not contain protective covenant restrictions. Furthermore, in calculating financial ratios under existing covenants, it is sometimes possible to exclude lease payments from the firm's debt commitments. Once again, the extent to which lack of restrictions benefits a lessee will depend on the price it must pay. If a lessor views its security position to be superior to that of a lender, it may not require a higher return on the lease to compensate for the lack of restrictions on the lessee. Conversely, if the prospective lessee is viewed as a marginal credit risk, a higher rate may be charged.

Avoidance of Risk of Obsolescence

Similar reasoning applies to another popular argument for leasing. This argument states that a lease is advantageous because it allows the firm to avoid the risk that the equipment will become obsolete. In actuality, the risk of obsolescence is passed on to the lessee in any financial lease. Because the original cost of the asset is fully amortized over the basic lease term, all of the risk is borne by the lessee. Only in a cancelable operating lease is it sometimes possible to avoid the risk of obsolescence.

A related argument in favor of leasing states that a lessor will generally provide the firm with better and more reliable service to maintain the resale value of the asset. The extent to which this is true depends on the lessor's own cost-benefit tradeoff. If the lessor is a manufacturing or a leasing company that specializes in a particular type of equipment, it may be profitable to maintain the equipment's resale value by ensuring that it is properly repaired and maintained. Because of their technical and marketing expertise, these types of lessors may be able to operate successfully in the secondary market for the equipment. Conversely, bank lessors or independent financial leasing companies would probably find it too expensive to follow this approach.

Conservation of Working Capital

One of the oldest and most widely used arguments in favor of leasing is the assertion that a lease conserves the firm's working capital. Indeed, many managers within the leasing industry consider this to be the number one advantage of leasing. The conservation argument runs as follows: Because a lease does not require an immediate outflow of cash to cover the full purchase price of the asset, funds are retained in the business.

It is clear that a lease does require a lower initial outlay than a cash purchase. However, the cash outlay associated with the purchase option can be reduced or eliminated by borrowing the downpayment from another source. This argument leads us directly into the next purported advantage of lease financing.

One Hundred Percent Financing

Another alleged benefit of leasing is embodied in the argument that a lease provides the firm with 100 percent financing. It is pointed out that the borrow-and-buy alternative generally involves a downpayment, whereas leasing does not. Given that investors and creditors are reasonably intelligent, however, it is sensible to conclude that they consider similar amounts of lease and debt financing to add equivalent amounts of risk to the firm. Thus, a firm uses up less of its capacity to raise nonequity funds with debt than with leasing. In theory, it could issue a second debt instrument to make up the difference—that is, the downpayment.

Tax Savings

It is also argued that leasing offers an economic advantage in that the tax shield generated by the lease payments usually exceeds the tax shield from depreciation that would be available if the asset were purchased. The extent to which leasing provides a tax-shield benefit is a function of many factors. The *NAL* equation (9-4), discussed earlier, is the basis for weighing these differences in tax shields.

Ease of Obtaining Credit

Another purported advantage of leasing is that firms with poor credit ratings are able to obtain assets through leases when they are unable to finance the acquisitions with debt capital. The counterargument is that the firm will certainly face a high lease interest rate to compensate the lessor for bearing this higher risk of default.

WHY DO FIRMS LEASE?

Several researchers have asked firms why they use financial leases as opposed to purchasing. For example, in a study by Ferrara, Thies, and Dirsmith[6] the following factors were found to affect the leasing decision:

Factor	Rank	Percent of Respondents
Implied interest rate	1	52
Threat of obsolescence	2	37
Income taxes	3	33
Maintain flexibility	4	12
Conserve working capital	5	12
Less restrictive financing	6	6
Off balance sheet finance	7	7

Interestingly, the factor most often mentioned was the implied cost of financing. That is, 52 percent of the lessees considered the cost of lease financing to be an important factor in determining their decision to use lease financing. This factor was followed by concern over the risk of obsolescence followed by tax considerations. In light of the theoretical significance given to tax considerations in the theo-

---

[6]W. L. Ferrara, J. B. Thies, and M. W. Dersmith, "The Lease-Purchase Decision," National Association of Accountants, 1980. Cited in "Leasing—A Review of the Empirical Studies," *Managerial Finance* 15, 1 and 2 (1989): 13–20.

Financial Executive (July/August 1994): 53–56.

How to Lease in Peace

Today, almost every company leases some of its equipment—and with good reason. Leasing can be a convenient financing alternative, partly because it doesn't involve capital-budget financing. Another advantage is the ability to match costs with the revenues the equipment generates. And if you structure your lease financing properly, you can account for it off the balance sheet and shift your tax deducitions to the lessor, which lowers your after-tax cost compared with buying.(A)

This benefit can help your company maintain its debt-to-equity ratio. And leases can protect against inflation because leased equipment usually retains its productive capacity, even as the dollars used to pay the rent lose their purchasing power. Interest-rate fluctuations won't affect the fixed leasing rate. Of course, leasing also offers you a hedge against technological change and obsolescence, because by upgrading to new equipment when your lease expires, you can shift to the lessor the risk of getting stuck with outdated equipment.(B)

Given these advantages, how do you get the most financial leverage possible out of your leasing transactions? First, when you're at the negotiating table

with your lessor, try to anticipate your needs before you sign the lease, because it's tough to get lessors to make changes later on. This reluctance stems from the fact that the lessor actually finances the purchase price of the equipment through a nonrecourse loan from (or discounted rental-stream assignment to) a bank or other funding source, which will then take a security interest in the lease, the lease rentals and the equipment. This normally doesn't create a risk for you, since the lender's primary interest is maintaining cash flow. But it does create some distance between you and the assignee of the lessor.(C)

Quiet Enjoyment and Other Protections

Although the lessor will probably want to make these assignments without your consent, you should at least insist on being notified. You'll also want the lease to stipulate that your company has the right to "quietly enjoy" uninterrupted use of equipment as long as you continue to pay the leasing fees and comply with the lease terms. You ask that assignees of the lessor's interest confirm this in writing.

The next thing you need to know is that most equipment leased in the United States today

is covered by a "triple net" lease.(D) Generally, this means that all essential risks and obligations relating to the equipment during the lease term including the risk of loss or damage to the equipment and responsibility for taxes, are your sole responsibility. Property, sales and use taxes, as well as any miscellaneous taxes, are also usually your responsibility. Since you're responsible for insurance and maintenance, as well as all wear and tear to the equipment, consider self-insurance as an option. If you can self-insure, you may be able to get the lessor to remove the standard insurance requirements in the lease.

Also, almost all leases address the subject of returning the leased property, including refurbishment, modification, storage, shipping, and crating responsibilities. Before signing the lease, you must consider if you want an option to buy the equipment at the end of the lease term for a nominal price, a predetermined price or a price equal to the property's then-current fair-market value.

Nominal-purchase options are particularly useful in instances where the cost of removing and shipping the leased equipment may well exceed its fair-market value, such as with telephone systems and restaurant or store fixtures. If you have a similar situation and your lease doesn't contain this you may face potentially burdensome return penalties. You don't want to find yourself in the position of being forced to purchase equipment you no longer need and losing the benefit of your lease transaction simply to avoid paying these penalties.

Don't delay about returning your equipment, either. Leases often contain automatic renewal, or "evergreen," provisions. This means you're still liable for the equipment after the lease expires or, in the case of an initial lease term, for "renewal" of the lease term, usually for up to one year. Establish monitoring systems to ensure that you return or purchase the leased equipment when the lease term expires. Of course, that also goes for your rental payments. Leasing compa-

nies may not always invoice you for your monthly rentals, but that won't stop them from charging substantial penalties for late payments.

As your company grows, you may need to relocate the leased equipment to another location, subsidiary or other affiliated company in a distant city. Generally, the lessor won't provide absolute freedom to sublease the equipment or to move the equipment from one location to another, so if moving or subleasing your equipment is a possibility, talk it over with your lessor before signing the lease. You should be ready to assure the lessor that you'll respect its interests by giving appropriate notice before you move a piece of equipment and by refiling Uniform Commercial Code financing statements if necessary. When

agreeing to permit the equipment to be used by a subsidiary or affiliate company, the lessor will also require a guarantee from you that your responsibility won't be diluted in any way, and that you'll continue to remain fully and primarily liable for all your obligations.(E)

The Lowdown on Upgrades

Similarly, if you think you may need to upgrade or modify the equipment during the lease term, you should ask for provisions that grant your company reasonable permission in advance to alter the equipment. It's customary for the lessor to keep any modifications to its equipment. But if you want to retain the rights to the upgrade, you can structure the lease to

---

ANALYSIS AND IMPLICATIONS...

A. Be careful! The "potential" advantages of leasing when compared to purchasing do include many of the considerations listed here. However, it's not quite this simple. Let's consider some of the reasons cited here for leasing. First, is leasing better than purchasing because it doesn't involve capital-budget financing? Perhaps. If the firm has very rigid policies regarding purchases that restrict its ability to acquire equipment but allow it to be leased, then leasing may prove to be advantageous. Note that leasing is not the first best solution here, but second best. The first best solution would be to have the option to consider the lowest

cost method of acquiring the leased asset (that is, not have the restriction on purchasing that lead to the necessity of choosing a lease). What about off balance sheet financing? Why is it advantageous to have an asset and its financing not appear on the firm's balance sheet? One possible answer is to avoid the scrutiny of an unsuspecting lender or to avoid violating a prior loan covenant. In a world where analysts are aware of the availability of off balance sheet financing, this isn't likely to fool many and consequently should not be considered a strong reason for lease financing. What about shifting the tax burden of ownership to the

lessor? Now we're finding a real reason for leasing. If your firm is not paying taxes or is doing so at very low marginal tax rates, then shifting the tax benefits of asset ownership (tax-deductible interest and depreciation as well as any investment tax credits were they available) to a lessor whose marginal tax rates are higher than yours makes good sense. Here the source of the benefit comes from the government coffers since the savings in taxes the lessee accrues comes directly from reduced taxes to the lessor.

B. Does leasing serve as a hedge against the risks of equipment

reflect this without increasing the lessor's risk.

For example, the lease can specify that the lessor has the right of first refusal for any proposed upgrades. This means it doesn't have to finance the upgrades that you request. And you can guarantee that any upgrades you make will be removable without damage to the equipment. If you can't get your lessor's cooperation to permit an upgrade, you may have to negotiate to avoid paying the entire lease rental balance in order to relieve yourself from contractual liability.

Warranties are another aspect of your leasing arrangements to which you should pay close attention. In most lease financing (other than a warranty of good title), the lessor will disclaim every type of warranty, representation or obligation on its part. Therefore, get the appropriate warranties and protection from the vendor or distributor furnishing the equipment. Most leases contain "hell or high water" provisions, which means your company must pay the rental fees regardless of the circumstances—even if the equipment is defective. Since the protections you get from the vendor or manufacturer are so important, the lease should assign to you all the lessor's rights against the manufacturer and vendor of the equipment for any express and implied warranties. Also, keep copies of all express warranties.

A Final Caution

One final caution for any kind of leasing transaction: It's important to investigate the rep-utation of the leasing company and the equipment vendor. Many leasing companies are small businesses whose entire operation may consist of a single employee, a desk and a telephone.

To ensure that you're dealing with a reputable company, contact some trade associations for information, get referrals from other companies and contact the company's previous customers. Often, manufacturers will provide a list of the lessors they recommend. But don't limit yourself only to those companies, since they may not be as competitive as independent third-party lessors.

SOURCE: Michael A. Leichtling, 1994, "How to Lease in Peace," *Financial Executive* (July/August 1994): 53–56.

obsolescence? Perhaps. What leasing does is shift the risk of obsolescence from the lessee to the lessor. If the lessor is willing and able to bear this risk at lower cost (due to expertise in buying and selling used equipment of the type being leased), it may pass along these cost savings to the lessee. The point here is that someone bears the risk of obsolescence. Whether there are savings to the lessee or not depends on whether the lessor can bear those risks at lower cost and, if so, whether the lessor will pass a part of those savings on to the lessee.

C. This discussion points out an important attribute of leasing.

Someone purchases and finances the leased asset. Thus, when a firm chooses to lease rather than purchase and finance, it is simply entering into an agreement whereby another firm purchases and finances the asset (the lessor). The basic economic question regarding leasing versus purchasing is "who can purchase and finance the asset under the most favorable terms, the lessee or the lessor?"

D. There are many different types of leasing arrangements. However, the triple net or "net, net, net" lease agreement is the most common in use. This agreement places a great deal of "own-ership burden" back on the lessee. In this instance, the lease agreement is purely financial and the lessee must provide all other owner-related services such as maintenance, insurance, tax-payment, and even return the equipment at the end of the agreement in some predetermined state or working condition.

E. There's more to leasing than signing a set agreement. Here the author emphasizes the importance of negotiation of the specific lease terms to reflect the firm's current and intended future needs.

retical literature on lease financing, it is interesting to note that only 33 percent of the respondents felt that tax considerations were a factor in their decision to lease.

Ferrara, Thies, and Dirsmith also provide evidence concerning the motives underlying a firm's decision to use lease financing and its financial characteristics. Specifically, they observed that smaller and financially weaker firms tended to justify the use of lease financing based on qualitative benefits. These included flexibility, the conservation of working capital, financing restrictions, off balance sheet financing, and transference of the risk of obsolescence. Conversely, larger and financially stronger firms tended to base their leasing decisions on more quantitative considerations. That is, this latter group tended to use more formal comparisons of the cost of leasing versus other forms of intermediate-term financing.

SUMMARY

Intermediate credit, or simply term credit, is any source of financing with a final maturity greater than one year but less than ten. The two major sources of term credit are term loans and financial leases.

Term loans are available from commercial banks, life insurance companies, and pension funds. Although the specifics of each agreement vary, they share a common set of general characteristics. These include

1. A final maturity of one to ten years
2. A requirement of some form of collateral
3. A body of restrictive covenants designed to protect the security interests of the lender
4. A loan amortization schedule whereby periodic loan payments, comprised of both principal and interest components, are made over the life of the loan.

Installment loans generally require the borrower to repay them by making level monthly (quarterly or annual) payments or installments. These payments include two components: (1) the interest owed on the loan balance outstanding at the time of the last loan payment, and (2) the difference in the installment payment and the interest component. This difference goes toward reducing the principal amount of the loan.

Installment payments are calculated using present value analysis. They constitute the periodic (monthly, quarterly, annual, and so on) payment whose present value, when discounted back to the present using the loan rate of interest, equals the face amount of the loan.

There are three basic types of lease arrangements:

1. Direct lease
2. Sale and leaseback
3. Leveraged lease

The lease agreement can further be classified as a financial or operating lease; we focused on the financial lease. Current reporting requirements of the FASB virtually ensure the inclusion of all financial leases in the body of the lessee firm's balance sheet.

The lease-versus-purchase decision is a hybrid capital-budgeting problem wherein the analyst must consider both the investment and financing aspects of the decision. The method we recommend for analyzing the lease versus purchase choice involves first calculating the net present value of the asset if it were purchased. Next we calculate the net advantage of leasing over purchasing.

Many and varied factors are often claimed as advantages of leasing the firm's usual debt-equity financing mix. Many of the arguments have been found to be at least partly fallacious. However, a complete lease-purchase analysis, using a model similar to the one discussed here, should provide a rational basis for uncovering the true advantages of lease financing.

STUDY QUESTIONS

9-1. What characteristics distinguish intermediate-term debt from other forms of debt instruments?

9-2. List and discuss the major types of restrictions generally found in the covenants of term loan agreements.

9-3. Define each of the following:
   a. Direct leasing
   b. Sale and leaseback arrangement
   c. Leveraged leasing
   d. Operating lease

9-4. How are financial leases handled in the financial statements of the lessee firm?

9-5. List and discuss each of the potential benefits from lease financing.

SELF-TEST PROBLEMS

ST-1. (Analyzing a Term Loan) Calculate the annual installment payment and the principal and interest components of a five-year loan carrying a 10 percent rate of interest. The loan amount is $50,000.

ST-2. (Analyzing an Installment Loan) The S. P. Sargent Sales Company is contemplating the purchase of a new machine. The total cost of the machine is $120,000 and the firm plans to make a $20,000 cash downpayment. The firm's bank has offered to finance the remaining $100,000 at a rate of 14 percent. The bank has offered two possible loan repayment plans. Plan A involves equal annual installments payable at the end of each of the next five years. Plan B requires five equal annual payments plus a balloon payment of $20,000 at the end of year 5.
   a. Calculate the annual payment on the loan in plan A.
   b. Calculate the principal and interest components of the plan A installment loan.
   c. Calculate the annual installments for plan B where the loan carries a 14 percent rate.

ST-3. (Lease versus Purchase Analysis) Jensen Trucking, Inc., is considering the possibility of leasing a $100,000 truck-servicing facility. This newly developed piece of equipment facilitates the cleaning and servicing of diesel tractors used on long-haul runs. The firm has evaluated the possible purchase of the equipment and found it to have an $8,000 net present value. However, an equipment leasing company has approached Jensen with an offer to lease the equipment for an annual rental charge of $24,000 payable at the beginning of each of the next five years. In addition, should Jensen lease the equipment it would receive insurance and maintenance valued at $4,000 per year (assume that this amount would be payable at the beginning of each year if purchased separately from the lease agreement). Also, for simplicity you may assume that tax savings are realized immediately. Additional information pertaining to the lease and purchase alternatives is found in the following table:

Acquisition price	$100,000
Useful life (used in analysis)	5 years
Salvage value (estimated)	$0
Depreciation method	Straight-line
Borrowing rate	12%
Marginal tax rate	40%
Cost of capital (based on a target debt/total asset ratio of 30%)	16%

a. Calculate the net advantage of leasing (*NAL*) the equipment.

b. Should Jensen lease the equipment?

STUDY PROBLEMS (SET A)

9-1A. (Calculation of Balloon Payment for a Term Loan) The First State Bank has offered to lend $325,000 to Jamie Tulia to help him purchase a group home for mentally retarded persons. The bank loan officer (Chris Turner) has structured the loan to include four installments of $50,000 each followed in year five by a balloon payment. The loan is to carry a 10 percent rate of interest with annual compounding. What is the fifth year balloon payment?

9-2A. (Calculating Lease Payments) Apple Leasing, Inc. calculates its lease payments such that they provide the firm with a 12 percent pre-tax return. The firm has been asked to quote rental payments on a $100,000 piece of equipment which is to include ten payments spread over the next nine years (the first payment is made immediately upon signing of the agreement with the remaining payments coming at the end of each of the next nine years). What amount should Apple quote on the lease?

9-3A. (Installment Payments) Compute the annual payments for an installment loan carrying an 18 percent rate of interest, a five-year maturity, and a face amount of $100,000.

9-4A. (Principal and Interest Components of an Installment Loan) Compute the annual principal and interest components of the loan in problem 9-3A.

9-5A. (Cost of an Intermediate-Term Loan) The J. B. Marcum Company needs $250,000 to finance a new minicomputer. The computer sales firm has offered to finance the purchase with a $50,000 down payment followed by five annual installments of $59,663.11 each. Alternatively, the firm's bank has offered to lend the firm $250,000 to be repaid in five annual installments based on an annual rate of interest of 16 percent. Finally, the firm has arranged to finance the needed $250,000 through a loan from an insurance company requiring a lump-sum payment of $385,080, in five years.

a. What is the effective annual rate of interest on the loan from the computer sales firm?

b. What will the annual payments on the bank loan be?

c. What is the annual rate of interest for the insurance company term loan?

d. Based on cost considerations only, which source of financing should Marcum select?

9-6A. (Cost of Intermediate-Term Credit) Charter Electronics is planning to purchase a $400,000 burglar alarm system for its southwestern Illinois plant. Charter's bank has offered to lend the firm the full $400,000. The note would be paid in one payment at the end of four years and would require payment of interest at a rate of 14 percent compounded annually. The manufacturer of the alarm system has offered to finance the $400,000 purchase with an installment loan. The loan would require four annual installments of $140,106 each. Which method of financing should Charter select?

9-7A. (Lease versus Purchase Analysis) S. S. Johnson Enterprises (SSJE) is evaluating the acquisition of a heavy-duty forklift with 20,000- to 24,000-pound lift capacity. SSJE can purchase the forklift through the use of its normal financing mix (30 percent debt and 70 percent common equity) or lease it. Pertinent details follow:

Acquisition price of the forklift	$20,000
Useful life	4 years
Salvage value (estimated)	$4000
Depreciation method	Straight-line
Annual before-tax and depreciation cash savings from the forklift	$6000
Rate of interest on a 4-year installment loan	10 percent
Marginal tax rate	50 percent
Annual rentals (4-year lease)	$6000
Annual operating expenses included in the lease	$1000
Cost of capital	12 percent

   a. Evaluate whether the forklift acquisition is justified through normal purchase financing.
   b. Should SSJE lease the asset?

9-8A. (Installment Loan Payment) Calculate the annual installment payments for the following loans:

   a. A $100,000 loan carrying a 15 percent annual rate of interest and requiring ten annual payments.
   b. A $100,000 loan carrying a 15 percent annual rate of interest with quarterly payments over the next five years. (*Hint:* Refer to chapter 5 for discussion of semiannual compounding and discounting.)
   c. A $100,000 loan requiring annual installments for each of the next five years at a 15 percent rate of interest. However, the annual installments are based on a thirty-year loan period. In year 5, the balance of the loan is due in a single (balloon) payment. (*Hint:* Calculate the installment payments using $n = 30$ years. Next use the procedure given in Table 9-1 to determine the remaining balance of the loan at the end of the fifth year.)

Problem

Early in the spring of 1995, the Jonesboro Steel Corporation (JSC) decided to purchase a small computer. The computer is designed to handle the inventory, payroll, shipping, and general clerical functions for small manufacturers like JSC. The firm estimates that the computer will cost $60,000 to purchase and will last four years, at which time it can be salvaged for $10,000. The firm's marginal tax rate is 50 percent, and its cost of capital for projects of this type is estimated to be 12 percent. Over the next four years, the management of JSC thinks the computer will reduce operating expenses by $27,000 a year before depreciation and taxes. JSC uses straight-line depreciation .

JSC is also considering the possibility of leasing the computer. The computer sales firm has offered JSC a four-year lease contract with annual payments of $18,000. In addition, if JSC leases the computer, the lessor will absorb insurance and maintenance expenses valued at $2,000 per year. Thus JSC will save $2,000 per year if it leases the asset (on a before-tax basis).

   a. Evaluate the net present value of the computer purchase. Should the computer be acquired via purchase? (*Hint:* Refer to Tables 9-3 and 9-4.)
   b. If JSC uses a 40 percent target debt to total assets ratio, evaluate the net present value advantage of leasing. JSC can borrow at a rate of 8 percent with annual installments paid over the next four years. (*Hint:* Recall that the interest tax shelter lost through leasing is based on a loan equal to the full purchase price of the asset or $60,000.)

EVALUATING PROJECT RISK

10.1 RISK SPECIFIC TO INDIVIDUAL PROJECTS

Chapter 6 investigated risk related to portfolios of projects. Chapter 10 delves into the specific elements of risk associated with each project. Project managers rely upon empirical support for risk assessment and evaluations. They formally seek ways to mitigate or reduce the risks. There is a growing research base of specific actions that affect projects and increase the probability of project success, or inversely, increase the risk of failure. During the planning stage, a formal effort should be made to define, "What can go wrong?" and "What is the effect of the risk?" If these actions can be further identified, quantified, and combined into a predictive model, the probability of achieving project goals can be measurably improved. Most importantly, contingency plans can be developed to minimize the risk.

10.2 PROJECT RISK EVALUATION

Following is a generic project risk evaluation form. Every factor on the form has been scientifically correlated with project success or failure.

RISK ANALYSIS MATRIX
KEY RISK FACTORS AFFECTING PROJECT SUCCESS

(Will This Project Be Successful?)

Listed below are a series of statements about the project. Research has shown that these are the critical variables that determine the success of a project. Read each statement and evaluate the degree of risk associated with the statement. For statements that you feel represent high risk (4 & 5) describe the response you plan to react to the risk.

PROJECT NAME: _____

PROJECT MANAGER: _____

	SUBJECTIVE RISK ESTIMATES		RISK EXPLANATION & RESPONSE PLANS
	HIGHEST PROBABILITY OF PROJECT SUCCESS	HIGHEST RISK OF PROJECT FAILURE	Explain 4 & 5 Answers. How do you expect to respond? (Accept, Mitigate, Deflect, Develop Contingency Plan)
	1 2 3	4 5	
	|———|———|———|———|		

OVERALL RISK FACTORS

	SUCCESS	FAILURE

The Overall Evaluation of Project Success is that:

There is a high probability of success \|———\|———\|———\|———\| There is a high risk of failure _____

The Size of the Risk is such that:

It will have no impact on organizational finances \|———\|———\|———\|———\| Project failure could cripple or destroy the organization.

_____

PROJECT OUTPUT (PRODUCT OR SERVICE) RISK FACTORS

The project product or service:

Is unique in the customer's eyes	|———|———|———|———|	Is the same as competition _____
Fits the organization's core competence	|———|———|———|———|	Differs from the company's core competence _____
Concept is clear and easily understood	|———|———|———|———|	Is unclear and hard to understand _____
Has intrinsic value to the customer	|———|———|———|———|	Offers no intrinsic value _____
Offers innovative features	|———|———|———|———|	No innovative features _____
Solves customer problems	|———|———|———|———|	Solves no customer problems _____
Is unique	|———|———|———|———|	Is commonplace _____
Is consistent with the corporate image	|———|———|———|———|	Is inconsistent with the corporate image _____

Compared to competition, the project product or service:

Is clearly superior	|———|———|———|———|	Is clearly inferior _____
Has superior technical performance	|———|———|———|———|	Has inferior technical performance _____
Has lower cost	|———|———|———|———|	Has higher cost _____
Is more reliable	|———|———|———|———|	Is less reliable _____
Has higher quality	|———|———|———|———|	Has poorer quality _____

MARKET RISK FACTORS

The market for the project product or service:

Is attractive	|———|———|———|———|	Is unattractive _____
Has low overall intensity of competition	|———|———|———|———|	Is highly competitive _____
Is growing	|———|———|———|———|	Is declining _____
Is non-competitive	|———|———|———|———|	Is highly competitive _____
Has unsatisfied customer demand	|———|———|———|———|	Has satisfied customer demand _____

The project output represents early entry

into the market	|———|———|———|———|	Late entry into the market _____
Customers are intimately involved in project actions	|———|———|———|———|	are not involved _____

	SUCCESS	FAILURE
Suppliers are intimately involved in project actions	|——-|——-|——-|——|	are not involved _____
Users needs have been identified and understood	|——-|——-|——-|——|	are not identified nor understood _____

INTERNAL ORGANIZATION RISK FACTORS

Project has visible, top management commitment & support	|——-|——-|——-|——|	has top management opposition _____
Project is built on existing corporate strengths	|——-|——-|——-|——|	is built on corporate weaknesses _____
Project has adequate resources (time, labor, materials, and money) available	|——-|——-|——-|——|	has no resources _____
Senior management works closely with project leadership to develop the project concept	|——-|——-|——-|——|	top management is not involved _____

TEAM RISK FACTORS

Members represent all functional areas affected by the project	|——-|——-|——-|——|	Are from one functional area only _____
The Project Team works together to: Smoothly execute all project phases	|——-|——-|——-|——|	Execution is disorganized _____
Define goals, develop workable plans, prioritize work	|——-|——-|——-|——|	Does not work as a team _____
Frequently communicate with outsiders	|——-|——-|——-|——|	Never communicates with outsiders _____
Increase the amount and variety of task-oriented information	|——-|——-|——-|——|	Ignores task-oriented information

_____

Be thoroughly trained in multifunctional areas pertinent to the project	|——-|——-|——-|——|	Is untrained _____
Bring conflicts to the surface early	|——-|——-|——-|——|	Do not bring conflicts to the surface _____
Resolve conflicts at lower levels	|——-|——-|——-|——|	Do not resolve conflicts _____
Have a high degree of internal communication	|——-|——-|——-|——|	Have no internal communications _____

PROJECT LEADER RISK FACTORS

The Project Leader: Has a history of high performance on projects	|——-|——-|——-|——|	Has a history of project failure _____
Has significant decision-making accountability	|——-|——-|——-|——|	Is not accountable _____

Is an excellent politician who lobbies for product
    support, ensures resources, and buffers the
    team from outside pressure
	|——-|——-|——-|——|	Is a poor politician _____

Encourages team communications outside the group	|——-|——-|——-|——|	Discourages team communications with outsiders _____
Gives team members the freedom to work autonomously within the constraints of the project vision	|——-|——-|——-|——|	Gives no freedom _____
Synthesizes and communicates a complex variety of factors to create a portrait of the total picture	|——-|——-|——-|——|	Fails to paint a vision _____
Is an effective manager of the group	|——-|——-|——-|——|	Cannot manage _____
Is a senior and respected manager with authority	|——-|——-|——-|——|	Has no authority _____
Attracts top team members to the group	|——-|——-|——-|——|	Repels prospective team members _____
The Project Leader Communicates: A clear vision of the project objectives to the team	|——-|——-|——-|——|	Fails to communicate a vision _____
Gathers, facilitates, and translates external information for team members	|——-|——-|——-|——|	Fails to gather external information _____

RISK ANALYSIS MATRIX
KEY RISK FACTORS AFFECTING PROJECT SUCCESS

(continued)

PLANNING RISK FACTORS

	SUCCESS	FAILURE
The Project:		
Will be a financial success	|———-|———-|———-|———-|	Will lose money _____
Has frequent milestones	|———-|———-|———-|———-|	Has no milestones _____
Predevelopment activities are carefully planned	|———-|———-|———-|———-|	Are not planned _____
Target market is well defined	|———-|———-|———-|———-|	Is undefined _____
Planning accounts for all expected events	|———-|———-|———-|———-|	There is no planning _____
Variables that correlate with the success of this project have been identified	|———-|———-|———-|———-|	No critical success variables have been identified _____
Supplier network is integrated into the development process	|———-|———-|———-|———-|	Suppliers are not included _____
Specifications are thorough, complete, and reflect the target market	|———-|———-|———-|———-|	Specifications do not exist _____
Concept is clear and easy to understand	|———-|———-|———-|———-|	Is not understandable_____

SUMMARY OF FINDINGS: _____ PROCEED; _____ PROCEED WITH RESERVATIONS; _____ RESOLVE PROBLEMS BEFORE PROCEEDING; _____ ABANDON.
EXPLAIN YOUR CONCLUSION:

_____

_____

10.3   USING THE RISK EVALUATION FORM

A user of the Risk Evaluation Form would complete the chart and fill in risk categories and checklist items. The end product gives a visual picture of the high risk categories and items. A risk mitigation, diversion, or minimization plan would be developed for items in the checklist that represent significant risk to the project.

The risk analysis evaluation should be a periodic and ongoing process and would be reviewed at each project milestone. At each review, the relative risk of various factors should be evaluated and updated.

The risk analysis form can be summarized with the factors listed below. All of the factors have been positively correlated with project success. In other words, if all these activities are carried out and, barring unforeseen events, the project will have the highest probability of goal achievement.

356   SECTION III: PROJECT FINANCIAL PLANNING

PROJECT RELATED RISK FACTORS THAT RESULT IN PROJECT SUCCESS

(Scientifically Correlated)

- The project is the result of a rational plan, communications web, and disciplined problem solving.
- The product or service is superior and focused toward an attractive market.
- The project team is well coordinated and competent. The project has senior management support.
- The project team closely monitors the market and stakeholder interests.
- The product or service has a clear advantage to the user, is of high quality, attractive cost, and has innovative features. It is reliable and unique.
- Predevelopment planning is emphasized. The market is well defined, and there should be a clear technical assessment of the product.
- Top management support is given and the project is built on existing corporate strengths.
- Cross-functional skills on the part of project members are mandatory. Cross-functional teams give access to more varied information. Cross-functional teams also make possible the overlap of development phases; hence, project lead times are reduced. In addition, cross-functional teams recognize problems earlier when they are easier to resolve.
- Reducing lead time is important, particularly if it provides entry into large growing markets.
- Involvement of vendors and customers in the development process.
- Good communications by the team. Clear connections with outsiders. A project leader who communicates with superiors and communicates information to team leaders. Project leaders should also be good politicians and ambassadors for the project. They should buffer the team from outside influences. They should engage in presenting a positive but realistic picture to their client and ensure resources are made available.
- Internal team communication results in better goal definition, more workable plans, and superior performance.
- The project manager is the pivotal member of the team. He/she serves as the bridge with the client. The project manager must have significant decision making authority to be successful. He/she should have high organizational authority as well. The project manager should command respect. The project manager should articulate his/her vision of the project. He/she should have excellent management and leadership skills.
- Good project planning results in conflicts being identified at an early point.
- Frequent milestones improve project success.

Once risk is identified, it is necessary to make plans to mitigate or respond to the risk. A few guidelines are listed below.

RISK REDUCTION TECHNIQUES

- Include several decision points, milestones, or go-no-go points.
- Include capability plans to shut down, terminate, spin off, or find alternative uses if the project gets into trouble.
- Keep fixed costs minimal and minimize financial leverage.
- Diversify.
- Evaluate project success at arm's length (e.g., don't get emotionally involved).
- Emphasize fast payback. Pull out seed money early.
- Have an audit plan. Define problems early, remedy them, and avoid them in the future.
- Pre-identify major risk factors in the project. Monitor closely.
- Modularize by breaking the project into independent components.
- Purchase insurance for insurable risks.
- Have partners to share the risk.
- Transfer risk to others (i.e., use outside contractors).

SECTION IV
MONITORING AND CONTROLLING THE PROJECT

CHAPTER 11

PROJECT FINANCIAL CONTROL

11.1 IMPORTANCE OF PROJECT FINANCIAL CONTROL

Once the project is underway, the attention of the project team shifts from emphasis on planning to monitoring and controlling the project. Specifically, project control includes all the formal and informal methods of ensuring that the project goes where the stakeholders want it to go. The control process is often compared to a thermostat that detects ambient temperature, assesses the significance of change, and then makes appropriate adjustments. The control process is important for any or all of the following purposes:

- Identify problems
- Evaluate management
- Make decisions about continuing
- Reward management
- Rank performance

One of the most important control tools in project management is the use of milestones and go-no-go decision points. Both establish a discipline for evaluating the project before proceeding to the next step and incurring additional expenses. It is important to note that project control pertains to both project strategy as well as project tasks.

The readings from Horngren that follow introduce cost management systems and activity-based costing. A common question is why the chapters discuss costing in manufacturing environments rather than in service, retail, or project applications. The reason is that manufacturing costing is the most complicated. It includes flows of paperwork and goods as well as several different types of raw materials, inventory, work in process, and finished goods. Typically, if a person understands costing in an industrial setting, it is an easy matter to adapt the concepts to a project.

As you can see, all kinds of organizations—manufacturing firms, service companies, and nonprofit organizations—need some form of **cost accounting**, that part of the accounting system that measures costs for the purposes of management decision making and financial reporting. Because it is the most general case, embracing production, marketing, and general administration functions, we will focus on cost accounting in a manufacturing setting. Remember, though, that you can apply this framework to any organization.

In this chapter we introduce the concepts of cost and management accounting appropriate to any manufacturing company. We also consider recent changes that have led to what is called the *new manufacturing environment*. Manufacturing companies are in the midst of great changes. The need to compete in global markets has changed the types of information useful to managers. At the same time, technology has changed both the manufacturing processes and information-processing capabilities. Although the basic *concepts* of management accounting have not changed, their *application* is significantly different in many companies than it was a decade ago. Management accountants today must be able to develop systems to support globally oriented, technology-intensive companies, often called *world-class manufacturing companies*.

In addition, we discuss how cost accounting affects and is affected by financial reporting, and how the need to use costs for reported income statements and balance sheets influences the way cost accounting systems are structured.

CLASSIFICATIONS OF COSTS

Costs may be classified in many ways—far too many to be covered in a single chapter. This chapter concentrates on the big picture of how manufacturing costs are accumulated and classified.

Cost Accumulation and Cost Objectives

A **cost** may be defined as a sacrifice or giving up of resources for a particular purpose. Costs are frequently measured by the monetary units (for example, dollars or francs) that must be paid for goods and services. Costs are initially recorded in elementary form (for example, repairs or advertising). Then these costs are grouped in different ways to help managers make decisions, such as evaluating subordinates and subunits of the organization, expanding or deleting products or territories, and replacing equipment.

To aid decisions, managers want to know the cost of something. This "something" is called a **cost objective** or **cost object**, defined as *any activity or resource for which a separate measurement of costs is desired*. Examples of cost objectives include departments, products, territories, miles driven, bricks laid, patients seen, tax bills sent, checks processed, student hours taught, and library books shelved.

The cost accounting system typically includes two processes:

1. **Cost accumulation:** Collecting costs by some "natural" classification, such as materials or labor.
2. **Cost allocation:** Tracing and reassigning costs to one or more cost objectives, such as departments, customers, or products.

Exhibit 11-1 illustrates these processes. First, the costs of all raw materials are *accumulated*. Then they are *allocated* to the departments that use them and further to the specific items made by these departments. The total raw materials cost of a particular product is the sum of the raw materials costs allocated to it in the various departments.

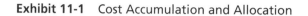

Exhibit 11-1   Cost Accumulation and Allocation

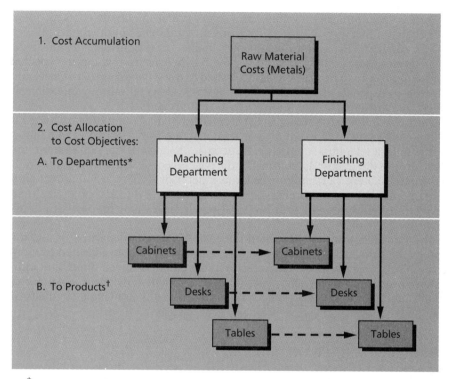

* Purpose: to evaluate performance of manufacturing departments.
† Purpose: to obtain costs of various products for valuing inventory, determining income, and judging product profitability.

To make intelligent decisions, managers want reliable measurements. An extremely large U.S. grocery chain, A&P, ran into profit difficulties. It began retrenching by closing many stores. Management's lack of adequate cost information about individual store operations made the closing program a hit-or-miss affair. A news story reported the following:

> Because of the absence of detailed profit-and-loss statements and a cost-allocation system that did not reflect true costs, A&P's strategists could not be sure whether an individual store was really unprofitable. For example, distribution costs were shared equally among all the stores in a marketing area without regard to such factors as a store's distance from the warehouse. Says one close observer of the company: "When they wanted to close a store, they had to wing it. They could not make rational decisions because they did not have a fact basis."

Direct and Indirect Costs

A major feature of costs in both manufacturing and nonmanufacturing activities is whether the costs have a direct or an indirect relationship to a particular cost objective. **Direct costs** can be identified specifically and exclusively with a given cost objective in an economically feasible way. In contrast, **indirect costs** cannot be identified specifically and exclusively with a given cost objective in an economically feasible way.

Whenever it is "economically feasible," managers prefer to classify costs as direct rather than indirect. In this way, managers have greater confidence in the reported costs of products and services. "Economically feasible" means "cost effective," in the sense that managers do not want cost accounting to be too expensive in relation to expected benefits. For example, it may be economically feasible to trace the exact cost of steel and fabric (direct cost) to a specific lot of desk chairs, but it may be economically infeasible to trace the exact cost of rivets or thread (indirect costs) to the chairs.

Other factors also influence whether a cost is considered direct or indirect. The key is the particular cost objective. For example, consider a supervisor's salary in the maintenance department of a telephone company. If the cost objective is the department, the supervisor's salary is a direct cost. In contrast, if the cost objective is a service (the "product" of the company) such as a telephone call, the supervisor's salary is an indirect cost. In general, many more costs are direct when a department is the cost objective than when a service (a telephone call) or a physical product (a razor blade) is the cost objective.

Frequently, managers want to know both the costs of running departments and the costs of products, services, activities, or resources. Costs are inevitably allocated to more than one cost objective. Thus, a particular cost may simultaneously be direct and indirect. As you have just seen, a supervisor's salary can be both direct (with respect to his or her department) and indirect (with respect to the department's individual products or services).

Categories of Manufacturing Costs

Any raw material, labor, or other input used by any organization could, in theory, be identified as a direct or indirect cost, depending on the cost objective. In manufacturing operations, which transform materials into other goods through the use of labor and factory facilities, products are frequently the cost objective. As a result, manufacturing costs are most often divided into three major categories: (1) direct materials, (2) direct labor, and (3) factory overhead.

1. **Direct-material costs** include the acquisition costs of all materials that are physically identified as a part of the manufactured goods and that may be traced to the manufactured goods in an economically feasible way. Examples are iron castings, lumber, aluminum sheets, and subassemblies. Direct materials often do not include minor items such as tacks or glue because the costs of tracing these items are greater than the possible benefits of having more precise product costs. Such items are usually called *supplies* or *indirect materials*, which are classified as a part of the factory overhead described in this list.

2. **Direct-labor costs** include the wages of all labor that can be traced specifically and exclusively to the manufactured goods in an economically feasible way. Examples are the wages of machine operators and assemblers. Much labor, such as that of janitors, forklift truck operators, plant guards, and storeroom clerks, is considered to be *indirect labor* because it is impossible or economically infeasible to trace such activity to specific products. Such indirect labor is classified as a part of factory overhead. In highly automated factories, there may be no direct labor costs. Why? Because it may be economically infeasible to physically trace any labor cost directly to specific products.

3. **Factory-overhead costs** include all costs associated with the manufacturing process that are not classified as direct material or direct labor. Other terms used to describe this category are **factory burden** and **manufacturing overhead**. Examples are power, supplies, indirect labor, supervisory salaries, property taxes, rent, insurance, and depreciation.

In traditional accounting systems, all manufacturing overhead costs are considered to be indirect. However, computers have allowed modern systems to physically trace many overhead costs to products in an economically feasible manner. For example, meters wired to computers can monitor the electricity used to produce each product, and costs of setting up a batch production run can be traced to the items produced in the run. In general, the more overhead costs that can be traced directly to products, the more accurate the product cost.

Prime Costs, Conversion Costs, and Direct-Labor Costs

Exhibit 11-2 shows that direct labor is sometimes combined with one of the other types of manufacturing costs. The combined categories are **prime costs**—direct labor plus direct materials—or **conversion costs**—direct labor plus factory overhead.

The twofold categorization, direct materials and conversion costs, has replaced the threefold categorization, direct materials, direct labor, and factory overhead, in many modern, automated manufacturing companies. Why? Because direct labor in such a company is a small part of costs and not worth tracing directly to the products. In fact, some companies call their two categories direct materials and factory overhead, and simply include direct labor costs in the factory overhead category.

Exhibit 11-2   Relationships of Key Categories of Manufacturing Costs for Product-Costing Purposes

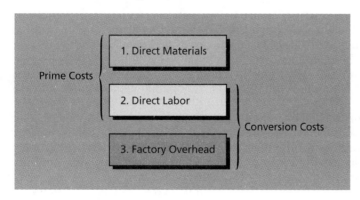

Why so many different systems? As mentioned earlier, accountants and managers weigh the costs and benefits of additional categories when they design their cost accounting systems. When the costs of any single category or item become relatively insignificant, separate tracking may no longer be desirable. For example, in highly automated factories direct labor is often less than 5% of total manufacturing costs. In such cases, it may make economic sense to combine direct-labor costs with one of the other major cost categories. Such is the case at several Hewlett-Packard plants, which collect direct labor as just another subpart of factory overhead.

To recap, the three major categories for manufacturing product costs are direct material, direct labor, and factory overhead. Some companies, however, have only two categories: direct materials and conversion costs. As information technology improves, some companies may have four or more. For instance, a company might have direct materials, direct labor, other direct costs (such as specifically metered power), and factory overhead.

In addition to direct-material, direct-labor, and factory-overhead costs, all manufacturing companies also incur selling and administrative costs. These costs are accumulated by departments such as advertising and sales departments. However, as you will see later in this chapter, most firms *financial statements* do not allocate these costs to the physical units produced. In short, these costs do not become a part of the reported inventory cost of the manufactured products. To aid in decisions, however, managers often want to know the selling and administrative costs associated with each product. Therefore, *management reports* often include such costs as product costs.

COST ACCOUNTING FOR FINANCIAL REPORTING

Regardless of the type of cost accounting system used, the resulting costs are used in a company's financial statements. This section discusses how financial reporting requirements influence the design of cost accounting systems.

Costs are reported on both the income statement, as cost of goods sold, and the balance sheet, as inventory amounts.

Product Costs and Period Costs

When preparing both income statements and balance sheets, accountants frequently distinguish between *product costs* and *period costs*. **Product costs** are costs identified with goods produced or purchased for resale. Product costs are initially identified as part of the inventory on hand. These product costs (inventoriable costs) become expenses (in the form of *cost of goods sold*) only when the inventory is sold. In contrast, **period costs** are costs that are deducted as expenses during the current period without going through an inventory stage.

For example, look at the top half of Exhibit 11-3. A merchandising company (retailer or wholesaler) acquires goods for resale without changing their basic form. The only product cost is the purchase cost of the merchandise. Unsold goods are held as merchandise inventory cost and are shown as an asset on a balance sheet. As the goods are sold, their costs become expenses in the form of "cost of goods sold."

A merchandising company also has a variety of selling and administrative expenses. These costs are period costs because they are deducted from revenue as expenses without ever being regarded as a part of inventory.

The bottom half of Exhibit 11-3 illustrates product and period costs in a manufacturing firm. Note that direct materials are transformed into salable form with the help of direct labor and factory overhead. All these costs are product costs because they are allocated to inventory until the goods are sold. As in merchandising accounting, the selling and administrative expenses are not regarded as product costs but are treated as period costs.

Be sure you are clear on the differences between merchandising accounting and manufacturing accounting for such costs as insurance, depreciation, and wages. In merchandising accounting, all such items are period costs (expenses of the current period). In manufacturing accounting, many of these items are related to production activities and, thus, as factory overhead, are product costs (become expenses in the form of cost of goods sold as the inventory is sold).

In both merchandising and manufacturing accounting, selling and general administrative costs are period costs. Thus, the inventory cost of a manufactured product *excludes* sales salaries, sales commissions, advertising, legal, public relations, and the president's salary. *Manufacturing overhead* is traditionally regarded as a part of finished-goods inventory cost, whereas *selling* expenses and *general administrative* expenses are not.

Balance Sheet Presentation

Examining both halves of Exhibit 11-3 together, you can see that the balance sheets of manufacturers and merchandisers differ with respect to inventories. The merchandiser's "inventory account" is supplanted in a manufacturing concern by three inventory classes that help managers trace all product costs through the production process to the time of sales.

These classes are:

- *Direct-materials inventory*: Materials on hand and awaiting use in the production process.
- *Work-in-process inventory*: Goods undergoing the production process but not yet fully completed. Costs include appropriate amounts of the three major manufacturing costs (direct material, direct labor, and factory overhead).
- *Finished-goods inventory*: Goods fully completed but not yet sold.

The only essential difference between the structure of the balance sheet of a manufacturer and that of a retailer or wholesaler would appear in their respective current asset sections:

Current Asset Sections of Balance Sheets

Manufacturer			Retailer or Wholesaler	
Cash		$ 4,000	Cash	$ 4,000
Receivables		25,000	Receivables	25,000
Finished goods	$32,000			
Work in process	22,000			
Direct material	23,000			
Total inventories		77,000	Merchandise inventories	77,000
Other current assets		1,000	Other current assets	1,000
Total current assets		$107,000	Total current assets	$107,000

Exhibit 11-3   Relationships of Product Costs and Period Costs

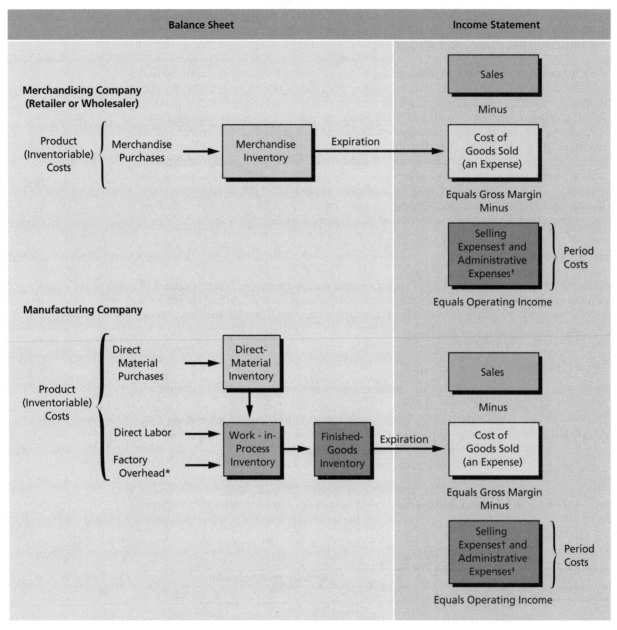

*   Examples: indirect labor, factory supplies, insurance, and depreciation on plant.

†   Examples: insurance on salespersons' cars, depreciation on salespersons' cars, salespersons' salaries.

‡ Examples: insurance on corporate headquarters building, depreciation on office equipment, clerical salaries.

Note particularly that when insurance and depreciation relate to the manufacturing function, they are inventoriable, but when they relate to selling and administration, they are not inventoriable.

Unit Costs for Product Costing

Reporting cost of goods sold or inventory values requires costs to be assigned to units of product. Assume the following:

Total cost of goods manufactured	$40,000,000
Total units manufactured	10,000,000
Unit cost of product for inventory purposes ($40,000,000 ÷ 10,000,000)	$ 4

If some of the 10 million units manufactured are still unsold at the end of the period, a part of the $40 million cost of goods manufactured will be "held back" as a cost of the ending inventory of finished goods (and shown as an asset on a balance sheet). The remainder becomes "cost of goods sold" for the current period and is shown as an expense on the income statement.

Costs and Income Statements

In income statements, the detailed reporting of selling and administrative expenses is typically the same for manufacturing and merchandising organizations, but the cost of goods sold is different:

Manufacturer	Retailer or Wholesaler
Manufacturing cost of goods produced and then sold, usually composed of the three major categories of cost: direct materials, direct labor, and factory overhead.	Merchandise cost of goods sold, usually composed of the purchase cost of items, including freight in, that are acquired and then resold.

Consider the additional details as they are presented in the model income statement of a manufacturing company in Exhibit 11-4. The $40 million cost of goods manufactured is subdivided into the major components of direct materials, direct labor, and factory overhead. In contrast, a wholesale or retail company would replace the entire "cost-of-goods-manufactured" section with a single line, "cost of goods purchased."

The terms "costs" and "expenses" are often used loosely by accountants and managers. "Expenses" denote all costs deducted from (matched against) revenue in a given period. On the other hand, "costs" is a much broader term and is used to describe both an asset (the cost of inventory) and an expense (the cost of goods sold). Thus, manufacturing costs are funneled into an income statement as an expense (in the form of cost of goods sold) via the multi-step inventory procedure shown earlier in Exhibit 11-3. In contrast, selling and general administrative costs are commonly deemed expenses immediately as they are incurred.

Transactions Affecting Inventories

The three manufacturing inventory accounts are affected by the following transactions:

- Direct Materials Inventory
    Increased by purchases of direct materials
    Decreased by use of direct materials

Exhibit 11-4 Model Income Statement, Manufacturing Company

Sales (8,000,000 units @ $10)			$80,000,000
Cost of goods manufactured and sold			
Beginning finished-goods inventory		$ —0—	
Cost of goods manufactured			
Direct materials used	$20,000,000		
Direct labor	12,000,000		
Factory overhead	8,000,000	40,000,000	
Cost of goods available for sale		$40,000,000	
Ending finished-goods inventory, 2,000,000 units @ $4		8,000,000	
Cost of goods sold (an expense)			32,000,000
Gross margin or gross profit			$48,000,000
Less: other expenses			
Selling costs (an expense)		$30,000,000	
General and administrative costs (an expense)		8,000,000	38,000,000
Operating income*			$10,000,000

*Also net income in this example because other expenses such as interest and income taxes are ignored here for simplicity.

- Work-in-Process Inventory
  Increased by use of direct materials, direct labor, or factory overhead
  Decreased by transfer of completed goods to finished-goods inventory
- Finished-Goods Inventory
  Increased by transfers of completed goods from work-in-process inventory
  Decreased by the amount of cost of goods sold at time of sale

Direct labor and factory overhead are used at the same time they are acquired. Therefore, they are entered directly into work-in-process inventory and have no separate inventory account. In contrast, direct materials are often purchased in advance of their use and held in inventory for some time.

Exhibit 11-5 Inventory Transactions (in millions)

Transaction	Direct-Materials Inventory	Work-in-Process Inventory	Finished-Goods Inventory
Beginning balance	$ 0	$ 0	$ 0
Purchase direct materials	+30	—	—
Use direct materials	−20	+20	—
Acquire and use direct labor	—	+12	—
Acquire and use factory overhead	—	+8	—
Complete production	—	−40	+40
Sell goods and record cost of goods sold	—	—	$−32
Ending balance	$ 10	$ 0	$ 8

Exhibit 11-5 traces the effects of each transaction. It uses the dollar amounts from Exhibit 11-4, with one exception. Purchases of direct materials totaled $30 million, with $20 million used in production (as shown in Exhibit 11-4) and $10 million left in inventory at the end of the period. As the bottom of Exhibit 11-5 indicates, the ending balance sheet amounts would be:

Direct-material inventory	$10,000,000
Work-in-process inventory	0
Finished-goods inventory	8,000,000
Total inventories	$18,000,000

COST BEHAVIOR AND INCOME STATEMENTS

In addition to differences between manufacturing and merchandising firms, manufacturers differ among themselves in accounting for costs on income statements, with some favoring an *absorption* approach and others using a *contribution* approach. To highlight the different effects of these approaches, we will assume that in 19X2 the Samson Company has direct-material costs of $7 million and direct-labor costs of $4 million. Assume also that the company incurred the factory overhead illustrated in Exhibit 11-6 and the selling and administrative expenses illustrated in Exhibit 11-7. Total sales were $20 million. Finally, assume that the units produced are equal to the units sold. That is, there is no change in inventory levels. (In this way, we avoid some complications that are unnecessary and unimportant at this stage.)

Exhibit 11-6   Samson Company

Schedules of Factory Overhead (Product Costs) for the Year Ended December 31, 19X2 (thousands of dollars)

Schedule 1: Variable Costs

Supplies (lubricants, expendable tools, coolants, sandpaper)	$ 150	
Material-handling labor (forklift operators)	700	
Repairs	100	
Power	50	$1,000

Schedule 2: Fixed Costs

Managers' salaries	$ 200	
Employee training	90	
Factory picnic and holiday party	10	
Supervisory salaries	700	
Depreciation, plant and equipment	1,800	
Property taxes	150	
Insurance	50	3,000
Total manufacturing overhead		$4,000

Exhibit 11-7 Samson Company

Schedules of Selling and Administrative Expenses (Period Costs) for the Year Ended December 31, 19X2 (thousands of dollars)

Schedule 3: Selling Expenses

Variable		
Sales commissions	$ 700	
Shipping expenses for products sold	300	$1,000
Fixed		
Advertising	$ 700	
Sales salaries	1,000	
Other	300	2,000
Total selling expenses		$3,000

Schedule 4: Administrative Expenses

Variable		
Some clerical wages	$ 80	
Computer time rented	20	$ 100
Fixed		
Office salaries	$ 100	
Other salaries	200	
Depreciation on office facilities	100	
Public-accounting fees	40	
Legal fees	100	
Other	360	900
Total administrative expenses		$1,000

Note that Exhibits 11-6 and 11-7 subdivide costs as variable or fixed. Many companies do not make such subdivisions in their income statements. Furthermore, when such subdivisions are made, sometimes arbitrary decisions are necessary as to whether a given cost is variable, fixed, or partially fixed (for example, repairs). Nevertheless, to aid decision making, many companies are attempting to report the extent to which their costs are approximately variable or fixed.

Absorption Approach

Exhibit 11-8 presents Samson's income statement using the **absorption approach** (*absorption costing*), the approach used by most companies. Firms that take this approach consider all factory overhead (both variable and fixed) to be product (inventoriable) costs that become an expense in the form of manufacturing cost of goods sold only as sales occur.

Note in Exhibit 11-8 that gross profit or gross margin is the difference between sales and the *manufacturing* cost of goods sold. Note, too, that the *primary classifications* of costs on the income statement are by three major management *functions*: manufacturing, selling, and administrative.

Exhibit 11-8 Samson Company

Absorption Income Statement for the Year Ended December 31, 19X2
(thousands of dollars)

Sales		$20,000
Less: manufacturing costs of goods sold		
Direct material	$7,000	
Direct labor	4,000	
Factory overhead (Schedules 1 plus 2)*	4,000	15,000
Gross margin or gross profit		$ 5,000
Selling expenses (Schedule 3)	$3,000	
Administrative expenses (Schedule 4)	1,000	
Total selling and administrative expenses		4,000
Operating income		$ 1,000

* Note: Schedules 1 and 2 are in Exhibit 11-6. Schedules 3 and 4 are in Exhibit 11-7.

Contribution Approach

In contrast, Exhibit 11-9 presents Samson's income statement using the **contribution approach** (*variable costing* or *direct costing*). The contribution approach is not allowed for external financial reporting. However, many companies use this approach for internal (management accounting) purposes and an absorption format for external purposes because they expect the benefits of making better decisions to exceed the extra costs of using different reporting systems simultaneously.

For decision purposes, the major difference between the contribution approach and the absorption approach is that the former emphasizes the distinction between variable and fixed costs. Its primary classifications of costs are by variable and fixed *cost behavior patterns*, not by *business functions*.

The contribution income statement provides a *contribution margin*, which is computed after deducting from revenue all variable costs including variable selling and administrative costs. This approach makes it easier to understand the impact of changes in sales demand on operating income. It also dovetails neatly with the CVP analysis.

The contribution approach stresses the lump-sum amount of fixed costs to be recouped before net income emerges. This highlighting of total fixed costs focuses management attention on fixed-cost behavior and control in making both short-run and long-run plans. Remember that advocates of the contribution approach do not maintain that fixed costs are unimportant or irrelevant. They do stress, however, that the distinctions between behaviors of variable and fixed costs are crucial for certain decisions.

The difference between the gross margin (from the absorption approach) and the contribution margin (from the contribution approach) is striking in manufacturing companies. Why? Because fixed manufacturing costs are regarded as a part of cost of goods sold, and these fixed costs reduce the gross margin accordingly. However, *fixed* manufacturing costs do not reduce the contribution margin, which is affected solely by revenues and *variable* costs.

Exhibit 11-9 Samson Company

Contribution Income Statement for the Year Ended December 31, 19X2 (thousands of dollars)

Sales		$20,000
Less: variable expenses		
Direct material	$ 7,000	
Direct labor	4,000	
Variable indirect manufacturing costs (Schedule 1)*	1,000	
Total variable manufacturing cost of goods sold	$12,000	
Variable selling expenses (Schedule 3)	1,000	
Variable administrative expenses (Schedule 4)	100	
Total variable expenses		13,100
Contribution margin		$ 6,900
Less: fixed expenses		
Manufacturing (Schedule 2)	$ 3,000	
Selling (Schedule 3)	2,000	
Administrative (Schedule 4)	900	5,900
Operating income		$ 1,000

* Note: Schedules 1 and 2 are in Exhibit 11-6. Schedules 3 and 4 are in Exhibit 11-7.

ACTIVITY-BASED ACCOUNTING, VALUE-ADDED COSTING, AND JUST-IN-TIME PRODUCTION

In the past decade, many companies in the United States, struggling to keep up with competitors from Japan, Germany, and other countries, adopted new management philosophies and developed new production technologies. In many cases, these changes prompted corresponding changes in accounting systems.

For example, Borg-Warner's Automotive Chain Systems Operation transformed its manufacturing operation to a just-in-time manufacturing system with work cells. This change in the way manufacturing was done made the traditional accounting system obsolete. A new cost accounting system coupled with the new production systems "improved the overall reporting, controls, and efficiency dramatically."[1]

Activity-Based Accounting

The primary focus of the changes in operations and accounting has been an increased attention to the cost of the *activities* undertaken to design, produce, sell, and deliver a company's products or services. **Activity-based accounting (ABA)** or **activity-based-costing (ABC)** systems first accumulate overhead costs for each of the *activities* of an organization and then assign the costs of activities to the products, services, or other cost objects that caused that activity.

Consider the Salem manufacturing plant of a major appliance producer. Exhibit 11-10 contrasts the traditional costing system with an ABC system. In the traditional

---

[1] A. Phillips and Don Collins, "How Borg-Warner Made the Transition From Pile Accounting to JIT," *Management Accounting*, October 1990, pp. 32–35.

Contribution Approach and Activity-Based Costing

Since the 1950s a growing number of firms have used the contribution approach for internal income statements. However, with the emergence of activity-based costing (ABC) in the late 1980s, some ABC proponents suggested that absorption costing information from an ABC system was more appropriate than contribution-based information for decision making. Now in the 1990s, according to Robert Koehler, "the combination of activity-based costing . . . and the contribution-margin approach will give a true overview of the whole cost picture."

One company that has combined ABC with the contribution approach is the Elgin Sweeper Company, the leading manufacturer of motorized street sweepers in North America, with annual sales of $50 million. In the late 1980s Elgin set out to install a cost-management system so that the effects of management decisions on costs could be pinpointed. The first step was to perform a cost-behavior study to identify the costs of Elgin's various activities. The company compiled a list of cost drivers that included actual labor dollars, actual labor hours, units shipped, units produced, purchase orders, service parts sales dollars, service orders shipped, workdays, calendar days, completed engineering change notices, engineering hours worked, and many others. Then costs that varied with each cost driver were identified and measured.

After measuring cost behavior, product-line contribution statements were prepared. These were designed to help managers see the results of their resource-allocation decisions and to assess the outcomes of strategic decisions. Each statement had three sections for each product line: (1) contribution margin, (2) direct margin, and (3) pretax income.

To measure *contribution margin*, costs driven by volume-related cost drivers were deducted from revenues to show the effects of volume on profits. The *direct margin* included a deduction of costs directly related to the product line but not necessarily related to volume. This provided a measure of the economic results of the full product line. Finally, pretax income included a deduction of all remaining fixed costs.

Elgin is still in the process of improving its cost-management system. Refinements of its product line contribution statements are planned, as are increased involvement of production supervisors with the cost-driver concept and the elimination of non-value-added activity. Elgin expects the result of its cost-management system to be "people making intelligent, informed, and cost-effective decisions." ■

Source: Adapted from R. W. Koehler, "Triple-Threat Strategy," Management Accounting, *October 1991, pp. 30–34; and J. Callan, W. Tredup, and R. Wissinger, "Elgin Sweeper Company's Journey Toward Cost Management,"* Management Accounting, *July 1991, pp. 24–27.*

cost system, the portion of *total overhead* allocated to a product depends on the proportion of *total direct-labor-hours* consumed in making the product. In the ABC system, significant overhead activities (machining, assembly, quality inspection, etc.) and related resources are separately identified and traced to products using cost drivers— machine hours, number of parts, number of inspections, etc. In the ABC system, the amount of overhead costs allocated to a product depends on the proportion of total machine hours, total parts, total inspections, and so on, consumed in making the product. One large overhead cost pool has been broken into several pools, each associated with a key activity. We now consider a more in-depth illustration of the design of an ABC system.

Illustration of Activity-Based Costing

Consider the Billing Department at Portland Power Company (PPC), an electric utility. The Billing Department (BD) at PPC provides account inquiry and bill-printing services for two major classes of customers—residential and commercial. Currently, the BD services 120,000 residential and 20,000 commercial customer accounts.

Exhibit 11-10   Traditional and Activity-Based Cost Systems

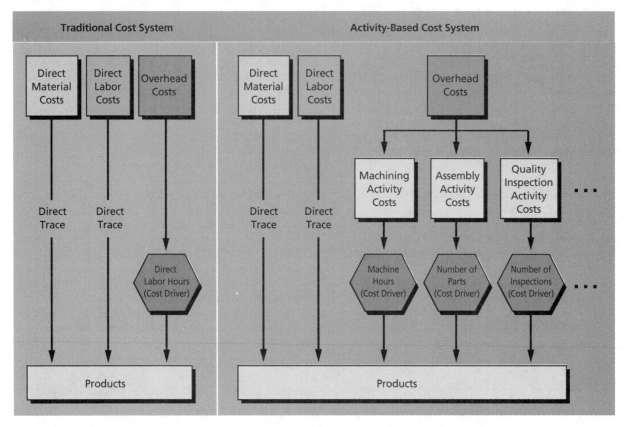

Two factors are having a significant impact on PPC's profitability. First, deregulation of the power industry has led to increased competition and lower rates, so PPC must find ways of reducing its operating costs. Second, the demand for power in PPC's area will increase due to the addition of a large housing development and a shopping center. The marketing department estimates that residential demand will increase by almost 50% and commercial demand will increase by 10% during the next year. Since the BD is currently operating at full capacity, it needs to find ways to create capacity to service the expected increase in demand. A local service bureau has offered to take over the BD functions at an attractive lower cost (compared to the current cost). The service bureau's proposal is to provide all the functions of the BD at $3.50 per account regardless of the type of account.

Exhibit 11-11 depicts the residential and commercial customer classes (cost objects) and the resources used to support the BD. The costs associated with the BD are all indirect—they cannot be identified specifically and exclusively with either customer class in an economically feasible way. The BD used a traditional costing system that allocated all support costs based on the number of account inquiries of the two customer classes. Exhibit 11-11 shows that the cost of the resources used in the BD last month was $565,340. BD received 23,000 account inquiries during the month, so the cost per inquiry was $565,340 ÷ 23,000 = $24.58. There were 18,000 residential account inquiries, 78.26% of the total. Thus, residential accounts were charged with 78.26% of the support costs, while commercial accounts were charged with 21.74%. The resulting cost, per account is $3.69 and $6.15 for residential and commercial accounts, respectively.

Exhibit 11-11   Current (Traditional) Costing System: Portland Power Company—Billing Department

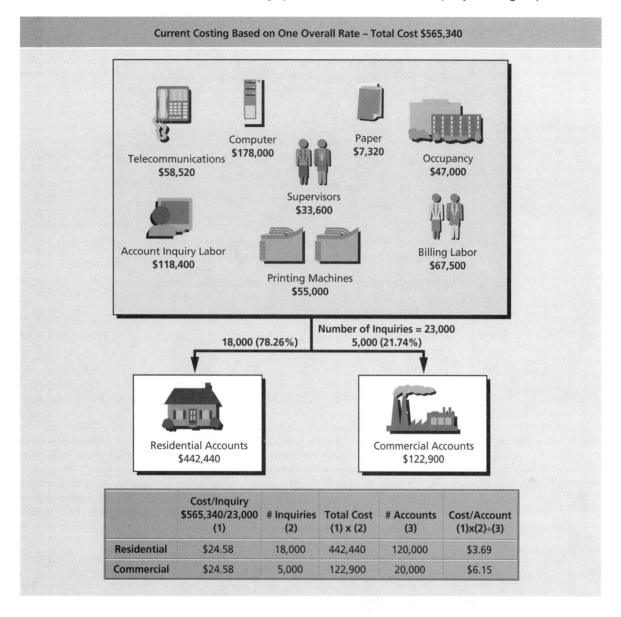

Current Costing Based on One Overall Rate – Total Cost $565,340

Telecommunications $58,520

Computer $178,000

Paper $7,320

Occupancy $47,000

Supervisors $33,600

Account Inquiry Labor $118,400

Printing Machines $55,000

Billing Labor $67,500

Number of Inquiries = 23,000

18,000 (78.26%)   5,000 (21.74%)

Residential Accounts $442,440

Commercial Accounts $122,900

	Cost/Inquiry $565,340/23,000 (1)	# Inquiries (2)	Total Cost (1) x (2)	# Accounts (3)	Cost/Account (1)x(2)÷(3)
Residential	$24.58	18,000	442,440	120,000	$3.69
Commercial	$24.58	5,000	122,900	20,000	$6.15

Management believed that the actual consumption of support resources was much greater than 22% for commercial accounts because of their complexity. For example, commercial accounts average 50 lines per bill compared with only 12 for residential accounts. Management was also concerned about activities such as correspondence (and supporting labor) resulting from customer inquiries because these activities are costly but do not add value to PPC's services from the customer's perspective. However, management wanted a more thorough understanding of key BD activities and their interrelationships before making important decisions that would impact PPC's profitability. The company decided to perform a study of the BD using activity-based costing. The following is a description of the study and its results.

The activity-based-costing study was performed by a team of managers from the BD and the chief financial officer from PPC. The team followed a four-step procedure to conduct the study.

Step 1: Determine cost objectives, key activity centers, resources, and related cost drivers. Management had set the objective for the study—determine the BD cost per account for each customer class. The team identified the following activities, and related cost drivers for the BD through interviews with appropriate personnel.

Activity Centers	Cost Drivers
Account billing	Number of lines
Bill verification	Number of accounts
Account inquiry	Number of labor hours
Correspondence	Number of letters

The four key BD activity centers are *account billing, bill verification, account inquiry, and correspondence.* The resources shown in Exhibit 11-11 support these major activity centers. Cost drivers were selected based on two criteria:

1. There had to be a reasonable cause-effect relationship between the driver unit and the consumption of resources and/or the occurrence of supporting activities.
2. Data on the cost-driver units had to be available.

Step 2: Develop a process-based map representing the flow of activities, resources, and their interrelationships. An important phase of any activity-based analysis is identifying the interrelationships between key activities and the resources consumed. This is typically done by interviewing key personnel. Once the linkages between activities and resources are identified, a process map is drawn that provides a visual representation of the operations of the BD.

Exhibit 11-12 is a process map that depicts the flow of activities and resources at the BD. Note that there are no costs on Exhibit 11-12. The management team first focused on understanding business processes. Costs were not considered until Step 3, after the key interrelationships of the business were understood.

Consider residential accounts. Three key activities support these accounts: account inquiry, correspondence, and account billing. Account inquiry activity consumes account inquiry labor time. Account inquiry laborers, in turn, use telecommunication and computer resources, occupy space, and are supervised. Correspondence is sometimes necessary as a result of inquiries. This activity requires account inquiry laborers who are supervised. The account billing activity is performed by billing laborers using printing machines. The printing machines occupy space, and require paper and computer resources. Billing laborers also occupy space, use telecommunucations, and are supervised. The costs of each of the resources consumed were determined during Step 3—data collection.

Step 3: Collect relevant data concerning costs and the physical flow of the cost-driver units among resources and activities. Using the process map as a guide, BD accountants collected the required cost and operational data by further interviews with relevant personnel. Sources of data include the accounting records, special studies, and sometimes "best estimates of managers."

Exhibit 11-13 is a graphical representation of the data collected for the four activity centers identified in Step 1. For each activity center, data collected included traceable costs and the physical flow of cost-driver units. For example, Exhibit 11-13 shows traceable costs of $235,777 for the account billing activity. Traceable costs include the costs of the printing machines ($55,000 from Exhibit 11-11) plus portions of the costs of all other

Exhibit 11-12 Process Map of Billing Department Activities

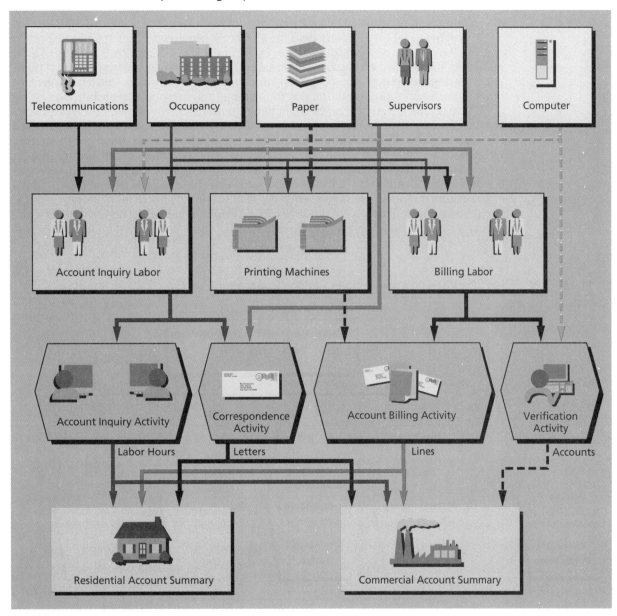

resources that support the billing activity (paper, occupancy, computer, and billing labor). Notice that the total traceable costs of $205,332 + $35,384 + $235,777 + $88,847 = $565,340 in Exhibit 11-13 equals the total indirect costs in Exhibit 11-11. Next, the physical flow of cost-driver units was determined for each activity or cost object. For each activity center, the traceable costs were divided by the sum of the physical flows to establish a cost per cost-driver unit.

Step 4: Calculate and interpret the new activity-based information. The activity-based cost per account for each customer class can be determined from the data in Step 3. Exhibit 11-14 shows the computations.

Examine the last two items in Exhibit 11-14. Notice that traditional costing overcosted the high-volume residential accounts and substantially undercosted the low-volume, complex commercial accounts. The cost per account for residential accounts using ABC is $2.28, which is $1.41 (or 38%) less than the $3.69 cost generated by the traditional costing system. The cost per account for commercial accounts is $14.57, which is $8.42 (or 137%) more than the $6.15 cost from the traditional cost system. Management's belief that traditional costing was undercosting commercial accounts was confirmed. PPC's management now has more accurate cost information for planning and decision-making purposes.

These results are common when companies perform activity-based-costing studies—high volume cost objects with simple processes are overcosted when only one volume-based cost driver is used. In the BD, this volume-based cost-driver was the number of inquiries. Which system makes more sense—the existing allocation system that "spreads" all support costs to customer classes based solely on the number of inquiries, or the activity-based-costing system that identifies key activities and assigns costs based on the consumption of units of cost drivers chosen for each key activity? For PPC, the probable benefits of the new activity-based-costing system appear to outweigh the costs of implementing and maintaining the new cost system. However, the cost-benefit balance must be assessed on a case-by-case basis.

Exhibit 11-13 ABC System: Portland Power Company—Billing Department

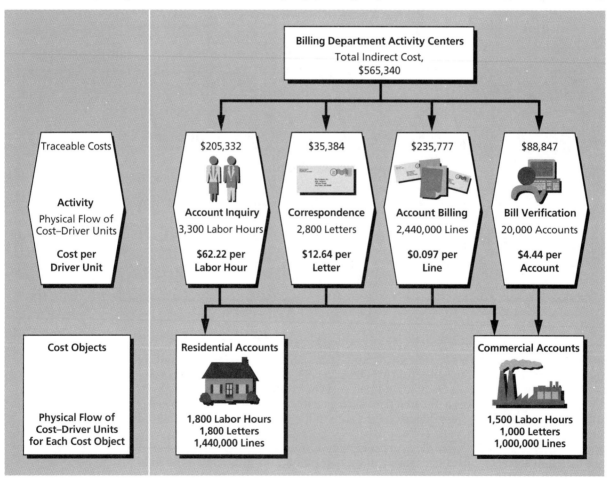

Exhibit 11-14 Key Results of Activity-Based-Costing Study

Driver Costs

Activity/Resource (Driver Units)	Traceable Costs (From Exhibit 11-13) (1)	Total Physical Flow of Driver Units (From Exhibit 4-13) (2)	Cost per Driver Unit (1)÷(2)
Account inquiry (labor hours)	$205,332	3,300 Hours	$62.2218
Correspondence (letters)	35,384	2,800 Letters	12.6371
Account billing (lines)	235,777	2,440,000 Lines	0.09663
Bill verification (accounts)	88,847	20,000 Accounts	4.44235

Cost per Customer Class

		Residential		Commercial	
	Cost per Driver Unit	Physical Flow of Driver Units	Cost	Physical Flow of Driver Units	Cost
Account inquiry	$62.2218	1,800 Hrs.	$111,999	1,500 Hrs.	$ 93,333
Correspondence	$12.6371	1,800 Ltrs.	22,747	1,000 Ltrs.	12,637
Account billing	$0.09663	1,440,000 Lines	139,147	1,000,000 Lines	96,630
Bill verification	$4.44235	0	0	20,000 Accts.	88,847
Total cost			$273,893		$291,447
Number of accounts			120,000		20,000
Cost per account			$2.28		$14.57
Cost per account, traditional system from Exhibit 11-11			$3.69		$6.15

Summary of Activity-Based Costing

Activity-based accounting systems can turn many indirect manufacturing overhead costs into direct costs, costs identified specifically with given cost objectives. Appropriate selection of activities and cost drivers allows managers to trace many manufacturing overhead costs to cost objectives just as specifically as they have traced direct-material and direct-labor costs. Because activity-based accounting systems classify more costs as direct than do traditional systems, managers have greater confidence in the accuracy of the costs of products and services reported by activity-based systems.

Activity-based accounting systems are more complex and costly than traditional systems, so not all companies use them. But more and more organizations in both manufacturing and nonmanufacturing industries are adopting activity-based systems for a variety of reasons:

- Fierce competitive pressure has resulted in shrinking profit margins. Companies may know their overall margin, but they often do not believe in the accuracy of the margins for *individual* products or services. Some are winners and some are losers—but which ones? Accurate costs are essential for answering this question.

- Business complexity has increased, resulting in greater diversity in the types of products and services as well as customer classes. Therefore, the consumption of a company's shared resources also varies substantially across products and customers.

Activity-Based Management

What's the next step beyond activity-based costing? Activity-based management. According to Peter Turney, one of the leaders in activity-based costing (ABC), ABC "can supply useful information, but what a company does with that information is what counts." In activity-based management, managers apply the information gathered using ABC to make better decisions.

In the broadest terms, activity-based management aims "to improve the value received by customers" and "to improve profits by providing this value," states Turney. How does activity-based management achieve these objectives?

Activity-based management focuses on managing activities—including identifying non-value-added activities that can be eliminated—and making sure that needed activities are carried out efficiently. Of course, each organization has its own set of activities. To improve operations, management must search out unnecessary or inefficient activities, determine the cost drivers for the activities, and change those cost drivers. For example, moving a partly finished product from the end of one production process to the start of another provides no value to the customer, but it is a necessary step. The distance between the processes drives this particular cost. By decreasing the distance, the cost can be reduced, if not eliminated.

Focusing on activities alerts managers to opportunities to save costs. Peter Turney cites Stockham Valve and Fittings, which used ABC to

- produce parts with the lowest cost process,
- design parts to minimize manufacturing costs,
- modify equipment to reduce costs,
- increase prices of products priced below ABC cost, and
- drop unprofitable products.

Using ABC information to improve operating decisions often justifies the added expense of an ABC system. ■

Source: Adapted from Peter B. B. Turney, "Activity-Based Management," Management Accounting, *January 1992, pp. 20–25.*

- New production techniques have increased the proportion of indirect costs—that is, indirect costs are far more important in today's world-class manufacturing environment. In many industries direct labor is being replaced by automated equipment. Indirect costs are sometimes over 50 percent of total cost.

- The rapid pace of technological change has shortened product life cycles. Hence, companies do not have time to make price or cost adjustments once costing errors are discovered.

- The costs associated with bad decisions that result from inaccurate cost determinations are substantial (bids lost due to overcosted products, hidden losses from undercosted products, failure to detect activities that are not cost effective, etc.). Companies with accurate costs have a huge advantage over those with inaccurate costs.

- Computer technology has reduced the costs of developing and operating cost systems that track many activities.

Cost-Management Systems and Value-Added Costing

To support managers' decisions better, accountants go beyond simply determining the cost of products and services. They develop cost-management systems. A **cost-management system** identifies how management's decisions affect costs. To do so, it first measures the resources used in performing the organization's activities and then assesses the effects on costs of changes in those activities. Cost management makes extensive use of *activity analysis.*

The cornerstone of cost management is distinguishing between value-added costs and non-value-added costs. A **value-added cost** is the cost of an activity that cannot be eliminated without affecting a product's value to the customer. Value-added costs are

Identifying Activities, Resources, and Cost Drivers

Arkansas Blue Cross Blue Shield (ABCBS) is the largest health insurer in the state of Arkansas with annual revenue of more than $450 million. Recently, ABCBS implemented activity-based management (ABM). ABM is using activity-based information in the decision-making process. The identification of key activities, resources, and cost drivers was one of the early steps performed.

- A pilot study was performed on one area of the firm—information management. The criteria for selection of a pilot area included significant costs, the possibility of improving the existing cost-allocation system, access to data, and a receptive staff.

- The cost objectives were defined—the internal customers of information management.

- Activities, resources, and cost drivers were identified based on meetings with managers. Examples of key activities are Production (job scheduling, production control), Electronic Media Claims Processing, Printing, and Mail Processing. Resources include Systems Programmers, Mail Labor, Print Labor, Tape Labor, Data Base Administrators, 3080 CPU, 3090 CPU, LSM (robotic cartridge system), DASD (hard disk storage), and Telecommunications. Cost drivers included CPU minutes, single-density volumes (DASD), number of tape/cartridge mounts (LSM), number of jobs, and number of CRTs (telecommunications).

- Once the key activities, resources, and drivers were identified, a process map of the operations of the information management function was developed by the project team. This map reflected the flow of activities and resources in support of the cost centers. The map also identified the data that needed to be collected to complete the study. (Note that the process map is very similar to Exhibit 11-12 in appearance.)

- Once the ABC model was built and validated, the results were interpreted and recommendations for improvement were made.

As a result of the ABC study, the following actions were taken by management:

- A separate utility meter was placed on the computer room.

- CRT purchases are now charged directly to the user. Maintenance costs for CRTs are now assigned based on CRT count.

- Three new cost centers were created: EMC Systems, Change Control, and Production Control.

- CPU was upgraded.

ABCBS is now in the process of expanding the new ABM system corporate-wide to include purchasing, actuarial, advertising, and claims processing. The company is also using the new ABM system for activity-based budgeting. ∎

Source: From "Implementing Activity-Based Costing— The Model Approach," Institute of Management Accountants and Sapling Corporation, Orlando, November 1994.

necessary (as long as the activity that drives such costs is performed efficiently). In contrast, companies try to minimize **non-value-added costs**, costs that *can* be eliminated without affecting a product's value to the customer. Activities such as handling and storing inventories, transporting partly finished products from one part of the plant to another, and changing the setup of production-line operations to produce a different model of the product are all non-value-adding activities that can be reduced, if not eliminated, by careful redesign of the plant layout and the production process. Often accounting is regarded as a non-value-adding activity. Although it cannot be eliminated, organizations should be sure that the benefits derived from accounting information exceed the costs.

JIT Systems

Attempts to minimize non-value-added costs have led many organizations to adopt JIT systems to eliminate waste and improve quality. In a **just-in-time (JIT) production system**, an organization purchases materials and parts and produces components *just* when they are needed in the production process. Goods are not produced until it is time for them to be shipped to a customer. The goal is to have zero inventory because holding inventory is a non-value-added activity.

JIT companies are customer-oriented because customer orders drive the production process. An order triggers the immediate delivery of materials, followed by production and delivery of the goods. Instead of producing inventory and hoping an order will come, a JIT system produces products directly for received orders. Several factors are crucial to the success of JIT systems:

1. *Focus on quality*: JIT companies try to involve all employees in controlling quality. Although any system can seek quality improvements, JIT systems emphasize *total quality control (TQC)* and *continuous improvement in quality.* Having all employees striving for zero defects minimizes non-value-added activities such as inspection and rework for defective items.

2. *Short **production cycle times**, the time from initiating production to delivering the goods to the customer*: Keeping production cycle times short allows timely response to customer orders and reduces the level of inventories. Many JIT companies have achieved remarkable reductions in production cycle times. For example, applying JIT methods in one AT&T division cut production cycle time by a factor of 12.

3. *Smooth flow of production*: Fluctuations in production rates inevitably lead to delays in delivery to customers and excess inventories. To achieve smooth production flow, JIT companies simplify the production process to reduce the possibilities of delay, develop close relationships with suppliers to assure timely delivery and high quality of purchased materials, and perform routine maintenance on equipment to prevent costly break-downs.

   Many companies help achieve these objectives by improving the physical layout of their plants. In conventional manufacturing, similar machines (lathes, molding machines, drilling machines, etc.) are grouped together. Workers specialize in only one machine operation (operating either the molding or the drilling machine). There are at least two negative effects of such a layout. First, products must be moved from one area of the plant to another for required processing. This increases material handling costs and results in work-in-process inventories that can be substantial. These are non-value-added activities and costs. Second, the specialized labor resource is often idle—waiting for work-in-process. This wasted resource—labor time—is also non-value-added.

   In a JIT production system, machines are often organized in cells according to the specific requirements of a product family. This is called **cellular manufacturing**. Only the machines that are needed for the product family are in the cell, and these machines are located as close to each other as possible. Workers are trained to use all the cellular machines. Each cell (often shaped in the form of a "U") is a mini-factory or focused factory. Many problems associated with the conventional production layout are eliminated in cellular manufacturing. Work-in-process inventories are reduced or eliminated because there is no need for moving and storing inventory. Idle time is reduced or eliminated because workers are capable of moving from idle machine activity to needed activities. As a result, cycle times are reduced.

4. *Flexible production operations*: Two dimensions are important: facilities flexibility and employee flexibility. Facilities should be able to produce a variety of components and products to provide extra capacity when a particular product is in high demand and to avoid shut-down when a unique facility breaks down. Facilities should also require short setup times, the time it takes to switch from producing one product to another. Cross-training employees—training employees to do a variety of jobs—provides further flexibility. Multiskilled workers can fill in when a particular operation is overloaded and can reduce setup time. One company reported a reduction in setup time from 45 minutes to 1 minute by training production workers to perform the setup operations.

Accounting for a JIT system is often simpler than for other systems. Most cost accounting systems focus on determining product costs for inventory valuation. But JIT systems have minimal inventories, so there is less benefit from an elaborate inventory costing system. In true JIT systems, material, labor and overhead costs can be charged directly to cost of goods sold because inventories are small enough to be ignored. All costs of production are assumed to apply to products that have already been sold.

Highlights To Remember

Many new terms were introduced in this chapter. Review them to make sure you know their exact meaning. Basic terms, such as cost, cost objective, cost accumulation, and cost allocation are especially important.

A major feature of costs for both manufacturing and nonmanufacturing organizations is whether the costs have a direct or an indirect relationship to cost objectives such as a department or product. Manufacturing costs (direct material, direct labor, and factory overhead) are traditionally regarded as product costs (inventoriable costs). In contrast, selling and administrative costs are period costs; hence, they are typically deducted from revenue as expenses in the period incurred.

Financial statements for manufacturers differ from those of merchandisers. Costs such as utilities, wages, and depreciation, which are treated as period costs by a merchandising company, are product costs (part of factory overhead) for a manufacturing company if they are related to the manufacturing process. Balance sheets of manufacturers may include three inventory accounts: direct materials, work in process, and finished goods.

The contribution approach to preparing an income statement emphasizes the distinction between fixed and variable costs and is a natural extension of the CVP analysis used in decisions. In contrast, the absorption approach emphasizes the distinction between manufacturing costs and selling and administrative costs.

Activity-based costing (ABC) and just-in-time (JIT) production systems are two approaches used by modern companies to improve their competitiveness. The focus of activity-based costing is on more accurate product or service costing. Management can then use ABC information to manage costs better. To manage costs, they try to eliminate non-value-added activities. The JIT approach focuses on improving operating efficiencies by reducing waste. JIT and ABC can be used separately or together—many modern companies use both.

Summary Problem for Your Review

Problem

1. Review the illustrations in Exhibits 11-6 through 11-9. Suppose that all variable costs fluctuate in direct proportion to units produced and sold, and that all fixed costs are unaffected over a wide range of production and sales. What would operating income have been if sales (at normal selling prices) had been $20.9 million instead of $20.0 million? Which statement, the absorption income statement or the contribution income statement, did you use as a framework for your answer? Why?

2. Suppose employee training (Exhibit 11-6) was regarded as a variable rather than a fixed cost at a rate of $90,000 ÷ 1,000,000 units, or $.09 per unit. How would your answer in part 1 change?

Solution

1. Operating income would increase from $1,000,000 to $1,310,500, computed as follows:

Increase in revenue	$ 900,000
Increase in total contribution margin:	
Contribution-margin ratio in contribution income statement	
(Exhibit 11-9) is $6,900,000 ÷ $20,000,000 = .345	
Ratio times revenue increase is .345 × $900,000	$ 310,500
Increase in fixed expenses	—0—
Operating income before increase	1,000,000
New operating income	$1,310,500

Computations are easily made by using data from the contribution income statement. In contrast, the traditional absorption costing income statement must be analyzed and divided into variable and fixed categories before the effect on operating income can be estimated.

2. The original contribution-margin ratio would be lower because the variable costs would be higher by $.09 per unit: ($6,900,000 − $90,000) ÷ $20,000,000 = .3405.

	Given Level	Higher Level	Difference
Revenue	$20,000,000	$20,900,000	$900,000
Variable expense ($13,100,000 + $90,000)	13,190,000	13,783,550	593,550
Contribution margin at .3405	$ 6,810,000	$ 7,116,450	$306,450
Fixed expenses ($5,900,000 − $90,000)	5,810,000	5,810,000	—
Operating income	$ 1,000,000	$ 1,306,450	$306,450

Appendix: More on Labor Costs

Classifications of Labor Costs

The terms used to classify labor costs are often confusing. Each organization seems to develop its own interpretation of various labor-cost classifications. We begin by considering some commonly encountered labor-cost terms:

- Direct labor (already defined)
- Factory overhead (examples of prominent labor components of these indirect manufacturing costs follow)
    Indirect labor (wages)
        Forklift truck operators (internal handling of materials)
        Maintenance (to set up for production runs)
        Janitors

Expediting (overseeing special orders, usually on a rush basis)

Plant guards

Rework labor (time spent by direct laborers redoing defective work)

Overtime premium paid to all factory workers

Idle time

Managers' salaries

Payroll fringe costs (for example, health care premiums, pension costs)

All factory labor wages, other than those for direct labor and manager salaries, are usually classified as **indirect labor** costs, a major component of factory overhead. The term *indirect labor* is usually divided into many subsidiary classifications. The wages of forklift truck operators are generally not commingled with janitors' salaries, for example, although both are regarded as indirect labor.

Costs are classified in a detailed fashion primarily to associate a specific cost with its specific cost driver. Two classes of indirect labor deserve special mention: overtime premium and idle time.

Overtime premium paid to all factory workers is usually considered a part of overhead. If a lathe operator earns $8 per hour for straight time and time and one-half for overtime, the premium is $4 per overtime hour. If the operator works 44 hours, including 4 overtime hours, in 1 week, the gross earnings are classified as follows:

Direct labor: 44 hours × $8	$352
Overtime premium (factory overhead): 4 hours × $4	16
Total earnings for 44 hours	$368

Why is overtime premium considered an indirect cost rather than direct? After all, it can usually be traced to specific batches of work. It is usually not considered a direct charge because the scheduling of production jobs is generally random. Suppose that at 8:00 A.M. you bring your automobile to a shop for repair. Through random scheduling, your auto is repaired between 5:00 and 6:00 P.M., when technicians receive overtime pay. Then, when you come to get your car, you learn that all the overtime premium had been added to your bill. You probably would not be overjoyed.

Thus, in most companies, the overtime premium is not allocated to any specific job. Instead, the overtime premium is considered to be attributable to the heavy overall volume of work, and its cost is thus regarded as part of the indirect manufacturing costs (factory overhead). The latter approach does not penalize a particular batch of work solely because it happened to be worked on during the overtime hours.

Another subsidiary classification of indirect-labor costs is **idle time**. This cost typically represents wages paid for unproductive time caused by machine breakdowns, material shortages, sloppy production scheduling, and the like. For example, if the same lathe operator's machine broke down for 3 hours during the week, the operator's earnings would be classified as follows:

Direct labor: 41 hours × $8	$328
Overtime premium (factory overhead): 4 hours × $4	16
Idle time (factory overhead): 3 hours × $8	24
Total earnings for 44 hours	$368

Manager salaries usually are not classified as a part of indirect labor. Instead, the compensation of supervisors, department heads, and all others who are regarded as part of manufacturing management are placed in a separate classification of factory overhead.

Payroll Fringe Costs

A type of labor cost that is growing in importance is **payroll fringe costs,** such as employer contributions to employee benefits like social security, life insurance, health insurance, and pensions. Most companies classify these as factory overhead. In some companies, however, fringe benefits related to direct labor are charged as an additional direct-labor cost. For instance, a direct laborer, such as a lathe operator or an auto mechanic, whose gross wages are computed on the basis of $10 an hour, may enjoy fringe benefits totaling $4 per hour. Most companies classify the $10 as direct-labor cost and the $4 as factory overhead. Other companies classify the entire $14 as direct-labor cost. The latter approach is conceptually preferable because these costs are a fundamental part of acquiring labor services.

Accountants and managers need to pinpoint exactly what direct labor includes and excludes. Such clarity may avoid disputes regarding cost reimbursement contracts, income tax payments, and labor union matters. For example, some countries offer substantial income tax savings to companies that locate factories there. To qualify, these companies' "direct labor" in that country must equal at least a specified percentage of the total manufacturing costs of their products. Disputes have arisen regarding how to calculate the direct-labor percentage for qualifying for such tax relief. Are payroll fringe benefits on direct labor an integral part of direct labor, or are they a part of factory overhead? Depending on how companies classify costs, you can readily see that the two identical firms may show different percentages of total manufacturing costs. Consider a company with $10,000 of payroll fringe costs:

Classification A			Classification B		
Direct materials	$ 80,000	40%	Direct materials	$ 80,000	40%
Direct labor	40,000	20	Direct labor	50,000	25
Factory overhead	80,000	40	Factory overhead	70,000	35
Total manufacturing costs	$200,000	100%	Total manufacturing costs	$200,000	100%

Classification A assumes that payroll fringe costs are part of factory overhead. In contrast, Classification B assumes that payroll fringe costs are part of direct labor.

Fundamental Assignment Material

11-A1   Straightforward Income Statements
The Goldsmith Company had the following manufacturing data for the year 19X6 (in thousands of dollars):

Beginning and ending inventories	None
Direct material used	$425
Direct labor	350
Supplies	20
Utilities—variable portion	45
Utilities—fixed portion	15
Indirect labor—variable portion	100
Indirect labor—fixed portion	50
Depreciation	110
Property taxes	20
Supervisory salaries	50

Selling expenses were $325,000 (including $70,000 that were variable) and general administrative expenses were $148,000 (including $24,000 that were variable). Sales were $1.9 million.

Direct labor and supplies are regarded as variable costs.

1. Prepare two income statements, one using the contribution approach and one using the absorption approach.

2. Suppose that all variable costs fluctuate directly in proportion to sales, and that fixed costs are unaffected over a very wide range of sales. What would operating income have been if sales had been $2.2 million instead of $1.9 million? Which income statement did you use to help obtain your answer? Why?

11-A2 Meaning of Technical Terms

Refer to the absorption income statement of your solution to the preceding problem. Give the amounts of the following: (1) prime cost, (2) conversion cost, (3) factory burden, (4) factory overhead, and (5) manufacturing overhead.

11-A3 Activity-Based Costing

Quality Machining Products (QMP) is an automotive component supplier. QMP has been approached by General Motors to consider expanding its production of part G108 to a total annual quantity of 2,000 units. This part is a low-volume, complex product with a high gross margin that is based on a proposed (quoted) unit sales price of $7.50. QMP uses a traditional costing system that allocates factory-overhead costs based on direct-labor costs. The rate currently used to allocate factory-overhead costs is 400% of direct-labor cost. This rate is based on the $3,300,000 annual factory overhead divided by $825,000 annual direct-labor cost. To produce 2,000 units of G108 requires $5,000 of direct materials and $1,000 of direct labor. The unit cost and gross margin percentage for Part G108 based on the traditional cost system are computed as follows:

	Total	Per Unit (÷2,000)
Direct material	$ 5,000	$2.50
Direct labor	1,000	.50
Factory overhead:		
[400% X direct labor]	4,000	2.00
Total cost	$10,000	$5.00
Sales price quoted		7.50
Gross margin		$2.50
Gross margin percentage		33.3%

The management of QMP decided to examine the effectiveness of their traditional costing system versus an activity-based-costing system. The following data have been collected by a team consisting of accounting and engineering analysts:

Activity Center	Traceable Factory Overhead Costs (Annual)
Quality	$ 800,000
Production scheduling	50,000
Setup	600,000
Shipping	300,000
Shipping administration	50,000
Production	1,500,000
Total factory overhead cost	$3,300,000

Activity Center: Cost Drivers	Annual Cost-Driver Quantity
Quality: number of pieces scrapped	10,000
Production scheduling and setup:	
number of setups	500
Shipping: number of containers shipped	60,000
Shipping administration: number of shipments	1,000
Production: number of machine hours	10,000

The accounting and engineering team has performed activity analysis and provides the following estimates for the total quantity of cost drivers to be used to produce 2,000 units of part G108:

Cost Driver	Cost-Driver Consumption
Pieces scrapped	120
Setups	4
Containers shipped	10
Shipments	5
Machine hours	15

1. Prepare a schedule calculating the unit cost and gross margin of Part G108 using the activity-based-costing approach.
2. Based on the ABC results, which course of action would you recommend regarding the proposal by General Motors? List the benefits and costs associated with implementing an activity-based-costing system at QMP.

11-B1   Contribution and Absorption Income Statements
The following information is taken from the records of the Queensland Company for the year ending December 31, 19X5. There were no beginning or ending inventories.

Sales	$11,000,000	Long-term rent, factory	$ 110,000
Sales commissions	550,000	Factory superintendent's	
Advertising	225,000	salary	32,000
Shipping expenses	310,000	Supervisors' salaries	105,000
Administrative executive		Direct material used	4,100,000
salaries	100,000	Direct labor	2,200,000
Administrative clerical		Cutting bits used	60,000
salaries (variable)	450,000	Factory methods research	40,000
Fire insurance on		Abrasives for machining	100,000
factory equipment	2,000	Indirect labor	810,000
Property taxes on		Depreciation on	
factory equipment	10,000	equipment	300,000

1. Prepare a contribution income statement and an absorption income statement. If you are in doubt about any cost behavior pattern, decide on the basis of whether the total cost in question will fluctuate substantially over a wide range of volume. Prepare a separate supporting schedule of indirect manufacturing costs subdivided between variable and fixed costs.

2. Suppose that all variable costs fluctuate directly in proportion to sales, and that fixed costs are unaffected over a wide range of sales. What would operating income have been if sales had been $12.5 million instead of $11 million? Which income statement did you use to help get your answer? Why?

11-B2   JIT and Non-Value-Added Activities

A motorcycle manufacturer was concerned with declining market share because of foreign competition. To become more efficient, the company was considering changing to a JIT production system. As a first step in analyzing the feasibility of the change, the company identified its major activities. Among the 120 activities were the following:

Materials receiving and inspection

Production scheduling

Production setup

Rear-wheel assembly

Movement of engine from fabrication to assembly building

Assembly of handlebars

Paint inspection

Reworking of defective brake assemblies

Installation of speedometer

Placement of completed motorcycle in finished goods storage

1. From the preceding list of 10 activities, prepare two lists: one of value-added activities and one of non-value-added activities.

2. For each non-value-added activity, explain how a JIT production system might eliminate, or at least reduce, the cost of the activity.

11-B3   Activity-Based Costing

The cordless phone manufacturing division of a consumer electronics company uses activity-based accounting. For simplicity, assume that its accountants have identified only the following three activities and related cost drivers for manufacturing overhead:

Activity	Cost Driver
Materials handling	Direct materials cost
Engineering	Engineering change notices
Power	Kilowatt hours

Three types of cordless phones are produced: CL3, CL5, and CL9. Direct costs and cost-driver activity for each product for a recent month are as follows:

	CL3	CL5	CL9
Direct materials cost	$25,000	$50,000	$125,000
Direct labor cost	$4,000	$1,000	$3,000
Kilowatt hours	50,000	200,000	150,000
Engineering change notices	13	5	2

Manufacturing overhead for the month was:

Materials handling	$10,000
Engineering	30,000
Power	24,000
Total manufacturing overhead	$64,000

1. Compute the manufacturing overhead allocated to each product with the activity-based accounting system.
2. Suppose all manufacturing overhead costs had been allocated to products in proportion to their direct-labor costs. Compute the manufacturing overhead allocated to each product.
3. In which product costs, those in requirement 1 or those in requirement 2, do you have the most confidence? Why?

Additional Assignment Material

Questions

11-1. Name four cost objectives or cost objects.

11-2. "Departments are not cost objects or objects of costing." Do you agree? Explain.

11-3. What is the major purpose of detailed cost-accounting systems?

11-4. "The same cost can be direct and indirect." Do you agree? Explain.

11-5. "Economic feasibility is an important guideline in designing cost-accounting systems." Do you agree? Explain.

11-6. How does the idea of economic feasibility relate to the distinction between direct and indirect costs?

11-7. "The typical accounting system does not allocate selling and administrative costs to units produced." Do you agree? Explain.

11-8. Distinguish between prime costs and conversion costs.

11-9. "For a furniture manufacturer, glue or tacks become an integral part of the finished product, so they would be direct material." Do you agree? Explain.

11-10. Many cost-accounting systems have a twofold instead of a threefold category of manufacturing costs. What are the items in the twofold category?

11-11. "Depreciation is an expense for financial statement purposes." Do you agree? Explain.

11-12. Distinguish between "costs" and "expenses."

11-13. "Unexpired costs are always inventory costs." Do you agree? Explain.

11-15. Why is there no direct-labor inventory account on a manufacturing company's balance sheet?

11-16. What is the advantage of the contribution approach as compared with the absorption approach?

11-17. Distinguish between manufacturing and merchandising companies.

11-18. "The primary classifications of costs are by variable- and fixed-cost behavior patterns, not by business functions." Name three commonly used terms that describe this type of income statement.

11-19. Name 4 steps in the design and implementation of an activity-based-costing system.

11-20. Refer to the Portland Power Company illustration on pages 136–142. Which BD resource costs depicted in Exhibit 11-11 would have variable cost behavior?

11-21. Why are more and more organizations adopting activity-based-costing systems?

11-22. Why do managers want to distinguish between value-added activities and non-value-added activities?

11-23. Name four factors crucial to the success of JIT production systems.

11-24. "ABC and JIT are alternative techniques for achieving competitiveness." Do you agree?

11-25 Meaning of Technical Terms

Refer to Exhibit 11-4. Give the amounts of the following with respect to the cost of goods available for sale: (1) prime costs, (2) conversion costs, (3) factory burden, and (4) indirect manufacturing costs.

11-26 Presence of Ending Work in Process

Refer to Exhibits 11-4 and 11-5. Suppose manufacturing costs were the same, but there was an ending work-in-process inventory of $3 million. The cost of the completed goods would therefore be $37 million instead of $40 million. Suppose also that the cost of goods sold is unchanged.

1. Recast the income statement of Exhibit 11-4.
2. What lines and ending balances would change in Exhibit 11-5 and by how much?

11-27 Relating Costs to Cost Objectives

A company uses an absorption cost system. Prepare headings for two columns: (1) assembly department and (2) products assembled. Fill in the two columns with a *D* for direct and an *I* for indirect for each of the costs below. For example, if a specific cost is direct to the department but indirect to the product, place a *D* in column 1 and an *I* in column 2. The costs are: materials used, supplies used, assembly labor, material-handling labor (transporting materials between and within departments), depreciation—building, assembly supervisor's salary, and the building and grounds supervisor's salary.

11-28 Classification of Manufacturing Costs

Classify each of the following as direct or indirect (*D* or *I*) with respect to product and as variable or fixed (*V* or *F*) with respect to whether the cost fluctuates in total as activity or volume changes over wide ranges of activity. You will have two answers, *D* or *I* and *V* or *F*, for each of the 10 items.

1. Food for a factory cafeteria
2. Workers' compensation insurance in a factory
3. Supervisor training program
4. Salary of a factory storeroom clerk
5. Paper towels for a factory washroom
6. Steel scrap for a blast furnace
7. Factory rent
8. Cutting bits in a machinery department
9. Cement for a roadbuilder
10. Abrasives (sandpaper, etc.)

11-29   Variable Costs and Fixed Costs; Manufacturing and Other Costs

For each of the numbered items, choose the appropriate classifications for a manufacturing company. If in doubt about whether the cost behavior is basically variable or fixed, decide on the basis of whether the total cost will fluctuate substantially over a wide range of volume. Most items have two answers among the following possibilities with respect to the cost of a particular job:

a. Selling cost

b. Manufacturing costs, direct

c. Manufacturing costs, indirect

d. General and administrative cost

e. Fixed cost

f. Variable cost

g. Other (specify)

Sample answers:

Direct material	e, f
President's salary	d, e
Bond interest expense	e, g (financial expense)

Items for your consideration:

1. Company picnic costs
2. Overtime premium, punch press
3. Idle time, assembly
4. Freight out
5. Property taxes
6. Paint for finished products
7. Heat and air conditioning, factory
8. Material-handling labor, punch press
9. Straight-line depreciation, salespersons' automobiles storeroom
10. Factory power for machines
11. Salespersons' commissions
12. Salespersons' salaries
13. Welding supplies
14. Fire loss
15. Sandpaper
16. Supervisory salaries, production control
17. Supervisory salaries, assembly department
18. Supervisory salaries, factory

11-30   Inventory Transactions

Review Exhibit 11-9. Assume that the Jenkins Company had no beginning inventories. The following transactions occurred in 19X6 (in thousands):

1.	Purchase of direct materials	$400
2.	Direct materials used	310
3.	Acquire direct labor	180
4.	Acquire factory overhead	210
5.	Complete all goods that were started	?
6.	Cost of goods sold (half of the goods completed were sold)	?

Prepare an analysis similar to Exhibit 11-9. What are the ending balances of direct materials, work-in-process, and finished-goods inventories?

11-31   Inventory Transactions

Refer to the preceding problem. Suppose goods were still in process that cost $90,000. Half the goods completed were sold. What are the balances of all the accounts in the ending balance sheet?

11-32   Straightforward Absorption Statement

The Gomez Company had the following data (in thousands) for a given period:

Sales	$900
Direct materials	250
Direct labor	180
Indirect manufacturing costs	150
Selling and administrative expenses	170

There were no beginning or ending inventories. Compute the (1) manufacturing cost of goods sold, (2) gross profit, (3) operating income, (4) prime cost, and (5) conversion cost.

11-33   Straightforward Contribution Income Statement

Yoko Ltd. had the following data (in millions of yen) for a given period:

Sales	¥750
Direct materials	280
Direct labor	150
Variable factory overhead	50
Variable selling and administrative expenses	90
Fixed factory overhead	100
Fixed selling and administrative expenses	50

There were no beginning or ending inventories. Compute the (1) variable manufacturing cost of goods sold, (2) contribution margin, and (3) operating income.

11-34   Straightforward Absorption and Contribution Statement

Martinez Company had the following data (in millions) for a recent period. Fill in the blanks. There were no beginning or ending inventories.

a.	Sales	$950
b.	Direct materials used	360
c.	Direct labor	200
	Factory overhead	
d.	Variable	110
e.	Fixed	50
f.	Variable manufacturing cost of goods sold	——
g.	Manufacturing cost of goods sold	——
	Selling and administrative expenses	
h.	Variable	100
i.	Fixed	50
j.	Gross profit	——
k.	Contribution margin	——
l.	Prime costs	——
m.	Conversion costs	——
n.	Operating income	——

11-35 Absorption Statement

Richard's Jewelry had the following data (in thousands) for a given period. Assume there are no inventories. Fill in the blanks.

Sales	$___
Direct materials	400
Direct labor	___
Factory overhead	___
Manufacturing cost of goods sold	800
Gross margin	130
Selling and administrative expenses	___
Operating income	40
Conversion cost	___
Prime cost	610

11-36 Contribution Income Statement

Nottingham Company had the following data (in thousands) for a given period. Assume there are no inventories.

Direct labor	$190
Direct materials	200
Variable factory overhead	140
Contribution margin	210
Fixed selling and administrative expenses	110
Operating income	20
Sales	980

Compute the (1) variable manufacturing cost of goods sold, (2) variable selling and administrative expenses, and (3) fixed factory overhead.

11-37 Classifications of Direct Labor Cost

Study Appendix 4. A division of a machinery manufacturer has the following cost of goods manufactured:

Direct materials	$240,000	60%
Direct labor	60,000	15
Factory overhead	100,000	25
Cost of goods manufactured	$400,000	100%

The fringe benefits related to direct labor are 30% of the nominal direct-labor costs. They are currently included in factory overhead. If these benefits were regarded as part of direct labor rather than factory overhead, what percentage of cost of goods manufactured would direct labor represent?

11-38 Overtime Premium

Study Appendix 4. Downtown Auto has a service department. You have brought your car for repair at 8:00 A.M. When you come to get your car after 6:00 P.M., you notice that your bill contains a charge under "labor" for "overtime premium." When you inquire about the reason for the charge, you are told, "We worked on your car from 5:00 P.M. to 6:00 P.M. Our union contract calls for wages to be paid at time-and-a-half after 8 hours. Therefore our ordinary labor charge of $40 per hour was billed to you at $60."

1. Should Downtown Auto allocate the overtime premium only to cars worked on during overtime hours? Explain.
2. Would your preceding answer differ if Downtown Auto arranged to service your car at 8:00 P.M. as a special convenience to you? Explain.

11-39 Value-Added Analysis in a Service Company

Refer to the Portland Power Company illustration and Exhibit 11-12.Some companies that perform value-added cost analysis subdivide non-value-added activities into two categories—essential and discretionary. An example of an essential but non-value-added activity is setting up the company's computer system for a billing run. An example of a discretionary non-value-added activity is monitoring telephone inquiries. Most non-value-added discretionary activities should be eliminated. Non-value-added essential activities are reduced through continuous improvement efforts. For each resource and activity listed below, indicate whether it is value-added (VA), non-value-added essential (NVA-E), or non-value-added discretionary (NVA-D). Also indicate appropriate managerial actions to control costs for each type of resource and activity based on its classification.

Resource/Activity
Telecommunications
Paper
Computer
Supervisors
Account inquiry activity
Billing labor

11-40 Cost Allocation and Activity-Based Costing

Refer to the Portland Power Company illustration and Exhibit 11-14. The data used in the BD study are averages for each customer class. Based on the study results, the company conducted a thorough investigation of all commercial customers that received correspondence. On average, these accounts consumed 5 minutes of inquiry labor time and had 75 lines on the electric bill. What was the cost per account to service this customer class? (Assume only 1 letter per customer and that commercial accounts are verified only one time.)

11-41 Cost Accumulation and Allocation

Wang Manufacturing Company has two departments, machining and finishing. For a given period, the following costs were incurred by the company as a whole: direct material, $130,000; direct labor, $75,000; and manufacturing overhead, $80,000. The grand total costs were $285,000.

The machining department incurred 70% of the direct-material costs, but only 33⅓% of the direct-labor costs. As is commonplace, manufacturing overhead incurred by each department was allocated to products in proportion to the direct-labor costs of products within the departments.

Three products were produced.

Product	Direct Material	Direct Labor
X-1	40%	30%
Y-1	30%	30%
Z-1	30%	40%
Total for the machining department	100%	100%
X-1	33 ⅓ %	40%
Y-1	33 ⅓%	40%
Z-1	33 ⅓%	20%
Total added by finishing department	100%	100%

The manufacturing overhead incurred by the machining department and allocated to all products therein amounted to: machining, $38,000; finishing, $42,000.

1. Compute the total costs incurred by the machining department and added by the finishing department.
2. Compute the total costs of each product that would be shown as finished-goods inventory if all the products were transferred to finished stock on completion. (There were no beginning inventories.)

11-42 Cost Allocation and Activity-Based Accounting

Quality Machining Products (QMP) is a discrete automotive component supplier. QMP has been approached by Chrysler with a proposal to significantly increase production of Part T151A to a total annual quantity of 100,000. Chrysler believes that by increasing the volume of production of Part T151A, QMP should realize the benefits of economies of scale and hence should accept a lower price than the current $6.00 per unit. Currently, QMP's gross margin on Part T151A is 3.3%, computed as follows:

	Total	Per Unit (÷ 100,000)
Direct materials	$150,000	$1.50
Direct labor	86,000	.86
Factory overhead (400% X direct labor)	344,000	3.44
Total cost	$580,000	$5.80
Sales price		6.00
Gross margin		$ .20
Gross margin percentage		3.3%

Part T151A seems to be a marginal profit product. If additional volume of production of Part T151A is to be added, QMP management believes that the sales price must be increased, not reduced as requested by Chrysler. The management of QMP sees this quoting situation as an excellent opportunity to examine the effectiveness of their traditional costing system versus an activity-based-costing system. Data have been collected by a team consisting of accounting and engineering analysts.

Activity Center: Cost Drivers	Annual Cost-Driver Quantity
Quality: number of pieces scrapped	10,000
Production scheduling and setup: number of setups	500
Shipping: number of containers shipped	60,000
Shipping administration: number of shipments	1,000
Production: number of machine hours	10,000

Activity Center	Traceable Factory Overhead Costs (Annual)
Quality	$ 800,000
Production scheduling	50,000
Setup	600,000
Shipping	300,000
Shipping administration	50,000
Production	1,500,000
Total costs	$3,300,000

The accounting and engineering team has provided the following cost-driver consumption estimates for the production of 100,000 units of Part T151A:

Cost Driver	Cost-Driver Consumption
Pieces scrapped	1,000
Setups	12
Containers shipped	500
Shipments	100
Machine hours	500

1. Prepare a schedule calculating the unit cost and gross margin of Part T151A using the activity-based-costing approach.
2. Based on the ABC results, what course of action would you recommend regarding the proposal by Chrysler? List the benefits and costs associated with implementing an activity-based-costing system at QMP.

11-43 Financial Statements for Manufacturing and Merchandising Companies
Mountain Equipment Company (MEC) and Outdoor Supplies Inc. (OSI) both sell tents. MEC purchases its tents from a manufacturer for $100 each and sells them for $130. It purchased 10,000 tents in 19X6.

OSI produces its own tents. In 19X6 OSI produced 10,000 tents. Costs were as follows:

Direct materials purchased		$ 585,000
Direct materials used		570,000
Direct labor		300,000
Factory overhead		
Depreciation	$40,000	
Indirect labor	60,000	
Other	30,000	130,000
Total cost of production		$1,000,000

Assume that OSI had no beginning inventory of direct materials. There was no beginning inventory of finished tents, but ending inventory consisted of 1,000 finished tents. Ending work-in-process inventory was negligible.

Each company sold 9,000 tents for $1,170,000 in 19X6 and incurred the following selling and administrative costs:

Sales salaries and commissions	95,000
Depreciation on retail store	30,000
Advertising	25,000
Other	10,000
Total selling and administrative cost	$160,000

1. Prepare the inventories section of the balance sheet for December 31, 19X6, for MEC.
2. Prepare the inventories section of the balance sheet for December 31, 19X6, for OSI.
3. Using Exhibit 11-4 as a model, prepare an income statement for the year 19X6 for MEC.
4. Using Exhibit 11-4 as a model, prepare an income statement for the year 19X6 for OSI.
5. Summarize the differences between the financial statements of MEC, a merchandiser, and OSI, a manufacturer.

11-44   Library Research in JIT or Activity-Based Accounting

Select an article from *Management Accounting* or *Journal of Cost Management* (available in most libraries) that describes a particular company's application of either (1) a JIT production system or (2) an activity-based accounting system. Prepare a summary of 300 words or less that includes the following:

Name of the company (if given)

Industry of the company

Description of the particular application

Assessment of the benefits the company received from the application

Any difficulties encountered in implementation

11-45   Review

The Dames Shoe Manufacturing Company provides you with the following miscellaneous data regarding operations in 19X5:

Gross profit	$ 30,000
Net loss	(10,000)
Sales	125,000
Direct material used	40,000
Direct labor	30,000
Fixed manufacturing overhead	15,000
Fixed selling and administrative expenses	15,000

There are no beginning or ending inventories.

Compute the (1) variable selling and administrative expenses, (2) contribution margin in dollars, (3) variable manufacturing overhead, (4) break-even point in sales dollars, and (5) manufacturing cost of goods sold.

11-46 Review

Sullivan Corporation provides you with the following miscellaneous data regarding operations for 19X6:

Break-even point (in sales dollars)	$125,000
Direct material used	40,000
Gross profit	25,000
Contribution margin	30,000
Direct labor	43,000
Sales	150,000
Variable manufacturing overhead	20,000

There are no beginning or ending inventories.

Compute the (1) fixed manufacturing overhead, (2) variable selling and administrative expenses, and (3) fixed selling and administrative expenses.

11-47 Review

(D. Kleespie.) U. Grant Company manufactured and sold 1,000 sabres during October. Selected data for this month follow:

Sales	$160,000
Direct materials used	42,000
Direct labor	38,000
Variable manufacturing overhead	22,000
Fixed manufacturing overhead	14,000
Variable selling and administrative expenses	?
Fixed selling and administrative expenses	?
Contribution margin	40,000
Operating income	19,000

There were no beginning or ending inventories.

1. What were the variable selling and administrative expenses for October?
2. What were the fixed selling and administrative expenses for October?
3. What was the cost of goods sold under absorption costing during October?
4. Without prejudice to your earlier answers, assume that the fixed selling and administrative expenses for October amounted to $12,000.
   a. What was the break-even point in units for October?
   b. How many units must be sold to earn a target operating income of $14,000?
   c. What would the selling price per unit have to be if the company wanted to earn an operating income of $14,500 on the sale of 900 units?

11-48 Payroll Fringe Costs

Study the Appendix in this chapter. Direct labor is often accounted for at the gross wage rate, and the related "fringe costs," such as employer payroll taxes and employee contributions to health care plans, are accounted for as part of overhead. Suppose Amy O'Keefe, a direct laborer, works 40 hours during a particular week as an auditor for a public accounting firm. She receives $18 gross pay per hour plus related fringe costs of $10 per hour.

1. What would be the weekly cost of O'Keefe's direct labor? Of related general overhead?

2. Suppose O'Keefe works 30 hours for Client A and 10 hours for Client B, and the firm allocates costs to each client. What would be the cost of O'Keefe's "direct labor" on the Client A job? The Client B job?

3. How would you allocate general overhead to the Client A job? The Client B job?

4. Suppose O'Keefe works a total of 50 hours (30 for Client A and 20 for Client B), 10 of which are paid on a time-and-one-half basis. What would be the cost of O'Keefe's "direct labor" on the Client A job? The Client B job? The addition to general overhead?

Cases

11-49 Identifying Activities, Resources, and Cost Drivers in Manufacturing
Extrusion Plastics is a multinational, diversified organization. One of its manufacturing divisions, Northeast Plastics Division, has become less profitable due to increased competition. The division produces three major lines of plastic products within its single plant. Product Line A is high-volume, simple pieces produced in large batches. Product Line B is medium-volume, more complex pieces. Product Line C is low-volume, small-order, highly complex pieces.

Currently, the division allocates indirect manufacturing costs based on direct labor. The V.P. Manufacturing is uncomfortable using the traditional cost figures. He thinks the company is under-pricing the more complex products. He decides to conduct an activity-based costing analysis of the business.

Interviews were conducted with the key managers in order to identify activities, resources, cost drivers, and their interrelationships.

Interviewee: Production Manager

Q1: What activities are carried out in your area?

A1: *All products are manufactured using three similar, complex, and expensive molding machines. Each molding machine can be used in the production of the three product lines. Each setup takes about the same time irrespective of the product.*

Q2: Who works in your area?

A2: *Last year, we employed thirty machine operators, two maintenance mechanics, and two supervisors.*

Q3: How are the operators used in the molding process?

A3: *It requires nine operators to support a machine during the actual production process.*

Q4: What do the maintenance mechanics do?

A4: *Their primary function is to perform machine setups. However, they were also required to provide machine maintenance during the molding process.*

Q5: Where do the supervisors spend their time?

A5: *They provide supervision for the machine operators and the maintenance mechanics. For the most part, the supervisors appear to spend the same amount of time with each of the employees that they supervise.*

Q6: What other resources are used to support manufacturing?

A6: *The molding machines use energy during the molding process and during the setups. We put meters on the molding machines to get a better understanding of their energy consumption. We discovered that for each hour that a machine ran, it used 6.3 kilowatts of energy. The machines also require consumable shop supplies (e.g., lubricants, hoses, etc.). We have found a direct correlation between the amount of supplies used and the actual processing time.*

Q7: How is the building used, and what costs are associated with it?

A7: *We have a 100,000-square-foot building. The total rent and insurance costs for the year were $675,000. These costs are allocated to production, sales, and administration based on square footage.*

1. Identify the activities, resources, and cost drivers for the division.
2. For each resource identified in requirement 1, indicate its cost behavior with respect to the activities it supports (assume a planning period of 1 month).

11-50 Analysis with Contribution Income Statement

The following data have been condensed from Chateau Corporation's report of 19X5 operations (in millions of French francs [FF]):

	Variable	Fixed	Total
Manufacturing cost of goods sold	FF420	FF200	FF620
Selling and administrative expenses	150	70	220
Sales			950

1. Prepare the 19X5 income statement in contribution form, ignoring income taxes.
2. Chateau's operations have been fairly stable from year to year. In planning for the future, top management is considering several options for changing the annual pattern of operations. You are asked to perform an analysis of their estimated effects. Use your contribution income statement as a framework to compute the estimated operating income (in millions) under each of the following separate and unrelated assumptions.
   a. Assume that a 10% reduction in selling prices would cause a 40% increase in the physical volume of goods manufactured and sold.
   b. Assume that an annual expenditure of FF30 million for a special sales promotion campaign would enable the company to increase its physical volume by 10% with no change in selling prices.
   c. Assume that a basic redesign of manufacturing operations would increase annual fixed manufacturing costs by FF80 million and decrease variable manufacturing costs by 15% *per product unit*, but with no effect on physical volume or selling prices.
   d. Assume that a basic redesign of selling and administrative operations would double the annual fixed expenses for selling and administration and increase the variable expenses for selling and administration by 25% *per product unit*, but would also increase physical volume by 20%. Selling prices would be increased by 5%.
   e. Would you prefer to use the absorption form of income statement for the preceding analyses? Explain.
3. Discuss the desirability of alternatives *a* through *d* in requirement 2. If only one alternative could be selected, which would you choose? Explain.

COST ALLOCATION IN GENERAL

Cost allocation is fundamentally a problem of linking some cost or group of costs with one or more *cost objectives*, such as products, departments, customer classes, activities, and divisions. Ideally, cost allocation should assign each cost to the cost objective that *caused* it.

The linking of costs with cost objectives is accomplished by selecting cost drivers, activities that cause costs. When used for allocating costs, a cost driver is often called a **cost-allocation base**. Major costs, such as newsprint for a newspaper and direct professional labor for a law firm, may be allocated to departments, jobs, and projects on an item-by-item basis using obvious cost drivers such as tons of newsprint consumed or direct-labor-hours used. Other costs, taken one at a time, are not important enough to justify being allocated individually. These costs are *pooled* and then allocated together. A **cost pool** is a group of individual costs that is allocated to *cost objectives* using a single cost driver. For example, building rent, utilities cost, and janitorial services may be in the same cost pool because all are allocated on the basis of square footage of space occupied. Or a university could pool all the operating costs of its registrar's office and allocate them to its colleges on the basis of the number of students in each college. In summary, all costs in a given cost pool should be caused by the same factor. That factor is the cost driver.

Many different terms are used to describe cost allocation in practice. You may encounter terms such as *allocate, attribute, reallocate, trace, assign, distribute, redistribute, load, burden, apportion,* and *reapportion* being used interchangeably to describe the allocation of costs to cost objectives. The terms *apply* or *absorb* tend to have the narrower meaning of costs allocated to products rather than to departments or divisions.

Four Purposes of Allocation

What logic should be used for allocating costs? This question bothers many internal users and suppliers of services in all organizations. The answer depends on the principal purpose(s) of the cost allocation.

Costs are allocated for four major purposes.

1. *To predict the economic effects of planning and control decisions*: Managers within an organizational unit should be aware of all the consequences of their decisions, even consequences outside of their unit. Examples are the addition of a new course in a university that causes additional work in the registrar's office, the addition of a new flight or an additional passenger on an airline that requires reservation and booking services, and the addition of a new specialty in a medical clinic that produces more work for the medical records department.

2. *To obtain desired motivation*: Cost allocations are sometimes made to influence management behavior and, thus, promote goal congruence and managerial effort. Consequently, in some organizations there is no cost allocation for legal or internal auditing services or internal management consulting services because top management wants to encourage their use. In other organizations there is a cost allocation for such items to spur managers to make sure the benefits of the specified services exceed the costs.

3. *To compute income and asset valuations*: Costs are allocated to products and projects to measure inventory costs and cost of goods sold. These allocations frequently serve finan-

cial accounting purposes. However, the resulting costs also are often used by managers in planning and performance evaluation.

4. *To justify costs or obtain reimbursement*: Sometimes prices are based directly on costs. For example, government contracts often specify a price that includes reimbursement for costs plus some profit margin. In these instances, cost allocations become substitutes for the usual working of the marketplace in setting prices.

The first two purposes specify planning and control uses for allocation. Purposes 3 and 4 show how cost allocations may differ for inventory costing (and cost of goods sold) and for setting prices. Moreover, different allocations of costs to products may be made for the various purposes. Thus, full costs may guide pricing decisions (purpose 1), manufacturing costs may be proper for asset valuations (purpose 3), and some "in-between" cost may be negotiated for a government contract (purpose 4).

Ideally, all four purposes would be served simultaneously by a single cost allocation. But thousands of managers and accountants will testify that for most costs this ideal is rarely achieved. Instead, cost allocations are often a major source of discontent and confusion to the affected parties. Allocating fixed costs usually causes the greatest problems. When all four purposes cannot be attained simultaneously, the manager and the accountant should start attacking a cost-allocation problem by trying to identify which of the purposes should dominate in the particular situation at hand.

Often inventory-costing purposes dominate by default because they are externally imposed. When allocated costs are used in decision making and performance evaluation, managers should consider adjusting the allocations used to satisfy inventory-costing purposes. Often the added benefit of using separate allocations for planning and control and inventory-costing purposes is much greater than the added cost.

Three Types of Allocations

As Exhibit 11-16 shows, there are three basic types of cost allocations.

1. *Allocation of costs to the appropriate organizational unit*: Direct costs are physically traced to the unit, but costs used jointly by more than one unit are allocated based on cost-driver activity in the unit. Examples are allocating rent to departments based on floor space occupied, allocating depreciation on jointly used machinery based on machine-hours, and allocating general administrative expense based on total direct cost.

2. *Reallocation of costs from one organizational unit to another*: When one unit provides products or services to another, the costs are transferred along with the products or services. Some units, called **service departments**, exist only to support other departments, and their costs are totally reallocated. Examples include personnel departments, laundry departments in hospitals, and legal departments in industrial firms.

3. *Allocation of costs of a particular organizational unit or activity to products or services*: The pediatrics department of a medical clinic allocates its costs to patient visits, the assembly department of a manufacturing firm to units assembled, and the tax department of a CPA firm to clients served. The costs allocated to products or services include those allocated to the organizational unit in allocation types 1 and 2.

The major focus of this chapter is on type 2, the reallocation of costs from one organizational unit to another. However, all three types of allocations are fundamentally similar. Let us look first at how service department costs are allocated to production departments.

Exhibit 11-16   Three Types of Cost Allocations

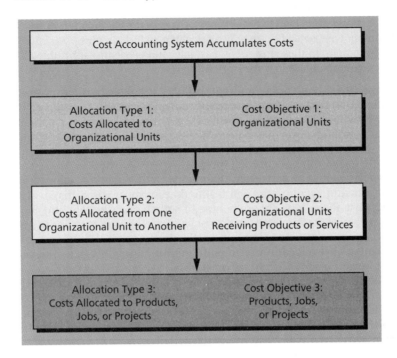

ALLOCATION OF SERVICE DEPARTMENT COSTS

Ideally, costs are allocated to organizational units because some activity in the unit caused the cost to be incurred. Therefore, a cost allocation system should focus on the causes of costs—the cost drivers.

General Guidelines

What causes costs? Organizations incur costs to produce goods and services and to provide the support services required for that production. Essentially, costs are *caused* by the very same activities that are usually chosen as cost objectives. Examples are products produced, patients seen, orders processed, and legal consultations. The ultimate *effects* of these activities are various costs. It is important to understand how cost behavior relates to activities and the consumption of resources. To perform activities, resources are required. These resources have costs. Some costs vary in direct proportion to the consumption of resources. Examples are energy and supplies. Other costs do not vary (in the short run) with resource use. Examples are depreciation, supervisory salaries, and occupancy (rent, insurance). So we say that activities consume resources and the costs of these resources follow various behavioral patterns. When the manager and accountant search for cost drivers, they should focus on the relationship between activities and the consumption of resources. It is important to understand that cost drivers relate activities to the consumption of resources. Therefore, the manager and the accountant should search for some cost driver that establishes a convincing relationship between the cause (activities being performed) and the effect (consumption of resources and related costs) and that permits *reliable predictions* of how costs will be affected by decisions regarding the activities.

To illustrate this important principle, we will consider allocation of service department costs. The preferred guidelines for allocating service department costs are as follows:

1. *Evaluate performance using budgets* for each service (staff) department, just as for each production or operating (line) department. The performance of a service department is evaluated by comparing actual costs with a budget, independent of how the costs are later allocated. From the budget, variable-cost pools and fixed-cost pools can be identified for use in allocation.

2. *Allocate variable- and fixed-cost pools separately* (sometimes called the dual method of allocation). Note that one service department (such as a computer department) can contain multiple cost pools if more than one cost driver causes the department's costs. At a minimum, there should be a variable-cost pool and a fixed-cost pool.

3. *Establish part or all of the details regarding cost allocation in advance* of rendering the service rather than after the fact. This approach establishes the "rules of the game" so that all departments can plan appropriately.

Consider a simplified example of a computer department of a university that serves two major users, the School of Business and the School of Engineering. The computer mainframe was acquired on a 5-year lease that is not cancelable unless prohibitive cost penalties are paid.

How should the costs of the computer department (salaries, depreciation, energy, materials, etc.) be allocated to the user departments? Suppose there are two major purposes for the allocation: (1) predicting economic effects of the use of the computer, and (2) motivating departments and individuals to use its capabilities more fully.

To apply the first of the preceding guidelines, we need to analyze the costs of the computer department in detail. The primary activity performed is computer processing. Resources consumed include processing time, operator time, consulting time, energy, materials, and building space. Suppose cost behavior analysis has been performed and the budget formula for the forthcoming year is $100,000 monthly fixed cost plus $200 variable cost per hour of computer time used. Applying both guidelines 2 and 3 is the topic of the next two sections.

Variable-Cost Pool

The cost driver for the variable-cost pool is *hours of computer time used*. Therefore, variable costs should be allocated as follows:

budgeted unit rate × actual hours of computer time used

The cause-and-effect relationship is clear: The heavier the usage, the higher the total costs. In this example, the rate used would be the budgeted rate of $200 per hour.

The use of *budgeted* cost rates rather than *actual* cost rates for allocating variable costs of service departments protects the using departments from intervening price fluctuations and also often protects them from inefficiencies in the service departments. When an organization allocates *actual* total service department cost, it holds user department managers responsible for costs beyond their control and provides less incentive for service departments to be efficient. Both effects are undesirable.

Consider the allocation of *variable* costs to a department that uses 600 hours of computer time. Suppose inefficiencies in the computer department caused the variable costs to be $140,000 instead of the 600 hours × $200, or $120,000 budgeted. A good cost-allocation scheme would allocate only the $120,000 to the consuming departments and would let the $20,000 remain as an unallocated, unfavorable budget variance of the computer department. This scheme holds computer department managers responsible for the $20,000 variance and reduces the resentment of user managers. User department managers sometimes complain more vigorously about uncertainty over allocations and the poor management of a service department than about the choice of a cost driver (such as direct-labor dollars or number of employees). Such complaints are less likely if the service department managers have budget responsibility and the user departments are protected from short-run price fluctuations and inefficiencies.

Most consumers prefer to know the total price in advance. They become nervous when an automobile mechanic or contractor undertakes a job without specifying prices. As a minimum, they like to know the hourly rates that they must bear. Therefore, predetermined unit prices (at least) should be used. When feasible, predetermined total prices should be used for various kinds of work based on budgets and standards.

To illustrate, consider an automobile repair and maintenance department for a state government. Agencies who use the department's service should receive firm prices for various services. Imagine the feelings of an agency head who had an agency automobile repaired and was told, "Normally your repair would have taken 5 hours. However, we had a new employee work on it and the job took him 10 hours. Therefore, we must charge you for 10 hours of labor time."

Fixed-Cost Pool

The cost driver for the fixed-cost pool is the amount of capacity required when the computer facilities were acquired. Therefore, fixed costs should be allocated as follows:

budgeted percent of capacity available for use × total budgeted fixed costs

Consider again our example of the university computer department. Suppose the deans had originally predicted the long-run average monthly usage by Business at 210 hours, and by Engineering at 490 hours, a total of 700 hours. The fixed-cost pool would be allocated as follows:

	Business	Engineering
Fixed costs per month		
210/700, or 30% of $100,000	$30,000	
490/700, or 70% of $100,000		$70,000

This predetermined lump-sum approach is based on the long-run capacity *available* to the user, regardless of actual usage from month to month. The reasoning is that the level of fixed costs is affected by *long-range* planning regarding the overall level of service and the *relative expected* usage, not by *short-run* fluctuations in service levels and *relative actual* usage.

A major strength of using capacity *available* rather than capacity *used* when allocating *budgeted* fixed costs is that short-run allocations to user departments are not affected by the *actual* usage of *other* user departments. Such a budgeted lump-sum approach is more likely to have the desired motivational effects with respect to the ordering of services in both the short run and the long run.

In practice, fixed-cost pools often are inappropriately allocated on the basis of capacity used, not capacity available. Suppose the computer department allocated the total actual costs after the fact. At the end of the month, total *actual* costs would be allocated in proportion to the *actual* hours used by the consuming departments. Compare the costs borne by the two schools when Business uses 200 hours and Engineering 400 hours:

Total costs incurred, $100,000 + 600($200) = $220,000	
Business: 200/600 × $220,000 =	$ 73,333
Engineering: 400/600 × $220,000 =	146,667
Total cost allocated	$220,000

What happens if Business uses only 100 hours during the following month, and Engineering still uses 400 hours?

Total costs incurred, $100,000 + 500($200) = $200,000	
Business: 100/500 × $200,000 =	$ 40,000
Engineering: 400/500 × $200,000 =	160,000
Total cost allocated	$200,000

Engineering has done nothing differently, but it must bear higher costs of $13,333, an increase of 9%. Its short-run costs depend on what other consumers have used, not solely on its own actions. This phenomenon is caused by a faulty allocation method for the *fixed* portion of total costs, a method whereby the allocations are highly sensitive to fluctuations in the actual volumes used by the various consuming departments. This weakness is avoided by using a predetermined lump-sum allocation of fixed costs, based on budgeted usage.

Consider another example, the automobile repair shop example introduced on page 408. You would not be happy if you came to get your car and were told, "Our daily fixed overhead is $1,000. Yours was the only car in our shop today, so we are charging you the full $1,000. If we had processed 100 cars today, your charge would have been only $10."

Troubles with Using Lump Sums

Using lump-sum allocations can cause problems, however. If fixed costs are allocated on the basis of long-range plans, there is a natural tendency on the part of consumers to underestimate their planned usage and thus obtain a smaller fraction of the cost allocation. Top management can counteract these tendencies by monitoring predictions and by following up and using feedback to keep future predictions more honest.

In some organizations there are even definite rewards in the form of salary increases for managers who make accurate predictions. Moreover, some cost-allocation methods provide for penalties for underpredictions. For example, suppose a manager predicts usage of 210 hours and then demands 300 hours. The manager either doesn't get the hours or pays a dear price for every hour beyond 210 in such systems.

Allocation of Central Costs

The seeming need to allocate central costs is a manifestation of a widespread, deep-seated belief that all costs must somehow be fully allocated to the revenue-producing (operating) parts of the organization. Such allocations are neither necessary from an accounting viewpoint nor useful as management information. However, most managers accept them as a fact of a manager's life—as long as all managers seem to be treated alike and thus "fairly."

Whenever possible, the preferred cost driver for central services is usage, either actual or estimated. But the costs of such services as public relations, top corporate management overhead, a real estate department, and a corporate-planning department are the least likely to be allocated on the basis of usage. Data processing, advertising, and operations research are the most likely to choose usage as a cost driver.

Companies that allocate central costs by usage tend to generate less resentment. Consider the experience of J. C. Penney Co. as reported in *Business Week*:

> The controller's office wanted subsidiaries such as Thrift Drug Co. and the insurance operations to base their share of corporate personnel, legal, and auditing costs on their revenues. The subsidiaries contended that they maintained their own personnel and legal departments, and should be assessed far less. . . . The subcommittee addressed the issue by asking the corporate departments to approximate the time and costs involved in servicing the subsidiaries. The final allocation plan, based on these studies, cost the divisions less than they were initially assessed but more than they had wanted to pay. Nonetheless, the plan was implemented easily.

Usage is not always an economically viable way to allocate central costs, however. Also, many central costs, such as the president's salary and related expenses, public relations, legal services, income tax planning, company-wide advertising, and basic research, are difficult to allocate on the basis of cause and effect. As a result, some companies use cost drivers, such as the revenue of each division, the cost of goods sold by each division, the total assets of each division, or the total costs of each division (before allocation of the central costs) to allocate central costs.

The use of the foregoing cost drivers might provide a *rough* indication of cause-and-effect relationship. Basically, however, they represent an "ability to bear" philosophy of cost allocation. For example, the costs of company-wide advertising, such as the goodwill sponsorship of a program on a noncommercial television station, might be allocated to all products and divisions on the basis of the dollar sales in each. But such costs precede sales. They are discretionary costs as determined by management policies, not by sales results. Although 60 percent of the companies in a large survey treat sales revenue as a cost driver for cost allocation purposes, it is seldom truly a cost driver in the sense of being an activity that *causes* the costs.

Use of Budgeted Sales for Allocation

If the costs of central services are to be allocated based on sales even though the costs do not vary in proportion to sales, the use of *budgeted* sales is preferable to the use of *actual* sales. At least this method means that the short-run costs of a given consuming department will not be affected by the fortunes of other consuming departments.

For example, suppose $100 of fixed central advertising costs were allocated on the basis of potential sales in two territories:

| | Territories | | | |
	A	B	Total	Percent
Budgeted sales	$500	$500	$1,000	100
Central advertising allocated	$ 50	$ 50	$ 100	10

Consider the possible differences in allocations when actual sales become known:

| | Territories | |
	A	B
Actual sales	$300	$600
Central advertising		
1. Allocated on basis of budgeted sales	$ 50	$ 50
or		
2. Allocated on basis of actual sales	$ 33	$ 67

Compare allocation 1 with 2. Allocation 1 is preferable. It indicates a low ratio of sales to advertising in territory A. It directs attention where it is deserved. In contrast, allocation 2 soaks territory B with more advertising cost because of the *achieved* results and relieves territory A despite its lower success. This is another example of the analytical confusion that can arise when cost allocations to one consuming department depend on the activity of other consuming departments.

Reciprocal Services

Service departments often support other service departments in addition to producing departments. Consider a manufacturing company with two producing departments, molding and finishing, and two service departments, facilities management (rent, heat, light, janitorial services, etc.) and personnel. All costs in a given service department are assumed to be caused by, and therefore vary in proportion to, a single cost driver. The company has decided that the best cost driver for facilities management costs is square footage occupied and the best cost driver for personnel is the number of employees.

Exhibit 11-2b shows the direct costs, square footage occupied, and number of employees for each department. Note that facilities management provides services for the personnel department in addition to providing services for the producing departments, and that personnel aids employees in facilities management as well as those in production departments.

Exhibit 11-2b Cost Drivers

| | Service Departments | | Production Departments | |
	Facilities Management	Personnel	Molding	Finishing
Direct department costs	$126,000	$24,000	$100,000	$160,000
Square feet	3,000	9,000	15,000	3,000
Number of employees	20	30	80	320
Direct-labor hours			2,100	10,000
Machine-hours			30,000	5,400

There are two popular methods for allocating service department costs in such cases: the direct method and the step-down method.

Direct Method

As its name implies, the **direct method** ignores other service departments when any given service department's costs are allocated to the revenue-producing (operating) departments. In other words, the fact that facilities management provides services for personnel is ignored, as is the support that personnel provides to facilities management. Facilities management costs are allocated based on the relative square footage occupied *by the production departments only*:

- Total square footage in production departments: 15,000 + 3,000 = 18,000
- Facilities management cost allocated to molding = (15,000 ÷ 18,000) × $126,000 = $105,000
- Facilities management cost allocated to finishing = (3,000 ÷ 18,000) × $126,000 = $21,000

Likewise, personnel department costs are allocated *only to the production departments* on the basis of the relative number of employees in the production departments:

- Total employees in production departments = 80 + 320 = 400
- Personnel costs allocated to molding = (80 ÷ 400) × $24,000 = $4,800
- Personnel costs allocated to finishing = (320 ÷ 400) × $24,000 = $19,200

Step-down Method

The **step-down method** recognizes that some service departments support the activities in other service departments as well as those in production departments. A sequence of allocations is chosen, usually by starting with the service department that renders the greatest service (as measured by costs) to the greatest number of other service departments. The last service department in the sequence is the one that renders the least service to the least number of other service departments. Once a department's costs are allocated to other departments, no subsequent service department costs are allocated back to it.

In our example, facilities management costs are allocated first. Why? Because facilities management renders more support to personnel than personnel provides for facilities management. Examine Exhibit 11-3b. After facilities management costs are allocated, no costs are allocated back to facilities management, even though personnel does provide some services for facilities management. The personnel costs to be allocated to the production departments include the amount allocated to personnel from facilities management ($42,000) in addition to the direct personnel department costs of $24,000.

Examine the last column of Exhibit 11-3b. Before allocation, the four departments incurred costs of $410,000. In step 1, $126,000 was deducted from facilities management and added to the other three departments. There was no net effect on the total cost. In step 2, $66,000 was deducted from personnel and added to the remaining two departments. Again, total cost was unaffected. After allocation, all $410,000 remains, but it is all in molding and finishing. None was left in facilities management or personnel.

Exhibit 11-3b Step-Down Allocation

	Facilities Management	Personnel	Molding	Finishing	Total
Direct department costs before allocation $410,000	$ 126,000	$ 24,000	$100,000	$160,000	
Step 1					
Facilities management	$(126,000)	$(9 \div 27) \times \$126,000$ = $ 42,000	$(15 \div 27) \times \$126,000$ = $ 70,000	$(3 \div 27) \times \$126,000$ = $ 14,000	0
Step 2					
Personnel		$(66,000)	$(80 \div 400) \times \$66,000$ = $ 13,200	$(320 \div 400) \times \$66,000$ = $ 52,800	0
Total cost after allocation	$ 0	$ 0	$ 183,200	$ 226,800	$

Compare the costs of the production departments under direct and step-down methods, as shown in Exhibit 11-4b. Note that the method of allocation can greatly affect the costs. Molding appears to be a much more expensive operation to a manager using the direct method than to one using the step-down method. Conversely, finishing seems more expensive to a manager using the step-down method.

Which method is better? Generally, the step-down method. Why? Because it recognizes the effects of the most significant support provided by service departments to other service departments. In our example, the direct method ignores the following possible cause-effect link: If the cost of facilities management is caused by the space used, then the space used by personnel causes $42,000 of facilities management cost. If the space used in personnel is caused by the number of production department employees supported, then the number of production department employees, not the square footage, causes $42,000 of the facilities management cost. The producing department with the most employees, not the one with the most square footage, should bear this cost.

Exhibit 11-4b Direct Versus Step-Down Method

	Molding		Finishing	
	Direct	*Step-down*	*Direct*	*Step-down*
Direct department costs	$100,000	$100,000	$160,000	$160,000
Allocated from facilities management	105,000	70,000	21,000	14,000
Allocated from personnel	4,800	13,200	19,200	52,800
Total costs	$209,800	$183,200	$200,200	$226,800

The greatest virtue of the direct method is its simplicity. If the two methods do not produce significantly different results, many companies elect the direct method because it is easier for managers to understand.

Costs Not Related to Cost Drivers

Our example illustrating direct and step-down allocation methods assumed that a single cost driver caused all costs in a given service department. For example, we assumed that square footage occupied caused all facilities management costs. Additional square footage would result in additional facilities management cost. But what if some of the costs in facilities management are independent of square footage?

Three alternative methods of allocation should be considered:

1. Identify additional cost drivers. Divide facilities management costs into two or more different cost pools and use a different cost driver to allocate the costs in each pool.

2. Divide facilities management costs into two cost pools, one with costs that vary in proportion to the square footage (variable costs) and one with costs not affected by square footage (fixed costs). Allocate the former using the direct or step-down method, but do not allocate the latter. Costs not allocated are period costs for the organization but are not regarded as a cost of a particular production department.

3. Allocate all costs by the direct or step-down method using square footage as the cost driver. This alternative implicitly assumes that, in the long run, square footage causes all facilities management costs—even if a short-term causal relationship is not easily identifiable. In other words, using more square footage may not cause an immediate increase in all facilities management costs, but eventually such costs will creep up in proportion to increases in square footage.

Suppose that most costs in a service department are caused by a single cost driver. Then alternatives 2 and 3 have much appeal. Only a small portion of costs would be unallocated (in alternative 2) or arbitrarily allocated (in alternative 3). But if large amounts of cost are not related to the single cost driver, alternative 1 should be seriously considered.

ALLOCATION OF COSTS TO OUTPUTS

Up to this point, we have concentrated on cost allocation to divisions, departments, and similar segments of an entity. Cost allocation is almost always carried one step further—to the outputs of these departments, however defined. Examples are *products*, such as automobiles, furniture, and newspapers, and *services*, such as banking, health care, and education. Sometimes the allocation of total departmental costs to the revenue-producing products or services is called **cost application** or *cost attribution*.

Costs are allocated to products for inventory valuation purposes and for decision purposes such as pricing, adding products, and promoting products. Cost allocation is also performed for cost-reimbursement purposes. As noted earlier, many defense contractors are reimbursed for the "costs" of producing products for the government.

General Approach

The general approach to allocating costs to final products or services is the following:

1. Allocate production-related costs to the operating (line), or production or revenue-producing departments. This includes allocating service department costs to the production departments. The production departments then contain all the costs: their direct department costs and the service department costs.

2. Select one or more cost drivers in each production department. Historically most companies have used only one cost driver per department. Recently a large number of companies have started using multiple cost pools and multiple cost drivers within a department. For example, a portion of the departmental costs may be allocated on the basis of direct-labor hours, another portion on the basis of machine-hours, and the remainder on the basis of number of machine setups.

3. Allocate (apply) the total costs accumulated in step 1 to products or services that are the outputs of the operating departments using the cost drivers specified in step 2. If only one cost driver is used, two cost pools should be maintained, one for variable costs and one for fixed costs. Variable costs should be allocated on the basis of actual cost-driver activity. Fixed costs should either remain unallocated or be allocated on the basis of budgeted cost-driver activity.

Consider our manufacturing example, and assume that the step-down method was used to allocate service department costs. Exhibit 11-3b showed total costs of $183,200 accumulated in molding and $226,800 in finishing. Note that all $410,000 total manufacturing costs reside in the production departments. To allocate these costs to the products produced, cost drivers must be selected for each department. We will use a single cost driver for each department and assume that all costs are caused by that cost driver. Suppose machine-hours is the best measure of what causes costs in the molding department, and direct-labor hours drive costs in finishing. Exhibit 11-2b showed 30,000 total machine-hours used in molding and 10,000 direct-labor hours in finishing. Therefore, costs are allocated to products as follows:

Molding: $183,200 ÷ 30,000 machine-hours = $6.11 per machine-hour
Finishing: $226,800 ÷ 10,000 direct-labor hours = $22.68 per direct-labor hour

A product that takes 4 machine-hours in molding and 2 direct-labor hours in finishing would have a cost of

$$(4 \times \$6.11) + (2 \times \$22.68) = \$24.44 + \$45.36 = \$69.80$$

ACTIVITY-BASED COSTING (ABC)

In the past, most departments used direct-labor hours as the only cost driver for applying costs to products. But the use of direct-labor hours is not a very good measure of the cause of costs in modern, highly automated departments. Labor-related costs in an automated system may be only 5% to 10% of the total manufacturing costs and often are not related to the causes of most manufacturing overhead costs. Therefore, many companies are implementing *activity-based costing* to develop measures that better reflect the consumption of resources and related costs in their environment.

Principles of Activity-Based Costing

Many managers in modern manufacturing firms and automated service companies believe it is inappropriate to allocate all costs based on measures of volume. Using direct-labor hours or cost—or even machine-hours—as the only cost driver seldom meets the cause-effect criterion desired in cost allocation. If many costs are caused by non-volume-based cost drivers, activity-based costing (ABC) should be considered. Recall that activity-based costing is a system that first accumulates the costs of each activity of an organization and then applies the costs of activities to the products, services, or other cost objects using appropriate cost drivers.

The goal of activity-based costing is to trace costs to products or services instead of arbitrarily allocating them. Direct materials and direct labor are directly traced to products because there is a physical measure of their consumption by a particular product. In activity-based costing, by using appropriate cost drivers, many manufacturing overhead costs can be accurately traced to products or services. For example, in traditional systems, engineering design costs are often part of an overhead cost pool that is allocated based on direct-labor hours. In many activity-based costing systems, such costs are assigned to products in proportion to the engineering design services received by the products.

To apply activity-based costing, an organization must first engage in *activity analysis*. Managers identify the major activities undertaken by each department, as well as the resources consumed and select a cost driver for each activity. The cost driver should be a quantifiable measure of what causes resources to be used. In essence, the costs of the resources used to support a particular activity become a cost pool, and the cost driver is used to allocate the costs to products or services.

Most cost drivers are measures of the number of transactions involved in a particular activity. Therefore, activity-based costing is also called **transaction-based costing**. Examples of transactions that serve as cost drivers are production orders, material requisitions, machine setups, product inspections, material shipments received, and orders shipped. Low-volume products usually cause more transactions per unit of output than do high-volume products. Highly complex manufacturing processes have more transactions than do simple processes. If resources are used as a result of the number of transactions, allocations based totally on volume will assign too much cost to high-volume, low-complexity products and vice versa.

In activity-based costing systems, costs are not classified as either direct or indirect. They can fall at any point on a spectrum between a direct physical tracing and arbitrary allocation. Sophisticated and costly systems identify many activities, resources, and cost drivers so that most costs can be physically traced to products or services. Because of cost-benefit considerations, other activity-based costing systems have fewer activities, resources, and cost drivers. Such systems physically trace more costs to products than do traditional systems, but many costs continue to be allocated based on cost drivers that are only partly related to the consumption of resources.

Why are activity-based costing systems becoming popular? For two main reasons. First, the profitability of products and customers is more accurately measured by an activity-based costing system. As global competition increases, product mix, pricing, and other decisions require better product cost information.

In addition, many managers have discovered that control of costs is best accomplished by focusing directly on efficient use of activities, not by focusing on products. For example, savings might be possible in the material-handling activity. This opportunity is seen most readily from activity-based costs, and incentives for improvement are more effective if the costs of the activity are being specifically measured and reported. Identifying cost drivers also reveals the possible cost reductions from limiting the number of transactions. For instance, if some costs are driven by the number of components in a final product, costs can be reduced by designing products with fewer components.

Notice that the main advantages of an activity-based costing system come from its use for planning and control.

Illustration of Activity-Based Costing

A previous section introduced a four-step procedure for the design and implementation of activity-based-costing systems. We consider this same four-step procedure for the Molding Department of a manufacturing company that produces plastic parts using injection molding machines. The molding process produces three product lines with diverse demands on various activities and resources. Product line A consists of simple products that are produced in high volume (tape holders). Line B products are of medium volume and complexity (flashlight casings). Product line C consists of complex products that are produced in small lots (small camera casings). The former costing system allocated factory overhead costs based on the amount of direct-labor hours used to produce each product. The rate used to allocate factory overhead was $27 per direct-labor hour. This rate was calculated by dividing the total expected factory overhead ($1,080,000) by the total expected direct-labor hours (40,000). Product line C was allocated $6 \div 40 = 15\%$ of total overhead resource costs since 6,000 of the 40,000 total direct-labor hours were required to produce 150,000 units of C. The use of this volume-based driver to allocate factory overhead (indirect) cost resulted in the unit cost for the three product lines shown in Exhibit 11-5b.

Management changed to activity-based costing in this manufacturing department. Product line C is typical of complex products that require relatively more indirect resources from setup and machining activity. Management believed that the former costing system may have undercosted such products. A study was performed to determine the activity-based costs for the three product lines.

Exhibit 11-5b   Product Cost Based on Former Costing System

	Product Line A	Product Line B	Product Line C
Direct material	$1,050,000	$ 575,000	$240,000
Direct labor (operators)	344,000	303,000	123,000
Factory overhead @ $27 per DLH			
Product line A (18,000 DLH)	486,000		
Product line B (16,000 DLH)		432,000	
Product line C (6,000 DLH)			162,000
Total cost	$1,880,000	$1,310,000	$525,000
Units produced	1,000,000	500,000	150,000
Unit cost	$ 1.88	$ 2.62	$ 3.50

Step 1: Determine the cost objective, key activity centers, resources, and related cost drivers. The costing objective is to determine the costs of product lines A, B, and C. Direct material and direct labor (machine operators) are traced directly to each product. The remaining overhead resources are listed in Exhibit 11-6b together with the two activity centers and chosen cost drivers.

Step 2: Develop a process-based map representing the flow of activities, resources, and their interrelationships. Based on interviews with key personnel, the interrelationships between activities and resources were determined. Exhibit 11-7b depicts the flow of activities and resources. Note that the cost behavior for each resource is also shown. Understanding the cost behavior of resources is vital during the planning process. For example, if the volume of product line A is expected to increase (within the relevant range of activity), machine-hours and the number of setups would increase. However, the only costs that would be expected to increase are direct materials, supplies, and energy since they are variable-cost resources (*VR*). Since the remaining resources are fixed-cost resources (*FR*), their costs would not increase in response to increased setups or machine hours.

Exhibit 11-6b   Activity Centers, Cost Drivers, and Resources Molding Department

Activity Center	Cost Driver	Resources Consumed
Setup	Number of setups	Maintenance mechanic time
		Supervisor time
		Energy (machines had to remain on during setup activity)
		Occupancy space
		Molding machine time
Molding process	Machine hours	Supplies
		Energy
		Supervisor time
		Molding machine time
		Occupancy space
		Maintenance mechanic time

Exhibit 11-7b Process-Based Map of the Molding Department Operations

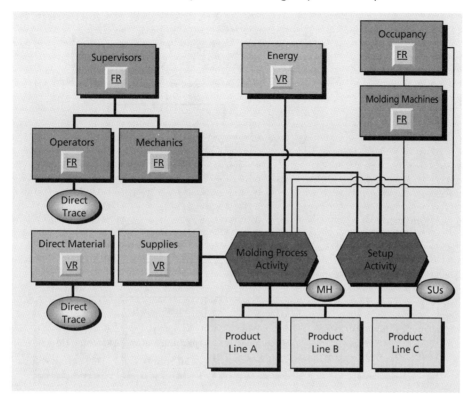

Step 3: Collect relevant data concerning costs and the physical flow of cost-driver units among resources and activities. Using the process map as a guide, accountants collected the required cost and operational data by further interviews with relevant personnel.

Exhibit 11-8b is a graphical representation and summary of the data collected for the two activity centers identified in Step 1. For each activity center, data collected included traceable overhead costs and the physical flow of cost-driver units.

Step 4: Calculate and interpret the new activity-based information. Exhibit 11-9b shows the computations to determine the cost per unit for each product line. The results of the study confirmed management's belief—product line C was being under-costed by ($4.86 – $3.50) ÷ $3.50, or 39%. Exhibit 11-10b compares the allocation of factory overhead using the former costing system with the activity-based-costing system. Product line A's allocation of overhead decreased from 45% to 23.1% while product line C's allocation increased from 15% to 33.9%. Notice that the use of just two additional cost drivers (machine-hours and setups) can make a significant difference in product costing. Many companies use more than 20 different cost drivers to improve the accuracy of their costing system, but the costs associated with using many activity centers can be high. The benefit-cost criteria must be applied in each case.

Effect of Activity-Based Costing

Many companies have adopted activity-based costing in recent years. For example, consider Schrader Bellows, which increased the number of cost drivers used to allocate costs to products. Several of the new cost drivers are essentially measures of the

Exhibit 11-8b Activity-Based Costing System

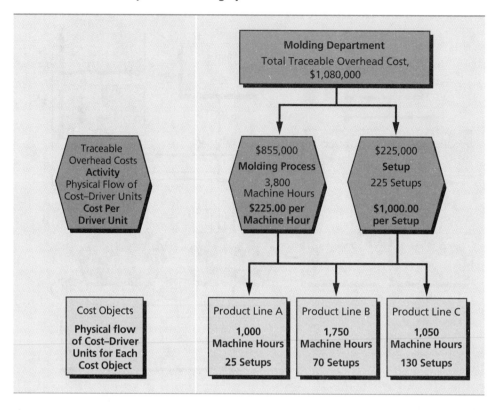

Exhibit 11-9b Key Results of Activity-Based-Costing Study

Activity/Resource (Driver Units)	Traceable Costs (1)	Total Physical Flow of Driver Units (2)	Cost per Driver Unit (1)÷(2)
Setup [number of setups]	$225,000	225 Setups	$1,000
Molding process [machine-hours]	$855,000	3,800 Machine Hours	$ 225

		Product Line A		Product Line B		Product Line C	
	Cost per Driver Unit	Physical Flow of Driver Units	Cost	Physical Flow of Driver Units	Cost	Physical Flow of Driver Units	Cost
Direct material			$1,050,000		$ 575,000		$240,000
Direct labor			344,000		303,000		123,000
Setup costs	$1,000	25	25,000	70	70,000	130	130,000
Molding process	$ 225	1,000	225,000	1,750	393,750	1,050	236,250
Total			$1,644,000		$1,341,750		$729,250
Units produced			1,000,000		500,000		150,000
Cost per unit			$ 1.64		$ 2.68		$ 4.86

Exhibit 11-10b Comparison of Costing Systems

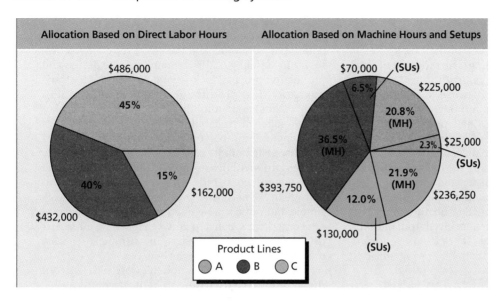

number of transactions rather than measures of volume. The cost driver having the largest effects on unit costs is *number of machine setups*. The resulting changes in unit costs for the company's seven products were dramatic, as shown in Exhibit 11-11b. Except for product 7, the products with low volume and a high number of setups per unit had large increases in unit costs. The products with high volume and fewer setups per unit had decreases in unit costs. Although product 7 had low volume, its unit cost dropped because it was assembled from components used in large volumes in other products. The unit cost of the components decreased because of their high volume and relatively few setups.

Exhibit 11-11b Schrader Bellows* Costs Before and After Activity-Based Costing System

| | | Unit Cost | | |
Product	Sales Volume	Old System	Activity-based System	Percent Change
1	43,562 units	$ 7.85	$ 7.17	(8.7)
2	500	8.74	15.45	76.8
3	53	12.15	82.49	578.9
4	2,079	13.63	24.51	79.8
5	5,670	12.40	19.99	61.2
6	11,169	8.04	7.96	(1.0)
7	423	8.47	6.93	(18.2)

*This example is from "How Cost Accounting Systematically Distorts Product Costs" by R. Cooper and R. Kaplan, in *Accounting and Management: Field Study Perspectives* by W. Bruns, Jr., and R. Kaplan (Boston, MA: Harvard Business School Press, 1987), pp. 204–28.

Activity-Based Costing at Hewlett-Packard

The Roseville Network Division (RND) of Hewlett-Packard was one of the first groups to use activity-based costing. The producer of computer-networking devices referred to its system as "cost-driver accounting." Because RND's products were increasing in number and decreasing in length of product life, the design of new products and their production processes was especially important to the division's success. But the old accounting system did not produce information helpful in comparing the production costs of different designs.

RND's new system focused on the costs of each production process—essentially, the different activities of the division. The system evolved from one with only two cost drivers—direct-labor hours and number of insertions—to one with the following nine cost drivers:

1. Number of axial insertions
2. Number of radial insertions
3. Number of DIP insertions
4. Number of manual insertions
5. Number of test hours
6. Number of solder joints
7. Number of boards
8. Number of parts
9. Number of slots

The increase in the number of cost drivers came about as accountants and managers developed a better understanding of the economics of the design and production process. By knowing the costs of the various activities, product designers could develop designs that would minimize costs for a given level of functionality and reliability.

Recognizing the average product life cycle of 24 months, RND built its cost system around its strategy to keep product lines as up-to-date as possible. RND also recognized a trade-off between accuracy and complexity. The initial two-cost-driver system was simple, but not accurate enough. But with the current nine cost drivers, concern grows that adding more cost drivers may make the system too complex—that is, make its costs greater than its benefits.

Engineering managers at RND were pleased with the activity-based-costing system. It greatly influenced the design of new products. For example, once it became clear that manual insertion was three times as expensive as automatic insertion, designs could be modified to include more automatic insertions. The system clearly had the desired effect of influencing the behavior of product designers. ■

Source: Adapted from R. Cooper and P. B. B. Turney, "Internally Forced Activity-Based Cost Systems," in R. S. Kaplan, ed., Measures for Manufacturing Excellence. Boston, MA: Harvard Business School Press, 1990.

ALLOCATION OF JOINT COSTS AND BY-PRODUCT COSTS

Joint costs and by-product costs create especially difficult cost-allocation problems. By definition, such costs relate to more than one product and cannot be separately identified with an individual product.

Joint Costs

So far we have assumed that cost drivers could be identified with an individual product. For example, if costs are being allocated to products or services on the basis of machine-hours, we have assumed that each machine-hour is used on a single final product or service. However, sometimes inputs are added to the production process before individual products are separately identifiable (i.e., before the *split-off point*). Recall that such costs are called *joint costs*. Joint costs include all inputs of material, labor, and overhead costs that are incurred before the split-off point.

Suppose a department has more than one product and some costs are joint costs. How should such joint costs be allocated to the products? Allocation of joint costs should not affect decisions about the individual products. Nevertheless, joint product costs are routinely allocated to products for purposes of *inventory valuation* and *income determination*.

Consider the example of joint product costs. A department in Dow Chemical Company produces two chemicals, X and Y. The joint cost is $100,000, and production is 1,000,000 liters of X and 500,000 liters of Y. X can be sold for $.09 per liter and Y for $.06 per liter. Ordinarily, some part of the $100,000 joint cost will be allocated to the inventory of X and the rest to the inventory of Y. Such allocations are useful for inventory purposes only. Joint cost allocations should be ignored for decisions such as selling a joint product or processing it further.

Two conventional ways of allocating joint costs to products are widely used: *physical units* and *relative sales values*. If physical units were used, the joint costs would be allocated as follows:

	Liters	Weighting	Allocation of Joint Costs	Sales Value at Split-Off
X	1,000,000	10/15 × $100,000	$ 66,667	$ 90,000
Y	500,000	5/15 × $100,000	33,333	30,000
	1,500,000		$100,000	$120,000

This approach shows that the $33,333 joint cost of producing Y exceeds its $30,000 sales value at split-off, seemingly indicating that Y should not be produced. However, such an allocation is not helpful in making production decisions. Neither of the two products could be produced separately.

A decision to produce Y must be a decision to produce X *and* Y. Because total revenue of $120,000 exceeds the total joint cost of $100,000, both will be produced. The allocation was not useful for this decision.

The physical-units method requires a common physical unit for measuring the output of each product. For example, board feet is a common unit for a variety of products in the lumber industry. However, sometimes such a common denominator is lacking. Consider the production of meat and hides from butchering a steer. You might use pounds as a common denominator, but pounds is not a good measure of the output of hides. As an alternative, many companies use the *relative-sales-value method* for allocating joint costs. The following allocation results from applying the relative-sales-value method to the Dow Chemical department:

	Relative Sales Value at Split-Off	Weighting	Allocation of Joint Costs
X	$ 90,000	90/120 × $100,000	$ 75,000
Y	30,000	30/120 × $100,000	25,000
	$120,000		$100,000

The weighting is based on the sales values of the individual products. Because the sales value of X at split-off is $90,000 and total sales value at split-off is $120,000, X is allocated 90/120 of the joint cost.

Now each product would be assigned a joint cost portion that is less than its sales value at split-off. Note how the allocation of a cost to a particular product such as Y depends not only on the sales value of Y but also on the sales value of X. For example, suppose you were the product manager for Y. You planned to sell your 500,000 liters for $30,000, achieving a profit of $30,000 − $25,000 = $5,000. Everything went as expected except that the price of X fell to $.07 per liter for revenue of $70,000 rather than $90,000. Instead of 30/120 of the joint cost, Y received 30/100 × $100,000 = $30,000 and had a profit of $0. Despite the fact that Y operations were exactly as planned, the cost-allocation method caused the profit on Y to be $5,000 below plan.

The relative-sales-value method can also be used when one or more of the joint products cannot be sold at the split-off point. To apply the method, we approximate the sales value at split-off as follows:

Sales value at split-off = Final sales value − Separable costs

For example, suppose the 500,000 liters of Y requires $20,000 of processing beyond the split-off point, after which it can be sold for $.10 per liter. The sales value at split-off would be ($.10 × 500,000) − $20,000 = $50,000 − $20,000 = $30,000.

By-Product Costs

By-products are similar to joint products. A **by-product** is a product that, like a joint product, is not individually identifiable until manufacturing reaches a split-off point. By-products differ from joint products because they have relatively insignificant total sales values in comparison with the other products emerging at split-off. In contrast, joint products have relatively significant total sales values at split-off in comparison with the other jointly produced items. Examples of by-products are glycerine from soap making and mill ends of cloth and carpets.

If an item is accounted for as a by-product, only separable costs are allocated to it. All joint costs are allocated to the main products. Any revenues from by-products, less their separable costs, are deducted from the cost of the main products.

Consider a lumber company that sells sawdust generated in the production of lumber to companies making particle board. Suppose the company regards the sawdust as a by-product. In 19X6 sales of sawdust totaled $30,000, and the cost of loading and shipping the sawdust (that is, costs incurred beyond the split-off point) was $20,000. The inventory cost of the sawdust would consist of only the $20,000 separable cost. None of the joint cost of producing lumber and sawdust would be allocated to the sawdust. The difference between the revenue and separable cost, $30,000 − $20,000 = $10,000, would be deducted from the cost of the lumber produced.

Highlights to Remember

Costs are allocated for four major purposes: (1) prediction of economic effects of decisions, (2) motivation, (3) income and asset measurement, and (4) pricing.

Costs to be allocated are assigned to cost pools, preferably keeping variable costs and fixed costs in separate pools. Fixed costs of service departments should be allocated by using predetermined monthly lump sums for providing a basic capacity to serve. Variable costs should be allocated by using a predetermined standard unit rate for the services actually used. Often it is best to allocate only those central costs of an organization for which measures of usage by departments are available. Service department costs can be allocated using either the direct method or the step-down method.

Activity-based costing is growing in popularity. It first assigns costs to the activities of an organization. Then costs are allocated to products or services based on cost drivers that measure the causes of the costs of a particular activity.

Joint costs are often allocated to products for inventory valuation and income determination using the physical-units or relative-sales-value method. However, such allocations should not affect decisions.

Summary Problem for Your Review

Problem

Nonmanufacturing organizations often find it useful to allocate costs to final products or services. Consider a hospital. The output of a hospital is not as easy to define as the output of a factory. Assume the following measures of output in three revenue-producing departments:

Department	Measures of Output*
Radiology	X-ray films processed
Laboratory	Tests administered
Daily Patient Services†	Patient-days of care (i.e., the number of patients multiplied by the number of days of each patient's stay)

* These become the "product" cost objectives, the various revenue-producing activities of a hospital.
† There would be many of these departments, such as obstetrics, pediatrics, and orthopedics. Moreover, there may be both inpatient and outpatient care.

Budgeted output for 19X7 is 60,000 x-ray films processed in Radiology, 50,000 tests administered in the Laboratory, and 30,000 patient-days in Daily Patient Services.

In addition to the revenue-producing departments, the hospital has three service departments: Administrative and Fiscal Services, Plant Operations and Maintenance, and Laundry. (Of course, real hospitals have more than three revenue-producing departments and more than three service departments. This problem is simplified to keep the data manageable.)

The hospital has decided that the cost driver for Administrative and Fiscal Services costs is the direct department costs of the other departments. The cost driver for Plant Operations and Maintenance is square feet occupied, and for Laundry is pounds of laundry. The pertinent budget data for 19X7 are:

	Direct Department Costs	Square Feet Occupied	Pounds of Laundry
Administrative and Fiscal Services	$1,000,000	1,000	—
Plant Operations and Maintenance	800,000	2,000	—
Laundry	200,000	5,000	—
Radiology	1,000,000	12,000	80,000
Laboratory	400,000	3,000	20,000
Daily Patient Services	1,600,000	80,000	300,000
Total	$5,000,000	103,000	400,000

1. Allocate service department costs using the direct method.
2. Allocate service department costs using the step-down method. Allocate Administrative and Fiscal Services first, Plant Operations and Maintenance second, and Laundry third.
3. Compute the cost per unit of output in each of the revenue-producing departments using (a) the costs determined using the direct method for allocating service department costs (requirement 1) and (b) the costs determined using the step-down method for allocating service department costs (requirement 2).

Solution

1. The solutions to all three requirements are shown in Exhibit 11-12b. The direct method is presented first. Note that no service department costs are allocated to another service department. Therefore allocations are based on the relative amounts of the cost driver in the revenue-producing department only. For example, in allocating Plant Operations and Maintenance, square footage occupied by the service departments is ignored. The cost driver is the 95,000 square feet occupied by the revenue-producing departments.

   Note that the total cost of the revenue-producing departments after allocation, $1,474,386 + $568,596 + $2,957,018 = $5,000,000, is equal to the total of the direct department costs in all six departments before allocation.

2. The step-down method is shown in the lower half of Exhibit 11-12b. The costs of Administrative and Fiscal Services are allocated to all five other departments. Because a department's own costs are not allocated to itself, the cost driver consists of the $4,000,000 direct department costs in the five departments excluding Administrative and Fiscal Services.

   Plant Operations and Maintenance is allocated second on the basis of square feet occupied. No cost will be allocated to itself or back to Administrative and Fiscal Services. Therefore the square footage used for allocation is the 100,000 square feet occupied by the other four departments.

   Laundry is allocated third. No cost would be allocated back to the first two departments, even if they had used laundry services.

   As in the direct method, note that the total costs of the revenue-producing departments after allocation, $1,430,000 + $545,000 + $3,025,000 = $5,000,000, equals the total of the direct department costs before allocation.

3. The solutions are labeled 3a and 3b in Exhibit 11-12b. Compare the unit costs derived from the direct method with those of the step-down method. In many instances, the final product costs may not differ enough to warrant investing in a cost-allocation method that is any fancier than the direct method. But sometimes even small differences may be significant to a government agency or anybody paying for a large volume of services based on costs. For example, in Exhibit 11-12b the "cost" of an "average" laboratory test is either $11.37 or $10.90. This may be significant for the fiscal committee of the hospital's board of trustees, who must decide on hospital prices. Thus cost allocation often is a

Exhibit 11-12b Allocation of Service Department Costs: Two Methods

Accumulated Base	Administrative and Fiscal Services	Plant Operations and Maintenance	Laundry	Radiology	Laboratory	Daily Patient Services
	Accumulated Costs	Sq. Footage	Pounds			
1. Direct Method						
Direct departmental costs before allocation	$1,000,000	$ 800,000	$ 200,000	$1,000,000	$400,000	$1,600,000
Administrative and Fiscal Services	(1,000,000)	—	—	333,333*	133,333	533,334
Plant Operations and Maintenance		(800,000)		101,053†	25,263	673,684
Laundry			(200,000)	40,000‡	10,000	150,000
Total costs after allocation				$1,474,386	$568,596	$2,957,018
3a. Product output in films, tests, and patient-days, respectively				60,000	50,000	30,000
Cost per unit of output				$24.573	$11.372	$98.567
2. Step-down Method						
Direct departmental costs before allocation	$1,000,000	$ 800,000	$ 200,000	$1,000,000	$400,000	$1,600,000
Administrative and Fiscal Services	(1,000,000)	200,000§	50,000	250,000	100,000	400,000
Plant Operations and Maintenance		(1,000,000)	50,000¶	120,000	30,000	800,000
Laundry			(300,000)	60,000#	15,000	225,000
Total costs after allocation				$1,430,000	$545,000	$3,025,000
3b. Product output in films, tests, and patient-days, respectively				60,000	50,000	30,000
Cost per unit of output				$23.833	$10.900	$100.833

* $1,000,000 ÷ ($1,000,000 + $400,000 + $1,600,000) = 33⅓%; 33⅓% × $1,000,000 = $333,333; etc.
† $800,000 ÷ (12,000 + 3,000 + 80,000) = $8.4210526; $8.4210526 × 12,000 sq. ft. = $101,053; etc.
‡ $200,000 ÷ (80,000 + 20,000 + 300,000) = $.50; $.50 × 80,000 = $40,000; etc.
§ $1,000,000 ÷ ($800,000 + $200,000 + $1,000,000 + $400,000 + $1,600,000) = 25%; 25% × $800,000 = $200,000; etc.
¶ $1,000,000 ÷ (5,000 + 12,000 + 3,000 + 80,000) = $10.00; $10.00 × 5,000 sq. ft. = $50,000; etc.
# $300,000 ÷ (80,000 + 20,000 + 300,000) = $.75; $.75 × 80,000 = $60,000; etc.

technique that helps answer the vital question, "Who should pay for what, and how much?"

Fundamental Assignment Material

11-A4 Allocation of Central Costs

The Central Railroad allocates all central corporate overhead costs to its divisions. Some costs, such as specified internal auditing and legal costs, are identified on the basis of time spent. However, other costs are harder to allocate, so the revenue achieved by each division is used as an allocation base. Examples of such costs were executive salaries, travel, secretarial, utilities, rent, depreciation, donations, corporate planning, and general marketing costs.

Allocations on the basis of revenue for 19X5 were (in millions):

Division	Revenue	Allocated Costs
Northern	$120	$ 6
Mesa	240	12
Plains	240	12
Total	$600	$30

In 19X6, Northern's revenue remained unchanged. However, Plains' revenue soared to $280 million because of unusually bountiful crops. The latter are troublesome to forecast because unpredictable weather has a pronounced influence on volume. Mesa had expected a sharp rise in revenue, but severe competitive conditions resulted in a decline to $200 million. The total cost allocated on the basis of revenue was again $30 million, despite rises in other costs. The president was pleased that central costs did not rise for the year.

1. Compute the allocations of costs to each division for 19X6.
2. How would each division manager probably feel about the cost allocation in 19X6 as compared with 19X5? What are the weaknesses of using revenue as a basis for cost allocation?
3. Suppose the budgeted revenues for 19X6 were $120, $240, and $280, respectively, and the budgeted revenues were used as a cost driver for allocation. Compute the allocations of costs to each division for 19X6. Do you prefer this method to the one used in requirement 1? Why?
4. Many accountants and managers oppose allocating any central costs. Why?

11-A5 Direct and Step-Down Methods of Allocation

Pinney Tool and Die has three service departments:

	Budgeted Department Costs
Cafeteria, revenue of $100,000	
less expenses of 250,000	$ 150,000
Engineering	2,500,000
General factory administration	950,000

Cost drivers are budgeted as follows:

Production Departments	Employees	Engineering Hours Worked for Production Departments	Total Labor Hours
Machining	100	50,000	250,000
Assembly	450	20,000	600,000
Finishing and painting	50	10,000	100,000

1. All service department costs are allocated directly to the production departments without allocation to other service departments. Show how much of the budgeted costs of each service department are allocated to each production department. To plan your work, examine requirement 2 before undertaking this question.
2. The company has decided to use the step-down method of cost allocation. General factory administration would be allocated first, then cafeteria, then engineering. Cafeteria employees worked 30,000 labor hours per year. There were 50 engineering employees with 100,000 total labor hours. Recompute the results in requirement 1, using the step-down method. Show your computations. Compare the results in requirements 1 and 2. Which method of allocation do you favor? Why?

11-A6   Activity-Based Costing

Chen Company makes printed circuit boards in a suburb of Tokyo. The production process is automated with computer-controlled robotic machines assembling each circuit board from a supply of parts. Chen has identified four activities:

Activity	Cost Driver	Rate
Materials handling	Cost of direct materials	5% of materials cost
Assembly	Number of parts used	¥50 per part
Soldering	Number of circuit boards	¥1,500 per board
Quality assurance	Minutes of testing	¥350 per minute

Chen makes three types of circuit boards, models A, B, and C. Requirements for production of each circuit board are:

	Model A	Model B	Model C
Direct materials cost	¥4,000	¥6,000	¥8,000
Number of parts used	60	40	20
Minutes of testing	5	3	2

1. Compute the cost of production of 100 of the three types of circuit boards and the cost per circuit board for each type.
2. Suppose the design of model A could be simplified so that it required only 30 parts (instead of 60) and took only 3 minutes of testing time (instead of 5). Compute the cost of 100 model A circuit boards and the cost per circuit board.

11-A7   Joint Products

Benjamin Metals, Inc., buys raw ore on the open market and processes it into two final products, A and B. The ore costs $12 per pound, and the process separating it into A and B has a cost of $4 per pound. During 19X6 Benjamin plans to produce 200,000 pounds of A and 600,000 pounds of B from 800,000 pounds of ore. A sells for $30 a pound and B for $15 a pound. The company allocated joint costs to the individual products for inventory valuation purposes.

1. Allocate all the joint costs to A and B using the physical-units method.
2. Allocate all the joint costs to A and B using the relative-sales-value method.
3. Suppose B *cannot be sold* in the form in which it emerges from the joint process. Instead, it must be processed further at a fixed cost of $300,000 plus a variable cost of $1 per pound. Then it can be sold for $21.50 a pound. Allocate all the joint costs to A and B using the relative-sales-value method.

11-B4 Allocation of Computer Costs

Review the section "Allocation of Service Department Costs," pages 406–414, especially the example of the use of the computer by the university. Recall that the budget formula was $100,000 fixed cost monthly plus $200 per hour of computer time used. Based on long-run predicted usage, the fixed costs were allocated on a lump-sum basis, 30% to Business and 70% to Engineering.

1. Show the total allocation if Business used 210 hours and Engineering used 390 hours in a given month. Assume that the actual costs coincided exactly with the budgeted amount for total usage of 700 hours.
2. Assume the same facts as in requirement 1 except that the fixed costs were allocated on the basis of actual hours of usage. Show the total allocation of costs to each school. As the dean of Business, would you prefer this method or the method in requirement 1? Explain.

11-B5 Allocation of Service Department Costs

Chief Cleaning, Inc. provides cleaning services for a variety of clients. The company has two producing divisions, Residential and Commercial, and two service departments, Personnel and Administrative. The company has decided to allocate all service department costs to the producing departments—Personnel on the basis of number of employees, and Administrative on the basis of direct department costs. The budget for 19X6 shows:

	Personnel	Administrative	Residential	Commercial
Direct department costs	$70,000	$90,000	$240,000	$400,000
Number of employees	6	10	24	36
Direct-labor hours			30,000	45,000
Square feet cleaned			4,500,000	9,970,000

1. Allocate service department costs using the direct method.
2. Allocate service department costs using the step-down method. The Personnel Department costs should be allocated first.
3. Suppose the company prices by the hour in the Residential Department and by the square foot cleaned in Commercial. Using the results of the step-down allocations in requirement 2:
   a. Compute the cost of providing one direct-labor hour of service in the Residential Department.
   b. Compute the cost of cleaning one square foot of space in the Commercial Department.

11-B6 Activity-Based Costing

The Cunningham Novelty company makes a variety of souvenirs for visitors to New Zealand. The Beebee Division manufactures stuffed kiwi birds using a highly automated operation. A recently installed activity-based-costing system has four activity centers.

Activity Center	Cost Driver	Cost per Driver Unit
Materials receiving and handling	Kilograms of materials	$1.20 per kg
Production setup	Number of setups	$50 per setup
Cutting, sewing, and assembly	Number of units	$.40 per unit
Packing and shipping	Number of orders	$10 per order

Two products are called "standard kiwi" and "giant kiwi." They require .20 and .40 kg of materials, respectively, at a materials cost of $1.30 for standard kiwis and $2.20 for giant kiwis. One computer-controlled assembly line makes all products. When a production run of a different product is started, a setup procedure is required to reprogram the computers and make other changes in the process. Normally, 500 standard kiwis are produced per setup, but only 200 giant kiwis. Products are packed and shipped separately, so a request from a customer for, say, three different products is considered three different orders.

Ausiland Waterfront Market just placed an order for 100 standard kiwis and 50 giant kiwis.

1. Compute the cost of the products shipped to Ausiland Waterfront Market.
2. Suppose the products made for Ausiland Waterfront Market required "AWM" to be printed on each kiwi. Because of the automated process, printing the initials takes no extra time or materials, but it requires a special production setup for each product. Compute the cost of the products shipped to the Ausiland Waterfront Market.
3. Explain how the activity-based-costing system helps Cunningham Novelty to measure costs of individual products or orders better than a traditional system that allocates all non-materials costs based on direct labor.

11-B7 Joint Products

Manhattan Milling buys oats at $.50 per pound and produces MM Oat Flour, MM Oat Flakes, and MM Oat Bran. The process of separating the oats into oat flour and oat bran costs $.30 per pound. The oat flour can be sold for $1.50 per pound, the oat bran for $2.00 per pound. Each pound of oats has .2 pounds of oat bran and .8 pounds of oat flour. A pound of oat flour can be made into oat flakes for a fixed cost of $240,000 plus a variable cost of $.50 per pound. Manhattan Milling plans to process 1 million pounds of oats in 19X6, at a purchase price of $500,000.

1. Allocate all the joint costs to oat flour and oat bran using the physical-units method.
2. Allocate all the joint costs to oat flour and oat bran using the relative-sales-value method.
3. Suppose there were no market for oat flour. Instead, it must be made into oat flakes to be sold. Oat flakes sell for $2.80 per pound. Allocate the joint cost to oat bran and oat flakes using the relative-sales-value method.

Additional Assignment Material
Questions

11-51. "A cost pool is a group of costs that is physically traced to the appropriate cost objective." Do you agree? Explain.

11-52. Give five terms that are sometimes used as substitutes for the term *allocate*.

11-53. What are the four purposes of cost allocation?

11-54. What are the three types of allocations?

11-55. Give three guides for the allocation of service department costs.

11-56. "Allocation is based on cause-effect." Explain.

11-57. Why should budgeted cost rates, rather than actual cost rates, be used for allocating the variable costs of service departments?

11-58. Why do many companies allocate fixed costs separately from variable costs?

11-59. "We used a lump-sum allocation method for fixed costs a few years ago, but we gave it up because managers always predicted usage below what they actually used." Is this a common problem? How might it be prevented?

11-60. "A commonly misused basis for allocation is dollar sales." Explain.

11-61. How should national advertising costs be allocated to territories?

11-62. Briefly describe the two popular methods for allocating service department costs.

11-63. "The step-down method allocates more costs to the producing departments than does the direct method." Do you agree? Explain.

11-64. How does the term *cost application* differ from *cost allocation*?

11-65. Many companies that previously applied costs to final products based on direct-labor hours have changed to another cost driver, such as machine hours. Why?

11-66. Why is activity-based costing also called transaction-based costing?

11-67. "Activity-based costing is useful for product costing, but not for planning and control." Do you agree? Explain.

11-68. Give five examples of transactions that can be used as cost drivers for transaction-based allocations.

11-69. Chapter 6 explained that joint costs should not be allocated to individual products for decision purposes. For what purposes are such costs allocated to products?

11-70. Briefly explain each of the two conventional ways of allocating joint costs of products.

11-71. What are by-products and how do we account for them?

11-72   Fixed- and Variable-Cost Pools

The city of Cedarwood signed a lease for a photocopy machine at $2,000 per month and $.02 per copy. Operating costs for toner, paper, operator salary, and so on are all variable at $.03 per copy. Departments had projected a need for 50,000 copies a month. The Public Works Department predicted its usage at 18,000 copies a month. It made 21,000 copies in August.

1. Suppose one predetermined rate per copy was used to allocate all photocopy costs. What rate would be used and how much cost would be allocated to the Public Works Department in August?

2. Suppose fixed- and variable-cost pools were allocated separately. Specify how each pool should be allocated. Compute the cost allocated to the Public Works Department in August.

3. Which method, the one in requirement 1 or the one in requirement 2, do you prefer? Explain.

11-73   Sales-Based Allocations

Pioneer Markets has three grocery stores in the metropolitan Topeka area. Central costs are allocated using sales as the cost driver. Following are budgeted and actual sales during November:

	Sunnyville	Wedgewood	Capitol
Budgeted sales	$600,000	$1,000,000	$400,000
Actual sales	600,000	700,000	500,000

Central costs of $180,000 are to be allocated in November.

1. Compute the central costs allocated to each store with *budgeted* sales as the cost driver.

2. Compute the central costs allocated to each store with *actual* sales as the cost driver.

3. What advantages are there to using *budgeted* rather than *actual* sales for allocating the central costs?

11-74 Joint Costs
Robinson Company's production process for its two solvents can be diagrammed as follows:

solvent A = 10,000 gallons

joint input = 15,000 gallons

split-off point   solvent B = 5,000 gallons

The cost of the joint input, including processing costs before the split-off point, is $200,000. Solvent A can be sold at split-off for $10 per gallon and solvent B for $30 per gallon.

1. Allocate the $200,000 joint cost to solvents A and B by the physical-units method.
2. Allocate the $200,000 joint cost to solvents A and B by the relative-sales-value method.

11-75 By-Product Costing
The Jones Press Company buys apples from local orchards and presses them to produce apple juice. The pulp that remains after pressing is sold to farmers as livestock food. This livestock food is accounted for as a by-product.

During the 19X5 fiscal year, the company paid $800,000 to purchase 8 million pounds of apples. After processing, 1 million pounds of pulp remained. Jones spent $30,000 to package and ship the pulp, which was sold for $50,000.

1. How much of the joint cost of the apples is allocated to the pulp?
2. Compute the total inventory cost (and therefore the cost of goods sold) for the pulp.
3. Assume that $130,000 was spent to press the apples and $150,000 was spent to filter, pasteurize, and pack the apple juice. Compute the total inventory cost of the apple juice produced.

11-76 Hospital Allocation Base
Jade Soon, the administrator of Saint Jude Hospital, has become interested in obtaining more accurate cost allocations on the basis of cause and effect. The $150,000 of laundry costs had been allocated on the basis of 600,000 pounds processed for all departments, or $.25 per pound.

Soon is concerned that government health care officials will require weighted statistics to be used for cost allocation. She asks you, "Please develop a revised base for allocating laundry costs. It should be better than our present base, but not be overly complex either."

You study the situation and find that the laundry processes a large volume of uniforms for student nurses and physicians and for dietary, housekeeping, and other personnel. In particular, the coats or jackets worn by personnel in the radiology department take unusual handwork.

A special study of laundry for radiology revealed that 7,500 of the 15,000 pounds were jackets and coats that were five times as expensive to process as regular laundry items. Several reasons explained the difference, but it was principally because of handwork involved.

Assume that no special requirements were needed in departments other than radiology. Revise the cost-allocation base and compute the new cost-allocation rate. Compute the total cost charged to radiology using pounds and using the new base.

11-77 Cost of Passenger Traffic
Northern Pacific Railroad (NP) has a commuter operation that services passengers along a route between San Jose and San Francisco. Problems of cost allocation were highlighted in a news story about NP's application to the Public Utilities Commission (PUC) for a rate increase. The PUC staff claimed that the "avoidable annual cost" of running the operation was $700,000, in contrast to NP officials' claim of a loss of $9 million. PUC's estimate was based on what NP would be able to save if it shut down the commuter operation.

The NP loss estimate was based on a "full-allocation-of-costs" method, which allocates a share of common maintenance and overhead costs to the passenger service.

If the PUC accepted its own estimate, a 25% fare increase would have been justified, whereas NP sought a 96% fare increase.

The PUC stressed that commuter costs represent less than 1% of the system-wide costs of NP and that 57% of the commuter costs are derived from some type of allocation method—sharing the costs of other operations.

NP's representative stated that "avoidable cost" is not an appropriate way to allocate costs for calculating rates. He said that "it is not fair to include just so-called above-the-rail costs" because there are other real costs associated with commuter service. Examples are maintaining smoother connections and making more frequent track inspections.

1. As public utilities commissioner, what approach toward cost allocation would you favor for making decisions regarding fares? Explain.
2. How would fluctuations in freight traffic affect commuter costs under the NP method?

11-78 Allocation of Automobile Costs

The motor pool of a major city provides automobiles for the use of various city departments. Currently, the motor pool has 50 autos. A recent study showed that it costs $2,400 of annual fixed cost per automobile plus $.10 per mile variable cost to own, operate, and maintain autos such as those provided by the motor pool.

Each month, the costs of the motor pool are allocated to the user departments on the basis of miles driven. On average, each auto is driven 24,000 miles annually, although wide month-to-month variations occur. In April 19X6, the 50 autos were driven a total of 50,000 miles. The motor pool's total costs for April were $19,000.

The chief planner for the city always seemed concerned about her auto costs. She was especially upset in April when she was charged $5,700 for the 15,000 miles driven in the department's five autos. This is the normal monthly mileage in the department. Her memo to the head of the motor pool stated, "I can certainly get autos at less than the $.38 per mile you charged in April." The response was, "I am under instructions to allocate the motor pool costs to the user departments. Your department was responsible for 30% of the April usage (15,000 miles ÷ 50,000 miles), so I allocated 30% of the motor pool's April costs to you (.30 × $19,000). That just seems fair."

1. Calculate the city's average annual cost per mile for owning, maintaining, and operating an auto.
2. Explain why the allocated cost in April ($.38 per mile) exceeds the average in requirement 1.
3. Describe any undesirable behavioral effects of the cost-allocation method used.
4. How would you improve the cost-allocation method?

11-79 Allocation of Costs

The Vigil Transportation Company has one service department and two regional operating departments. The budgeted cost behavior pattern of the service department is $750,000 monthly in fixed costs plus $.75 per 1,000 ton-miles operated in the North and South regions. (Ton-miles are the number of tons carried times the number of miles traveled.) The actual monthly costs of the service department are allocated using ton-miles operated as the cost driver.

1. Vigil processed 500 million ton-miles of traffic in April, half in each operating region. The actual costs of the service department were exactly equal to those predicted by the budget for 500 million ton-miles. Compute the costs that would be allocated to each operating region on an actual ton-miles basis.
2. Suppose the North region was plagued by strikes, so that the freight handled was much lower than originally anticipated. North moved only 150 million ton-miles of traffic. The South region handled 250 million ton-miles. The actual costs were exactly as budgeted for this lower level of activity. Compute the costs that would be allo-

cated to North and South on an actual ton-miles basis. Note that the total costs will be lower.

3. Refer to the facts in requirement 1. Various inefficiencies caused the service department to incur total costs of $1,250,000. Compute the costs to be allocated to North and South. Are the allocations justified? If not, what improvement do you suggest?

4. Refer to the facts in requirement 2. Assume that assorted investment outlays for equipment and space in the service department were made to provide a basic maximum capacity to serve the North region at a level of 360 million ton-miles and the South region at a level of 240 million ton-miles. Suppose fixed costs are allocated on the basis of this capacity to serve. Variable costs are allocated by using a predetermined standard rate per 1,000 ton-miles. Compute the costs to be allocated to each department. What are the advantages of this method over other methods?

11-80 Hospital Equipment

Many states have a hospital commission that must approve the acquisition of specified medical equipment before the hospitals in the state can qualify for cost-based reimbursement related to that equipment. That is, hospitals cannot bill government agencies for the use of the equipment unless the commission originally authorized the acquisition.

Two hospitals in one such state proposed the acquisition and sharing of some expensive x-ray equipment to be used for unusual cases. The depreciation and related fixed costs of operating the equipment were predicted at $15,000 per month. The variable costs were predicted at $30 per patient procedure.

The commission asked each hospital to predict its usage of the equipment over its expected useful life of 5 years. Premier Hospital predicted an average usage of 75 x-rays per month; St. Mary's Hospital of 50 x-rays. The commission regarded this information as critical to the size and degree of sophistication that would be justified. That is, if the number of x-rays exceeded a certain quantity per month, a different configuration of space, equipment, and personnel would be required that would mean higher fixed costs per month.

1. Suppose fixed costs are allocated on the basis of the hospitals' predicted average use per month. Variable costs are allocated on the basis of $30 per x-ray, the budgeted variable-cost rate for the current fiscal year. In October, Premier Hospital had 50 x-rays and St. Mary's Hospital had 50 x-rays. Compute the total costs allocated to Premier Hospital and to St. Mary's Hospital.

2. Suppose the manager of the equipment had various operating inefficiencies so that the total October costs were $19,500. Would you change your answers in requirement 1? Why?

3. A traditional method of cost allocation does not use the method in requirement 1. Instead, an allocation rate depends on the actual costs and actual volume encountered. The actual costs are totaled for the month and divided by the actual number of x-rays during the month. Suppose the actual costs agreed exactly with the budget for a total of 100 actual x-rays. Compute the total costs allocated to Premier Hospital and to St. Mary's Hospital. Compare the results with those in requirement 1. What is the major weakness in this traditional method? What are some of its possible behavioral effects?

4. Describe any undesirable behavioral effects of the method described in requirement 1. How would you counteract any tendencies toward deliberate false predictions of long-run usage?

11-81 Direct Method for Service Department Allocation

Sanders Instruments Company has two producing departments, Mechanical Instruments and Electronic Instruments. In addition, there are two service departments, Building Services and Materials Receiving and Handling. The company purchases a variety of component parts from which the departments assemble instruments for sale in domestic and international markets.

The Electronic Instruments division is highly automated. The manufacturing costs depend primarily on the number of subcomponents in each instrument. In contrast, the Mechanical Instruments division relies primarily on a large labor force to hand-assemble instruments. Its costs depend on direct-labor hours.

The costs of Building Services depend primarily on the square footage occupied. The costs of Materials Receiving and Handling depend primarily on the total number of components handled.

Instruments M1 and M2 are produced in the Mechanical Instruments department, and E1 and E2 are produced in the Electronic Instruments department. Data about these products follow:

	Direct-Material Cost	Number of Components	Direct-Labor Hours
M1	$74	25	4.0
M2	86	21	8.0
E1	63	10	1.5
E2	91	15	1.0

Budget figures for 19X5 include:

	Building Services	Materials Receiving and Handling	Mechanical Instruments	Electronic Instruments
Direct department costs (excluding direct materials cost)	$180,000	$120,000	$680,000	$548,000
Square footage occupied		5,000	50,000	25,000
Number of final instruments produced			8,000	10,000
Average number of components per instrument			10	16
Direct-labor hours			30,000	8,000

1. Allocate the costs of the service departments using the direct method.
2. Using the results of requirement 1, compute the cost per direct-labor hour in the Mechanical Instruments Department and the cost per component in the Electronic Instruments Department.
3. Using the results of requirement 2, compute the cost per unit of product for instruments M1, M2, E1, and E2.

11-82 Step-Down Method for Service Department Allocation
Refer to the data in Problem 11-81.

1. Allocate the costs of the service departments using the step-down method.
2. Using the results of requirement 1, compute the cost per direct-labor hour in the Mechanical Instruments Department and the cost per component in the Electronic Instruments Department.
3. Using the results of requirement 2, compute the cost per unit of product for instruments M1, M2, E1, and E2.

11-83 Direct and Step-Down Methods of Allocation
The Maton Company has prepared departmental overhead budgets for normal activity levels before reapportionments, as follows:

Building and grounds	$ 20,000	
Personnel	1,200	
General factory administration*	28,020	
Cafeteria operating loss	1,430	
Storeroom	2,750	
Machining	35,100	
Assembly	56,500	
	$145,000	

* To be reapportioned before cafeteria.

Management has decided that the most sensible product costs are achieved by using departmental overhead rates. These rates are developed after appropriate service department costs are allocated to production departments.

Cost drivers for allocation are to be selected from the following data:

Department	Direct-Labor Hours	Number of Employees	Square Feet of Floor Space Occupied	Total Labor Hours	Number of Requisitions
Building and grounds	—	—	—	—	—
Personnel*	—	—	2,000	—	—
General factory administration	—	35	7,000	—	—
Cafeteria operating loss	—	10	4,000	1,000	—
Storeroom	—	5	7,000	1,000	—
Machining	5,000	50	30,000	8,000	3,000
Assembly	15,000	100	50,000	17,000	1,500
	20,000	200	100,000	27,000	4,500

* Basis used is number of employees.

1. Allocate service department costs by the step-down method. Develop overhead rates per direct-labor hour for machining and assembly.
2. Same as in requirement 1, using the direct method.
3. What would be the plantwide factory-overhead application rate, assuming that direct-labor hours are used as a cost driver?
4. Using the following information about two jobs, prepare three different total overhead costs for each job, using rates developed in requirements 1, 2, and 3.

	Direct-Labor Hours	
	Machining	*Assembly*
Job K10	19	2
Job K12	3	18

11-84 Joint Costs and Decisions

A petrochemical company has a batch process whereby 1,000 gallons of a raw material are transformed into 100 pounds of Z-1 and 400 pounds of Z-2. Although the joint costs of their production are $1,000, both products are worthless at their split-off point. Additional separable costs of $350 are necessary to give Z-1 a sales value of $900 as product A. Similarly, additional separable costs of $200 are necessary to give Z-2 a sales value of $900 as product B.

You are in charge of the batch process and the marketing of both products. (Show your computations for each answer.)

1. a. Assuming that you believe in assigning joint costs on a physical basis, allocate the total profit of $250 per batch to products A and B.

b. Would you stop processing one of the products? Why?

2. a. Assuming that you believe in assigning joint costs on a net-realizable-value (relative-sales-value) basis, allocate the total operating profit of $250 per batch to products A and B. If there is no market for Z-1 and Z-2 at their split-off point, a net realizable value is usually imputed by taking the ultimate sales values at the point of sale and working backward to obtain approximated "synthetic" relative sales values at the split-off point. These synthetic values are then used as weights for allocating the joint costs to the products.

b. You have internal product-profitability reports in which joint costs are assigned on a net-realizable-value basis. Your chief engineer says that, after seeing these reports, he has developed a method of obtaining more of product B and correspondingly less of product A from each batch, without changing the per-pound cost factors. Would you approve this new method? Why? What would the overall operating profit be if 50 pounds more of B were produced and 50 pounds less of A?

Cases

11-85 Allocation, Department Rates, and Direct-Labor Hours Versus Machine-Hours

The Tolbert Manufacturing Company has two producing departments, machining and assembly. Mr. Tolbert recently automated the machining department. The installation of a CAM system, together with robotic workstations, drastically reduced the amount of direct labor required. Meanwhile the assembly department remained labor-intensive.

The company had always used one firmwide rate based on direct-labor hours as the cost driver for applying all costs (except direct materials) to the final products. Mr. Tolbert was considering two alternatives: (1) continue using direct-labor hours as the only cost driver, but use different rates in machining and assembly, and (2) using machine-hours as the cost driver in the machining department while continuing with direct-labor hours in assembly.

Budgeted data for 19X6 are:

	Machining	Assembly	Total
Total cost (except direct materials), after allocating service department costs	$525,000	$420,000	$945,000
Machine-hours	105,000	*	105,000
Direct-labor hours	15,000	30,000	45,000

* Not applicable.

1. Suppose Tolbert continued to use one firmwide rate based on direct-labor hours to apply all manufacturing costs (except direct materials) to the final products. Compute the cost-application rate that would be used.

2. Suppose Tolbert continued to use direct-labor hours as the only cost driver but used different rates in machining and assembly:

a. Compute the cost-application rate for machining.

b. Compute the cost-application rate for assembly.

3. Suppose Tolbert changed the cost accounting system to use machine-hours as the cost driver in machining and direct-labor hours in assembly:

    a. Compute the cost-application rate for machining.

    b. Compute the cost-application rate for assembly.

4. Three products use the following machine-hours and direct-labor hours:

	Machine-Hours in Machining	Direct-Labor Hours in Machining	Direct-Labor Hours in Assembly
Product A	10.0	1.0	14.0
Product B	17.0	1.5	3.0
Product C	14.0	1.3	8.0

    a. Compute the manufacturing cost of each product (excluding direct materials) using one firm-wide rate based on direct-labor hours.

    b. Compute the manufacturing cost of each product (excluding direct materials) using direct-labor hours as the cost driver, but with different cost-application rates in machining and assembly.

    c. Compute the manufacturing cost of each product (excluding direct materials) using a cost-application rate based on direct-labor hours in assembly and machine-hours in machining.

    d. Compare and explain the results in requirements 4a, 4b, and 4c.

11-86 Multiple Allocation Bases

The Cozzetta Electronics Company produces three types of circuit boards; call them L, M, and N. The cost accounting system used by Cozzetta until 1994 applied all costs except direct materials to the products using direct-labor hours as the only cost driver. In 1994 the company undertook a cost study. The study determined that there were six main factors causing costs to be incurred. A new system was designed with a separate cost pool for each of the six factors. The factors and the costs associated with each are as follows:

1. Direct-labor hours—direct-labor cost and related fringe benefits and payroll taxes

2. Machine-hours—depreciation and repairs and maintenance costs

3. Pounds of materials—materials receiving, handling, and storage costs

4. Number of production setups—labor used to change machinery and computer configurations for a new production batch

5. Number of production orders—costs of production scheduling and order processing

6. Number of orders shipped—all packaging and shipping expenses

The company is now preparing a budget for 1996. The budget includes the following predictions:

	Board L	Board M	Board N
Units to be produced	10,000	800	5,000
Direct-material cost	£66/unit	£88/unit	£45/unit
Direct-labor hours	4/unit	18/unit	9/unit
Machine-hours	7/unit	15/unit	7/unit
Pounds of materials	3/unit	4/unit	2/unit
Number of production setups	100	50	50
Number of production orders	300	200	70
Number of orders shipped	1,000	800	2,000

The total budgeted cost for 1996 is £3,712,250, of which £955,400 was direct-materials cost, and the amount in each of the six cost pools defined above is:

Cost Pool*	Cost
1	£1,391,600
2	936,000
3	129,600
4	160,000
5	25,650
6	114,000
Total	£2,756,850

* Identified by the cost driver used.

1. Prepare a budget that shows the total budgeted cost and the unit cost for each circuit board. Use the new system with six cost pools (plus a separate direct application of direct-materials cost).
2. Compute the budgeted total and unit costs of each circuit board if the old direct-labor-hour-based system had been used.
3. How would you judge whether the new system is better than the old one?

11-87 Case of Allocation of Data Processing Costs

(CMA, adapted.) The International Underwriters Insurance Co. (IUI) established a Systems Department two years ago to implement and operate its own data processing systems. IUI believed that its own system would be more cost-effective than the service bureau it had been using.

IUI's three departments—Claims, Records, and Finance—have different requirements with respect to hardware and other capacity-related resources and operating resources. The system was designed to recognize these differing needs. In addition, the system was designed to meet IUI's long-term capacity needs. The excess capacity designed into the system would be sold to outside users until needed by IUI. The estimated resource requirements used to design and implement the system are shown in the following schedule:

	Hardware and Other Capacity-Related Resources	Operating Resources
Records	25%	60%
Claims	50	15
Finance	20	20
Expansion (outside use)	5	5
Total	100%	100%

IUI currently sells the equivalent of its expansion capacity to a few outside clients.

At the time the system became operational, management decided to redistribute total expenses of the Systems Department to the user departments based on actual computer time used. The actual costs for the first quarter of the current fiscal year were distributed to the user departments as follows:

Department	Percentage Utilization	Amount
Records	60%	$330,000
Claims	15	82,500
Finance	20	110,000
Outside	5	27,500
Total	100%	$550,000

The three user departments have complained about the cost distribution method since the Systems Department was established. The Records Department's monthly costs have been as much as three times the costs experienced with the service bureau. The Finance Department is concerned about the costs distributed to the outside user category because these allocated costs form the basis for the fees billed to the outside clients.

Jerry Owens, IUI's controller, decided to review the cost-allocation method. The additional information he gathered for his review is reported in Tables 1 to 3.

Table 1 Systems Department Costs and Activity Levels

	Annual Budget		First Quarter			
			Budget		Actual	
	Hours	Dollars	Hours	Dollars	Hours	Dollars
Hardware and other capacity-related costs	—	$ 600,000	—	$150,000	—	$155,000
Software development	18,750	562,500	4,725	141,750	4,250	130,000
Operations						
Computer related	3,750	750,000	945	189,000	920	187,000
Input/output related	30,000	300,000	7,560	75,600	7,900	78,000
		$2,212,500		$556,350		$550,000

Table 2 Historical Usage

	Hardware and Other Capacity Needs	Software Development		Operations			
				Computer		Input/Output	
		Range	Average	Range	Average	Range	Average
Records	25%	0-30%	15%	55-65%	60%	10-30%	15%
Claims	50	15-60	40	10-25	15	60-80	75
Finance	20	25-75	40	10-25	20	3-10	5
Outside	5	0-25	5	3-8	5	3-10	5
	100%		100%		100%		100%

Table 3 Usage of Systems Department's Services First Quarter (in hours)

	Software Development	Operations Computer Related	Input/Output
Records	450	540	1,540
Claims	1,800	194	5,540
Finance	1,600	126	410
Outside	400	60	410
Total	4,250	920	7,900

Owens has concluded that the method of cost allocation should be changed. He believes that the hardware and capacity-related costs should be allocated to the user departments in proportion to the planned long-term needs. Any difference between actual and budgeted hardware costs would not be allocated to the departments but remain with the Systems Department.

The costs for software development and operations would be charged to the user departments based on actual hours used. A predetermined hourly rate based on the annual budget data would be used. The hourly rates that would be used for the current fiscal year are as follows:

Function	Hourly Rate
Software development	$ 30
Operations	
Computer related	200
Input/output related	10

Owens plans to use first-quarter activity and cost data to illustrate his recommendations. The recommendations will be presented to the Systems Department and the user departments for their comments and reactions. He then expects to present his recommendations to management for approval.

1. Calculate the amount of data processing costs that would be included in the Claims Department's first-quarter *budget* according to the method Jerry Owens has recommended.
2. Prepare a schedule to show how the actual first-quarter costs of the Systems Department would be charged to the users if Owens' recommended method were adopted.
3. Explain whether Owens' recommended system for charging costs to the user departments will:
   a. Improve cost control in the Systems Department
   b. Improve planning and cost control in the user departments

CHAPTER 12

EARNED VALUE CONCEPTS AND FORMULAS

12.1   PROJECT APPLICATIONS OF EARNED VALUE

Earned value is primarily used by the U.S. government to monitor projects. A survey of 60 corporate participants in the Fortune 500 Benchmarking Forum concludes that none of them use earned value in the same format as that utilized by the government. The major complaint is that earned value is complicated and difficult to understand. In particular, the conversion of schedule time delays into dollars and cents is a particularly troublesome concept to visualize. Most companies resolve the schedule control problem by planning projects with numerous milestones and measurement points. Upon arriving at the milestone, it is a simple matter to observe whether the project is ahead or behind schedule. Despite the criticisms, earned value remains a cornerstone of the Project Management Institute's Body of Knowledge and several questions on the Project Management Professional Certification Exam pertain to earned value. It is also an integral part of most government project management related contracts.

The following reading by J. Davidson Frame presents the concept, its application, and its benefits in a clear fashion.

12.2   INTEGRATING COST AND SCHEDULE CONTROL TO MEASURE WORK PERFORMANCE

A well-known joke in project management circles states that the last 10 percent of a project typically takes 50 percent of the effort. We often encounter projects that are stuck at the 90 percent mark for months. It happens so frequently that I have given it a special name: the 90 percent hang-up. The problem is not that project staff are suddenly encountering insurmountable obstacles; rather, it is that the reporting on the amount of work achieved has been incorrect. On most projects, staff do not know how to measure work performance effectively.

Perhaps the most important control information project managers have is data on the amount of work that has been done. If they do not know how much work they have accomplished, they cannot really know whether they are overspending or underspending, or whether they are near to meeting their schedule objectives. Effective project control requires that project organizations generate accurate measures of work performance.

Traditionally, work performance data are collected by having project staff report on "percent of task complete" month by month. Staff are usually left to interpret what this means on their own. Most report percent complete based on gut feeling. I call this the "dartboard school" of work performance measurement since one has the sense that the data are chosen by throwing darts at a board. Their reliability is low. It is likely that five people reporting on percent of work complete will offer five different assessments.

Occasionally, staff may review their budget expenditures and report the percent of budget spent as their estimate of work complete. Unfortunately, in the real world of project management, the correlation between money spent and work done is weak, so this is not a good measure. Furthermore, with this approach project staff are not providing new insights to the organization since the accounting department already knows how much of the budget has been spent.

So how does one measure work performance? This question is the key concern of this chapter. As we shall see, the answer centers on the concepts of earned value and integrated cost/schedule control.

A Graphical Approach to Integrated Cost Schedule Control

The interpretation of cost and schedule variance data must be undertaken cautiously. If the project accounts show that we have a positive cost variance of 10 percent in March, we should not jump to the conclusion that we have saved money. Perhaps the positive variance reflects the fact that we have not done much work. If we have not done the job, it may be that we have not spent our money. Similarly, a negative variance of 10 percent does not necessarily mean that we have overspent. It may reflect the fact that we did more work than planned in March.

Common sense suggests that to have an accurate perception of project status, we should look at cost and schedule variances concurrently. A 10 percent positive cost variance actually reflects a true savings if we are on or ahead of schedule. A negative 10 percent cost variance indicates overspending if we are slipping our schedule, or even if we are on schedule.

An effective way to examine cost and schedule variance is to use cumulative cost curves (also called S-curves) and Gantt charts. Employment of these control tools allows staff and manager to assess overall project status at a glance. This is seen in Figure12.1, which employs Gantt charts and cumulative cost curves to illustrate three different scenarios. The Gantt chart in Figure 12.1a shows that the project is fundamentally on schedule, and the cumulative cost curve shows that money is being spent in conformance with the budget. This reflects a situation where progress appears to be going according to the plan.

Figure 12.lb shows that tasks are being accomplished earlier than planned. At the same time, more money is being spent than budgeted in the time period under review. This reflects a situation of "crashing," in which extra resources are thrown into a project to either maintain or accelerate schedule.

Figure 12.lc shows the worst possible situation. The project is experiencing both schedule slippage and a cost overrun.

The beauty of the simultaneous use of Gantt charts and cumulative cost curves is that managers can determine at a glance what their project status is. Furthermore, integrated cost/schedule control portrayed through graphical means is an effective communication tool. As such, it can be employed to report project status both to upper management and project staff in a way that is easy to understand. Another advantage of the graphical approach is that today's project scheduling

Figure 12.1 Integrated Cost/Schedule Reporting

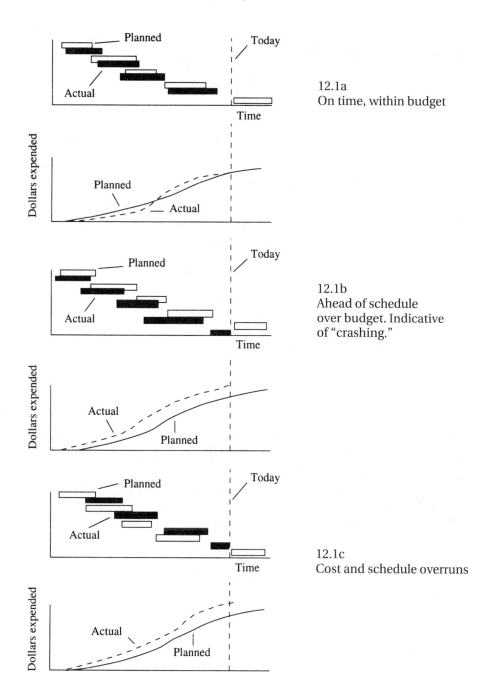

12.1a
On time, within budget

12.1b
Ahead of schedule over budget. Indicative of "crashing."

12.1c
Cost and schedule overruns

packages typically generate good-looking cost and schedule charts so that producing the graphics is no problem.

The principal deficiency of the graphical approach is that it is cumbersome from an analytical perspective. The graphs provide a visual impression of project status. By themselves, they do not offer other important information, such as the rate at which the budget is being spent vis-a-vis the amount of work being accomplished, the contribution of individual tasks to budget and schedule performance, or the percent of the work that has been carried out. In addition, on projects of moderate or substantial size, the number of Gantt and cost curves that must be generated can be overwhelming.

In the next section, we examine an analytical approach to reviewing budget and schedule status called the *earned-value approach*. It is one of the more clever techniques developed in the arena of management. Although it has its origins in the late 1960s, its early use lay exclusively in the domain of large defense programs. Today, project managers have discovered that it can be usefully employed in small projects as well as large ones, and its popularity on projects of all sizes is growing rapidly.

The Fifty-Fifty Rule for Measuring Work Performance

Here we introduce the earned-value approach by examining one method cost accountants have developed to measure work performance. It is called the *fifty-fifty rule*.

Employment of the fifty-fifty rule is quite straightforward. At the moment a task begins, we assume we have achieved half its value, where value is measured by the budgeted cost of the task. Thus, for a $1,000 budgeted task, we assume $500 in work has been accomplished the moment the task begins. We do not assume that the full value of the work has been achieved until the task actually ends. Thus, once our hypothetical $1,000 task has been completed—whether it is completed early, late, or on time—we say we have achieved $1,000 worth of work.

The utility of the fifty-fifty rule in measuring work performance can be seen in Figure 12.2. This figure portrays the Gantt chart for a very simple, four-task project. To keep the arithmetic simple, each task has a budgeted value of $100.

Task I begins on time, and when it begins, we assume we have accomplished $50 in work. Task l finishes on schedule, and upon its completion we note that the full $l00 value of the task has been achieved.

Task 2 begins on time, so we assume we have done $50 of work. At the time of its scheduled finish, work remains to be done, so we do not close the books on it. We note that the task has achieved its full $100 value only when it is complete.

Task 3 begins late. We do not indicate the accomplishment of any work until the task actually begins. At that time we note the achievement of $50 in work. The task slips its deadline. Not until it actually finishes do we state that it has achieved its full $100 value.

Finally, we see that Task 4 begins late and that as of today it is still incomplete. Consequently, we report that it has only achieved half its value, that is, $50.

In making a status report, we compute that as of today we have achieved $350 worth of work out of a planned $400 of effort. The measure of the $350 of work performed is called *earned value*. The fact that $350 of work out of a planned $400 of work has been achieved suggests that we have reached 87.5 percent of our target.

Notice that we have said nothing about how much it cost us to accomplish our work. Let's assume that a tally of time sheets and invoices tells us that we spent $700 to achieve $350 of work. Thus, for each dollar actually spent, we attained fifty cents of value. If this project has a $10,000 total budget, and if we continue to get fifty cents of value for each dollar spent, the final cost of this project will reach $20,000!

This simple example demonstrates the power of the earned-value approach. It gives us a method for calculating the percent of the job that has been achieved. It

Figure 12.2 The Fifty-Fifty Rule

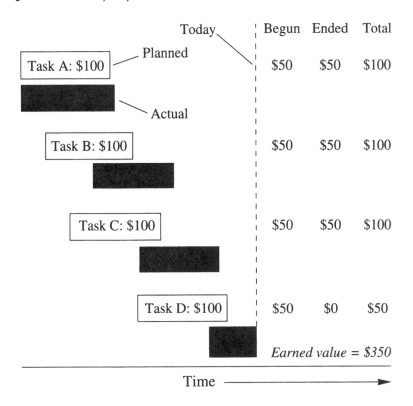

	Begun	Ended	Total
Task A: $100	$50	$50	$100
Task B: $100	$50	$50	$100
Task C: $100	$50	$50	$100
Task D: $100	$50	$0	$50

Earned value = $350

also enables us to measure the "burn rate" of our expenditures, thus allowing us to calculate the budget impact of our performance. Earned value computations can be carried out at any level of the work breakdown structure (WBS): we can examine project performance from the perspective of the whole project down to the level of individual work packages (that is, the lowest level of the WBS). In other words, the earned-value approach allows us to conduct integrated cost/schedule control analyses analytically, in contrast to the graphical approach discussed earlier.

Other Ways to Calculate Earned Value

There are several ways to calculate earned value beyond the fifty-fifty rule. Data processing personnel tend to be very conservative. To them, the fifty-fifty rule is recklessly optimistic because it is based on the premise that the work is half-finished the moment it is begun. Anyone who has written software code realizes that half-finished software has no value. Consequently, they employ the zero-one hundred rule in calculating earned value. That is, when a task begins, it is not assumed that anything has been accomplished. Only when the task is complete is it given its full value. In the example provided in Figure 12.2, the total earned value as of today is $300 with the zero-one hundred rule. This means that the project has achieved only 75 percent of its target.

The favored way to calculate earned value is to make computations based on historical experience. I will illustrate this with a simplified example of a company that assembles computers. The assembly process involves five steps. First, auxiliary memory chips are installed on the motherboard. Experience suggests that when this step is complete, the assembly process has achieved the 25-percent mark.

Then, the motherboard is installed in the chassis (the 30-percent mark). After this, a hard drive is installed in the hard drive slot (the 70-percent mark). All cables are linked to their appropriate connectors (the 85-percent mark), and then the chassis is slipped into the computer housing (the 100-percent mark).

To calculate earned value status each month, a tabulation is made of the number of computers found at each stage of the assembly process, and a weighted average is computed estimating the total value of work achieved during the month. For example, suppose the work value of a complete assembly operation is $100. If during the review of work in progress it is found that five computers have had auxiliary memory installed, then the value of work achieved for these computers is $100 × 5 × 0.25 = $125.

Calculating earned value based on "gut feeling" is permitted but is the least preferred approach. In this case, a task leader might guess that she has achieved 85 percent of her $1,000 assigned effort, indicating that she has accomplished an earned value of $850 worth of work.

A New Look at Cost and Schedule Variance

The traditional approach to measuring cost variance has been to subtract actual costs from planned costs. A negative variance suggests that more has been spent than planned; a positive variance indicates that less has been spent than planned. For example, suppose that for the month of March we planned to spend $1,000 but actually spent $900. This would yield a positive cost variance of $100. As we saw earlier, this cost variance cannot be interpreted meaningfully by itself. It must be examined in conjunction with information on schedule status.

With the earned value approach, we take a different tack to calculating cost variance. It is computed by subtracting actual costs from earned value. Staying with the example offered in the paragraph above, if earned value is computed to be $850, then cost variance will be $850 - $900 = -$50. This means that we paid $900 to do $850 in work. For the work we have done, we have overspent by $50. *Note that cost variance here is being assessed against the value of the work that has been performed.* In this case, it is not necessary to look at the Gantt chart to determine that we have overspent our money. By itself, the cost variance data indicate that we have spent too much. Any negative cost variance figure suggests overspending and positive cost variance indicates cost saving.

Schedule variance is defined as earned value minus planned cost. In our example, this is $850 - $1,000 = -$150. In words, this says that although we were supposed to have achieved $1,000 in work, we only accomplished $850, giving us a work shortfall valued at $150.

Note that schedule variance is being measured in monetary units, not time units. At first this appears peculiar because people normally think of schedules in the context of time. However, the logic of the approach takes on meaning when we realize that *earned value measures work performance,* and that when less work is performed than planned, schedule slippages ensue.

The viability of earned value in measuring schedule variance is seen clearly when earned value schedule variance is mapped to the Gantt chart. This is illustrated in Figures 12.3a, 12.3b, and 12.3c.

The Gantt chart in Figure 12.3a shows a two-task project that is experiencing schedule slippage. The first task (valued at $700) is complete, but the second task (valued at $300) is only half complete. Although the planned amount of effort to be accomplished is $l,000, earned value is only $850. Schedule slippage is thus $850 - $1,000 = -$150. In general, a negative schedule variance figure indicates schedule slippage and reflects a Gantt chart that shows such slippage, whether the Gantt chart has two tasks, twenty tasks, or two hundred tasks!

Figure 12.3b shows a project on which the planned work has been achieved. As of today, $1,000 in work was supposed to have been accomplished, and $1,000 in

Figure 12.3   Earned Value: Examining Schedule Variance

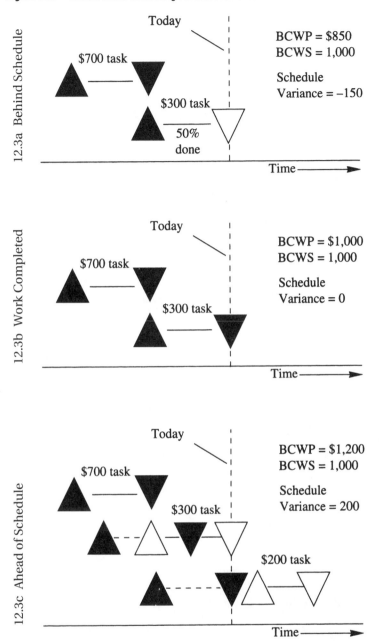

12.3a Behind Schedule

Today

$700 task

$300 task

50% done

BCWP = $850
BCWS = 1,000

Schedule
Variance = –150

Time ⟶

12.3b Work Completed

Today

$700 task

$300 task

BCWP = $1,000
BCWS = 1,000

Schedule
Variance = 0

Time ⟶

12.3c Ahead of Schedule

Today

$700 task

$300 task

$200 task

BCWP = $1,200
BCWS = 1,000

Schedule
Variance = 200

Time ⟶

work has actually been finished. Schedule variance is $1,000 - $1,000 = 0. In general, a zero variance indicates that the planned effort has been accomplished.

Figure 12.3c shows a project on which work has been accelerated so that more work has been accomplished as of today than originally planned. The first task (valued at $700) is finished early, so work on the second task begins. This second task (valued at $300) is also finished early, so work on the third task (valued at $200) begins early. As of today, $1,000 of work was supposed to have been accomplished, whereas $1,200 has actually been achieved. Schedule variance is

$1,200 - $1,000 = $200. In general, a positive schedule variance indicates that more work has been accomplished than planned.

Integrated cost/schedule control occurs when cost and schedule variances are examined concurrently. This is done in Table 12.1, which shows seven different cost/schedule variance scenarios that might be encountered. With Project A, cost and schedule targets have been achieved, yielding zero cost and schedule variances. In Project B, the value of work performed ($600) is less than what was planned ($800). In addition, the actual cost of this work ($800) was greater than the value achieved. Thus, with Project B we encounter a cost overrun and a schedule slippage. The other projects can be examined in like fashion.

Table 12.1. Different Cost and Schedule Variance Scenarios

	Planned cost	Actual costs	Earned value	Cost variance	Schedule variance
Project A	800	800	800	0	0
Project B	800	800	600	-200	-200
Project C	800	600	1000	200	200
Project D	800	1000	1000	0	200
Project E	800	600	800	200	0
Project F	800	1200	1000	-200	200
Project G	800	400	600	200	-200

Developing a New Vocabulary

One of the confusing features of the fully developed earned-value approach is that it has its own terminology, and this does not conform with the commonsense understanding of words. I find when teaching the earned-value approach that students spend more energy trying to master the vocabulary than the concepts.

With the earned-value approach, planned cost is called *budgeted cost of work scheduled* (BCWS). Actual cost is called *actual cost of work performed* (ACWP). Both BCWS and ACWP correspond exactly to traditional understandings of the meanings of planned and actual cost respectively. Earned value itself is called *budgeted cost of work performed* (BCWP).

With this new vocabulary, we define schedule variance as:

$$SV = BCWP - BCWS$$

We define cost variance as:

$$CV = BCWP - ACWP$$

The percent of a job achieved is computed as:

$$\% \text{ Complete} = 100 \times BCWP/BCWS$$

The "burn rate" at which we are spending money—it can also be interpreted as an efficiency rate—is called the *cost performance index* (CPI) and is computed as:

$$CPI = BCWP/ACWP$$

The estimate of final project cost is called *estimate at complete* (EAC) and is computed as:

$$EAC = BAC/CPI$$

where BAC stands for *budgeted at completion*, which is the total budgeted value of the project. EAC allows us to forecast final project costs on the basis of the efficiency with which work performance is achieved for each dollar actually spent. If a project is budgeted to cost $500,000 (that is, BAC = $500,000) and eighty cents of work is being generated for each dollar spent (that is, CPI = 0.8), the final estimated cost of the project will be $500,000/0.8 or $625, 000 (that is, EAC = $625,000).

Case Study: The Bora Bora Officers Club

The power of the earned-value approach as an analytical tool is best seen through an example. The example employed here is a project to build the hypothetical Bora Bora Officers Club. Data on progress to date are provided in Table 12.2. The bottom line of this table shows that as of today, three phases of the construction project should have been completed, for a budgeted cost of $96,300 (BCWS). As of today, $87,100 has actually been spent (ACWP). The value of the work achieved is only $78,650 (BCWP). The data on schedule and cost variance tell us that this project is behind schedule and over cost. Schedule variance (BCWP - BCWS) is -$17,650 and cost variance (BCWP - ACWP) is -$8,450. The project has achieved 81.7 percent of the planned effort (78,650/96,300). The burn rate (cost performance index) for the expenditure of funds is .903 (78,650/ 87,100)—that is, for every dollar spent, the project is achieving ninety cents of value. Given this burn rate, the final project cost (that is, estimate at completion) of this $115,000 budgeted project could be $127,353 (115,000/0.903).

The analysis of the bottom line gives us a good sense of progress on this project. The verdict is that it is not doing very well. It has a substantial schedule variance, and its final cost will be greater than what has been budgeted.

A strength of the earned value approach is that we are not restricted to an aggregate overview of the project. Budget and schedule analysis can occur at any level of the work breakdown structure. To see this, consider the data on Phase I of the Bora Bora Officers' Club project. The schedule variances of zero for individual tasks shows that work on this phase is complete. At the end of the work, a small cost overrun of -$500 exists.

The Phase II data suggest some problems. Three tasks have negative schedule variances (finish roof, install plumbing, and attach siding), indicating that more work must be done before the phase is complete. The overall cost overrun for the phase is -$7,175. The lion's share of the cost overrun is tied to problems in framing the house (a -$6,000 overrun).

Phase III is in even greater trouble. Schedule variance data reveal that a whopping $16,075 of work remains undone. Although the cost variance appears small (-$775), the project is so far behind schedule that it is likely that it will incur substantial cost overruns before it is completed.

Collecting Data

On very large, complex projects, data collection on work performed can become quite complicated. The way companies handle data collection is by assigning cost account managers (CAMs) the responsibility for gathering data. On large projects, an individual CAM may have responsibility for millions of dollars of effort.

The principal data CAMs focus on are figures that will enable them to estimate the amount of work performed (that is, earned value). They do this by walking around the organization asking task leaders how much of their work they have achieved. The CAMs know what the milestones are, so their inquiries focus largely on the achievement of planned milestones.

CAMs also have responsibility for taking the raw data and fashioning them into earned value reports. They are the first line of defense in identifying deficiencies in

Table 12.2 Subcontractor Report on Progress-to-Date. Project: Bora Bora Officers Club.

	Planned costs	Actual costs	Estimated percent complete	BCWP	Schedule variance	Cost variance
PHASE I						
Clear 1/4th acre site	1,500	1,500	100	1,500	0	0
Excavate site	2,500	2,600	100	2,500	0	(100)
Pour concrete foundation	3,500	3,600	100	3,500	0	(100)
Emplace basic plumbing	1,000	1,200	100	1,000	0	(200)
Erect cinderblock foundation	2,500	2,500	100	2,500	0	0
Waterproof foundation	800	900	100	800	0	(100)
Total, Phase I	11,800	12,300		11,800	0	(500)
PHASE II						
Frame house	35,000	41,000	100	35,000	0	(6,000)
Finish roof	6,500	7,300	95	6,175	(325)	(1,125)
Insulate house	3,500	3,200	100	3,500	0	300
Install electrical wiring	3,000	3,000	100	3,000	0	0
Install plumbing	3,500	3,100	90	3,150	(350)	50
Attach siding	4,500	4,000	80	3,600	(900)	400
Total, Phase II	56,000	61,600		54,425	(1,575)	(7,175)
PHASE III						
Put up dry wall	12,000	6,000	50	6,000	(6,000)	0
Finish floor	6,000	5,200	80	4,800	(1,200)	(400)
Finish interior woodwork	6,500	2,000	25	1,625	(4,875)	(375)
Paint interior	300	0	0	0	(3,000)	0
Paint exterior	1,000	0	0	0	(1,000)	0
Total, Phase III	28,500	13,200		12,425	(16,075)	(775)
Total Project to Date	96,300	87,100		78,650	(17,650)	(8,450)
Total budget (BAC): $115,000.						

Note: All tasks listed were to have been completed by the time of this report.

meeting the plan. Each month they highlight these deficiencies, alerting management to their existence.

On smaller projects, it is not cost effective to hire CAMs to track data. Work performance can be tracked a number of ways without incurring major administrative costs. By employing something like the fifty-fifty rule or the zero-one hundred rule, all that needs to be tracked is: Has a task begun? Has it ended? The clever use of milestones can also facilitate measurement of work performance (for example, "We have achieved twenty out of thirty milestones, where each milestone represents one hundred person-hours of work. Thus, we have achieved two-thirds of our target"). As a last resort, work performance can be measured by guesswork (for example, "Experience tells me we have done about 85 percent of our planned effort").

Trend Analysis with the Earned-Value Approach

Earned-value analysis can be employed to determine general trends in work performance. This is illustrated in Figure 12.5, which shows trends in actual costs (ACWP), earned value (BCWP), and planned costs (BCWS). If everything is going exactly according to plan, the lines reflecting these three measures should be pictured as a single line. Deviations of the ACWP line from the earned value line indicate cost variance. Deviations of the BCWS line from the earned value line indicate schedule variance.

Figure 12.4 shows that in the early months of this project, there are abundant cost and schedule variances. Both ACWP and BCWS are substantially larger than BCWP, indicating negative variances. However, as time goes on, the size of these variances shrinks, and by Month 8 the variances have virtually disappeared, indicating that the project is under control.

Use of a chart such as this can offer managers a high-level view of project status at a glance. If the chart indicates that the project is generally faring well, there is no need to burden managers with detailed tables of numerical data. If the chart indicates problems, this might suggest a review of more detailed data.

Figure 12.4 Earned-Value Analysis over Time

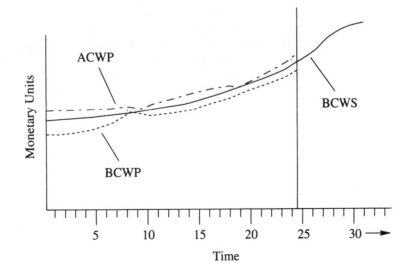

When Is the Earned-Value Approach Appropriate?

The earned-value approach was originally devised to provide government contractors and government program managers with guidance on how to track progress on large complex projects (see the historical note offered in the appendix to this chapter). Because the fully developed earned-value system is governed by detailed instructions that create a substantial administrative burden, the assumption has been that this approach is only appropriate on projects in the range of $100,000,000 or larger. Using it on smaller projects would be like trying to kill a mosquito with a shotgun.

The Bora Bora Officers Club case demonstrates that—stripped of unnecessary administrative requirements—the earned-value approach can give project managers valuable insights into project progress even on small projects. If a project has information on planned costs and if actual cost data are being reported accurately and promptly, the earned-value approach can be employed usefully. It offers a numerical substitute for the use of Gantt charts and cumulative cost curves. Although these graphic tools serve the purpose of communicating project progress visually, the earned-value approach is far more powerful analytically.

With well-maintained data, an earned-value system can measure precisely work performed, the proportion of our effort we have achieved, and the "burn rate" for the expenditures of project funds. It can even offer rough forecasting capabilities through the computation of the EAC. Note that these analyses can be carried out at any level of the WBS.

Use of the earned-value approach has two key limitations. One is the availability of accurate and timely cost data. Unfortunately, the majority of the organizations with which I work have not established systems to collect such data. I suspect that these organizations represent not the exception but the rule. It is difficult to fathom how an organization expects to manage its projects effectively without such data.

A second limitation is educational. For the earned value approach to work properly, everyone in the organization who touches the project management function should have an understanding of its mechanics. For example, they should be able to read and understand an earned value-based status report. "Everyone" includes upper management. If they do not study this approach and learn how it can yield improved insights into project performance, then much of its impact is lost.

A Historical Note

The earned-value approach was developed in the United States in the 1960s to help manage very large defense projects. Most of the effort in its development was driven by the U.S. Air Force. During the heyday of defense contracting in the 1950s and 1960s, it became apparent to the Defense Department that as projects get larger and more complex, it grows increasingly difficult to track what is happening on them. This problem is compounded by the fact that these large projects are being carried out in multiple contractor organizations, each of which employs its own peculiar planning and control system.

By the early 1960s, it was obvious that the Defense Department was no longer able to track adequately the efforts of its contractors. It decided that contractors on large, complex projects should be required to report their project efforts in a consistent fashion. It worked to develop rules for reporting project progress and in 1967 issued DODI, 7000.2, known also as the *Cost/Schedule Control System Criteria* (C/SCSC). In 1991, DODI 7000.2 was superseded by DODI 5000.2, which is virtually identical to DODI 7000.2. DODI 5000.2 tends to be a bit dry and abstract, so in order to put more meat on the bones, the Defense Department produced a document called the *Joint Implementation Guide,* which offers detailed and reasonably practical instructions on how to satisfy C/SCS requirements.

Today, DODI 5000.2 and the *Joint Implementation Guide* continue to offer the key guidance on how to report progress on large, complex projects. They focus on developing consistency and a tight management discipline in five areas:

- *Organization.* Instructions are provided on the development of work breakdown structures and organizational breakdown structures.
- *Planning.* Key planning requirements are highlighted—for example, the establishment of performance baselines.
- *Accounting.* Requirements are specified for the collection and maintenance of cost accounting data.
- *Analysis.* Guidance is offered on use of earned-value techniques for reporting budget variances, schedule variance, and EAC.
- *Reporting.* Instructions are given on reporting project status through cost performance reports (CPRs), which are required on very large projects, or cost/schedule status reports (C/SSRs), which are less burdensome to generate than CPRs and are required on smaller projects.

Because of the big-project focus of DODI 5000.2, coupled with its arcane nature, organizations outside of the defense community were unaware of its potential use to them on nondefense projects. This situation began to change in the late 1980s. As the Bora Bora Officer's Club example demonstrates, the earned-value approach can be used effectively on small projects when bureaucratic requirements—such as those found in DODI 5000.2—are stripped away. Non-U.S. project organizations have been studying DODI 5000.2 and the *Joint Implementation Guide* carefully in order to garner insights to help them manage their large, complex projects more effectively. One of the most savvy managers I know in the use of DODI 5000.2 is a Japanese fellow working on large construction projects in Japan.

Conclusions

There cannot be much accountability on projects if no one is sure how much work has been done. If project staff's rigor in reporting progress is restricted to "I think we're basically on target," they are not likely to know they are in trouble until it is too late.

This chapter argues that special effort must be made to measure work performance. Knowing how much work has been done is certainly one of the most important pieces of information a project manager can have. The good news is that well-tested methods exist for measuring work performed. These methods focus on what is called *integrated cost/schedule control.* They can entail something as simple as generating and comparing Gantt charts and cumulative cost curves. Or they may involve following the detailed instructions of Department of Defense Instruction (DODI) 5000.2 in order to track the world's largest, most complex projects. In any case, measuring work performed is vital if project staff desire to spot problems when they are little and can be fixed with few resources. The alternative is to be ignorant of problems until they are large and damaging.

CHAPTER 13

JOB ORDER COSTING AS IT APPLIES TO PROJECTS

13.1. JOB ORDER COSTING AND PROJECT MANAGEMENT

Job order costing applies costing concepts to jobs that have a specific beginning, ending, and include clearly definable units of production. In a project environment it could pertain to the activities or segments between each milestone, individual work packages, or even the total project. Note that the following reading by Horngren addresses job order costing in a manufacturing environment. Again the reason is that manufacturing represents the most complicated form of costing.

13.2. JOB-COSTING SYSTEMS

DISTINCTION BETWEEN JOB COSTING AND PROCESS COSTING

Recall that a *cost objective* is any activity or resource for which a separate measurement of costs is desired. Cost accounting systems have a twofold purpose fulfilled by their day-to-day operations: (1) to allocate costs to departments for planning and control, hereafter for brevity's sake often called *control*, and (2) to allocate costs to units of product for *product costing*.

Two extremes of product costing are *job-order costing* and *process costing*. **Job-order costing** (or simply **job costing**) allocates costs to products that are readily identified by individual units or batches, each of which requires varying degrees of attention and skill. Industries that commonly use job-order methods include construction, printing, aircraft, furniture, special-purpose machinery, and any manufacture of tailor-made or unique goods.

Process costing averages costs over large numbers of nearly identical products. It is most often found in such industries as chemicals, oil, textiles, plastics, paints, flour, canneries, rubber, lumber, food processing, glass, mining, cement, and meat packing. These industries involve mass production of like units, which usually pass in continuous fashion through a series of uniform production steps called *operations* or *processes*.

The distinction between the job-cost and the process-cost methods centers largely on how product costing is accomplished. Job costing applies costs to specific jobs, which may consist of either a single physical unit (such as a custom sofa) or a few like units (such as a dozen tables) in a distinct batch or job lot. In contrast, process costing deals with great masses of like units and broad averages of unit costs.

The most important point is that product costing is an *averaging* process. The unit cost used for inventory purposes is the result of taking some accumulated cost that has been allocated to production departments and dividing it by some measure of production. The basic distinction between job-order costing and process costing is the breadth of the denominator: In job-order costing, the denominator is small (e.g., one painting, 100 advertising circulars, or one special packaging machine); however, in process costing, the denominator is large (e.g., thousands of pounds, gallons, or board feet).

Job costing and process costing are extremes along a continuum of potential costing systems. Each company designs its own accounting system to fit its underlying production activities. Many companies use *hybrid* costing systems, which are blends of ideas from both job costing and process costing.

ILLUSTRATION OF JOB-ORDER COSTING

Job costing is best learned by example. But first we examine the basic records used in a job-cost system.

Basic Records

The centerpiece of a job-costing system is the job-cost record (also called a job-cost sheet or job order), shown in Exhibit 13-1. All costs for a particular product, service, or batch of products are recorded on the job-cost record. A file of job-cost records for partially completed jobs provides supporting details for the Work-in-Process Inventory account, often simply called Work in Process (WIP). A file of completed job-cost records comprises the Finished-Goods Inventory account.

As Exhibit 13-1 shows, the job-cost record summarizes information contained on source documents such as *materials requisitions* and *labor time tickets*. **Materials requisitions** are records of materials issued to particular jobs. **Labor time tickets** (or **time cards**) record the time a particular direct laborer spends on each job.

Today job-cost records and source documents are likely to be computer files, not paper records. In fact, with on-line data entry, barcoding, and optical scanning, much of the information needed for such records enters the computer without ever being written on paper. Nevertheless, whether records are on paper or on computer files, the accounting system must collect and maintain the same basic information.

As each job begins, a job-cost record is prepared. As units are worked on, entries are made on the job-cost record. Three classes of costs are applied to the units as they pass through the departments: material requisitions are the source of direct-material

Implementing Activity-Based Costing in a Job-Order and Process-Manufacturing Environment: Tredegar Molded Products

Tredegar Molded Products Company, a subsidiary of Tredegar Industries, Inc., is a diversified custom injection molder of plastics and metal products. Tredegar has six injection molding plants and one tooling facility and uses both job and process production and cost accounting systems. Examples of products manufactured are:

Job Order Production	Process Production
Steel molds	Deodorant canisters
Medical devices	Lip balm
	Closures (various sizes)
	Plugs and fitments

Recently, Tredegar began implementing activity-based costing (ABC) at three of its plants. The business issues leading to the implementation of ABC included the need for

- More accurate product costing
- Better understanding of key business processes
- Better utilization of resources

Specific applications of the new ABC information include:

- Activity-based budgeting
- Support for process improvement
- New product pricing
- Capital spending justification

Future uses of ABC at Tredegar include:

- Make or buy decisions
- Pricing of existing products ■

Source: From Janet B. Wynn, "Beyond the Pilot at Tredegar," NetProphet User Conference, September 1994, Sapling Corporation, Toronto.

costs, time tickets provide direct-labor costs, and budgeted overhead rates are used to apply factory overhead to products. (The computation of these budgeted rates will be described later in this chapter.)

Data for Illustration

To illustrate the functioning of a job-order costing system, we will use the basic records and journal entries of the Enriquez Electronics Company. On December 31, 19X5, the firm had the following inventories:

Direct materials (12 types)	$110,000
Work in process	—
Finished goods (unsold units from two jobs)	12,000

The following is a summary of pertinent transactions for the year 19X6:

	Machining	Assembly	Total
1. Direct materials purchased on account	—	—	$1,900,000
2. Direct materials requisitioned for manufacturing	$1,000,000	$890,000	1,890,000
3. Direct-labor costs incurred	200,000	190,000	390,000
4a. Factory overhead *incurred*	290,000	102,000	392,000
4b. Factory overhead *applied*	280,000	95,000	375,000
5. Cost of goods completed and transferred to finished-goods inventory	—	—	2,500,000
6a. Sales on account	—	—	4,000,000
6b. Cost of goods sold	—	—	2,480,000

Exhibit 13-1 Completed Job-Cost Record and Sample Source Documents

Job Cost Record: _____ Machining _____ Department					

Date Started _____ 1/7/X6 _____   Job No. _____ 963 _____
Date Completed _____ 1/14/X6 _____   Units Completed ___ 12 ___

Cost	Date	Ref.	Quantity	Amount	Summary
Direct Materials:					
6" Bars	1/7/X6	N41	24	120.00	
Casings	1/9/X6	K56	12	340.00	460.00
Direct Labor:					
Drill	1/8/X6	7Z4	7.0	105.00	
	1/9/X6	7Z5	5.5	82.50	
Grind	1/13/X6	9Z2	4.0	80.00	267.50
Factory Overhead:					
Applied	1/14/X6		9.0 Mach. Hrs.	180.00	180.00
Total Cost					907.50
Unit Cost					75.625

Direct Materials Requisition: No. ___ N41 ___
Job No. ___ 963 ___   Date ___ 1/7/X6 ___
Department ___ Machining ___

Descript	Quantity	Unit Cost	Amount
6" Bars	24	5.00	120.00

Authorization _____ J. Hays _____

Time Ticket: No. _____ Z74 _____
Employee No. _____ 464-89-7265 _____
Department _____ Machining _____
Date _____ 1/8/X6 _____

Start	End	Hours	Rate	Amount	Job
8:00	11:30	3.5	15.00	52.50	963
12:30	4:00	3.5	15.00	52.50	963
4:00	5:00	1.0	15.00	15.00	571
Totals		8.0		120.00	

Supervisor _____ M. Butler _____

We explain the nature of *factory overhead applied* later in this chapter. First, however, we need to consider the accounting for these transactions.

Exhibit 13-2 is an overview of the general flow of costs through the Enriquez Electronics Company's job-order-costing system. The exhibit summarizes the effects of transactions on the key manufacturing accounts in the firm's books. As you proceed through the detailed explanation of transactions, keep checking each explanation against the overview in Exhibit 13-2.

Explanation of Transactions

The following transaction-by-transaction summary analysis will explain how product costing is achieved. Entries are usually made as transactions occur. However, to obtain a sweeping overview, our illustration uses a summary for the entire year 19X6. Further, explanations for the journal entries are omitted.

Exhibit 13-2   Job-Order Costing, General Flow of Costs (Thousands)

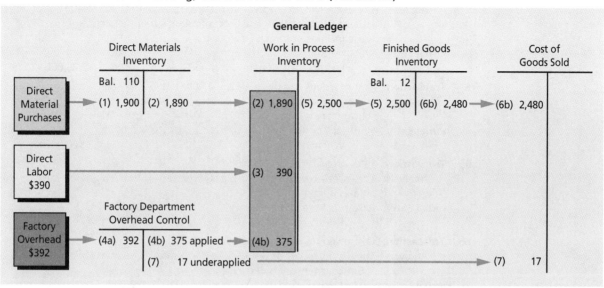

1. **Transaction:** Direct materials purchased, $1,900,000.
   Analysis: The asset Direct-Materials Inventory is increased. The liability
   Accounts Payable is increased.
   Journal Entry: Direct-Materials Inventory 1,900,000
   Accounts Payable   1,900,000

2. **Transaction:** Direct materials requisitioned, $1,890,000.
   Analysis: The asset Work-in-Process (WIP) Inventory is increased. The asset
   Direct-Materials Inventory is decreased.
   Journal Entry: WIP Inventory 1,890,000
   Direct-Materials Inventory   1,890,000

3. **Transaction:** Direct-labor cost incurred, $390,000.
   Analysis: The asset WIP Inventory is increased. The liability Accrued
   Payroll is increased.
   Journal Entry: WIP Inventory 390,000
   Accrued Payroll   390,000

4a. **Transaction:** Factory overhead incurred, $392,000.
   Analysis: These actual costs are first charged to departmental overhead
   accounts, which may be regarded as assets until their amounts are
   later "cleared" or transferred to other accounts. Each department has detailed overhead accounts such as indirect labor, utilities, repairs, depreciation, insurance, and property taxes. These
   details support a summary Factory Department Overhead Control
   account. The managers are responsible for regulating these costs,
   item by item. As these costs are charged to the departments, the
   other accounts affected will be assorted assets and liabilities.
   Examples include cash, accounts payable, accrued payables, and
   accumulated depreciation.
   Journal Entry: Factory Department Overhead Control .. 392,000
   Cash, Accounts Payable, and various
   other balance sheet accounts   392,000

4b. **Transaction:** Factory overhead applied, \$95,000 + \$280,000 = \$375,000.

Analysis: The asset WIP Inventory is increased. The asset Factory Department Overhead Control is decreased. (A fuller explanation occurs later in this chapter.)

Journal Entry:

WIP Inventory	375,000	
Factory Department Overhead Control		375,000

5. **Transaction:** Cost of goods completed, \$2,500,000.

Analysis: The asset Finished Goods Inventory is increased. The asset WIP Inventory is decreased.

Journal Entry:

Finished Goods Inventory	2,500,000	
WIP Inventory		2,500,000

6a. **Transaction:** Sales on account, \$4,000,000.

Analysis: The asset Accounts Receivable is increased. The revenue account Sales is increased.

Journal Entry:

Accounts Receivable	4,000,000	
Sales		4,000,000

6b. **Transaction:** Cost of goods sold, \$2,480,000.

Analysis: The expense Cost of Goods Sold is increased. The asset Finished Goods Inventory is decreased.

Journal Entry:

Cost of Goods Sold	2,480,000	
Finished Goods Inventory		2,480,000

Summary of Transactions

Exhibit 13-2 summarizes the Enriquez transactions for the year, focusing on the inventory accounts. WIP Inventory receives central attention. The costs of direct material used, direct labor, and factory overhead applied to product are brought into WIP. In turn, the costs of completed goods are transferred from WIP to Finished Goods. As goods are sold, their costs become expense in the form of Cost of Goods Sold. The year-end accounting for the \$17,000 of underapplied overhead is explained later.

ACCOUNTING FOR FACTORY OVERHEAD

In the Enriquez Company example, factory overhead of \$375,000 was applied to the WIP account. This section describes how to determine the amount of applied factory overhead.

Cost Application or Absorption

Recall that cost allocation refers to identifying or tracing accumulated costs to departments and products, and cost application (cost absorption) refers to allocation to products, as distinguished from allocation to departments.

Few companies wait until the actual factory overhead is finally known before computing the costs of products. Instead, they compute a budgeted (predetermined) overhead rate at the beginning of a fiscal year and use it to apply overhead costs as products are manufactured. Most managers want a close approximation of the costs of various products continuously, not just at the end of a year. Managers desire those costs for various ongoing uses including choosing which products to emphasize or de-emphasize, pricing products, producing interim financial statements, and managing inventories.

Budgeted Overhead Application Rates

The following steps summarize how to account for factory overhead:

1. Select one or more cost drivers to serve as a base for applying overhead costs. Examples include direct-labor hours, direct-labor costs, machine-hours, and production setups. The cost driver should be an activity that is the common denominator for systematically relating a cost or a group of costs, such as machinery cost, set-up costs, or energy cost, with products. The cost driver(s) should be the best available measure of the cause-and-effect relationships between overhead costs and production volume.

2. Prepare a factory-overhead budget for the planning period, ordinarily a year. The two key items are (1) budgeted overhead and (2) budgeted volume of the cost driver. There will be a set of budgeted overhead costs and an associated budgeted cost-driver level for each component of total overhead. In businesses with simple production systems there may be just one set.

3. Compute the **budgeted factory-overhead rate(s)** by dividing the budgeted total overhead by the budgeted cost-driver activity.

4. Obtain actual cost-driver data (such as machine-hours) as the year unfolds.

5. Apply the budgeted overhead to the jobs by multiplying the budgeted rate(s) times the actual cost-driver data.

6. At the end of the year, account for any differences between the amount of overhead actually incurred and overhead applied to products.

ILLUSTRATION OF OVERHEAD APPLICATION

To understand how to apply factory overhead to jobs, consider the Enriquez illustration again.

The following manufacturing-overhead budget has been prepared for the coming year, 19X7:

	Machining	Assembly
Indirect labor	$ 75,600	$ 36,800
Supplies	8,400	2,400
Utilities	20,000	7,000
Repairs	10,000	3,000
Factory rent	10,000	6,800
Supervision	42,600	35,400
Depreciation on equipment	104,000	9,400
Insurance, property taxes, etc.	7,200	2,400
	$277,800	$103,200

As products are worked on, Enriquez applies the factory overhead to the jobs. A budgeted overhead rate is used, computed as follows:

$$\text{budgeted overhead application rate} = \frac{\text{total budgeted factory overhead}}{\substack{\text{total budgeted amount of cost driver} \\ \text{(such as direct-labor costs or machine-hours)}}}$$

Simplifying Product Costing at Harley-Davidson

When Harley-Davidson, the motorcycle manufacturer, adopted a just-in-time (JIT) philosophy in the early 1980s, it quickly discovered that its accounting system needed revision. The main focus of the accounting system was direct labor, which not only made up a part of product cost itself, but also functioned as an all-purpose base for allocating overhead. However, by the mid-1980s, direct labor was only 10% of total product cost. It certainly did not generate a majority of overhead costs. As Harley-Davidson's production process had changed, the accounting system had remained static.

The first point that became apparent with the JIT system was that detailed information on direct-labor costs was not useful to managers. It was costly to have each direct laborer record the time spent on each product or part and then enter the information from these time cards into the accounting system. For example, if each of 500 direct laborers works on 20 products per day, the system must record 10,000 entries per day, which is 200,000 entries per month. The time spent by direct laborers to record the time, by clerks to enter the data into the system, and by the accountants to check the data's accuracy is enormous—and all to produce product cost information that was used for financial reporting but was useless to managers.

The JIT system forced manufacturing managers to focus on satisfying customers and minimizing non-value-added activities. Gradually, accountants began to focus on the same objectives. Accounting's customers were the managers who used the accounting information, and effort put into activities that did not help managers was deemed counterproductive. Therefore, eliminating the costly, time-consuming recording of detailed labor costs became a priority. Direct labor was eliminated as a direct cost, and consequently it could not be used for overhead allocation. After considering process hours, flow-through time, material value, and individual cost per unit as possible cost drivers for allocating overhead, the company selected process hours. Direct labor and overhead were combined to form *conversion costs*, which were applied to products on the basis of total process hours. This did not result in costs significantly different than the old system, but the new system was much simpler and less costly. Only direct material was traced directly to the product. Conversion costs were applied at completion of production based on a simple measure of process time.

Accounting systems should generate benefits greater than their costs. More sophisticated systems are not necessarily better systems. Harley-Davidson's main objective in changing its accounting system was simplification—eliminating unnecessary tasks and streamlining others. These changes resulted in a revitalized accounting system. ■

Source: Adapted from W. T. Turk, "Management Accounting Revitalized: The Harley-Davidson Experience," in B. J. Brinker, ed., Emerging Practices in Cost Management, *Warren, Gorham & Lamont, Boston, 1990, pp. 155–66.*

Suppose machine-hours are chosen as the only cost driver in the Machining Department, and direct-labor cost is chosen in the Assembly Department. The overhead rates are as follows:

	Year 19X7	
	Machining	*Assembly*
Budgeted manufacturing overhead	$277,800	$103,200
Budgeted machine-hours	69,450	
Budgeted direct-labor cost		$206,400
Budgeted overhead rate, per machine-hour: $277,800 ÷ 69,450 =	$4	
Budgeted overhead rate, per direct-labor dollar: $103,200 ÷ $206,400 =		50%

Note that the overhead rates are budgeted; they are estimates. These rates are then used to apply overhead based on *actual* events. That is, the total overhead applied in our illustration is the result of multiplying *actual* machine-hours or labor cost by the *budgeted* overhead rates:

Machining: actual machine-hours of 70,000 × $4 = $280,000
Assembly: actual direct-labor cost of $190,000 × .50 =   95,000
Total factory overhead applied $375,000

The summary journal entry for the application (entry 4b) is:

4b. WIP Inventory   375,000
        Factory Department Overhead Control   375,000

Choice of Cost Drivers

Factory overhead is a conglomeration of manufacturing costs that, unlike direct material or direct labor, cannot conveniently be applied on an individual job basis. But such overhead is an integral part of a product's total cost. Therefore, it is applied indirectly, using as a base a cost driver that is common to all jobs worked on and is the best available index of the product's relative use of, or benefits from, the overhead items. In other words, there should be a strong cause-and-effect relationship between the factory overhead cost incurred (the effect) and the cost driver chosen for its application.

As we have noted several times in this text, no one cost driver is right for all situations. The goal is to find the driver that best links cause and effect. In the Enriquez Machining Department, two or more machines can often be operated simultaneously by a single direct laborer. Use of machines causes most overhead cost in the Machining Department, for example, depreciation and repairs. Therefore, machine-hours is the cost driver and the appropriate base for applying overhead costs. Thus, Enriquez must keep track of the machine-hours used for each job, creating an added data collection cost. That is, both direct-labor costs and machine-hours must be accumulated for each job.

In contrast, direct labor is a principal cost driver in the Enriquez Assembly Department. It is an accurate reflection of the relative attention and effort devoted to various jobs. The workers are paid equal hourly rates. Therefore, all that is needed is to apply the 50% overhead rate to the cost of direct labor already entered on the job-cost records. No separate job records have to be kept of the labor-hours. If the hourly labor rates differ greatly for individuals performing identical tasks, the hours of labor, rather than the dollars spent for labor, might be used as a base. Otherwise a $9-per-hour worker would cause more overhead applied than an $8-per-hour worker, even though the same time would probably be taken and the same facilities used by each employee for the same work.

Sometimes direct-labor cost is the best overhead cost driver even if wage rates vary within a department. For example, higher-skilled labor may use more costly equipment and have more indirect labor support. Moreover, many factory-overhead costs include costly labor fringe benefits such as pensions and payroll taxes. The latter are often more closely driven by direct-labor cost than by direct-labor hours.

If a department identifies more than one cost driver for overhead costs, these costs ideally should be put into as many cost pools as there are cost drivers. In practice, such a system is too costly for many organizations. Instead, these organizations select a few cost drivers (often only one) to serve as a basis for allocating overhead costs. The 80–20 rule can be used in these situations. In many cases, 80% of total overhead cost can be accounted for with just a few drivers (20% of all the drivers identified). For example, a company may identify 10 separate overhead pools with 10 different drivers. Often, approximately 80% of the total cost can be applied with only 2 drivers.

The selected cost drivers should be the ones that cause most of the overhead costs. For example, suppose machine-hours cause 70% of the overhead costs in a particular department, number of component parts cause 20%, and five assorted cost drivers cause the other 10%. Instead of using seven cost pools allocated on the basis of the seven cost drivers, most managers would use one cost driver, machine-hours, to allocate all overhead costs. Others would assign all cost to two cost pools, one allocated on the basis of machine-hours and one on the basis of number of component parts.

No matter which cost drivers are chosen, the overhead rates are applied day after day throughout the year to cost the various jobs worked on by each department. All overhead is applied to all jobs worked on during the year on the appropriate basis of machine-hours or direct-labor costs of each job. Suppose management predictions coincide exactly with actual amounts (an extremely unlikely situation). Then the total overhead applied to the year's jobs via these budgeted rates would be equal to the total overhead costs actually incurred.

PROBLEMS OF OVERHEAD APPLICATION

Normalized Overhead Rates

Basically, our illustration has demonstrated the *normal costing* approach. Why the term "normal"? Because an annual average overhead rate is used consistently throughout the year for product costing, *without altering it from day to day and from month to month*. The resultant "normal" product costs include an average or normalized chunk of overhead.

As actual overhead costs are incurred by departments from month to month, they are charged to the departments. On a weekly or monthly basis, these actual costs are then compared with budgeted costs to obtain budget variances for performance evaluation. This *control* process is distinct from the *product-costing* process of applying overhead to specific jobs.

During the year and at year-end, the actual overhead amount incurred will rarely equal the amount applied. This variance between incurred and applied cost can be analyzed. The most common—and important—contributor to these variances is operating at a different level of volume than the level used as a denominator in calculating the budgeted overhead rate (e.g., using 100,000 budgeted direct-labor-hours as the denominator and then actually working only 80,000 hours). Other frequent contributory causes include: poor forecasting, inefficient use of overhead items, price changes in individual overhead items, erratic behavior of individual overhead items (e.g., repairs made only during slack time), and calendar variations (e.g., 20 workdays in one month, 22 in the next).

All these peculiarities of overhead are mingled in an *annual* overhead pool. Thus, an annual rate is budgeted and used regardless of the month-to-month peculiarities of specific overhead costs. Such an approach is more defensible than, say, applying the actual overhead for *each month*. Why? Because a *normal* product cost is more useful for decisions, and more representative for inventory-costing purposes, than an "actual" product cost that is distorted by month-to-month fluctuations in production volume and by the erratic behavior of many overhead costs. For example, the employees of a gypsum plant using an "actual" product cost system had the privilege of buying company-made items "at cost." Employees joked about the benefits of buying "at cost" during high-volume months, when unit costs were lower because volume was higher:

	Actual Overhead			Direct-Labor Hours	Actual Overhead Application Rate* per Direct-Labor Hour
	Variable	*Fixed*	*Total*		
Peak-volume month	$60,000	$40,000	$100,000	100,000	$1.00
Low-volume month	30,000	40,000	70,000	50,000	1.40

* Divide total overhead by direct-labor hours. Note that the presence of fixed overhead causes the fluctuation in unit costs from $1.00 to $1.40. The variable component is $.60 an hour in both months, but the fixed component is $.40 in the peak-volume month ($40,000 ÷ 100,000) and $.80 in the low-volume month ($40,000 ÷ 50,000).

Disposition of Underapplied or Overapplied Overhead

Our Enriquez illustration contained the following data:

Transaction	
4a. Factory overhead incurred	$392,000
4b. Factory overhead applied	375,000
Underapplied factory overhead	$ 17,000

Total costs of $392,000 must eventually be charged to expense in some way. The $375,000 will become part of the Cost of Goods Sold expense when the products to which it is applied are sold. The remaining $17,000 must also become expense by some method.

When budgeted rates are used, the difference between incurred and applied overhead is typically allowed to accumulate during the year. When the amount applied to product *exceeds* the amount incurred by the departments, the difference is called **overapplied overhead.** When the amount applied is *less than* incurred, the difference is called **underapplied overhead.** At year-end, the difference ($17,000 underapplied in our illustration) is disposed of either through a *write-off* or through *proration*.

Immediate Write-Off

This is the most widely used approach. The $17,000 is regarded as a reduction in current income by adding the underapplied overhead to the cost of goods sold. The same logic is followed for overapplied overhead except that the result would be a decrease in cost of goods sold.

The theory underlying the direct write-off is that most of the goods worked on have been sold, and a more elaborate method of disposition is not worth the extra trouble. Another justification is that the extra overhead costs represented by underapplied overhead do not qualify as part of ending inventory costs because they do not represent assets. They should be written off because they largely represent inefficiency or the underutilization of available facilities in the current period.

The immediate write-off eliminates the $17,000 difference with a simple journal entry, labeled as transaction 7 in Exhibit 13-2.

```
7. Cost of Goods Sold (or a separate
      charge against revenue) .........................   17,000
              Factory Department Overhead Control ...........            17,000
   To close ending underapplied overhead directly to Cost of
      Goods Sold.
```

Proration Among Inventories

This method *prorates* underapplied overhead among three accounts. Theoretically, if the objective is to obtain as accurate a cost allocation as possible, all the overhead costs of the individual jobs worked on should be recomputed, using the actual, rather than the budgeted, rates. This approach is rarely feasible, so a practical attack is to prorate on the basis of the ending balances in each of three accounts (WIP, $155,000; Finished Goods, $32,000; and Cost of Goods Sold, $2,480,000). To **prorate** underapplied overhead means to assign it in proportion to the sizes of the ending account balances.

	(1) Unadjusted Balance, End of 19X2*	(2) Proration of Underapplied Overhead	(3) Adjusted Balance, End of 19X2
WIP	$ 155,000	$155/2,667 \times 17,000 = $ 988$	$ 155,988
Finished Goods	32,000	$32/2,667 \times 17,000 = 204$	32,204
Cost of Goods Sold	2,480,000	$2,480/2,667 \times 17,000 = 15,808$	2,495,808
	$2,667,000	$17,000	$2,684,000

* See pages 461–62 for details.

The journal entry for the proration follows:

```
WIP ...................................................     988
Finished Goods  .......................................     204
Cost of Goods Sold  ................................... 15,808
        Factory Department Overhead Control .............           17,000
   To prorate ending underapplied overhead among
      three accounts.
```

The amounts prorated to inventories here are not significant. In actual practice, prorating is done only when inventory valuations would be materially affected. Exhibit 13-3 provides a schematic comparison of the two major methods of disposing of underapplied (or overapplied) factory overhead.

The Use of Variable and Fixed Application Rates

As we have seen, overhead application is the most troublesome aspect of product costing. The presence of fixed costs is a major reason for the costing difficulties. Most companies have made no distinction between variable- and fixed-cost behavior in the design of their accounting systems. For instance, the Machining Department at Enriquez Electronics Company developed the following rate:

$$\text{budgeted overhead application rate } = \frac{\text{budgeted total overhead}}{\text{budgeted machine-hours}}$$

$$= \frac{\$277,800}{69,450} = \$4 \text{ per machine-hour}$$

Some companies distinguish between variable overhead and fixed overhead for product costing as well as for control purposes. If the Machining Department had made this distinction, then rent, supervision, depreciation, and insurance would have been considered the fixed portion of the total manufacturing overhead, and two rates would have been developed:

$$\text{budgeted variable-overhead application rate } = \frac{\text{budgeted total variable overhead}}{\text{budgeted machine-hours}}$$

$$= \frac{\$114,000}{69,450}$$

$$= \$1.64 \text{ per machine-hour}$$

$$\text{budgeted fixed-overhead application rate } = \frac{\text{budgeted total fixed overhead}}{\text{budgeted machine-hours}}$$

$$= \frac{\$163,800}{69,450}$$

$$= \$2.36 \text{ per machine-hour}$$

Exhibit 13-3 Year-end Disposition of Underapplied Factory Overhead (COGS = Cost of Goods Sold)

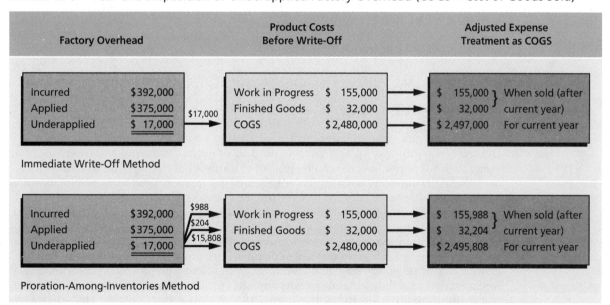

Such rates can be used for product costing. Distinctions between variable- and fixed-overhead incurrence can also be made for control purposes.

Actual Costing Versus Normal Costing

The overall system we have just described is sometimes called an *actual costing system* because every effort is made to trace the *actual* costs, as incurred, to the physical units benefited. However, it is only partly an actual system because overhead, by definition, cannot be traced to physical products. Instead, overhead is applied on an average or normalized basis to get representative or normal inventory valuations. Hence we shall label the system a **normal costing system.** The cost of the manufactured product is composed of *actual* direct material, *actual* direct labor, and *normal* applied overhead.

The two job-order costing approaches may be compared as follows:

	Actual Costing	Normal Costing
Direct materials	Actual	Actual
Direct labor	Actual	Actual
Manufacturing overhead	Actual	Budgeted rates*

* Actual inputs (such as direct-labor hours or direct-labor costs) multiplied by budgeted overhead rates (computed by dividing total budgeted manufacturing overhead by a budgeted cost driver such as direct-labor hours).

In a true actual costing system, overhead would not be applied as jobs were worked on, but only after all overhead costs for the year were known. Then, using an "actual" average rate(s) instead of a budgeted rate(s), costs would be applied to all jobs that had been worked on throughout the year. All costs incurred would be exactly offset by costs applied to the WIP Inventory. However, increased accuracy would be obtained at the serious sacrifice of timeliness in using costs for measuring operating efficiency, determining selling prices, and producing interim financial statements.

Normal costing has replaced actual costing in many organizations precisely because the latter approach fails to provide costs of products as they are worked on during the year. It is possible to use a normal costing system plus year-end adjustments to produce final results that closely approximate the results under actual costing. To do so in our illustration, the underapplied overhead is prorated among WIP, Finished Goods, and Cost of Goods Sold, as shown in Exhibit 13-3.

PRODUCT COSTING IN SERVICE AND NONPROFIT ORGANIZATIONS

This chapter has concentrated on how to apply costs to manufactured products. However, the job-costing approach is used in nonmanufacturing situations too. For example, universities have research "projects," airlines have repair and overhaul "jobs," and public accountants have audit "engagements." In such situations, the focus shifts from the costs of products to the costs of services.

In nonprofit organizations the "product" is usually not called a "job order." Instead, it may be called a program or a class of service. A "program" is an identifiable group of activities that frequently produces outputs in the form of services rather than goods. Examples include a safety program, an education program, and a family counseling program. Costs or revenues may be traced to individual hospital patients, individual social welfare cases, and individual university research projects. However, departments often work simultaneously on many programs, so the "job-order" costing challenge is to "apply" the various department costs to the various programs. Only then can managers make wiser decisions regarding the allocation of limited resources among competing programs.

In service industries—such as repairing, consulting, legal, and accounting services—each customer order is a different job with a special account or order number. Sometimes only costs are traced directly to the job, sometimes only revenue is traced, and sometimes both. For example, automobile repair shops typically have a repair order for each car worked on, with space for allocating materials and labor costs. Customers are permitted to see only a copy showing the retail prices of the materials, parts, and labor billed to their orders. If the repair manager wants cost data, a system may be designed so that the "actual" parts and labor costs of each order are traced to a duplicate copy of the repair order. That is why you often see auto mechanics "punching in" and "punching out" their starting and stopping times on "time tickets" as each new order is worked on.

Budgets and Control of Engagements

In many service organizations and some manufacturing operations, job orders are used not only for product costing, but also for planning and control purposes. For example, a public accounting firm might have a condensed budget for 19X1 as follows:

Revenue	$10,000,000	100%
Direct labor (for professional hours charged to engagements)	2,500,000	25%
Contribution to overhead and operating income	$ 7,500,000	75%
Overhead (all other costs)	6,500,000	65%
Operating income	$ 1,000,000	10%

In this illustration:

$$\text{budgeted overhead rate} = \frac{\text{budgeted overhead}}{\text{budgeted direct labor}}$$

$$= \frac{\$6,500,000}{\$2,500,000} = 260\%$$

As each engagement is budgeted, the partner in charge of the audit predicts the expected number of necessary direct-professional hours. Direct-professional hours are those worked by partners, managers, and subordinate auditors to complete the engagement. The budgeted direct-labor cost is the pertinent hourly labor costs multiplied by the budgeted hours. Partners' time is charged to the engagement at much higher rates than subordinates' time.

How is overhead applied? Accounting firms usually use either direct-labor cost or direct-labor hours as the cost driver for overhead application. In our example, the firm uses direct-labor cost. Such a practice implies that partners require proportionately more overhead support for each of their hours charged.

The budgeted total cost of an engagement is the direct-labor cost plus applied overhead (260% of direct-labor cost in this illustration) plus any other direct costs.

The engagement partner uses a budget for a specific audit that includes detailed scope and steps. For instance, the budget for auditing cash or receivables would specify the exact work to be done, the number of hours, and the necessary hours of partner time, manager time, and subordinate time. The partner monitors progress by comparing the hours logged to date with the original budget and with the estimated hours remaining on the engagement. Obviously, if a fixed audit fee has been quoted, the profitability of an engagement depends on whether the audit can be accomplished within the budgeted time limits.

Accuracy of Costs of Engagements

Suppose the accounting firm has costs on an auditing engagement as follows:

Direct-professional labor	$ 50,000
Applied overhead, 260% of $50,000	130,000
Total costs excluding travel costs	$180,000
Travel costs	14,000
Total costs of engagement	$194,000

Two direct costs, professional labor and travel costs, are traced to the jobs. But only direct-professional labor is a cost driver for overhead. (Note that costs reimbursed by the client—such as travel costs—do not add to overhead costs and should not be subject to any markups in the setting of fees.)

Managers of service firms, such as auditing and consulting firms, frequently use either the budgeted or "actual" costs of engagements as guides to pricing and to allocating effort among particular services or customers. Hence, the accuracy of costs of various engagements may affect decisions.

Activity-Based Costing: Shifting Overhead to Direct Costs

Our accounting firm example described a widely used, relatively simple job-costing system. Only two direct-cost items (direct-professional labor and travel costs) are used and only a single overhead application rate is used.

In recent years, to obtain more accurate costs, many professional service firms have refined their data processing systems and adopted activity-based costing. Computers help accumulate information that is far more detailed than was feasible a few years ago. As noted in earlier chapters, firms that use activity-based costing generally shift costs from being classified as overhead to being classified as direct costs. Using our previously assumed numbers for direct labor ($50,000) and travel ($14,000), we recast the costs of our audit engagement as follows:

Direct-professional labor	$ 50,000
Direct-support labor, such as secretarial costs	10,000
Fringe benefits for all direct labor*	24,000
Telephone calls	1,000
Photocopying	2,000
Computer time	7,000
Total direct costs	94,000
Applied overhead†	103,400
Total costs excluding travel costs	197,400
Travel costs	14,000
Total costs of engagement	$211,400

* 40% assumed rate multiplied by ($50,000 + $10,000) = $24,000.
† 110% assumed rate multiplied by total direct costs of $94,000 = $103,400.

Costs such as direct-support labor, telephone calls, photocopying, computer time, and travel costs are applied by directly measuring their usage on each engagement. The remaining costs to be allocated are assigned to cost pools based on their cause. The cost driver for fringe benefits is labor cost, and the cost driver for other overhead is total direct costs.

The more detailed approach of activity-based costing will nearly always produce total costs that differ from the total costs in the general approach shown earlier: $211,400 compared with $194,000. Of course, any positive or negative difference is attributable to having more types of costs traced directly to the engagement. For instance, secretarial time is directly tracked in the second but not the first example. Moreover, the fringe benefits are separately tracked. Some firms include such fringe benefits as an integral part of their direct-labor costs. Therefore, if fringe benefits are 40% of an auditor's hourly compensation of $25, some firms cost their labor at $25 plus 40% of $25, or $25 + $10 = $35. Other firms do as implied in the tabulation, compiling direct-professional labor at the $25 rate and separately compiling the related fringe benefits at the 40% rate.

Effects of Classifications on Overhead Rates

The activity-based-costing approach also has a lower overhead application rate, assumed at 110% of total direct costs instead of the 260% of direct labor used in the first example, for two reasons. First, there are fewer overhead costs because more costs are traced directly. Second, the application base is broader including all direct costs rather than only direct labor.

Even with activity-based costing, some firms may prefer to continue to apply their overhead based on direct-labor costs rather than total direct costs. Why? Because the partners believe that overhead is dominantly affected by the amount of direct-labor costs rather than other direct costs such as telephone calls. But at least the activity-based-costing firm has made an explicit decision that direct-labor costs are the best cost driver.

Whether the overhead cost driver should be total direct costs, direct-professional labor costs or hours, or some other cost driver is a knotty problem for many firms including most professional service firms. Ideally, activity analysis should uncover the principal cost drivers, and they should all be used for overhead application. In practice, only one or two cost drivers are usually used.

Multiple Overhead Rates

A growing minority of service and manufacturing organizations use more than one overhead rate to apply costs to engagements or jobs. For example, a professional services firm might apply some overhead on the basis of direct professional labor and other overhead on the basis of computer time. The latter cost driver is becoming more widely used as expensive computers assume a more prominent role in rendering service to clients or customers.

As might be expected, the activity-based-costing approach results in different total costs. Depending on how prices are set, these costs may lead to a different total revenue for the engagement. The activity-based-costing approach demonstrates a trend in both service and manufacturing industries. That is, as data processing becomes less expensive, more costs than just direct materials and direct labor will be classified as direct costs when feasible. Moreover, more than one cost driver will be used for overhead application. In these ways, there will be more accurate tracking of costs to specific jobs or engagements. Then managers will have improved information to guide their decisions.

Highlights to Remember

Accounting systems are designed to help satisfy control and product-costing purposes simultaneously. Costs are initially charged to departments; then they are applied to products to get inventory costs for balance sheets and income statements, to guide pricing, and to evaluate product performance.

Product costing is an averaging process. Process costing deals with broad averages and great masses of like units. Job costing deals with narrow averages and a unique unit or a small batch of like units. The job-cost sheet summarizes the costs of a particular job and holds the underlying detail for the WIP Inventory account.

Indirect manufacturing costs (factory overhead) are often applied to products using budgeted overhead rates. The rates are computed by dividing total budgeted overhead by a measure of cost-driver activity such as expected labor-hours or machine-hours. These rates are usually annual averages. The resulting product costs are normal costs, consisting of actual direct material plus actual direct labor plus applied overhead using budgeted rates. When actual overhead differs from applied overhead, overapplied or underapplied overhead arises, which is either written off at the end of the year or prorated to the inventory accounts.

Exhibit 13-4   Relation of Costs to Financial Statements

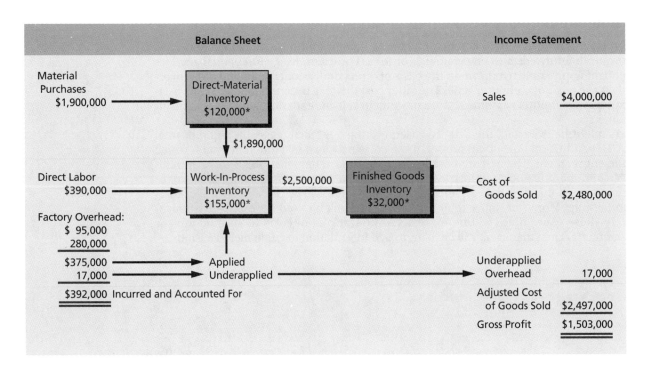

The job-costing approach is used in nonmanufacturing as well as in manufacturing. Examples include costs of services such as auto repair, consulting, and auditing. For example, the job order is a key device for planning and controlling an audit engagement by a public accounting firm.

Summary Problem for Your Review

Problem

Review the Enriquez illustration, especially Exhibits 13-2 and 13-3. Prepare an income statement for 19X6 through the gross profit line. Use the immediate write-off method for overapplied or underapplied overhead.

Solution

Exhibit 13-4 recapitulates the final impact of the Enriquez illustration on the financial statements. Note how the immediate write-off means that the $17,000 is added to the cost of goods sold. As you study Exhibit 13-4, trace the three major elements of cost (direct material, direct labor, and factory overhead) through the accounts.

Fundamental Assignment Material

13-A1 Basic Journal Entries

The following data (in thousands) summarize the factory operations of the Lewis Manufacturing Co. for the year 19X5, its first year in business:

a.	Direct materials purchased for cash	$360
b.	Direct materials issued and used	330
c.	Labor used directly on production	125
d1.	Indirect labor	80
d2.	Depreciation of plant and equipment	55
d3.	Miscellaneous factory overhead (ordinarily would be detailed)	40
e.	Overhead applied: 180% of direct labor	?
f.	Cost of production completed	625
g.	Cost of goods sold	400

1. Prepare summary journal entries. Omit explanations. For purposes of this problem, combine the items in *d* as "overhead incurred."
2. Show the T-accounts for all inventories, Cost of Goods Sold, and Factory Department Overhead Control. Compute the ending balances of the inventories. Do not adjust for underapplied or overapplied factory overhead.

13-A2 Accounting for Overhead, Budgeted Rates

McFarland Aeronautics Co. uses a budgeted overhead rate in applying overhead to individual job orders on a *machine-hour* basis for Department A and on a *direct-labor-hour* basis for Department B. At the beginning of 19X6, the company's management made the following budget predictions:

	Department A	Department B
Direct-labor cost	$1,500,000	$1,200,000
Factory overhead	$1,820,000	$1,000,000
Direct-labor hours	90,000	125,000
Machine-hours	350,000	20,000

Cost records of recent months show the following accumulations for Job Order No. 455:

	Department A	Department B
Material placed in production	$12,000	$32,000
Direct-labor cost	$10,800	$10,000
Direct-labor hours	900	1,250
Machine-hours	3,500	150

1. What is the budgeted overhead *rate* that should be applied in Department A? In Department B?
2. What is the *total overhead* cost of Job Order No. 455?
3. If Job Order No. 455 consists of 120 units of product, what is the *unit cost* of this job?
4. At the *end* of 19X6, actual results for the year's operations were as follows:

	Department A	Department B
Actual overhead costs incurred	$1,300,000	$1,200,000
Actual direct-labor hours	80,000	120,000
Actual machine-hours	300,000	25,000

Find the underapplied or overapplied overhead for each department and for the factory as a whole.

13-A3 Disposition of Overhead

Shoreline Marine Manufacturing applies factory overhead using machine-hours and number of component parts as cost drivers. In 19X5, actual factory overhead incurred was $134,000 and applied factory overhead was $126,000. Before disposition of underapplied or overapplied factory overhead, the cost of goods sold was $525,000, gross profit was $60,000, and ending inventories were:

Direct materials	$ 25,000
WIP	75,000
Finished goods	150,000
Total inventories	$250,000

1. Was factory overhead overapplied or underapplied? By how much?
2. Assume that Shoreline writes off overapplied or underapplied factory overhead as an adjustment to cost of goods sold. Prepare the journal entry, and compute adjusted gross profit.
3. Assume that Shoreline prorates overapplied or underapplied factory overhead based on end-of-the-year unadjusted balances. Prepare the journal entry, and compute adjusted gross profit.

4. Assume that actual factory overhead was $124,000 instead of $134,000, and that Shoreline writes off overapplied or underapplied factory overhead as an adjustment to cost of goods sold. Prepare the journal entry, and compute adjusted gross profit.

13-B1 Basic Journal Entries

Consider the following data for a London printing company (in thousands):

Inventories, December 31, 19X4	
Direct materials	£ 18
Work in process	25
Finished goods	100

Summarized transactions for 19X5:

a.	Purchases of direct materials	£109
b.	Direct materials used	95
c.	Direct labor	105
d.	Factory overhead incurred	90
e.	Factory overhead applied, 80% of direct labor	?
f.	Cost of goods completed and transferred to finished goods	280
g.	Cost of goods sold	350
h.	Sales on account	600

1. Prepare summary journal entries for 19X5 transactions. Omit explanations.
2. Show the T-accounts for all inventories, Cost of Goods Sold, and Factory Department Overhead Control. Compute the ending balances of the inventories. Do not adjust for underapplied or overapplied factory overhead.

13-B2 Disposition of Overhead

Baker Mfg. Co. had overapplied overhead of $50 in 19X6. Before adjusting for overapplied or underapplied overhead, the ending inventories for Direct Materials, WIP, and Finished Goods were $75, $100, and $150, respectively. Unadjusted cost of goods sold was $250.

1. Assume that the $50 was written off solely as an adjustment to cost of goods sold. Prepare the journal entry.
2. Management has decided to prorate the $50 to the appropriate accounts (using the unadjusted ending balances) instead of writing it off solely as an adjustment of cost of goods sold. Prepare the journal entry. Would gross profit be higher or lower than in requirement 1? By how much?

13-B3 Application of Overhead Using Budgeted Rates

The Mesa Clinic computes a cost of treating each patient. It allocates costs to departments and then applies departmental overhead costs to individual patients using a different budgeted overhead rate in each department. Consider the following predicted 19X7 data for two of Mesa's departments:

	Pharmacy	Medical Records
Department overhead cost	$180,000	$300,000
Number of prescriptions filled	90,000	
Number of patient visits		60,000

The cost driver for overhead in Pharmacy is *number of prescriptions filled*; in Medical Records it is *number of patient visits*.

In June 19X7, Luke Ashton paid two visits to the clinic and had four prescriptions filled at the pharmacy.

1. Compute departmental overhead rates for the two departments.
2. Compute the overhead costs applied to the patient Luke Ashton in June 19X7.
3. At the end of 19X7 actual overhead costs were:

Pharmacy	$175,000
Medical records	$325,000

The pharmacy filled 85,000 prescriptions, and the clinic had 63,000 patient visits during 19X7. Compute the overapplied or underapplied overhead in each department.

Additional Assignment Material

Questions

13-1. "There are different product costs for different purposes." Name at least two purposes.

13-2. Distinguish between job costing and process costing.

13-3. "The basic distinction between job-order costing and process costing is the breadth of the denominator." Explain.

13-4. How does hybrid costing relate to job costing and process costing?

13-5. Describe the subsidiary ledger for work in process in a job-cost system.

13-6. "The general ledger entries are only a small part of the accountant's daily work." Explain.

13-7. "Cost application or absorption is terminology related to the product-costing purpose." Explain.

13-8. "Job costs are accumulated for purposes of inventory valuation and income determination." State two other purposes.

13-9. Give four examples of cost drivers.

13-10. "Each department must choose one cost driver to be used for cost application." Do you agree? Explain.

13-11. "There should be a strong relationship between the factory overhead incurred and the cost driver chosen for its application." Why?

13-12. "Sometimes direct-labor cost is the best cost driver for overhead allocation even if wage rates vary within a department." Do you agree? Explain.

13-13. What are some reasons for differences between the amounts of *incurred* and *applied* overhead?

13-14. "Under actual overhead application, unit costs soar as volume increases and vice versa." Do you agree? Explain.

13-15. "Overhead application is overhead allocation." Do you agree? Explain.

13-16. Define *normal costing*.

13-17. What is the best theoretical method of allocating underapplied or overapplied overhead, assuming that the objective is to obtain as accurate a cost application as possible?

13-18. State three examples of service industries that use the job-costing approach.

13-19. "Service firms trace only direct-labor costs to jobs. All other costs are applied as a percentage of direct-labor cost." Do you agree? Explain.

13-20. "As data processing becomes more economical, more costs than just direct material and direct labor will be classified as direct costs wherever feasible." Give three examples of such costs.

13-21 Direct Materials

For each of the following independent cases, fill in the blanks (in millions of dollars):

	1	2	3	4
Direct-materials inventory, Dec. 31, 19X5	8	8	5	–
Purchased	5	9	–	8
Used	7	–	7	3
Direct-materials inventory, Dec. 31, 19X6	–	6	9	7

13-22 Direct Materials

Genesis Athletic Shoes had an ending inventory of direct materials of $8 million. During the year the company had acquired $15 million of additional direct materials and had used $12 million. Compute the beginning inventory.

13-23 Use of WIP Inventory Account

September production resulted in the following activity in a key account of Colebury Casting Company (in thousands):

WIP Inventory		
September 1 balance	12	
Direct material used	50	
Direct labor charged to jobs	25	
Factory overhead applied to jobs	55	

Job Orders 13N and 37Q, with total costs of $70,000 and $54,000, respectively, were completed in September.

1. Journalize the completed production for September.
2. Compute the balance in WIP Inventory, September 30, after recording the completed production.
3. Journalize the credit sale of Job 13N for $98,000.

13-24 Job-Cost Record

Yale University uses job-cost records for various research projects. A major reason for such records is to justify requests for reimbursement of costs on projects sponsored by the federal government.

Consider the following summarized data regarding Project No. 76 conducted by some physicists:

- Jan. 5   Direct materials, various metals, $825
- Jan. 7   Direct materials, various chemicals, $780
- Jan. 5–12   Direct labor, research associates, 120 hours
- Jan. 7–12   Direct labor, research assistants, 180 hours

Research associates receive $32 per hour; assistants, $19. The overhead rate is 80% of direct-labor cost.

Sketch a job-cost record. Post all the data to the project-cost record. Compute the total cost of the project through January 12.

13-25 Analysis of Job-Cost Data

Job-cost records for Naomi's Remodeling, Inc., contained the following data:

Job No.	Started	Finished	Sold	Total Cost of Job at May 31
1	April 19	May 14	May 15	$2,800
2	April 26	May 22	May 25	8,800
3	May 2	June 6	June 8	7,200
4	May 9	May 29	June 5	8,100
5	May 14	June 14	June 16	3,900

Compute Naomi's (1) WIP Inventory at May 31, (2) Finished-Goods Inventory at May 31, and (3) Cost of Goods Sold for May.

13-26 Analysis of Job-Cost Data

The Cortez Construction Company constructs houses on speculation. That is, the houses are begun before any buyer is known. Even if the buyer agrees to purchase a house under construction, no sales are recorded until the house is completed and accepted for delivery. The job-cost records contained the following (in thousands):

Job No.	Started	Finished	Sold	Total Cost of Job at Sept. 30	Total Construction Cost Added in Oct.
43	4/26	9/7	9/8	$180	
51	5/17	9/14	9/17	170	
52	5/20	9/30	10/4	150	
53	5/28	10/14	10/18	200	$50
61	6/3	10/20	11/24	115	20
62	6/9	10/21	10/27	175	25
71	7/7	11/6	11/22	118	36
81	8/7	11/24	12/24	106	52

1. Compute Cortez's cost of (a) construction-in-process inventory at September 30 and October 31, (b) finished-houses inventory at September 30 and October 31, and (c) cost of houses sold for September and October.
2. Prepare summary journal entries for the transfer of completed houses from construction in process to finished houses for September and October.
3. Record the cash sale and cost of house sold of Job 53 for $350,000.

13-27 Discovery of Unknowns

Kleen Plastics has the following balances on December 31, 19X5. All amounts are in millions:

Factory overhead applied	$200
Cost of goods sold	500
Factory overhead incurred	210
Direct-materials inventory	40
Finished-goods inventory	160
WIP inventory	110

The cost of goods completed was $420. The cost of direct materials requisitioned for production during 19X5 was $200. The cost of direct materials purchased was $225. Factory overhead was applied to production at a rate of 160% of direct-labor cost.

Compute the beginning inventory balances of direct materials, WIP, and finished goods. Make these computations before considering any possible adjustments for overapplied or underapplied overhead.

13-28 Discovery of Unknowns

The Chickadee Manufacturing Company has the following balances (in millions) as of December 31, 19X6:

WIP inventory	$ 14
Finished-goods inventory	175
Direct-materials inventory	65
Factory overhead incurred	180
Factory overhead applied	
at 150% of direct-labor cost	150
Cost of goods sold	350

The cost of direct materials purchased during 19X6 was $275. The cost of direct materials requisitioned for production during 19X6 was $235. The cost of goods completed was $493, all in millions.

Before considering any year-end adjustments for overapplied or underapplied overhead, compute the beginning inventory balances of direct materials, WIP, and finished goods.

13-29 Journal Entries for Overhead

Consider the following summarized data regarding 19X6:

	Budget	Actual
Indirect labor	$ 310,000	$ 325,000
Supplies	35,000	30,000
Repairs80,000	75,000	
Utilities	110,000	103,000
Factory rent	125,000	125,000
Supervision	60,000	70,000
Depreciation, equipment	220,000	220,000
Insurance, property taxes, etc.	40,000	42,000
a.Total factory overhead	$ 980,000	$ 990,000
b.Direct materials used	$1,650,000	$1,570,000
c. Direct labor	$1,225,000	$1,200,000

Omit explanations for journal entries.
1. Prepare a summary journal entry for the actual overhead incurred for 19X6.
2. Prepare summary journal entries for direct materials used and direct labor.
3. Factory overhead was applied by using a budgeted rate based on budgeted direct-labor costs. Compute the rate. Prepare a summary journal entry for the application of overhead to products.

4. Post the journal entries to the T-accounts for WIP and Factory Department Overhead Control.
5. Suppose overapplied or underapplied factory overhead is written off as an adjustment to cost of goods sold. Prepare the journal entry. Post the overhead to the overhead T-account.

13-30 Relationships Among Overhead Items
Fill in the unknowns:

	Case A	Case B	Case C
Budgeted factory overhead	$3,600,000	?	$1,500,000
Budgeted cost drivers			
Direct-labor cost	$2,000,000		
Direct-labor hours		450,000	
Machine-hours			250,000
Overhead application rate	?	$5	?

13-31 Relationship Among Overhead Items
Fill in the unknowns:

	Case 1	Case 2
a. Budgeted factory overhead	$600,000	$420,000
b. Cost driver, budgeted direct-labor cost	400,000	?
c. Budgeted factory-overhead rate	?	120%
d. Direct-labor cost incurred	570,000	?
e. Factory overhead incurred	830,000	425,000
f. Factory overhead applied	?	?
g. Underapplied (overapplied) factory overhead	?	35,000

13-32 Underapplied and Overapplied Overhead
Starr Welding Company applies factory overhead at a rate of $8.50 per direct-labor hour. Selected data for 19X6 operations are (in thousands):

	Case 1	Case 2
Direct-labor hours	30	36
Direct-labor cost	$220	$245
Indirect-labor cost	32	40
Sales commissions	20	15
Depreciation, manufacturing equipment	22	32
Direct-material cost	230	250
Factory fuel costs	35	47
Depreciation, finished-goods warehouse	5	17
Cost of goods sold	420	510
All other factory costs	138	204

Compute for both cases:
1. Factory overhead applied.
2. Total factory overhead incurred.
3. Amount of underapplied or overapplied factory overhead.

13-33 Disposition of Overhead
Assume the following at the end of 19X4 (in thousands):

Cost of goods sold	$250
Direct-materials inventory	80
WIP	100
Finished goods	150
Factory department overhead control (credit balance)	50

1. Assume that the underapplied or overapplied overhead is regarded as an adjustment to cost of goods sold. Prepare the journal entry.
2. Assume that the underapplied or overapplied overhead is prorated among the appropriate accounts in proportion to their ending unadjusted balances. Show computations and prepare the journal entry.
3. Which adjustment, the one in requirement 1 or 2, would result in the higher gross profit? Explain, indicating the amount of the difference.

13-34 Disposition of Overhead
A French manufacturer uses a job-order system. At the end of 19X6 the following balances existed (in millions of French francs):

Cost of goods sold	FF150
Finished goods	120
WIP	30
Factory overhead (actual)	70
Factory overhead (applied)	50

1. Prepare journal entries for two different ways to dispose of the underapplied overhead.
2. Gross profit, before considering the effects in requirement 1, was FF50 million. What is the adjusted gross profit under the two methods demonstrated?

13-35 Disposition of Year-End Underapplied Overhead
Gloria Cosmetics uses a normal cost system and has the following balances at the end of its first year's operations:

WIP inventory	$200,000
Finished-goods inventory	200,000
Cost of goods sold	400,000
Actual factory overhead	409,000
Factory overhead applied	453,000

Prepare journal entries for two different ways to dispose of the year-end overhead balances. By how much would gross profit differ?

13-36 Relationships of Manufacturing Costs
(CMA adapted.) Selected data concerning the past fiscal year's operations of the Wallis Manufacturing Company are (in thousands):

	Inventories	
	Beginning	*Ending*
Raw materials	$ 70	$ 90
WIP	75	35
Finished goods	100	120
Other data		
Raw materials used		$ 468
Total manufacturing costs charged to production during the year (includes raw materials, direct labor, and factory overhead applied at a rate of 80% of direct-labor cost)		864
Cost of goods available for sale		1,026
Selling and general expenses		50

Select the best answer for each of the following items:
1. The cost of raw materials purchased during the year amounted to
   a. $430   **c.** $488   **e.** None of these
   b. $458   **d.** $468
2. Direct-labor costs charged to production during the year amounted to
   a. $162   **c.** $396   **e.** None of these
   b. $230   **d.** $220
3. The cost of goods manufactured during the year was
   a. $926   **c.** $951   **e.** None of these
   b. $914   **d.** $906
4. The cost of goods sold during the year was
   a. $991   **c.** $906   **e.** None of these
   b. $926   **d.** $914

13-37 Relationship of Subsidiary and General Ledgers, Journal Entries
The following summarized data are available on three job-cost records of Weeks Company, a manufacturer of packaging equipment:

	412		413		414
	September	*October*	*September*	*October*	*October*
Direct materials	$8,000	$2,500	$12,000	—	$13,000
Direct labor	4,000	1,500	5,000	2,500	2,000
Factory overhead applied	8,000	?	10,000	?	?

The company's fiscal year ends on October 31. Factory overhead is applied as a percentage of direct-labor costs. The balances in selected accounts on September 30 were: direct-materials inventory, $19,000; and finished-goods inventory, $18,000.

Job 412 was completed during October and transferred to finished goods. Job 413 was still in process at the end of October, as was Job 414, which had begun on October 24. These were the only jobs worked on during September and October.

Job 412 was sold along with other finished goods by October 30. The total cost of goods sold during October was $32,000. The balance in Cost of Goods Sold on September 30 was $450,000.

1. Prepare a schedule showing the balance of the WIP Inventory, September 30. This schedule should show the total costs of each job record. Taken together, the job-cost records are the subsidiary ledger supporting the general ledger balance of work in process.
2. What is the overhead application rate?
3. Prepare summary general journal entries for all costs added to WIP during October. Also prepare entries for all costs transferred from WIP to Finished Goods and from Finished Goods to Cost of Goods Sold. Post to the appropriate T-accounts.
4. Prepare a schedule showing the balance of the WIP Inventory, October 31.

13-38 Straightforward Job Costing
The Scott Custom Furniture Company has two departments. Data for 19X8 include the following:

Inventories, January 1, 19X8:

Direct materials (30 types)	$75,000
WIP (in assembly)	50,000
Finished goods	40,000

Manufacturing overhead budget for 19X8:

	Machining	Assembly
Indirect labor	$220,000	$ 410,000
Supplies	45,000	40,000
Utilities	95,000	75,000
Repairs	140,000	110,000
Supervision	105,000	215,000
Factory rent	75,000	75,000
Depreciation on equipment	160,000	105,000
Insurance, property taxes, etc.	60,000	70,000
	$900,000	$1,100,000

Budgeted machine-hours were 90,000; budgeted direct-labor cost in Assembly was $2,200,000. Manufacturing overhead was applied using budgeted rates on the basis of machine-hours in Machining and on the basis of direct-labor cost in Assembly.

Following is a summary of actual events for the year:

	Machining	Assembly	Total
a. Direct materials purchased			$ 1,900,000
b. Direct materials requisitioned	$1,100,000	750,000	1,850,000
c. Direct-labor costs incurred	900,000	2,800,000	3,700,000
d1. Factory overhead incurred	1,100,000	1,100,000	2,200,000
d2. Factory overhead applied	900,000	?	?
e. Cost of goods completed	—	—	7,820,000
f1. Sales	—	—	13,000,000
f2. Cost of goods sold	—	—	7,800,000

The ending work in process (all in Assembly) was $80,000.

1. Compute the budgeted overhead rates.
2. Compute the amount of the machine-hours actually worked.
3. Compute the amount of factory overhead applied in the Assembly Department.
4. Prepare general journal entries for transactions *a* through *f*. Work solely with the total amounts, not the details for Machining and Assembly. Explanations are not required.

Show data in thousands of dollars. Present T-accounts, including ending inventory balances, for direct materials, WIP, and finished goods.

5. Prepare a partial income statement similar to the one illustrated in Exhibit 13-4, page 550. Overapplied or underapplied overhead is written off as an adjustment of current cost of goods sold.

13-39 Nonprofit Job Costing

Job-order costing is usually identified with manufacturing companies. However, service industries and nonprofit organizations also use the method. Suppose a social service agency has a cost accounting system that tracks cost by department (for example, family counseling, general welfare, and foster children) and by case. In this way, Heather Long, the manager of the agency, is better able to determine how its limited resources (mostly professional social workers) should be allocated. Furthermore, the manager's interactions with superiors and various politicians are more fruitful when she can cite the costs of various types of cases.

The condensed line-item budget for the general welfare department of the agency for 19X7 showed:

Professional salaries		
Level 12	5 @ $35,000 = $ 175,000	
Level 10	21 @ $26,000 = 546,000	
Level 8	34 @ $18,000 = 612,000	$1,333,000
Other costs		479,880
Total costs		$1,812,880

For costing various cases, the manager favored using a single overhead application rate based on the ratio of total overhead to direct labor. The latter was defined as those professional salaries assigned to specific cases.

The professional workers filled out a weekly "case time" report, which approximated the hours spent for each case.

The instructions on the report were: "Indicate how much time (in hours) you spent on each case. Unassigned time should be listed separately." About 20% of available time was unassigned to specific cases. It was used for professional development (for example, continuing education programs). "Unassigned time" became a part of "overhead," as distinguished from the direct labor.

1. Compute the "overhead rate" as a percentage of direct labor (that is, the assignable professional salaries).
2. Suppose that last week a welfare case, Client No. 537, required two hours of Level 12 time, four hours of Level 10 time, and nine hours of level 8 time. How much job cost should be allocated to Client No. 537 for the week? Assume that all professional employees work a 1,800-hour year.

13-40 Job Costing in a Consulting Firm

Link Engineering Consultants is a firm of professional civil engineers. It mostly does surveying jobs for the heavy construction industry throughout New England. The firm obtains its jobs by giving fixed-price quotations, so profitability depends on the ability to predict the time required for the various subtasks on the job. (This situation is similar to that in the auditing profession, where times are budgeted for such audit steps as reconciling cash and confirming accounts receivable.)

A client may be served by various professional staff, who hold positions in the hierarchy from partners to managers to senior engineers to assistants. In addition, there are secretaries and other employees.

Link Engineering has the following budget for 19X6:

Compensation of professional staff	$3,600,000
Other costs	1,300,000
Total budgeted costs	$4,900,000

Each professional staff member must submit a weekly time report, which is used for charging hours to a client job-order record. The time report has seven columns, one for each day of the week. Its rows are as follows:

- Chargeable hours
    - Client 156
    - Client 183
    - Etc.
- Nonchargeable hours
    - Attending seminar on new equipment
    - Unassigned time
    - Etc.

In turn, these time reports are used for charging hours and costs to the client job-order records. The managing partner regards these job records as absolutely essential for measuring the profitability of various jobs and for providing an "experience base for improving predictions on future jobs."

1. This firm applies overhead to jobs at a budgeted percentage of the professional compensation charged directly to the job ("direct labor"). For all categories of professional personnel, chargeable hours average 85% of available hours. Nonchargeable hours are regarded as additional overhead. What is the overhead rate as a percentage of "direct labor," the chargeable professional compensation cost?
2. A senior engineer works 48 weeks per year, 40 hours per week. His compensation is $60,000. He has worked on two jobs during the past week, devoting 10 hours to Job 156 and 30 hours to Job 183. How much cost should be charged to Job 156 because of his work there?

13-41 Choice of Cost Drivers in Accounting Firm

Nicole Cookie, the managing partner of N&T Cookie Accounting, is considering the desirability of tracing more costs to jobs than just direct labor. In this way, the firm will be able to justify billings to clients.

Last year's costs were:

Direct-professional labor	$ 5,000,000
Overhead	10,000,000
Total costs	$15,000,000

The following costs were included in overhead:

Computer time	$ 950,000
Secretarial cost	900,000
Photocopying	350,000
Fringe benefits to direct labor	1,000,000
Phone call time with clients (estimated but not tabulated)	800,000
Total	$4,000,000

The firm's data processing techniques now make it feasible to document and trace these costs to individual jobs.

As an experiment, in December Nicole Cookie arranged to trace these costs to six audit engagements. Two job records showed the following:

	Engagement	
	Zeandale Milling	*Kaw Valley Bank*
Direct-professional labor	$15,000	$15,000
Fringe benefits to direct labor	3,000	3,000
Phone call time with clients	1,500	500
Computer time	3,000	700
Secretarial costs	2,000	1,500
Photocopying	500	300
Total direct costs	$25,000	$21,000

1. Compute the overhead application rate based on last year's costs.
2. Suppose last year's costs were reclassified so that $4 million would be regarded as direct costs instead of overhead. Compute the overhead application rate as a percentage of direct labor and as a percentage of total direct costs.
3. Using the three rates computed in requirements 1 and 2, compute the total costs of engagements for Zeandale Milling and Kaw Valley Bank.
4. Suppose that client billing was based on a 30% markup of total job costs. Compute the billings that would be forthcoming in requirement 3.
5. Which method of job costing and overhead application do you favor? Explain.

13-42 Reconstruction of Transactions

(This problem is more challenging than the others in this chapter.)

You are asked to bring the following incomplete accounts of a printing plant acquired in a merger up to date through January 31, 19X6. Also consider the data that appear after the T-accounts.

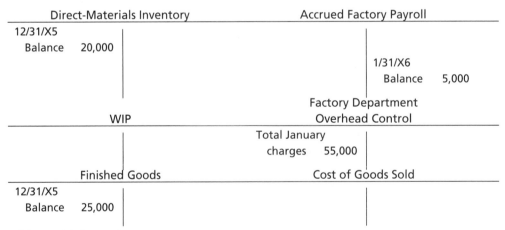

Additional information:

1. The overhead is applied using a budgeted rate that is set every December by forecasting the following year's overhead and relating it to forecasted direct-labor costs. The budget for 19X6 called for $640,000 of direct labor and $800,000 of factory overhead.
2. The only job unfinished on January 31, 19X6, was No. 419, on which total labor charges were $3,000 (200 direct-labor-hours), and total direct-material charges were $21,000.

3. Total materials placed into production during January totaled $140,000.
4. Cost of goods completed during January was $260,000.
5. January 31 balances of direct materials totaled $25,000.
6. Finished-goods inventory as of January 31 was $35,000.
7. All factory workers earn the same rate of pay. Direct-labor hours for January totaled 3,000. Indirect labor and supervision totaled $12,000.
8. The gross factory payroll paid on January paydays totaled $55,000. Ignore withholdings.
9. All "actual" factory overhead incurred during January has already been posted.

a. Direct materials purchased during January
b. Cost of goods sold during January
c. Direct-labor costs incurred during January
d. Overhead applied during January
e. Balance, Accrued Factory Payroll, December 31, 19X5
f. Balance, WIP, December 31, 19X5
g. Balance, WIP, January 31, 19X6
h. Overapplied or underapplied overhead for January

Cases

13-43 Overhead Accounting for Control and for Product Costing

The games department of a major toy manufacturer has an overhead rate of $5 per direct-labor hour, based on expected variable overhead of $150,000 per year, expected fixed overhead of $350,000 per year, and expected direct-labor hours of 100,000 per year.

Data for the year's operations follow:

	Direct-Labor Hours Used	Overhead Costs Incurred*
First six months	55,000	$262,000
Last six months	41,000	236,500

* Fixed costs incurred were exactly equal to budgeted amounts throughout the year.

1. What is the underapplied or overapplied overhead for each six-month period? Label your answer as underapplied or overapplied.
2. Explain *briefly* (not more than 50 words for each part) the probable causes for the under-applied or overapplied overhead. Focus on variable and fixed costs separately. Give the exact figures attributable to the causes you cite.

13-44 Multiple Overhead Rates and Activity-Based Costing

A division of Hewlett-Packard assembles and tests printed circuit (PC) boards. The division has many different products. Some are high volume; others are low volume. For years, manufacturing overhead was applied to products using a single overhead rate based on direct-labor dollars. However, direct labor has shrunk to 6% of total manufacturing costs.

Managers decided to refine the division's product-costing system. Abolishing the direct-labor category, they included all manufacturing labor as a part of factory overhead. They also identified several activities and the appropriate cost driver for each. The cost driver for the first activity, the start station, was the number of raw PC boards. The application rate was computed as follows:

$$\text{application rate for start station activity} = \frac{\text{budgeted total factory overhead at the activity}}{\text{budgeted raw PC boards for the year}}$$

$$= \frac{\$150,000}{125,000} = \$1.20$$

Each time a raw PC board passes through the start station activity, $1.20 is added to the cost of a product. The product cost is the sum of costs directly traced to the product plus the indirect costs (factory overhead) accumulated at each of the manufacturing activities undergone.

Using assumed numbers, consider the following data regarding PC Board 74:

Direct materials	$70.00
Factory overhead applied	?
Total manufacturing product cost	?

The activities involved and the related cost drivers chosen were:

Activity	Cost Driver	Factory-Overhead Costs Applied for Each Activity
1. Start station	No. of raw PC boards	1 × $ 1.20 = $1.20
2. Axial insertion	No. of axial insertions	42 × .07 = ?
3. Dip insertion	No. of dip insertions	? × .20 = 5.60
4. Manual insertion	No. of manual insertions	15 × ? = 6.00
5. Wave solder	No. of boards soldered	1 × 3.20 = 3.20
6. Backload	No. of backload insertions	8 × .60 = 4.80
7. Test	Standard time board is in test activity	.15 × 80.00 = ?
8. Defect analysis	Standard time for defect analysis and repair	.05 × ? = 4.50
Total		$?

1. Fill in the blanks.
2. How is direct labor identified with products under this product-costing system?
3. Why would managers favor this multiple-overhead rate, activity-based costing system instead of the older system?

13-45 One or Two Cost Drivers

The Zoe Tool Co. in Geneva, Switzerland, has the following 19X7 budget for its two departments in Swiss francs (SF):

	Machining	Finishing	Total
Direct labor	SF 300,000	SF 800,000	SF 1,100,000
Factory overhead	SF 960,000	SF 800,000	SF 1,760,000
Machine-hours	60,000	20,000	80,000

In the past, the company has used a single plantwide overhead application rate based on direct-labor cost. However, as its product line has expanded and as competition has intensified, Mr. Zoe, the company president, has questioned the accuracy of the profits or losses shown on various products.

Zoe makes custom tools on special orders from customers. To be competitive and still make a reasonable profit, it is essential that the firm measure the cost of each customer order. Mr. Zoe has focused on overhead allocation as a potential problem. He knows that changes in costs are more heavily affected by machine-hours in the machining department and by direct-labor costs in the finishing department. As company controller, you have gathered the following data regarding two typical customer orders:

	Order Number	
	100361	*100362*
Machining		
Direct materials	SF 4,000	SF 4,000
Direct labor	SF 3,000	SF 1,500
Machine-hours	1,200	100
Finishing		
Direct labor	SF 1,500	SF 3,000
Machine-hours	120	120

1. Compute six factory overhead application rates, three based on direct-labor cost and three based on machine-hours for machining, finishing, and for the plant as a whole.
2. Use the application rates to compute the total costs of orders 100361 and 100362 as follows: (a) plantwide rate based on direct-labor cost and (b) machining based on machine-hours and finishing based on direct-labor cost.
3. Evaluate your answers in requirement 2. Which set of job costs do you prefer? Why?

CHAPTER 14

PROCESS COSTING
APPLIED TO PROJECTS

14.1   PROCESS COSTING AND PROJECT MANAGEMENT

The difference between job order and process costing is that job order costing measures the cost of a group of *units of production* and process costing measures units produced in *a specific period of time*. Process costing is used in operations such as mining and petroleum production. Many observers conclude that process costing has little application to projects. However, if a project has few milestones, over a period of time it begins to take on the attributes of a process flow operation. Further, if one considers the earned value calculations discussed in chapter 11, it will be noted that the schedule related calculations apply more to projects with continuous flows rather than many small, segmented milestones. In a way, the schedule calculations associated with earned value could be considered an attempt to measure progress in a process flow working environment.

In the reading that follows, Horngren gives an overview of process costing.

14.2   PROCESS-COSTING SYSTEMS

INTRODUCTION TO PROCESS COSTING

All product costing uses averaging to determine costs per unit of production. The average unit cost may be relatively narrow, as in the production of a particular printing order in job-order costing. In contrast, the average may be broad, as in the production of beverages in process costing. *Process-costing systems* apply costs to like products that are usually mass produced in continuous fashion through a series of production *processes*. These processes are often organized as separate departments, although a single department sometimes contains more than one process.

Process Costing Compared with Job Costing

Job costing and process costing are used for different types of products. Firms in industries such as printing, construction, and furniture manufacturing, in which each unit or batch (job) of product is unique and easily identifiable, use job-order costing. Process costing is used when there is mass production through a sequence of several processes, such as mixing and cooking. Examples include chemicals, flour, glass, and toothpaste.

Exhibit 14-1 Comparison of Job-Order and Process Costing

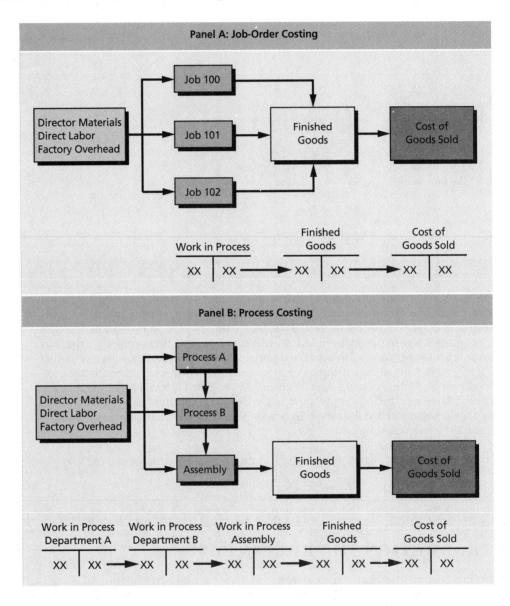

Exhibit 14-1 shows the major differences between job-order costing and process costing. Process costing requires several work-in-process accounts, one for each process or department. As goods move from process to process, their costs are transferred accordingly.

Process manufacturing systems vary in design. The design shown in panel B of Exhibit 14-1 is sequential—units pass from process A to process B. Many other designs are found in practice—each tailored to meet specific product requirements. For example, processes can be operated in parallel until final assembly. In this case process A and process B might simultaneously each produce a subcomponent of the final product. Whatever the specific layout, the basic principles of process costing are the same.

The process-costing approach does not distinguish among individual units of product. Instead, accumulated costs for a period are divided by quantities produced during that period to get broad, average unit costs. Process costing is applied to nonmanufacturing activities as well as manufacturing activities. Examples include dividing the costs of giving state automobile driver's license tests by the number of tests given and dividing the cost of a post office sorting department by the number of items sorted.

Process-costing systems are usually simpler and less expensive than job-order costing. Individual jobs do not exist. There are no job-cost records. The unit cost for inventory purposes is calculated by accumulating the costs of each processing department and dividing the total cost by an appropriate measure of output.

To get a rough feel for process costing, consider Magenta Midget Frozen Vegetables. It quick-cooks tiny carrots, beans, and so on before freezing them. As shown below, the costs of cooked vegetables (in millions of dollars) are transferred from the Cooking Department to the Freezing Department:

Work in Process—Cooking			Work in Process—Freezing		
Direct materials	14	Transfer cost of goods completed to next department 24	Cost transferred in from cooking 24	Transfer cost of goods completed to finished goods 25	
Direct labor	4		Additional costs 3		
Factory overhead	88		27		
	26				
Ending inventory	2		Ending inventory 2		

The amount of cost to be transferred is determined by dividing the accumulated costs in the Cooking Department by the pounds of vegetables processed. The resulting cost per pound is then multiplied by the pounds of vegetables physically transferred to the Freezing Department.

The journal entries are similar to those for the job-order-costing system. That is, direct materials, direct labor, and factory overhead are accounted for as before. However, now there is more than a single work-in-process account for all units being manufactured. There is one work-in-process account for each processing department, Work in Process—Cooking and Work in Process—Freezing, in our example. The foregoing data would be recorded as follows:

1.	Work in Process—Cooking 14	
	Direct-materials inventory	14
	To record direct materials used	
2.	Work in Process—Cooking 4	
	Accrued payroll	4
	To record direct labor	
3.	Work in Process—Cooking 8	
	Factory overhead	8
	To record factory overhead applied to product	
4.	Work in Process—Freezing 24	
	Work in Process—Cooking	24
	To transfer goods from the cooking process	
5.	Work in Process—Freezing 3	
	Accrued payroll	1
	Factory overhead	2
	To record direct labor and factory overhead applied to product	
6.	Finished goods 25	
	Work in Process—Freezing	25
	To transfer goods from the freezing process	

The central product-costing problem is how each department should compute the cost of goods transferred out and the cost of goods remaining in the department. If an identical amount of work was done on each unit transferred and on each unit in ending inventory, the solution is easy. Total costs are simply divided by total units. However, if the units in the inventory are each partially completed, the product-costing system must distinguish between the fully completed units transferred out and the partially completed units not yet transferred.

APPLICATION OF PROCESS COSTING

Consider another illustration. Suppose Oakville Wooden Toys, Inc., buys wood as a direct material for its Forming Department. The department processes only one type of toy, marionettes. The marionettes are transferred to the Finishing Department, where hand shaping, strings, paint, and clothing are added.

The Forming Department manufactured 25,000 identical units during April, and its costs that month were:

Direct materials		$ 70,000
Conversion costs		
Direct labor	$10,625	
Factory overhead	31,875	42,500
Costs to account for		$112,500

The unit cost of goods completed would simply be $112,500 \div 25,000 = \$4.50$. An itemization would show:

Direct materials, $70,000 ÷ 25,000	$2.80
Conversion costs, $42,500 ÷ 25,000	1.70
Unit cost of a whole completed marionette	$4.50

But what if not all 25,000 marionettes were completed during April? For example, assume that 5,000 were still in process at the end of April—only 20,000 were started and fully completed. All direct materials had been placed in process, but on average only 25% of the conversion costs had been applied to the 5,000 marionettes that remain in process. How should the Forming Department calculate the cost of goods transferred and the cost of goods remaining in the ending work-in-process inventory? The answer lies in the following five key steps:

- **Step 1:** Summarize the flow of physical units.
- **Step 2:** Calculate output in terms of equivalent units.
- **Step 3:** Summarize the total costs to account for, which are the costs applied to work in process.
- **Step 4:** Calculate unit costs.
- **Step 5:** Apply costs to units completed and to units in the ending work in process.

Physical Units and Equivalent Units (Steps 1 and 2)

Step 1, as the first column in Exhibit 14-2 shows, tracks the physical units of production. How should the output for April be measured? Not as 25,000 units. Instead, the output was 20,000 fully completed units and 5,000 partially completed units. A partially completed unit is not a perfect substitute for a fully completed unit. Accordingly, output is usually stated in *equivalent units*, not physical units.

Equivalent units are the number of completed units that could have been produced from the inputs applied. For example, four units each one-half completed represent two equivalent units. If each had been one-fourth completed, they would have represented one equivalent unit.

In our example, as step 2 in Exhibit 14-2 shows, the output would be measured as 25,000 equivalent units of direct-materials cost but only 21,250 equivalent units of *conversion costs*. Conversion costs include all manufacturing costs other than direct materials. Direct labor is usually not a major part of total costs, so it is combined with factory-overhead costs (such as the costs of energy, repairs, and material handling) as a major classification called conversion costs. Why only 21,250 equivalent units of conversion costs but 25,000 of direct-materials cost? Because direct materials had been added to all 25,000 units. In contrast, the conversion costs applied to the 5,000 partially completed units would have been sufficient to complete 1,250 units in addition to the 20,000 units that were actually completed.

Computation of equivalent units requires estimates of degrees of completion for inventories in process. The accuracy of these estimates depends on the care and skill of the estimator and the nature of the process. Estimating the degree of completion is usually easier for materials than for conversion costs. The conversion sequence usually consists of a number of standard operations or a standard number of hours, days, weeks, or months for mixing, heating, cooling, aging, curing, and so forth. Thus, the degree of completion for conversion costs depends on what proportion of the total effort needed to complete one unit or one batch has been devoted to units still in process. In industries where no exact estimate is possible, or, as in textiles, where vast quantities in process prohibit costly physical estimates, all work in process in every department is assumed to be one-third or one-half or two-thirds complete. In other cases, continuous processing entails little change of work-in-process levels from month to month. Consequently, in such cases, work in process is safely ignored, and monthly production costs are assigned solely to goods completed.

Exhibit 14-2   Forming Department Output in Equivalent Units for the Month Ended April 30, 19X1

Flow of Production	(Step 1) Physical Units	(Step 2) Equivalent Units	
		Direct Materials	Conversion Costs
Started and completed	20,000	20,000	20,000
Work in process, ending inventory	5,000	5,000	1,250*
Units accounted for	25,000		
Work done to date		25,000	21,250*

* 5,000 physical units × .25 degree of completion of conversion costs.

Measures in equivalent units are not confined to manufacturing situations. Such measures are a popular way of expressing workloads in terms of a common denominator. For example, radiology departments measure their output in terms of weighted units. Various x-ray procedures are ranked in terms of the time, supplies, and related costs devoted to each. A simple chest x-ray may receive a weight of one. But a skull x-ray may receive a weight of three because it uses three times the resources (e.g., technicians' time) as a procedure with a weight of one. Another example is the expression by universities of students enrolled in terms of full-time enrollment equivalents.

CALCULATION OF PRODUCT COSTS (STEPS 3 TO 5)

Exhibit 14-3 is a production-cost report. It shows steps 3 to 5 of process costing. Step 3 summarizes the total costs to account for (i.e., the total costs in, or debits to, Work in Process—Forming). Step 4 obtains unit costs by dividing total costs by the appropriate measures of equivalent units. The unit cost of a completed unit—material cost plus conversion costs—is $2.80 + $2.00 = $4.80. Step 5 then uses these unit costs to apply costs to products.

Concentrate in Exhibit 14-3 on how the costs are applied to obtain an ending work in process of $16,500. The 5,000 physical units are fully completed in terms of direct materials. Therefore, the direct materials applied to work in process are 5,000 equivalent units times $2.80, or $14,000. In contrast, the 5,000 physical units are 25% completed in terms of conversion costs. Therefore, the conversion costs applied to work in process are 1,250 equivalent units (25% of 5,000 physical units) times $2.00, or $2,500.

Exhibit 14-3 Forming Department Production Cost Report Month Ended April 30, 19X1

	Total Costs	Details	
		Direct Materials	Conversion Costs
(Step 3) Costs to account for	$112,500	$70,000	$42,500
(Step 4) Divide by equivalent units		÷25,000	÷ 21,250
Unit costs	$ 4.80	$ 2.80	$ 2.00
(Step 5) Application of costs			
To units completed and transferred to the Finishing Department, 20,000 units @$4.80	$ 96,000		
To units not completed and still in process, April 30, 5,000 units			
Direct materials	$ 14,000	5,000 ($2.80)	
Conversion costs	2,500		1,250 ($2.00)
Work in process, April 30	$ 16,500		
Total costs accounted for	$112,500		

Journal entries for the data in our illustration would appear as:

1.	Work in Process	70,000	
	Direct-materials inventory		70,000
	Materials added to production in April		
2.	Work in Process—Forming	10,625	
	Accrued payroll		10,625
	Direct labor in April		
3.	Work in Process—Forming	31,875	
	Factory overhead		31,875
	Factory overhead applied in April		
4.	Work in Process—Finishing	96,000	
	Work in Process—Forming		96,000
	Cost of goods completed and transferred in April from Forming to Assembly		

The $112,500 added to the Work in Process—Forming account less the $96,000 transferred out leaves an ending balance of $16,500:

Work in Process—Forming			
1. Direct materials	$ 70,000	4. Transferred out	
2. Direct labor	10,625	to finishing	$96,000
3. Factory overhead	31,875		
Costs to account for	112,500		
Bal. April 30	16,500		

Summary Problem for Your Review

Problem One

Taylor Plastics makes a variety of plastic products. Its Extruding Department had the following output and costs:

Units
  Started and completed: 30,000 units
  Started and still in process: 10,000 units; 100% completed for direct materials,
    but 60% completed for conversion costs
Costs applied
  Total: $81,600; direct materials, $60,000; conversion, $21,600

Compute the cost of work completed and the cost of the ending inventory of work in process.

Solution to Problem One

	(Step 1)	(Step 2) Equivalent Units	
Flow of Production	Physical Units	Direct Materials	Conversion
Started and completed	30,000	30,000	30,000
Ending work in process	10,000	10,000*	6,000*
Units accounted for	40,000		
Work done to date		40,000	36,000

* 10,000 x 100% = 10,000; 10,000 x 60% = 6,000.

		Total Costs	Details	
			Direct Materials	Conversion Costs
(Step 3)	Costs to account for	$81,600	$60,000	$21,600
(Step 4)	Divide by equivalent units		÷40,000	÷36,000
	Unit costs	$ 2.10*	$ 1.50	$ .60
(Step 5)	Application of costs			
	To units completed and transferred, 30,000 units @$2.10	$63,000		
	To ending work in process, 10,000 units			
	Direct materials	$15,000	10,000 ($1.50)	
	Conversion costs	3,600		6,000 ($.60)
	Work in process, ending inventory	$18,600		
	Total costs accounted for	$81,600		

* Unit cost ($2.10) = direct materials costs ($1.50) + conversion costs ($.60).

EFFECTS OF BEGINNING INVENTORIES

When beginning inventories are present, product costing becomes more complicated. Suppose Oakville Wooden Toys had 3,000 marionettes in work in process in its Forming Department on March 31. All direct materials had been placed in process, but on the average only 40% of the conversion costs had been applied to the 3,000 units. Because 25,000 units were worked on during April (20,000 units completed plus 5,000 still in process at the end of the month) and because there were 3,000 units in beginning inventory, 22,000 units must have been started in production during April.

The accompanying table presents the data we use in our illustrations:

Units		
Work in process, March 31: 3,000 units; 100% completed for materials, but only 40% completed for conversion costs		
Units started in April: 22,000		
Units completed in April: 20,000		
Work in process, April 30: 5,000 units; 100% completed for materials, but only 25% completed for conversion costs		
Costs		
Work in process, March 31		
Direct materials	$7,320	
Conversion costs	2,119	$ 9,439
Direct materials added during April		70,180
Conversion costs added during April		
($10,625 + $31,881)		42,506
Total costs to account for		$122,125

Note that the $122,125 total costs to account for include the $9,439 of beginning inventory in addition to the $112,686 added during April.

In this section, we discuss common inventory methods: the weighted-average method and the first-in, first-out method. The five-step approach is recommended for both methods.

WEIGHTED-AVERAGE METHOD

The **weighted-average (WA) process-costing method** adds the cost of (1) all work done in the current period to (2) the work done in the preceding period on the current period's beginning inventory of work in process. This total is divided by the equivalent units of work done to date, whether that work was done in the current period or previously.

Why is the term *weighted-average* used to describe this method? Primarily because the unit costs used for applying costs to products are affected by the *total cost incurred to date*, regardless of whether those costs were incurred during or before the current period.

Exhibit 14-4 shows the first two steps in this method, computation of physical units and equivalent units. Note that this illustration differs from the previous illustration in only one major respect, the presence of beginning work in process.

The computation of equivalent units ignores whether all 25,000 units to account for came from beginning work in process, or all were started in April, or some combination thereof. Thus, both Exhibits 14-2 and 14-4 show the total work done to date, 25,000 equivalent units of direct materials and 21,250 units of conversion costs. The equivalent units for work done to date, which is the divisor for unit costs, is unaffected by whether all work was done in April or some before April on the March 31 inventory of work in process.

Exhibit 14-5 presents a production-cost report. Its pattern is similar to that in Exhibit 14-3. That is, the report summarizes steps 3 to 5 regarding computations of product costs.

The unit costs in Exhibit 14-5 are higher than those in Exhibit 14-3. Why? Because the equivalent units are the same, but the total costs include the costs incurred before April on the units in beginning inventory as well as those costs added during April.

Exhibit 14-4 Forming Department Output in Equivalent Units
Month Ended April 30, 19X1 (Weighted-Average Method)

| | | (Step 2) Equivalent Units | |
| | (Step 1) Physical | *Direct* | *Conversion* |
Flow of Production	Units	*Materials*	*Costs*
Work in process, March 31	3,000 (40%)*		
Started in April	22,000		
To account for	25,000		
Completed and transferred out		20,000	20,000
during current period	20,000		
Work in process, April 30	5,000 (25%)*	5,000	1,250†
Units accounted for	25,000		
Work done to date		25,000	21,250

* Degrees of completion for conversion costs at the dates of inventories.
† .25 × 5,000 = 1,250.

To recap what has happened so far in this chapter:

1. In the first simple example, we assumed no beginning or ending inventories of work in process. Thus, when the $112,500 of costs incurred during April were applied to the 25,000 units worked on and fully completed during April, the unit cost (p. 496) was $2.80 + $1.70 = $4.50.
2. However, in the next example, we assumed that some of the units were not fully completed by the end of the month. This reduced the equivalent units and thus increased the unit cost (Exhibit 14-3) to $2.80 1 $2.00 = $4.80.
3. Then, in this latest example, we assumed that some of the units had also been worked on before April. The costs of that work are carried in work-in-process inventory, March 31. The addition of these costs (with no change in the equivalent units) increased the unit cost of work completed in April to $3.10 + $2.10 = $5.20.

FIRST-IN, FIRST-OUT METHOD

The **first-in, first-out (FIFO) process-costing method** sharply distinguishes the current work done from the previous work done on the beginning inventory of work in process. The calculation of equivalent units is confined to the work done in the current period (April in this illustration).

Exhibit 14-6 presents steps 1 and 2. The easiest way to compute equivalent units under the FIFO method is, first, compute the work done to date. Exhibit 14-6 shows these computations, which are exactly the same as in Exhibit 14-4. Second, deduct the work done *before* the current period. The remainder is the work done *during* the current period, which is the key to computing the unit costs by the FIFO method.

Exhibit 14-5 Foming Department Production-Cost Report for the Month Ended April 30, 19X1 (Weighted-Average Method)

		Totals	Direct Materials	Conversion Costs
			Details	
(Step 3)	Work in process, March 31	$ 9,439	$ 7,320	$ 2,119
	Costs added currently	112,686	70,180	42,506
	Total costs to account for	$122,125	$77,500	$44,625
(Step 4)	Divisor, equivalent units for work done to date*		25,000	21,250
	Unit costs (weighted averages)	$ 5.20	$ 3.10	$ 2.10
(Step 5)	Application of costs			
	Completed and transferred, 20,000 units ($5.20)	$104,000		
	Work in process, April 30, 5,000 units			
	Direct materials	$ 15,500	5,000 ($3.10)	
	Conversion costs	2,625		1,250* ($2.10)
	Total work in process	$ 18,125		
	Total costs accounted for	$122,125		

* Equivalent units of work done. For more details, see Exhibit 14-4.

Exhibit 14-6 Forming Department Output in Equivalent Units for the Month Ended April 30, 19X1 (FIFO Method)

Same as Exhibit 14-4

Flow of Production	(Step 1) Physical Units	(Step 2) Equivalent Units	
		Direct Materials	Conversion Costs
Work in process, March 31	3,000 (40%)*		
Started in April	22,000		
To account for	25,000		
Completed and transferred out	20,000	20,000	20,000
Work in process, April 30	5,000 (25%)*	5,000	1,250†
Units accounted for	25,000		
Work done to date		25,000	21,250
Less: equivalent units of work from previous periods included in beginning inventory		3,000‡	1,200§
Work done in current period only		22,000	20,050

* Degrees of completion for conversion costs at the dates of inventories.
† 5,000 × .25 = 1,250 equivalent units.
‡ 3,000 × 1.00 = 3,000 equivalent units.
§ 3,000 × .40 = 1,200 equivalent units.

FIFO is really a small step in the direction of job-order costing. Why? Because FIFO recognizes a distinct batch of production each period, whereas the weighted-average method does not. The divisor equivalent units for computing a unit cost are the equivalent units of only *current* work done.

Exhibit 14-7 is the production-cost report. It presents steps 3 to 5. The $9,439 beginning inventory balance is kept separate from current costs. The calculations of equivalent unit costs are confined to costs added in April only.

The bottom half of Exhibit 14-7 shows two ways to compute the costs of goods completed and transferred out. The first and faster way is to compute the $18,600 ending work in process and then deduct it from the $122,125 total costs to account for, obtaining $103,525. As a check on accuracy, it is advisable to use a second way: compute the cost of goods transferred in the detailed manner displayed in the footnote in Exhibit 14-7.

Exhibit 14-7 Forming Department Production-Cost Report for the Month Ended April 30, 19X1 (FIFO Method)

		Totals	Details Direct Materials	Details Conversion Costs
(Step 3)	Work in process, March 31	$ 9,439	(work done before April)	
	Costs added currently	112,686	$70,180	$42,506
	Total costs to account for	$122,125		
(Step 4)	Divisor, equivalent units of work done in April only		22,000*	20,050*
	Unit costs (for FIFO basis)	$ 5.31	$ 3.19	$ 2.12
(Step 5)	Application of costs			
	Work in process, April 30			
	Direct materials	$ 15,950	5,000 ($3.19)	
	Conversion costs	2,650		1,250* ($2.12)
	Total work in process (5,000 units)	18,600		
	Completed and transferred out (20,000 units), $122,125 − $18,600	103,525†		
	Total costs accounted for	$122,125		

* Equivalent units of work done. See Exhibit 14-6 for more details.

† Check: Work in process, March 31 $ 9,439

     Additional costs to complete, conversion costs of 60% of

       3,000 × $2.12 =   3,816

     Started and completed, 22,000 − 5,000 = 17,000;

       17,000 × $5.31 =   90,270

     Total cost transferred $103,525

     Unit cost transferred, $103,525 ÷ 20,000 = $5.17625

Differences Between FIFO and Weighted-Average Methods

The key difference between the FIFO and weighted-average computations is equivalent units:

- FIFO—Equivalent units are the work done in the current period only.
- Weighted-average—Equivalent units are the work done to date including the earlier work done on the current period's beginning inventory of work in process.

These differences in equivalent units lead to differences in unit costs. Accordingly, there are differences in costs applied to goods completed and still in process. In our example, the FIFO method results in a larger work-in-process inventory on April 30 and a smaller April cost of goods transferred out:

	Weighted Average*	FIFO†
Cost of goods transferred out	$104,000	$103,525
Ending work in process	18,125	18,600
Total costs accounted for	$122,125	$122,125

* From Exhibit 14-5.
† From Exhibit 14-7.

Differences in unit costs between FIFO and weighted-average methods are ordinarily insignificant because (1) changes in material prices, labor wage rates, and other manufacturing costs from month to month tend to be small, and (2) changes in the volume of production and inventory levels also tend to be small.

The FIFO method involves more detailed computations than the weighted-average method. That is why FIFO is almost never used in practice in process costing *for product-costing purposes.* However, the FIFO *equivalent units* for current work done are essential *for planning and control purposes.* Why? Because they isolate the output for one particular period. Consider our example. The FIFO computations of equivalent units help managers to measure the efficiency of April's performance independently from March's performance. Thus, budgets or standards for each month's departmental costs can be compared against actual results in light of the actual work done during any given month.

Transferred-in Costs

Many companies that use process costing have sequential production processes. For example, Oakville Wooden Toys transfers the items completed in its Forming Department to the Finishing Department. The Finishing Department would call the costs of the items it receives **transferred-in costs**—costs incurred in a previous department for items that have been received by a subsequent department. They are similar to but not identical to additional direct-material costs. Because transferred-in costs are a combination of all types of costs (direct-material and conversion costs) incurred in previous departments, they should not be called a direct-material cost in a subsequent department.

We account for transferred-in costs just as we account for direct materials, with one exception: Transferred-in costs are kept separate from the direct materials added in the department. Therefore, reports such as Exhibits 14-5 and 14-7 will include three columns of costs instead of two: transferred-in costs, direct-material costs, and conversion costs. The total unit cost will be the sum of all three types of unit costs.

Summary Problem for Your Review

Problem One appeared earlier in this chapter.

Problem Two

Consider the Cooking Department of Middleton Foods, a British food-processing company. Compute the cost of work completed and the cost of the ending inventory of work in process, using both the (1) weighted-average (WA) method and (2) FIFO method.

Units
  Beginning work in process: 5,000 units; 100% completed
    for materials, 40% completed for conversion costs
  Started during month: 28,000 units
  Completed during month: 31,000 units
  Ending work in process: 2,000 units; 100% completed
  for materials, 50% for conversion costs

Costs		
Beginning work in process		
Direct materials	£8,060	
Conversion costs	1,300	£ 9,360
Direct materials added in current month		41,440
Conversion costs added in current month		14,700
Total costs to account for		£65,500

Solution to Problem Two

		(Step 2) Equivalent Units	
Flow of Production	(Step 1) Physical Units	Material	Conversion Cost
Completed and transferred out	31,000	31,000	31,000
Ending work in process	2,000	2,000*	1,000*
1. Equivalent units, WA	33,000	33,000	32,000
Less: beginning work in process	5,000	5,000†	2,000†
2. Equivalent units, FIFO	28,000	28,000	30,000

* 2,000 × 100% = 2,000; 2,000 × 50% = 1,000.
† 5,000 × 100% = 5,000; 5,000 × 40% = 2,000.

Note especially that the work done to date is the basis for computing the equivalent units under the weighted-average method. In contrast, the basis for computing the equivalent units under the FIFO method is the work done in the current period only.

1.

Weighted-Average Method	Total Cost	Direct Materials	Conversion Costs
Beginning work in process	£ 9,360	£ 8,060	£ 1,300
Costs added currently	56,140	41,440	14,700
Total costs to account for	£65,500	£49,500	£16,000
Equivalent units, weighted-average		÷33,000	÷32,000
Unit costs, weighted-average	£ 2.00	£ 1.50	£ 0.50
Transferred out, 31,000 × £2.00	£62,000		
Ending work in process			
Direct materials	£ 3,000	(£ 1.50) 2,000	
Conversion cost	500		1,000 (£.50)
Total work in process	£ 3,500		
Total costs accounted for	£65,500		

2.

FIFO Method	Total Cost	Direct Materials	Conversion Costs
Beginning work in process	£ 9,360	(work done before month)	
Costs added currently	56,140	£41,440	£14,700
Total costs to account for	£65,500		
Equivalent units, FIFO		÷28,000	÷30,000
Unit costs, FIFO	£1.97	£1.48	£0.49
Ending work in process			
Direct materials	£ 2,960	2,000 (£1.48)	
Conversion cost	490		1,000 (£.49)
Total work in process	£ 3,450		
Transferred out,			
£65,500 − £3,450	£62,050*		
Total costs accounted for	£65,500		

* Check:

Beginning work in process	£ 9,360
Costs to complete, 60% × 5,000 × £.49	1,470
Started and completed,	
(31,000 − 5,000) (£1.48 + £.49)	51,220
Total cost transferred	£62,050

Unit cost transferred, £62,050 ÷ 31,000 = £2.00161

PROCESS COSTING IN A JIT SYSTEM: BACKFLUSH COSTING

Tracking costs through various stages of inventory—raw materials, work-in-process, and finished-goods inventories—makes accounting systems complex. If there were no inventories, all costs would be charged directly to cost of goods sold, and accounting systems would be much simpler. Organizations using JIT production systems usually have very small inventories and they may not want to bear the expense of a system that traces costs through all the inventory accounts. Such firms can use **backflush costing,** an accounting system that applies costs to products only when the production is complete.

Principles of Backflush Costing

Backflush costing has only two categories of costs: materials and conversion costs. Its unique feature is an absence of a work-in-process account. Actual material costs are entered into a *materials inventory* account, and actual labor and overhead costs are entered into a *conversion costs* account. Costs are transferred from these two temporary accounts directly into finished-goods inventories. Some backflush systems even eliminate the finished-goods inventory accounts and transfer costs directly to cost of goods sold, especially if goods are not kept in inventory but are shipped immediately on completion. Backflush systems rely on the assumption that completion of production follows so soon after the application of conversion activities that balances in the conversion costs accounts always should remain near zero. Costs are transferred out almost immediately after being initially recorded.

Example of Backflush Costing

Speaker Technology Inc. (STI) produces speakers for automobile stereo systems. STI recently introduced a JIT production system and backflush costing. Consider the July production for speaker model AX27. The standard material cost per unit of AX27 is $14, and the standard unit conversion cost is $21. During July, STI purchased materials for $5,600, incurred conversion costs of $8,400, which included all labor costs and manufacturing overhead, and completed and sold 400 units of AX27.
   Backflush costing is accomplished in three steps:

1. Record actual materials and conversion costs. For simplicity, we assume for now that actual materials and conversion costs were identical to the standard costs. As materials are purchased, backflush systems add their cost to the materials inventory account:

Materials inventory	5,600	
Accounts payable (or cash)		5,600
To record material purchases		

   Similarly, as direct labor and manufacturing overhead costs are incurred, they are added to the conversion-costs account:

Conversion costs	8,400	
Accrued wages and other accounts		8,400
To record conversion costs incurred		

2. Apply costs to completed units. When production is complete, costs from materials inventory and conversion-costs accounts are transferred directly to finished goods based on the number of units completed and a *standard cost* of each unit:

Finished-goods inventory (400 × $35)	14,000	
Materials inventory		5,600
Conversion costs		8,400
To record costs of completed production		

Because of short production cycle times, there is little lag between additions to the conversion-costs account and transfers to finished goods. The conversion-costs account, therefore, remains near zero.

3. Record cost of goods sold during the period. The standard cost of the items sold is transferred from finished goods inventory to cost of goods sold:

```
Cost of goods sold . . . . . . . . . . . . . . . . . . . . . . . . . . . . . . . . . . . . .    14,000
        Finished goods inventory  . . . . . . . . . . . . . . . . . . . . . . .                14,000
To record cost of 400 units sold @$35 per unit
```

Suppose completed units are delivered immediately to customers, so that finished goods inventories are negligible. Steps 2 and 3 can then be combined and the finished goods inventory account eliminated:

```
Cost of goods sold . . . . . . . . . . . . . . . . . . . . . . . . . . . . . . . . . . . . .    14,000
        Material inventory  . . . . . . . . . . . . . . . . . . . . . . . . . . . . .                5,600
        Conversion costs  . . . . . . . . . . . . . . . . . . . . . . . . . . . . . .                8,400
```

What if actual costs added to the conversion-costs account do not equal the standard amounts that are transferred to finished-goods inventory? Variances are treated like overapplied or underapplied overhead. Backflush systems assume that conversion-costs account balances should be approximately zero at all times. Any remaining balance in the account at the end of an accounting period is charged to cost of goods sold. Suppose actual conversion costs for July had been $8,600 and the amount transferred to finished goods (i.e., applied to the product) was $8,400. The $200 balance in the conversion-costs account at the end of the month would be written off to cost of goods sold:

```
Cost of goods sold . . . . . . . . . . . . . . . . . . . . . . . . . . . . . . . . . . . . . .    200
        Conversion costs  . . . . . . . . . . . . . . . . . . . . . . . . . . . . . . . .                200
To recognize underapplied conversion costs
```

Highlights to Remember

Process costing is used for inventory costing when there is continuous mass production of like units. The key concept in process costing is that of equivalent units, the number of fully completed units that could have been produced from the inputs applied. The concept of equivalent units is widely applied in both manufacturing and nonmanufacturing settings. For example, universities use the concept to measure full-time equivalent enrollment.

Five basic steps may be used to solve process-cost problems:

1. Summarize the flow of physical units.
2. Calculate output in terms of equivalent units.
3. Summarize the total costs to account for.
4. Calculate unit costs.
5. Apply costs to units completed and to units in the ending work in process.

Process costing is complicated by the presence of beginning inventories. Two methods can be used when these complications are present: the *weighted-average* and *first-in, first-out* methods. The FIFO method focuses on the work done only in the current period, whereas the weighted-average method focuses on the work done in previous periods on the current period's beginning inventory in addition to work done in the current period.

Many companies with JIT production systems use backflush costing. Such systems have no work-in-process inventory account and apply costs to products only after the production process is complete.

Summary Problem for Your Review

Problems One and Two appeared earlier in the chapter.

Problem Three

The most extreme (and simplest) version of backflush costing makes product costing entries at only one point. Suppose Speaker Technology Inc. (STI) had no materials inventory account (in addition to no work-in-process inventory account). Materials are not "purchased" until they are needed for production. Therefore, STI enters both material and conversion costs directly into its finished goods inventory account.

Prepare journal entries (without explanations) and T-accounts for July's production of 400 units. As given earlier, materials purchases totaled $5,600, and conversion costs were $8,400. Why might a company use this extreme type of backflush costing?

Solution to Problem Three

In one step, material and conversion costs are applied to finished goods inventories:

Finished goods inventories	14,000	
Accounts payable		5,600
Wages payable and other accounts		8,400

Finished Goods Inventories		Accounts Payable, Wages Payable, and Other Accounts	
Materials 5,600			5,600
Conversion			
costs 8,400			8,400

This example of backflush costing illustrates a system that is simple and inexpensive. It provides reasonably accurate product costs if (1) materials inventories are low (most likely because of JIT delivery schedules), and (2) production cycle times are short, so that at any time only inconsequential amounts of material costs or conversion costs have been incurred for products that are not yet complete.

APPENDIX: HYBRID SYSTEMS—OPERATION COSTING

Job costing and process costing are extremes along a continuum of potential costing systems. Each company designs its own accounting system to fit its underlying production activities. Many companies use **hybrid-costing systems,** which are blends of ideas from both job costing and process costing. This appendix discusses one of many possible hybrid-costing systems, *operation costing.*

Nature of Operation Costing

Operation costing is a hybrid-costing system often used in the batch or group manufacturing of goods that have some common characteristics plus some individual characteristics. Examples of such goods include personal computers, clothing, and semiconductors. Such products are specifically identified by work orders. The goods are often variations of a single design but require a varying sequence of standardized operations. For instance, suits of clothes may differ, requiring various materials and hand operations. Similarly, a textile manufacturer may apply special chemical treatments (such as waterproofing) to some fabrics but not to others.

Operation costing may entail mass production, but there is sufficient product variety to have products scheduled in different batches or groups, each requiring a particular sequence of operations.

An *operation* is a standardized method or technique that is repetitively performed, regardless of the distinguishing features of the finished product. Examples include cutting, planing, sanding, painting, and chemical treating. Products proceed through the various operations in groups as specified by work orders or production orders. These work orders list the necessary direct materials and the step-by-step operations required to make the finished product.

Suppose a clothing manufacturer produces two lines of blazers. The wool blazers use better materials and undergo more operations than the polyester blazers, as follows:

	Wool Blazers	Polyester Blazers
Direct materials	Wool Satin lining Bone buttons	Polyester Rayon lining Plastic buttons

Operations	1. Cutting cloth
	2. Checking edges
	3. Sewing body
	4. Checking seams
	5. —
	
	6. Sewing collars and
	    lapels by hand
		1. Cutting cloth
		—
		3. Sewing body
		—
		5. Sewing collars and
		    lapels by machine
		
		—

The costs of the blazers are compiled by work order. As in job costing, the direct materials—different for each work order—are specifically identified with the appropriate order. Conversion costs—direct labor plus factory overhead—are initially compiled for each operation. A cost driver, such as the number of units processed or minutes or seconds used, is identified for each operation, and a conversion cost per unit of cost driver activity is computed. Then conversion costs are applied to products in a manner similar to the application of factory overhead in a job-cost system.

Example of Operation-Costing Entries

Suppose our manufacturer has two work orders, one for 100 wool blazers and the other for 200 polyester blazers, as follows:

	Wool Blazers	Polyester Blazers
Number of blazers	100	200
Direct materials	$2,500	$3,100
Conversion costs		
1. Cutting cloth	600	1,200
2. Checking edges	300	—
3. Sewing body	500	1,000
4. Checking seams	600	—
5. Sewing collars and lapels by machine	—	800
6. Sewing collars and lapels by hand	700	—
Total manufacturing costs	$5,200	$6,100

Direct labor and factory overhead vanish as separate classifications in an operation-costing system. The sum of these costs is most frequently called conversion cost. The conversion cost is applied to products based on the company's budgeted rate for performing each operation. For example, suppose the conversion costs of operation 1, cutting cloth, are driven by machine hours and are budgeted for the year as follows:

$$\text{budgeted rate for applying conversion costs for cutting cloth to product} = \frac{\text{budgeted conversion cost for cutting cloth for the year (direct labor, power, repairs, supplies, other factory overhead of this operation)}}{\text{budgeted machine-hours for the year for cutting cloth}}$$

$$\text{rate per machine-hours} = \frac{\$150,000 + \$450,000}{20,000 \text{ hours}} = \$30 \text{ per machine-hour}$$

As goods are manufactured, conversion costs are applied to the work orders by multiplying the $30 hourly rate times the number of machine-hours used for cutting cloth.

If 20 machine-hours are needed to cut the cloth for the 100 wool blazers, then the conversion cost involved is $600 (20 hours × $30 per hour). For the 200 polyester blazers, the conversion cost for cutting cloth is twice as much, $1,200 (40 hours × $30), because each blazer takes the same cutting time, and there are twice as many polyester blazers.

Summary journal entries for applying costs to the polyester blazers follow. (Entries for the wool blazers would be similar.)

The journal entry for the requisition of direct materials for the 200 polyester blazers is:

Work-in-process inventory (polyester blazers)	3,100	
Direct-materials inventory		3,100

Direct labor and factory overhead are subparts of a conversion-costs account in an operation-costing system. Suppose actual conversion costs of $3,150 were entered into the conversion-costs account:

Conversion costs	3,150	
Accrued payroll, accumulated depreciation,		
accounts payable, etc.		3,150

The application of conversion costs to products in operation costing is similar to the application of factory overhead in job-ordering costing. A *budgeted* rate per unit of cost-driver activity is used. To apply conversion costs to the 200 polyester blazers, the following summary entry is made for operations 1, 3, and 5 (cutting cloth, sewing body, and sewing collars and lapels by machine):

Work-in-process inventory (polyester blazers)	3,000	
Conversion costs, cutting cloth		1,200
Conversion costs, sewing body		1,000
Conversion costs, sewing collars		
and lapels by machine		800

After posting, work-in-process inventory has the following debit balance:

Work-in-Process Inventory (polyester blazers)

Direct materials	$3,100	
Conversion costs applied	3,000	
Balance	$6,100	

As the blazers are completed, their cost is transferred to finished-goods inventory in the usual manner.

Any overapplication or underapplication of conversion costs is disposed of at the end of the year in the same manner as overapplied or underapplied overhead in a job-order costing system. In this case, conversion costs have been debited for actual cost of $3,150 and credited for costs applied of $3,000. The debit balance of $150 indicates that conversion costs are underapplied.

Fundamental Assignment Material

14-A1 Basic Process Costing

Rockmania, Inc., produces portable compact disk (CD) players in large quantities. For simplicity, assume that the company has two departments, assembly and testing. The manufacturing costs in the Assembly Department during February were:

Direct materials added		$ 60,800
Conversion costs		
Direct labor	$50,000	
Factory overhead	40,000	90,000
Assembly costs to account for		$150,800

There was no beginning inventory of work in process. Suppose work on 19,000 CD players was begun in the assembly department during February, but only 17,000 CD players were fully completed. All the parts had been made or placed in process, but only half the labor had been completed for each of the CD players still in process.

1. Compute the equivalent units and unit costs for February.
2. Compute the costs of units completed and transferred to the Testing Department. Also compute the cost of the ending work in process. (For journal entries, see Problem 14-21.)

14-A2 Weighted-Average Process-Costing Method

The Lucero Company manufactures electric drills. Material is introduced at the beginning of the process in the Assembly Department. Conversion costs are applied uniformly throughout the process. As the process is completed, goods are immediately transferred to the Finishing Department.

Data for the Assembly Department for the month of July 19X5 follow:

Work in process, June 30: $175,500 (consisting of $138,000 materials and $37,500 conversion costs); 100% completed for direct materials, but only 25% completed for conversion costs	10,000 units
Units started during July	80,000 units
Units completed during July	70,000 units
Work in process, July 31: 100% completed for direct materials, but only 50% completed for conversion costs	20,000 units
Direct materials added during July	$852,000
Conversion costs added during July	$634,500

1. Compute the total cost of goods transferred out of the Assembly Department during July.
2. Compute the total costs of the ending work in process. Prepare a production-cost report or a similar orderly tabulation of your work. Assume weighted-average product costing. (For the FIFO method and journal entries, see Problems 14-31 and 14-37.)

14-A3 Backflush Costing

Thermo Controls, Inc., makes electronic thermostats for homes and offices. The Westplains Division makes one product, Autotherm, which has a standard cost of $37, consisting of $22 of materials and $15 of conversion costs. In January, actual purchases of materials totaled $45,000, labor payroll costs were $11,000, and manufacturing overhead was $19,000. Completed output was 2,000 units.

The Westplains Division uses a backflush-costing system that records costs in materials inventory and conversion costs accounts and applies costs to products at the time production is completed. There were no finished goods inventories on January 1 and 20 units on January 31.

1. Prepare journal entries (without explanations) to record January's costs for the Westplains Division. Include the purchase of materials, incurrence of labor and manufacturing overhead costs, application of product costs, and recognition of cost of goods sold.
2. Suppose January's actual manufacturing overhead costs had been $22,000 instead of $19,000. Prepare the journal entry to recognize underapplied conversion costs at the end of January.

14-B1 Basic Process Costing

McClure Company produces digital watches in large quantities. The manufacturing costs of the Assembly Department were:

Direct materials added		$1,620,000
Conversion costs		
Direct labor	$415,000	
Factory overhead	260,000	675,000
Assembly costs to account for		$2,295,000

For simplicity, assume that this is a two-department company, assembly and finishing. There was no beginning work in process.

Suppose 900,000 units were begu n in the Assembly Department. There were 600,000 units completed and transferred to the Finishing Department. The 300,000 units in ending work in process were fully completed regarding direct materials but half-completed regarding conversion costs.

1. Compute the equivalent units and unit costs in the Assembly Department.
2. Compute the costs of units completed and transferred to the Finishing Department. Also compute the cost of the ending work in process in the Assembly Department.

14-B2 Weighted-Average Process-Costing Method

The Rainbow Paint Co. uses a process-cost system. Materials are added at the beginning of a particular process, and conversion costs are incurred uniformly. Work in process at the beginning is assumed 40% complete; at the end, 20%. One gallon of material makes 1 gallon of product. Data follow:

Beginning inventory	550 gal
Direct materials added	7,150 gal
Ending inventory	400 gal
Conversion costs incurred	$35,724
Cost of direct materials added	$65,340
Conversion costs, beginning inventory	$ 1,914
Cost of direct materials, beginning inventory	$ 3,190

Use the weighted-average method. Prepare a schedule of output in equivalent units and a schedule of application of costs to products. Show the cost of goods completed and cost of ending work in process. (For journal entries see Problem 14-30. For the FIFO method see Problem 14-36.)

14-B3 Backflush Costing

ACME Auto Parts recently installed a backflush-costing system in its Audio Components Department. One cost center in the department makes 4-inch speakers with a standard cost as follows:

Materials	$ 9.80
Conversion costs	4.20
Total	$14.00

Speakers are scheduled for production only after orders are received, and products are shipped to customers immediately on completion. Therefore, no finished goods inventories are kept, and product costs are applied directly to cost of goods sold.

In October, 1,500 speakers were produced and shipped to customers. Materials were purchased at a cost of $15,500, and actual conversion costs (labor plus manufacturing overhead) of $6,300 were recorded.

1. Prepare journal entries to record October's costs for the production of 4-inch speakers.
2. Suppose October's actual conversion costs had been $6,000 instead of $6,300. Prepare a journal entry to recognize overapplied conversion costs.

Additional Assignment Material

Questions

14-1. Give three examples of industries where process-costing systems are probably used.

14-2. Give three examples of nonprofit organizations where process-costing systems are probably used.

14-3. Give three examples of equivalent units in various organizations.

14-4. Under what conditions can significant amounts of work in process be safely ignored in process costing?

14-5. What is the central product-costing problem in process costing?

14-6. "There are five key steps in process-cost accounting." What are they?

14-7. "Equivalent units are the work done to date." What method of process costing is being described?

14-8. Identify the major distinction between the first two and the final three steps of the five major steps in accounting for process costs.

14-9. Present an equation that describes the physical flow in process costing.

14-10. Why is "work done in the current period only" a key measurement of equivalent units?

14-11. "The beginning inventory is regarded as if it were a batch of goods separate and distinct from the goods started *and* completed by a process during the current period." What method of process costing is being described?

14-12. "Ordinarily, the differences in unit costs under FIFO and weighted-average methods are insignificant." Do you agree? Explain.

14-13. "The total conversion costs are divided by the equivalent units for the work done to date." Does this quotation describe the weighted-average method or does it describe FIFO?

14-14. "Backflush-costing systems work only for companies using a JIT production system." Do you agree? Explain.

14-15. Explain what happens in a backflush-costing system when the amount of actual conversion cost in a period exceeds the amount applied to the products completed that period.

14-16. Give three examples of industries that probably use operation costing.

14-17. "In operation costing, average conversion costs are applied to products in a manner similar to the application of factory overhead in a job-cost system." Do you agree? Explain.

14-18. Prepare journal entries reflecting the application of conversion costs of $90,000 to work in process.

14-19 Basic Process Costing

A department of Mayberry Textiles produces cotton fabric. All direct materials are introduced at the start of the process. Conversion costs are incurred uniformly throughout the process.

In May there was no beginning inventory. Units started, completed, and transferred: 650,000. Units in process, May 31: 220,000. Each unit in ending work in process was 60% converted. Costs incurred during May: direct materials, $3,654,000; conversion costs, $860,200.

1. Compute the total work done in equivalent units and the unit cost for May.
2. Compute the cost of units completed and transferred. Also compute the cost of units in ending work in process.

14-20 Uneven Flow

One department of Wamego Technology Company manufactures basic hand-held calculators. Various materials are added at various stages of the process. The outer front shell and the carrying case, which represent 10% of the total material cost, are added at the final step of the assembly process. All other materials are considered to be "in process" by the time the calculator reaches a 50% stage of completion.

Seventy-four thousand calculators were started in production during 19X2. At year-end, 6,000 calculators were in various stages of completion, but all of them were beyond the 50% stage and on the average they were regarded as being 70% completed.

The following costs were incurred during the year: direct materials, $205,520; conversion costs, $397,100.

1. Prepare a schedule of physical units and equivalent units.
2. Tabulate the unit costs, cost of goods completed, and cost of ending work in process.

14-21 Journal Entries
Refer to the data in Problem 14-A1. Prepare summary journal entries for the use of direct materials, direct labor, and factory overhead applied. Also prepare a journal entry for the transfer of goods completed and transferred. Show the postings to the Work-in-Process account.

14-22 Journal Entries
Refer to the data in Problem 14-B1. Prepare summary journal entries for the use of direct materials, direct labor, and factory overhead applied. Also prepare a journal entry for the transfer of goods completed and transferred. Show the posting to the Work-in-Process—Assembly Department account.

14-23 Physical Units
Fill in the unknowns in physical units:

	Case	
Flow of Production	*A*	*B*
Work in process, beginning inventory	1,500	4,000
Started	6,000	?
Completed and transferred	?	8,000
Work in process, ending inventory	2,000	3,000

14-24 Flow of Production, FIFO
Fill in the unknowns in physical or equivalent units:

		Equivalent Units	
Flow of Production	**Physical Units**	*Direct Materials*	*Conversion Costs*
Beginning work in process	1,000 (50%)*		
Started	?		
To account for	36,000		
Completed and transferred out	33,000	33,000	33,000
Ending work in process	? (30%)*	?	?
Units accounted for	?		
Work done to date		?	?
Equivalent units in beginning inventory		?	?
Work done in current period only		?	?

* Degree of completion of conversion costs at dates of inventory. Assume that all materials are added at the beginning of the process.

14-25 Multiple Choice

The Preparation Department of Blackburn, Inc., had the following flow of latex paint production (in gallons) for the month of April:

Units completed	
From work in process on April 1	5,000
From April production	25,000
	30,000

Direct materials are added at the beginning of the process. Units of work in process at April 30 were 10,000. The work in process at April 1 was 30% complete as to conversion costs, and the work in process at April 30 was 50% complete as to conversion costs. What are the equivalent units of production for the month of April using the FIFO method? Choose one of the following combinations:

	Direct Materials	Conversion Costs
a.	40,000	40,000
b.	35,000	33,500
c.	35,000	35,000
d.	40,000	35,000

14-26 Equivalent Units, FIFO

Fill in the unknowns:

		(Step 2) Equivalent Units	
Flow of Production in Units	(Step 1) Physical Units	Direct Materials	Conversion Costs
Work in process, beginning inventory	30,000*		
Started	45,000		
To account for	75,000		
Completed and transferred out	?	?	?
Work in process, ending inventory	2,000†	?	?
Units accounted for	75,000		
Work done to date		?	?
Less: Equivalent units of work from previous periods included in beginning inventory		?	?
Work done in current period only (FIFO method)		?	?

* Degree of completion: direct materials, 80%; conversion costs, 40%.
† Degree of completion: direct materials, 40%; conversion costs, 10%.

14-27 Compute Equivalent Units
Consider the following data for February:

	Physical Units
Started in February	80,000
Completed in February	90,000
Ending inventory, work in process	10,000
Beginning inventory, work in process	20,000

The beginning inventory was 80% complete regarding direct materials and 40% complete regarding conversion costs. The ending inventory was 20% complete regarding direct materials and 10% complete regarding conversion costs.

Prepare a schedule of equivalent units for the work done to date and the work done during February only.

14-28 FIFO and Unit Direct-Material Costs
The Lindberg Company uses the FIFO process-cost method. Consider the following for July:

- Beginning inventory, 15,000 units, 70% completed regarding direct materials, which cost $89,250
- Units completed, 80,000
- Cost of materials placed in process during July, $580,000
- Ending inventory, 5,000 units, 60% completed regarding materials

Compute the direct-material cost per equivalent unit for the work done in July only.

14-29 FIFO Method, Conversion Cost
Given the following information, compute the unit conversion cost for the month of June for the Abraham Company, using the FIFO process-cost method. Show details of your calculation.

- Units completed, 45,000
- Conversion cost in beginning inventory, $30,000
- Beginning inventory, 10,000 units with 75% of conversion cost
- Ending inventory, 15,000 units with 30% of conversion cost
- Conversion costs put into production in June, $180,600

14-30 Journal Entries
Refer to the data in Problem 14-B2. Prepare summary journal entries for the use of direct materials and conversion costs. Also prepare a journal entry for the transfer of goods completed, assuming that the goods are transferred to another department.

14-31 Journal Entries
Refer to the data in Problem 14-A2. Prepare summary journal entries for the use of direct materials and conversion costs. Also prepare a journal entry for the transfer of the goods completed and transferred from the Assembly Department to the Finishing Department.

14-32 Process and Activity-Based Costing
Consider the potato chip production process at a company such as Frito-Lay. Frito-Lay uses a continuous flow technology that is suited for high volumes of product. At the Plano, Texas, facility, between 6 and 7 thousand pounds of potato chips are produced each hour. The plant operates 24 hours a day. It takes 30 minutes to completely produce a bag of potato chips from the raw potato to the packed end-product.

1. What product and process characteristics of potato chips dictate the cost accounting system used? Describe the costing system best suited to Frito-Lay.
2. What product and process characteristics dictate the use of an activity-based-costing system? What implications does this have for Frito-Lay?
3. When beginning inventories are present, product costing becomes more complicated. Estimate the relative magnitude of beginning inventories at Frito-Lay compared to total production. What implication does this have for the costing system?

14-33 Nonprofit Process Costing

The IRS must process millions of income tax returns yearly. When the taxpayer sends in a return, documents such as withholding statements and checks are matched against the data submitted. Then various other inspections of the data are conducted. Of course, some returns are more complicated than others, so the expected time allowed to process a return is geared to an "average" return.

Some work-measurement experts have been closely monitoring the processing at a particular branch. They are seeking ways to improve productivity.

Suppose 3 million returns were received on April 15. On April 22, the work-measurement teams discovered that all supplies (punched cards, inspection check-sheets, and so on) had been affixed to the returns, but 40% of the returns still had to undergo a final inspection. The other returns were fully completed.

1. Suppose the final inspection represents 20% of the overall processing time in this process. Compute the total work done in terms of equivalent units.
2. The materials and supplies consumed were $600,000. For these calculations, materials and supplies are regarded just like direct materials. The conversion costs were $4,830,000. Compute the unit costs of materials and supplies and of conversion.
3. Compute the cost of the tax returns not yet completely processed.

14-34 Two Materials

The following data pertain to the Mixing Department at Foster Chemicals for April:

Units	
Work in process, March 31	0
Units started	60,000
Completed and transferred	
to finishing department	40,000
Costs	
Materials	
Plastic compound	$300,000
Softening compound	$ 80,000
Conversion costs	$192,000

The plastic compound is introduced at the start of the process, while the softening compound is added when the product reaches an 80% stage of completion. Conversion costs are incurred uniformly throughout the process.

The ending work in process is 40% completed for conversion costs. None of the units in process reached the 80% stage of completion.

1. Compute the equivalent units and unit costs for April.
2. Compute the total cost of units completed and transferred to finished goods. Also compute the cost of the ending work in process.

14-35 Materials and Cartons

A Manchester, England, company manufactures and sells small portable tape recorders. Business is booming. Various materials are added at various stages in the assembly department. Costs are accounted for on a process-cost basis. The end of the process involves conducting a final inspection and adding a cardboard carton.

The final inspection requires 5% of the total processing time. All materials besides the carton are added by the time the recorders reach an 80% stage of completion of conversion.

There were no beginning inventories. One hundred fifty thousand recorders were started in production during 19X6. At the end of the year, which was not a busy time, 5,000 recorders were in various stages of completion. All the ending units in work in process were at the 95% stage. They awaited final inspection and being placed in cartons.

Total direct materials consumed in production, except for cartons, cost £2,250,000. Cartons used cost £319,000. Total conversion costs were £1,198,000.

1. Present a schedule of physical units, equivalent units, and unit costs of direct materials, cartons, and conversion costs.
2. Present a summary of the cost of goods completed and the cost of ending work in process.

14-36 FIFO Computations

Refer to Problem 14-B2. Using FIFO, answer the same questions.

14-37 FIFO Methods

Refer to Problem 14-A2. Using FIFO costing, answer the same questions.

14-38 Backflush Costing

Everest Controls manufactures a variety of meters and other measuring instruments. One product is an altimeter used by hikers and mountain climbers. Everest adopted a JIT philosophy with an automated, computer-controlled, robotic production system. Production is scheduled after an order is received, materials and parts arrive just as they are needed, the production cycle time for altimeters is less than 1 day, and completed units are packaged and shipped as part of the production cycle.

Everest's backflush costing system has only three accounts related to production of altimeters: materials and parts inventory, conversion costs, and finished goods inventory. At the beginning of April (as at the beginning of every month) each of the three accounts had a balance of zero. Following are the April transactions related to the production of altimeters:

Materials and parts purchased	$287,000
Conversion costs incurred	$ 92,000
Altimeters produced	11,500 units

The budgeted (or standard) cost for one altimeter is $24 for materials and parts and $8 for conversion costs.

1. Prepare summary journal entries for the production of altimeters in April.
2. Compute the cost of goods sold for April. Explain any assumptions you make.
3. Suppose the actual conversion costs incurred during April were $95,000 instead of $92,000, and all other facts were as given. Prepare the additional journal entry that would be required at the end of April. Explain why the entry was necessary.

14-39 Basic Operation Costing

Study the Appendix to this chapter. Hudson Co. manufactures a variety of wooden chairs. The company's manufacturing operations and costs applied to products for April were:

	Cutting	Assembly	Finishing
Direct labor	$ 60,000	$30,000	$ 90,000
Factory overhead	115,500	37,500	141,000

Three styles of chairs were produced in April. The quantities and direct material cost were:

Style	Quantity	Direct Materials
Standard	6,000	$108,000
Deluxe	4,500	171,000
Unfinished	3,000	63,000

Each unit, regardless of style, required the same cutting and assembly operations. The unfinished chairs, as the name implies, had no finishing operations whatsoever. Standard and deluxe styles required the same finishing operations.

1. Tabulate the total conversion costs of each operation, the total units produced, and the conversion cost per unit.
2. Tabulate the total costs, the units produced, and the cost per unit.

14-40 Operation Costing with Ending Work in Process

Study the Appendix to this chapter. Squire Co. uses three operations in sequence to make video cameras. Using the information on the next page, complete the following:

1. Operation 2 was highly automated. Product costs depended on a budgeted application rate for conversion costs based on machine-hours. The budgeted costs for 19X5 were $120,000 direct labor and $480,000 factory overhead. Budgeted machine-hours were 20,000. Each camera required 6 minutes of time in operation 2. Compute the costs of processing 1,000 cameras in operation 2.
2. Compute the total manufacturing costs of 1,000 cameras and the cost per standard-quality camera and better-quality camera.
3. Suppose that at the end of the year 500 standard-quality cameras were in process through operation 1 only and 600 better-quality cameras were in process through operation 2 only. Compute the cost of the ending work-in-process inventory. Assume that no direct materials are applied in operation 2, but that $10,000 of the $100,000 direct-material cost of the better-quality cameras are applied to each 1,000 cameras processed in operation 3.

CHAPTER 15

STANDARD COSTS AND VARIANCE ANALYSIS

15.1 STANDARD COSTS RELATED TO PROJECT COSTS

During the project planning process, the costs for each of the tasks comprising project work packages is estimated. These estimated costs become the "standard" costs of the project. They have counterparts in nearly every industry. In the auto service business they are termed flat rates. The primary reason they are used is because (a) it is easier to use an estimate than to calculate actual rates, and (b) actual costs are not known. Once the project is underway, actual costs begin to be accumulated. Comparing the actual costs with the estimated or standard costs results in "variances". The reading that follows is by Calvin Engler and discusses all these subjects.

15.2 STANDARD COSTS AND PERFORMANCE EVALUATION

Standards, the expected levels of performance, play an important part in our daily lives. When attending high school or college, a student must perform at a certain level of scholarship to graduate and earn a diploma or a degree. When dining in a restaurant, a patron expects a certain level of quality in the food served, and when purchasing a product, a consumer demands a certain level of dependability and service. Thus, standards pervade all areas of human activity, including, as we shall see, the field of management, where it is vital that clear and quantitative standards be used to measure performance.

A firm is usually concerned with producing its product at the lowest possible cost consistent with the quality it wishes to maintain. Thus, the firm will monitor the prices it pays for its direct materials, direct labor, and manufacturing overhead.

Not only must it monitor these items, it must also control the quantities of these factors used in its production process. Because of the volume of transactions that a firm has in an accounting period, such as one month, it is extremely impractical and costly to monitor every transaction during the period. Thus, firms group large numbers of similar transactions and then compare the grouping to a norm set in advance of the actual occurrence of the transactions. The setting of norms to be used for the controlling of costs is known as *standard costing*. This chapter is concerned with the setting of predetermined (standard) costs and their use in a firm's accounting system, the identification of the differences between a firm's actual costs and standard costs, the analysis of these differences, and their interpretation. The use of standard costs is not a cost accounting system in and of itself; rather, standard costs are used in conjunction with job order costs or process costs.

Actual costs vary from predetermined costs for two reasons: the actual price paid for a good or service may differ from its estimated price, and the quantity consumed may differ from the amount predicted. These differences may be classified as favorable when the price paid or the quantity consumed is less than expected, or they may be classified as unfavorable when the reverse is true. For cost-control purposes, managers need timely performance reports showing the differences between standard costs and actual costs with analyses showing the causes of the differences and whether the differences are favorable or unfavorable.

PERFORMANCE EVALUATION

Management by Exception

Very often, one person may expect a standard of behavior from another person, but the actual behavior is different from the expectation. For example, you may expect an easy exam from a certain professor, but when you take the exam, it is more difficult than you expected. In the same manner, the actual performance of an employee, machine, or a product is usually different from its expected performance. Differences between actual performance and expected performance can range in size from infinitesimal to extremely large. Since it is quite likely that a variance will occur between actual performance and expected performance, should a manager investigate every variance? It is obvious that the answer is "no." Thus, a manager of a firm must decide what variances should be investigated. When management chooses to investigate and take action on only those variances that depart significantly from prescribed standards, their approach is called **management by exception.** The critical aspect of management by exception lies in the choice of variances to investigate. Thus, each firm must develop decision rules for selecting which variances to investigate. Practices vary from firm to firm. The criteria used in selecting variances to investigate are discussed later in this chapter.

Everyone at one time or another is evaluated on his or her performance. Terms like *effective* and *efficient* are often used to rate favorable performance, while *ineffective* and *inefficient* are used to rate unfavorable performance. **Effectiveness** relates to whether an objective is achieved. **Efficiency,** on the other hand, is a measure of the means by which an objective is achieved—that is, whether it is achieved with the least amount of effort and the least possible cost. For example, if a sales representative is required to make a trip from New York to Florida to attend a sales convention, she may choose a direct flight from New York to Florida, which would be both efficient and effective. Alternatively, she could take a flight from New York to California and then take another flight from California to Florida. Although this route would be effective—the objective is to attend a sales convention in Florida—the means by which it is achieved is inefficient. Evaluating the effectiveness and efficiency of an employee's performance requires the setting of expected levels of performance, or standards.

STANDARDS

A *standard* is an established criterion used to measure the quality of performance. Unless a firm develops standards for measuring employee performance, a manager's evaluations are likely to be biased, subjective, and ineffective. Moreover, if employees are not told what level of performance is expected, they cannot be expected to take their manager's evaluations seriously. On the other hand, when an appropriate level of performance is clearly defined and when that level is reasonable and fair to both the employer and the employee, companies should give rewards for superior performance and penalties for inferior performance. Thus, it is important for managers to clearly define the levels of performance they expect of employees. These levels should be relatively free from bias and scientifically determined, when possible.

Standards may be developed to measure both effectiveness and efficiency. If a firm's factory is capable of producing 10,000 units of product per month and the firm's objective is to produce the full 10,000 units, this would be a standard of effectiveness. If 10,000 units are actually produced, then production is effective. If only 9,500 are produced, then production is ineffective. An efficiency standard relates to the *cost* of the units produced. If a particular task should take five hours of direct labor to perform and the rate of pay is $8 per hour, the cost of this task for direct labor is expected to be $40. However, if an employee works at a slower pace than normal and takes seven hours to complete the task, the cost for direct labor is $56 (7 hours × $8), and performance is inefficient. In effect, seven hours of direct labor were put into production and only five hours of output were received, leading to a waste of two hours at a cost of $8 per hour, or $16 of inefficiency. Efficiency standards are usually referred to as *standard costs*.

Standard Costs

A **standard cost** is a carefully predetermined cost used in evaluating performance. Because budgeted costs are also predetermined costs, one may ask, "What is the difference between standard costs and budgeted costs?" The answer is relatively simple. Standard cost applies to *one unit of output* efficiently produced, and budgeted cost relates to *total output* for a period of time. If the standard cost for one unit of production is multiplied by the expected number of units to be produced during a period of time, the result is the **budgeted cost** for the period.

Because the setting of standards tends to extend beyond the scope of any individual, companies usually have a committee to set standards in accordance with the firms' goals and objectives.

The Standards Committee A company's **standards committee** normally includes its controller, industrial engineer, purchasing manager, management accountants, marketing manager, factory superintendent, and line supervisors. Each member provides needed information within his or her area of expertise. The committee is directly responsible for the setting of standards.

Setting Standards Standard costs are determined for direct materials, direct labor, and manufacturing overhead. For standard costs to be an effective control mechanism, they must reflect what *future* costs should be and *not* what *past* costs were. Past costs may contain inefficiencies, and if they are automatically used as a starting point for the current year, the inefficiencies will be perpetuated. Furthermore, standard costs must be kept current. Even if the previous year's standard costs contain little or no inefficiencies, they may still be useless for the current year if there have been changes in prices, product quality, or operating practices and procedures. Firms use standards to control the behavior of their employees.

When setting the standard cost for direct materials, the committee must consider both the *quantity* of each direct material and its price. The quantities of direct materials needed for one unit may be determined by having the firm's engineering staff prepare a bill of materials. A **bill of materials** is a detailed listing, right down to the smallest bolt and nut (although nuts and bolts are often classified as indirect materials), of every item and quantity of direct material needed to manufacture one unit of finished product. The bill of materials is then priced out by asking the firm's purchasing department to quote the best prices available for each item, multiplying the quantities by the prices, and summarizing the results to obtain the total standard cost for direct materials.

A similar procedure may be used to obtain the standard cost for direct labor. However, although the quantities of direct labor may be obtained from engineering estimates, line supervisors can corroborate the estimates by observing and timing employees performing the task. The company's wage rates are then used to price out the standard direct labor cost for a unit of product.

Many firms now construct computer models of the operations to be performed, and through simulation studies, the standards committee can obtain additional corroboration of what standard costs should be.

Once standard costs are determined by the standards committee, managers and employees responsible for operating efficiency usually accept them as reasonable.

Bases of Standard Costs

Ideal Standards versus Practical Standards Standard costs may be used to motivate employees to achieve organizational goals. However, when standards are selected, great care must be given to evaluating their attainability. If standards are too tight, they will discourage employee performance. If they are too loose, they will lead to inefficient operations. An **ideal standard** is a measurement for evaluating performance that is theoretically possible but impractical to attain because it does not allow for machine breakdowns, rest periods, and the like, and requires employees to work at a constant rate of peak performance without any interruptions. In contrast, **practical (attainable) standards** are set high enough to motivate employees and low enough to allow for normal interruptions.

Some firms mistakenly use ideal standards so that employees will always have something to strive for. However, when employees realize it is impossible to reach the ideal, they usually lose both faith and interest in the system. Instead of being motivated, they become cynical and disgruntled. Consequently, most firms use practical standards that set realistic demands and reward employees for desired levels of performance.

After the standards committee has decided the question of attainability, it can turn to setting specific standards.

Uses of Standard Costs

Managers utilize standard costs in a variety of ways. Among the most important uses are:
1. Control through performance reports.
2. Critical cost analysis when setting standards.
3. Pricing.
4. Inventory valuation.
5. Budget preparation.
6. Simplified record-keeping.

1. Control through Performance Reports   By comparing actual performance results with planned operations, managers are able to monitor subordinates' results. When employees know their performance is being monitored, they are more likely to recognize the importance of meeting specified standards. When performance reports are prepared fairly and humanely, they should not be offensive to employees who understand the need for control.

2. Critical Cost Analysis When Setting Standards   When setting or updating standards each year, the standards committee reexamines prior costs, which should lead to increased efficiencies. In many cases, the setting of proper standards is an extremely difficult task.

3. Pricing   Many firms believe setting a long-run, stable selling price based on what costs should be (normal costs) is superior to constantly adjusting prices to reflect fluctuations in actual costs. Proponents of this strategy believe customers prefer to purchase their goods knowing that in the foreseeable future the price will remain unchanged and that they will not obtain a better price by waiting. General Motors, Ford, and Chrysler have been practicing this strategy for many years. Occasionally, the automobile manufacturers have been known to offer rebates on certain slow-selling models, but their overall policy has been to price their products using long-run standard costs rather than actual costs.

4. Inventory Valuation   If a firm does not use standard costs, it must price its inventories at actual costs. This necessitates the use of a cost-flow assumption (such as FIFO, LIFO, or average) and the maintenance of a record-keeping system for inventories and cost of goods sold that is unnecessarily complex. With standard costs, all inventories (with the possible exception of direct materials) and cost of goods sold are priced at standard, and thus all units of the same kind are priced the same regardless of their actual costs. As a result, the need for a cost-flow assumption is obviated, and the record-keeping for inventories and cost of goods sold is simplified.

5. Budget Preparation   When standard costs are used as part of a firm's accounting system, standard costs are also used for budget preparation. Instead of basing the coming year's budget on the preceding year's costs, standard costs for the expected level of activity are used. In this manner, the budget is based on *what costs should be* rather than on *what they were in the past.* From a control standpoint, comparing actual costs to standard costs is superior to comparing actual costs to estimated costs based on a previous year's actual results because, as noted earlier, built-in inefficiencies tend to be weeded out when standard costs are used.

6. Simplified Record-Keeping   When actual costs are used, records like materials requisitions must be priced out using a cost-flow assumption. This entails using the actual purchase prices, which differ over time, on material requisitions for the same item. Clearly, a different cost for direct materials will be used whenever the price of a direct material changes and the firm uses FIFO, LIFO, or average unit costs for its direct materials prices on material requisitions. When standard costs are used, only one price—the standard unit price—is used even if the materials are issued from two batches purchased at different prices. In fact, the materials requisitions may have the prices preprinted on them because only one price is used until a new standard price is adopted.

Standards for Direct Materials

Each amount of material listed in the bill of materials prepared by the engineering department must be adjusted to account for normal spoilage, waste, shrinkage, and the like. For example, if a firm is manufacturing wooden bookcases, the amount of lumber required must be adjusted to account for saw cuts, trimming of ends, and random defects, such as knots, planing, and sanding. The bill of materials plus the sum of all such adjustments for each direct material equal the **standard quantity of direct materials.**

When the prices of direct materials are obtained from the purchasing department, they must be adjusted for such items as freight-in, insurance while in transit, cash discounts allowed, and import duties. After adjustment, the prices equal the **standard price of direct materials.**

The **standard cost of direct materials** per unit may be expressed as:

$$\begin{array}{c} \text{Standard quantity of direct material per unit} \\ \times \text{ Standard price per unit of direct material} \\ = \text{Standard cost of direct material per unit} \end{array}$$

If a bookcase requires 30 board feet (bd. ft.) of clear pine lumber and the lumber's standard cost is $1 per board foot, the standard cost for direct materials is $30 (30 feet × $1).

Normally, a tabulation is prepared by listing the quantity, price and total cost of the required direct materials, as shown in Illustration 15-1.

Standards for Direct Labor

The estimates of required direct-labor hours obtained from engineers and factory supervisors must be adjusted for reasonable personal needs, coffee breaks, machine breakdowns and maintenance, and the like. If the required time to manufacture a bookcase is 55 minutes and the adjustment for personal needs and the like is 40 minutes per eight-hour day, the **standard quantity of direct labor** is 60 minutes (55 + $\frac{40}{8}$ = 60 minutes).

If an employee who works on bookcases earns $8 per hour, the standard direct labor rate is $8 per hour. A **standard direct labor rate** is the normal rate of pay per hour paid to employees for a particular kind of work. The **standard cost of direct labor** per unit may be expressed as:

$$\begin{array}{c} \text{Standard quantity of direct labor per unit} \\ \times \text{ Standard direct labor rate} \\ = \text{Standard cost of direct labor per unit} \end{array}$$

Illustration 15-1

FOREMOST FURNITURE COMPANY
Standard Cost of Direct Materials and Direct Labor
Product: Pine unfinished bookcase

Description	Quantity	Price or Rate	Total
Direct materials—1" clear pine*	30 board feet	$1	$30
Direct labor	1 hour	8	8
Total			$38

* Although glue is also used, it is not listed here because it is considered an indirect material.

Using the one-hour quantity and the $8 rate, the standard cost of direct labor at Foremost Furniture would be $8 (1 hour × $8), as summarized in Illustration 15-1.

Once the standard cost per unit is decided upon, work may proceed toward the construction of a budget.

Standard Quantity Allowed

As noted previously, a standard cost refers to only *one unit* of product. Because firms usually manufacture their products in batches, the standard cost per unit must be converted into budgeted data. This is accomplished by multiplying the expected number of units to be produced in an accounting period by the standard cost per unit. For example, the standard cost of direct materials for the Foremost Furniture Company's bookcase is $30 per unit. If the company expects to manufacture 100 bookcases for the month of January 19x1, its budgeted cost for direct materials is $3,000 (100 units × $30). A budgeted cost may be computed by multiplying the *estimated* production by the standard cost per unit:

$$\text{Budgeted cost} = \text{Estimated units} \times \text{Standard cost per unit} \qquad (1)$$

The budgeted cost for direct materials is useful for planning purposes. It provides a measure of the expected activity and how much direct materials will be needed for the month. However, it may not be useful for controlling purposes. In this case, if exactly 100 bookcases are produced in January, then the $3,000 budgeted amount is useful for comparing the actual materials cost with the estimated cost to determine if the actual cost is higher than it should be (an unfavorable event) or lower than it should be (a favorable event). For example, if the actual direct materials cost for the bookcases during January is $3,200 and 100 bookcases were manufactured, then the actual cost is $200 greater than it should be—an unfavorable event. But if 110 bookcases were *actually* produced and the direct materials cost amounted to $3,200, a manager's conclusion that the additional cost of $200 is unfavorable might be erroneous. Before a conclusion can be reached about the $3,200 actual cost, it is necessary to adjust the budgeted cost of $3,000 to reflect the *actual* number of units produced. This is accomplished by computing the **standard quantity allowed** using the formula:

$$\begin{aligned}\text{Standard quantity allowed} = \text{Standard quantity of one unit} \\ \times \text{Actual number of units produced}\end{aligned} \qquad (2)$$

If 110 bookcases were manufactured, the standard quantity allowed for materials would be 3,300 board feet (110 units × 30 bd. ft. per unit).

The standard quantity allowed, sometimes called the *flexible budget quantity*, is then used to compute the total standard cost. The formula to find the **total standard cost** for direct materials is:

$$\begin{aligned}\text{Total standard cost}_{dm} = \text{Standard quantity allowed} \\ \times \text{Standard unit price of direct material}\end{aligned} \qquad (3)$$

Because Foremost normally pays $1 per board foot of lumber, its total standard cost for direct materials would be $3,300 (3,300 bd. ft. × $1). The same result may be achieved by multiplying the number of units produced by the standard cost per unit (110 units × $30 = $3,300). Although this calculation of the total standard cost is simpler to compute than the standard-quantity-allowed approach, we will see later that the standard quantity allowed provides some useful information for control purposes that is not found in this simpler calculation. However, the simpler calculation may be used as a check on the standard-quantity-allowed calculations.

It is now possible to make a valid comparison between the actual cost of $3,200 for direct materials and the total standard cost of $3,300. This comparison indicates that a favorable cost difference exists, instead of the unfavorable one indicated by the comparison of the budgeted cost with the actual cost. Thus, whenever actual production differs from estimated production, it is necessary to first compute the total standard cost for comparison with the actual cost. The budgeted cost should only be used for comparison when actual production coincides with estimated production.

Similar equations are used for analyzing direct labor, except direct labor is substituted for direct materials. Therefore, Equation 3 for direct labor becomes:

$$\text{Total standard cost}_{dl} = \text{Standard quantity allowed} \times \text{Standard rate per direct labor-hour} \qquad (4)$$

Using Equation 2 for direct labor, the standard quantity allowed is 110 hours (110 units $\times$ 1 hour), and the total standard cost, using Equation 4, is $880 (110 hours $\times$ $8 per hour). This amount should be used for comparison with the actual cost to determine if a favorable or unfavorable condition occurred during January 19xl.

When comparing actual costs with total standard costs, it is important for managers to recognize that a difference between the two costs is really composed of two factors, a quantity-used factor and a price factor. The individuals responsible for each factor are normally different, and thus it is necessary to analyze these factors to attribute the cause of a difference to the individual(s) responsible for it.

Input and Output

Input is a quantity of goods or services entered into production that is expected to yield a certain quantity of finished goods, and **output** is all completed units (or equivalent completed units) of product. Suppose that at Foremost, the input of 4,000 board feet of lumber and 130 direct labor-hours were used to produce the output of 110 bookcases. Based on standard quantity allowed, the 4,000 board feet of lumber should have produced 133 bookcases (4,000 bd. ft. $\div$ 30 bd. ft.). Thus, the fact that only 110 bookcases were produced indicates that management should investigate the reason(s) for the difference. Similarly, 130 hours of direct labor should produce 130 units of output (130 hours $\div$ 1 hour), so this difference, too, requires investigation.

PROGRESS CHECK

1. Why do firms use standard cost accounting?
2. What is meant by *management by exception?* Why is it used?
3. What is the difference between effectiveness and efficiency?
4. How are standards for direct materials and direct labor determined?
5. What is the difference between an ideal standard and a practical standard?
6. For what purposes do managers use standard costs?
7. How is the standard cost of direct materials computed?
8. How is the standard cost of direct labor computed?
9. What does the *standard quantity allowed* mean?

VARIANCE ANALYSIS

In **variance analysis,** the difference between an actual cost and its budgeted, or standard, counterpart is segregated into price and quantity components. As noted before, these components are needed to properly assess responsibility. For example, responsibility for a direct materials price variance should rest with the manager of the purchasing department; responsibility for a direct labor quantity variance, sometimes called an *efficiency variance,* should lie with the line supervisor whose employees created the variance. A **favorable variance** occurs when *output exceeds input* or when the price paid for a good or service is less than expected. An **unfavorable variance** arises when *output is less than input* or when the price paid for a good or service is greater than expected. Although an unfavorable variance is generally unsatisfactory, this is not always the case. An example of an unfavorable variance that is not unsatisfactory appears in the next three paragraphs.

If your roommates went to the supermarket to buy two cans of tuna fish that normally cost $1.25 each, you would expect them to spend $2.50. If you discover that they spent $3.00 on tuna fish, you might conclude that this was an unfavorable transaction, because an extra $.50 was actually expended. Your mental analysis would be:

Actual cost	$3.00
Planned (budgeted) cost	2.50
Unfavorable	$ .50

However, on questioning your roommates you may learn that the tuna fish was on sale for $.75 per can and that they bought four cans instead of the two you requested. Having completed a course in managerial accounting, your roommates then explain how important it is to analyze a seemingly unfavorable result before rushing to a conclusion that may be wrong. To help you understand the results, they present the following analysis:

Price difference:
4 cans at $.50 ($1.25 − $.75) . . . . . . $2.00 favorable
Quantity difference:
2 additional cans at $1.25 . . . . 2.50 unfavorable
Net difference expended . . . . . . $ .50 unfavorable

However, although the net difference in the amount spent is unfavorable, a proper analysis shows that there was a savings of 50 cents per can on the two originally requested and that you actually received two additional cans at a unit cost savings of 50 cents.

A manager who compares only actual and total standard costs without segregating them into their quantity and price components may also come to a wrong conclusion. Therefore, formulas have been developed to compare the components of actual and total standard costs so that managers can determine if a variance is detrimental or beneficial to their firm.

Direct Materials Variance Analysis

The Foremost Furniture Company's budgeted costs, total standard costs, and actual costs for direct materials and direct labor for the bookcases are summarized in Illustration 15-2. The actual data are assumed and 110 units are produced. Under these circumstances, the total standard cost for direct materials amounts to $3,300 (30 budgeted board feet × $1 budgeted cost per board foot × 110 bookcases). Now let us assume the actual cost of direct materials is $3,200 (4,000 board feet at 80 cents per board foot). A comparison of the actual with the total standard cost indicates a savings of $100, an apparently favorable condition. However, this figure does not provide Foremost's managers with all the information they need to control their firm's operations. To be optimally helpful, the **total variance**—the difference between the actual cost and the total standard cost—needs to be broken down into price and quantity segments. A **price variance** is the actual quantity of a

Illustration 15-2   Foremost Furniture Company

Budgeted Data

Direct materials	—100 units × 30 bd. ft.	×	$1.00	=	$3,000
Direct labor	—100 units × 1 hour	×	8.00	=	800
Total					$3,800

Total Standard Cost

Direct materials	—110 units × 30 bd. ft.	×	$1.00	=	$3,300
Direct labor	—110 units × 1 hour	×	8.00	=	880
Total					$4,180

Actual Cost

Direct materials	—4,000 bd. ft.	×	$0.80	=	$3,200
Direct labor	—130 hours	×	8.10	=	1,053
Total					$4,253

good or service used multiplied by the difference between the actual and standard prices. For direct materials, the price variance may be stated as:

$$\text{Price variance}_{dm} = \text{Actual quantity of direct material}$$
$$\times \ (\text{Actual price per unit} - \text{Standard price per unit}) \qquad (5)$$

A **quantity variance** is the difference between the input quantity of a good or service and the corresponding output quantity (standard quantity allowed) multiplied by the standard price per unit of input. For direct materials, the quantity variance may be stated as:

$$\text{Quantity variance}_{dm} = \text{Standard price}$$
$$\times \ (\text{Actual quantity} - \text{Standard quantity allowed}) \qquad (6)$$

Inserting Foremost's numbers, the results are:

Direct materials price variance:
4,000 bd. ft. × ($.80 − $1)..........$800 favorable
Direct materials quantity variance:
$1 × (4,000 bd. ft. − 3,300 bd. ft.).... 700 unfavorable
Net variance.....................$100 favorable

The combined $100 favorable variance assumes new importance when it is analyzed into price and quantity components. On investigation, Foremost's general manager found that the purchasing agent bought a lower grade of lumber at 20 cents per board foot below the clear pine price. Because this grade of lumber has occasional knots, significant amounts of lumber were wasted to avoid flaws in the finished shelves. A lower grade of direct materials may also affect the amount of direct labor used.

The Diagrammatic Approach

Another format for analyzing variances into price and quantity components is shown in Illustration 15-3. Referred to as the *diagrammatic approach*, it is extremely useful for analyzing variances because it is systematic and highlights the relationships of the data to be analyzed. The **diagrammatic approach** shows the actual cost at the extreme left arrow, the total standard cost at the extreme right arrow,

Illustration 15-3   Analysis of Direct Materials Variances

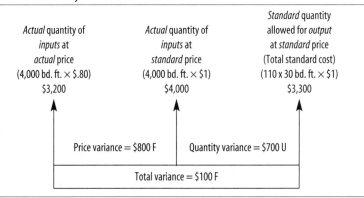

Actual quantity of
inputs at
actual price
(4,000 bd. ft. × $.80)
$3,200

Actual quantity of
inputs at
standard price
(4,000 bd. ft. × $1)
$4,000

Standard quantity
allowed for *output*
at *standard* price
(Total standard cost)
(110 x 30 bd. ft. × $1)
$3,300

Price variance = $800 F   Quantity variance = $700 U

Total variance = $100 F

and the actual quantity of inputs at the standard price per input in the center. The price variance is computed by subtracting the actual cost of inputs from the dollar amount above the center arrow. If the actual cost is less than the center amount, the price variance is favorable; otherwise, it is unfavorable. A similar subtraction is made between the total standard cost and the amount above the center arrow. If the total standard cost is less than the center amount, the variance is unfavorable; otherwise, it is favorable.

Under certain conditions, a firm may wish to analyze its direct materials variance into three components, which includes a joint price-quantity variance.

Direct Labor Variance Analysis

When analyzing direct labor variances into their price and quantity components, most accountants, including this author, prefer to use the terms *rate variance* in place of *price variance* and *efficiency variance* in place of *quantity variance.* The reason for this is that employees earn a *rate* of pay and are either *efficient* or inefficient. The **direct labor rate variance** is computed in the same way as the material price variance and may be stated as:

$$\text{Rate variance}_{dl} = \text{Actual number of direct labor-hours}$$
$$\times (\text{Actual rate per hour} - \text{Standard rate per hour}) \qquad (7)$$

The **direct labor efficiency variance** is the standard rate of pay per direct labor-hour multiplied by the difference between the input number of direct labor-hours and the corresponding output (standard quantity allowed). It may be stated as follows:

$$\text{Efficiency variance}_{dl} = \text{Standard rate per hour}$$
$$\times (\text{Actual number of hours} - \text{Standard quantity allowed}) \qquad (8)$$

Using the information provided in Illustration 15-2, the direct labor rate and efficiency variances for the Foremost Furniture Company are:

Direct labor rate variance:
130 hours × ($8.10 − $8.00) . . . . $ 13 unfavorable
Direct labor efficiency variance:
$8 × (130 hours − 110 standard allowed hours). . 160 unfavorable
Total labor variance . . . . $173 unfavorable

Although the variances themselves do not provide specific information, they do indicate when and where to investigate further. In this case, the rate variance of $13 would not require investigation or action because it is too small to warrant further attention. On the other hand, the $160 efficiency variance is worthy of investigation because it represents an 18 percent deviation ($160 ÷ $880) from the total standard direct labor cost.

On investigation, Foremost found that the additional 20 hours of direct labor were spent on screening the lumber for knots and deciding where saw cuts should be made to minimize materials waste. Also, because 700 extra board feet of lumber were used due to the knots, additional cutting was needed to complete the 110 bookcases.

Based on the results of his investigation, the general manager concluded that the $800 saved by purchasing lower-grade lumber was not beneficial to the company as a whole because there was $700 of wasted material and $160 of wasted direct labor, or a total of $860 of additional costs, attributable to the attempt to save on direct materials. Moreover, the extra 20 hours of direct labor would normally require that additional variable manufacturing overhead costs be incurred. What may have at first seemed a smart move by the purchasing agent turned out to be an added cost for the firm as a whole.

The diagrammatic approach to isolating direct labor rate and efficiency variances appears in Illustration 15-4. Note that it is similar to Illustration 15-3 except direct labor costs are substituted for direct materials costs.

Performance Reports

A **performance report** is a detailed comparison of *budgeted,* or *total standard, costs* with *actual costs.* Variances between the two are segregated into price and quantity components, and when a variance is significant, its source is explained. Although performance reports may differ in format from firm to firm, their purpose remains the same. They provide information and, when possible, explanations to assist managers in deciding what, if any, remedial action is needed when a significant unfavorable variance occurs. The remedial action should be taken as soon as possible after the triggering event. Otherwise, the negative situation is likely to continue and grow more costly. Furthermore, as time passes, people may forget details about the problem, making a solution more difficult to formulate.

As shown in Illustration 15-5, a performance report typically contains standard cost data, actual data, the difference between the two segregated into price and

Illustration 15-4   Analysis of Direct Labor Variances

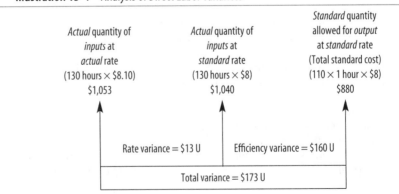

quantity components, and explanations of the variances, if they are available. The steps needed to prepare a performance report are:

Step 1

Compute the standard quantity allowed for direct materials and direct labor. Insert these amounts in the first column.

Step 2

Enter the actual quantities for direct materials and direct labor in the second column and place the respective standard prices in the third column.

Step 3

Determine the actual price for direct materials and the actual rate of pay for direct labor and insert these amounts in column 4.

Step 4

Compute the direct materials price variance using Equation 5, the direct materials quantity variance using Equation 6, the direct labor rate variance using Equation 7, and the direct labor efficiency variance using Equation 8. (The variances may also be computed using the diagrammatic approach instead of the equations.) Insert the variances in the fifth column and label each F (if favorable) or U (if unfavorable).

Step 5

Investigate the reasons for the significant variances and report the findings in the final column.

Illustration 15-5

FOREMOST FURNITURE DESCRIPTION
Performance Report
For the month of January 19x1

Description	Standard Quantity Allowed	Actual Quantity	Standard Price	Actual Price	Variance F—Favorable U—Unfavorable	Explanation
Direct materials:						
Quantity variance	3,300 bd. ft	4,000 bd. ft	$1		$700 U	Inferior materials—waste
Price variance		4,000	1	$ .80	800 F	Cheaper grade of material
Total direct materials variance					$100 F	
Direct labor:						
Efficiency variance	110 hours	130 hours	8		$160 U	Inferior materials— extra cutting
Rate variance		130	8	$8.10	13 U	
Total direct labor variance					$173 U	

VARIANCE INVESTIGATION

Selecting Variances for Investigation

The cost/benefit rule controls variance investigation. An attempt to determine the cause of a variance will be made only if the cost of such investigation does not exceed the benefits to be gained from eliminating the variance. Thus, each firm must develop decision rules for selecting which variances to investigate. Although practices vary from firm to firm, the following factors should be considered:

1. Size of variance.
2. Frequency of occurrence.
3. Nature of item.
4. Kind of variance (unfavorable versus favorable).

1. Size of Variance When assessing the significance of the size of a variance, two measures are usually used—a specified dollar amount and a specified percentage of standard (or budgeted) cost. For example, if total standard cost is $50 and a $10 unfavorable variance occurs, the difference would amount to 20 percent of standard. Although 20 percent is a significant variation, $10 is not a significant amount of money, so investigation would not be justified. To avoid such unjustifiable investigations, a percentage cutoff point is usually used in conjunction with a dollar value. Let us assume, for example, that a variance must exceed both 2 percent and $300. Then, if the total standard cost of an item is $50,000 and the variance is $1,100 (that is, 2.2 percent), the variance should be investigated. On the other hand, if the variance is $500 (1 percent), the item should not be investigated. In practice, many firms prefer to investigate any dollar variance greater than a set amount, regardless of its percentage of total standard cost. In such cases, the decision rule would be to investigate any variance that is at least $300 *or* at least 2 percent of total standard cost, whichever is smaller. This decision rule may be illustrated as follows:

Case 1

Total standard cost is $10,000, and variance is $150. *Action:* Do not investigate. The rationale for this decision might be that a variance of 1.5 percent is a normal variance—one that is expected and due to random events. The manager's conclusion might be that there is nothing wrong and that $150 is too small an amount to worry about.

Case 2

Total standard cost is $20,000, and variance is $350. *Action:* Investigate. The rationale for this decision might be that although the variance, at 1.75 percent, is below the 2 percent threshold, $350 is a significant amount of money and justifies a manager's time to investigate. Through further study, the manager might find a control mechanism that would prevent the recurrence of this kind of unfavorable variance in the future.

Case 3

Total standard cost is $5,000, and variance is $150. *Action:* Investigate. Here the manager might decide that although $150 is not a significant amount of money, because it amounts to 3 percent of total standard cost the deviation might not be normal or random. In such a case, the manager should take corrective action before the condition becomes more serious and a significant amount of money is lost.

2. Frequency of Occurrence This author was associated with a steel fabricating firm where daily performance reports were prepared by computer. One particular supervisor's performance report was an ongoing concern for the firm's accountants. The report consistently showed an unfavorable direct labor efficiency variance, but the amount was always lower than the firm's investigative cutoff point. When such a condition exists, management may wish to investigate and take corrective action even though the variances are below the specified cutoff point. The fact that the variances are always unfavorable may be symptomatic of leadership problems or wasteful practices. The cumulative effect of consistently small unfavorable variances may be just as damaging to a firm's cost efficiency as an occasional large one. The supervisor in this steel fabricating firm was ultimately replaced when it became clear that the unfavorable variances were likely to continue despite his attempts to correct them.

3. Nature of Item   Some variances require closer surveillance than others. For example, a supervisor may have an unfavorable variance due to unexpected repairs to machinery and may attempt to compensate for it by forgoing required maintenance. Although this tactic may temporarily negate the unfavorable variance, the forgone maintenance may cause more expensive repairs in the future that could have been avoided. Thus, favorable repair variances in one time period may lead to unfavorable repair variances in a subsequent period.

Another critical variance is light and power. If an unfavorable variance is due to a utility company's rate increase, it is uncontrollable and must be accepted. However, if the variance is due to an unreasonable number of kilowatt-hours having been consumed, it is possible that machines were left running when not in use. Other variances that require close surveillance are (1) the direct materials price variance, (2) the direct materials quantity variance, and (3) the direct labor efficiency variance.

4. Kind of Variance (Unfavorable versus Favorable)   Significant unfavorable variances require a manager's attention, but favorable variances should not be ignored. Significant favorable variances, on investigation, may reveal outdated standards, inferior direct materials, inferior workmanship, neglected maintenance or research and development, or exemplary performance. Thus, both favorable and unfavorable variances should be investigated when indicated by size, frequency of occurrence, and kind of item.

Once managers determine which variances are significant and warrant investigation, they must decide which variances require action and what kind of action to take.

Management Action

Based on the performance report shown in Illustration 15-5, the manager in charge of the purchasing department should investigate the reasons for the purchase of lower-grade lumber. The purchasing agent might have erroneously believed the $800 savings in price would more than compensate for the waste of $700 and the firm would receive $100 in overall savings. If so, he should be made aware of the additional $160 in labor-hours that was spent. Another possibility is that clear pine lumber was not available from the firm's suppliers at the time of purchase. The manager should determine if the reasons are excusable. If they are, the variances are not charged to anyone. If the variances are due to errors in judgment by the purchasing agent, the resulting efficiency variance for direct labor should be charged to the purchasing department and *not* to the line supervisors in charge of direct labor.

STANDARD COSTING FOR SERVICE INDUSTRIES

Service industries also use standard cost accounting. For example, a word processing business can have a standard direct materials cost for its paper supplies and a standard direct labor cost per typewritten page. Similarly, a public accounting firm can have a standard direct labor cost for each of the different kinds of tax returns prepared, and a law firm can have standard costs for each of the different kinds of wills and trust agreements prepared by staff attorneys. Automobile repair service centers very often charge customers for the services performed by using a standard amount of allotted time per service performed, rather than the actual time used to perform the service. These standard times are published by Chilton. Hospitals also use standard costs.

Standard Costs for Hospitals

Hospitals use standard costs in a manner similar to manufacturing firms, but there are significant differences. For certain procedures, such as laboratory tests and X rays, hospitals use a concept called a **relative value unit,** which is a weighted-average measurement based on the time used to perform a task, the degree of skill needed, and the resources used. In a variety of functions performed by hospitals, standards can be developed for direct materials and direct labor. Examples of these standards include (1) patients' meals; (2) diagnostic procedures, such as X rays, CAT scans, and MRIs; (3) blood tests; (4) hospital laundry; and (5) nursing services. Once the standards are computed, the analysis of the variances into price and efficiency components is prepared in the same manner as for manufacturing firms.

STANDARD COSTING IN THE NEW MANUFACTURING ENVIRONMENT

The manufacturing environment is undergoing dynamic changes. Standard costs and their analyses, while still relevant, are not so important in the new manufacturing environment as they are in the traditional manufacturing environment. In a highly automated manufacturing environment, labor costs are significantly reduced and replaced with large infusions of automated machinery and computers. Primary manufacturing costs now consist of direct materials cost—a variable cost—and large amounts of fixed costs. Thus, for firms in this new manufacturing environment, standard costs for direct materials are now more important than direct labor standard costs. Because of the shift in cost structure from a predominantly variable cost structure to a predominantly fixed cost structure, highly automated firms now pay greater attention to manufacturing overhead costs.

New Performance Measures

Highly automated firms have developed new performance measures in place of traditional ones. Since firms strive for a zero-defects process, quality control is now accorded a higher performance measure. In addition, nonvalue-added costs, such as those assigned to inspection time, move time, and wait time, are always reviewed with an eye to minimizing or eliminating them. The performance measure used to evaluate the measure of success the firm has achieved with regard to non-value-added costs is the manufacturing cycle efficiency (MCE). Firms that are moving in the direction of the new manufacturing environment rely more heavily on these newer performance measures and less on the traditional standard costing ones. Nevertheless, Hewlett-Packard, a firm that has adopted the JIT philosophy in its manufacturing operations, continues to use some standard cost accounting in its accounting system.

Example

For both planning and product costing, much of the accounting activity at (POD) [HP Personal Office Computer Division] was organized within two six-month cycles comprising the October 31 fiscal year. POD used a standard cost system *together with other target systems* to formulate a six-month operating budget; the six-month target production volume implied a total standard production cost, which, when combined with period cost targets, yielded a semi-annual net income goal. Monthly production plans provided intermediate targets from which monthly variance reports were generated (emphasis added).[1]

SUMMARY

For control purposes, managers employ the principle of **management by exception,** which means they investigate only significant variances of actual costs compared with standard (or budgeted) costs. The factors that influence a manager's decision to investigate a variance are the size of the variance, the frequency of its occurrence, the kind of item creating the variance, and the kind of variance. Some items, such as machine maintenance, require more scrutiny than others, such as direct labor, which may vary only slightly due to union contracts and/or employment policies.

Estimated costs are based on historical costs and, thus, may contain inefficiencies based on past performance. When estimated historical costs are adjusted to eliminate inefficiencies, they become **standard costs,** which are carefully predetermined to reflect what costs *ought* to be rather than what they were in prior periods. Because the setting of standards extends beyond any one department, standard costs are determined by a **standards committee** composed of engineers, management accountants, and various managers who base their decisions on **bills of materials,** prices of direct materials, time-and-motion studies, and direct labor wage rates.

Using standard costs, a firm can evaluate the efficiency of each segment's operations. **Efficiency** is a measure of whether an objective was accomplished with a minimum amount of effort and cost. Standard costs are especially suited for measuring efficiency, but they may also help in measuring **effectiveness**—that is, whether an objective was actually achieved.

Standard costs are used for (1) controlling through the use of performance reports, (2) critical cost analysis when the standards are set, (3) pricing, (4) inventory valuation, (5) budget preparation, and (6) simplified record-keeping.

---

[1] James M. Patell, "Cost Accounting, Process Control, and Product Design: A Case Study of the Hewlett-Packard Personal Office Computer Division," *The Accounting Review*, October 1987, p. 823.

REVIEW PROBLEM

Computation of Price and Quantity Variances

The Mercer Company manufactures redwood window boxes. Each box requires the following direct materials and direct labor:

	Standard Quantity	Price (Rate)	Standard Cost
1" clear redwood............................	5 bd. ft.	$ 1.10 per bd. ft.	$5.50
Direct labor................................	.5 hour	10.00 per hour	5.00

During January 19x2, the following transactions occurred:

1. Purchases of lumber amounted to $27,540. The price paid was $1.08 per board foot. There was no direct materials inventory at the beginning or end of the month.
2. The direct labor cost was $28,050. The hourly rate of pay was $10.20.
3. There was no work in process inventory on January 31, 19x2, and 5,000 window boxes were manufactured.

Using *both* the formula and diagrammatic approaches, compute the appropriate price (rate) and quantity (efficiency) variances, and indicate if they are favorable or unfavorable.

SOLUTION TO REVIEW PROBLEM

Formula approach—Direct materials:

$MPV = AQ(AP - SP)$

Materials price variance—25,500($1.08 - $1.10) .... $510 F

$MQV = SP(AQ - SQ)$

Materials quantity variance—$1.10(25,500* - 25,000†)....................................... 550 U

* $27,540 ÷ $1.08 = 25,500 bd. ft.
† 5,000 units × 5 bd. ft. = 25,000 bd. ft.

Diagrammatic approach—Direct materials:

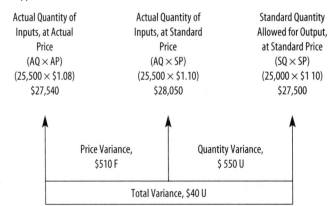

Formula approach—Direct labor:

    LRV = AH(AR−SR)
Labor rate variance—2,750($10.20 − $10.00) . . . . $550 U
    LEV = SR(AH−SH)
Labor efficiency variance—$10.00(2,750‡ − 2,500§) . . . . 2.500 U

‡ $28,050 ÷ $10.20 = 2,750 DLH.
§ 5,000 units × .5 hr. = 2,500 DLH.

Diagrammatic approach—Direct labor:

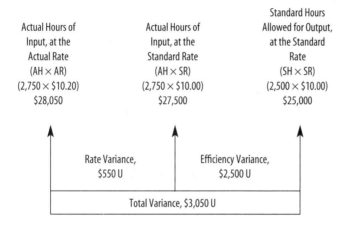

Actual Hours of Input, at the Actual Rate (AH × AR) (2,750 × $10.20) $28,050	Actual Hours of Input, at the Standard Rate (AH × SR) (2,750 × $10.00) $27,500	Standard Hours Allowed for Output, at the Standard Rate (SH × SR) (2,500 × $10.00) $25,000
	Rate Variance, $550 U	Efficiency Variance, $2,500 U
	Total Variance, $3,050 U	

SELF-TEST

True or False

1. A manager choosing to investigate only the significant variances between standard and actual costs is practicing management by exception.
2. A supervisor of a production line had to have the line work overtime to meet a rush order and was successful in getting the order out on time. In this instance, the supervisor was efficient.
3. Standard costs are really budgeted costs that are carefully predetermined.
4. The reason that a standards committee is used is that the preparation of standards requires input from individuals with different abilities.
5. Standard costs are used for a variety of reasons, but the most important one is that it helps managers better understand the firm's record-keeping.
6. A standard bill of materials is a listing of the most important components of the product being manufactured.
7. The difference between a standard cost and an actual cost for direct materials can be analyzed into price and quantity components.
8. The standard quantity allowed is the standard units multiplied by the standard cost per unit.
9. The difference between a standard cost and an actual cost for direct labor can be analyzed into rate and efficiency components.
10. A performance report is used to summarize favorable and unfavorable variances and the reasons for their occurrence.
11. It is never necessary to investigate unfavorable variances as long as they are less than the cutoff point established for variance investigation.
12. Firms that use the new performance measures in the new manufacturing environment have no need for standard costs.

Multiple Choice

1. Home Company manufactures tables with vinyl tops. The standard material cost for the vinyl used per type R table is $7.80 based on six square feet of vinyl at a cost of $1.30 per square foot. A production run of 1,000 tables in January 19x0 resulted in usage of 6,400 square feet of vinyl at a cost of $1.20 per square foot, a total cost of $7,680. The quantity variance resulting from the above production run was
   a. $120 favorable.
   b. $480 unfavorable.
   c. $520 unfavorable.
   d. $640 favorable.

Items 2 and 3 are based on the following information.
   Data on Goodman Company's direct labor costs are given below:

Standard direct labor-hours	30,000
Actual direct labor-hours	29,000
Direct labor usage (efficiency) variance—favorable	$4,000
Direct labor rate variance—favorable	$5,800
Total payroll	$110,200

2. What was Goodman's actual direct labor rate?
   a. $3.60.
   b. $3.80
   c. $4.00
   d. $5.80.
3. What was Goodman's standard direct labor rate?
   a. $3.54.
   b. $3.80.
   c. $4.00.
   d. $5.80.
4. Perkins Company, which has a standard cost system, had 500 units of direct material X in its inventory at June 1, 19x2, purchased in May for $1.20 per unit and carried at a standard cost of $1. The following information pertains to direct material X for the month of June 19x2:

Actual number of units purchased	1,400
Actual number of units used	1,500
Standard number of units allowed for actual production	1,300
Standard cost per unit	$1.00
Actual cost per unit	$1.10

The unfavorable materials purchase price variance for direct material X for June was
   a. $0.
   b. $130.
   c. $140.
   d. $150.
5. Information on Kennedy Company's direct material costs is as follows:

Standard unit price	$3.60
Actual quantity purchased	1,600
Standard quantity allowed for actual production	1,450
Materials purchase price variance—favorable	$240

What was the actual purchase price per unit, rounded to the nearest penny?
- *a.* $3.06.
- *b.* $3.11.
- *c.* $3.45.
- *d.* $3.75.

(AICPA Adapted)

QUESTIONS

1. What is management by exception?
2. What is the difference between effectiveness and efficiency? Use an example to demonstrate each.
3. What standards are used by businesses?
4. What is a standard for efficiency? Give an example to illustrate its use.
5. What is a standards committee, and why do firms generally use one?
6. What are some of the uses of standard costs? Explain each one.
7. Explain the difference between ideal standards and practical standards. Which one would you use? Why?
8. What is the difference between a budgeted cost and a standard cost?
9. What is the standard quantity allowed? How is it used?
10. Differentiate input and output. Use an example to illustrate their use.
11. What is a quantity (efficiency) variance? How is it computed? Is it important? Why?
12. What is a price (rate) variance? How is it computed? Is it important? Why?
13. What is a performance report? What purpose does it serve?
14. Are all variances investigated? If not, how do managers select which variances to investigate?
15. Do service industries use standard costs? If so, explain how they are used.
16. What is a relative value unit? How is it used by hospitals?
17. Does the new manufacturing environment use standard costs? If so, do firms in this environment limit their performance measures to standard costs? Explain.

EXERCISES

Computations of Variances

The Martin Company manufactures tables with glass tops. Each table requires the following direct materials for glass and direct labor:

	Standard Quantity	Price (Rate)	Standard Cost
¼" plate glass	10 sq. ft.	$ 4 per sq. ft.	$40
Direct labor	2 hours	14 per hour	28

During January 19x2, the following transactions occurred:

1. Purchases of plate glass amounted to $6,510. The amount of glass purchased was 1,550 square feet. There was no direct materials inventory at the beginning or end of the month.
2. The direct labor cost was $4,560. The hourly rate of pay was $14.25.
3. There was no work in process inventory on January 31, 19x2, and 150 tables were manufactured.

Using *both* the formula and diagrammatic approaches, compute the appropriate price (rate) and quantity (efficiency) variances, and indicate if they are favorable or unfavorable.

Computation of Data from Variances

The Crest Company manufactures redwood umbrella stands. Each stand requires the following direct materials and direct labor:

	Standard Quantity	Price (Rate)	Standard Cost
2" clear redwood	12 bd. ft.	$ 2.10 per bd. ft.	$25.20
Direct labor	1.5 hours	14.00 per hour	21.00

During March 19x2, the following was determined:

1. There was no work in process or direct materials inventory at the beginning or end of March, and 6,000 stands were manufactured.
2. The total direct materials variance was $6,180 unfavorable, and the materials quantity variance was $2,520 unfavorable.
3. The direct labor cost for the month amounted to $127,875, and the direct labor rate variance was $2,325 favorable.
4. Bolts and screws are considered indirect materials.

   a. How many board feet of lumber were purchased?
   b. What was the price paid per board foot?
   c. What was the actual cost of the direct materials purchased?
   d. How many hours were actually worked?
   e. What was the hourly rate of pay?

Standard Process Costs with Equivalent Production

The following data apply to items 1 through 6.

Dash Company adopted a standard cost system several years ago. The standard costs for the prime costs of its single product are as follows:

Material (8 kilograms at $5 per kilogram) $40.00
Labor (6 hours at $8.20 per hour) 49.20

The following operating data were taken from the records for November:

In-process beginning inventory .... None
In-process ending inventory .... 800 units, 75% complete as to labor; material is issued at the beginning of processing
Units completed .... 5,600 units
Budgeted output .... 6,000 units
Purchases of materials .... 50,000 kilograms
Total actual labor costs. $300,760
Actual hours of labor. .... 36,500 hours
Material usage variance .... $1,500 unfavorable
Total material variance. .... $750 unfavorable

1. The labor rate variance for November is
    a. $1,460 U.
    b. $1,460 F.
    c. $4,120 U.
    d. $4,120 F.
    e. Some amount other than those shown above.
2. The labor efficiency variance for November is
    a. $4,100 U.
    b. $5,740 F.
    c. $15,580 F.
    d. $23,780 U.
    e. Some amount other than those shown above.
3. The actual kilograms of material used in the production process during November are
    a. 45,100 kg.
    b. 49,900 kg.
    c. 50,000 kg.
    d. 51,500 kg.
    e. Some amount other than those shown above.
4. The actual price paid per kilogram of material during November is
    a. $4.495.
    b. $4.985.
    c. $5.015.
    d. $5.135.
    e. Some amount other than those shown above.
5. The total amounts of material and labor cost transferred to the finished goods account for November is
    a. $499,520.
    b. $535,200.
    c. $550,010.
    d. $561,040.
    e. Some amount other than those shown above.

6. The total amount of material and labor cost in the ending balance of work in process inventory at the end of November is
   a. $0.
   b. $9,840.
   c. $61,520.
   d. $71,360.
   e. Some amount other than those shown above.

(CMA Adapted)

Computation of Price and Quantity Variances

Stackum Company manufactures cedar storage boxes. Each box requires the following direct materials and direct labor:

	Standard Quantity	Price (Rate)	Standard Cost
1"clear cedar........................	10 bd. ft.	$ 1.20 per bd. ft.	$12
Direct labor..........................	1 hour	12.00 per hour	12

During January 19x2, the following transactions occurred:

1. Purchases of lumber amounted to $100,500. The price paid was $1.25 per board foot. There was no direct materials inventory at the beginning or end of the month.
2. The direct labor cost was $99,225. The hourly rate of pay was $12.25.
3. There was no work in process inventory on January 31, 19x2, and 8,000 storage boxes were manufactured.

Using *both* the formula and diagrammatic approaches, compute the appropriate price (rate) and quantity (efficiency) variances, and indicate if they are favorable or unfavorable.

Computation of Data from Variance

The Broome Company manufactures redwood flowerpots. Each flowerpot requires the following direct materials and direct labor:

	Standard Quantity	Price (Rate)	Standard Cost
1" clear redwood	3 bd. ft.	$1.20 per bd. ft.	$3.60
Direct labor..........................	.5 hour	12.00 per hour	6.00

During March 19x2, the following was determined:

1. There was no work in process or direct materials inventory at the beginning or end of March, and 6,000 flowerpots were manufactured.
2. The total direct materials variance was $555 favorable, and the materials quantity variance was $360 unfavorable.
3. The direct labor cost for the month amounted to $37,975, and the direct labor rate variance was $775 unfavorable.
   a. How many board feet of lumber were purchased?

b. What was the price paid per board foot?
c. What was the actual cost of the direct materials purchased?
d. How many hours were actually worked?
e. What was the hourly rate of pay?

Computation of Standard Cost per Unit from Variances and Actual Data

The Prince Company manufactures redwood outdoor furniture sets. The direct material consists of one item, 2" x 4" redwood. Screws and bolts may be ignored.

The following information is available for the month of April 19x3:

1. Two thousand sets of furniture were produced. There are no beginning or ending inventories.
2. The actual cost of lumber purchased amounted to $285,200 for 184,000 board feet of redwood. The materials price variance amounted to $9,200 unfavorable, and the materials quantity variance amounted to $6,000 unfavorable.
3. The direct labor payroll for the month amounted to $121,520, and the labor rate variance was $3,920 unfavorable. The labor efficiency variance was $2,400 favorable. The actual hours worked were 9,800.

Compute the following:

a. The standard cost of one board foot of lumber.
b. The standard quantity of board feet per one set of furniture.
c. The actual cost per board foot.
d. The standard rate per hour of direct labor.
e. The standard quantity of hours needed per one set of furniture.
f. The actual labor rate per hour.

Computation of Price and Quantity Variances for an X-Ray Lab

The X-Tra Careful X ray Lab is an X-ray laboratory. Each chest X ray requires the following direct materials and direct labor:

	Standard Quantity	Price (Rate)	Standard Cost
X-ray film.	2 exposures	$ 2 per film	$4
Direct labor	.25 hour	20 per hour	5

During January 19x2, the following transactions occurred:

1. Purchases of film amounted to $4,290. The price paid was $1.95 per X-ray film. There was no direct materials inventory at the beginning or end of the month.
2. The direct labor cost was $5,460. The hourly rate of pay was $21 per hour.
3. There was no work in process inventory on January 31, 19x2, and 1,000 chest X rays were taken during the month. (Each X ray requires two exposures.)

Using *both* the formula and diagrammatic approaches, compute the appropriate price (rate) and quantity (efficiency) variances, and indicate if they are favorable or unfavorable.

Computation of Variances and Information from Variances

1. The following information pertains to Bates Company's direct labor for March 19x2:

Standard direct labor-hours 21,000
Actual direct labor-hours 20,000
Favorable direct labor rate variance $8,400
Standard direct labor rate per hour $6.30

What was Bates's total actual direct labor cost for March 19x2?
 a. $117,600.
 b. $118,000.
 c. $134,000.
 d. $134,400.

2. Throop Company had budgeted 50,000 units of output using 50,000 units of direct materials at a total material cost of $100,000. Actual output was 50,000 units of product requiring 45,000 units of direct materials at a cost of $2.10 per unit. The direct material price variance and usage variance were

Price	Quantity (Usage)
a. $ 4,500 unfavorable	$10,000 favorable
b. $ 5,000 favorable	$10,500 unfavorable
c. $ 5,000 unfavorable	$10,500 favorable
d. $10,000 favorable	$ 4,500 unfavorable

3. Lab Corporation uses a standard cost system. Direct labor information for product CER for the month of October is as follows:

Standard rate .... $6 per hour
Actual rate paid .... $6.10 per hour
Standard hours allowed for actual production .... 1,500 hours
Labor efficiency variance .... $600 unfavorable

What are the actual hours worked?
 a. 1,400.
 b. 1,402.
 c. 1,598.
 d. 1,600.

(AICPA Adapted)

Computation of Price and Quantity Variances

The Marder Company manufactures shoeshine boxes. Each box requires the following direct materials and direct labor:

	Standard Quantity	Price (Rate)	Standard Cost
1" clear oak	3 bd. ft.	$ 2 per bd. ft.	$6
Direct labor	4 hour	12 per hour	4

During January 19x2, the following transactions occurred:

1. Purchases of lumber amounted to $38,220. The price paid was $2.10 per board foot. There was no direct materials inventory at the beginning or end of the month.
2. The direct labor cost was $30,625. The hourly rate of pay was $12.25.
3. There was no work in process inventory on January 31, 19x2, and 6,000 shoeshine boxes were manufactured.

Using *both* the formula and diagrammatic approaches, compute the appropriate price (rate) and quantity (efficiency) variances, and indicate if they are favorable or unfavorable.

Computation of Variances with Possible Explanations for Their Occurrence

The Saxonel Company manufactures draperies with the following standard costs:

Direct materials (20 yards at $2.40 per yard) $48
Direct labor (4 hours at $12 per hour) 48

The following transactions occurred during the month of July 19x2:

1. Production of finished goods amounted to 5,000 pairs.
2. There were no beginning or ending inventories of direct materials or work in process.
3. Purchases of direct materials were 101,000 yards at $2.50 per yard.
4. The direct labor cost was for 20,500 hours at $13 per hour.

   a. Compute the materials price and quantity variances, and indicate if they are favorable or unfavorable.
   b. Compute the labor rate and efficiency variances, and indicate if they are favorable or unfavorable.
   c. Write a brief explanation of why the labor efficiency variance is unfavorable.

Computation of Data from Variances

The Brisk Company manufactures redwood picnic tables. Each table requires the following direct materials and direct labor:

	Standard Quantity	Price (Rate)	Standard Cost
2" clear redwood	14 bd. ft.	$ 1.10 per bd. ft.	$15.40
Direct labor	1 hour	10.00 per hour	10.00

During March 19x2, the following was determined:

1. There was no work in process or direct materials inventory at the beginning or end of March, and 8,000 tables were manufactured.
2. The total direct materials variance was $3,500 favorable, and the materials quantity variance was $2,200 unfavorable.
3. The direct labor cost for the month amounted to $81,340, and the direct labor rate variance was $1,660 favorable.
4. Bolts and screws are considered indirect materials.

   a. How many board feet of lumber were purchased?
   b. What was the price paid per board foot?
   c. What was the actual cost of the direct materials purchased?
   d. How many hours were actually worked?
   e. What was the hourly rate of pay?

Computation of Variances with Possible Explanations for Their Occurrence

The Chambers Company manufactures a product with the following standard costs:

Direct materials (20 yards at $2 per yard)............................$40
Direct labor (2 hours at $16 per hour)................................32

The following transactions occurred during the month of July 19x2:

1. Production of finished goods amounted to 4,000 units.
2. There were no beginning or ending inventories of direct materials or work in process.
3. Purchases of direct materials were 86,000 yards at $1.70 per yard.
4. The direct labor cost was for 9,000 hours at $15 per hour.

   a. Compute the materials price and quantity variances, and indicate if they are favorable or unfavorable.
   b. Compute the labor rate and efficiency variances, and indicate if they are favorable or unfavorable.
   c. Write a brief explanation of why the labor efficiency variance is unfavorable.

Setting Standards for Direct Materials

Danson Company is a chemical manufacturer that supplies industrial users. The company plans to introduce a new chemical solution and needs to develop a standard product cost for it.

The new chemical solution is made by combining a chemical compound (nyclyn) and a solution (salex), boiling the mixture, adding a second compound (protet), and bottling the resulting solution in 10-liter containers. The initial mix, which is 10 liters in volume, consists of 12 kilograms of nyclyn and 9.6 liters of salex. A 20 percent reduction in volume occurs during the boiling process. The solution is then cooled slightly before five kilograms of protet are added; the addition of protet does not affect the total liquid volume.

The purchase prices of the direct materials used in the manufacture of this new chemical solution are as follows:

Nyclyn	$1.30 per kilogram
Salex	1.80 per liter
Protet	2.40 per kilogram

Determine the standard quantity for each of the direct materials needed to produce a 10-liter container of Danson Company's new chemical solution and the standard materials cost of a 10-liter container of the new product.

(CMA Adapted)

Computations of Variances

The following information pertains to the month of June 19x1:
1. Pyle Company manufactures a product with the following standard costs:

Direct materials (30 yards at $1.35 per yard)	$40.50
Direct labor (6 hours at $11 per hour)	66.00

2. Direct materials purchased were $39,200 (28,000 yards at $1.40 per yard).
3. There was no beginning direct materials inventory.
4. The ending direct materials inventory amounted to 3,000 yards.
5. Direct labor was $56,000 (5,000 hours at $11.20 per hour).
6. During the month of June, 800 units were manufactured. There was no work in process at the beginning or end of the month.

Compute the following:

a. Materials price variance (based on purchases).
b. Materials quantity variance.
c. Labor rate variance.
d. Labor efficiency variance.

Computation of Variances

The Carberg Corporation manufactures and sells a single product. The company uses a standard cost system. The standard cost per unit of product is shown below:

Material (one pound plastic at $2)	$2.00
Direct labor (1.6 hours at $4)	6.40

The charges to the manufacturing department for November, when 5,000 units were produced, are given below:

Material (5,300 pounds at $2) $10,600
Direct labor (8,200 hours at $4.10) 33,620

The purchasing department normally buys about the same quantity as is used in production during a month. In November, 5,200 pounds were purchased at a price of $2.10 per pound.

a. Calculate the following variances from standard costs for the data given:
   (1) Materials purchase price.
   (2) Materials quantity.
   (3) Direct labor wage rate.
   (4) Direct labor efficiency.
b. The company has divided its responsibilities such that the purchasing department is responsible for the price at which materials and supplies are purchased. The manufacturing department is responsible for the quantities of materials used. Does this division of responsibilities solve the conflict between price and quantity variances? Explain your answer.

(CMA Adapted)

Computation of Variances with Two Direct Materials

Eastern Company manufactures special electrical equipment and parts. Eastern employs a standard cost accounting system with separate standards established for each product.

A special transformer is manufactured in the transformer department. Production volume is measured by direct labor-hours in this department.

Standard costs for the special transformer are determined annually in September for the coming year. The standard cost of a transformer for 19x7 was computed as shown below:

Direct materials:
Iron .... 5 sheets at $2 $10
Copper .... 3 spools at $3   9
Direct labor .... 4 hours at $7   28

During October 19x7, 800 transformers were produced. This was below expectations because a work stoppage occurred during contract negotiations with the labor force. Once the contract was settled, the department scheduled overtime in an attempt to catch up to expected production levels.

CHAPTER 16

PROJECT VALUE ANALYSIS

16.1   THE NEED FOR VALUE ANALYSIS

Value analysis refers to the formal process of eliminating cost from the project or the project's product and service. The process is necessary because often cost is not the major consideration during the project planning process. Generally planners focus on including every element, work package, and activity. The emphasis is on establishing time and budget definitions. If a new product is being designed, the perspective is usually on performance and meeting specifications. During all these activities cost is a secondary element. If the project is of long duration, say several years, the constant influence of external economic factors encourages higher labor rates, more expensive materials, and increases in the overall cost of doing business. There is a tendency for costs to increase even more as unforeseen events occur and schedules change. Often in the haste to get underway or to design a product against a deadline, quality features and activities may be added that contribute to the product's or project's overall suitability.

From this view, the extra quality, detail, and features represent wasted expenditures. More so, the cause of the cost may result in continuation of the problem. The value analysis is a formal process to review the project and/or its associated product or service with the objective of reducing costs without impairing efficiency, effectiveness, or suitability of the product or service.

16.2   HOW VALUE ANALYSIS RESOLVES PROBLEMS

The review must be a formal process because it takes time, special attention, and even creative talents on the part of the reviewers. The process particularly lends itself to a team effort. It requires a critical approach on the part of the reviewers to ensure that the project stakeholders receive the best value from the project team efforts.

553

Value analysis is a goal oriented method for improving project, product, or service value by comparing elements of project, product, or service value or worth with their corresponding elements of cost. The objective of value analysis is to accomplish the goals of the project, product, or service at the minimal amount of cost.

16.3   VALUE ANALYSIS LESSONS FROM THE PURCHASING PROFESSION

The application of value analysis is probably most common and highly developed in the field of purchasing. Astute purchasing managers have learned that they can greatly reduce the cost of purchased items without compromising the functions, capabilities, or specifications of the item being purchased. Purchasing managers have learned through experience that an important element of the process is approval from the department requesting the product. The same is true in a project environment where the project stakeholders need to understand the changes being made. Without this, the perception can be that the project is being "cheapened" or compromised. In addition, stakeholders may point out overlooked impractical aspects of the change and other factors that outweigh the potential cost savings. Most seasoned purchasing managers advise that the value analysis team can challenge existing procedures and specifications but should always obtain the approval of stakeholders before proceeding with the change.

Experienced value analysis team members also stress to stakeholders that the changes being suggested are not a criticism of the skill and judgment of the original planners of the project. It is simply a process of refining the project planning and implementation process. It represents continuous improvement through systematic analysis. The value analysis approach should also not become a process of squeezing concessions or cost reductions from suppliers or other stakeholders.

It is also important to resist the temptation to make change for the sake of change. If any element of the project or project product or service is satisfactory, there should be no inclination on the part of the review team to make modifications.

The question arises about how large cost savings should be before being addressed by the value analysis team. Essentially, it is a judgment call. The cost savings should be significant enough to exceed the time expended in making the change. For example, in a mass production environment such as automobile manufacturing, a small savings of a dollar or two per auto will accumulate to a sizable amount of money over time. On a non-repetitive project, a savings of a few dollars is probably not worth the effort involved in making the change.

Value analysis teams report that typical savings from the efforts far exceed the cost. Black and Decker, for example, reported a value analysis savings of $1.2 million from a value analysis program that added only $12,000 in departmental expense.

In projects of extended duration, experience indicates that the value analysis program continues to pay dividends if repeated at periodic intervals. There appear to be few diminishing returns but continuing positive results.

One approach to value analysis is to investigate the cause of the cost. The corrective action then is directed toward minimizing the cause of the cost, which in turn reduces or eliminates the cost itself.

16.4   THE VALUE ANALYSIS TEAM

Value analysis is typically a function of the project team rather than an outside auditing function. The project team is closest to the details of the project and in the best position to analyze procedures and processes. The project team can be challenged to question wasteful and avoidable costs. Value analysis training can multiply the results of the team effort. The primary qualification for the most successful value analysis team members is a critical, imaginative, questioning mind supported by knowledge of cost accounting and project processes.

Once a mind set is instilled, the formal team analysis can carry over to the day-to-day project activities of individual project team members. The project team can become cost conscious about materials and labor that is used on a daily basis. Each project team member is continually confronted with the cost elements of a project. Often cost savings can be made without effort simply by being aware of the need.

Often there are numerous cost savings that result simply as a benefit of the experience of project team members. Over time they conduct price analysis and comparisons, evaluate alternative materials and labor sources and methodologies for accomplishing complex tasks. This knowledge is enhanced by the project team members' daily exposure to the application of these goods and processes. As new opportunities arise, all this experience is translated into greater efficiency and lower costs for the project. The project team is in the best strategic position to impact costs by applying their experience. The team members intuitively recognize the areas where value analysis will give the greatest rewards.

16.5   ATTAINING STAKEHOLDER INVOLVEMENT

One of the most valuable sources of information and ideas in improving project value is from the project's stakeholders. Often there are numerous experts around the periphery of the project whose observations and views represent an arm's length opinion of potential project improvements. Enlisting the support of these individuals can generate rich rewards for the project team.

Some value analysis teams have organized stakeholder workshops to formalize the process. Side benefits accrue as the stakeholders can see the detail involved in the project process and the approaches being taken to provide the maximum amount of stakeholder benefit at the minimal amount of cost.

16.6   VALUE ANALYSIS TECHNIQUES

There are any number of approaches to the value analysis process. The most common approach is to look at the project, product, or service as a complete unit composed of numerous individual components. From here, the analysis proceeds to increasingly smaller units.

Another approach is to use a team-based brainstorming session. Best results are obtained from teams composed of members from several different functional areas. The problem is presented to the group and every idea for improvement is noted. Some groups use adhesive notes to write down their ideas. These can then be posted and grouped according to subject areas. After the initial flow of ideas has slowed, the group can then begin exploring and discussing individual suggestions in detail. Often this discussion will generate new ideas for improvement.

Some groups prefer a more structured approach to the value analysis process. They can use any form of logical progession. This approach to value analysis is a reasonably simple concept that lends itself to a checklist approach. One such checklist is as follows:

VALUE ANALYSIS CHECKLIST

Consider elimination of any project activity, product, or service component that does not satisfy these evaluation questions

YES   NO

☐   ☐   1. It clearly contributes to value.
             Suggestions: _____

☐   ☐   2. Its cost is proportionate to its usefulness.
             Suggestions: _____

☐   ☐   3. All the activities and features are needed.
             Suggestions: _____

☐   ☐   4. It is the best available for the intended use.
             Suggestions: _____

☐   ☐   5. It represents the lowest cost method of attaining the objective.
             Suggestions: _____

☐   ☐   6. It is a lower cost than a standard product or contract service.
             Suggestions: _____

☐   ☐   7. It uses the proper tooling, equipment, and procedures considering the volumes involved.
             Suggestions: _____

☐   ☐   8. Material, reasonable labor, overhead, and profit are lower than the project cost of the work package, product, or service.
             Suggestions: _____

☐   ☐   9. It is a lower cost than comparable goods or services provided by suppliers.
             Suggestions: _____

☐   ☐   10. Our costs are the lowest in the industry.
              Suggestions: _____

☐   ☐   11. Its specifications are the least restrictive needed to achieve the objective.
              Suggestions: _____

☐   ☐   12. There are no ways to reduce cost that we have not considered.
              Suggestions: _____

16.8 THE STANDARDIZATION CONCEPT AS APPLIED TO PROJECTS

In a mass production setting, the concept of uniformity, interchangeability, and standardization are fundamental cost reduction concepts. Most manufacturing organizations embrace the concept of standardization as an intuitive approach to management. In the project environment the concept is not as clear but does generate significant benefits. It can take the form of standardizing on one brand of machinery or equipment, using all metric (or SAE) specifications, using common supplies as were used on prior projects, or selecting fewer sizes of components such as screws and fasteners. Standardization can take the form of eliminating unnecessary types and varieties of items; utilizing nationally recognized technical industry standards and regularly produced items. It can include procedures such as a common marking system for supplies and components and standardized testing procedures.

Standardization can be a powerful tool for reducing costs. The process lends itself to being identified by value analysis teams. Standardizing products and processes effectively establishes quality standards. Combined with the other benefits of standardization is the greater availability and faster delivery of standardized components and services. Such items are typically carried in stock by vendors. Inventory is reduced because fewer special items must be carried in stock. There is also greater flexibility in meeting changing demands as the project schedule changes or is adjusted.

16.9 REPORTING THE BENEFITS OF VALUE ANALYSIS

Various reports and recommendations are the end result of value analysis. The benefits of value analysis are typically reported to stakeholders. In all cases the result of value analysis should be quantified into money saved, if possible. If changes to project scope or specifications are suggested as a result of the analysis, these should be communicated as well. Communication of value analysis results in increased awareness throughout the organization of value analysis process benefits, as well as increased cost consciousness by all stakeholders. It also improves understanding and generates enthusiasm for the concept.

16.10 STUDY QUESTIONS

1. Give a definition of value analysis.
2. Explain the practical benefit of value analysis for the superior project manager.
3. List ten tests of value.
4. Give an example from your workplace in which value analysis would generate benefits.
5. Apply the value analysis checklist to a project, product, or service.
6. Discuss the stakeholders' role in the value analysis process.
7. Explain why stakeholders might encourage a project team to conduct a value analysis.
8. Explain the importance of standardization in the value analysis process.
9. Give examples of standardization and its benefits in typical projects.

SECTION V
PROJECT TERMINATION AND FOLLOW UP

CHAPTER 17

FINANCIAL PLANNING FOR PROJECT TERMINATION

17.1   ORDERLY TERMINATION

One of the most overlooked activities in planning for a project is the termination process. As the project begins to wind down, it is necessary to develop a cost and resource estimate needed to complete project activities. Surprisingly, many project plans fail to include termination costs or even the steps necessary to terminate the project. If a project is sizable and its duration is lengthy, the termination can be stressful. Many seasoned project executives judge the termination process as one of the most critical elements of successful project leadership. The manner in which the termination process is handled directly impacts the residual attitudes of stakeholders about the project and the project team. Although the many human emotional elements dominate the termination process, the financial and accounting aspects of the termination impact the perception of success or failure.

The termination phase of the project includes developing plans to transfer all assets back into the host organization or to another project. Ideally, the project will be financially successful and terminated in an orderly fashion. Accounts are closed; all moneys are accounted for; and property and equipment is inventoried. Contracts and agreements with vendors will be terminated, and purchasing and other functional areas are notified of the project's termination. Many project organizations require an audit of the accounting and financial records.

The termination phase of the project also includes making plans for project follow up. The project follow up planning process includes consideration of such items as setting up new accounts for the goods or services generated by the project and the development of a project follow up budget.

PROJECT TERMINATION FINANCIAL & ACCOUNTING CHECKLIST

1. Financial and accounting documents have been closed and recorded.
2. Final charges and costs have been audited.
3. Audit has been completed of all the financial and accounting records.
4. Final project financial report has been completed.
5. Receivables have been collected.
6. Payables have been paid.
7. Vendor contracts have been reviewed to ensure all terms have been satisfied.
8. All contractual deliverables and completion dates have been met.
9. Work orders and contracts closed out.
10. Financial reporting procedures terminated.
11. Financial reports submitted to pertinent stakeholders.
12. Pertinent licenses and permits terminated.
13. Non-essential project records destroyed.
14. Essential project records stored.
15. Electricity turned off, doors closed and locked, say "goodbye."

Premature Termination

Occasionally a project goes astray. In an ideal situation the decision to terminate will be made on a timely basis. The judgment to terminate any project is generally subjective, although financial performance is invariably a critical element in the decision process. Financial and accounting analysis and supporting data are important tools in answering the following questions:

- Is the project meeting its original goals?
- Is organizational resource support adequate?
- Could the project be contracted to outside vendors?
- Could the project's product or service be purchased or subcontracted?
- Is the project profitable?
- Is the project cost effective?
- Could the project be integrated with an on-going operation of the host organization?
- Are there more profitable applications of the funds being expended on the project?
- Have any profitability or return on investment elements of the project changed?

CHAPTER 18

PROJECT FOLLOW UP

After the conclusion of the project, the lessons learned are prepared as well as the project performance evaluation and communication. Warranty costs are tracked and compared with estimates.

18.1   LESSONS LEARNED

Superior project managers evaluate the project's successes and failures. From these, lessons learned are recorded for the benefit of future projects. The lessons learned are the method of transferring knowledge from project to project. Some project groups use a generalized "Lessons Learned" template to guide a structured review of the project. Others wait four or five months after completion to ensure there is more information available. At that point, they can draw arm's length conclusions and more accurately identify things that went wrong. They also look at factors that can't be changed. Lessons learned can be tied to the project assessment process and should be prepared at each milestone.

The financial management approach to lessons learned is to quantify or convert to dollars and cents each of the lessons. The review team can start with an overview comparison of total project costs with estimated costs. Reasons for the variances can be discussed and recorded. The variances can be ranked in terms of financial impact on the project. The team can then attempt to identify the cost of errors and problems. All of this information is used to place a price on future risk items. The transfer of knowledge process results in a more precise risk weighting process.

Superior project managers and best-practice project organizations measure the impact of the project on the host organization's bottom line. Measurement of the project group's performance is crucial to ensure that the benefits of project groups are recognized and that continuous improvements are made. To project managers, the benefits and positive results of the project effort seem clear, but the portrait is often opaque to senior executives and others in the organization. The situation is accentuated because, historically, project management groups have not always quantified and measured the bottom line benefits of implementing cross-functional project management groups in their organizations. Listed below are various approaches companies take to measure project benefits. Any or all of these measurement methods can be tailored to optimize and articulate project benefits with the host organization's goals.

Create a measurement manual or set of standard performance measurements to evaluate project performance.

Best-practice companies build performance measurement devices to fit their specific needs. They start with basic questions and build measurable critical success factors needed to solve the business problem. Then, they measure the project performance against the critical success factors.

One best-practice company utilizes eighteen different ways of measuring project performance. Their primary evaluation tool is a " value measurement model". Their project leader says, "We start with the problem and ask, 'What is the standard that we measure against?'" From this a value measurement model is developed. The model sets a baseline for project cost and then a ratio is established of what is built compared to marketplace value.

Often an organization will have performance records from similar projects executed in prior years. If sufficient examples are available, cost and performance trend lines can be developed and compared with the results of the current project. In every case, to measure the practical value of the project, it is necessary to agree upon critical success factors that result in measuring bottom line contributions and project goal achievement. Best-practice project management organizations use some or all of the following good practice examples when measuring project contribution.

Identify customer requirements and measure project performance against those requirements and customer satisfaction.

There is general agreement that the true measure of project performance is customer satisfaction. There is also agreement that customer satisfaction should be measured continually after project termination.

Measure accuracy in achieving time and budget goals.

Several best-practice organizations evaluate projects on the basis of accuracy in meeting goals. For example, a project might be under *or over* by say, 5%. Either result would be equally accurate and would receive the same management response.

Measure productivity and efficiency by comparing work output and resources used.

Project work output can be compared with cost and/or resources used (e.g., labor). One concern with this method is that it carries the danger that costs will be cut to the point that output is also reduced.

Measure reduction in project cycle time (e.g., lead time to market).

One of the most dramatic results of cross-functional project management is the significant reduction in time to complete projects. When a new product is involved, the practical benefit is that the product enters the market sooner. Generally, the historical time to develop new products is well known within a company. It is probably never precisely quantified, but experienced executives will have a general idea of traditional "lead times to market." One measurement of project performance is to compare the former lead times to market with those achieved by the current project.

Although the method of investigation was not precise, it did tend to give quantitative numbers for evaluating the effectiveness of an action. One company in the Fortune 500 Project Management Benchmarking Forum used this measurement method to measure the results of dramatically reducing lead time to market. Two years before the project group was started, new product development time to market was 52 months. The projects being managed by the cross functional group have a lead time to market averaging 18 months. The dollar value of projects the group is directly responsible for is approximately $1.4 billion per year.

The value of reducing time to market by one day is phenomenal. Each day time to market is reduced adds one more day of sales. By shortening lead time from 52 to 18 months, sales occur nearly three years earlier than they would have without the project approach. A quick calculation indicates that if the company obtained incremental sales of approximately $1.4 billion per year, this would amount to $4 billion for the 34-month lead time reduction.

Benefits accrue to the company in other ways. By generating sales sooner, money is made available for other investments. The time value of money is maximized. Furthermore, shortened time to market means that market position is established earlier. Incremental sales are obtained and higher profits occur by applying pricing techniques to capitalize on the market niche, limited competition, and initial high demand for the new product. Finally, marginal products are identified earlier in the design process.

If one considers solely the impact of the time value of money, the results are dramatic. The money generated by the product sales can be invested in other income producing opportunities. At a 10% interest rate and on a compounded basis, the incremental interest revenue available to the company amounts to approximately $597 million over the 34-month period.

Reducing lead time to market offers other, more subtle benefits. Its effects are similar to increasing inventory turnover. A high inventory turnover means that the investment in inventory is small compared to the amount of resultant sales. By reducing time to market, the same number of people can complete more projects. Where previously a person might be involved in a project for say, a year or so, now they will complete one in a few months and then move on to another. The cash investment in each project is reduced. Savings occur from (a) making project managers and team members available for other, higher potential projects, and (b) eliminating the investment associated with the project development expenses for the extra months of development time.

Reducing lead time to market enables the company to react faster to market changes. The organization has the confidence of knowing they can respond to market changes faster than competition and consistently be the first in the market.

It could be asserted that the sales are not incremental—that all that has happened is the sales occurred three years sooner than they would have otherwise. To support this form of logic requires an assumption that competition would not rush in and fill the marketing void. In other words, that everyone would wait while the slower companies took time to develop their product.

The consensus is that competition would supply the product demand. Hence, reducing lead time to market does generate incremental sales. Companies that are first to market obtain those prime sales that are only available early in the product's life cycle. Higher profits and market share are achieved.

The first products to be introduced enjoy the benefits of high demand and low supply, or scarcity, of the product. Consequently, an astute pricing policy will capitalize on this set of circumstances and maximize profits. As the market matures and competition begins to enter, then pricing becomes more competitive and profit margins decline.

Products that are early in the market also have potential to carve out a niche and establish a stronger competitive position. Late-comers are relegated to the reduced and declining profits reflective of the maturity and obsolescence stages of the product life cycle.

It is important to note that the profits and market dominance described above are available only once in a typical product life cycle. The company that is first into the market achieves the benefit of strategic life cycle positioning.

Measure the impact of problem identification and corrective action.

One advantage of continuous measurement and monitoring of project performance is that marginal projects are identified and culled earlier in the development process. One project management group indicates that they identify and terminate projects on the average of three months. At the inception of their performance measurement efforts, it takes approximately one year to terminate a clearly losing project. Other groups report that they measure the time to identify problems and the number of project problems corrected.

Measure cost of quality—getting it right the first time, rework, scrap, cost of nonconformance.

Measuring cost of quality is a noble goal, but difficult to do. A few best-practice companies have anecdotal estimates of its value. One company formally queries customers about the degree of satisfaction with project quality.

Measure the cost of professional project managers.

In theory, the use of professional project managers should improve project performance well in excess of its cost. This issue is of particular importance because the professional project manager is generally more expensive than the non-professional. Consequently, best-practice project groups measure the cost of professional project management. The cost is then compared with project output. Several project organizations have a line item "cost for project management" or "construction management." They measure the percentage amount of the project that is management. Project management groups quote that the cost of professional project management ranges from 1.5 to 7% of total project cost. On some government managed projects, it is common to observe the costs of project management as high as 40% of total project cost.

Aggregate profitability and/or benefits of projects.

All of the measurement methods used by a project organization can be totaled over a period of time and numerous projects. The aggregation of measurements gives the project organization capability to measure improvement and to set goals for future projects. Some participating organizations roll up the aggregates of all their projects for the year. They show the results of each specific project as well as all projects in total. Status and performance measurements are graphically portrayed for all stakeholders to evaluate.

18.3 WARRANTY

Many projects produce a product or service. Often companies agree to provide free service on units that are defective or fail to perform properly. When these costs or "warranties" are expected to be minor in nature, the project team will need to allocate little attention to their implications. However, if the warranty costs are expected to be sizeable, it is necessary to estimate the size of the obligation. It is not uncommon for excessive warranty costs to have an impact on the perception of stakeholders about the overall success of the project.

Warranty costs are usually estimated based on past experience. In situations involving a totally new product or service, the warranty estimate can be based on an analysis of individual components and experience gained during the project development process.

Often preplanning for warranty cost gives the company time to develop a mitigation strategy. Customers can be sold a service contract which results in shifting some of the financial burden. In effect, the service contract is an insurance contract executed with the customer. Warranty preplanning also gives the company time to develop education programs to prepare customers for the expected result. Finally, warranty preplanning provides information needed to budget the cost into future financial statements.

GLOSSARY

absorption approach A costing approach that considers all factory overhead (both variable and fixed) to be product (inventoriable) costs that become an expense in the form of manufacturing cost of goods sold only as sales occur.

account Each item in a financial statement.

accounts payable Amounts owed on open accounts whereby the buyer pays cash some time after the date of sale.

accounts receivable Amounts owed to a company by customers who buy on open account.

accrual basis A process of accounting that recognizes the impact of transactions on the financial statements in the time periods when revenues and expenses occur instead of when cash is received or disbursed.

accrue To accumulate a receivable or payable during a given period even though no explicit transaction occurs.

activity-based accounting (ABA) (activity-based costing [ABC]) A system that first accumulates overhead costs for each of the activities of an organization, and then assigns the costs of activities to the products, services, or other cost objects that caused that activity.

adjustments Recording of implicit transactions, in contrast to the explicit transactions that trigger nearly all day-to-day routine entries.

amortized loan A loan paid off in equal installments.

analytical income statement A financial statement used by internal analysts that differs in composition from audited or published financial statements.

annual percentage yield (APY) or effective annual rate The annual compound rate that produces the same return as the nominal or quoted rate.

annuity A series of equal dollar payments for a specified number of years.

annuity due An annuity in which the payments occur at the beginning of each period.

assets Economic resources that are expected to benefit future activities.

audit An examination or in-depth inspection that is made in accordance with generally accepted auditing standards. It culminates with the accountant's testimony that management's financial statements are in conformity with generally accepted accounting principles.

avoidable costs   Costs that will not continue if an ongoing operation is changed or deleted.

backflush costing   An accounting system that applies costs to products only when the production is complete.

balance sheet (statement of financial position, statement of financial condition)   A snapshot of financial status at an instant of time.

bill of materials   A detailed listing of every item and quantity of direct material needed to manufacture one unit of finished product.

book value (net book value)   The original cost of equipment less accumulated depreciation, which is the summation of depreciation charged to past periods.

budgeted cost   The estimated production multiplied by the standard cost per unit.

budgeted factory-overhead rate   The budgeted total overhead divided by the budgeted cost driver activity.

business risk   The relative dispersion in the firm's expected earnings before interest and taxes.

by-product   A product that, like a joint product, is not individually identifiable until manufacturing reaches a split-off point, but has relatively insignificant total sales value.

capital budgeting   The decision-making process with respect to investment in fixed assets. Specifically, it involves measuring the incremental cash flows associated with investment proposals and evaluating those proposed investments.

capital rationing   The placing of a limit by the firm on the dollar-size of the capital budget.

cash basis   A process of accounting where revenue and expense recognition would occur when cash is received and disbursed.

cash breakeven analysis   A variation from traditional breakeven analysis that removes (deducts) noncash expenses from the cost items.

cash budget   A detailed plan of future cash receipts and disbursements.

cellular manufacturing   A production system in which machines are organized in cells according to specific requirements of a product family.

certainty equivalent approach   A technique for incorporating risk into the capital-budgeting decision in which the decision maker substitutes a set of equivalent riskless cash flows for the expected cash flows and then discounts these cash flows back to the present.

certainty equivalents   The amount of cash a person would require with certainty to make him or her indifferent between this certain sum and a particular risky or uncertain sum.

common costs   Those costs of facilities and services that are shared by users.

compound annuity   Depositing an equal sum of money at the end of each year for a certain number of years and allowing it to grow.

compound interest   Interest that occurs when interest paid on the investment during the first period is added to the principal, then, during the second period, interest is earned on this new sum.

conservatism convention   Selecting the method of measurement that yields the gloomiest immediate results.

continuity convention (going concern convention)   The assumption that in all ordinary situations an entity persists indefinitely.

contribution approach   A method of internal (management accounting) reporting that emphasizes the distinction between variable and fixed costs for the purpose of better decision making.

contribution margin   Unit sales price minus unit variable cost.

conversion costs   Direct labor costs plus factory overhead costs.

corporation   A business organized as a separate legal entity and owned by its stockholders.

cost A sacrifice or giving up of resources for a particular purpose, frequently measured by the monetary units that must be paid for goods and services.

cost accounting That part of the accounting system that measures costs for the purposes of management decision making and financial reporting.

cost accounting systems The techniques used to determine the cost of a product, service, or other cost objective by collecting and classifying costs and assigning them to cost objects.

cost accumulation Collecting costs by some natural classification such as materials or labor.

cost allocation Tracing and reassigning costs to one or more cost objectives such as departments, customers, or products.

cost-allocation base A cost driver when it is used for allocating costs.

cost application The allocation of total departmental costs to the revenue-producing products or services.

cost objective (cost object) Any activity or resource for which a separate measurement of costs is desired. Examples include departments, products, and territories.

cost pool A group of individual costs that is allocated to cost objectives using a single cost driver.

cost recovery A concept in which assets such as inventories, prepayments, and equipment are carried forward as assets because their costs are expected to be recovered in the form of cash inflows (or reduced cash outflows) in future periods.

cost-benefit criterion An approach that implicitly underlies the decisions about the design of accounting systems. As a system is changed, its potential benefits should exceed its additional costs.

cost-management system Identifies how management's decisions affect costs by first measuring the resources used in performing the organization's activities, and then assessing the effects on costs of changes in those activities.

credit An entry on the right side of an account.

debit An entry on the left side of an account.

decision model Any method for making a choice, sometimes requiring elaborate quantitative procedures.

depreciation The periodic cost of equipment which is spread over (or charged to) the future periods in which the equipment is expected to be used.

diagrammatic approach A method of analyzing variances in which the actual cost is shown at the extreme left, the total standard cost is shown at the extreme right, and the actual quantity of inputs at the standard price per input is shown in the center. The price and quantity variances are found by subtracting each end figure from the center figure.

differential cost (incremental cost) The difference in total cost between two alternatives.

direct costs Costs that can be identified specifically and exclusively with a given cost objective in an economically feasible way.

direct-labor costs The wages of all labor that can be traced specifically and exclusively to the manufactured goods in an economically feasible way.

direct labor efficiency variance The standard rate of pay per direct labor-hour multiplied by the difference between the input number of direct labor-hours and the corresponding output (standard quantity allowed).

direct labor rate variance The actual number of direct labor-hours multiplied by the difference between the actual rate of pay per hour and the standard rate of pay per hour.

direct material costs The acquisition costs of all materials that are physically identified as a part of the manufactured goods and that may be traced to the manufactured goods in an economically feasible way.

direct method   A method for allocating service department costs that ignores other service departments when any given service department's costs are allocated to the revenue-producing (operating) departments.

discounted payback period   A variation of the payback period defined as the number of years required to recover the initial cash outlay from the discounted net cash flows.

discretionary financing   Sources of financing that require an explicit decision on the part of the firm's management every time funds are raised. An example is a bank note, which requires that negotiations be undertaken and an agreement signed setting forth the terms and conditions for the financing.

discriminatory pricing   Charging different prices to different customers for the same product or service.

dividends   Distributions of assets to stockholders that reduce retained income.

double-entry system   A method of record keeping in which at least two accounts are affected by each transaction.

effectiveness   A measure of whether an objective is achieved.

efficiency   A measure of the means by which an objective is achieved—that is, whether it is achieved with the least amount of effort and the least possible cost.

equities   The claims against, or interests in, an organization's assets.

equivalent annual annuity (EAA)   An annual cash flow that yields the same present value as the project's NPV. It is calculated by dividing the project's NPV by the appropriate $PVIFA_{i, n}$.

equivalent units   The number of completed units that could have been produced from the inputs applied.

expenses   Gross decreases in assets from delivering goods or services.

factory-overhead costs (factory burden, manufacturing overhead)   All costs other than direct material or direct labor that are associated with the manufacturing process.

favorable variance   A case in which output exceeds input or the price paid for a good or service is less than expected.

Financial Accounting Standards Board (FASB)   The primary regulatory body over accounting principles and practices. Consisting of seven full-time members, it is an independent creation of the private sector.

financial lease   A noncancelable contractual commitment on the part of the firm leasing the asset (the lessee) to make a series of payments to the firm that actually owns the asset (the lessor) for the use of the asset over the period of the agreement.

financial leverage   Financing a portion of the firm's assets with securities bearing a fixed or limited rate of return.

financial risk   The additional variability in earnings available to the firm's common stockholder, and the additional chance of insolvency borne by the common stockholder caused by the use of financial leverage.

first-in, first-out (FIFO) process-costing method   A process-costing method that sharply distinguishes the current work done from the previous work done on the beginning inventory of work in process.

fixed costs (indirect costs)   Costs that do not vary in total dollar amount as sales volume or quantity of output changes.

full cost (fully allocated cost)   The total of all manufacturing costs plus the total of all selling and administrative costs.

future-value interest factor (FVIF$_{i,n}$)   The value $(1 + i)^n$ used as a multiplier to calculate an amount's future value.

future-value interest factor of an annuity (FVIFA$_{i,n}$)   The value $\left[\sum_{t=0}^{n-1}(1 + i)^t\right]$ used as a multiplier to calculate the future value of an annuity.

general ledger   A collection of the group of accounts that supports the items shown in the major financial statements.

hybrid-costing system   An accounting system that is a blend of ideas from both job costing and process costing.

ideal standard   A measurement for evaluating performance that is theoretically possible but impractical to attain because it does not allow for machine breakdowns, rest periods, and the like, and requires employees to work at a constant rate of peak performance without interruptions.

idle time   An indirect labor cost consisting of wages paid for unproductive time caused by machine breakdowns, material shortages, and sloppy scheduling.

imperfect competition   A market in which a firm's price will influence the quantity it sells.

income statement   A statement that measures the performance of an organization by matching its accomplishments (revenue from customers, which is usually called sales) and its efforts (cost of goods sold and other expenses).

incremental cash flows   The cash flows that result from the acceptance of a capital-budgeting project.

indirect costs   Costs that cannot be identified specifically and exclusively with a given cost objective in an economically feasible way.

indirect labor   All factory labor wages, other than those for direct labor and manager salaries.

initial outlay   The immediate cash outflow necessary to purchase the asset and put it in operating order.

input   A quantity of goods or services entered into production that is expected to yield a certain quantity of manufactured finished goods.

internal rate of return (IRR)   A capital-budgeting technique that reflects the rate of return a project earns. Mathematically, it is the discount rate that equates the present value of the inflows with the present value of the outflows.

inventory turnover   The number of times the average inventory is sold per year.

job-cost record (job-cost sheet, job order)   A document that shows all costs for a particular product, service, or batch of products.

job-order costing (job costing)   The method of allocating costs to products that are readily identified by individual units or batches, each of which requires varying degrees of attention and skill.

joint costs   The costs of manufacturing joint products prior to the split-off point.

joint probability   The probability of two different sequential outcomes occurring.

joint products   Two or more manufactured products that (1) have relatively significant sales values and (2) are not separately identifiable as individual products until their split-off point.

just-in-time (JIT) production system   A system in which an organization purchases materials and parts and produces components just when they are needed in the production process, the goal being to have zero inventory because holding inventory is a non-value-added activity.

labor time tickets (time cards)   The record of the time a particular direct laborer spends on each job.

ledger accounts   A method of keeping track of how multitudes of transactions affect each particular asset, liability, revenue, and expense.

liabilities   The entity's economic obligations to nonowners.

limiting factor (scarce resource)   The item that restricts or constrains the production or sale of a product or service.

management by exception   An approach in which management chooses to investigate and take action on only those variances that depart significantly from prescribed standards.

marginal cost   The additional cost resulting from producing and selling one additional unit.

marginal revenue The additional revenue resulting from the sale of an additional unit.

markup The amount by which price exceeds cost.

matching The relating of accomplishments or revenues (as measured by the selling prices of goods and services delivered) and efforts or expenses (as measured by the cost of goods and services used) to a particular period for which a measurement of income is desired.

materiality The accounting convention that justifies the omission of insignificant information when its omission or misstatement would not mislead a user of the financial statements.

materials requisitions Records of materials issued to particular jobs.

modified internal rate of return (MIRR) A variation of the IRR capital-budgeting criterion defined as the discount rate that equates the present value of the project's annual cash outlays with the present value of the project's terminal value, where the terminal value is defined as the sum of the future value of the project's cash inflows compounded to the project's termination at the project's required rate of return.

mutually exclusive projects A set of projects that perform essentially the same task, so that acceptance of one will necessarily mean rejection of the others.

net and net-net leases In a net lease agreement the lessee assumes the risk and burden of ownership over the term of the lease. This means that the lessee must pay insurance and taxes on the asset as well as maintain the operating condition of the asset. In a net-net lease the lessee must, in addition to the requirements of a net lease, return the asset to the lessor at the end of the lease still worth a preestablished value.

net present value (NPV) A capital-budgeting technique defined as the present value of the future net cash flows after taxes less the project's initial outlay.

net worth A synonym for owner's equity.

nominal or quoted interest rate The stated rate of interest on the contract.

non-value-added costs Costs that can be eliminated without affecting a product's value to the customer.

normal costing system The cost system in which overhead is applied on an average or normalized basis, in order to get representative or normal inventory valuations.

objectivity (verifiability) Accuracy supported by a high extent of consensus among independent measures of an item.

operation costing A hybrid-costing system often used in the batch or group manufacturing of goods that have some common characteristics plus some individual characteristics.

operating lease A lease agreement (see financial lease) in which the lessee can cancel the agreement at any time after giving proper notice to the lessor.

operating leverage The incurrence of fixed operating costs in the firm's income stream.

opportunity cost The maximum available contribution to profit forgone (or passed up) by using limited resources for a particular purpose.

ordinary annuity An annuity in which the payments occur at the end of each period.

outlay cost A cost that requires a cash disbursement.

output All completed units (or equivalent completed units) of product.

overapplied overhead The excess of overhead applied to products over actual overhead incurred.

overtime premium An indirect labor cost, consisting of wages paid to all factory workers in excess of their straight-time wage rate.

owners' equity The excess of the assets over the liabilities.

paid-in capital The ownership claim against, or interest in, the total assets arising from any paid-in investment.

partnership   An organization that joins two or more individuals together as co-owners.

payback period   A capital-budgeting criterion defined as the number of years required to recover the initial cash investment.

payroll fringe costs   Employer contributions to employee benefits such as social security, life insurance, health insurance, and pensions.

perfect competition   A market in which a firm can sell as much of a product as it can produce, all at a single market price.

performance report   A detailed comparison of budgeted, or total standard, costs with actual costs. Variances between the two are segregated into price and quantity components, and when a variance is significant, its source is explained.

period costs   Costs that are deducted as expenses during the current period without going through an inventory stage.

practical (attainable) standard   A measurement for evaluating performance that is set high enough to motivate employees and low enough to allow for normal machine breakdowns, rest periods, and the like.

predatory pricing   Establishing prices so low that competitors are driven out of the market so that the predatory pricer then has no significant competition and can raise prices dramatically.

present value   The current value of a future sum.

present-value interest factor ($PVIF_{i,n}$)   The value $[1/(1 + i)^n]$ used as a multiplier to calculate an amount's present value.

present-value interest factor for an annuity ($PVIFA_{i,n}$)   The value $\left[\sum_{t=1}^{n} \dfrac{1}{(1 + i)^t} \right]$ used as a multiplier to calculate the present value of an annuity.

price elasticity   The effect of price changes on sales volumes.

price variance   The actual quantity of a good or service used multiplied by the difference between the actual and standard prices.

prime costs   Direct labor costs plus direct materials costs.

probability tree   A schematic representation of a problem in which all possible outcomes are graphically displayed.

process costing   The method of allocating costs to products by averaging costs over large numbers of nearly identical products.

product costs   Costs identified with goods produced or purchased for resale.

production cycle time   The time from initiating production to delivering the goods to the consumer.

profitability index (PI or Benefit/Cost Ratio)   A capital-budgeting criterion defined as the ratio of the present value of the future net cash flows to the initial outlay.

profits (earnings, income)   The excess of revenues over expenses.

project standing alone risk   The risk of a project standing alone is measured by the variability of the asset's expected returns. That is, it is the risk of a project ignoring the fact that it is only one of many projects within the firm, and the firm's stock is but one of many stocks within a stockholder's portfolio.

project's contribution-to-firm risk   The amount of risk that a project contributes to the firm as a whole. That is, a project's risk considering the effects of diversification among different projects within the firm, but ignoring the effects of shareholder's diversification within his or her portfolio.

prorate   To assign underapplied overhead or overapplied overhead in proportion to the sizes of the ending account balances.

pure play method   A method of estimating a project's beta that attempts to identify a publicly traded firm that is engaged solely in the same business as the project and uses that beta as a proxy for the project's beta.

quantity variance   The difference between the input quantity of direct materials and the corresponding output quantity (standard quantity allowed) multiplied by the standard price per unit of input.

relative value unit   A weighted-average measurement used by hospitals. It is based on the time used to perform a task, the degree of skill needed, and the resources used.

relevant information   The predicted future costs and revenues that will differ among alternative courses of action.

residual value   The predicted sales value of a long-lived asset at the end of its useful life.

retained income (retained earnings)   The ownership claim arising as a result of profitable operations.

revenue   A gross increase in assets from delivering goods or services.

risk   The likely variability associated with expected revenue or income streams.

risk-adjusted discount rate   A method for incorporating the project's level of risk into the capital-budgeting process, in which the discount rate is adjusted upward to compensate for higher than normal risk or downward to adjust for lower than normal risk.

sale and leaseback arrangement   An arrangement arising when a firm sells land, buildings, or equipment that it already owns and simultaneously enters into an agreement to lease the property back for a specific period, under specific terms.

scenario analysis   Simulation analysis that focuses on an examination of the range of possible outcomes.

Securities and Exchange Commission (SEC)   By federal law, the agency with the ultimate responsibility for specifying the generally accepted accounting principles for U.S. companies whose stock is held by the general investing public.

semivariable costs (semifixed costs)   Costs that exhibit the joint characteristics of both fixed and variable costs over different ranges of output.

sensitivity analysis   The process of determining how the distribution of possible returns for a particular project is affected by a change in one particular input variable.

separable costs   Any cost beyond the split-off point.

service departments   Units that exist only to support other departments.

simulation   The process of imitating the performance of an investment project under evaluation using a computer. This is done by randomly selecting observations from each of the distributions that affect the outcome of the project, combining those observations to determine the final output of the project, and continuing with this process until a representative record of the project's probable outcome is assembled.

skewed distribution   A distribution that has a longer "tail" to the right or the left.

sole proprietorship   A business entity with a single owner.

source documents   Explicit evidence of any transactions that occur in the entity's operation, for example, sales slips and purchase invoices.

split-off point   The juncture of manufacturing where the joint products become individually identifiable.

spontaneous financing   Sources of financing that arise naturally during the course of business. Accounts payable is a primary example.

standard cost   A carefully predetermined cost, usually per unit, used to evaluate performance.

standard cost of direct labor   The standard quantity of direct labor multiplied by the standard direct labor rate.

standard cost of direct materials   The standard quantity of direct materials multiplied by the standard price per unit of direct materials.

standard direct labor rate   The normal rate of pay per hour paid to employees for a particular kind of work.

standard price of direct materials   The price of a direct material quoted by the purchasing department and adjusted for such items as freight-in, insurance during transit, cash discounts allowed, and import duties.

standard quantity allowed The standard quantity of one unit multiplied by the actual number of units produced.

standard quantity of direct labor The estimated required direct labor-hours provided by engineers and factory supervisors adjusted for reasonable personal needs, coffee breaks, machine breakdowns, and the like.

step-down method A method for allocating service department costs that recognizes that some service departments support the activities in other service departments as well as those in production departments.

standard quantity of direct materials The required direct material listed in the bill of materials adjusted for normal spoilage, waste, shrinkage, and the like.

standards committee A committee directly responsible for the setting of standards, composed of the company's controller, industrial engineer, purchasing manager, management accountants, factory superintendent, and the line supervisors.

stockholders' equity The excess of assets over liabilities of a corporation.

sunk cost A cost that has already been incurred and, therefore, is irrelevant to the decision making process. Synonyms are *historical cost* and *past cost*.

sustainable rate of growth The maximum rate of growth in sales that the firm can sustain while maintaining its present capital structure (debt and equity mix) and without having to sell new common stock.

systematic risk The risk of a project measured from the point of view of a well-diversified shareholder. That is, a project's risk taking into account the fact that this project is only one of many projects within the firm, and the firm's stock is but one of many stocks within a stockholder's portfolio.

target costing A strategy in which companies first determine the price at which they can sell a new product or service and then design a product or service that can be produced at a low enough cost to provide an adequate profit margin.

total revenue Total sales dollars.

total standard cost The standard quantity allowed multiplied by the standard price of direct material or direct labor.

total variance The difference between the actual cost and the total standard cost.

transaction Any event that affects the financial position of an organization and requires recording.

transaction-based costing Activity-based costing.

transferred-in costs In process costing, costs incurred in a previous department for items that have been received by a subsequent department.

unavoidable costs Costs that continue even if an operation is halted.

underapplied overhead The excess of actual overhead over the overhead applied to products.

unearned revenue (deferred revenue) Collections from customers received and recorded before they are earned.

unexpired cost Any asset that ordinarily becomes an expense in future periods, for example, inventory and prepaid rent.

unfavorable variance A case in which output is less than input or the price paid for a good or service is greater than expected.

value-added cost The necessary cost of an activity that cannot be eliminated without affecting a product's value to the customer.

variable costs (direct costs) Costs that are fixed per unit of output but vary in total as output changes.

variance analysis Segregating the difference between an actual cost and its budgeted counterpart into price (rate) and quantity (efficiency) components.

volume of output The firm's level of operations expressed either in sales dollars or as units of output.

weighted-average (WA) process-costing method   A process-costing method that adds the cost of (1) all work done in the current period to (2) the work done in the preceding period on the current period's beginning inventory of work in process and divides the total by the equivalent units of work done to date.

COMPOUND SUM OF $1

n	1%	2%	3%	4%	5%	6%	7%	8%	9%	10%
1	1.010	1.020	1.030	1.040	1.050	1.060	1.070	1.080	1.090	1.100
2	1.020	1.040	1.061	1.082	1.102	1.124	1.145	1.166	1.188	1.210
3	1.030	1.061	1.093	1.125	1.158	1.191	1.225	1.260	1.295	1.331
4	1.041	1.082	1.126	1.170	1.216	1.262	1.311	1.360	1.412	1.464
5	1.051	1.104	1.159	1.217	1.276	1.338	1.403	1.469	1.539	1.611
6	1.062	1.126	1.194	1.265	1.340	1.419	1.501	1.587	1.677	1.772
7	1.072	1.149	1.230	1.316	1.407	1.504	1.606	1.714	1.828	1.949
8	1.083	1.172	1.267	1.369	1.477	1.594	1.718	1.851	1.993	2.144
9	1.094	1.195	1.305	1.423	1.551	1.689	1.838	1.999	2.172	2.358
10	1.105	1.219	1.344	1.480	1.629	1.791	1.967	2.159	2.367	2.594
11	1.116	1.243	1.384	1.539	1.710	1.898	2.105	2.332	2.580	2.853
12	1.127	1.268	1.426	1.601	1.796	2.012	2.252	2.518	2.813	3.138
13	1.138	1.294	1.469	1.665	1.886	2.133	2.410	2.720	3.066	3.452
14	1.149	1.319	1.513	1.732	1.980	2.261	2.579	2.937	3.342	3.797
15	1.161	1.346	1.558	1.801	2.079	2.397	2.759	3.172	3.642	4.177
16	1.173	1.373	1.605	1.873	2.183	2.540	2.952	3.426	3.970	4.595
17	1.184	1.400	1.653	1.948	2.292	2.693	3.159	3.700	4.328	5.054
18	1.196	1.428	1.702	2.026	2.407	2.854	3.380	3.996	4.717	5.560
19	1.208	1.457	1.753	2.107	2.527	3.026	3.616	4.316	5.142	6.116
20	1.220	1.486	1.806	2.191	2.653	3.207	3.870	4.661	5.604	6.727
21	1.232	1.516	1.860	2.279	2.786	3.399	4.140	5.034	6.109	7.400
22	1.245	1.546	1.916	2.370	2.925	3.603	4.430	5.436	6.658	8.140
23	1.257	1.577	1.974	2.465	3.071	3.820	4.740	5.871	7.258	8.954
24	1.270	1.608	2.033	2.563	3.225	4.049	5.072	6.341	7.911	9.850
25	1.282	1.641	2.094	2.666	3.386	4.292	5.427	6.848	8.623	10.834
30	1.348	1.811	2.427	3.243	4.322	5.743	7.612	10.062	13.267	17.449
40	1.489	2.208	3.262	4.801	7.040	10.285	14.974	21.724	31.408	45.258
50	1.645	2.691	4.384	7.106	11.467	18.419	29.456	46.900	74.354	117.386

n	11%	12%	13%	14%	15%	16%	17%	18%	19%	20%
1	1.110	1.120	1.130	1.140	1.150	1.160	1.170	1.180	1.190	1.200
2	1.232	1.254	1.277	1.300	1.322	1.346	1.369	1.392	1.416	1.440
3	1.368	1.405	1.443	1.482	1.521	1.561	1.602	1.643	1.685	1.728
4	1.518	1.574	1.630	1.689	1.749	1.811	1.874	1.939	2.005	2.074
5	1.685	1.762	1.842	1.925	2.011	2.100	2.192	2.288	2.386	2.488
6	1.870	1.974	2.082	2.195	2.313	2.436	2.565	2.700	2.840	2.986
7	2.076	2.211	2.353	2.502	2.660	2.826	3.001	3.185	3.379	3.583
8	2.305	2.476	2.658	2.853	3.059	3.278	3.511	3.759	4.021	4.300
9	2.558	2.773	3.004	3.252	3.518	3.803	4.108	4.435	4.785	5.160
10	2.839	3.106	3.395	3.707	4.046	4.411	4.807	5.234	5.695	6.192
11	3.152	3.479	3.836	4.226	4.652	5.117	5.624	6.176	6.777	7.430
12	3.498	3.896	4.334	4.818	5.350	5.936	6.580	7.288	8.064	8.916
13	3.883	4.363	4.898	5.492	6.153	6.886	7.699	8.599	9.596	10.699
14	4.310	4.887	5.535	6.261	7.076	7.987	9.007	10.147	11.420	12.839
15	4.785	5.474	6.254	7.138	8.137	9.265	10.539	11.974	13.589	15.407
16	5.311	6.130	7.067	8.137	9.358	10.748	12.330	14.129	16.171	18.488
17	5.895	6.866	7.986	9.276	10.761	12.468	14.426	16.672	19.244	22.186
18	6.543	7.690	9.024	10.575	12.375	14.462	16.879	19.673	22.900	26.623
19	7.263	8.613	10.197	12.055	14.232	16.776	19.748	23.214	27.251	31.948
20	8.062	9.646	11.523	13.743	16.366	19.461	23.105	27.393	32.429	38.337
21	8.949	10.804	13.021	15.667	18.821	22.574	27.033	32.323	38.591	46.005
22	9.933	12.100	14.713	17.861	21.644	26.186	31.629	38.141	45.923	55.205
23	11.026	13.552	16.626	20.361	24.891	30.376	37.005	45.007	54.648	66.247
24	12.239	15.178	18.788	23.212	28.625	35.236	43.296	53.108	65.031	79.496
25	13.585	17.000	21.230	26.461	32.918	40.874	50.656	62.667	77.387	95.395
30	22.892	29.960	39.115	50.949	66.210	85.849	111.061	143.367	184.672	237.373
40	64.999	93.049	132.776	188.876	267.856	378.715	533.846	750.353	1051.642	1469.740
50	184.559	288.996	450.711	700.197	1083.619	1670.669	2566.080	3927.189	5988.730	9100.191

COMPOUND SUM OF $1 (continued)

n	21%	22%	23%	24%	25%	26%	27%	28%	29%	30%
1	1.210	1.220	1.230	1.240	1.250	1.260	1.270	1.280	1.290	1.300
2	1.464	1.488	1.513	1.538	1.562	1.588	1.613	1.638	1.664	1.690
3	1.772	1.816	1.861	1.907	1.953	2.000	2.048	2.097	2.147	2.197
4	2.144	2.215	2.289	2.364	2.441	2.520	2.601	2.684	2.769	2.856
5	2.594	2.703	2.815	2.932	3.052	3.176	3.304	3.436	3.572	3.713
6	3.138	3.297	3.463	3.635	3.815	4.001	4.196	4.398	4.608	4.827
7	3.797	4.023	4.259	4.508	4.768	5.042	5.329	5.629	5.945	6.275
8	4.595	4.908	5.239	5.589	5.960	6.353	6.767	7.206	7.669	8.157
9	5.560	5.987	6.444	6.931	7.451	8.004	8.595	9.223	9.893	10.604
10	6.727	7.305	7.926	8.594	9.313	10.086	10.915	11.806	12.761	13.786
11	8.140	8.912	9.749	10.657	11.642	12.708	13.862	15.112	16.462	17.921
12	9.850	10.872	11.991	13.215	14.552	16.012	17.605	19.343	21.236	23.298
13	11.918	13.264	14.749	16.386	18.190	20.175	22.359	24.759	27.395	30.287
14	14.421	16.182	18.141	20.319	22.737	25.420	28.395	31.691	35.339	39.373
15	17.449	19.742	22.314	25.195	28.422	32.030	36.062	40.565	45.587	51.185
16	21.113	24.085	27.446	31.242	35.527	40.357	45.799	51.923	58.808	66.541
17	25.547	29.384	33.758	38.740	44.409	50.850	58.165	66.461	75.862	86.503
18	30.912	35.848	41.523	48.038	55.511	64.071	73.869	85.070	97.862	112.454
19	37.404	43.735	51.073	59.567	69.389	80.730	93.813	108.890	126.242	146.190
20	45.258	53.357	62.820	73.863	86.736	101.720	119.143	139.379	162.852	190.047
21	54.762	65.095	77.268	91.591	108.420	128.167	151.312	178.405	210.079	247.061
22	66.262	79.416	95.040	113.572	135.525	161.490	192.165	228.358	271.002	321.178
23	80.178	96.887	116.899	140.829	169.407	203.477	244.050	292.298	349.592	417.531
24	97.015	118.203	143.786	174.628	211.758	256.381	309.943	374.141	450.974	542.791
25	117.388	144.207	176.857	216.539	264.698	323.040	393.628	478.901	581.756	705.627
30	304.471	389.748	497.904	634.810	807.793	1025.904	1300.477	1645.488	2078.208	2619.936
40	2048.309	2846.941	3946.340	5455.797	7523.156	10346.879	14195.051	19426.418	26520.723	36117.754
50	13779.844	20795.680	31278.301	46889.207	70064.812	104354.562	154942.687	229345.875	338440.000	497910.125

n	31%	32%	33%	34%	35%	36%	37%	38%	39%	40%
1	1.310	1.320	1.330	1.340	1.350	1.360	1.370	1.380	1.390	1.400
2	1.716	1.742	1.769	1.796	1.822	1.850	1.877	1.904	1.932	1.960
3	2.248	2.300	2.353	2.406	2.460	2.515	2.571	2.628	2.686	2.744
4	2.945	3.036	3.129	3.224	3.321	3.421	3.523	3.627	3.733	3.842
5	3.858	4.007	4.162	4.320	4.484	4.653	4.826	5.005	5.189	5.378
6	5.054	5.290	5.535	5.789	6.053	6.328	6.612	6.907	7.213	7.530
7	6.621	6.983	7.361	7.758	8.172	8.605	9.058	9.531	10.025	10.541
8	8.673	9.217	9.791	10.395	11.032	11.703	12.410	13.153	13.935	14.758
9	11.362	12.166	13.022	13.930	14.894	15.917	17.001	18.151	19.370	20.661
10	14.884	16.060	17.319	18.666	20.106	21.646	23.292	25.049	26.924	28.925
11	19.498	21.199	23.034	25.012	27.144	29.439	31.910	34.567	37.425	40.495
12	25.542	27.982	30.635	33.516	36.644	40.037	43.716	47.703	52.020	56.694
13	33.460	36.937	40.745	44.912	49.469	54.451	59.892	65.830	72.308	79.371
14	43.832	49.756	54.190	60.181	66.784	74.053	82.051	90.845	100.509	111.120
15	57.420	64.358	72.073	80.643	90.158	100.712	112.410	125.366	139.707	155.567
16	75.220	84.953	95.857	108.061	121.713	136.968	154.002	173.005	194.192	217.793
17	98.539	112.138	127.490	144.802	164.312	186.277	210.983	238.747	269.927	304.911
18	129.086	148.022	169.561	194.035	221.822	253.337	289.046	329.471	375.198	426.875
19	169.102	195.389	225.517	260.006	299.459	344.537	395.993	454.669	521.525	597.625
20	221.523	257.913	299.937	348.408	404.270	468.571	542.511	627.443	724.919	836.674
21	290.196	340.446	398.916	466.867	545.764	637.256	743.240	865.871	1007.637	1171.343
22	380.156	449.388	530.558	625.601	736.781	865.668	1018.238	1194.900	1400.615	1639.878
23	498.004	593.192	705.642	838.305	994.653	1178.668	1394.986	1648.961	1946.854	2295.829
24	652.385	783.013	938.504	1123.328	1342.781	1602.988	1911.129	2275.564	2706.125	3214.158
25	854.623	1033.577	1248.210	1505.258	1812.754	2180.063	2618.245	3140.275	3761.511	4499.816
30	3297.081	4142.008	5194.516	6503.285	8128.426	10142.914	12636.086	15716.703	19517.969	24201.043
40	49072.621	66519.313	89962.188	121388.437	163433.875	219558.625	294317.937	393684.687	525508.312	700022.688

PRESENT VALUE OF $1

n	1%	2%	3%	4%	5%	6%	7%	8%	9%	10%
1	.990	.980	.971	.962	.952	.943	.935	.926	.917	.909
2	.980	.961	.943	.925	.907	.890	.873	.857	.842	.826
3	.971	.942	.915	.889	.864	.840	.816	.794	.772	.751
4	.961	.924	.888	.855	.823	.792	.763	.735	.708	.683
5	.951	.906	.863	.822	.784	.747	.713	.681	.650	.621
6	.942	.888	.837	.790	.746	.705	.666	.630	.596	.564
7	.933	.871	.813	.760	.711	.665	.623	.583	.547	.513
8	.923	.853	.789	.731	.677	.627	.582	.540	.502	.467
9	.914	.837	.766	.703	.645	.592	.544	.500	.460	.424
10	.905	.820	.744	.676	.614	.558	.508	.463	.422	.386
11	.896	.804	.722	.650	.585	.527	.475	.429	.388	.350
12	.887	.789	.701	.625	.557	.497	.444	.397	.356	.319
13	.879	.773	.681	.601	.530	.469	.415	.368	.326	.290
14	.870	.758	.661	.577	.505	.442	.388	.340	.299	.263
15	.861	.743	.642	.555	.481	.417	.362	.315	.275	.239
16	.853	.728	.623	.534	.458	.394	.339	.292	.252	.218
17	.844	.714	.605	.513	.436	.371	.317	.270	.231	.198
18	.836	.700	.587	.494	.416	.350	.296	.250	.212	.180
19	.828	.686	.570	.475	.396	.331	.277	.232	.194	.164
20	.820	.673	.554	.456	.377	.312	.258	.215	.178	.149
21	.811	.660	.538	.439	.359	.294	.242	.199	.164	.135
22	.803	.647	.522	.422	.342	.278	.226	.184	.150	.123
23	.795	.634	.507	.406	.326	.262	.211	.170	.138	.112
-14	.788	.622	.492	.390	.310	.247	.197	.158	.126	.102
25	.780	.610	.478	.375	.295	.233	.184	.146	.116	.092
30	.742	.552	.412	.308	.231	.174	.131	.099	.075	.057
40	.672	.453	.307	.208	.142	.097	.067	.046	.032	.022
50	.608	.372	.228	.141	.087	.054	.034	.021	.013	.009

n	11%	12%	13%	14%	15%	16%	17%	18%	19%	20%
1	.901	.893	.885	.877	.870	.862	.855	.847	.840	.833
2	.812	.797	.783	.769	.756	.743	.731	.718	.706	.694
3	.731	.712	.693	.675	.658	.641	.624	.609	.593	.579
4	.659	.636	.613	.592	.572	.552	.534	.516	.499	.482
5	.593	.567	.543	.519	.497	.476	.456	.437	.419	.402
6	.535	.507	.480	.456	.432	.410	.390	.370	.352	.335
7	.482	.452	.425	.400	.376	.354	.333	.314	.296	.279
8	.434	.404	.376	.351	.327	.305	.285	.266	.249	.233
9	.391	.361	.333	.308	.284	.263	.243	.225	.209	.194
10	.352	.322	.295	.270	.247	.227	.208	.191	.176	.162
11	.317	.287	.261	.237	.215	.195	.178	.162	.148	.135
12	.286	.257	.231	.208	.187	.168	.152	.137	.124	.112
13	.258	.229	.204	.182	.163	.145	.130	.116	.104	.093
14	.232	.205	.181	.160	.141	.125	.111	.099	.088	.078
15	.209	.183	.160	.140	.123	.108	.095	.084	.074	.065
16	.188	.163	.141	.123	.107	.093	.081	.071	.062	.054
17	.170	.146	.125	.108	.093	.080	.069	.060	.052	.045
18	.153	.130	.111	.095	.081	.069	.059	.051	.044	.038
19	.138	.116	.098	.083	.070	.060	.051	.043	.037	.031
20	.124	.104	.087	.073	.061	.051	.043	.037	.031	.026
21	.112	.093	.077	.064	.053	.044	.037	.031	.026	.022
22	.101	.083	.068	.056	.046	.038	.032	.026	.022	.018
23	.091	.074	.060	.049	.040	.033	.027	.022	.018	.015
24	.082	.066	.053	.043	.035	.028	.023	.019	.015	.013
25	.074	.059	.047	.038	.030	.024	.020	.016	.013	.010
30	.044	.033	.026	.020	.015	.012	.009	.007	.005	.004
40	.015	.011	.008	.005	.004	.003	.002	.001	.001	.001
50	.005	.003	.002	.001	.001	.001	.000	.000	.000	.000

PRESENT VALUE OF $1 (continued)

n	21%	22%	23%	24%	25%	26%	27%	28%	29%	30%
1	.826	.820	.813	.806	.800	.794	.787	.781	.775	.769
2	.683	.672	.661	.650	.640	.630	.620	.610	.601	.592
3	.564	.551	.537	.524	.512	.500	.488	.477	.466	.455
4	.467	.451	.437	.423	.410	.397	.384	.373	.361	.350
5	.386	.370	.355	.341	.328	.315	.303	.291	.280	.269
6	.319	.303	.289	.275	.262	.250	.238	.227	.217	.207
7	.263	.249	.235	.222	.210	.198	.188	.178	.168	.159
8	.218	.204	.191	.179	.168	.157	.148	.139	.130	.123
9	.180	.167	.155	.144	.134	.125	.116	.108	.101	.094
10	.149	.137	.126	.116	.107	.099	.092	.085	.078	.073
11	.123	.112	.103	.094	.086	.079	.072	.066	.061	.056
12	.102	.092	.083	.076	.069	.062	.057	.052	.047	.043
13	.084	.075	.068	.061	.055	.050	.045	.040	.037	.033
14	.069	.062	.055	.049	.044	.039	.035	.032	.028	.025
15	.057	.051	.045	.040	.035	.031	.028	.025	.022	.020
16	.047	.042	.036	.032	.028	.025	.022	.019	.017	.015
17	.039	.034	.030	.026	.023	.020	.017	.015	.013	.012
18	.032	.028	.024	.021	.018	.016	.014	.012	.010	.009
19	.027	.023	.020	.017	.014	.012	.011	.009	.008	.007
20	.022	.019	.016	.014	.012	.010	.008	.007	.006	.005
21	.018	.015	.013	.011	.009	.008	.007	.006	.005	.004
22	.015	.013	.011	.009	.007	.006	.005	.004	.004	.003
23	.012	.010	.009	.007	.006	.005	.004	.003	.003	.002
24	.010	.008	.007	.006	.005	.004	.003	.003	.002	.002
25	.009	.007	.006	.005	.004	.003	.003	.002	.002	.001
30	.003	.003	.002	.002	.001	.001	.001	.001	.000	.000
40	.000	.000	.000	.000	.000	.000	.000	.000	.000	.000
50	.000	.000	.000	.000	.000	.000	.000	.000	.000	.000

n	31%	32%	33%	34%	35%	36%	37%	38%	39%	40%
1	.763	.758	.752	.746	.741	.735	.730	.725	.719	.714
2	.583	.574	.565	.557	.549	.541	.533	.525	.518	.510
3	.445	.435	.425	.416	.406	.398	.389	.381	.372	.364
4	.340	.329	.320	.310	.301	.292	.284	.276	.268	.260
5	.259	.250	.240	.231	.223	.215	.207	.200	.193	.186
6	.198	.189	.181	.173	.165	.158	.151	.145	.139	.133
7	.151	.143	.136	.129	.122	.116	.110	.105	.100	.095
8	.115	.108	.102	.096	.091	.085	.081	.076	.072	.068
9	.088	.082	.077	.072	.067	.063	.059	.055	.052	.048
10	.067	.062	.058	.054	.050	.046	.043	.040	.037	.035
11	.051	.047	.043	.040	.037	.034	.031	.029	.027	.025
12	.039	.036	.033	.030	.027	.025	.023	.021	.019	.018
13	.030	.027	.025	.022	.020	.018	.017	.015	.014	.013
14	.023	.021	.018	.017	.015	.014	.012	.011	.010	.009
15	.017	.016	.014	.012	.011	.010	.009	.008	.007	.006
16	.013	.012	.010	.009	.008	.007	.006	.006	.005	.005
17	.010	.009	.008	.007	.006	.005	.005	.004	.004	.003
18	.008	.007	.006	.005	.005	.004	.003	.003	.003	.002
19	.006	.005	.004	.004	.003	.003	.003	.002	.002	.002
20	.005	.004	.003	.003	.002	.002	.002	.002	.001	.001
21	.003	.003	.003	.002	.002	.002	.001	.001	.001	.001
22	.003	.002	.002	.002	.001	.001	.001	.001	.001	.001
23	.002	.002	.001	.001	.001	.001	.001	.001	.001	.000
24	.002	.001	.001	.001	.001	.001	.001	.000	.000	.000
25	.001	.001	.001	.001	.001	.000	.000	.000	.000	.000
30	.000	.000	.000	.000	.000	.000	.000	.000	.000	.000
40	.000	.000	.000	.000	.000	.000	.000	.000	.000	.000

SUM OF AN ANNUITY OF $1 FOR n PERIODS

n	1%	2%	3%	4%	5%	6%	7%	8%	9%	10%
1	1.000	1.000	1.000	1.000	1.000	1.000	1.000	1.000	1.000	1.000
2	2.010	2.020	2.030	2.040	2.050	2.060	2.070	2.080	2.090	2.100
3	3.030	3.060	3.091	3.122	3.152	3.184	3.215	3.246	3.278	3.310
4	4.060	4.122	4.184	4.246	4.310	4.375	4.440	4.506	4.573	4.641
5	5.101	5.204	5.309	5.416	5.526	5.637	5.751	5.867	5.985	6.105
6	6.152	6.308	6.468	6.633	6.802	6.975	7.153	7.336	7.523	7.716
7	7.214	7.434	7.662	7.898	8.142	8.394	8.654	8.923	9.200	9.487
8	8.286	8.583	8.892	9.214	9.549	9.897	10.260	10.637	11.028	11.436
9	9.368	9.755	10.159	10.583	11.027	11.491	11.978	12.488	13.021	13.579
10	10.462	10.950	11.464	12.006	12.578	13.181	13.816	14.487	15.193	15.937
11	11.567	12.169	12.808	13.486	14.207	14.972	15.784	16.645	17.560	18.531
12	12.682	13.412	14.192	15.026	15.917	16.870	17.888	18.977	20.141	21.384
13	13.809	14.680	15.618	16.627	17.713	18.882	20.141	21.495	22.953	24.523
14	14.947	15.974	17.086	18.292	19.598	21.015	22.550	24.215	26.019	27.975
15	16.097	17.293	18.599	20.023	21.578	23.276	25.129	27.152	29.361	31.772
16	17.258	18.639	20.157	21.824	23.657	25.672	27.888	30.324	33.003	35.949
17	18.430	20.012	21.761	23.697	25.840	28.213	30.840	33.750	36.973	40.544
18	19.614	21.412	23.414	25.645	28.132	30.905	33.999	37.450	41.301	45.599
19	20.811	22.840	25.117	27.671	30.539	33.760	37.379	41.446	46.018	51.158
20	22.019	24.297	26.870	29.778	33.066	36.785	40.995	45.762	51.159	57.274
21	23.239	25.783	28.676	31.969	35.719	39.992	44.865	50.422	56.764	64.002
22	24.471	27.299	30.536	34.248	38.505	43.392	49.005	55.456	62.872	71.402
23	25.716	28.845	32.452	36.618	41.430	46.995	53.435	60.893	69.531	79.542
24	26.973	30.421	34.426	39.082	44.501	50.815	58.176	66.764	76.789	88.496
25	28.243	32.030	36.459	41.645	47.726	54.864	63.248	73.105	84.699	98.346
30	34.784	40.567	47.575	56.084	66.438	79.057	94.459	113.282	136.305	164.491
40	48.885	60.401	75.400	95.024	120.797	154.758	199.630	295.052	337.872	442.580
50	64.461	84.577	112.794	152.664	209.341	290.325	406.516	573.756	815.051	1163.865

n	11%	12%	13%	14%	15%	16%	17%	18%	19%	20%
1	1.000	1.000	1.000	1.000	1.000	1.000	1.000	1.000	1.000	1.000
2	2.110	2.120	2.130	2.140	2.150	2.160	2.170	2.180	2.190	2.200
3	3.342	3.374	3.407	3.440	3.472	3.506	3.539	3.572	3.606	3.640
4	4.710	4.779	4.850	4.921	4.993	5.066	5.141	5.215	5.291	5.368
5	6.228	6.353	6.480	6.610	6.742	6.877	7.014	7.154	7.297	7.442
6	7.913	8.115	8.323	8.535	8.754	8.977	9.207	9.442	9.683	9.930
7	9.783	10.089	10.405	10.730	11.067	11.414	11.772	12.141	12.523	12.916
8	11.859	12.300	12.757	13.233	13.727	14.240	14.773	15.327	15.902	16.499
9	14.164	14.776	15.416	16.085	16.786	17.518	18.285	19.086	19.923	20.799
10	16.722	17.549	18.420	19.337	20.304	21.321	22.393	23.521	24.709	25.959
11	19.561	20.655	21.814	23.044	24.349	25.733	27.200	28.755	30.403	32.150
12	22.713	24.133	25.650	27.271	29.001	30.850	32.824	34.931	37.180	39.580
13	26.211	28.029	29.984	32.088	34.352	36.786	39.404	42.218	45.244	48.496
14	30.095	32.392	34.882	37.581	40.504	43.672	47.102	50.818	54.841	59.196
15	34.405	37.280	40.417	43.842	47.580	51.659	56.109	60.965	66.260	72.035
16	39.190	42.753	46.671	50.980	55.717	60.925	66.648	72.938	79.850	87.442
17	44.500	48.883	53.738	59.117	65.075	71.673	78.978	87.067	96.021	105.930
18	50.396	55.749	61.724	68.393	75.836	84.140	93.404	103.739	115.265	128.116
19	56.939	63.439	70.748	78.968	88.211	98.603	110.283	123.412	138.165	154.739
20	64.202	72.052	80.946	91.024	102.443	115.379	130.031	146.626	165.417	186.687
21	72.264	81.698	92.468	104.767	118.809	134.840	153.136	174.019	197.846	225.024
22	81.213	92.502	105.489	120.434	137.630	157.414	180.169	206.342	236.436	271.028
23	91.147	104.602	120.203	138.295	159.274	183.600	211.798	244.483	282.359	326.234
24	102.173	118.154	136.829	158.656	184.166	213.976	248.803	289.490	337.007	392.480
25	114.412	133.333	155.616	181.867	212.790	249.212	292.099	342.598	402.038	471.976
30	199.018	241.330	293.192	356.778	434.738	530.306	647.423	790.932	966.698	1181.865
40	581.812	767.080	1013.667	1341.979	1779.048	2360.724	3134.412	4163.094	5529.711	7343.715
50	1668.723	2399.975	3459.344	4994.301	7217.488	10435.449	15088.805	21812.273	31514.492	45496.094

SUM OF AN ANNUITY OF $1 FOR n PERIODS (continued)

n	21%	22%	23%	24%	25%	26%	27%	28%	29%	30%
1	1.000	1.000	1.000	1.000	1.000	1.000	1.000	1.000	1.000	1.000
2	2.210	2.220	2.230	2.240	2.250	2.260	2.270	2.280	2.290	2.300
3	3.674	3.708	3.743	3.778	3.813	3.848	3.883	3.918	3.954	3.990
4	5.446	5.524	5.604	5.684	5.766	5.848	5.931	6.016	6.101	6.187
5	7.589	7.740	7.893	8.048	8.207	8.368	8.533	8.700	8.870	9.043
6	10.183	10.442	10.708	10.980	11.259	11.544	11.837	12.136	12.442	12.756
7	13.321	13.740	14.171	14.615	15.073	15.546	16.032	16.534	17.051	17.583
8	17.119	17.762	18.430	19.123	19.842	20.588	21.361	22.163	22.995	23.858
9	21.714	22.670	23.669	24.712	25.802	26.940	28.129	29.369	30.664	32.015
10	27.274	28.657	20.113	31.643	33.253	34.945	36.723	38.592	40.556	42.619
11	34.001	35.962	38.039	40.238	42.566	45.030	47.639	50.398	53.318	56.405
12	42.141	44.873	47.787	50.895	54.208	57.738	61.501	65.510	69.780	74.326
13	51.991	55.745	59.778	64.109	68.760	73.750	79.106	84.853	91.016	97.624
14	63.909	69.009	74.528	80.496	86.949	93.925	101.465	109.611	118.411	127.912
15	78.330	85.191	92.669	100.815	109.687	119.346	129.860	141.302	153.750	167.285
16	95.779	104.933	114.983	126.010	138.109	151.375	165.922	181.867	199.337	218.470
17	116.892	129.019	142.428	157.252	173.636	191.733	211.721	233.790	258.145	285.011
18	142.439	158.403	176.187	195.993	218.045	242.583	269.885	300.250	334.006	371.514
19	173.351	194.251	217.710	244.031	273.556	306.654	343.754	385.321	431.868	483.968
20	210.755	237.986	268.783	303.598	342.945	387.384	437.568	494.210	558.110	630.157
21	256.013	291.343	331.603	377.461	429.681	489.104	556.710	633.589	720.962	820.204
22	310.775	356.438	408.871	469.052	538.101	617.270	708.022	811.993	931.040	1067.265
23	377.038	435.854	503.911	582.624	673.626	778.760	900.187	1040.351	1202.042	1388.443
24	457.215	532.741	620.810	723.453	843.032	982.237	1144.237	1332.649	1551.634	1805.975
25	554.230	650.944	764.596	898.082	1054.791	1238.617	1454.180	1706.790	2002.608	2348.765
30	1445.111	1767.044	2160.459	2640.881	3227.172	3941.953	4812.891	5873.172	7162.785	8729.805
40	9749.141	12936.141	17153.691	22728.367	30088.621	39791.957	52570.707	69376.562	91447.375	120389.375

n	31%	32%	33%	34%	35%	36%	37%	38%	39%	40%
1	1.000	1.000	1.000	1.000	1.000	1.000	1.000	1.000	1.000	1.000
2	2.310	2.320	2.330	2.340	2.350	2.360	2.370	2.380	2.390	2.400
3	4.026	4.062	4.099	4.136	4.172	4.210	4.247	4.284	4.322	4.360
4	6.274	6.362	6.452	6.542	6.633	6.725	6.818	6.912	7.008	7.104
5	9.219	9.398	9.581	9.766	9.954	10.146	10.341	10.539	10.741	10.946
6	13.077	13.406	13.742	14.086	14.438	14.799	15.167	15.544	15.930	16.324
7	18.131	18.696	19.277	19.876	20.492	21.126	21.779	22.451	23.142	23.853
8	24.752	25.678	26.638	27.633	28.664	29.732	30.837	31.982	33.167	34.395
9	33.425	34.895	36.429	38.028	39.696	41.435	43.247	45.135	47.103	49.152
10	44.786	47.062	49.451	51.958	54.590	57.351	60.248	63.287	66.473	69.813
11	59.670	63.121	66.769	70.624	74.696	78.998	83.540	88.335	93.397	98.739
12	79.167	84.320	89.803	95.636	101.840	108.437	115.450	122.903	130.822	139.234
13	104.709	112.302	120.438	129.152	138.484	148.474	159.166	170.606	182.842	195.928
14	138.169	149.239	161.183	174.063	187.953	202.925	219.058	236.435	255.151	275.299
15	182.001	197.996	215.373	234.245	254.737	276.978	301.109	327.281	355.659	386.418
16	239.421	262.354	287.446	314.888	344.895	377.690	413.520	452.647	495.366	541.985
17	314.642	347.307	383.303	422.949	466.608	514.658	567.521	625.652	689.558	759.778
18	413.180	459.445	510.792	567.751	630.920	700.935	778.504	864.399	959.485	1064.689
19	542.266	607.467	680.354	761.786	852.741	954.271	1067.551	1193.870	1334.683	1491.563
20	711.368	802.856	905.870	1021.792	1152.200	1298.809	1463.544	1648.539	1856.208	2089.188
21	932.891	1060.769	1205.807	1370.201	1556.470	1767.380	2006.055	2275-982	2581.128	2925.862
22	1223.087	1401.215	1604.724	1837.068	2102.234	2404.636	2749.294	3141.852	3588.765	4097.203
23	1603.243	1850.603	2135.282	2462.669	2839.014	3271.304	3767.532	4336.750	4989.379	5737.078
24	2101.247	2443.795	2840.924	3300.974	3833.667	4449.969	5162.516	5985.711	6936.230	8032.906
25	2753.631	3226.808	3779.428	4424.301	5176.445	6052.957	7073.645	8261.273	9642.352	11247.062
30	10632.543	12940.672	15737.945	19124.434	23221.258	28172.016	34148.906	41357.227	50043.625	60500.207

APPENDIX D

PRESENT VALUE OF AN ANNUITY OF $1 FOR n PERIODS

n	1%	2%	3%	4%	5%	6%	7%	8%	9%	10%
1	990	.980	.971	.962	.952	.943	.935	.926	.917	.909
2	1.970	1.942	1.913	1.886	1.859	1.833	1.808	1.783	1.759	1.736
3	2.941	2.884	2.829	2.775	2.723	2.673	2.624	2.577	2.531	2.487
4	3.902	3.808	3.717	3.630	3.546	3.465	3.387	3.312	3.240	3.170
5	4.853	4.713	4.580	4.452	4.329	4.212	4.100	3.993	3.890	3.791
6	5.795	5.601	5.417	5.242	5.076	4.917	4.767	4.623	4.486	4.355
7	6.728	6.472	6.230	6.002	5.786	5.582	5.389	5.206	5.033	4.868
8	7.652	7.326	7.020	6.733	6.463	6.210	5.971	5.747	5.535	5.335
9	8.566	8.162	7.786	7.435	7.108	6.802	6.515	6.247	5.995	5.759
10	9.471	8.983	8.530	8.111	7.722	7.360	7.024	6.710	6.418	6.145
11	10.368	9.787	9.253	8.760	8.306	7.887	7.499	7.139	6.805	6.495
12	11.255	10.575	9.954	9.385	8.863	8.384	7.943	7.536	7.161	6.814
13	12.134	11.348	10.635	9.986	9.394	8.853	8.358	7.904	7.487	7.103
14	13.004	12.106	11.296	10.563	9.899	9.295	8.746	8.244	7.786	7.367
15	13.865	12.849	11.938	11.118	10.380	9.712	9.108	8.560	8.061	7.606
16	14.718	13.578	12.561	11.652	10.838	10.106	9.447	8.851	8.313	7.824
17	15.562	14.292	13.166	12.166	11.274	10.477	9.763	9.122	8.544	8.022
18	16.398	14.992	13.754	12.659	11.690	10.828	10.059	9.372	8.756	8.201
19	17.226	15.679	14.324	13.134	12.085	11.158	10.336	9.604	8.950	8.365
20	18.046	16.352	14.878	13.590	12.462	11.470	10.594	9.818	9.129	8.514
21	18.857	17.011	15.415	14.029	12.821	11.764	10.836	10.017	9.292	8.649
22	19.661	17.658	15.937	14.451	13.163	12.042	11.061	10.201	9.442	8.772
23	20.456	18.292	16.444	14.857	13.489	12.303	11.272	10.371	9.580	8.883
24	21.244	18.914	16.936	15.247	13.799	12.550	11.469	10.529	9.707	8.985
25	22.023	19.524	17.413	15.622	14.094	12.783	11.654	10.675	9.823	9.077
30	25.808	22.397	19.601	17.292	15.373	13.765	12.409	11.258	10.274	9.427
40	32.835	27.356	23.115	19.793	17.159	15.046	13.332	11.925	10.757	9.779
50	39.197	31.424	25.730	21.482	18.256	15.762	13.801	12.234	10.962	9.915

n	11%	12%	13%	14%	15%	16%	17%	18%	19%	20%
1	.901	.893	.885	.877	.870	.862	.855	.847	.840	.833
2	1.713	1.690	1.668	1.647	1.626	1.605	1.585	1.566	1.547	1.528
3	2.444	2.402	2.361	2.322	2.283	2.246	2.210	2.174	2.140	2.106
4	3.102	3.037	2.974	2.914	2.855	2.798	2.743	2.690	2.639	2.589
5	3.696	3.605	3.517	3.433	3.352	3.274	3.199	3.127	3.058	2.991
6	4.231	4.111	3.998	3.889	3.784	3.685	3.589	3.498	3.410	3.326
7	4.712	4.564	4.423	4.288	4.160	4.039	3.922	3.812	3.706	3.605
8	5.146	4.968	4.799	4.639	4.487	4.344	4.207	4.078	3.954	3.837
9	5.537	5.328	5.132	4.946	4.772	4.607	4.451	4.303	4.163	4.031
10	5.889	5.650	5.426	5.216	5.019	4.833	4.659	4.494	4.339	4.192
11	6.207	5.938	5.687	5.453	5.234	5.029	4.836	4.656	4.487	4.327
12	6.492	6.194	5.918	5.660	5.421	5.197	4.988	4.793	4.611	4.439
13	6.750	6.424	6.122	5.842	5.583	5.342	5.118	4.910	4.715	4.533
14	6.982	6.628	6.303	6.002	5.724	5.468	5.229	5.008	4.802	4.611
15	7.191	6.811	6.462	6.142	5.847	5.575	5.324	5.092	4.876	4.675
16	7.379	6.974	6.604	6.265	5.954	5.669	5.405	5.162	4.938	4.730
17	7.549	7.120	6.729	6.373	6.047	5.749	5.475	5.222	4.990	4.775
18	7.702	7.250	6.840	6.467	6.128	5.818	5.534	5.273	5.033	4.812
19	7.839	7.366	6.938	6.550	6.198	5.877	5.585	5.316	5.070	4.843
20	7.963	7,469	7.025	6.623	6.259	5.929	5.628	5.353	5.101	4.870
21	8.075	7.562	7.102	6.687	6.312	5.973	5.665	5.384	5.127	4.891
22	8.176	7.645	7.170	6.743	6.359	6.011	5.696	5.410	5.149	4.909
23	8.266	7.718	7.230	6.792	6.399	6.044	5.723	5.432	5.167	4.925
24	8.348	7.784	7.283	6.835	6.434	6.073	5.747	5.451	5.182	4.937
25	8.442	7.843	7.330	6.873	6.464	6.097	5.766	5.467	5.195	4.948
30	8.694	8.055	7.496	7.003	6.566	6.177	5.829	5.517	5.235	4.979
40	8.951	8.244	7.634	7.105	6.642	6.233	5.871	5.548	5.258	4.997
50	9.042	8.305	7.675	7.133	6.661	6.246	5.880	5.554	5.262	4.999

PRESENT VALUE OF AN ANNUITY OF $1 FOR *n* PERIODS (continued)

n	21%	22%	23%	24%	25%	26%	27%	28%	29%	30%
1	.826	.820	.813	.806	.800	.794	.787	.781	.775	.769
2	1.509	1.492	1.474	1.457	1.440	1.424	1.407	1.392	1.376	1.361
3	2.074	2.042	2.011	1.981	1.952	1.923	1.896	1.868	1.842	1.816
4	2.540	2.494	2.448	2.404	2.362	2.320	2.280	2.241	2.203	2.166
5	2.926	2.864	2.803	2.745	2.689	2.635	2.583	2.532	2.483	2.436
6	3.245	3.167	3.092	3.020	2.951	2.885	2.821	2.759	2.700	2.643
7	3.508	3.416	3.327	3.242	3.161	3.083	3.009	2.937	2.868	2.802
8	3.726	3.619	3.518	3.421	3.329	3.241	3.156	3.076	2.999	2.925
9	3.905	3.786	3.673	3.566	3.463	3.366	3.273	3.184	3.100	3.019
10	4.054	3.923	3.799	3.682	3.570	3.465	3.364	3.269	3.178	3.092
11	4.177	4.035	3.902	3.776	3.656	3.544	3.437	3.335	3.239	3.147
12	4.278	4.127	3.985	3.851	3.725	3.606	3.493	3.387	3.286	3.190
13	4.362	4.203	4.053	3.912	3.780	3.656	3.538	3.427	3.322	3.223
14	4.432	4.265	4.108	3.962	3.824	3.695	3.573	3.459	3.351	3.249
15	4.489	4.315	4.153	4.001	3.859	3.726	3.601	3.483	3.373	3.268
16	4.536	4.357	4.189	4.033	3.887	3.751	3.623	3.503	3.390	3.283
17	4.576	4.391	4.219	4.059	3.910	3.771	3.640	3.518	3.403	3.295
18	4.608	4.419	4.243	4.080	3.928	3.786	3.654	3.529	3.413	3.304
19	4.635	4.442	4.263	4.097	3.942	3.799	3.664	3.539	3.421	3.311
20	4.657	4.460	4.279	4.110	3.954	3.808	3.673	3.546	3.427	3.316
21	4.675	4.476	4.292	4.121	3.963	3.816	3.679	3.551	3.432	3.320
22	4.690	4.488	4.302	4.130	3.970	3.822	3.684	3.556	3.436	3.323
23	4.703	4.499	4.311	4.137	3.976	3.827	3.689	3.559	3.438	3.325
24	4.713	4.507	4.318	4.143	3.981	3.831	3.692	3.562	3.441	3.327
25	4.721	4.514	4.323	4.147	3.985	3.834	3.694	3.564	3.442	3.329
30	4.746	4.534	4.339	4.160	3.995	3.842	3.701	3.569	3.447	3.332
40	4.760	4.544	4.347	4.166	3.999	3.846	3.703	3.571	3.448	3.333
50	4.762	4.545	4.348	4.167	4.000	3.846	3.704	3.571	3.448	3.333

n	31%	32%	33%	34%	35%	36%	37%	38%	39%	40%
1	.763	.758	.752	.746	.741	.735	.730	.725	.719	.714
2	1.346	1.331	1.317	1.303	1.289	1.276	1.263	1.250	1.237	1.224
3	1.791	1.766	1.742	1.719	1.696	1.673	1.652	1.630	1.609	1.589
4	2.130	2.096	2.062	2.029	1.997	1.966	1.935	1.906	1.877	1.849
5	2.390	2.345	2.302	2.260	2.220	2.181	2.143	2.106	2.070	2.035
6	2.588	2.534	2.483	2.433	2.385	2.339	2.294	2.251	2.209	2.168
7	2.739	2.677	2.619	2.562	2.508	2.455	2.404	2.355	2.308	2.263
8	2.854	2.786	2.721	2.658	2.598	2.540	2.485	2.432	2.380	2.331
9	2.942	2.868	2.798	2.730	2.665	2.603	2.544	2.487	2.432	2.379
10	3.009	2.930	2.855	2.784	2.715	2.649	2.587	2.527	2.469	2.414
11	3.060	2.978	2.899	2.824	2.752	2.683	2.618	2.555	2.496	2.438
12	3.100	3.013	2.931	2.853	2.779	2.708	2.641	2.576	2.515	2.456
13	3.129	3.040	2.956	2.876	2.799	2.727	2.658	2.592	2.529	2.469
14	3.152	3.061	2.974	2.892	2.814	2.740	2.670	2.603	2.539	2.477
15	3.170	3.076	2.988	2.905	2.825	2.750	2.679	2.611	2.546	2.484
16	3.183	3.088	2.999	2.914	2.834	2.757	2.685	2.616	2.551	2.489
17	3.193	3.097	3.007	2.921	2.840	2.763	2.690	2.621	2.555	2.492
18	3.201	3.104	3.012	2.926	2.844	2.767	2.693	2.624	2.557	2.494
19	3.207	3.109	3.017	2.930	2.848	2.770	2.696	2.626	2.559	2.496
20	3.211	3.113	3.020	2.933	2.850	2.772	2.698	2.627	2.561	2.497
21	3.215	3.116	3.023	2.935	2.852	2.773	2.699	2.629	2.562	2.498
22	3.217	3.118	3.025	2.936	2.853	2.775	2.700	2.629	2.562	2.498
23	3.219	3.120	3.026	2.938	2.854	2.775	2.701	2.630	2.563	2.499
24	3.221	3.121	3.027	2.939	2.855	2.776	2.701	2.630	2.563	2.499
25	3.222	3.122	3.028	2.939	2.856	2.776	2.702	2.631	2.563	2.499
30	3.225	2.124	3.030	2.941	2.857	2.777	2.702	2.631	2.564	2.500
40	3.226	3.125	3.030	2.941	2.857	2.778	2.703	2.632	2.564	2.500
50	3.226	3.125	3.030	2.941	2.857	2.778	2.703	2.632	2.564	2.500

INDEX

direct-materials inventory, 367, 461, 479–481, 483–484, 488, 496, 499, 512
discount rate, 60–61, 64–69, 71, 73–74, 76, 78–86, 90, 92–93, 182–183, 186–187, 189, 191–196, 200–201, 226, 246, 248–249, 251–254, 262–263, 265, 267, 335, 337, 571–573
discounted cash flow, 187, 199, 217, 222–223, 225, 227–228, 239, 300
discounted cash flow analysis, 199
discounted cash flow capital-budgeting criteria, 228
discounted cash flow criteria, 187, 217, 222–223, 225, 227
discounted cash flow evaluation, 300
discounted cash flow methods, 199, 217, 239
discounted net cash flows, 182, 200, 570
discounted payback period, 182–184, 200, 203–205, 570
discounting, 77–78, 83, 86–87, 93, 187, 195, 213, 251, 339, 351
discounting annuities, 86
discretionary costs, 410
discretionary financing, 277, 279–281, 290–291, 293–294, 296, 570
discriminatory pricing, 115, 570
dispersion, 242–243, 261, 297, 299, 570
disposal value, 56, 153–156, 158, 161–162, 164, 168, 170–171, 177
distribution, 34, 36, 151, 198, 243, 246, 250, 254–255, 257–258, 260–264, 269, 297, 363, 441, 573
distributions of profits, 35, 51
distributions of retained income, 35
dividend payout, 280–282, 288
dividend payout ratios, 280
dividend policy, 36, 221, 280
dividends, 14, 22, 28, 30, 34–36, 40–42, 49–55, 57–58, 188, 276–281, 288, 291–296, 317, 554, 571
DODI 5000.2, 454–455
DODI 7000.2, 454
double-entry system, 46, 571
driver activity, 463, 511
dual method of allocation, 407

earned revenue, 31
earned value, 6–7, 359, 443–451, 453–455, 493
earned value approach, 448, 451, 454
earned-value analysis, 453
earned-value system, 454
earnings per share, 300, 312–315, 317–318, 320
earnings stream, 300, 320
earnings stream variability, 300
earnings-per-share criterion, 313
EBIT stream, 299
economies of scale, 280, 283, 288, 295, 398

effectiveness, 390, 398, 524–525, 530, 539, 543, 553, 565
efficiency, 15, 122, 143, 246, 259, 374, 450–451, 470, 505, 524–526, 530–531, 533–535, 537–553, 555, 565
efficiency standard, 525
efficiency variance, 531, 533–535, 537, 541–543, 545, 547–551
electronic spreadsheets, 287
end-to-end project team involvement, 97
ending work in process, 393, 485, 497–498, 500, 504–507, 509, 513–517, 520–522
entities, 16, 42, 115
equities, 17–18, 20–21, 27, 29–30, 35, 37, 39, 46, 51–52, 57, 571
equity project financing, 59
equivalent certain cash flow, 247
equivalent units, 497–507, 509, 513, 515–521
estimated costs, 523, 527, 539, 563
ethics, 15–16, 135, 197–198, 200, 206, 269, 287
excess of revenue over expense, 24
expected coefficient of variation, 299
expected EBIT, 299
expected future cost, 99, 125
expected performance, 524
expected value, 247, 252, 261, 264, 299
expenditures, 72, 132, 181, 210, 237, 259, 284, 286, 292, 294, 297, 444, 447, 454, 553
expense accounts, 14, 21–22, 47
expenses, 9, 12–13, 16, 18–19, 21–27, 30–31, 33–34, 38–43, 46, 48–54, 57–58, 101–103, 108–109, 124, 126–130, 136–139, 144–146, 151, 162, 165–166, 172–175, 206, 208–209, 211–214, 216, 218, 227, 275–278, 280, 284–286, 288–290, 293, 297, 308, 336–337, 339–340, 351, 360, 366–367, 369–374, 385–386, 389, 391–392, 395–396, 400–401, 403, 410, 428, 439–440, 484, 565, 569–572
expiration of unexpired costs, 24–25, 31, 34, 42
explicit transactions, 24, 32–33, 569

facilities, 18, 23, 108–109, 112, 134, 138, 140–141, 147–149, 158–160, 167, 170, 177, 190, 209, 211, 236–238, 248, 255, 270, 289, 330, 349, 364, 372, 384, 408, 411–414, 459, 465, 467, 519, 570
factory burden, 365, 389, 393
factory overhead, 138, 140, 144, 147–148, 159–160, 163, 165, 170, 174, 364–367, 369–373, 385–390, 394–396, 398–399, 417–419, 459–463, 465, 467–469, 474–485, 488–491, 495–496, 499, 511–514, 516–517, 522
factory overhead applied, 459–460, 462, 465, 467, 477, 479–485, 490, 496, 499, 517
fair value, 335
favorable variance, 531–532
FIFO, 502–507, 509, 514–519, 521, 527